BOLTON'S AMERICAN ARMORY

BOLTON'S
AMERICAN ARMORY

A RECORD OF COATS OF ARMS WHICH HAVE BEEN IN USE
WITHIN THE PRESENT BOUNDS OF
THE UNITED STATES

BY

CHARLES KNOWLES BOLTON

"We ourselves have been content to record the arms which
have been in use by the families whose names are attached
to them."—*Oswald Barron.*

CLEARFIELD COMPANY
REPRINTS & REMAINDERS

IN A LAND OF CHIVALRY
HERALDRY AND HER SISTER ARTS
WILL EVER FLOURISH

THAT THE SOUTH IS WELL REPRESENTED IN THESE PAGES
IS DUE IN NO SMALL MEASURE
TO THE UNTIRING ZEAL OF

MARGUERITE HIGGS EVERETT

WIFE OF WILLIAM ROBERT EVERETT OF
PALMYRA, NORTH CAROLINA

CLARKE ARMS

Part of the floor of the eastern parlor of the Clarke-Frankland House, Boston,
where Sir Charles Henry Frankland, Baronet, lived, having married
Agnes Surriage, whom he first saw barefooted scrubbing
the Tavern floor at Marblehead

Table of Contents

INTRODUCTION

This is a record of those coats of arms only that have been in use (some of them from the earliest Colonial times) within the bounds of the present United States. Readers whose chief interest is in "authentic" arms or the right to bear arms must look elsewhere.

Heraldry, as we know it, can be traced back to about 1164, and by the time of the third crusade (1189) it was a recognized art. The Stewart arms — or a fess chequy azure and argent — appeared at this period. For centuries to follow, leaders of men assumed coats. Not infrequently brothers had different arms, just as Jewish brothers today assume different surnames, and a husband sometimes appropriated a wife's coat. There was then, as now, a disposition to resent the use by one person of arms long associated with another's family, as we find in Hewlett's delightful heraldic romance, "The Forest Lovers," but it was not often the tragic affair that our learned pundits of today would have us believe. The Scropes, to be sure, objected in 1385 to the use of azure a bend or by the Grosvenors, producing a hundred or more witnesses to assert that these arms went with the name Scrope. On the other side, the Grosvenors produced an equal number of good men to swear the contrary.

In 1483 the College of Arms was chartered, although grants of arms from great nobles and the Crown began much earlier. The attitude of ancient families toward this College has not always been friendly, since descendants of men who won or assumed arms at the time of service on historic mediaeval battlefields will never look with favor upon arms granted by authority on payment of a fee.

One of the greatest of English authorities on this subject, Mr. Oswald Barron, in the Introduction to "Hertfordshire Families" (London, 1907) has this to say;—and I have italicized one significant sentence: "In considering the qualification of the families admitted by us we have put away all question of their right to armorial bearings. With the quaint fancies of certain popular writers that the bearing of officially authorized arms is a condition of nobility we are unconcerned. Armorial bearings, at best an accident of nobility, are in England no true proof of nobility, and the assertion that nobility derives itself from the bearing of them has fled before the first scouting party of inquirers. Indeed we have but to open one of such writers' books to find the newest of new men flaunting his newly acquired coat and exalted as its bearer above the county squire whose recognized social status is infinitely higher than his own. Were we indeed to set up the possession of rightfully borne arms as a condition for inclusion in our volumes we should bar the door to some of the greatest names in England, for even in high places it is possible to discover shields of arms borne under official direction which when set beside the true genealogy of their bearers show themselves as false assumptions. *We ourselves have been content to record the arms which have been in use by the families whose names are attached to them,* reserving to ourselves the right to comment upon the sufficiency of the reasons which have influenced their assumption or recognition."

In fairness the opposite point of view should be recorded. Mr. Charles A. H. Franklin, in his "The Bearing of Coat-Armour by Ladies," writes:

"I want to emphasize this point: everyone has not got a coat of arms; indeed, very few have. The possession of arms is not constituted by wearing a signet ring, or by having at home a painting of arms and some device engraved upon family silver."

Mr. Franklin suggests an appeal to the heraldic officers in England, Scotland, or Ireland, for he is writing for Englishmen. Here we have no arbiter in such matters. It will be said that the "very few" who have an undoubted right to bear arms may display them or not, as they choose, but that those who in three centuries have risen to the armigerous station in society out of a population of one hundred millions should on account of our conditions here bear no arms. However right this view may be, it will be increasingly difficult for it to prevail. Even in Colonial days when we were subject to the mother country, arms were assumed.

Every Colonial Governor used an official seal, and on this seal were arms, whether his or not did not seem much to concern him. These arms are recorded here, with whatever facts have been ascertained regarding their origin. The aristocratic Page family of Virginia looked with complaisance on a deceased father resting under a "table tomb" bearing the Paget arms. The sleeper was more concerned about Heaven and so are most of us.

It has long seemed to me desirable to gather and preserve the fleeting records of use on tombstones, now fast going to decay, on portraits, old silver, bookplates, seal rings, and on ancient framed water-colors. These water-color coats of arms were no doubt taken very often from Guillim's famous book on heraldry. In some cases they were used of right, but the owner of the painting cared little about "right."

Before the days of stationers, arms were drawn by carriage painters and wandering "heraldic artists." At the very least, it may be said that the man who paid ten dollars or gave bed and breakfast for a painted coat of arms had some gentlemanly aspirations. A few such artists in New England were:

Thomas Johnson (1708–1767).
Francis Garden from London, 1745.
James Turner, about 1750.
Benjamin Hurd, Jr., about 1750.
Nathaniel Hurd (1729–1777).
George Searle, Newburyport, 1773.
S. Blyth, about 1780.
John Coles, in Boston, 1800–1813.
  Helmet on the left or open side yellow or gold, on the right
  or back side blue.   Mantling red.   Below are palm branches
  (like cornstalks) heavy stemmed, with scroll smooth lined.
  Under the coat: "He beareth," etc.
John Coles, Jr., in Boston, 1806–1826.
  Shield wide and squat.   All are alike.   The left palm branch
  has one leaf turned, and between two straight branches.
  The three lobes or arcs at the top of the shield are uniform.
  The scroll is crinkly.
The names of Southern artists whenever known have been
recorded in these pages.
  Bookplates are not often reliable heraldically.   If Mr. French,
one of the best known of American bookplate engravers, had an
accurate knowledge of heraldry, there is little to prove it in his
handsome bookplates.   While I have recorded his and other bookplates as they are engraved, I have attempted in every case to show
between brackets the recognized tinctures of the coats.
  Heraldry appeals to a deep rooted love for symbolism and
for design.   As we today "follow the flag," so the men of old fol-
lowed a coat of arms embroidered on a surcoat worn over a coat
of mail, for this symbol stood for home leadership.   The closed
helmet left this the only means of identification.
  Humor and play upon surnames also looms large in heraldry.
Play upon the name in a design — standing dishes for Standish,
for example — was an early manifestation of that love of a joke
which is so inseparable a part of cathedral carving in chapter house
and in misericords.   The Wynkoop arms here recorded are of
this type.
  Many writers have contributed to the study of American
heraldry.   The late William Sumner Appleton compiled a short
but authoritative list of New England families entitled to bear
arms (see N. E. Hist. and Gen. Register, July, 1891, and April,
1898).   W. A. Crozier covered Virginia families in his Virginia
Heraldica.   For the whole country there are E. DeV. Vermont's
America Heraldica, with colored plates and some critical notes;
Crozier's General Armory;   Matthews' American Armoury;   and
Eugene Zieber's "Heraldry in America," a comprehensive book
issued by the Bailey, Banks and Biddle Company, Philadelphia
(2d edition. 1909).   Reference to these works in the text does

not mean necessarily that the record here is based on one of the above works.

Even with their aid, this collection of coats of arms that have been in use is very far from complete. Many genealogies and biographies refer to family arms, but when use is not shown the arms are not recorded.

Clearly one's obligation to others cannot be adequately recorded here, although innumerable acknowledgments will be found throughout the book. The late Lawrence Park of Groton, Massachusetts, sketched with remarkable skill many gravestones in Virginia and South Carolina for my use. They form an invaluable record. I am much indebted for aid to Mr. Clarence S. Brigham of the American Antiquarian Society, to Dr. Harold Bowditch of Brookline, Massachusetts, to Mrs. William Robert Everett and Miss Harriet Herring of North Carolina, the late J. B. Ludlow of New York and his secretary, Miss Rose Rediker, Mrs. Robert H. Bancroft of Boston and the South, George William Maslin of Maryland, Mrs. Tilghman Earle of Maryland, Frederic Winthrop of Boston, Mrs. John P. Hollingsworth of Pennsylvania, Miss Mabel L. Webber of South Carolina, Mrs. Milnor Ljungstedt of Maryland, Francis H. Bigelow of Cambridge, Robert D. Weston of Boston, Mrs. C. K. Bolton of Shirley, and to Mrs. Norman T. Thomas, who as Miss Florence Light helped me at the outset of my undertaking. My secretary, Miss Evelyn Marguerite Coker, has rendered intelligent help which appears on every page. The staff of the Riverdale Press have added materially to the value of the book by their unselfish and untiring efforts to meet the difficulties inherent in so unfamiliar a subject. These friends are not to be held responsible for the scope, purpose, or errors here to be found.

C. K. B.

Pound Hill Place,
    Shirley, Massachusetts.

THE ELEMENTS OF HERALDRY

It is not the purpose of this book to give a treatise on heraldry, but a few elementary statements may be of service. The *shape of the shield* has little significance today, except that the arms of a woman are in a lozenge. The eleventh century kite shaped shield (seen in the Bayeux tapestry) gave way in time to a shield nearly triangular, and this gradually widened in the middle. *Above the shield* is often a helmet — side view for untitled people — on the top of which is a wreath or skein of twisted silk of the chief color and metal of the arms, supporting a *crest*. The helmet is not always present.

Mantling may serve as a background for the shield, but its form has no significance as to dignity or rank. *Supporters* on either side of the shield are rarely granted to untitled people.

A *motto* may be added at the choice of the owner of the arms.

The *furs*, *colors*, and *metals* used on shields are often indicated in black and white for convenience.

In Copinger's "Heraldry Simplified" will be found pictures of most of the objects or charges to be seen on shields. In Fairbairn's "Crests" a collection of crests may be consulted.

A LIST OF FAMILIAR TERMS USED IN THESE RECORDS

Addorsed. Back to back.
Affronté. Full-faced.
Annulet. A ring. In cadency for the fifth son.
Antique crown. Triangular points rising from the band.
Argent. Silver. Often indicated by white.
At bay. A stag with head lowered.
At gaze. A stag with face to the spectator is at gaze.
Attired. Said of horns of stags when different in tincture from the body.
Azure. Blue. Indicated by horizontal lines.

Bar. A thin fess. Never used singly.
Bar sinister. An error for *Baton.*
Bars-gemelles. Thin bars in pairs.
Barrulet. A thin bar.
Barry. A shield of bars alternately tinctured.
Base. The lower part of the shield.
Baton. A thin bend sinister not long enough to touch either side of the shield. Often denoting illegitimacy.
Belled. A falcon with bells attached to its legs is "belled."
Bend. A band diagonally from the upper left (dexter) side of the shield to the lower right or sinister side. Properly one-third the width, but often less.
Bewet. Ring or strap which attaches the bells to a hawk's leg.
Bezant. A golden disc or roundel.
Billet. An oblong rectangle.
Bird-bolt. A blunt-headed arrow.
Bordure. The outer fifth of the shield. A border.
Botonné. See *Cross.*

Cabossed. The face of a horned beast, without the neck.
Canton. A square in the dexter chief, less than a quarter.
Cap of Maintenance or Chapeau. Of crimson velvet turned up to show ermine. Used under a crest.
Chequy. A checker-board of colors and metals alternating.
Chevron. A bend and a bend sinister springing from the lower sides and meeting.
Chief. The top third of the shield.
Cinquefoil. A five-lobed conventional leaf.
Close. Said of a bird with wings at rest.
Cockatrice. A monster with head, wings, and legs of a fowl and tail ended like an arrow head. A cock-headed wyvern.
Combatant. Rampant and face to face.
Compony. A single row of squares alternating color and metal.
Conjoined. Touching one another. Of wings, with the points down.
Contourné. Facing the sinister side of the shield — the beholder's right.
Cotised. Having diminutives on either side. As a bend cotised.
Couchant. Lying down with head raised.
Counter-changed. Part of the shield metal on color and the corresponding part color on metal.
Counter compony. Two rows of squares, metal adjoining color.
Counter-embattled. The projection on one side opposite the indentation on the other side.
Counter passant. Going in opposite directions.
Couped. Cut off clean.
Courant. Running.

Crenellé. Embattled.
Crescent. A crescent moon with horns up.   In cadency for the second son.
Crest. A device above the helmet and shield.   Used by men only.
Crined. Colored.   Said of hair when differing in color from the body.
Cross. Botonné, Trefoil ends.
      Calvary. A cross on three steps.
      Crosslet fitché.   Three ends crossed, and one pointed.
      Fleury. Ending in three leaves or a fleurs-de-lys top.
      Forme. See Patté.
      Moline. The ends with two leaves or foils.
      Patonce. Fleury but with extremities enlarged.
      Patté. As if a square with diagonal slits from the corners.
      Potent. The ends capped by bars at right angles.
      St. Andrews. A saltire.
Crusilly. The field strewn with small crosses.
Cubit arm. Hand with arm cut off at elbow.

Dancetté. Deep indentations.
Debruised. Partly covered.
Decrescent. A crescent with horns toward the sinister side.
Dexter. The side of the shield near the right arm as worn, or the left side as
    seen by the spectator.   All faces are turned to the dexter unless otherwise
    described.
Diapering. Faint decorations on large surfaces for looks only.   Not now much
    used.
Dismembered. Cut in pieces but left in position.
Displayed. The underside of the body exposed and the wings extended.
Dormant. With head between paws.
Double-queued. With two ends to a tail.
Dragon. A monster with scaly body, four birds claws, bat's wings, and head
    with barbed tongue.

Embattled. Alternating square projections and spaces on a line.
Embowed. Bent, especially of an arm and of a dolphin.
Endorse. One-quarter the width of a pale.
Enfiled. Pierced by a sword, arrow, etc.
Engrailed. An edge with semi-circular incisions, close together.
Eradicated. Torn up by the roots.
Ermine. A fur.   The nose and front paws (it is said) shown by three sable dots
    on a field argent; the tail and hind legs conjoined below the dots or perhaps
    a tail erased.
Ermines. Silver ermine spots on a black field.
Erminois. Black ermine spots on a gold field.
Estoile. A star with six or more wavy points.

Face. Usually a full face without neck; cabossed.
Fess. A band across the shield.   One-third as wide as the height of the shield
    in theory.
Fessways. Arranged across the shield.
Fimbriated. Bordered with a different tinctured narrow band.
Fire ball. A bomb spouting flames from the top.
Fitché. Pointed, as one arm of a cross.
Flaunches. A section from each side of the shield enclosed by a convex line.
Fleur-de-lys. A conventionalized lily.   In cadency for the sixth son.
Fleury. ⎫
Flory. ⎬ A fleur-de-lys end.
Formé. See *Cross.*
Fountain. A roundel or disc covered by six wavy bars alternating argent and
    azure.

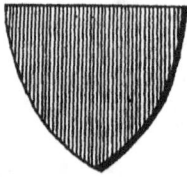

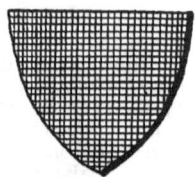

| Red–Gules | Blue–Azure | Green–Vert | Black–Sable |

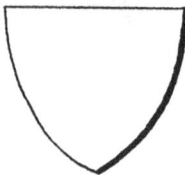
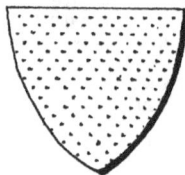

| Purple–Purpure | Silver–Argent | Gold–Or | Ermine |

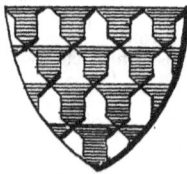
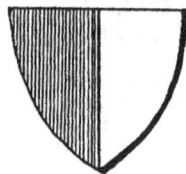
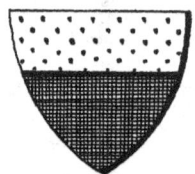

| Erminois | Vair | Per Pale | Per Fess |

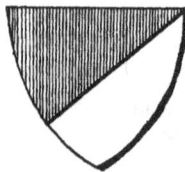

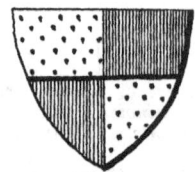

| Per Bend | Per Bend Sinister | Per Chevron | Quarterly |

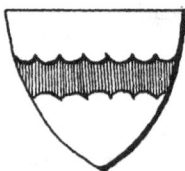
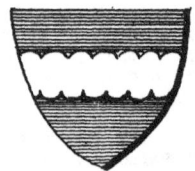

| Per Saltire | Gyronny | Fess Engrailed | Fess Invected |

Fret. A narrow saltire and mascle interlaced.
Fructed. With fruit or seeds.
Fulgent. Showing rays.
Furs. *See* the Introduction.
Fusil. A long narrow lozenge or a spinning wheel spindle.

Galley. An ancient ship, usually of 2 or 3 masts.
Gamb. A beast's leg.
Garb. A sheaf of grain.
Garnished. Ornamented.
Gauntlet. An armored glove.
Gaze. See *At gaze.*
Gemels. See *Bars-gemelles.*
Gilly-flower. A crimson species of pink.
Gobony. See *Compony.*
Gold. See *Or.*
Gorge. A whorl argent and azure, supposed to represent a whirlpool.
Gouttês. Drops; *Gouttée,* sprinkled with drops; *de sang* with red drops of blood.
Griffin or *Gryphon.* A monster with the front half an eagle, the hinder half a lion.
Guardant. With the face full.
Gules. Red. Shown in black by perpendicular lines.
Gyronny. A shield divided per pale, per fess, and per saltire into gyrons.

Habited. Clothed.
Harpy. A monster, the upper half of a woman attached to the body of a vulture.
Hatchment. A shield of arms on a sable lozenge displayed after death. In the
   case of impaled arms only the section back of the arms of the deceased is
   sable.
Hauriant. A fish when erect or in pale — breathing at the surface.
Head. Usually indicating head and neck.
Helmet. An esquire's or gentleman's helmet is of steel, faces the dexter, and has
   the visor closed.
Humetté. Objects cut off so that they do not reach the edges of the shield.
Hurt. A blue roundel.

Impaled. The shield may be divided per pale, with the husband's arms on the
   dexter side (impaling) the wife's arms on the sinister side.
In bend. Running or lying in the direction of the bend.
In chief. At the top of the shield.
In fess. Horizontally in relation to the shield.
In pale. Upright.
In her piety. A pelican is "in her piety" when she is feeding her young with blood
   pecked from her breast.
In splendor. The sun with rays all around it.
Increscent. A crescent with horns pointing to the dexter.
Ink moline. See *Mill-rind.*
Inescutcheon. See *Pretence.*
Invected. An engrailed line upside down.
Issuant. Rising out of. Usually the upper half only is shown.

Jellop. Wattles and comb of a cock.
Jessant. Springing forth.
Jess. Strap attached to a hawk's leg. If a ring or varvel is on the end, the
   swivel of a leash can be snapped on.

Label. A strip of silk or linen with 3 pendants. In cadency the eldest son, and
   said to have been worn by him as part of a collar in tourneys.
Lambrequin. See *Mantle.*

Pale

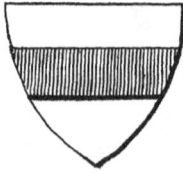

Fess

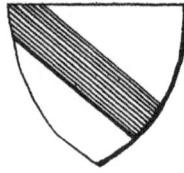

Bend

Bend Sinister

Chevron

Cross

Saltire

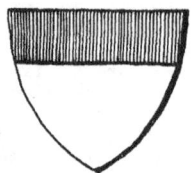

Chief

Pile

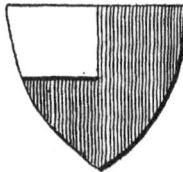

Quarter

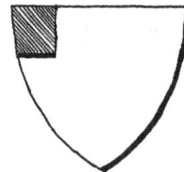

Canton

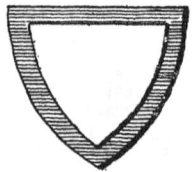

Bordure

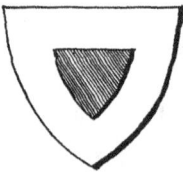

Inscutcheon

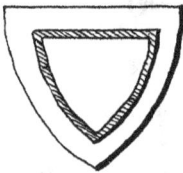

Orle

Tressure

Flaunches

Lozenge

Mascle

Fusil

Fret

Langued. The tongue when colored (usually red), and different from the body.
Leopard. See *Lion.*
Lion. In old heraldry "lions" were always rampant or rearing. When passant or statant they were "leopards."
Lioncel. A young lion or of four or more lions on one shield.
Lodged. Deer lying down. Lions lying down are "couchant."
Lozenge. A diamond-shaped figure. A shield for women.
Lucie. A pike fish.
Lure. A decoy. See also *Conjoined in lure.*
Lymphad. A galley, usually with one mast.

Maintenance. See *Cap.*
Maltese cross. A cross patté with the ends indented.
Mantle or Mantling. Ornamental drapery (often like foliage) about the helmet and shield.
Martlet. A small bird with two feathers in place of legs. In cadency for the fourth son.
Mascle. A lozenge voided to show the field through the lozenge-shaped opening.
Masoned. Lined to represent stone construction.
Maunche. A sleeve very full at the wrist.
Metals. Gold (or) and silver (argent).
Mill-rind. An iron sunk in a stone.
Moline. See *Cross.*
Moor-cock. Grouse. Looks like a cock with two long tail-feathers.
Moor's head. A negro (in profile?) couped at the neck, a wreath about the temples and ear-rings.
Mullet. A five-pointed star. In cadency for the third son. Some mullets are pierced.
Mural crown. The circular band masoned and the top embattled.

Naiant. Swimming. A fish in fess is naiant.
Naissant. Issuing from the center of a fess, chevron, etc., not from the edge as in issuant.
Nebuly. A partition line like a silhouette of rounded nail heads fitted together alternating one up one down, or potent fur devices rounded at the corners.
Noded or *Nowed.* Knotted. Often an animal's tail.

Of the field. When tinctures are named more than twice if the third mentioned is the same as the shield it is said to be "of the field" or "of the first."
Ogress. A black roundel.
Ondé. Wavy.
Oppressed. See *Debruised.*
Or. Gold or yellow. In engraving shown by dots on a white ground.
Orle. A narrow band within but following the form of the shield.
Over all. See *Debrusied.*

Pale. A band one-third the width of the shield and perpendicular.
Pall. An archi-episcopal robe shaped like a Y.
Panache. Three or more rows of feathers, like a pyramid. Used as a crest.
Party per pale, etc. A partition line perpendicular, horizontal, etc. "Party" is not now used.
Paschal Lamb. Knights' Templars device. A lamb passant argent, carrying a banner charged with the cross of St. George (argent a cross gules).
Passant. Beast walking with the dexter paw raised. When guardant the head is full-faced. When reguardant the head is turned back to the sinister.
Patonce. See *Cross.*
Patté. See *Cross.*
Pean. A fur, with gold ermine spots on a black field.

Escallop

Maunche

Pheon

Water Bouget

Lance

Lymphad

Barnacle

Bird Bolt

Cross Patté

Mill-rind

Trefoil slipped

Roundle

Cross Botonné

Cross Flory

Cross Patonce

Cross Crosslet
Fitché

Pegasus. A horse with wings.
Pelican. A fish-eating bird with large bill. See also "*In her piety.*"
Pellet. A black roundle.
Pheon. The barbed point of an arrow, the inner edge commonly engrailed.
Phoenix. A sacred bird that burned itself on the altar at Heliopolis and rose
     more beautiful from its ashes.
Pile. A triangle, issuing from the middle chief of the shield and its point extend-
     ing toward the middle base.
Plate. A silver roundle.
Pomme. A green roundle.
Potent. A fur of azure and argent T shapes each azure T next to an argent T
     upside down, and fitting closely to it. In counter potent the Ts are tinc-
     tured alternately by perpendicular rows and not individually.
Pretence, escutcheon of. A shield at the center of a larger shield, bearing the
     arms of a married heiress or co-heiress.
Proper. Shown in natural color, and given as "ppr."
Purpure. Purple, and shown by bend sinister lines.

Quarter. A square occupying the dexter upper quarter of the shield.
Quarterly. The shield divided to allow (after the man's arms) display of arms
     indicating alliances of his ancestors with heiresses.
Quatrefoil. A four-lobed conventional leaf.

Raguly. Embattlement where the angles are not right angles.
Rampant. An animal standing on his left hind leg, his forepaws raised, the right
     higher than the left.
Reflexed. Curved backward.
Reguardant. Looking backward.
Reversed. Turned contrary to the usual.
Riband. A narrow bend, sometimes couped.
Rompu. Broken.
Rose. Five petals (tincture given), between each two a leaf or barb, and if
     double five smaller petals or lobes within, each lobe centered on a barb. The
     barbs are green, and the seeds at the center gold. When "slipped" it is
     more natural and has a stem.
Roundles. Circular figures.
          When of gold — a bezant.
          When of blue — a hurt.
          When of red — a torteau.
          When of white — a plate.
          When of black — a pellet or ogress.
          When of green — a pomme.
          When of purple — a golpe.
          When barry wavy of six white and blue — a fountain.
Rowel. A pierced mullet or wheel spur
Rustre. A lozenge with a round hole.

Sable. Black. Shown by cross hatched vertical and horizontal lines.
Salamander. A lizard-like amphibian fabled to live in fire. Blazoned green.
Salient. Springing.
Saltire or Saltorel. A bend and a bend sinister intersected. A St. Andrew's
     cross.
Sanglant. Bloody where torn off.
Sanguine. Dark red.
Savage. A wild-man with leaves about the loins and holding a club.
Scimitar. A sword with narrow curved blade.
Sea-lion. A fabled animal, half lion and half fish's tail.
Sergeant. Applied usually to the griffin when springing.

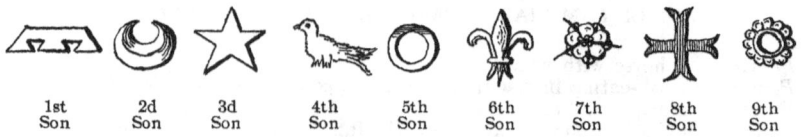

1st Son	2d Son	3d Son	4th Son	5th Son	6th Son	7th Son	8th Son	9th Son

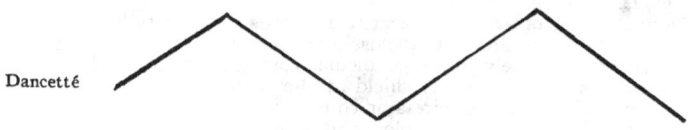

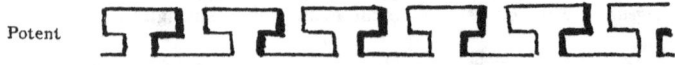

Wavy

Dancetté

Indented

Engrailed
Cut into

Invected

Nebuly

Raguly

Embattled

Fleury
Counter Fleury

Potent

Sejant. Sitting.
Semé. Strewn. Also "poudré."
Shoveler. A large duck frequenting rivers.
Sinister. The side of a shield at the *right* hand of the observer, but the left as
  worn by the soldier.
Sinople. Green or vert.
Slipped. Stems of plants when torn away.
Sphinx. A monster with a lion's body and a woman's head and breasts.
Staple. A squarish U of iron.
Starved. Stripped of leaves.
Statant. All feet on the ground.
Supporters. Figures supporting the shield on either side. Used by peers and
  knights, chiefs of clans, and by special grant.
Surcharged. One heraldic device upon another.

Talbot. A dog with long ears hanging down.
Tawney or *tenney.* Chestnut color, shown by perpendicular lines crossed by lines
  bend sinister ways.
Tiger. The heraldic tiger has a dragon's head and lion's tail.
Tinctures. Colors, metals, furs.
Torse. See *Wreath.*
Torteau. A red roundel.
Trefoil. A three-lobed leaf.
Tressure fleury, counter-fleury. Two orles, one within the other, eight or more
  fleurs-de-lys issuing outward from the larger, and eight issuing inward from
  the lesser, the portions of the fleurs-de-lys which ought to appear between
  the lines are omitted.
Tricked. Design and color indicated.
Trippant. Walking, with one foot raised. Of deer, etc.

Undé. Wavy.
Unicorn. A horse's head and body, lion's tail, legs, and cloven hoofs of a buck,
  a twisted horn from the forehead, and a goat's beard.

Vair. A fur. The bell shapes are placed point to point and base to base, one
  in each two being argent the other azure.
Vairé. The design as in Vair but the tinctures specified.
Vambraced. Encased in armor.
Vert. Green, and shown by lines bendways. Also called sinople.
Vested. Clothed.
Voided. All but the edges cut away to show the tincture of the field through the
  opening.
Vol. Two wings conjoined, the tips upward. See *Conjoined in lure.*
Volant. Flying.
Vulned. Wounded.

Water-bouget. Two leather bags on a stick, now drawn like a flowing M.
Wings. See *Conjoined in lure,* and *Vol.*
Wreath or *Torse.* A garland for the temples. A crest-wreath is made of two
  bands of silk or linen, one of the chief metal, the other of the chief color,
  twisted together into six sections, the first a metal.
Wyvern. A monster with two legs, wings, and head of a winged dragon, and the
  tail of an adder ended like an arrow head.

AN AMERICAN ARMORY

Alphabetically Arranged

A

Abbott Erm on a pale gu 3 pears or
Crest: a unicorn's head erased (?)
Motto: Festina lente
Bowdoin College. Abbott memorial collection bookplate

Abercrombie Arg a chev engr gu bet 3 boars' heads erased [az]. Impaling: Gu a bezant bet 3 demi-lions arg (Bennet)
Crest: a bee volant ppr
Mottoes: 1: Vive ut vivas; 2: Meus in ardues æqua
Bookplate James Abercrombie, Phil., 1758–1841. He married Margaret Bennet. Mentioned in Boswell's Johnson. Variations were used on ancient wine glasses. Amer. Heral., vol. 2, p. 24

Abernethy Arg a lion ramp gu surmounted by a ribbon sa
Framed painting owned by Misses Frank and Mary Blount Martin, Hickory, N. C.

Abrahall Az 3 hedgehogs or
Crest: a hedgehog ppr
Wax seal on deed dated 1690 from Col. Robert Abrahall of New Kent, Va., to William Bassett. Wm. & Mary Quar., Apr. 1894, p. 266

Acklom 1: Gu a maunch or bet 8 cinquefoils or (Acklom of Moreby, Co. York); 2: Arg on a bend az 3 mullets of 6 points or, in chief a label of 3 points gu (Morby); 3: Per chev embat sa and arg 3 buck's heads cabossed counterchanged; 4: Erm on a fess gu 3 fleurs de lis [or] (Herben?); 5: Arg a cross flory voided [az] (Melton); 6: Az 3 crescents or
Crest: Five oak leaves forming a star
Motto: Look through
Bookplate George Morbye Acklom, N. Y.

Adam Quart 1 and 4: Arg a mullet pierced az bet 3 crosses crosslet fitchée gu (Adam); 2 and 3: Arg 3 arrows [gu] 2 in saltire and 1 in pale feathered [or], bound by a ribbon, bet 6 trefoils slipped gu, 2 in chief, 2 in fess, and 2 in base (Littlejohn)
Crest: a cross crosslet of the arms surmounted of a sword in saltire ppr
Motto: Crux mihi grata quiès
Bookplate John Adam

Adams. Quart 1: A stag trippant by a pine tree above a fish naiant, all within a wreath of 13 mullets (Adams — devised by Pres. J. Q. Adams); 2: Sa a fess cotised or bet 3 martlets [or?] (Smith); 3: Gu seven mascles, 3, 3, 1 or (Quincy); 4: Gu 6 crosses crosslet fitchée arg 3, 2, 1; On a chief or 3 pellets, the center charged with a fleur-de-lis, those on either side with a lion pass guard (Boylston)
Crest: a lion pass guard hold in his dexter paw a cross crosslet fitchée
Motto: Fidem libertatem amicitiam retinebis (Tacitus?). Prest. John Quincy Adams bookplate

Adams Arg on a cross gu 5 mullets arg [or?]
Crest: out of a ducal cor a demilion [affrontée gu]
Motto: Loyal au mort
Bookplate Adrienne Adams Wickham. J. W. S., sc., 1899

Adams Arg on a cross gu 5 mullets or. Impaling: Arg a semée of cinquefoils gu a lion ramp sa (Pierpont?)
Crest: out of a ducal cor a demilion affrontée gu
Motto: Aspire persevere trust
Bookplate Thomas A. Adams. H. Hays engraver
On automobile Emma M. Adams, 568 Pine St., Lowell, 1916

Adams Az a crescent or, on a chief of the 2d 3 fleurs-de-lis of the first
Crest: Issuant from a chaplet of roses gu a demi-leopard ppr holding bet the paws an escallop or
Motto: Veritas liberabit
Grant for Daniel Adams, 1773–1863, of Pleasantville, N. J. Grandfather of Arthur Adams of Trinity College, Hartford

Adams Erm 3 cats pass in pale az
Seal of Thomas Adams of New Kent Co., Va. He was b. about 1730 in New Kent, d. 1788 in Augusta Co. Crozier's Va. Heral., p. 7

Adams For bookplates of John Adams, Charles Francis Adams, and John Quincy Adams, see Boylston

Addington Per pale erm and ermines on a chev bet 3 fleurs-de-lis 4 lozenges all counterchanged
Crest: a cat-a-mount pass guard bezantée

Engr. on caudle cup ex dono J[ohn] L[everett]. Owned by Mrs. D. H. Bradlee. Amer. Ch. Sil., M. F. A., 1911, pp. 29, 82

Addington Quartered by Wright

Addington *See also* Hatch

Addison Erm on a bend gu 3 annulets [or] on a chief arg 3 shields az, each charged with a leopard's face
Crest: a unicorn's head erased, pierced by an arrow in bend
Motto: Vulnus opemque fero
Notepaper Rev. Daniel Dulany Addison, Brookline, Mass. The old Tankard has no shields. Md. Hist. Mag. XIV, p. 388

Agnew Arg a chev gu bet in chief 2 cinquefoils gu 8 in base a saltire couped az, all within a bordure engr gu
Crest: an eagle rising
Motto: Consilio non impetu
Bookplate James Agnew of N. Y.

Ahmuty Arg a broken spear in bend sa bet 2 mullets az
Crest: a mailed dexter arm embowed holding a broken lance shaft
Motto: Dum spiro spero
Bookplate Thomas Ahmuty. Robert N. Auchmuty's coat has the mullets but pierced

Aitchison A double-headed eagle displ
Tomb of William Aitchison at Rose Hall, Princess Anne Co., Va. Nearly obliterated. He d. June, 1777. Crozier's Va. Heral., p. 9.

Alcott Gu a fess arg bet 3 cocks' heads erased [arg?] combed [or]
Crest: a cock
Motto: Semper vigilans
Bookplate John Sewall Pratt Alcott, Boston. Arms of Alcock. Engr. by E. H. Garrett.

Alden Gu 3 cresc arg within a bordure engr erm
Bookplate Hetty Gray Baker, by S. Harrod, 1923

Aldrich Az on a fess a bull pass guard
Notepaper Lilian, Mrs. Thomas Bailey Aldrich, 59 Mt. Vernon St., Boston

Alexander Quart 1 and 4: Per pale arg and sa a chev and in base a cresc all counterchanged; 2 and 3: Or a galley sails furled sa bet 3 cross crosslets fitchée gu
Crest: a beaver sejant
Water color of Alexander of Mecklenburg Co., N. C., owned by Miss Lena Smith, Scotland Neck, N. C.

Alexander Quart 1: a saltire; 2: a lymphad; 3: a garb; 4: a bend
Crest: a crescent
Supporters: lions
Motto: Sola bona quae honesta
Tomb of Ruth Alexander, d. 1796. Also other stones "beautifully cut." Old Sugaw Creek Presbyt. ch. yard near Charlotte, N. C. One with ship alone and doves (?) for supporters. Seen 1926 by Mrs. Milnor Ljungstedt

Allan Arg a pelican in her piety vulning herself. On a chief gu 3 mullets
Crest: a dexter hand holding a cutlas
Motto: Dirigat Deus
Bookplate of Richard Allan, M. D., So. Car.

Allcock Gu 3 demi-lions ramp couped or within a bordure erm. Perhaps: Per fess or and gu 3 demi-lions couped counterchanged within etc.
Crest: a unicorn's (?) head sa
Parchment 9 x 11¼ inches. Brought to Dorchester, Mass., by Dr. John Allcock (H. C. 1646). Owned by Dr. Bertha C. Downing of Kennebunk, Mass. On scroll: "Family of the Allcock." I do not find these arms in Burke

Alden Gu 3 crescents within a bordure engr erm
Crest: Out of a ducal cor a demi-lion ramp [or]
Bookplate with the John Coles type of mantling. Alden and Howland arms on bookplate of Miss Hetty Gray Baker, N. Y.

Allen [Az] a cross potent [or]
Crest: a demi-lion az holding in his 2 paws a ship's rudder or
Motto: Fortiter gerit crucem
Tombstone, Windsor, Conn.
Also Bookplate Charles Dexter Allen, writer, Hartford. Also notepaper Thomas Allen, Princeton, Mass. (b. 1849), Prest. trustees M. F. A. Boston. Artist. Also framed pedigree. His father (b. 1813) of St. Louis, Prest. Missouri Pac. R.R. Desc. of Samuel of Windsor

Allen Az a lion ramp holding a garb
Crest: a dexter hand holding open book inscribed "Nature"
Motto: Law and Right
Bookplate John Allen, 1763–1812, of Litchfield, Conn. R. Brunton, sc. Bates's Early Conn. Engr., p. 14

Allen Or on a chev az a rose gu bet 2 mullets arg
Crest: a demi-lion ramp [az?]
Mottoes: 1: Vita sine litteris mors est 2: Forti et fidele nihil difficile
Bookplate David William Allen

Allen Per bend rompu arg and sa 6 martlets counterchanged
Crest: a martlet or dove rising
Motto: Semper fidelis
Silver mug owned by Mrs. Lewis A. Barker, 40 Univ. Road, Brookline, Mass., made by W. Simpkins about 1720; once owned by Emily Stevens of Maine, wife of Thos. A. Hill of Bangor. Allen of Co. Pembroke? If Allyn, the annulet is missing. "M. A." engraved on the bottom of the mug on the front of which the arms appear

Allen Per chev arg and erm, in chief 2 lions' heads erased [or]
Bookplate Herbert Spencer Allen. F. G. Hall del.; J. W. Spenceley, sc., 1903

Allen Per chev gu and erm, in chief 2 lions' heads erased or
Crest: out of a ducal cor [or] a horse's head arg
Tombstone Elizabeth, wife of John Allen, Claremont, Surry Co., Va., has the arms of Allen impaling Bassett arg 3 bars wavy gu. Va. Heral., p. 7

Allen Per chev gu and erm, in chief 2 lions heads erased or. Impaling: Sa a chev or bet 3 lions' faces
Standing tray owned by Mrs. Chas. F. Dutch, Boston, made by T. Edwards abt. 1750-75. See Heral. Jour. IV, 110

Allen [Sa] a cross patonce [or], over all a bend, and in the sinister chief a bezant
Crest: an Indian affrontée; in the dexter hand a bow, in the sinister an arrow
Seal of Dr. Daniel Allen, Boston, 1689. N. E. Reg., Jan. 1877, p. 56

Alleyne Per chev [gu] and erm; in chief 2 lions' heads erased [or], langued [gu]
Crest: a unicorn's head [arg] ducally gorged
Bookplate Thomas Alleyne. N. H[urd], sculp. Also engr. on silver coffee pot by Jacob Hurd. Owned by Monroe Chickering. Amer. Ch. Sil., 1911, pp. 77, 124

Allison Az a chief erm, over all an eagle displ
Crest: a globe
Motto: Hinc labor et virtus
Bookplate ———— Allison, Phila. Sylvan City, 1883, p. 456

Allyn Arg on a chev a flail(?) A cresc for diff
On a doc., 1640, at the Mass. Hist. Soc. signed by Matthew Allyn of Conn.

Almy A chev bet 3 open books ppr
Bookplate Francis Almy, Buffalo

Almy Gu in chief a castle arg and in base 2 keys in saltire arg
Crest: a flag, spear, sword, and shield
Water color. "By the name of Almy" of R. I.

Alofsen Per pale arg and sa a chev couped counterchanged
Crest: a bull's horns partly arg and sa
Motto: Durate
Bookplate Solomon Alofsen, Brooklyn

Alsop Az a fess arg bet 3 doves
Crest: a dove holding an olive branch in the beak
Bookplate Richard Alsop of Conn. The visitation has sa 3 doves volant arg beaks and legs gu

Alston Az 10 estoiles of 6 points [or] 4, 3, 2, 1
Crest: a crescent [arg] charged with an estoile [or]
Motto: Immotus
Tombstone Georgetown, S. C. Zieber's Heral., p. 48

Alston Az 10 estoiles or; on a chief arg a crescent inverted gu bet 2 boars' heads couped sa. Impaling: Or 2 chev gu bet in chief 2 buckles az and in base a hunting horn az stringed gu (Orme Co. Fife)
Crest: a demi-swan wings expanded with a crescent reversed gu on each
Motto: In altum
Bookplate James Alston. John Ashe Alston and William Alston of Charleston, S. C., used the az 10 estoiles or; but for a crest: a crescent arg (not inverted), an estoile or bet its horns, and Immotus for motto

Alston Az 10 mullets 4, 3, 2, 1, or
Crest: a crescent enclosing a mullet, both arg
Motto: Immotus
Framed paintings owned by Ex-Gov. Wm. Walton Kitchen, Scotland Neck, N. C., also Mrs. Gertrude Kitchen McDowell, Mrs. James Harper Alexander. Noted by Mrs. W. R. Everett. The star in the crest is often or

Alward Az a fleur-de-lis bet 2 stars of 8 points or in bend, and 2 increscents or in saltire
Crest: from a ducal cor a vested and embowed dexter arm holding an anchor and cable
Motto: Verus et fidelis semper
Bookplate of Dennis Robinson Alward, Albany, N. Y.

Ambler Quart 1 and 4: Sa on a fess or bet 3 pheons arg a lion pass guard [gu] 2 and 3; Quart 1 and 4: Sable 3

horses' heads couped [or] Jaquelin;
2 and 3 arg on a bend [gu] 3 roses (Cary)
    Crest: a horse's head couped
    Mottoes: 1: Comme je trouve; 2:
Aduaces fortuna juvat timidosque
repellit
    Col. John Ambler d. 1836.   Richard
Ambler the emigrant married Elizabeth
Jaquelin
    On shaft in Schockoe Hill Cemetery,
Richmond, Va. Bellet's Some Prom.
Va. Families, vol 1.   Crozier says the
crest is: Two dexter hands conjoined,
holding a mural crown

Ambler   Quart 1 and 4: Sa on a fess or
bet 2 pheons [arg] a lion pass guard
[gu] ; 2 and 3: Sa 3 horses' heads
erased [or?] (Jaquelin)
    Crest: a horse's head
    Motto: Audaces fortuna juvat timi-
dosque repellit
    Bookplate of John Jaquelin Ambler,
Glenambler, Va.

Ames   Arg on a bend cotised [sa] 3
roses
    Motto: Fama candida rosa dulcior
    Bookplate Azel Ames, M. D.

Amory   Arg 3 bars wavy gu. Over all
a bend sa [az?]
    Crest: an eagle rising reguard, hold-
ing a serpent in its claws
    Motto: Avise le fin
    Bookplate J. Amory, Jr., Boston

Amory   Az on a bend arg 3 eagles displ
gu [sa?] within a bordure or
    Engr. on a tankard mentioned in will
of Mrs. Martha Amory of So. Car, 1699.
Bridgeman's Pilgrims of Boston, p. 74.
See Meredith's Hugh Amory, chapter
XVI

Amory   A barry of six nebulée arg and
gu over all a bend engr az
    Crest: out of a mural cor or a talbot's
head erased
    Motto: Amor y Amistad
    Bookplate Thomas C. Amory, 1812–
1899, Boston. His brother used "In
Deo Confido" and on a bend sa 3
bezants. The talbot's head was az
eared or

Anderson   Or on a chev gu bet 3 hawks'
heads erased sa, as many acorns slipped
[arg]. On a canton [sa] 3 martlets [arg].
    Crest: a hawk's head sa
    Motto: Vigila
    Bookplate Alexander Anderson, Jer-
sey City, b. 1775. First American
wood engraver

Andrews?   Arg on a chev engr gu bet
3 mullets of the last 3 quatrefoils
    Crest: a wolf's head(?) couped

Engr. on teapot made by Jacob Hurd,
a mug by Thomas Edwards, and a
chocolate pot by Zach. Brigden, the
1st and 2d given to the Museum of
Fine Arts, Boston, by Miss Georgiana
G. Eaton, the 3d owned by Wm. S.
Townsend

Andrews   Gu a saltire arg surmounted
of another az
    Crest: from out an Eastern crown a
blackamoor's head
    Bookplate James Andrews

Andrews   Gu a saltire or surmounted of
another vert
    Crest: a Saracen's head in profile
couped at the shoulders: ppr. From the
ear hangs a golden pendant
    Motto: Virtute et fortuna
    Tombstone in Old North Churchyard,
Providence, R. I. (1751). Vermont's
Amer. Heral., pp. 41, 156

Andros   1 and 6: Arg a chev [gu]
charged with 3 castles [or] bet 3 leopards' faces [sa] (De Saumarez); 2 and 5:
[Gu] a saltire [vert] fimbriated [or] on
a chief arg 3 mullets [sa] (Andros); 3
and 8: Erm a fess chequy arg and [sa]
(Crispe); 4 and 7: [Or] on a chev [sa]
5 horse shoes arg (Crispe)
    Crest: an eagle displ
    Supporters: unicorn and grey-hound
are for De Saumarez
    Engr. on a paten from Sir Edmund
Andros, 1694, to the old church in
Jamestown, Va. He was then Gov.
there. Given to the Diocese of Va.,
1856. E. A. Jones, Old Silver, p. 473.
Fine picture opposite p. 498

Andros   Quart 1 and 4: Arg a chev gu
charged with 3 towers or bet 3 leopards'
heads gu (De Saumarez); 2 and 3:
Arg a saltire or, and in chief 3 mullets
sa (Andros)
    Crest: an eagle displ
    Painted on canvas for use in 1886,
Bostonian Soc. Original in King's
Chapel, Boston

Anthony   Arg a leopard's head bet 2
flanches sa, each charged with a plate
    Crest: a goat's head erased
    Bookplate Henry B. Anthony, 1815–
84, U. S. senator and gov. R. I.

Antill   Gu a saltire or and in chief a
crescent
    Crest: a tree
    Motto: Opinionem vincere omnium
    Bookplate Lewis Antill, J. Smither
sc. Also of John Antill, Esq. with
label and motto: Honor et justitia.
Also of Edward Antill, Esq., A. M., az
a saltire arg and in chief a mullet and
motto: Probitas laudatur et alget

Appleton [Arg] a chev bet three apples [gu]
Crest: an apple of the field
Col. Samuel Appleton's altar tomb, Ipswich, Mass., 1653–1725. These are the arms of Appurley. Monum. mem. of the Appleton family

Appleton Arg a fess sa bet 3 apples gu leaved and stalked vert
Crest: an elephant's head couped sa, tusks and ears or, having a serpent vert issuing from the mouth and entwined round the trunk
Motto: Ne cede malis
Framed water color. Wm. S. Appleton, 5 Mt. Vernon Place, Boston, 1923

Appleton Arg a fess sa bet 3 apples gu leaved vert
Crest: an elephant's head sa
Bookplate Eben Appleton, also Nathan Appleton, Boston
Motto: Of Samuel Appleton, 1766–1853: Malis fortiter obsta; of Thomas Gold Appleton and William Hyde Appleton: Ex malo bonum; of Mrs. Everard J. Appleton of Cincinnati: Difficiles sed fructuosæ

Appleton Quart 1 and 4: Arg a griffin segreant (Griffin?); 2 and 3: Arg a fess sa bet 3 apples gu (Appleton)
Crest: a stag's head reguard erased
Motto: Je n'oublierai jamais
Bookplate James Appleton

Appleton Quartered by Oliver

Appleton See also Meyer

Ap Rhys Quartered by Betton

Apthorp Per pale nebule arg and az 2 rowels counterchanged. In chief a martlet (arms of Athorpe)
Crest: a mullet az
Motto: Nemo nisi Christus
Bookplate "East Apthorp, A. M.," 1733–1816. Dated 1761. Mass. Also of J. T. Apthorp with crest: a mullet arg, and no motto. Also of "Ste" of "Coll: Regal: Cant: Soc." Crest: a rowel az, but no motto. Also of "Steph" with the rowel arg and in sin chief a fleur-de-lis and no motto. Also Thomas Apthorp, d. 1741, with crest: a rowel arg, and motto: Juste rem para

Apthorp Per pale nebulé arg and az. Impaling: Chequy gu and erm (Garter?)
Wall tablet to Charles Apthorp, 1698–1758, Boston merchant, King's Chapel, Boston, north aisle. He married Griselda Eastwicke. There is no evidence on the shield of the usual "two mullets in pale counterchanged"

Apthorp Per pale nebulé arg and az 2 mullets counterchanged
Crest: a mullet arg pierced
Bookplate of [Jno.] Apthorp. In Milton's Paradise Lost, 1758

Apthorp Impaled by Wheelwright

Archdeacon Arg 3 chev sa
Crest: a dexter arm hold an arrow pointing to the dexter
Motto: Esse quam videri
Bookplate S. Archdeacon, signed W. S.

Archer Az 3 arrows arg
Motto: Fortitudo
Bookplate Col. William Archer, Va., a justice in 1743. Va. Heral., p. 71

Archer Gu on a fess az an arch (?)
On automobile of Frank M. Archer, Brookline, Mass.

Armour Quartered by Cabell and Mellon

Armstrong Gu 3 mailed arms erect, embowed, hands displ
Crest: a dexter hand holding a mailed and spurred leg at the bent knee
Motto: Vi et armis
Bookplate Armstrong, R. I.

Arnold Gu a chev erm bet 3 pheons or
Crest: a demi-leopard ramp or spotted sa with a ball of tar in the paws
Motto: Mihi gloria sursum
Seal owned by Arnold Talbot, Lincoln, R. I. Made for Richard James Arnold of R. I.

Arnold Gu a chev erm bet 3 pheons or
Crests: 1: A demi-tiger arg pelleté hold in its paws a fire-ball ppr; 2: A lion ramp gu holding bet its paws a lozenge or
Motto: Ut vivas vigila
Tomb of Oliver Arnold (d. 1770) in Old North Churchyard, Providence, R. I.

Arnold Gu on a bend or bet 2 lions ramp 3 clenched gauntlets
Crest: a gauntlet of the field
Motto: Be just and fear not
Bookplate Aaron Arnold, New York

Arnold Gu 3 pheons on a chief or a bar nebulée of the 2d
Impaled on bookplate arms of Lieut. Col. Pownoll Phipps of St. Kitts (1780–1858), who mar. Sophia Matilda, only dau. Gen. Benedict Arnold of Conn.
Oliver's West Ind. Bookplates, 1914, nos. 696, 697

Arnold Sa a chev bet 3 dolphins embowed, the two in chief confronté [arg]
Crest: a dolphin of the field
Motto: Morte triumpho
Bookplate Gustavus Arnold

Arran Quartered by Hamilton

Ascough Quartered by Candler

Ashenden Arg a lion ramp gu armed and langued az
Crest: a lion's gamb of the field erased holding a dagger
Motto: Suum cuique tributo
Notepaper Richard Edward Ashenden of Auburndale, Mass. brought by Mrs. Richard Ashenden from Chatham, Eng., in 1871

Ashton Arg a mullet sa
Tombstone Col. Henry Ashton, b. 1671 and d. 1731, Nominy Creek, Va. Crozier's Va. Heral., p. 11

Ashurst Quartered by Bowie

Ashwell Az 3 griffins' heads erased [or?]
Crest: a lion couchant
Whitwell arms?
Bookplate "Charles Ashwell of Grenada"

Aspinwall Gu 2 bars dancettée [or] within a bordure sa
Crest: a griffin's head erased
Motto: Finem respice
Bookplate Lloyd Aspinwall, Boston

Assheton Quart 1 and 4: [Arg] a mullet and canton sa; 2 and 3: Arg a mascle within a bordure engr sa (Shepley)
Crest: a man holding a scythe (costume about 1700)
Motto: In Domino confido
Bookplate Ralph Assheton, M. D., Phila. Also bookplate (very crude) of William Assheton of Barbados "of Gray's Inn, Judge of the Court of Admiralty of Pensilvania, 1718"

Athawes or **Athow** Sa on a chev bet 3 carpenters' squares, points to dexter or [arg?] a pillow
Crest: a demi-lion ramp
Bookplate Samuel Athawes, merchant, Va., 1799

Atkins *See also* Tyng

Atkinson Arg a bend az bet in chief an eagle's (?) head erased gu and in base a fleur-de-lis or
Crest: a lozenge
Framed water color, Essex Institute, Salem, Mass. No cornstalks. Of the Nath. Hurd type, 1729–77. The Whitmore painting is similar and has the same crest

Atkinson Arg an eagle displ with 2 heads sa, on a chief gu a rose bet 2 martlets or
Engr. on old silver salver formerly owned by Roger Atkinson and now by the Dutlow family of Charleston, W. Va. Wm. & Mary Quar., vol. 4, p. 270

Atkinson Az a cross voided bet 4 lions ramp or
Crest: an eagle displ
Motto: Vive et vivat
Bookplate Henry Atkinson. N. Hurd, sc.

Atkinson Vert a cross voided bet 4 lions ramp [or]
Crest: a dove displ
Bookplate Theodore Atkinson, about 1750. N. Hurd, sc. William King Atkinson, 1764–1820, had the same arms engraved by Callender. Lawyer, Portsmouth, N. H. *See* Heral. Jour., vol. 4, p. 119

Atkinson Vert a cross voided bet 4 lions ramp [or]
Crest: an eagle displ
Motto: Nil facimus non sponte Dei
Bookplate Theodore Atkinson, Boston, 1840

Atkinson Impaled by Broughton

Atlee Az a lion ramp [arg]
Bookplate William Augustus Atlee, Lancaster, Penn., judge Supreme Court, 1777–91
On a marble tablet to Col. Samuel John Atlee in Christ Church, Phila., 1883

Attwick Paly of 6 gu and or. On a chief az 3 eagles displ with double heads
Crest: a demi-eagle of the field
Bookplate William Attwick

Atwood Gu on a semée of acorns slipped [or] a lion ramp [arg]
Crest: a pheasant (?) crowned
Bookplate Harry Atwood

Auchmuty Impaled by Overing

Auchmuty *See also* Ahmuty

Austin Gu a chev bet 3 long crosses or
On old china owned by Samuel E. Morison, Boston

Avery Gu a chev bet 3 bezants
Crest: two lions' gambs or supporting a bezant
A hatchment of wood said to have been brought to N. E. by William Avery but first mentioned, 1750, in an inventory. Given to Dedham Hist. Soc., Mass., in 1919 by S. P. Avery. *See* Heral. Jour., vol. 2, p. 184, for acct. of seal used in 1721. Same arms. *See* "The Avery, Fairchild & Park Families," 1919

Avis Per pale gu and arg a lion ramp.
Impaling: Sa on a chev or bet 3 arrows
in pale, points in chief — 3 roundles
　　Crest: a dexter arm embowed and
vambraced, holding a battle axe
　　Arms on tankard made by Revere
about 1770 and formerly owned by

Thomas Avis of Boston. Heral. Jour.,
vol. 1, p. 88

Aylwin Arg a fess nebulée gu bet 3
lions ramp sa
　　Crest: a lion's gamb erect sa enfiled
with a mural crown [or]
　　Bookplate Thomas Aylwin, merchant, Boston

B

Bachert Gu a cross bet 4 stars of 8
points arg. On an inscutcheon az
crowned 3 fleurs-de-lis arg
　　Bookplate A. E. Bachert

Backhouse Per saltire or and az a
saltire erm
　　Crest: an eagle displ hold a serpent
nowed
　　Motto: Pax et amor
　　Bookplate W. Backhouse, M. A.

Backus Az a chev erm bet 3 doves
　　Crest: a dove close
　　Bookplate Elijah Backus, 1759-
1811, of New London, Conn., Marietta,
Ohio, and Kaskaskia, Ill. Bates's
Early Conn. Engr., p. 15

Bacon *See also* Tayloe

Bacon Gu on a chief arg 2 mullets sa
　　Crest: a boar statant
　　Motto: Mediocra firma
　　Bookplate Horace Bacon, Jr. John
Coles made a coat (with cornstalks)
the mullets being pierced and the crest
a dragon's head (?) erased. This is a
water color, 9 x 12 inches, owned by
Mrs. Edward Poor, Georgetown, Mass.
Daniel Bacon was in Woburn early.
See Essex Antiq., vol. 5, pp. 17, 25

Bacon Quart 1 and 4: Gu on a chief arg
2 mullets pierced sa (?); 2 and 3: Or
2 bars az, over all a bend gu (Quappelade)
　　Tomb of Col. Nathaniel Bacon of
King's Creek, York, Va. He d. 16
March, 1692. For his wife *see* Kingsmill. Va. Hist. Mag., vol. 2, p. 126

Baer Gu a chev bet 3 owls affrontée arg
[beaked or]
　　Crest: a demi-lion ramp [erm]
langued and crowned [or] hold a cross
crosslet fitchée [of the last]
　　Motto: Sapere aude
　　Arms of Sleigh, Ashe, Co. Derby, Eng.
　　Bookplate Frank House Baer

Bagot Quartered by Dumaresq

Bailey 3 towers
　　Bookplate Louis Jonathan Bailey,
Librarian at Gary, Indiana. C. F.
Norris, fec. '14

Baillie Sa a sun in splendor bet 9
mullets arg
　　Crest: a crescent

Supporters: 2 talbots
　　Motto: Major virtus quam splendor
　　Bookplate Wm. Elliot Baillie, Bridge-
port, Conn. Engr. by E. D. French

Bainbridge Arg on a chev bet 3 Cornish choughs [sa] 3 stags' heads
cabossed arg a mullet in chief for diff
　　Crest: a stag's head couped arg
attired [or]
　　Inlaid silverplate on dining room
chairs, now for sale (1923) by O'Hagan,
antique dealer, Meeting Street, Charleston, S. C. Seen by L. Park. Owned,
1925, by Ellery Sedgwick, Boston

Baird [Arg?] in chief 3 crescents 2 and
1 and in base 3 quatrefoils the same.
Impaling: [Arg?] a chev vert bet 3 lions
ramp contourné (sic)
　　Crest: a lion of the shield
　　Motto: Silenzio ad concordia
　　A Miss Baird who was married at
Saint Bartholomew's Church, N. Y.,
4 Oct. 1916, used this coat on her
invitation

Baker 3 falcons' heads
　　Used by Rev. Dr. James Baker,
Washington St. cor. Norfolk, Dorchester, Mass., 1800, on carriage, his
granddaughter Mrs. Taft says

Baker Arg on a fess nebulée bet 3 keys
sa, a tower triple towered of the first
　　Wax seal on deed of Henry Baker,
now in possession of Richard H. Baker,
Norfolk, Va. Wm. & Mary Quar., vol.
4, p. 269

Baker Arg on a fess gu 3 falcons' heads
erased of the field
　　Motto: Robor et agilitas
　　Notepaper Mrs. Frank Woods Baker,
Brookline, Mass.

Baker Arg a tower bet 3 keys erect [sa].
Impaling: On a bend sa 3 birds
　　Bookplate, old, Maryland (?)

Baker Sa a griffin segreant erm gorged
with a cor or
　　Crest: a lion's (?) head erased ppr
　　"By the name of Baker" and John
Coles's cornstalks. On old sheepskin
in the line of Wm. Baker. On gene-
alogy cover. Owned by Frank Dike
Baker of Sioux City

Baker [Sa] a griffin segreant [ermine]
Crest: a leopard's head gorged and erased
Seal of Alfred T. Baker, 14 Hopkins Road, Arlington, Mass. From a framed water color "By the name of Baker" and cornstalks (Coles), owned by —— Baker of Cincinnati

Balch Barry of six or and az on a bend engr gu 3 spear heads arg
Crest: a demi-griffin rising from a ducal crown
Motto: Not laws of man but laws of God
Bookplate Thomas Balch. Bookplate for gift of books to Harvard College from Edwin Swift Balch, Phila., has "Coeur et courage font l'ouvrage." The crest has no crown

Baldwin Gu a griffin sejant [or]
Crest: a lion ramp [az] hold in his paws a cross crosslet fitchée [or]
Motto: Je ne l'oublierai jamais
Bookplate A. Baldwin Charles

Baldwin [Arg?] 3 pairs of hazel leaves
Crest: a squirrel sejant holding a hazel sprig
Bookplate —— Baldwin

Baldwin Arg a chev ermines "bet 3 oaken branches" ppr. Impaling : Az a harpy with her wings distended, her hair flowing or (Huntington)
Crest: a lion's head erased
Framed water color (Coles type) owned by Edward R. Trowbridge of Providence. Arms of Rev. Thomas Baldwin, Baptist minister of Boston cir. 1825. Married Ruth Huntington of Conn.

Baldwin Arg a chev ermines bet 3 hazel sprigs vert
Crest: a squirrel sejant or holding a hazel sprig vert
Motto: Je n'oublierais pas
Tomb of Samuel Baldwin in St. Leonards, Md.? Notepaper F. Winthrop coll. has crest: a lion couchant and "Je n'oublierai pas"
Bookplate Miss Mary Baldwin Hamill, Princeton, N. J., by W. H. Ritter. Ancest. Rec. & Portr., vol. I, p. 80

Balfour Quartered by Bethune

Ball A bend bet 2 lions ramp hold a ball in the dexter paw
Crest: a lion ramp holding a ball
Seals of Richard, David, and Hannah Ball, Lancaster, Va., 1695. Wm. & Mary Quar., Jan. 1893, p. 119

Ball Arg a lion pass guard sa. On a chief sa 3 six-pointed stars
Motto: Coelum tueri
Joseph Ball's coat, framed. Mt. Vernon, Va.

Ball [Az] a chev bet 3 fire balls sa fired ppr
Crest: a dexter hand erect [or] holding a fire ball of the field
Bookplate Joseph Ball, Phila., 1790, partner of Robert Morris

Ball Arg a lion pass sa, on a chief of the second, 3 mullets of the first
Crest: out of the clouds ppr a demi-lion ramp sa, powdered with estoiles arg, holding a globe or
Motto: Coelumqui tueri
Painting on vellum brought to Va. by Wm. Ball, who d. in 1680. Crozier's Va. Heral., pp. 86, 87

Ball [Az] a lion pass sa, on a chief of the 2d 3 estoiles of 6 points of the first
Crest: a stag courant
Motto: Semper caveto
Bookplate Flamen Ball of N. Y. P. R. Maverick, sculp.

Ball *See also* Ballord

Ballagh Quart 1 and 4: Az on a bend engr or 3 martlets gu; 2 and 3: Az 3 torches erect ppr
Crest: an estoile of 6 points [or]
Motto: Toujours propice
Supporters: See Dawson, Viscount Cremorne, in Burke
Notepaper Mrs. James Henry Ballagh (Lillian Acer), 2010 Fifth Ave., Los Angeles, Cal.

Ballord Arg a lion ramp sa. On a chief az 3 stars of 6 points or
Crest: a lion's head couped
Bookplate William Ballord. Ball arms?

Ballou Sa fretty or
Crest: a dexter arm embowed vert holding an inverted cup gu dropping a shower of guttees d'eau
Motto: Tout d'en haut
Framed water color owned by R. A. Ballou, Boston

Balmanno [Arg?] a cross embattled sa
Crest: a dexter hand grasping a short sword in bend
Motto: Perseverando
Bookplate Robert Balmanno, F. S. A. of Brooklyn, N. Y., 1828

Bambridge Impaled by Winterbotham

Bancker Arg a figure 4 (merchant's mark) resting on an ornamented bar gu (called an old merchant's mark)
Crest: two wings expanded gu
Motto: Dieu defend le droit
Bookplate Evert Bancker, Jun; Charles N. Bancker, Phila., Jones, sculp; Evert I. Bancker, Dawkins, sculp; Abraham Bancker, Maverick, sc. (has motto: "Sublimiora petamus")

Bancroft Or on a bend az bet 6 crosses crosslet az 3 garbs in bend
Crest: a garb enclosed by 2 wings
Motto: Dat Deus incrementum
Bookplate —— Bancroft

Bancroft Or on a bend az bet 6 crosses crosslet of the 2d, 3 garbs of the first
Hotel Bancroft, Worcester, Mass. On china, with this confident motto: Deus dat incrementum

Bancroft Or on a bend az bet 6 crosses crosslet of the 2d, 3 garbs of the first
Framed. Formerly owned by Capt. Edmund Bancroft of Pepperell (1726–1806). Gen. Wm. A. Bancroft, Cambridge, Mass., 1900

Bangs Az on a cross arg bet 4 fleurs-de-lis 5 pheons gu
Crest: a man's face with a fleur-de-lis above his cap
Bookplate Francis Reginald Bangs, Boston

Banister Arg a cross flory sa. In chief a label of 3 points gu
Crest: a demi-lion ramp holding a cross of the field
Bookplate John Banister (d. 1787), a Revolutionary soldier, member Continental Congress

Banks Sa a cross engr or bet 4 fleurs-de-lis [arg]
Crest: a griffin holding a cross patée fitchée
Motto: Nullius in verba
Bookplate?

Banning *See* Binney

Barber Gu a St. Andrew's cross sa on another or (?)
Arms on automobile of Harry E. Barber, Dorchester, Mass.

Barberie Arg a chev bet 3 griffin's (eagle's?) heads erased [or]
Crest: a griffin's head erased
Seal of P. Barberie, N. Y. N. E. Reg., Jan. 1877, p. 56

Barclay Arg a chev bet 3 crosses pattée [gu]
Crest: a dagger erect
Motto: Crux Christi nostra corona
Bookplate Andrew Barclay, signer of Colonial bills of credit, 1759. E. Gallaudet, sc. Also memorial tablet to Col. Thomas Barclay, St. Paul's chapel, Broadway, N. Y. (no motto) He d. 1830. It is said the field is gu, the chev or, the crosses arg. "The chev should be arg." N. Y. G. B. Record, vol. 1, p. 21

Barbey Quart 1 and 4: Vert a masoned arch on which is a lion ramp bet 2 towers; 2 and 3: Per fess gu and (?) in chief a fish
Notepaper F. Winthrop coll., N. Y., 1885, in Bos. Ath.

Bard Sa on a chev bet 10 martlets contournées 4, 2 in chief and 1, 2, 1 in base arg 5 pellets
Crest: a lion's gamb holding a horse's leg erased sa
Motto: Fidite virtuti
Bookplate John Bard, Jr., M. D., and Samuel Bard, M. D., phys. to Geo. Washington

Barker Arg on a fess bet 3 crosses crosslet fitchée 3 cinquefoils
Motto: Liberte toute entiere
Bookplate E. H. L. Barker, Providence, R. I.

Barker Az 5 escallops in the form of a cross [or]
Crest: on a rock sa a hawk close or
Motto: In deo sola salus
Bookplate John Barker. Also at Wappaoolah, St. John's, Berkely Co., S. C., Mr. Nathaniel Heyward's place. Seen by L. Park, 1923

Barker Barry of 9 or and sa over all a bend gu
Crest: out of a ducal cor or a spread eagle sa membered gu
Framed water color owned by Mrs. Henry H. Edes, Cambridge, Mass. "T. W. pinx, 1902"

Barker Per fess nebulé az and sa 3 martlets 1 and 2 or a canton erm
Crest: a greyhound sejant with leash
Motto: Semper constans et fidelis
Notepaper F. Winthrop coll., N. Y., 1885, in Bos. Ath.

Barker Impaled by Shirley

Barksdale Major George A. Barksdale of Va. used the arms of Peyton, baronet of the Isle of Ely, on his bookplate. *See* Burke

Barlow Sa a double-headed eagle arg armed or
Crest: an eagle of the field erased or
Framed water color. A. E. Bodwell, 18 Tremont St., Boston, artist and owner

Barnard Arg a bear ramp [sa] muzzled or
Crest: a demi-bear couped [sa] and muzzled or
Motto: Foedere non vi
Engr. on flagon from Rev. John Barnard, 1748–49, First Church, Marblehead, Mass. Old Sil. Am. Ch., p. 262

Barney Gu a cross engr humettée erm
Crest: seven ostrich feathers
Bookplate Charles Norton Barney

Barnwell Erm a bordure engr gu
Crest: from a plume of 5 ostrich
feathers or, gu, arg, vert and arg a fal-
con rising of the last
Motto: Malo mori quam foedari
Seal of Col. John Barnwell, who came
to S. C. in 1701 from Dublin, Ire.
Ancest. Rec. & Portr., vol. 1, p. 378

Barradall On a bend 3 pheons [or
fleurs-de-lis] an annulet for diff. Impaling: [Az] 3 chev in base interlaced [or]
a chief of the last (Fitzhugh)
Tomb of Edward Barradall, attorney-
general of Va., who d. 1743. Bruton
Churchyard, Williamsburg, Va. Seen
by L. Park, 1922. Wm. & Mary
Quar., Oct. 1893, p. 79

Barrell Erm on a chief sa 3 talbots
heads erased arg [of the first?] an
annulet or in the center point for diff
Crest: a talbot's head of the field
Mottoes: Not always so. Indure,
but Hope
Bookplate Joseph Barrell, 1739-1804,
Boston merchant. Also in a window
at Mrs. C. H. Joy's, 86 Marlboro St.,
Boston, the chief az

Barrell Quart 1 and 4: Erm on a chief
az 3 talbots' heads erased arg (?); 2 and
3: Fitch (?)
Arms cut on vellum for Joseph Barrell in 1774, 1775, by his niece "Ruthy"
(Mrs. or Miss) Andrews. Is it still in
existence? See Heral. Jour., vol. 3, p.
45. A framed water color at York Co.
Jail, Maine, appears to be: Erm on a
chief vert 3 talbots' heads erased erm

Barrell See also Williams

Barrett Erm on a fess [gu] ? lions ramp
[or]
Crest: a lion passant
Tombstones Col. James Barrett, who
d. 1779, aged 69, and Col. Nathan
Barrett, who d. 1791. Arms of Blyth
family? From a drawing by Miss
Elizabeth Barrett of Concord, 1922.
Hill Burying Ground, Concord, Mass.
See Heral. Jour., vol. 3, pp. 155-6.
Dr. H. M. Buck says arms of George
Blyth, sec. to Council at York. See
Glover MS. Also similar to Person

Barrett Or a chev engr gu bet 3 bears'
heads sa muzzled or
Crest: a griffin segreant reguard gu
On automobile Harry W. Barrett,
28 Greystone Rd., Malden, Mass.

Barrett Erm on a fess az 3 lions ramp
Crest: a lion couchant
Engr. on silver tray by John Coburn.
Barrett Wendell, owner, Boston, 1920.

Also on a silver mug, impaling (Gerrish)*: Gu a pheon point down bet 3
escallops. John Barrett of Portsmouth, N. H., married Sarah, sister of
Col. Joseph Gerrish. Their son,
Samuel, owner about 1761, had dau.
Anna, who married Isaac Green, the
next owner (I. A. G.). Crest: a lion
passant

Barrett Impaled by Wendell

Barrington Arg 3 chev gu the upper
charged with a crescent. A label of 3
points az
Crest: a Capuchin friar affronté ppr
couped below the shoulders habited
[paly of 6 arg and gu on his head a cap
or]
Bookplate George Barrington

Barrington Quartered by Lunsford

Barron Gu a chev arg bet 3 garbs or
Crest: an eagle with wings expanded
sa
Colored framed arms at Mrs. Edward
R. Baird's, 544 Pembroke Ave., Nor-
folk, Va. Seen by L. Park, 1922

Barry [Az] an eagle displ with 2 heads
[arg] over all on a fess az [properly sa]
2 mullets arg
Crest: a wolf's head erased
Motto: Fortitudine
Seal ring, New York

Bartelot Impaled by Roane

Bartlet Az on a chev flory counter-
flory arg bet 3 doves of the last 3
trefoils slipped gu
Crest: out of a ducal cor or 2 demi-
dragons without wings back to back
az tied with a riband (See Burke)
Arms on porcelain (?) cuff-links in
the family of Mrs. Charles Fairchild,
Boston. Similar arms on automobile
Schuyler S. Bartlett, Wellesley Hills,
Mass.

Bartlett 3 crescents in pale
No crest
Motto: Deo favente cresco
Bookplate —— "Bartlett." Symes
arms?

Bartlett Sa 3 gauntlets pendent [arg]
Crest: a swan [arg] couched, wings
expanded or
Motto: Maturity
Bookplate John Russell Bartlett,
1902

Barton A barry of 3 az or and vert; on
the first a full-rigged ship, on the second
a plow; in base 3 garbs
Crest: a demi-eagle displ holding an
olive branch

---

*No Gerrish arms known. Garnishe
or Gerveis?

Motto: Virtue, liberty, and independence
Bookplate Alexander I. Barton, Phila.

Barton [Arg] 3 boars' heads couped [gu or sa]
Crest: a boar's head
Motto: Fide et fortitudine
Boston Public Library bookplate, 1873. Thomas Pennant Barton

Barton Erm on a fess gu 3 annulets or
Crest: a griffin's head erased
Motto: Fortis est veritas
Parchment brought from England, 1672, by Dr. John Barton to Salem, Mass., bears the arms; now owned by George Dean Phippen of Salem. On gravestone Dr. Thomas Barton, d. 1751, aged 71. Vermont's Amer. Heral., p. 118, 119, 157. Heral. Jour., vol. 4, p. 132

Barton Impaled by Heywood

Barton *See also* Fowler

Bartram Gu on an inscutcheon or bet an orle of 8 crosses pattée arg a thistle head sa
Crest: out of an antique crown or a ram's head arg
Mottoes: J'avance. Foy en Dieu
Bookplate John Bartram, botanist, Phila. Sylvan City, 1883, p. 446

Bassett Or 3 bars wavy gu
Crest: a unicorn's head couped arg
Motto: Pro rege et populo
Tomb of Col. William Bassett, who came to Va. previous to 1665, at Hollywood Cemetery, Richmond, Va. Also silver candlestick. *See* Buck's Old Plate, p. 123. Crozier's Va. Heral., p. 96. *See*, however, Va. Hist. Mag., vol. 23, p. 40

Bassett Impaled by Allen

Batcheldor A double-headed eagle displ
On a wax seal will of John Batcheldor of Va., 1685, at Urbanna. Wm. & Mary Quar., Ja. 1893, p. 121

Bates Sa a fess bet 3 dexter hands arg
Bookplate Albert C. Bates. J. W. Spenceley, sc.
"Arms of Bates of Denton, Co. Sussex"

Bates Sa a fess engr bet 3 dexter hands in bend arg couped at the wrist
In the new (1917) chapel at Ocean Point, Boothbay, Maine. Memorial window given by Lewis G. Wilson for his mother Lucy, daughter of Dr. Geo. Bates

Bathurst Az 2 bars and in chief 3 crosses pattée or
Crest: a horse passant tail and mane displ

Motto: Quod tibi vis alteri feceris
Bookplate Bathurst. *See* Crozier's Va. Heral.

Bathurst Quartered by Courtenay

Batterson Quart 1 and 4: Arg 3 bats, wings sa. On a chief gu a lion pass guard or: 2: Per fess sa and arg a lion ramp counterchanged; 3: Az 3 hunting horns 1 and 2, the first on a pile or
Crest: a bat's wing sa
Motto: Probitas verus honos
Bookplate Rev. H. G. Batterson, D. D., Phila.

Bay Erm a fess purpure. Over all a lion ramp facing the sinister
Crest: a pelican in her piety facing the sinister
Motto: Quo fata ocant
Bookplate John W. Bay, M. D. T. H. Cushman, sc.

Bayard Az a chev or bet 3 escallops arg
Crest: a demi-horse arg
Motto: Honor et justitia manet amicitia florebit semper que
Memorial window to James Asheton Bayard (1799–1880) and Anne Francis, his wife (1802–1864). Old Swedes' Church, Wilmington, Del. James Wilson Bayard, Germantown, has motto on notepaper: Amor, honor, justitia. Zieber's Heral., p. 65

Bayley Per pale gu and az
Bookplate Anselm Bayley

Bayley Impaled by Sherburne

Baynton [Sa] a bend lozengy [arg]
Tombstone Jane (d. 1822) and Rebecca (d. 1825), related to Peter Baynton. Christ Church graveyard, Phila. Also St. Mary's churchyard, Burlington, N. J. Zieber, pp. 39, 44.

Beal Quart 1 and 4: Sa on a chev bet 3 wolves' heads erased or 3 mullets pierced sa; 2 and 3: Gu 6 crosses crosslet fitchée arg 3, 2, 1. On a chief or 3 pellets, the center charged with a fleur-de-lis, the other two charged with a lion pass guard (Boylston)
Crest: a demi-wolf ramp sa holding a tilting spear in pale ppr
Bookplate Boylston Adams Beal of Boston and London. "C. W. S. 1898"

Beal Sa on a chev bet 3 griffins' heads or 3 cinquefoils sa
Crest: a demi-griffin sa holding in pale a tilting spear
Motto: Esse quam videri
Bookplate Thomas Prince Beal, Boston

Beale Sa on a chev bet 3 wolves' heads or 3 mullets arg
Crest: a unicorn's head erased
Motto: Malo mori quam foedari
Bookplate Charles F. T. Beale, Washington

Beale Sa on a chev bet 3 griffins' heads erased arg 3 estoiles gu
Crest: a unicorn's head erased or semee of estoiles gu
Tomb of Capt. Thomas Beale, Jr., at Chestnut Hill, Richmond County, Va., b. 1649, d. 1679. Wm. & Mary Quar., July, 1893, p. 25

Beale Sa on a chev [arg?] bet 3 griffins' heads erased or as many mullets of the first
Crest: a griffin's head erased or
"Wrongly engraved" on a cup in 1770. Given in 1900 to the First Church, Boston. F. H. Bigelow's Hist. Sil., p. 98

Beatty Arg a bee-hive surrounded with bees on the wing, all ppr
Crest: a demi-lion ramp holding a crescent
Bookplate Col. John Beatty, M. D., Princeton, N. J., 1749-1826. Curio, 1888, p. 114

Beck Quart 1: Or a black bird sa; 2 and 3: Sa a mullet of 6 points or; 4: Arg a dolphin hauriant
Crest: a raven ppr bet 2 wings erect [or]
Motto: Ad finem fidelis
Bookplate Francis W. Beck, Portland, Me. Arms of Bec or Beck, Vis. of London, I, p. 59

Beck Sa 2 quills in saltire, points down
Crest: from a ducal cor a child with ruff and sash over shoulder, holding 2 quills
Bookplate Charles Beck, Cambridge, Mass. N[ath.] D[earborn], sc.

Becket Arg a chev vert bet 3 garbs or [gu?]
Crest: a garb or?
Old framed water color "By the name of Becket." Owned by F. S. Whitwell, Boston. His ancestor Nathaniel Silsbee (born 1748) married in 1770 at Hampton Falls, N. H., Sarah Becket. Window, Blake Mem. Chapel, Salem, Mass.

Beckwith Arg a chev bet 3 hinds' heads erased gu
Crest: an antelope ppr in the mouth a branch vert
Motto: Jouir en bien
Silver waiter of Butler family, now in possession of Laurence Washington, has engraved upon it quarterly 1 and

4: "A chev bet 3 hinds' heads"; 2 and 3: A chief indented and a saltire with 3 covered cups (Butler). Crozier's Va. Heral., 1908, pp. 72, 79

Bedell Gu a chev bet 3 escallops arg
Crest: a mailed arm embossed holding a cutlass by the blade
Motto: Nil desperandum
Notepaper F. Winthrop coll., N. Y., 1885, in Bos. Ath.

Bedford [Arg] 3 lions' gambs couped erect within a bordure [engrailed?] [sa]
Crest: a lion's gamb of the field
Gunning Bedford's monument. He d. 1812. Perhaps bear's paws. Market Street churchyard, Wilmington, Del. Rev. Geo. T. Watkins of Durham, N. C., uses for crest: A demi-lion ramp sa murally crowned [or] holding between the gambs a globe [or]. Zieber's Heral., p. 42

Bedlow A fess wavy bet in chief a 3 towered castle and in base a monogram of B and L
Crest: two arms embowed and gloved, hold an anchor
Motto: My hope on high
Bookplate William Bedlow of Bedlow's Island, N. Y.

Bedon Az a chev or (?) bet 3 martlets
Crest: a boar's head couped ppr
Water color in So. Car. Hist. Soc.

Beekman Arg a bend wavy az bet 2 roses [or]
Crest: 2 wings addorsed
Motto: Mens conscia recti
Notepaper F. Winthrop coll., N. Y., 1885, in Bos. Ath.

Beekman Az a running brook, in bend, wavy, arg, bet 2 roses or
Crest: 2 wings addorsed
Motto: Mens conscia recti
On mantle in N. Y. Hist. Soc. of Jas. Beekman's house, 51st St. and 1st Ave. Official document of the immigrant, William Beekman, Gov. of South River, with Peter Stuyvesant, in New Amsterdam. Vermont's Amer. Heral., p. 157

Beeman Or a fox courant. On a chief az a lion ramp. Impaling: Gu 2 lions ramp addorsed [arg] (Rogers?)
Crest: on a crown a lion ramp
Motto: Certamine summo
Bookplate Allen Everett Beeman of Farmington, Conn., and Gardiner, Me. Tiffany engr.

Beere Quartered by Seabury

Belcher Or 3 pales gu a chief vairé [arg and az]
Crest: a greyhound's head erased and gorged
Motto: Loyal au mort

On a portrait of Gov. Jonathan Belcher: G. Phillips pinx. I. Faber, fec. 1724 or 1734. Old State House, Boston. The Governor's own seal on a letter to Secretary Waldron, about 1735, given by Barrett Wendell to the N. H. Hist. Soc., has the above arms and motto: "Loyal jusqu'a la mort." At the top "Labor ipse voluptas"

Belcher Or 3 pales gu. A chief vairé arg and az
Crest: a hound's head erased erm, collared sa and gu
Motto: Loyal au mort
On Price's Plan of Boston, 1769. Copy in Bostonian Soc. Also in a colored window, 3d floor, State House, Boston

Belcher Or 3 pales gu a chief vairé
Crest: a greyhound's head erased erm, with a collar gu and ring (or?)
Arms on Andrew Belcher's seal on his will. Heral. Jour., 1865, vol. 1, p. 125; vol. 2, pp. 62, 177

Belcher Or 3 pales gu a chief vairé arg and az
Crest: a greyhound's head erased erm, gorged gu
Mottoes: Sustine abstine. Loyal au mort
Bookplate Jonathan Belcher (born Boston, 1710), Halifax, N. S. E: Societate medij templi. Another of "J. Bel-Chier" with a label in chief and the motto: Loyal jusqu'a la mort
On canvas, 1886, for 200th anniv. of King's Chapel, Boston. The original hung in the wooden chapel before 1754. Bostonian Society, Boston

Belchier Or 3 pales gu a chief vairé arg and az. Impaling: Gu on a mount vert a castle supported bet 2 lions ramp [or]. On a chief or a tree vert bet 2 mullets az (Kelly)
Crest: a greyhound's head erased erm gorged gu
Mottoes: Sustine absinthe. Loyal au mort
Bookplate William Belchier

Bell Az a chev erm bet 3 bells or
Crest: a falcon with wings expanded erm
Motto: Nec quaerere honorem nec spernere
Tombstone in the Newport, R. I., churchyard (1737) erected to the memory of William Bell. Vermont's Amer. Heral., pp. 41, 157

Bell Az a fess erm bet 3 bells or
Crest: a falcon
Motto: Nec quaerere honorem nec spernere
Bookplate Charles H. Bell, Gov. N. H.

Bell Az 3 church-bells [or?]
Crest: figure of Justice holding sword in dexter and scales in sinister hand
Motto: Honor virtutis prœmium
Bookplate William Bell, N. H.

Bell Sa 3 bells 2 and 1, and 3 estoiles 1 and 2
Crest: an eagle rising
Bookplate John Bell. Also memorial tablet to Isaac Bell and his wife in Trinity Church, N. Y. Motto: Perseverance. See also Mott

Bell Quartered by Williams

Bellet Quartered by Blake

Bellingham Arg 3 bugle-horns sa stringed and garnished or
Crest: a stag's head cabossed arg attired or bet 2 branches vert
Motto: Amicus amico
Seal affixed to deed signed 1650 by William Bellingham, son of Gov. of Mass. M. H. S. Coll., vol. 37. Foster arms? Vermont's Amer. Heral., pp. 41, 157

Bellows [Sa] fretty [or]. On a chev [az] 3 lions' heads erased [of the second]
Crest: an arm embowed and habited pouring from a cup into a dish
Motto: Tout d'en haut
Cut on an obelisk over the grave of Charles C. Bellows, New Ipswich, N. H. He d. 1872

Belmont Per fess erm and gu. In chief a fox's head erased holding a sprig. In base an anchor. Impaling: Az an eagle volant toward the sun
Crest: ostrich feathers
Motto: Sans crainte
Bookplate —— Belmont

Benger Or a cross vert. Over all a bendlet gu
Crest: a cockatrice per pale or and vert with wings expanded counterchanged, combed gu
Benger of Kent. Painted arms in oval frame of period of 1780–1800. Owned by John B. Lightfoot of Richmond, Va. Seen by L. Park, 1922

Benjamin [Or] on a saltire sa 4 annulets [or] pierced sa, the center of the saltire voided and charged with an annulet sa pierced [or]
Crest: on a chapeau flames ppr
Motto: Poussez en avant
Bookplate Chas. H. Benjamin, Purdue Univ., Lafayette, Ind. Some Amer. Coll. Bookplate, 1915, p. 269

Bennet Impaled by Abercrombie

Bennet See also Craig

Bennett [Or] 3 demi-lions ramp [gu]. Impaling: [Az] a lion ramp [or] (Lloyd)
Ancient tomb on Greenberry's Point farm, Anne Arundel Co., Md. Picture in Zieber's Heral., p. 45; correction in Ridgely's Hist. Graves of Md., p. 7

Bennett Or 3 demi-lions ramp gu Impaled by Anne, dau. of Gov. Richard Bennett of Va. and wife of Theoderick Bland of Westover, 1671. Wm. & Mary Quar., Jan. 1894, p. 157

Bennett Impaled by Bland

Bennett *See also* Neale and Newman

Benson Arg on a chev sa a cross pattée arg
Crest: a sun in splendor
Bookplate Arthur F. Benson, N. Y.

Benson Gu a chev bet 3 crosses pattée
Crest: a goat's head erased
Bookplate Edwin N. Benson, Phila.

Benson Or on a saltire sa 4 annulets arg, the crossing voided and charged with an annulet sa (Leeke arms?)
Crest: a chapeau on fire
Motto: Trust in God
Bookplate Charles Coleman Benson, Phila.

Beram Quartered by Leigh

Beresford Quart 1 and 4: Arg a bear erect sa chained and muzzled [or]; 2 and 3: Per chev sa and or 3 pheons counterchanged. A crescent at the center point for diff (Hassell or Hinde?)
Crest: a dragon's head erased [az], pierced through the neck with a broken spear [or], the spear-head [arg] in its mouth
Bookplate Richard Beresford, Charleston, S. C., 1774

Berkeley Gu a chev bet 10 crosses pattée, 6 in chief and 4 in base
Crest: a unicorn's head
Motto: Dieu avec nous
Used by Edmund Berkeley of "Barn Elms," Middlesex Co., Va. Bellet's Some Prom. Va. Fam, vol. 2, p. 378. *See* photo, Va. Mag. of Hist., Jan. 1927, p. 34

Bernard Arg a bear ramp sa muzzled or
Crest: a demi-bear muzzled and collared or
Motto: Bear and forbear
Drawing of shield bearing arms of Bernards of Buckingham on deed o f rental from Capt. Thomas Harwood of Va. and others to Richard Bernard. The plantation rented was in York County and called "Pryor's Plantation." Wm. & Mary Quar., July, 1893, p. 25

Bernard Quart 1 and 4: Arg a bear ramp sa muzzled [or]; 2 and 3: Arg 3 lions' heads erased gu within a bordure engr vert (Winlow, Co. Lincoln). Over all an inscutcheon arg a cross flory az bet 4 Cornish choughs sa (Offley of London)
Crest: out of a ducal cor 4 fruited sprigs vert
Motto: Animus nisi paret imperat
Gov. Sir Francis Bernard, Boston. State House window, 3d floor, Boston. In color

Bernon Az a chev bet in chief 2 mullets or and in base a bear ppr a crescent for diff
Motto: Dieu te garde et regarde
Arms of Gabriel Bernon of R. I. on a bronze shield owned by Mrs. Wm. Ames of Providence

Berry Quart 1 and 4:——3 pales (dark); 2 and 3: Per fess (light and very dark) a fess bet a mullet in chief and 2 cresc in base
Crest: 3 battle axes diverging
Motto: Vincit veritas
Tintype of arms from Eng. forty years ago. Owned by Joseph Berry of Georgetown, Maine, then by Martin Van Buren Berry, b. 1834, then by Mrs. J. M. Everett, Chestnut Hill, Mass. Seen by Dr. H. Bowditch

Berry Vert a cross crosslet or
Crest: from a cor (set with crosses) a goat's head ppr
Framed water color 100 years old, owned by Frank J. Berry, Brookline, Mass., son of Charles P. Berry of Portsmouth, N. H. Seen by Dr. H. Bowditch

Bethune Quart 1 and 4: Az a fess bet 3 mascles or; 2 and 3: Arg a chev sa charged with an otter's head erased of the first (Balfour)
Crest: an otter's head erased ppr
Motto: Débonnaire
Seal on deed of partition of estates of Norden Pedrik, Marblehead (1723). Arms of George Béthune, the immigrant. Vermont's Amer. Heral., pp. 30, 157

Betton Quart 1 and 4: Arg 2 pales sa, each charged with 3 crosses crosslet fitchée [or]; 2 and 3: Sa 3 spear heads arg gutty de sang (Ap Rhys or Morgan?)
Crest: a demi-lion ramp ducally crowned
Motto: Nunquam non paratus
Bookplate Thomas Forrest Betton, Germantown, Pa. Another with an escallop over No. 1 for difference and impaling No. 2

Betts Sa on a bend arg 3 cinquefoils gu
Crest: out of a ducal cor [or] a buck's head [gu] attired [or] gorged [arg]
Bookplate William Betts. C. P. Harrison, sc.

Beverley Erm a rose gu barbed and seeded ppr
Crest: a unicorn's head
The tomb of Ursula (Byrd) Beverley, who d. in 1698, bears Beverley as above impaling Byrd
The will of the first Major Robert Beverley, Middlesex Court House, has a wax seal, "Quarterly arg and gu, a rose counterchanged, barbed vert." William Beverley of Blandfield in 1739 stated "That the arms his father used were red rose seeded and barbed in a field erm, with a unicorn's head for crest and not three bulls' heads." On a bond of William Beverley, 1736, in Essex County Court, there is a wax seal with "Arg a chev sa, on a chief of the second 3 bulls' heads cabossed of the first."
Beverley bookplates bear 3 bulls' heads and chev, but incorrectly.
Discussed in Crozier's Va. Heral., pp. 74 and 75

Bickerton Arg on a chev sa 3 anchors
Crest: a martlet sa
Bookplate Spencer Bickerton of Honolulu

Biddle Arg 3 brackets sa
Crest: "an heraldic tiger" ramp sa ducally gorged
Motto: Deus clypeus meus
Bookplate Arthur Biddle, 1897. Another of Biddle has a bordure sa. Sylvan City, 1883, p. 459

Bidwell Impaled by Nelson

Bigelow Az 3 lozenges 2 and 1 or
Crest: a ram's head couped, charged with 3 lozenges of the field
Bookplate Lewis Sherrill Bigelow. The Marlboro, Mass., Pub. Lib. "Hannah E. Bigelow Fund" bookplate by S. L. Smith has arg 3 lozenges 2 and 1 sa

Biggar Arg a bend az bet 3 mullets gu
Crest: a pelican's head couped ppr
Motto: Giving and forgiving
Notepaper Dr. H. F. Biggar, Cleveland

Bigger Four mullets in fess. On a chief per pale 8 mullets. A mullet in the center point
Crest: crossed swords
Supporters: Eagles erect (?)
Motto: Arma (?) Libertatis
Tombstone of Joseph Bigger, who d. Aug. 28, 1786, aged 64 years. Photo

lent by A. S. Salley, Jr., Columbia, So. Car. Not in Burke.

Bill Erm 2 bills in saltire sa, a chief az on a pale or bet 2 pelicans' heads arg a damask rose gu
Crest: a pelican's head arg
Water color (modern) framed, owned by Mrs. A. L. Bulluck (b. Bill), Cambridge, Mass. Seen by Dr. H. Bowditch, 1925. Family of Willimantic, Conn.

Billings Gu a fleur-de-lis or, a canton arg
Crest: a buck trippant ppr an arrow in its breast
"Wrought by Mrs. Eunice (Minot) Glover, mother of John I. Glover, when 15 years old, b. Sept. 28, 1781. Her mother's maiden name was Eunice Billings." Cross and Kensington stitches. Framed. C. F. Libbie & Co. auction, Boston, Dec. 6, 1915

Bingham The Bingham shield, crest, and motto of the Earl of Lucan, used on a bookplate by George P. Bingham

Bingley *See also* Broadhead

Binney Or 2 bars sa each charged with 2 escallops arg (Banning arms)
Crest: an ostrich holding a key in its beak
Motto: Tiens ta foy
Bookplate Wm. Binney

Bispham Gu a chev arg bet 3 lions' heads erased arg. On a canton or a rose gu [barbed and seeded arg]
Crest: on a chapeau gu a lion ramp with paw on a shield gu
Motto: Sola virtus invicta
Bookplate Wm. Bispham, N. Y.

Blachly Arg a beaver statant and toward the dexter a tree in leaf, the trunk nearly severed, all bet a chief dancettée az charged with 3 escallops and a base vert
Crest: a hawk (?)
Motto: Utere mundo
Bookplate Absalom Blachly of N. Y., 1780, Maverick, sc.

Black Arg a saltire sa a mullet in chief and a cresc in base of the second
Motto: Non crux sed lux
Bookplate Henry Van Deventer Black

Black Arg on a cross sa bet in chief a mullet and escallop and in base an escallop and mullet gu a crescent of the first
Motto: Deus vivat
Bookplate Rt. Rev. Jas. Black, protonotary apostolic and chancellor, Archdiocese of Oregon City, by P. de C. la Rose, 1924

Blackstock [Arg] 3 stumps with growing twigs 2 and 1 sa
Wm. Blackstock, Union Park, Boston, 1860. Framed water color. From Dumfriesshire. His daughter married Samuel Topliff

Blackwell [Arg] a greyhound courant [sa] collared [chequy or and gu and ringed or] on a chief dancettée [sa] 3 bezants
Crest: a demi-hound of the field [collared gu]
Motto: Malo Mori Quam Foedari
Seal in N. Y. Also seal of Joseph of Northumberland Co., Va. See Va. Hist. Mag., vol. 22, p. 438–9

Blackwell Paly of 6 arg and az; on a chief gu, a lion pass guard or
Crest: a swan's head and neck erased arg, ducally gorged or
Seal on letters of John Blackwell, Deputy Gov. of Penn., to William Penn [1688]

Bladen [Gu] 3 chevrons [arg]
Crest: a griffin pass holding an arrow (?) in its beak
Tomb of William Bladen (d. 1718), builder, father of Gov. Thomas Bladen of Maryland. Same arms as Bladen of Glastonbury, Co. Somerset, Eng., although William came from Hemsworth, Yorkshire. St. Ann's churchyard, Annapolis, Md. Zieber's Heral., p. 48

Bladen Impaled by Tasker

Blair Arg on a saltire bet a mullet in chief, a garb in base and 2 cresc in fess 5 mascles of the first
Crest: a stag courant
Motto: Amo probos
Robert Blair from Aghadowey, Ire., to Worcester, Mass., 1718. At Aghadowey "Miss Semple . . . found 11 tombstones with the arms of Blair cut on them." E. W. Leavitt. Bos. Transc., query 4671

Blake Arg a chev sa bet 3 garbs
Crest: on a chapeau gu turned up erm a martlet sa
Motto: Virtus sola nobilitat
Bookplate Francis Blake, Worcester, Mass., and George F. Blake, Jr., of Worcester (no motto). Also shield on cover of Blake Genealogy, 1881

Blake Quart 1 and 4: Arg a chev bet 3 garbs sa; 2: Sa a fess dancettée arg [or?] and in chief 3 fleurs-de-lis arg (Durant); 3: Arg on a chief gu 3 cinquefoils of the field (Bellet of Quemberford)
Crest: on a chapeau gu turned up erm a martlet sa
Motto: Virtus sola nobilitat
Bookplate George Baty Blake, Boston

Blanchard Arg a chev bet 3 crosses crosslet. Impaling: [Az?] a bend bet 6 leopards' faces or
Crest: a lion's head couped ppr
Embr. hatchment owned by R. C. Winthrop, Boston. Not the Blanchard arms recorded

Bland Arg on a bend sa 3 pheons of the field
Crest: out of a ducal cor or a lion's head ppr
Motto: Sperate et vivite fortes
Tombstone of Theodoric Bland, Westover, Va. Impaling: "Or, 3 demi-lions rampant gu (Bennett). See also Richard Bland's seal, M. H. S. Coll., vol. 41. Va. Hist. Mag., vol. 10, p. 373

Blatchford Az 2 bars wavy or. On a chief erm 3 pheons [az?]
Crest: a swan's head and neck erased [sa] bet 2 wings displayed arg
Motto: Providentia sumus
Bookplate Henry S. Blatchford, Cincinnati, Edgcumbe H., James W., and Paul Blatchford. Mary Edgcumbe Blatchford has on a chief or etc. The swan's head is or. This was engr. by Henry Mitchell, Boston

Blatchford Barry wavy of 6 [or] and gu. On a chief az 3 pheons or
Bookplate Thomas W. Blatchford, W. D. Smith, sc.

Blayney Sa 3 horses' heads 2 and 1 erased arg
Crest: a head of the arms bridled or
Embr. hatchment owned by Dr. Wm. Cogswell, Haverhill, Mass. This differs in details from that in Burke

Bleecker Quart below a chief az charged with a sword fessways piercing an ox-shoe (?) 1: 3 flaming hearts gu; 2: a cross crosslet az; 3: 3 guttees sang; 4: A sword, point down, piercing an ox shoe az. Impaling: [Or] on a chev gu bet 3 stags trippant 3 cinquefoils [of the first] (Robinson)
Crest: a stag lodged
Motto: Semper paratus
Bookplate I. Robinson Bleecker. Trested, sculp. Vermont gives: Per pale az and arg on the first 2 chevronels embattled counterembattled or, on the 2d a sprig of roses vert flowered gu (sometimes an oak branch with acorns)

Blight Arg a chev az bet 3 griffins' heads erased
Crest: a stag trippant
Motto: Finis coronat opus
Bookplate Atherton Blight, Phila.

Bliss Arg on a bend double cotised az 3 garbs or
Crest: a garb or
Motto: Quod severis metes

Framed water color by C. A. Hoppin, owned by Mrs. Emma L. Cummings, Shirley, Mass.

Blodgett Per pale erm and erminois an elephant ramp gu. In chief 3 fleurs-de-lis az
Crest: a coronet
Motto: Semper paratus
Water color given to N. E. Hist. Gen. Soc. by Mrs. Wm. Blodgett, Chestnut Hill, Mass.

Bloodgood Or 2 chev erm bet 3 fleurs-de-lis sa
Crest: a dragon's head ch with 2 chev erm
Motto: Dux vitae ratio
Bookplate John Van Schaick Bloodgood, engr. by A. W. Macdonald. Fanshaw arms?

Bloomfield Sa on a chev [or] 3 trefoils slipped. In a canton [or] a spear head rompu [sa]
Crest: a demi-wolf [az] holding a sword erect
Motto: Pro aris et focis
Bookplate [Gov. Joseph] Bloomfield [N. J. 1776]. I. Trenchard, sculp., on a teapot owned by relatives of M. A. de W. Howe in England

Blount [Or] 3 fruited twigs in pale fessways [sa]. Impaling: [Or] 3 chevrons [gu] (Claire)
Crests: 1: sun in splendor; 2: a stag's head cabossed
Seal owned by Mrs. Charles G. Irish of Utica, N. Y., used by her great grandfather Jacob Blount of North Car. Should be 3 bars nebulée?
Bookplate James Blount of Carolina about 1740. Painting owned by Miss Lena Smith, Scotland Neck, N. C.

Blount Or 3 bars nebulée sa (should be Barry nebulée or and sa). Impaling: 3 fleurs-de-lis (Montford?)
Crests: 1: a sun in splendor; 2: feathers
Painting owned by Miss Lena Smith, Scotland Neck, N. C.

Blyth *See also* Barrett

Boardman Erm 3 stringed bows erect 2 and 1
Crest: a mailed hand holding 3 arrows, 2 in saltire, 1 in pale
Motto: Vincit amor patriae
Bookplate David Sherman Boardman, 1768–1864, and Elijah B. Boardman, 1760–1823, U. S. Senator. New Milford, Conn.

Boas Or on a chev az 5 balls sa all bet 2 flaunches or (?). In the dexter chief a galleon sa, in the sin chief a lion ramp gu hold a sheaf of arrows. In base an anchor arg (?)
Crest: out of a ducal cor a demi-lion ramp hold a sheaf of arrows
Motto: Spes anchora vitae
Bookplate Emil Leopold Boas, engr. by E. D. French

Bodfish Or an eagle with two heads displ sa. Impaling: Per fess az and gu an estoile in chief and a fleur-de-lis in base (Gayer?)
Crest: a talbot guardant sejant
Bookplate Rev. Joshua P. Bodfish

Bogart Bet 3 trees an inscutcheon bearing per fess gu and or a lion ramp
Crest: a demi-lion ducally gorged
Motto: Fortitudini juncta fidelitas
Bookplate Bogart of N. Y.

Boker Or an eagle displ crowned and charged with a crescent or within a bordure az charged with 8 fleurs-de-lis
Crest: a swan collared and chained
Motto: Prorsum et sursum
Bookplate Charles S. Boker, M. D., Phila.

Bolles [Az] 3 cups [or] issuing boars' heads [couped arg?]. Impaling: A chev bet 3 swans (Swan?)
Bookplate Elizabeth Quincy Bolles

Bolling [Sa] an inscutcheon erm within an orle of 8 martlets [arg] a mullet in chief for diff
Bookplate Robert Bolling, Esq., Chillowe, Va. The same coat (with no crest) was exhibited in Washington, Oct. 1915, "as an heirloom of the family of Mrs. Galt" during her engagement to marry President Wilson. Randolph impaling Bolling: Va. Hist. Mag., vol. 22, p. 444

Bolling *See also* **Miller**

Bolton 3 bird bolts in tuns 2 and 1 ppr
Crest: a falcon jessed and belled
Bookplate Henry Carrington Bolton of N. Y. (b. 1843), prof. and writer, son of Jackson Bolton

Bolton Arg on a chev [gu] 3 lions statant guard [or], one in bend, 2 in fess, and 3 in bend sinister
Motto: Frange, lege, tege
Carved in slate over door at Pound Hill Place, Shirley, Mass. So carved in nave of Yorkminster. Motto used 31 March, 1292, by John de Bolton of Yorkshire. C. E. Bolton of Cleveland, 1890, used "Nulla dies sine linea"

Bolton [Arg] on a chev gu 3 lions pass guard [or]
Crest: a falcon jessed and belled [or]
Bookplate Robert Bolton, West Chester, N. Y. Also on font in Trinity Chapel, Shirley. Lions should be statant in chapel

Bolton   Arg on a chev or 3 lions ramp
Crest: a demi-dragon ramp
Bookplate W. W. Bolton

Bolton   Sa a falcon close, arg jessed and
belled [or].   In chief a label of 3 points
arg
Crest: a tun fessways ppr pierced by
a bird bolt paleways [or?]
Bookplate Thomas Bolton, N. Y.,
1801

Bolton   Six crosses crosslet fitchée 3, 2,
1.   On a chief 3 bullaces or wild
plums
Crest: a mailed arm with gauntlet
holding an arrow
Motto: Trewe
Notepaper of Mrs. Louis D. Bolton
(Dorothy Gray) of Detroit.   He was
son of Ogden Bolton, Jr., of Bolton
Steel Co., Canton, Ohio, and Jane
Bulley.   His father of Liverpool mar-
ried Charlotte von Mügen.   His father
Thomas of Wooler, Florida, and Chicago
married Frances Lewin

Bond   Arg on a chev sa 3 bezants
Crest: a demi-pegasus az semée of
estoiles or
Motto: Non sufficit orbis
Framed water color owned 1923 by
Misses Emma and Elizabeth Harris,
Holyoke Pl., Cambridge

Bond   Arg on a chev sa 3 [bezants]
Crest: a demi-lion couped
Seal, New York

Bond   Arg on a chev sa 3 bezants
Crest: a demi-Pegasus az winged and
guttée d'or
Signet ring of Phineas Bond, owned
by Travis Cochran, Phila.   Zieber's
Heral., p. 70

Bond   Arg on a chev sa 3 [bezants]
Crest: a lion sejant
Motto: Deus pro videbit
Bookplate T. Bond, surgeon, of Md.,
and Phila., 1712-1784.   Engr. by W.
Henshaw

Bonner   [Quart gu and sa] a cross
pattée quart [erm and or].   On a
chief a sun in splendor [in Burke a
demi-rose streaming rays] bet 2 pelicans
vulning themselves [of the first]
"Samuel Bonner, d. 1804."   Tomb
in Granary Burying Ground, Boston.
Heral. Jour., vol. 2, p. 120.   Capt.
John Bonner made maps

Boone   [Arg ?] on a bend cotised [gu?]
bet 6 lions ramp 3 escallops of the
first (?).   In chief a mullet
Seal of Thomas Boone, Gov. of S. C.
Seen by Dr. E. A. Jones.   Colors not
clear

Booth   Arg 3 boars' heads erect erased
sa
Crest: a demi- St. Catherine ppr
couped at the knees habited arg
crowned or; in the dexter hand a
Catherine wheel, in the sinister a
sword, point downward
Tomb of Thomas Booth of Gloucester Co., Va., impaling Cooke.   He d.
1736, aged 74.   *See* Genealogy.   *Also*
Crozier's Va. Heral., pp. 14, 30

Booth   Arg 3 boars' heads erect and
erased 2 and 1
Crest: a lion passant
Motto: Quod ero spero
On envelope with letter of Edwin
Booth, the actor, to Rufus Coffin, 15
May, 1877

Borland   Barry of 6 arg and sa [some-
times gu] a boar ramp ppr
Crest: a broken tilting spear ppr
Motto: Press through
Seal on will of John Borland (1726).
Vermont's Amer. Heral., p. 158

Bostwick   Sa a fess humettée arg
Crest: on a stump growing and erad-
icated arg a boar's head erased [sa
muzzled or]
Motto: Semper presto servire
Bostock-Bostwick arms used by H.
M. Bostwick of Thaxton, Va.   Used
also by Mrs. W. I. Hayes, Clinton,
Iowa, on notepaper

Boucher   Arg a cross engr gu bet
4 water bougets sa.   Impaling: Or a
cross patée fitchée az.   On a chief of
the second 3 fleurs-de-lis of the first
(Brockman?)
Crest: a man's head collared or,
crowned with a stocking cap
Motto: Linquenda tellus
The arms of Brockman of Beach-
borough, Kent, have sa instead of az.
Water color, framed?

Boucher   Party per pale arg and vert
3 coursing hounds paleways counterchanged
Crest: a demi-man bearded holding
a spear in the dexter hand
Motto: Non vi sed voluntate
Bookplate Jonathan Boucher, 1779,
loyalist clergyman of Va.

Boucher or **Bouchier**   Vert 3 coursing
hounds arg paleways
Crest: a demi-man bearded holding
a spear in the dexter hand
Motto: Non vi sed voluntate
Bookplate Rev. Jonathan Boucher,
Barton and Charles Bouchier

Bourchier   Quartered by Sears

Boudinot   Az a chev bet 2 mullets in
chief and a flaming heart in base or
Crest: a wreath of leaves and berries

Motto: Soli deo gloria et honor
Bookplate [Elias] Boudinot, 1740–
1821. Maverick, sculpt.

Boughton Quartered by Kingdon

Bourne Sa a chev party per pale arg
and or bet 3 griffins' heads erased arg
   Crest: a griffin's head ducally
gorged holding a rose
   Motto: Frangas non flectes
   Bookplate —— Bourne

Boush On a chev bet 3 trefoils slipped
as many mullets
   Engr. on a paten from Maximilian
Boush, 1728. Donation church, Lynn-
haven Parish, Princess Anne Co., Va.
E. A. Jones, Old Sil., p. 141. Col.
Boush was a lawyer

Boush On a chev bet 3 trefoils slipped
as many mullets
   Engr. on a chalice from Capt. Samuel
Boush, 1700. Capt. Boush was the
first mayor of Norfolk, Va. Christ
Church, Norfolk, Va. Old Sil. Am.
Ch., p. 341

Bowditch Arg a fess wavy bet 3 bows
paleways gu
   Crest: 7 arrows [or] 6 in saltire and
one in pale
   Motto: Spes durat avorum
   Seal ring, gold and bloodstone, by
McAuliffe & Hadley, Boston, for William Ingersoll Bowditch, 1920. Also
on furniture. Dr. Vincent Bowditch
first used an English seal so marked.
Dr. Harold Bowditch writes April,
1924, of these arms:
   "First use by N. I. Bowditch, son of
Nathaniel, on title page and covers of
second edition of 'Suffolk Surnames,'
1858 (not used in the first edition, 1857).
The bows are shown contournée, no
doubt an error. The seven arrows of
the crest all cross at one point and are
bound with a scarf with flying ends
   "Second use on third edition
   "Third use by Henry I. Bowditch, son
of Nathaniel, in a memorial window to
memory of son Nathaniel who died in
1863, in Emmanuel Church, Newbury
Street, Boston
   "Fourth use by Henry I. Bowditch
on title page of 'Memorial' to his son,
1865. The bows are shown turned to
the dexter (as they should be)
   I have a brass seal-matrix made for
me in Munich in 1911 showing the arms
with the fess wavy, the three bows, and
the crest as my father used it, as well
as the motto: 'Spes Durat Avorum''

Bowditch Arg a fess wavy bet 3 bows
paleways [gu]. Impaling: Az a fess
arg bet 3 swans rising (Swann)

   Crest: a bow fess ways crossed by
7 arrows [or] 6 in saltire and 1 in pale
   Motto: Spes durat avorum
   Bookplate Ernest William Bow-
ditch, Boston. Also William Inger-
soll Bowditch, by L. S. Ipsen. Also
Elizabeth Swann Bowditch, by L. S.
Ipsen

Bowdoin Az a chev or bet 3 teazels ppr.
Same coat impaled
   Crest: a swan
   Motto: Ut aquila versus coelum
   Slate slab reset in bronze, Granary
Burying Ground, also Bowdoin College
bookplate, both for Gov. James Bow-
doin. Engr. on tea caddy by Moulton,
owned 1922 by Mrs. F. B. Ingraham
of Wellesley, Mass. Also on her
pepper pot by John Edwards marked
$\begin{smallmatrix} M \\ IP \end{smallmatrix}$ Also on 2 wine coolers owned by
Mrs. J. G. Minot. Heral. Jour., vol.
2, p. 135

Bowdoin Quart arg and sa over all a
lion passant guardant
   "By the name of Bowdoin"
   Photograph from a water color by
John Coles, Sr. Imaginary?

Bowen Sa on a chev embattled arg bet
3 fleurs-de-lis or, 2 lions pass counter-
pass gu
   Crest: an eagle holding a fleur-de-lis
and rising from a ducal cor
   Bookplate Thomas Barton Bowen

Bowers Az 3 bulls' heads cabossed or
   Crest: an eagle rising, brown
   Framed water color, old. "By the
name of Bowers" and palm branches
(By Coles?). Miss Ellen A. Stone,
Lexington, Mass.

Bowes Erm 3 bows in fess [gu stringed
sa]. On a chief az a swan [ppr] bet
two leopards' faces [or]
   Crest: a demi-lion ramp hold 2
arrows in saltire, points down
   Bookplate —— Bowes

Bowie Arg on a bend sa 3 buckles or
   Crest: a demi-lion az, holding in the
dexter paw a dagger
   Motto: Quod non pro patria
   Old seal owned by John Bowie Gray
of "Travellers' Rest," Stafford Co.,
Va. Seal ring of Rev. W. Russell
Bowie, Richmond, Va., 1923

Bowie Quart 1 and 3: [Arg] on a bend
sa 3 buckles [or]; 2 and 4: Gu a cross
engrailed or bet 4 fleurs-de-lis [arg]
(Ashurst)
   Crest: an eagle rising from 5 curled
ostrich plumes
   Motto: Numine
   Bookplate Richard Ashurst Bowie,
Phila.

Bowlen   Quartered by Lewis

Bowles   *See also* Lewis

Bowly   Arg a chev or bet 3 lapwings' heads erased ppr (?)
Crest: a head of the shield
Water color in So. Car. Hist. Soc.

Bowman   Arg two bows in saltire [gu] stringed [or]
Motto: Quondam his vicimus armis
Notepaper Sarah Bowman Van Ness, Va. and Boston

Bowman   Or a chev arg bet 3 stringed bows paleways az
Crest: a quiver of arrows hung on a branching stump
Motto: Fenem respice
Bookplate Charles D. Bowman

Boyd   [Arg] a fess chequy [gu and or]
Crest: a falcon feeding
Arms a stone inlay, now cracked. North Burying Ground, Portsmouth, N. H.   George Boyd's altar tomb

Boyd   Az a fess chequy arg and gu
Crest: a dexter hand erect issuing out of the wreath pointing with the thumb and two fingers [ppr]
Motto: Confido
Bookplate Samuel John Boyd, Portland, Maine, 1808.   *See* Boyd of Kilmarnock in Burke

Boyd   Quart 1 and 4: Arg a fess chequy gu and or; 2 and 3 sa: A chevron erm bet 3 six-pointed estoiles arg (Brewster)
Tapestry hatchment, signed "Submit Boyd," daughter of Hon. Geo. Boyd of Portsmouth, N. H., and his wife, Jane Brewster.   Barrett Wendell, owner, Portsmouth, N. H., 1910. Framed

Boylston   Gu 6 crosses crosslet fitchée arg 3, 2, 1, on a chief or 3 pellets, the center charged with a fleur-de-lis, the other 2 each with a lion pass guard
Crest: a lion pass guard holding a cross crosslet of the field
Motto: Libertatem, amicitiam, retinebis et fidem
Bookplate John Adams, 1735–1826. Charles Francis Adams, 1807–1886, had the same bookplate with the motto: Crucem fer animose.   John Quincy Adams used a coat with the pellets not charged.   Bookplate Doctor Boylston, founder of the Boylston Medical Library, Cambridge, has these arms

Boylston   Quartered by Adams and Beal

Boys   Impaled by Read

Bozman   Arg a fess gu bet 3 eagles displ sa   (Leeds arms)
Crest: a staff raguly fessways vert, thereon a cockatrice

Motto: Sine virtute vani sunt honores
Bookplate John Leeds Bozman, Esq., of the Middle Temple, Maryland, b. 1757, d. 1823.   Copperplate owned by Mrs. G. W. Maslin of Princess Anne, Md., 1924.   Also John Leeds Kerr of Talbot Co., Md., 1780–1844

Brackett   Sa 3 garbs
Crest: a unicorn's head erased
Bookplate —— Brackett

Bradbury   Sa a chev erm bet 3 buckles tongues hanging down arg
Crest: a dove volant fretty [gu] holding in the beak a slip of barberry [vert] fructed [gu]
Gravestone Horace Dennison Bradbury, 1837–98, Mt. Auburn, Mass.

Bradford   Arg on a fess sa 3 bucks' heads erased or
Crest: a buck's head of the field
Motto: Virtus mille scuta
Bookplate Charles F. Bradford, Roxbury, Mass.

Bradford   Arg a wolf's head erased sa bet 3 hunting horns sa stringed [or]
Crest: a peacock's head ppr hold in the mouth a snake [vert] entwined about the neck
Bookplate George H. Bradford, 1899

Bradford   Quartered by Hoskins

Bradford   Quartered by Hodges

Bradley   Gu a chev arg bet 3 boars' heads couped or
Crest: a boar's head of the field
Motto: Liber ac sapiens esto
Arms on silver tankard owned by Dr. Coleman of Amherst.   His first wife was Sally Beecher Bradley, daughter of Eliphalet, son of Stephen of New Haven, Conn.   Same arms on a brass seal owned by Joseph Bradley, Fairfield, Conn.   Ex libris John Dorr and Frances Kales Bradley, W. S. sc., 1900; also Richards Merry and Amy Aldis Bradley, with the crest as above

Bradshaw   Quart 1 and 4: Gu 2 bends or; 2 and 3: Arg 2 lions (?) ducally gorged and chained.   On an inscutcheon sa a wolf ramp and in chief 3 estoiles [or] (Wilson)
Crest: a stag at gaze under a tree fructed ppr
Motto: Tune cede malis
Bookplate Thomas Bradshaw, Esq., Va.

Bradstreet   Arg a greyhound pass gu, on a chief sa 3 crescents or
Crest: an arm in armor embowed, the hand grasping a scimitar all ppr
Motto: Virtute et non vi

Seal of Simon Bradstreet, governor of Mass., 1679. Also on embroidery, N. E. Hist. Gen. Reg., vol. 8, p. 313. Perhaps owned, 1924, by Samuel Bradstreet of Marshfield. F. S. Whitwell of Boston has a pincushion with the arms in pins, dated 1772, and done for [Rev.] I[saac] S[tory] and R[ebecca] S[tory] his wife. She was a Bradstreet

Bradway *See* Phipps

Bragdon Barry of 10 arg and gu, over all a lion ramp crowned or
Crest: a lion's head erased gouttée gu (?)
Framed water color York (Maine) Jail. Brandon arms

Branch Quartered by Cabell

Brandford Az on a chev bet in chief 2 eagles rising and in base a lion pass all or 3 sprigs of oak fructed vert
Crest: an eagle rising or, a sprig of the arms in the dexter claw
Framed water color owned by Mrs. H. W. Montague, W. Cedar St., Boston, daughter of Jane Rebecca Brandford and Rev. Julius Waterbury. Rebecca's father John was desc. from William of London and Barbadoes, 1757

Brasher Arg 2 bars wavy gu on a chief of the 2d a rowel of 6 points
Crest: a portcullis surmounted by a demi-angel with wings expanded
Motto: Beata Domus, custodita sic cuja Deo, Domino est.
Bookplate Henry Brasher. Maverick, sc. (of N. Y.?)

Brattle [Gu] a chev engr [or] bet 3 battle axes erect [arg]
Engr. on baptismal basin from Rev. William Brattle, 1716–17, First Parish Church, Cambridge, Mass. Old Sil. Am. Ch., p. 109. On cover of "An Acct. of Some Desc. of Capt. Thos. Brattle," 1867

Brattle Gu a chev [sometimes engrailed] or bet 3 battle axes in pale arg
Seal of Thomas Brattle, for 20 years treas. Harvard College, d. 1713. Edward used the Smith arms. Erm a mullet bet 3 plates (N. E. Reg., Jan. '77, p. 57). Vermont's Amer. Heral., pp. 103, 158

Bray [Az] a chev bet 3 eagles legs erased a la Cuisse [sa] armed [gu]
Crest: an ounce ppr, tail bet legs
Tomb of Col. David Bray in Bruton churchyard, Williamsburg, Va. He d. 21 Oct., 1717, aged 52 and left wife, Judith, and son, David. Seen by L. Park, 1922

Brayton Az 2 chev bet as many mullets or
Bookplate Elizabeth Hitchcock Brayton. "J. W. Spenceley, Boston, 1901"

Brazer Gu a bend or bet 3 annulets arg
Crest: a dove with olive branch in her bill volant above other twigs
Motto: Try
Bookplate John Brazer, Salem, Mass.

Brearly Arg a cross potent gu. In the dexter point a fleur-de-lis gu
Crest: a demi-lion ramp gu
Motto: Honor virtutis praemium
Bookplate (old) David Brearly, Trenton, N. J.

Breck Gu on a chief per bend sinister indented or and arg 4 hurts 2 and 2
Engr on caudlecup, "the Joseph Hunt Breck family sugar bowl," made by Geo. Hanners (1696–1740) and marked ᴮ· Owned by Cleveland ɪₛ Museum. Arms said to have been inherited from Rev. Robt. Breck, Springfield, Mass., (1713–1784) had torteux instead of hurts and for crest: a dexter arm erect holding a sword. Sam. Breck's pamphlet "Notes," Omaha, 1887. Seen by Dr. Harold Bowditch

Breed Sa a two-tailed lion ramp arg
Bookplate C. Breed

Brent
Geo. Brent to brother Robert pieces of plate to have arms engraved thereon. Geo. was of Woodstock, Va., d. 1700. Va. Hist. Mag., vol. 18 ,p. 321

Brent Quartered by Dering

Brereton Arg 2 bars sa
Crest: out of a ducal cor a bear's head [or muzzled sa?]
Bookplate J. A. Brereton, Washington, D. C.

Brett Arg a lion ramp within an orle of crosses crosslet fitchée gu
Crest: on a chapeau a lion pass gu
Tomb of Catharyna, widow of Capt. Roger Brett, at Fishkill, N. Y., where she d. 1764. Modern tablet. He brought over the arms on a pewter plaque. Brett Geneal., 1915

Brewer Gu 2 bends wavy or, a chief vairé arg and az, a martlet for diff
Crest: a mermaid holding a comb and mirror
Motto: Memor et fidelis
Bookplate Gardner Brewer, b. 1806

Brewster Az a chev erm bet 3 estoiles of 8 points arg
Motto: Fortune, infortune, une fort une
Bookplate Anne M. H. Brewster

Brewster Az a chev erm bet 3 estoiles of 8 points arg
Crest: a leopard's head erased
Mottoes: Verite soit ma garde. Liberty above all things
Bookplate Benj. H. Brewster, Phila., Atty.-General. On Jessie Brewster's bookplate the crest is sa bezantée

Brewster Sa a chev erm bet 3 stars of 6 points [arg]
Crest: a bear's head (?) erased az
Motto: Verite soyez ma garde
Notepaper Mrs. Lucy H. Smith, Green St., Northampton, Mass. Framed water color Miss Ida B. Reed, Boston

Brewster Quartered by Boyd

Bridge Az a chief gu over all a bend engr sa charged in the dexter point with a chaplet [or]
Crest: two wings endorsed, arg; on each a chev engr sa charged with a chaplet [or]
Motto: Post hominem animus durst
Bookplate James Bridge, lawyer, Maine

Bridgen Az an arched and embat wall bet 3 sea lions or
Crest: a demi-sailor hold anchor and sphere
Motto: Probitate et industria
Bookplate Charles Bridgen

Bridgman Sa 6 plates 3, 2, 1. On a chief arg a lion pass of the first membered gu
Crest: a lion ramp arg holding in the paws a laurel wreath ppr
Motto: Nec timide nec temere
Framed water color owned by Rev. Howard A. Bridgman, Shirley, Mass., inherited from his father at Northampton, Mass.

Bridgman Impaled by Moat

Brigden Az a bridge of arches embattled at top in fess arg masoned sa bet 3 sea lions pass or
Crest: "a demi-mariner ppr habited in russet, round the waist a sash and on the head a cap gu. In the dexter hand a sphere held out or, the sinister arm resting on an anchor of the last"
Motto: Porbitate et industria
Bookplate Charles Brigden. Prob. Maverick, sc.

Briggs Quart 1 and 4: Gu 3 bars gemelles or, a canton sa; 2 and 3: Sa an estoile of 8 points or bet 2 flaunches or (Hobart)
Crest: a pelican vulning herself
Motto: Virtus est dei
Bookplate Henricus Briggs, S. T. D.

Briggs *See also* Brigham

Brigham Arg a crocus (?) with two buds proper, over all a saltire invected vert (Briggs arms)
Crest: out of a ducal cor 3 ostrich feathers
Motto: In cruce salus
Bookplate Wm. Tufts Brigham

Bright Sa a fess arg bet 3 escallops or
Crest: "a dragon's head gu vomiting flames ppr collared and lined or"
On cover of "The Brights of Suffolk . . . Henry Bright, Jun., of Watertown"

Brightley Or on a fess bet 3 boars pass az 3 annulets of the first (Hooper arms)
Crest: a boar's head erased az charged with 6 bezants 1, 2, 3
Motto: Cor unum, via una
Bookplate Frank Frederick Brightley, Phila.

Brimage Gu a chev embat or bet 3 helmets ppr. Impaling: Sa a leg couped at the thigh in armor bet 2 broken spears erect [or] headed [arg] (Gilbert)
Crest: out of a ducal cor an armed arm ppr holding in the gauntlet a sword all ppr
Motto: Deus dux certes
Bookplate William Brimage, perhaps the judge of Edenton, N. C. Owned by W. E. Baillie, Bridgeport, Conn.

Brinckerhoff Arg in base the sun's rays behind 3 hills az
Crest: 2 wings spread
Motto: Constans fides et integritas
Brinckerhoff bookplate, N. Y.

Brinley Per pale sa and or a chev bet 3 escallops counterchanged, all within a bordure arg charged with 8 hurts
Crest: an escallop gu
Seal of Francis Brinley of Newport, R. I., from Datchett, Co. Bucks. Whitmore's Elem. of Her., p. 88. In King's Church, Newport. The same arms without bordure or crest appear on the monument to Nathaniel Sylvester, Shelter Island, Long Island, N. Y. *See* Warner Papers, vol. 1, p. 48 (R. I. Hist. Soc.), 1661

Brisbane Sa a chev chequy or and gu bet in chief 2 cushions of the 2d and in base a garb of the last
Motto: Dabit otia deus
Used by James Brisbane of Charleston, S. C. Will, dated Oct. 25, 1821, of Wm. Brisbane, Charleston, mentions "watch seal with family coat of arms." S. C. Hist. and Gen. Mag., vol. 14, pp. 117, 132

Brisbane Sa a chev chequy [or and gu] bet in chief 2 pillows and in base a garb
Crest: a stork's head erased, holding in the beak a serpent entwined about the neck
Motto: Dabit otia deus
Bookplate William Brisbane

Britton Quartered by Cabell

Broadhead Erm a lion ramp collared and chained [or?]. In chief 2 eagles displ gu
Crest: a lion of the field holding a shield erm charged with an eagle displ gu
Bookplate Theodore Henry Broadhead, Esq. Another quarterly 1 and 4 as above; 2 and 3: Three mountain peaks; over all on a shield arg 2 bars sa, on a canton sa a pheon arg (Bingley)

Brockett Or a cross flory sa
Crest: a stag lodged [sa] ducally gorged and chained [or]
Motto: Crux mea lux
Bookplate Edward J. Brockett, N. J.

Brockman Impaled by Boucher

Brodnax Or 2 chev gu on a chief of the second 3 cinquefoils arg
Crest: out of mural crown arg a griffin's head or, winged and collared gu, charged with 3 cinquefoils arg
William Brodnax, who d. 1727, brought the family arms; also a seal with his arms. Crozier's Va. Heral., pp. 75 and 76

Bromfield Sa on a chev arg 3 broom sprigs vert; on a canton or a spear's head az embrued gu
Crest: a demi-tiger az, armed and tufted or, holding erect a broken sword arg, hilted or
Seal of Edward Bromfield, 1699, who came to Boston in 1675. Vermont's Amer. Heral., p. 158. Her. Jour., vol. 1, p. 187

Bromfield Impaled by Phillips

Brookings Gu 3 pitchers 2 and 1 or
Memorial tablet to Richard Brookings of Maryland, 1807–1852, desc. of Charles Broquin, 1761, in New Eng. Hist. Geneal. Soc., 9 Ashburton Place, Boston

Brooks Arg a bridge gu over a brook [az?] on the bridge an embattled tower vert flagged gu
Crest: a mailed sinister arm embowed, holding a scimitar
Motto: Sustinare
Bookplate Francis Brooks. Also of Abijah Brooks, 1752–1829, of Stratford, Conn. R. Brunton, sc. Bates's Early Conn. Engr., p. 16

Brooks Az a bridge of 3 arches chequy charged with 3 pellets. On the bridge an embattled tower purpure charged with 3 pellets, a pennant flying
Crest: a mailed arm emb, holding a scimitar
Motto: Sustinere
Bookplate Benj. N. S. Brooks. Doolittle, fec.

Brooks [Gu?] a castle arg standing in water [az]
Crest: an armed arm holding a cutlass. These appear to be the Rawson arms with "Brooks" engraved underneath
Engraved on the side of a Saltonstall tankard. Miss Elizabeth H. Brooks, owner

Brooks Or 8 fleurs-de-lis 3, 2, 3
Motto: Start in time
Bookplate James C. Brooks, C. P. Gray, Oct. 1905, A. W. Macdonald, engr.

Brooks Quart 1 and 4: Sa an estoile of 8 points arg; 2 and 3: Arg a pine tree
Crest: a broken ship, sails set
Bookplate I. Hobart Brooks, Boston

Broome Sa on a chev [or] 3 sprigs of broom vert
Crest: a demi-eagle [or] wings sa, in the beak a sprig of broom vert
Engr. on silver tankard in Met. Mus. of Art, N. Y., and inscribed S. P. B.

Broughton Arg 2 bars gu on a canton of the last a cross of the first. Impaling: Gu an eagle displ double-headed arg on a chief or a rose of the first bet 2 martlets (not so drawn) sa (Atkinson)
Crest: a sea-dog's head couped [gu] eared and finned arg
Bookplate

Brown Az 3 bucks trippant or
Crest: a stag's head erased
Motto: Nec timeo nec sperno
Bookplate Harold Winthrop Brown

Brown Arg 3 pheonix rising from the flames. Impaling: Gu 3 fleurs-de-lis arg on a chief or 3 hearts gu
Crest: a pheonix rising
Motto: Toujours loyal
Bookplate John Lewis Brown, Jr.

Brown Arg a two-headed eagle displ sa. Impaling: Or on a chief sa 3 crescents or (Preston)
Crest: a griffin' head erased
Motto: Fortiter et fideliter
Bookplate John Mason Brown

Brown Az 3 stags trippant ppr
Crest: a buck's head erased ppr [attired or?]
Motto: Nec timeo nec sperno
Bookplate Elisha Rhodes Brown. Also of Harold Winthrop Brown

Brown Gu a chev or bet 3 lions gambs arg on a chief or an eagle displ sa a bordure or
Crest: a griffin's head erased
Motto: Gaudeo
Bookplates John Carter Brown and John Nicholas Brown, R. I. Also seal ring of the latter. Also on façade of Jno. Carter Brown Library, Providence, with ermine symbols instead of gambs. Arms used also on Brown residence

Brown Sa 3 bends gemelles bet 3 lions pass
Crest: an eagle displ
Motto: Patria cara, carior libertas
Bookplate David Paul Brown, Phila. C. P. Harrison, sc.

Browne A lion ramp debruised by a bend charged with a cross
Crest: possibly a mascle. Later a demi-lion ramp was used
Seal of James Browne of Plymouth, 1668, son of John, on a deed. (Life, by Geo. Tilden Brown, p. 9.) Similar to Browne of Cheshire. Seal owned 1920 by Col. Cyrus P. Brown of St. Paul, Minn.

Browne Arg on a bend [sa] double cotised [of the same] 3 eagles displ of the field
Crest: an eagle of the field
Engr. on flagon from Hon. Samuel Browne, 1731, First Church, Salem, Mass. Old Sil. Am. Ch., p. 421
Bookplate I. Coffin Jones Brown, but the eagle of the crest has 2 bends sa in each wing. Also on two-handled cup from Col. Samuel Browne of Salem, 1731, to Harvard College (Curio, 1888, p. 21). Also on tray made by Hurd, owned by Mrs. Lucy T. Richardson, Jamaica Plain, Mass. Seen by L. Park, 1923

Browne Erm on a bend gu 3 lions ramp or
Crest: a griffin's head
Wax seal on will of Buckner Browne of Essex County, Va., probated at Tappahannock, 19 Aug., 1735. Wm. & Mary Quar., Jan. 1894, p. 157

Browne Gu a chev arg bet 3 lions gambs. On a chief arg an eagle displ sa
Crest: a lion's gamb
Bookplate A. G. Browne, Jr.

Browne Gu on a chev bet 3 leopards' faces or 3 escallops az
Crest: a cubit arm vested gu [hand gu also] holding erect a dagger arg hilted or enfiled with a face of the shield
Very old hatchment painted on wood 20 x 20 inches owned by Harry

Reed Draper, Ayer, Mass. His g. g. mother was Ruth Browne, desc. of Dea. Wm. Browne of Sudbury, Mass. Thos. and Rev. Edmund were his contemporaries there

Browne Gu on a chev arg bet 3 leopards' faces of the same 3 escallops ppr
Crest: a cubit arm habited gu holding a sword piercing a leopard's face through the neck
Oval water color (old), 3 x 2½ in., owned by Thomas Browne, Sr., of Portland, Me., 1790. Done in England. Now owned (1915) by Herbert Browne, 66 Beacon St., Boston. Another water color (abt. 1850), 8 x 5 in. framed

Browne Quart 1 and 4: Sa 3 mallets arg; 2 and 3: Per bend arg and sa 3 mascles in bend (Browne)
Crest: a demi-stork with wings expanded and neck nowed ppr
Motto: A prendre amourir
Bookplate Edward Ingersoll Browne, Boston. See Heral. Jour., vol. 4, p. 26

Browne (?) Sa 3 lions pass in bend bet 2 cotises (?)
Crest: a griffin's head erased vert (?)
Very old canvas hatchment owned 1923 by Misses Emma and Elizabeth Harris, Holyoke Pl., Cambridge. Benjamin Lynde married Mary Browne of Salem. Ancestors of the Harrises

Browne Sa 3 lions pass in bend bet 2 double cotises arg
Crest: a buck's head erased ppr attired and ducally gorged or
Motto: Suivez raison
Bust of Rev. Marmaduke Browne in Newport, R. I., burying ground, with arms at head of inscription

Browne Quartered by Lynde and Pownall

Brownell Erm on a chev cotised sa 3 escallops [arg]
Crest: out of a ducal cor a triple plume of ostrich feathers, 5, 4, 3
Motto: Vi et virtute
Bookplate Alfred Smith Brownell. E. B. Bird, des.

Bruce Or a saltire and chief gu
Framed painting owned by Mrs. Louis C. Arthur, Greenville, N. C.

Bruce See also Risley

Bruen Quart 1 and 4: Arg an eagle displ sa; 2 and 3: Or a chev sa bet 3 lions' faces
Crest: "a fisherman [per pale arg and sa?], in the right hand a fisherman's staff, in the sinister a landing net

[rolled?] thrown over the shoulder or [each article of dress counterchanged?]
Motto: Fides scutum
Bookplate Rev. Matthias Bruen, N. Y., 1810; also E. B. Bruen

Brune Arg a stag courant, issuing from a wood
Crest: a stag's horns
Bookplate John C. Brune, Baltimore

Bryan Or 3 piles in chief az
Crest: a chapeau gu turned up erm and above it a bugle horn [or tipped sa sans strings]
Motto: Esse quam videri
Christmas card Mr. and Mrs. Mahlon Reading Bryan, Brookline, Mass., 1917

Bryan Per pale or and arg 3 lions pass guard
Crest: a habited arm embowed holding a sword
Motto: Lamh laidir an uachdar
Framed painting owned by George Bryan, Scotland Neck, N. C. Noted by Mrs. Robert Everett

Bryan Impaled by Salter

Buchanan Or a lion ramp sa within a double tressure flory counter flory of the second
Crest: a cubit arm holding a chapeau gu turned up erm bet 2 leaved and fruited branches
Motto: Juvo audaces clarior hinc honos
Bookplate Wentworth J. Buchanan. That of Wm. Buchanan, Druid Hill Park, Balto., has motto: Leonis nobilis ira. It quarters Lenny: Gu on a chev bet 3 bears' heads erased bridled arg a cinquefoil sa. They intermarried before the migration

Buchanan [Or] a lion ramp [sa] armed and langued [gu] within a double tressure flory counter flory [gu]
Crest: a hand holding a cap [tufted on the top with a rose gu?] between 2 laurel branches ppr
Motto: Audaces juvo clarior hinc honos
On tomb of Andrew Buchanan, 1780. Zieber's Heral., p. 43

Buckle Sa a chev bet 3 chaplets arg and on a shield of pretence. Quart 1 and 4: Gu [sa?] on a chief or 3 heads couped and wreathed about the temples (Tanner); 2 and 3: Sa 3 covered cups
Crest: Out of a ducal cor or a demi-ounce arg
Motto: Sapere aude
Bookplate Thomas Buckle, S. C.

Buckler Sa bet 3 griffins' heads erased or, a fess of the last charged with 3 estoiles of 6 points sa
Crest: on a griffin's head erased sa 2 bars or
Motto: Fidelis ad mortem
Bookplate Riggin Buckler, M. D.

Bude Per fess nebulée arg and sa 3 bucks' horns counterchanged
Crest: a buck's horns or
Bookplate John H. Bude

Bulfinch Gu a chev arg bet 3 garbs or
Crest: a dexter arm couped below the elbow, erect and grasping a baton ppr
King's Chapel inscriptions, Boston. Vermont's Amer. Heral., p. 159

Bulkeley or **Bulkley** [Arg] a chev bet 3 bulls' heads cabossed [sa]
Arms without crest or motto on the seal of Peter Bulkley's letter dated 1642 (Mass. Archives, vol. 240, p. 43). He lived in Concord, Mass. Also on the tomb of Hon. Gershom Bulkley in the Westhersfield yard, Wethersfield, Conn. (where the chevron is couped?). Also on the tombstone of Capt. Edward Bulkley (ob. 1748) in Wethersfield (part known as Rocky Hill). Also on tomb of Col. John Bulkley (A. B. Yale, 1725) at Colchester, Conn., 1753. Also impaling Chetwode on a letter dated 1676 from Rev. Gershan Bulkeley of Wethersfield. Heral. Jour., vol. 1, pp. 76, 77. Arms engr. by Josiah Austin, Charlestown, Mass., 1775–1800, on teapot, Met. Mus. of Art, N. Y., has for crest demi-man clothed holding a staff or gun

Bulkeley Sa a chev bet 3 bulls' head cabossed arg
Crest: a bull's head
Framed painting, a hatchment, displayed at the death of "Hon. Col. Peter Bulkeley in Concord." Mrs. Geo. D. Sargent, Brookline, Mass., owner. Now at 9 Ashburton Place, Boston

Bulkley See also Sherburne

Bulkley Gu a chev bet 3 bulls' heads cabossed arg
Motto: Nec temere nec timide
On 2 pewter mugs from Odell, Beds., once owned by Rev. Peter Bulkley. So engr., but this is not the regular blazon. Miss Ellen Chase, Brookline, Mass.

Bulkley [Sa] a chev bet 3 bulls' heads cabossed [arg]
Crest: out of a ducal cor [or] a bull's head [arg] armed [or]
Motto: Nec temere nec timide

Arms of Rebecca Bulkley, wife of Noah P. Burr, Old Swedes' Churchyard, Wilmington, Del., 1878. *See* Zieber's Heral., p. 42.
Bookplate Samuel Bulkeley

Bull [Gu] a mailed cubit arm in fess from the sinister grasping a dagger in pale. In chief a mullet
Crest: a bull trippant ppr
Motto: "God is cortues"
On gravestone of Col. John Bull at Sheldon Church, Prince Williams Parish, S. C. He d. in 1767. N. L. Willet's Beaufort, S. C. Also drawing by Mr. Pat Wall of Port Royal. Henry M. Stuart writes that the silver has crest and motto. A tea caddy, however, owned by his sister, has the arm and sword for a crest with a shield above showing az a pale bet 2 eagles displayed (Woodward). The monument at Ashley Hall has: "Ducit amor Patrice." S. C. Hist. & Gen. Mag., Jan., 1900, p. 76, 85. Also Jan., 1907, p. 29

Bull Gu on a chev arg bet 3 bulls' heads couped of the second 3 roses [of the first]
Crest: a demi-eagle displ
Motto: Virtus basis vitae
Bookplate Martin Bull, Farmington, Conn. Engr. by himself

Bull Or 3 bulls' heads 2 and 1 cabossed sa (?)
Crest: a bull's head bet spread wings
Motto: Audax bona fide
Bookplate Wm. Lanman Bull. Engr. 1895 by E. D. French

Bullard Az on a chev arg 3 pierced mullets of the first
Lozenge on notepaper of Miss Ellen Bullard, 3 Commonwealth Ave., Boston

Bullard *See also* Day

Bult A gyronny of 8 az and or over all a cinquefoil gu
Crest: a mailed arm embowed and resting on the elbow, holding a club
Motto: Palmam qui meruit ferat
Bookplate Henry B. Bult, New York City

Burden Arg on a bend sa 3 [bezants]
Crest: a heart pierced by a dagger in bend sin
Notepaper F. Winthrop coll. N. Y., 1885

Burder Az 2 bars or each charged with 2 martlets sa. In chief a fleur-de-lis. A canton quart 1: Erm a cross flory sa; 2 and 3: Arg a hunting horn stringed sa; 4: Sa a pheon arg
Motto: Glorior in cruci Christi
Bookplate Thomas Harrison Burden, M. D.

Burdett Az 2 bars or
Crest: a lion's head erased
Bookplate E. W. Burdett

Burdon Quartered by Middleton

Burgess Or a fess chequy gu and or. In chief 3 crosses crosslet gu
Bookplate Wm. Burgess, Md.

Burnet Arg in chief 3 leaves vert and in base a hunting horn sa, stringed or
Crest: a sinister hand vested gu? issuing from a cloud az on the dexter side cutting a sprig of 3 leaves vert
Colored window, Gov. Wm. Burnet of Mass., 1728–1729, State House, Boston

Burnet Arg 3 holly leaves in chief [vert] and a hunting horn in base sa stringed and garnished [gu]
Crest: a hand from the sinister holding a pruning knife pruning a vine ppr
Motto: Virescit vulnere virtus
Bookplate John Burnet, Esq., New York. H. Dawkins, sculp., 1754

Burnet Arg in chief 3 leaves vert and in base a hunting horn sable
Gov. Wm. Burnet. Painted on canvas, 1886. Bostonian Society; original wooden, formerly in King's Chapel (*i. e.* before 1754)

Burnham Gu a chev or bet 3 leopards' heads erased [or]
Crest: a leopard's head of the shield
Motto: Ne tentes aut perfice
Bookplate Wm. Henry and Katharine Fernch Burnham. Engr. 1902 by E. D. French

Burnham Gu a chev or bet 3 lions' heads erased arg
Crest: a leopard's head erased or
Motto: Fortis et fidelis
Bookplate J. A. Burnham

Burrill Or a saltire gu. On a chief az a crescent bet 2 pierced stars of six points or
Engr. on tankard and baptismal basin from Col. Theophilus Burrill, 1737. First Church, Lynn, Mass. Amer. Ch. Sil., M. F. A., 1911, pp. 75, 120

Burrows Per fess [az? and erm?] a baton in bend bet 3 fleurs-de-lis [counterchanged?]. In chief the badge of Ulster
Crest: a bird rising holding a spear head in beak and a fleur-de-lis in the dexter claw
Motto: Et vi et virtute
Bookplate Charles W. Burrows, Cleveland

Burr Erm on a chief dancettée [sa] 2 lions ramp [arg]
Motto: Virtus honoris Janua
Arms of Noah Platz Burr on a monument in Old Swedes' Churchyard, Wilmington, Del., 1857. *See also* his wife's arms under Rebecca Bulkley. Zieber's Heral., p. 42

Burt Arg on a chev gu bet 3 bugle horns sa 3 crosses crosslet or
Crest: a bugle horn sa stringed gu
Motto: Fier mais sensible
Notepaper Clarence Edward Burt, M. D. New Bedford, Mass., 1922

Burwell A saltire bet 4 heads erased
Crest: a head holding in its mouth a twig
On tomb of Nathaniel Burwell, eldest son of Major Lewis Burwell. He married Elizabeth, daughter of Robert Carter. In Abington Churchyard, Gloucester Co., Va. MDCCXXI. Seen by L. Park, 1922. Burwell is pronounced Burrell
On tomb of Lewis Burwell, same place, son of Major Lewis Burwell and Lucy, his wife. He d. 19 Dec. 1710. Impaling: 3 cinquefoils in bend. He married (1) Abigail Smith, and (2) Mrs. Martha Cole (née Lear)
On tomb of Mary Burwell, same place, who d. 1658. Impaling: Per bend 3 crosses crosslet
On tomb of Abigail, wife of Major Lewis Burwell of Gloucester Co., Va., desc. of the Bacons and heiress of Hon. Nath. Bacon. Same place. She d. 12 Nov., 1692, aged 36. Impaling: [Gu?] on a chief [arg?] two mullets [sa?] (Bacon)

Burwell
Crest: a head in profile, the hair tied with a ribbon
All seen by L. Park, 1922
James Burwell of King's Creek has for crest a griffin's claw with 3 talons grasping a twig of 4 leaves. *See* Wm. & Mary Quar., vol. 2, p. 231
These arms are not in Burke. Possibly a variation of Burrell arms as the name is so pronounced. The heads look like lions, deer, bears, etc.

Burwell Paly of 6 arg and sa on a bend or, a teal's head erased az
Crest: a lion's gamb erect and erased or, grasping 3 burr leaves vert
Tomb of Lewis Burwell at Carter's Creek, Va. He d. 19 Nov. 1653. Also on the tomb of Benjamin Harrison of Berkeley. Crozier's Va. Heral., p. 33

Bushbury Quartered by Grosvenor

Butcher Vert an elephant [arg?] and on an inscutcheon arg a chev bet 3 griffins' heads erased sa (Cotton?)

Crest: a branch of a cotton tree fruited
Motto: Be steady
The arms of Button are like the above
Bookplate Robert Butcher

Butler Az a chev or bet 3 closed cups
Crest: a falcon displayed membered or
Motto: Nec virtus suprema fefellit
Bookplate Wm. Butler, S. Carolina

Butler Az 3 open cups or
Crest: a sinister hand cuffed grey and sable grasping a cup or
Framed water color
Wm. Butler Clarke, 26 Tremont St., Boston

Butler Quart 1 and 4: A chev bet 3 bottles erect (Butler); 2 and 3: 3 hunting horns
Crest: a gamb grasping a bottle (?)
Peter Butler's will, 1699, wax impression. Suffolk Co. Probate, Boston

Butler Per fess erm and az a lion ramp arg (?)
Crest: an eagle with wings extended, facing sinister
Bookplate Israel Butler. R. Brunton, sc. Bates Early Conn. Engr., p. 16

Butler Impaled by Washington

Butler Quartered by Beckwith

Button *See also* Butcher

Button *See also* Meath

Byfield Sa 5 [bezants] in saltire [or], a chief [or]
Crest: a demi-lion holding a [bezant
Engr. on baptismal basin by Hurd, Dorchester, Mass., First Church

Byfield [Sa] five bezants in saltire a chief [or]
Crest: broken off. The Heral. Jour., vol. 2, p. 126, has a demi-lion
On the chief are the letters L Y D E
Tomb of Nathaniel Byfield, Boston, 1674, Granary Burying Ground, Tremont St. side, Boston

Byrd Arg a cross flory, bet 4 martlets gu, on a canton az a crescent of the field
Crest: a bird rising gu
Bookplate Col. William Byrd of Westover, Va., who d. 1744
These arms are on the iron gate at Westover, Va.

Byrd Quart of 6: 1 and 6: Arg a cross flory bet 8 martlets gu, on a canton az a crescent or; 2: Az a lion ramp arg; 3: Arg a cross pattée fitchée gu; 4: Gu 3 bulls' heads cabossed arg; 5: Arg on a bend cotised az 3 crescents or
Crest: a dove with wings raised gu
Motto: Nulla Pallaescere Culpa

Framed water color at Brook Hill, Henrico Co., Va., the Miss Stewart, desc. of Col. Wm. Byrd and Lucy Parke. Seen by L. Park

Byrd Quart of 6: 1 and 6: Arg a cross flory bet 4 martlets gu, on a canton az a crescent arg and in 1 a crescent gu for diff; 2: Az a lion ramp arg collared or (Crew? Heiress married Dod); 3: Or a cross pattée fitchée sa (Broxton, Mabel, married David le Brid); 4: Arg 3 bulls' heads sa [sa 3 bulls' heads arg?] (Bulkeley of Broxon); 5: Arg on a bend bet two cotises sa three crescents of the first. (If intended for

Dod it should show a fess gu bet 2 cot wavy sa the cresc or)
Crest: a dove displ ppr
Motto: Nulla Pallescere Culpa
Bookplate Wm. Byrd, Westover, Va., 1674–1744; of Geo. H. Burd, N. Y., engr. by E. D. French; of Richard Evelyn Byrd of Winchester, Va.; Francis Otway Byrd and Wm. Byrd of N. Y., from electrotype
Framed water color at Mrs. Corbin Waller's, Boissevain Ave., Norfolk, Va., seen by L. Park, 1922. Ormerod's Cheshire, vol. 2, p. 675, etc., seems to indicate that these quarterings are from the ancient Bird or Brid pedigree there given

C

Cabell Quart of 16: 1: [Sa] a horse ramp [arg] bridled [or]; 2: [Az] a fleur-de-lis [or] (Gamble); 3: Arg a lion ramp gu armed az oppressed by a bend sa (Branch); 4: [Az] 3 butter churns [or] (Reade); 5: Sa on a bend arg 3 lozenges of the field (Carrington); 6: Per cross or and gu a bordure az (Gratten); 7, 11, 15: Arg guttée de sang a lion ramp gu on a chief of the last 3 escallops or (Patteson); 8: Arg a chev sa (Pride); 9: Arg a fess gu oppressed by 2 bendlets (?) (Caskie); 10: Two wings conjoined (Pincham); 12: Or on a bend engr [az] 3 cinquefoils [or] (Harris); 13: Arg on a chev [az] bet 3 arms ppr in armor fessways embowed [az] 3 mullets of the first (Armour); 14: Sa a griffin segreant [erm] (Sherwin); 16: Paly of 6 or and gu a bend sa guttee d'eau (Britton)
Crests: 1: a horse of the field (Cabell); 2: an armed arm embowed hold a dagger (Cabell); 3: out of a ducal cor or a cock's head [az] combed [gu] hold a branch vert (Branch)
Motto: Impavide
Notepaper James Branch Cabell, writer, Dumbarton, Va. Dr. Geo. Cabell, Richmond, has a bookplate which does not appear to be heraldic

Cabot Or 3 chabots erect 2 and 1 [gu?] backs to sinister
Crest: an escallop or
Bookplate Arthur Tracy Cabot, Boston, and Samuel Cabot. William Cabot's has the field vert. The chabot is a bull-head or sculpin. Heads gu?
On notepaper of Mrs. Godfrey L Cabot of Beverly Farms with motto: "Semper cor caput Cabot." At Essex Institute 2 seals with crest (1) 3 chabots erect 2 and 1 all backs to dexter, field or (2) 2 chabots in pale heads up, a third reversed, all backs to sinister no tinctures. One eye shows in each. In Rietstap 2 eyes show

Cadena Gu a castle debruised by a chain in bend [or?]
Crest: a helmet with 3 plumes
Motto: Fidem servat vinculae solvit
Bookplate Mariano Velasquez de la Cadena, prof. of Spanish in Columbia College, 1830–60. No 2 in a quarterly shield

Cadogan Quartered by Morris

Cahill Gyronny of 8 vert and arg over all 6 fleurs-de-lis 3 and 3 az
Crest: a lion's gamb holding a scimetar, both ppr
Arms painted on automobile of Dr. Eliza B. Cahill, Hotel Westminster, Boston. They differ from Burke

Caillaud Arg 3 doves. Impaling: Gu a lion ramp or. On a chief of the second 3 laurel sprigs erect ppr (Pechell?)
Crest: an eagle with chaplet in beak
Bookplate John Caillaud, Esq.

Caithness Quartered by Sinclair

Caldwell 3 wells 2 and 1
Crest: from a coronet a cubit hand grasping a cross
Motto: Fortiter! Ascende!
Bookplate Roxana Caldwell Cowles, desc. of John Caldwell of Ipswich, Mass., and Sarah Dillingham

Caldwell Az a chev arg bet in chief 2 doves and in base a garb or
Crest: a dove arg holding a branch vert
"By the name of Caldwell" and palm branches. Framed water color owned by Mrs. W. B. Stevens, Sr., 98 Mt. Vernon St., Boston, whose grandfather, Ezra Palmer (q. v.), married Elizabeth and then Susan Caldwell of Ipswich, Mass.

Calhoun Arg a saltire engr sa (Colquhoun)
Crest: a stag's head couped [gu]
Supporters: Two greyhounds collared sa

Plaster cast owned by Mrs. Louis Simonds, 48 Meeting Street, Charleston, S. C. Seen by L. Park, 1923. She was Mary Barnwell Rhett. Tablet to John Alfred Calhoun, 1807–1874, Episc. Ch., Trinity Parish, Abbeville, S. C. Seen March, 1924, by Mrs. Milnor Ljungstedt. Motto and tinctures not clear. Also his wife Sarah, 1814–1891

Callaway Or a chev gu bet 3 fleurs-de-lis
Motto: St. Callawy ora pro me
Bookplate Fuller E. Callaway, Vernon Road, La Grange, Ga.

Callaway Or 2 bars dancettée gu bet 3 fleurs-de-lis. Impaling: Or on a bend bet 2 lions ramp sa 3 doves [arg] (Dowes?)
Crest: on a mount a fleur-de-lis
Bookplate John Callaway

Callender Sa a bend or bet 6 half open rolls (or billets) arg
Crest: a dexter hand or holding erect a half open roll ppr
Bookplate John Callender the engraver

Callender Quartered by Livingston

Calthrop Impaled by Hutchinson

Calvert Paly of 6, or and sa, a bend counterchanged
Arms on a shilling issued by Cecil, second Lord Baltimore. Around it is the motto of the province: "Crescite et Multiplicamini. Also on bookplate of Benedict Leonard Calvert of Maryland with motto: "Fatti Maschii Parole Femine," and for crest: out of a ducal cor 2 pennants. Heral. Jour., vol. 3, p. 21

Cambridge Sa 4 garbs [or] in fess
Tomb of Tobias Cambridge, Goose Creek Church, Charleston, S. C. Seen 1926 by Miss Gertrude Gerrish

Camm Or a cross engr gu in the first quarter a crescent of the last
Crest: a cross gu charged with a crescent or
Bookplate John Camm, pres. of William and Mary College, 1771. Ancest. Rec. & Portr., vol. ?, p. 794, gives arms with motto: "Discite justitiam moniti"

Camp Sa a chev bet 3 griffins' heads erased or
"By the name of Camp." A framed water color owned by Henry Spelman, Brewster St., Cambridge, Mass. Not seen

Campbell Gyronny of 8 or and sa
Crest: a boar's head couped

Seal of Duncan Campbell, bookseller, postmaster, Boston, 1701. N. E. Reg., Jan. 1877, p. 57

Campbell Gyronny of 8 sa and or
Crest: a sinister hand holding a spear arg
Framed water color, A. E. Bodwell, 18 Tremont St., Boston, artist and owner

Campbell A gyronny of 6 gu and arg a bordure of the second
Crest: a dexter hand holding a spur
Motto: Forget not
Bookplate James Campbell of Maryland, lawyer. He also used a gyronny sa and or quarterly with arg a lymphad az flags fore and aft gu (Lorn) and for crest: a boar's head couped or

Campbell Gyronny of 8 sa and or a bordure of the second charged with 8 crescents of the first; a martlet sa on the dexter gyron or for diff
Crest: 2 oars of a galley in saltire ppr
Motto: By sea and land
Seal used by John Campbell of Boston (1696), postmaster and proprietor of the "Boston Newsletter." Vermont's Amer. Heral., p. 93

Cannon A man vested ppr holding a fuse to a cannon, the ground vert strewn with cannon ball sa. In the sinister chief a sun in glory bearing a human face
Crest: a mortar with a ball issuant, all ppr
Bookplate Philip A. Cannon, Conn. Kensett, sc.

Campbell Quart 1 and 4: A lymphad (Lorn); 2 and 3: A gyronny of 8 (Campbell)
Crest: a boar's head couped
Motto: Vix ea nostra voco
Supporters: Two lions ramp each holding a trident, the other a dagger
Gravestone John Campbell, Charleston, S. C., d. 10 July, 1790, aged 26. Seen by Mrs. Ljungstedt, 1925

Candler Quart 1 and 4: Parted in tierce per fess indented, the chief per pale arg and az, the base or a canton gu; 2 and 3: Sa a fess or bet 3 asses pass arg (Ascough)
Notepaper Leonard A. Vaughn, Winston-Salem, N. C.

Carbone Bendy of 6 vert and arg (?)
Carbone family, Boston florists, use on paper, door, etc.

Card Or a chev az bet 3 estoiles pierced of 6 points
Crest: a camel passant
Motto: Negata tentat iter via
Bookplate Samuel Card

Carmichael Arg a fess wreathed az and erm within a bordure of the last
Crest: a mailed arm emb holding a broken spear
Motto: Toviovrs prest
Bookplate Wm. Carmichael, Md., 1778

Carney *See also* Shober

Carpenter [Arg] a greyhound sa. A chief gu
Crest: a greyhound's head erased [and gorged?]
Motto: Celeritas viritus fidelitas
Notepaper Miss Rachel Carpenter, The Hermitage, Sandwich, Mass. Also Miss Agnes Z. Carpenter, 84 Homochitto St., Natchez, Miss., but no motto

Carpenter Arg a greyhound and a chief sa
Crest: a greyhound's head erased per fess sa and arg
Bookplate Edmund J. Carpenter, Milton, Mass.
On gravestone of Daniel Carpenter, 1767, at Rehoboth, Mass. Same arms used by Carpenters of Phila.

Carr [Gu] on a chev arg 3 estoiles of 6 points [sa], a crescent in the dexter chief for diff
Crest: a stag's head ppr (?)
Seal on letter from comm'rs to settle Plymouth and R. I. colony bounds, Mch. 11, 1664, to Gov. of Plymouth, signed by Robert Carr. MS in Boston Athenaeum

Carrington Arg a cross gu bet 4 peacocks az
Crest: a peacock's head issuing from a ducal coronet
Water color owned by Mrs. William Ames, Providence, R. I.

Carrington Quartered by Cabell

Carroll Arg 2 lions combatant gu supporting a sword arg hilt and pommel or
Crest: a falcon or [sometimes rising from a growing stump]
Bookplate "Charles Carroll of ye Inner Temple, Esqr."; emigrated to Maryland about 1686, grandfather of Charles the Signer. Ephraim Carroll used the stump and: "In fide et in bello fortes." The field appears to be az. John had field arg. James, Esquire, and Charles "Barrister at Law" had a field gu, the lions or, and the stump dead. C[harles] R[idgely] Carroll of Balto, the son of James, had a similar bookplate. Wm. Thomas's is not tricked. Heral. Jour., vol. 1, p. 39.
An act of the General Assembly of Maryland approved in May, 1783,

permitted Nicholas and James Maccubbin, nephew of Charles Carroll of Annapolis, to use the name and coat of arms of Carroll

Carter Arg a chev sa bet 3 catharine wheels [vert?]
Crest: on a mount [vert?] a greyhound sejant [arg] holding a shield [arg] charged with a wheel [vert?]
Notepaper of desc. of Rev. Samuel Carter, A. B. 1660, Harv. Coll. Son of Rev. Thos. Carter, M. A., St. John's, Camb., of Woburn, Mass. Rev. Thomas's daughter Judith married Samuel Converse, in whose family is a chest marked, 1684, with inverted Carter arms (?). *See* Converse Geneal., vol. 2, p. 902; *also* vol. 1, p. 12

Carter Arg a chev bet 3 cart wheels vert
Crest: on a mount vert a greyhound sejant arg sustaining a shield of the last charged with a cart wheel vert
Seal attached to deed of Landon Carter, 18S ept., 1752; also on tombstone of Hon. Robert Carter at Christ Church, Lancaster, Va.; also on tomb of Robert's wife, Judith Armistead; also on that of Hon. Mann Page, who married a daughter of said Robert Carter. For a crest *see* Va. Hist. Mag., vol. 12, p. 437. Crozier's Va. Heral., p. 97. William & Mary Quar., Jan. 1894, p. 157; Apr. 1894, p. 267

Carter Az a chev or bet 3 catharine wheels vert (?)
Crest: a greyhound sejant (arg?) holding under the dexter a shield az (arg?) charged with a wheel of the field
Motto: Purus sceleres
Bookplate Robert W. Carter, Va. Of Corotoman Creek. A memorial window, St. Mark's Church, Phila., to Maria Carter, has arms. Charles Carter of Shirley used: Nosce te ipsum. Over the door beyond the "hanging stair" at Shirley there is a hatchment, but of whose arms I know not. Amer. Heral., vol. 2, p. 28

Carter *See also* Dale and Renshaw

Carteret Quartered by Dumaresq

Cartwright Erm a fess [sa] bet 3 flaming fireballs [sa] a crescent on the fess for diff
Crest: a wolf's head [or] a spear [arg] through the neck
Seal on George Cartwright's letter from Boston, Dec. 27, 1664, to Governor Prince of Plymouth. In Boston Athenaeum MSS.

Cartwright *See also* Crown

Carver [Or] a chev sa. In base a fleur-de-lis
Crest: out of a ducal cor or a Saracen's face couped at the shoulders
Ex libris Clifford Nickels Carver, Sec. Amer. Embassy, London. A. N. Macdonald, sc. Some Amer. Coll. Bookplates, 1915, p. 274,

Cary Arg on a bend sa, 3 roses of the field leaved vert
Crest: a swan ppr wings elevated
Mottoes: (1) Comme je trove; (2) Sine Deo careo
Table tomb (now in ruins) of Miles Cary, who came to Va. about 1645. Tomb at Windmill Point, Warwick Co., Va. Also on his son Henry's document, and on family silver. *See* family history, 1919. Bellet's Some Prom. Va. Fam., vol. 2, p. 61

Cary Arg on a bend sa 3 roses arg
Crest: a swan rising
Motto: Cari Deo nihil carema
Bookplate Wilson Miles Cary, Md. There is a small bookplate marked "Cary" and bearing the motto: Virtute excerptae

Cary Arg on a bend sa 3 roses [of the field]
Crest: a swan rising or
Motto: In medio tutissimus ibis
Bookplate Rev. Thomas Cary, Charlestown, Mass., 1745–1808, and of Newburyport. Callender, sculp. Samuel Cary's, same arms and engraver, has: Virtute, non sanguine, non verbis

Cary Arg on a bend sa 3 roses [of the field]
Crest: a swan rising
Motto: In medio tutissimus ibis
Bookplate Thomas Cary. Callender, sculp. Samuel T. Cary had the same arms with a crescent in chief for diff

Cary [Arg] on a bend [sa] 3 roses [of the field]
Crest: a swan [ppr]
Samuel Cary, 1740–41. Tomb No. 12, Phipps St. Yard, Charlestown, Mass. Heral. Jour., vol. 1, p. 74. The two upper roses are now gone. Also embr. hatchment owned by Mrs. Robert S. Russell, 20 Com. Ave., Boston

Cary Per fess gu and arg, over all on a bend sa 3 roses
Crest: a swan
Bookplate Alpheus Cary, Jr. (d. 1867). A. Cary, del. H[azen] Morse, sculp.

Cary Quartered by Ambler

Case "He bareth Gules a unicorn's head, or"
Crest: a swan ppr, crowned or (facing the sinister)
Motto: Amator de virtus

"By the name of Case." Bookplate Harry Case. R. Brunton, sc. A. C. Bates's Early Conn. Engr., p. 18

Case Quartered by Gilman

Caskie Quartered by Cabell

Castle Az 2 chevronelles bet 3 towers [or?]
Crest: a flaming tower
Bookplate William Richards Castle, Jr., Boston. G. W. Eve, sc. 1911. Burke has arg and gu

Caswell Impaled by Southack

Catherwood Erm on a saltire gu bet 4 stalks 5 mascles or
Crest: a phoenix rising
Motto: Virtus sibi proemium
Bookplate H. Wilson Catherwood

Catlin Per chev az and or 3 lions pass guard counterchanged
Crest: a lion sejant or bet 2 wings endorsed charged barry of 6 or and az
Motto: Placidus semper timidus nunquam
Notepaper F. Winthrop coll., N. Y., 1885, in Boston Athenaeum

Caverly Gu a pegasus rising arg, mane, tail, and winged or, charged on the shoulder with a quatrefoil gu, all within a bordure compony arg and az
Crest: a horse's head contourné party colored sa and or, crowned with 3 feathers arg or and gu
Bookplate [Robert Boodey?] Caverly Lowell, Mass.

Cay Az a bend or debruised by a label of 3 points arg
Crest: a hawk ppr standing with a pennon [vert] attached to its collar, waving behind and charged with the arms
Bookplate John Cay (of Va.?)

Chalmers Arg a fess sa bet in chief a demi-lion issuant sa and in base a fleur-de-lis gu
Crest: an eagle rising
Motto: Spero
Bookplate George Chalmers, Md.

Chaloner Sa a chev bet 3 cherubim heads or
Crest: a wolf statant reguard arg, a broken spear half stuck through his body half in his mouth
Mottoes: A: Sicut quaercus; B: Garde la Foy
Seal owned by Walter Chaloner of Newport, R. I., who d. 1796. Owned 1916 by Mrs. Walker. Tombstone of "Ninyon" Chaloner (d. 1752) in the Newport, R. I., churchyard. Also on the bookplate of A. D. Chaloner, M. D. Wm. Challoner's crest is a lion pass guard with a broken spear, etc. Vermont's Amer. Heral., pp. 43, 160

Chamberlain Gu a chev bet 3 escallops or
Crest: a lion ramp or langued gu
Framed water color (old). "By the name of Chamberlain" and palm branches. (By Coles?) Dealer in antiques, Pemberton Square, Boston

Chamberlain Gu within an orle of 8 mullets arg an armillary sphere or
Crest: an eagle displ·ppr the dexter claw on an armillary sphere or
Motto: Spes et fides
Framed water color at Brook Hill, Henrico Co., Va., the Misses Stewart

Chambers Gu a chev bet 3 escallops or
Crest: a griffin ramp az holding an escallop gu
Motto: Vincit veritas
Bookplate John Chambers, chief justice, N. Y., 1754. E. Gallaudet, sculp.

Chambers Or a lion ramp (facing the sinister) bet 3 fleurs-de-lis
Crest: a dexter hand holding a scimitar [arg] hilt and pomel [or]
Bookplate Benjamin Chambers of Chambersburg, Penn.

Chambers See also Palmes

Champion Or on a fess gu bet 3 trefoils slipped an eagle displ of the first within a bordure engr az charged with 8 bezants
Crest: a cubit arm vested arg cuff [gu] holding in the hand ppr a chaplet [vert]
Motto: Pro rege et patria
Bookplate Epaphroditus Champion, Jr. P. Maverick, sc. Also of Richard C. with fess sa and bordure gu. Crest: a cubit arm holding a sprig with 3 roses and motto: Quod sis esse velis nilque malis. He was a potter, Eng. and So. Car. Ames, sc.

Chandler Chequy arg and az on a bend arg 3 lions passant or
Crest: a pelican in her piety [or?]
Motto: [Ad mortem fidelis]
Bookplate John Chandler, Junr., Esqr. N. Hurd, sculp. The bookplate of Gardiner Chandler, P. Revere, sculp.*
It appears to have the pelican or. Used also by Horace Parker Chandler of Boston, with the motto: Vivo et morior pro quibus amo. Samuel Chandler's has chequy arg and gu, the nest vert, the bird sa. See also Vermont's Amer. Heral., p. 137, 160. Arms engr. on a repoussé sugar bowl by Revere. See Dyer's Early Amer. Craftsmen, p. 214. Bigelow's Hist. Sil., p. 404.

*On the back of the G. C. plate Revere engraved the arms of the Freemasons

Chapin [Az] a full rigged ship sinister 3 topsails unfurled [arg] and a flag (az on a torteau a saltire or) at stern and mizzen peak
Crest: a cactus vert
Motto: Auxilio Dei supero
Arms of Howard M. Chapin, libn. R. I. Hist. Soc., Providence, on bookplate and bedspread. He formerly used as a bookplate arg a cactus vert with crest a cat's head sa. His great grandfather used the ship on a seal in 1809, but he assumed the crest and motto

Chapin Per bend arg and sa a capital C counterchanged
Bookplate —— Chapin. Used by Rev. James Henry Chapin

Chapman A chev or bet 3 caps of maintenance jessant-de-lis?
Seal of Capt. John Chapman, So. Carolina, 1712. Jeffries MSS. N. E. Reg., Jan. 1877, p. 58. Also Chapman of Jamaica

Chapman Per chev arg and az a crescent counterchanged and two in chief
Bookplate Randolph Cecil Chapman, by Sidney Hunt

Chapman Per chev arg and gu, in the center a crescent counterchanged
Crest: an arm embowed in armor, holding a broken spear encircled with a wreath
Mott: Crescit sub pondere virtus
In the will of Constantia Chapman, dated 2 Nov. 1768, is the following bequest: "I give and bequeath unto each of my three grandchildren, H. C. Weems, Wm. Locke Weems, and Sarah Louisa Weems, the sum of five guineas to be laid out for them in silver plate, as their mother shall think proper, the said plate to be engraved with the arms of the Chapman and Pearson families." On a silver salver, now owned by Mrs. Susan Swann Calvert of Alexandria, Va., the above combined arms are found as follows: As above for Chapman, and for Pearson," Per fess embattled az and gu, 3 suns or (see Pearson arms). Also on cover of Chapman Genealogy, 1854. Crozier's Va. Heral., p. 16

Charles ,Az a chev bet 3 lions ramp or
Crest: a boar's head couped sa
Motto: Volo et valeo
Bookplate Batsford Ralph Charles

Charles Bookplate A. Baldwin Charles. See Baldwin

Charnock Arg on a bend sa 3 crosses crosslet of the field. Impaling (King): Sa a lion ramp bet 3 crosses crosslet or
A hatchment, 1715, by Elizabeth, daughter of Capt. John Charnock of

Boston. Mrs. Mary Charnock was daughter of Capt. Ralph King, son of Daniel of Watford Herts and Lynn, Mass.

Chase Gu 4 crosses patonce arg. On a canton or a lion passant az
Crest: a lion ramp grasping a cross patée fitchée arg
Motto: Ne cede malis
Bookplate William L. Chase, Brookline, Mass. Wm. Henry Chase had on a canton az a lion passant or

Chase Gu 4 crosses patonce arg on a canton az a lion passant or
Crest: a demi-lion ramp or holding a cross of the field gu
Framed water color. Dr. Walter G. Chase, Brookline, Mass.

Chatterton Or a lion's head sa bet 3 mullets gu
Motto: Loyal au mort
Framed water color A. E. Bodwell, 18 Tremont Street, Boston, artist and owner

Chaumont Quartered by Middleton

Chauncey Arg a cross crosslet sa. On a chief gu a lion pass guard or
Crest: a demi-eagle displayed duc gorged
Bookplate Charles Chauncey, N. Y.

Chauncy Gu a cross crosslet arg on a chief az a lion pass or
Crest: a demi-eagle displ duc gorged
Bookplate J. St. Clair Chauncy, M. D., U. S. N.

Chauncy Gu a cross flory arg. On a chief az a lion pass or, a label for diff
Crest: a demi-griffin barred az and gu with a label on the neck
Motto: Sublimis per ardua tendo
Bookplate Charles Chauncy, M. D.

Checkley Or a chev gu bet 3 mullets of the same
Crest: a mullet gu
"By the name of Checkley." Richard Checkley of Boston d. 1742. The family from Preston-Capes, Northants. Granary Burying Ground, Tremont St. side, Boston. Also on tomb at Swan Point, Providence. Motto: Justi velut lumen astrarum. Heral. Jour., vol. 2, p. 131

Checkley Or a chev gu bet 3 mullets of the same
Bookcase home of Lawrence Park, Groton, Mass.

Checkley Or a chev gu bet 3 mullets of the same
Crest: a mullet gu

Painted on canvas, 1886. Bostonian Society. Formerly in King's Chapel. I found several of these in 1913 in a dusty closet under the eaves

Cheever Arg a chev gu bet 3 stags trip ppr (Rogers arms?)
Crest: a stag's head of the field couped
Motto: Industria et frugalitas
"By the name of Cheever." Embroidered hatchment by E. C., owned by Mrs. Alexander Whiteside, 192 Beacon St., Boston

Cheever Gu 3 goats (chèvres) saliant arg
Crest: a demi-goat saliant arg collared gu
Motto: En Dieu ma foy
Bookplate Dr. David W. Cheever, Boston. Engr. by J. W. Spenceley

Cheever Per bend dancettée [arg and az] three cinquefoils, 2 in chief and one in base [counterchanged]
Crest: a stag's head [erased] lozengy [arg and az]
Gravestone of Ezekiel Cheever, 1744, grandson of the schoolmaster. Phipps St. yard, Charlestown, Mass. Heral. Jour., vol. 1, p. 46. These are the arms of Chaytor of Spennithorne Hall, Co. York. Also an embr. hatchment owned by Mrs. Frank E. Peabody, Boston, in a lozenge and framed. Signed M[ary] C[heever], 1700. The stag's head is couped

Chesebrough [Gu] 3 crosses pattée, in fess arg, bet as many water bougets or
Crest: a demi-lion ramp gu, holding bet the paws a cross pattée or
Mottoes: [In England]: Fidei coticula crux; [In America]: Virtus vera nobilitas
Table tombs of David Chesebrough of Newport, R. I., in Stonington (Ct.) churchyard, d. 1782; and on that of his wife Margaret, d. 1780. Heral. Jour., vol. 2, pp. 86, 87

Chester Erm on a chief [sa] a griffin passant [or armed arg]
Crest: a griffin passant
Engr. on tankards from Richard Sprague, 1703. First Parish Church, Charlestown, Mass. Old Sil. Am. Ch., p. 120. Arms of Emma, wife of Richard Sprague and daughter of Leonard Chester of Connecticut

Chester Erm on a chief sa a griffin passant or armed arg
Crest: a dragon passant arg (or wyvern)
Motto: Vincit qui patitur
Bookplate and seal used by Colonel John Chester, distinguished at Bunker

Hill; also on tombstone of Leonard
Chester, who d. 1848, and was buried
at Wethersfield, Ct.
Framed water color. Horace Chester, Malden, Mass. An embroidered
hatchment sold by Miss Sarah Perkins
of Norwick, Conn., to W. N. Andrews,
a dealer there, about 1918, was seen by
Mrs. Coe of N. Y. Heral. Jour., vol. 2,
pp. 44, 45

Chew Az a catharine wheel [or] bet 3
griffins' heads erased [arg]
Crest: a griffin sejant [arg] holding
a catharine wheel [gu?] under the
dexter paw
Bookplate Joseph Chew, New London, Conn. The bookplate of Beverly
Chew engr. by French, 1895, has motto:
Esto quod esse videris

Chew Gu a chev arg on a chief az 3
leopards' faces or
Seal belonging to Samuel Chewe.
Crozier's Va. Heral., p. 33 and 34

Chew Gu a chev or, on a chief or 3
leopards' heads
Crest: a lion ramp guard
Bookplate —— Chew, Phila. Also
on silver. Sylvan City, 1883, p. 448

Chidson Arg on a chev vert 2 pierced
mullets or (Drury arms)
Crest: a greyhound courant ppr
[collared or]
Motto: Fidelitas vincit
Bookplate W. D. Chidson

Child [Gu] a chev engrailed erm bet
3 birds [i. e. eagles close arg]
Crest: an eagle rising entwined by a
snake
Motto: Fari aude
Bookplate Thomas Child of Edenton,
N. C., engr. by Nathaniel Hurd, also
in St. Paul's Church vestry room.
(From Miss Mary Pruden, Edenton.)
Seal of Dr. Robert Child, Corpus
Christi, 1631; of N. E., 1646–47. M.
H. S. Coll., vol. 41. Also of Wm.
Spencer Child, engr. by Thos. Chub-
bock, with motto: Imitari quam
invidere. Also Edward Patterson
Childs of N. Y. by Mrs. Harding, but
chev not engr

Chrystie Arg a chev sa bet 3 cold wells
gu
Crest: a phoenix rising from flames
ppr
Motto: Malo mori quam foedari
Bookplate Thomas Witter Chrystie,
attorney, N. Y.

Churchill Sa a lion ramp arg debruised
by a cottise gu
Crest: a dove hold in its beak a sprig
ppr

Framed water color after origina
by John Coles? Owned by George R.
Winsor, 36 Kilsyth Road, Brookline,
Mass. Seen by Dr. Harold Bowditch

Churchill Sa a lion rampant arg de-
bruised with a bendlet gu
Crest: out of a ducal cor or a demi-
lion ramp arg
Wax seal on deed of Benjamin
Churchill of Va. to his brother William
in 1772. Bellet's Some Prom. Va.
Fam., vol. 2, p. 499. In Wm. & Mary
Quar., vol. 10, p. 39, the field is
engraved azure

Churchill Impaled by Pownall

Chute Gu semée of mullets or 3 swords
arg hilted or barways, the center sword
encountering the other two. A canton
arg and vert (?) thereon a lion of
England
Crest: a dexter cubit arm in armor,
the hand grasping a broken sword
Gore roll of arms. Thomas Chute,
Marblehead, Mass., 1719

Claggett Erm on a fess sa 3 pheons
Crest: a crowned eagle's head to
sinister bet 2 wings
Bookplate Thos. Ino. Claggett, D. D.,
first bp. consecrated in America

Claghorn Per pale indented sa and arg,
on the sinister side a mullet sa
Crest: a hand issuing from a cloud
in the sinister holding a branch
Motto: Insperata floruit
Bookplate James L. Claghorn

Claiborne Arg 3 chevronels interlaced
in base sa, a chief and bordure of the
last
Crest: a dove and olive branch
Motto: Pax et copia
Tomb of Lieut.-Col. Thomas Claiborne, d. 7 Oct. 1683. At Romancoke,
King William Co., Va. Also on his
father's seal, quartering Bellingham.
Va. Hist. Mag., vol. 1, p. 317. J. H.
Claiborne's "Wm. Claiborne of Va.,"
1917, has on the cover Claiborne quartering Kirkbride of Kirkbride: Arg
a cross engrailed vert. Claiborne has
no bordure

Claire Impaled by Blount

Clapp Per saltire or and gu, over all a
castle arg
Crest: a lion's head erased arg
Framed water color with cornstalks
(by Coles?) owned by W. A. Butter-
field, Boston

Clapp Vairé gu and arg on a canton az
a sun in splendor
Crest: a pike naiant ppr
A sardonyx ring marked J. T. C.

F. E. Widmer, 31 West St., Boston. The bookplate of Eugene Howard Clapp has motto: Fais ce que dois advienne que pourra. That of Annie Mason Clapp has: The entrance to an enchanted world

Clark Arg an oak branch leaved and fruited slipped from the dexter lower corner
Crest: an American eagle displ with a mullet above
Motto: Semper idem
Bookplate D. Lawrence Clark

Clark Gu 3 broad swords points up
Crest: a swan rising, chained to a ducal coronet
Motto: Per ardua
Bookplate Henry G. Clark [medical writer?] and James Wilson Clark. Also water color. Essex Institute, Salem, Mass., with hand of Ulster for baronet. By Coles?

Clark Gu a cross arg
Seal of Thomas M. Clark, Bishop of R. I. Zieber's Heral., p. 201

Clark Per pale indented arg and gu 2 lions ramp counterchanged
Crest: a mailed arm emb holding a wavy sword
Motto: Manus haec inimica tyrannis
Bookplate James Clark

Clark Impaled by Shepard

Clark *See also* Shepard

Clarke A ragged staff in bend bet 3 roundels, a crescent in chief for diff
Crest: a swan [proper] crowned and chained [or?] with the dexter foot on a roundel
Tomb No. 15 for Hon. Wm. Clarke, merchant, who d. in Boston, 1742. These arms engr. on the watch of Clarence Howard Clark, 3d, of Phila. Herbert Lincoln Clark, Phila., has motto: Amat victoria curam

Clarke A ragged staff in bend bet 3 roundels
Crest: a swan [proper] crowned and chained [or?] with the dexter foot on a roundel
Engr. on tankard from Mrs. Cabot, daughter of Wm. Clarke, 1784. North Church, Salem, Mass. Old Sil. Am. Ch., p. 433

Clarke Arg 2 bars and in chief 3 mullets gu
Crest: from a ducal cor an eagle rising
Framed water color. W. B. Clarke, bookseller, Tremont St., Boston. A coat of arms with 3 escallops or instead of mullets is said to have been long in the Clarke family

Clarke Arg (?) on a bend gu bet 3 ogresses 3 swans of the first with wings elevated
No crest
Inlaid wood, parlor floor Wm. Clarke house, Garden Court St., Boston, 1712. Owned by Henry Warren, Newton Center, Mass. *See also* Clarke, Saltonstall, and Hubbard panels from same house.   The 4th (Whittingham?) appears to be lost. On silver candlestick. *See* Buck's Old Plate, p. 120

Clarke Arg on a bend gu bet 3 roundels (?) 3 swans. On a sinistercant on az 2 fleurs-de-lis in chief and a demi-lion rampant in base with a mace bendways or
Crest: a swan chained and holding a roundel
Motto: Saepe pro rege semper pro patria
Bookplate S. Clarke

Clarke Az a chev bet 3 lions ramp or (arms of Monastery of Lindisfarne)
Crest: a boar's head couped sa
Motto: Volo et valeo
Bookplate Botsford Ralph Clarke, 1881, by David M. Stauffer

Clarke [Gu] 3 swords erect in pale, arg points up, hilts or.   The middle sword bears on an inscutcheon a sinister hand
Crest: a dexter armed arm embowed
Engr. on baptismal basin owned by William Clarke of Boston (d. 1710). Given in his widow's will, 1728. Old South Church, Boston. Old Sil. Am. Ch., p. 58. Mr. F. H. Bigelow, Cambridge, Mass., has a coffee pot made about 1750 by Hurd with 3 swords erect in fess, points down; crest: a sword erect. *See also* Eckley

Clarke Or a ragged staff (bend raguly humetté) bet 3 ogresses
Crest: a swan [arg] crowned sa, beaked, gorged, and chained or, legged sa, with the dexter foot on an ogress and in the beak an olive branch vert
A variation of the arms of Clarke of Dublin, 1688. *See* N. E. H. G. Reg., vol. 33, pp. 19, 226. Shield with castle and cow painted on panel in Wm. Clark house, Garden Court St., Boston, 1712. Owned by Mrs. F. L. Gay. Stone in Copp's Hill yard, Boston. Heral. Jour., vol. 2, p. 74. Dr. John Clarke, d. 1728

Clarke Impaled by Freke

Clarke *See also* Eckley

Clarkson Arg on a bend engr sa 3 annulets or
Crest: an eagle's head erased bet 2 wings addorsed sa
Bookplate David Clarkson, 1694–1751, N. Y. Curio, 1888, p. 66

Claypoole   Or a chev az bet 3 herts
     Crest: a fleur-de-lis arg
     Arms granted to James Clepole of
Norborough, Eng., 1583, great grand-
father of James Claypoole of Phila.
Also on cover of Claypoole Genealogy,
Phila., 1893

Clayton   Arg a cross engr sa, bet 4
pellets
     Crest: a leopard's gamb erased and
erect arg grasping a pellet
     Tomb of Dr. Thomas Clayton, who
d. Oct. 12, 1739, and was buried in
Gloucester Co., Va. William and
Mary Quar., vol. 2, p. 236

Clayton   Quartered by Grosvenor

Cleborne   Arg 3 chevronelles interlaced
in base sa, bordured sa, a chief sa
     Crest: a lion's head erased sa
     Mottoes: Clibor ne sceame; Virtute
invidiam vincas
     Bookplate C. I. Cleborne, M. D.
Signed Jarrett, London

Cleborne   See also Claiborne

Clement   Arg a pale sa
     Crest: a demi-lion ramp couped gu
     Motto: Think well
     Bookplate Clara E skine Clement
(Mrs. Waters of Boston)

Clerk   Arg a fess chequy az and arg
bet in chief 2 crescents gu and in base
a boar's head couped sa within a bordure az
     Crest: a snake entwined about a
staff (?)
     Motto: Sat cito si sat tuto
     Bookplate James Clerk, Md.

Clifford   Quart 1 and 6: Chequy or and
az on a fess gu 3 cinquefoils [arg]; 2:
Gu a chev or bet 3 hounds' heads arg;
3: Per fess az and gu a lion ramp
(arg?) within a bordure or; 4: Arg 3
crosses crosslet; 5: Per pale gu and
az 3 fleurs-de-lis arg
     Crest: a griffin ramp
     Motto: Semper paratus
     Bookplate H. M. Clifford. English?

Clinton   Arg 6 crosses crosslet fitchée
3, 2, 1 [sa]. On a chief [az] 2 mullets
[or] pierced [gu]
     Crest: from a ducal cor [gu] 5
ostrich feathers [arg]
     Cut on the wall of the Capitol,
Albany, N. Y. Charles Clinton, who
came to America in 1728, had a seal.
Zieber's Heral., p. 62

Clinton   Arg 6 crosses crosslet fitchée
3, 2, and 1 sa, on a chief az 2 mullets
or pierced sa, a crescent for diff
     Seal of George Clinton, Gov. of N. Y.,
1777. Heral. Jour., vol. 4, p. 96

Clinton   Arg 6 crosses crosslet, fitchée
sa, on a chief az 2 mullets [or pierced gu]
     Crest: out of a ducal cor gu a plume
of 5 ostrich feathe.s arg, banded by a
ribbon az
     Mottoes: A: Loyalté n'a honte; B:
(Used by DeWitt Clinton) Cara patria
carior libertas
     Bookplate Gov. DeWitt Clinton.
Engr. by Maverick. Used also by
Charles A. Clinton. Vermont's Amer.
Heral., pp. 26, 161

Clopton   Sa a bend erm bet 2 cotises
dancetté or, a mullet for diff
     Crest: a wolf's head per pale [or] and
az Deed of William Clopton, Jr.,
dated 22 July, 1710, bears a wax seal.
Crozier's Va. Heral., p. 21

Clowes   Vert on a chev arg bet 3 unicorns' heads erased [or] as many crescents [gu]
     Bookplate John Clowes of N. Y.?

Coates   See a!so Coles

Cobb   Per chev or [gu?] and sa. In
chief 2 shovellers sa and in base a fish
[herring?] naiant or
     Crest: a bird's head or holding in the
beak a fish hauriant arg
     Framed water color. George N.
Black, 57 Beacon St., Boston

Cochran   Arg a chev gu bet 3 boars'
heads couped [az?]
     Crest: a horse pass arg
     Supporters: Two greyhounds arg
collared [or] leashed [gu]
     Arms of John Cochran, director-
general of military hospitals, b. Sads-
bury, Penn., 1730. A shield hanging
from the wall. See Godchild of Washington, p. 469

Cock   Arg a chev engr gu bet 3 eagles'
heads erased sa, on a canton az an
anchor or
     Tombstone Nicholas Cock, who d.
25 Oct. 1687. Crozier's Va. Heral.,
p. 83

Cock   Quarterly gu and arg
     Crest: an ostrich regardant gu
holding a key or
     Motto: Quod fieri non vis alter ne
feceris
     Bookplate Wm. Cock, N. Y. Mav-
erick, sc.

Cockayne   Gu a chev erm bet 3 cocks
     Crest; on a mural crown a cock
     Motto: Virtus in arduis
     Notepaper E. O. Cockayne, Wollas-
ton, Mass.

Cocke   Arg a fess sa bet 2 talbots pass
     Seal of Catesby Cocke, b. 1702,
living at Belmont, Fairfax Co., Va.,
4 Jan. 1724. Crozier's Va. Heral.,
p. 24

Coddington Arg a fess embattled counter-embattled sa bet 3 lions passant [gu or sa?]
Crest: a dragon's head gu bet 2 wings chequy or and az issuing out of a ducal coronet of the second
Motto: Immersabilis est vera virtus
Arms of Codrington on a seal used by William Coddington of R. I., to Gov. Leverett of Mass. Vermont's Amer. Heral., p. 106, 161

Coddington Gu a cross or within a fret az. Two trefoils slipped or in chief and 2 in base
Crest: a wolf's head erased or
A small color sketch in an old frame. Old South Church, Boston

Codman Az 2 wings conjoined ppr on a fess arg, over all 3 annulets of the first
Crest: a dove (?) holding in the bill a sprig
Motto: Pax in terris
Henry Sargent Codman's bookplate. Windsor Herald says arms of Cawoodley of Devon

Codman Arg 2 wings inverted and conjoined ppr. Over all a fess az charged with 3 annulets of the first
Crest: "a dove (?) or, in his bill a sprig of olive (?)
Bookplate John Codman, Warwick, sc., 145 Strand
Bookplate Codman Collection, Boston Public Library, in memory of Henry Sargent Codman and Philip Codman, 1896. Spenceley, sc. Also notepaper Edmund Dwight Codman, Boston, 1920. Miss Edith Codman's bookplate has a fess and the annulets gu. Motto: "Pax in terris"

Coffin Az 3 plates bet 14 crosses crosslet. Over all two batons in saltire within a wreath
Crest: the stern of a ship bearing a dove rising, a twig in its beak
Motto: Exstant recte factis proemia
Bookplate Hector Coffin of Newbury, Mass.? J. Akin, del. F. Kearny, sc.

Coffin [Az] 3 bezants bet 9 crosses crosslet [or]
Crest: a demi-griffin segreant
Engr. on paten with feet, made by John Allen and John Edwards. Mrs. R. H. Morgan. Amer. Ch. Sil., M. F. A. cat., 1911, p. 96

Coffin Vert 5 crosses crosslet arg, bet 4 plates
Crest: a pigeon close or
Arms in water color on velum in possession of Mrs. Arthur M. Merriam of Manchester, Mass., framed about 1760. This painting was done for

Dr. Nathaniel Coffin of Portland, Me., who d. in 1766. Also another painting where the arms of Hale are impaled. Heral. Jour., vol. 3, p. 51. Vermont's Amer. Heral., pp. 30, 161

Coffin Vert 5 crosses crosslet [arg] bet 4 roundels [plates]
Crest: a hawk
Motto: Post tenebris speramus lumen de lumine
Bookplate Hector Coffin. J. Akin, sc., Also of Charles A. Coffin, "S. L. S., sc., after J. Akin, sc., 1903"

Coffin Vert 5 crosses crosslet arg, bet 4 plates
On a sampler embr. by Miss Whippey, 1801. John Morrisey, owner, Nantucket

Coggeshall Arg a cross, bet 4 escallops sa
Crest: a stag, lodged sa, attired or
Seal affixed to a letter by John Coggeshall, sec. of Colony of R. I. (1677). Vermont's Amer. Heral., pp. 110, 161. Ancest. Rec. & Portr., vol. 1, p. 117, gives motto: "Nec sperno nec timeo"

Coggeshall Arg a cross bet four escallops sa
Crest: a stag lodged sa [attired or]
Motto: Veritas et fidelitas
Bookplate Frederic Coggeshall, M. D., Boston

Cohen Per chev inverted, the upper half per pale az and or, the lower half per chev purpure gu and arg, the chev points meeting. An inscutcheon barry of 4 and paly of 3, gu, or, gu; arg, az, vert; pur, per pale arg and gu, gu; per pale arg and gu, arg, vert. The shield held by golden chains to a larger arg shield
Crest: two human hands, palms shcwing, thumbs joined
Motto: (In Hebrew)
Bookplate Jacob Cohen, Charleston, S. C.

Colburn Sa 3 plates, each charged with an annulet
Crest: an owl guardant holding a mouse
Bookplate Burnham Standish Colburn

Colden Gu a chev arg bet 3 stags' heads and necks erased and cabossed or
Crest: A stag's head cabossed or
Motto: Fais bien, crains rien
Bookplate Cadwallader Colden. Heral. Jour., vol. 4, pp. 45, 95. Vermont's Amer. Heral., pp. 47, 162

Colden Vert a chev arg bet 3 stags' heads erased. Impaling: Arg 3 mullets pierced gu with an arrow in pale under each (Provost)
Crest: a stag's head erased
Motto: Fais bien, crains rien
Bookplate Cadwallader D. Colden, 1818, mayor N. Y.

Cole Arg a bull pass gu within a bordure sa charged with 10 bezants
Crest: a demi-dragon couped, holding an arrow [or] headed and feathered [arg] in his claw
Motto: Deum cole regem serva
Bookplate S. T. Cole

Cole Arg and vert a cross lozengy
Crest: out of a coronet a dexter hand
Tomb of Col. William Cole of Warwick Co., Va., who d. 1693–94, aged 56. Crozier's Va. Heral., p. 25

Cole Quart 1 and 4: Arg a bull sa within a bordure sa bezantée; 2 and 3: Chequy or and gu. On a chief az a fess wavy arg (Rayley)
Crest: a demi-dragon holding an arrow [or] armed [arg] point down
Motto: Parva segessatis est
Bookplate N. C.

Cole Per pale gu and arg a bull pass ppr on a chief sa 3 bezants
Crest: a demi-griffin with wings or
Framed water color at Lemon's Shop, Boston, 1917

Coles Quart 1 and 4: Erm 2 and 3: Paly of 6 or and gu
Crest: a cock
Bookplate Christopher Coles. Coates arms?

Collacutt A fess indented bet 3 crescents
Seal on a deed from Richard Collacutt, 1681, of Boston, to Thomas Swift of Milton, owned by Mrs. Lydia B. Taft, Milton, 1915

Collet Sa on a bend [arg] voided of the field bet 3 hinds statant 5 annulets [of the second]
Crest: a hind ppr supporting with his dexter paw an inscutcheon az
Motto: Dum spiro spero
Bookplate —— Collet, Phila.

Colleton Or 3 roebucks' heads couped ppr
Bookplate James Edward Colleton, A. M.

Collier Arg on a chev az bet 3 demi-unicorns courant [gu] as many acorn slips [or]
Crest: a demi-negro ppr with pearls in ears arg holding in the dexter hand an acorn branch fructed [or]
Greeting card of Jena Cuthbert Collier, Barnesville, Ga.

Collins Or a griffin ramp sa
Crest: a demi-griffin couped or collared gu
Motto: Favente deo et sedulitate
Bookplate James Collins

Colman Az upon a pale, rayonée or, a lion ramp gu
Crests: A: A demi-lion; B: A caltrap or bet 2 wings arg
In a volume of the Rev. Benjamin Colman (London, 1728). Also engr. on a silver bowl. Heral. Jour., vol. 1, p. 58

Colt Erm a fess sa bet 3 running colts [of the second]
Crest: a colt of the field holding in his mouth a broken tilting spear [or] headed [az], the handle lying bet the colt's hind legs
Motto: Vincit qui patitur
Stamped in gilt on the front cover of the Samuel Colt Memorial, N. Y., 1866. He made revolvers and guns. Also on dinner plates (crest contourné) and Impaling: Gu a plume of 6 feathers or? Owned by Mrs. Clement S. Houghton, Chestnut Hill, Mass.

Colton [Sa] a saltire bet 4 crosses crosslet [or]
Crest: a boar statant arg [armed or?] pierced by an arrow in the shoulder [gu?]
Motto: Never despair
Engr. on notepaper of Mrs. Hamilton Daughaday (née Colton), Chicago

Colville Quartered by Nelson

Colyear Impaled by Dawkins

Combe Erm 3 lions pass in pale [gu]
Crest: a mailed hand emb. holding a broken tilting spear
Motto: Nec temere, nec timide
Bookplate T. Combe

Comstock Arg [or?] on sword paleways point up impaling in base a crescent gu bet 2 bears ramp vert [sa?]
Crest: from a ducal cor [or] an elephant ramp ppr
Motto: Nid cyfoeth ond boddlondeh
Bookplate M. Louise Comstock; also Frederick H. Comstock. His has the sword gu point down. The bears are sa, muzzled and both to dexter

Conant Erm on a bend vert bet 3 dragons' heads erased az 3 fleurs-de-lis or
Crest: a stag holding under the dexter foot a shield
Bookplate William M. Conant, M. D., by E. H. Garrett

Conant Gu 10 billets 4, 3, 2, 1 [or]
Crest: a stag statant
Motto: Conanti nihil difficile est
Bookplate Prof. Grace Patten Conant, Littleton, Mass., and Milliken Univ., Decatur, Ill.

Water color by Victor H. Searles, owned by Miss Mary E. Ward, Brookline, Mass. Seen by Dr. H. Bowditch, 1925. Crest: among rushes a swan regardant. Mrs. Elizabeth Merrill, Portland, Me., impales Merrill and omits "est"

Conant Quart 1 and 4: Per saltire [az] and [gu] 13 billets [or] 3, 2, 3, 2, 3; 2 and 3: Arg a cross couped bet 2 bars sa and in chief 3 pellets. On an inscutcheon erm on a bend (?) bet in chief 2 griffins' heads erased and a dolphin in base 3 garbs
 Crest: a stag holding a shield of the arms
 Motto: Conanti dabitur
 Bookplate Lewis S. Conant

Conarroe Arg a fess dancette sa. In chief a crescent
 Crest: a griffin's head ducally gorged
 Motto: Jour de ma vie
 Bookplate George M. Conarroe, Phila.

Coney *See also* Foxcroft

Connolly Arg on a saltire sa 5 escallops of the field
 Crest: a mailed hand holding a wreath of 3 roses
 Motto: En Dieu est tout
 Bookplate Charles M. Connolly. Des. by J. G. Bolen, Broadway

Constable Quart 1 and 4: Vairé az and arg; 2 and 3: Gu; Over all a bend sinister or (*See* Burke, however)
 Crest: a ship under sail with St. Andrews cross on flag at stern
 Bookplate Wm. Constable, 1783. (Allen No. 181)

Constable Quartered by Maxwell

Contee Per chev gu and az a chev erm bet 3 lions (or wolves) passant or
 Engr. on silver owned by Douglas H. Thomas, desc. of Alexander Contée. Richardson's Sidelights on Md. Hist., vol. 1, p. 201; vol. 2, p. 72. Ancest. Rec. & Portr., vol. 2, p. 726. The above arms engr. on a silver teapot, cream jug, waiter, and large bowl with London Hall mark indicating date of manufacture, 1737–1739, which have been in the Contee, Hanson, and Thomas families for many generations. Letter from D. H. Thomas, 1917

Converse Arg on a bend sa bet 2 maunches 3 trefoils slipped and conjoined az
 Crest: a cubit arm issuing from an embat crown holding a trefoil of the field
 Motto: In Deo solo confido
 Bookplate Alfred Woods Converse, Windsor Locks, Conn.

Conway Sa on a bend arg cotised erm, a rose gu bet 2 annulets of the last
 Crest: a moor's head side faced ppr, banded round the temples arg and az
 Several deeds at Lancaster Court House, Va., made by Edwin Conway, who d. 1763.
 Bookplate Moncure Daniel Conway, writer, with motto: Fide et amore. Crozier's Va. Heral., pp. 68 and 69

Cooke Barry of 6 arg (?) and sa (?) and in chief 3 annulets of the last
 Crest: a griffin's head
 Seal (A. O. 13/80) of William Cooke, son of John Cooke of Prince George's Co., Md., adm. to the Inner Temple, 1768. Lawyer. Seen by E. A. Jones

Cooke Erm 2 bars
 This seal appears after the name of Francis Cooke of Boston, carterer, 1683. The witnesses are George Thomson, who wrote the bond, and Joseph Webb. Owned by C. P. Greenough

Cooke [Or] a fess bet 2 lions pass gu
 Crest: a wolf's head arg ducally gorged [gu]
 Tomb of Mary Booth, daughter of Mordecai Cooke, at Jarvis Farm, Ware River, Gloucester, Va., who d. 21 Jan. 1723. The above arms are impaled with Booth: "Arg 3 boars' heads erect sa." Cooke Genealogy

Cooke Paly of 6 gu and sa 3 eagles displ arg
 Crest: a demi-eagle per pale [gu and sa] with wings displ and ducally crowned [or]
 On bookplate of Miss Lyslie Moore Hawes of R. I. Arnold C. Hawes married Eliza, dau. James and Eliza (Cooke) Wardlow of Pawtucket, R. I.

Cooley Erm a lion ramp contourné bet 3 cinquefoils, all gu
 Crest: a unicorn contourné with paws on a mortar and pestle
 Motto: Candide et constanter
 Bookplate Saml. Cooley, b. 1755, Bolton, Conn. Removed to Northampton, O. Originated Cooley's Pills. R. Brunton, sc. Bates's Early Conn. Engr., p. 18

Cooley Or a lion ramp contourné gu bet 3 cinquefoils
 Crest: a mailed arm holding a scimitar
 Motto: Vivere recte est
 Bookplate Timothy M. Cooley. Bates's Early Conn. Engr., p. 18

Coolidge Arg 3 fleurs-de-lis az
 Crest: a lion's head erased az
 Motto: Cuneus genuem trudit
 Bookplate William H. Coolidge

Coolidge?   Vert a griffin segreant arg (?)
Crest: a demi-griffin
Seal of Isabel, dau. of Chas. A. Coolidge, 82 Marlboro St., Boston

Cooper   Arg a chev sa bet 3 doves ppr
Crest: a dove
Notepaper Walter I. Cooper, Phila.

Cooper   Gu on a chev bet 3 lions pass arg 3 lozenges gu
Crest: a hand couped holding a spear
Bookplate "Myles Cooper, LL.D., Coll. Regis Nov. Ebor. in America, Praeses," etc.

Cooper   Quartered by Phinney

Coote   Arg a chev sa bet 3 coots ppr
Seal of Richard Coote, Earl of Bellomont, Gov. of Mass.
For quarterings see Heral. Jour., vol. 1, p. 166; vol. 3, p. 24. King's Chapel, Boston. The Earl's arms hung in the wooden chapel

Coote   1 and 8: Arg a chev sa bet 3 coots ppr; 2: Or a fess sa bet 2 cotises dancettée sa; 3: Arg a chief gu; 4: Chequy or and az a fess erm; 5: Erm on a chief arg 3 crosses pattée sa; 6: Gu in chief and in base a lion passant erm crowned or; 7: Arg on a bend dancettée sa bet 2 bendlets gu, each charged with 3 bezants, 3 fleur-de-lis arg. Over all an inscutcheon Quart 1: Sa a chev erm bet 3 wings erect arg (Nanfan); 2: Arg a maunch sa (Hastings); 3: Sa 2 bars arg in chief 3 plates (Fleet?); 4: Per pale or and sa a saltire engr. counterchanged
Crest: an earl's crown above an escallop arg
Supporters: two wolves erm
Motto: Vincit veritas
Earl of Bellomont, Gov. of Mass. State House, Boston. In color in window, 3d floor. Heral. Jour., vol. 1, p. 166

Corbin   Quart 1 and 4: Arg on a chief gu 3 birds sa; 2 and 3: Per pale az and gu 3 couped saltires [or] (Lane). An inscutcheon quart 1 and 4: Arg 3 pales gu (?) (Goldsboro?); 2 and 3: Gu on a pale arg 3 stags' heads cabossed gu (Parke)
Motto: Probitas verus honos
Bookplate Richard Corbin, Laneville, Va. Framed coat owned by Mrs. Corbin Waller, Boissevain Ave., Norfolk, Va. Seen by L. Park, 1922. Arms of Francis Corbin, 1758, in St. Paul's Church vestry room, Edenton, N. C. Seen by Miss Mary Pruden, 1924

Corbin   See also Turberville and Lightfoot

Corey   Sa on a chev [or] bet 3 griffins' heads [or] 3 estoiles of 6 points [gu]
Crest: from a ducal cor a griffin's head gu [armed or] bet 2 wings erect or, each charged with a mullet [gu]
"The arms of Corey." Photograph of a water color. The late Ellery Corey, Cooperstown, N. Y. Also on notepaper of Mrs. J. Fred Frost, Belmont, Mass., no mullets but the motto: Virtus semper viridis

Cornbury, *Viscountess*   The heraldic coffin plate of Lady Cornbury of N. Y. with many quarterings is shown in Dr. Morgan Dix's History of the Parish of Trinity Church, part 1 (1898) opp. p. 164

Cory   Arg a saltire sa on a chief az 3 mullets or
Crest: a griffin's head gu armed or bet 2 wings erect or, each charged with a mullet gu
Motto: Virtus semper viridis
Water color, not very old. Owned by Mrs. J. Fred Frost, 480 Pleasant St., Belmont, Mass.

Cotes   See also Coles

Cotton   [Az] a chev bet 3 bundles of cotton yarn arg
Engr. on the side of a Saltonstall tankard. Miss Elizabeth H. Brooks, owner

Cotton   Sa a chev bet 3 griffins' heads erased arg
Crest: a griffin's head erased arg
Motto: Fidelitas vincit
Engr. on fluted circular silver tray owned by Mrs. Nathaniel Thayer of Boston. Bookplate of Philadelphia L. Cotton

Couchman   See Cushman

Courtenay   Quart 1 and 4: Or 3 torteaux; 2 and 3: Or a lion ramp gu (az?) (Redvers). Impaling: Sa 2 bars erm and in chief 3 crosses pattée (Bathurst?)
Crest: a dolphin embowed
Bookplate Henry Courtenay of Mass.

Covel   Or a chev bet 3 martlets sa
Crest: a greyhound sej arg
All figures are contourné. Painted on automobile door. Borden Covel, Boston

Covelle   Or on a fess gu 3 crosses crosslet or
Over the street clock of A. E. Covelle, optician, Boylston St., Boston

Cowell   Erm a hind trippant [gu]
Crest: a stag's head
Motto: Pax et amicitia
Bookplate Rev. David Cowell, 1704–60, Trenton, N. J.

Cox Arg 3 stag's attires az (?). Impaling: Greenleaf
Crest: a dove holding a twig
Old painting owned by Dr. Charles Harrod Vinton, Phila. Zieber's Heral., p. 69

Cox Or three bars az on a canton arg a lion's head erased gu
Crest: an antelope's head erased ppr, pierced through the neck by a spear
Seal in ring belonging to John Cox (Pa. & N. J.) and now in the possession of David R. Williams of Camden, S. C. Ancest. Rec. & Portr., vol. 1, p. 30

Coxe Quarterly gu and vert on each a bezant
Crest: a cock
Motto: Vigilantia praestat
Bookplate Richard S. Coxe, Atty.-Gen. U. S., Washington, D. C. Arms also of Daniel Coxe of New Jersey, loyalist, E. A. Jones says

Coxe Sa a rainbow ppr bet 3 crosses couped arg (diocesan). Impaling: arg a chev sa bet 3 cocks' heads erased ppr (Coxe)
Seal of Arthur Cleveland Coxe, Bishop of Western N. Y. Zieber's Heral., p. 209

Crabb Az a chev or bet in chief 2 fleurs-de-lis and in base a crab [or]
Crest: a gamb erased holding a short sword
Motto: Per ardua
Bookplate —— Crabb. H. Hays, sc.

Cradock Arg on a chev az, 3 garbs or
Crest: a bear's head erased sa billetée and muzzled or
Motto: Nec temere, nec timide
Seal of Matthew Cradock, early Gov. of Mass. I have seen the same arms stamped on wax attached to the calling card of Francis Brinley and marked "Seal of George Craddock." Vermont's Amer. Heral., pp. 55, 163

Craig Gu a bezant bet 3 demi-lions ramp arg (Bennet arms)
Crest: from a mural crown or a lion's head [gu] charged on the neck with a bezant
Bookplate John Craig, Boston, actor. Daniel Brewster, sc., 1915

Cram Gu 3 fleurs-de-lis arg
Crest: a crown encircl 3 feathers
Motto: Ecce ferunt calathis musae mihi lilia plenis
Bookplate Henry A. Cram. The same coat and perhaps crest of Geo. Washington Cram, Norwalk, Conn.

Cram Gu 3 fleurs-de-lis arg
Crest: out of a tower gu bet 2 fleurs-de-lis arg a panache of peacock plumes ppr
Motto: Stolz und treu

Seal ring of Ralph Adams Cram, architect, Boston, descended from John Cram, a founder of Exeter, N. H. Also carved in office 248 Boylston St., Boston, and in windows

Cram *See also* Harris

Cranston Gu 3 cranes within a bordure, embattled arg
Crest: a crane passant
Motto: Dum vigilo curo
Tombstone John Cranston [or Cranstoun], Gov. of R. I. (ob. 1680), and his son, John Cranston, also Gov. (ob. 1727), both buried in the Old Newport (R. I.) Burial Ground. Also MS confirmation in R. I. Hist. Soc., Prov. Also in tankard made by John Coney. (F. H. Bigelow.) Vermont's Amer. Heral., pp. 101, 163

Craven Arg a fess bet 6 crosses crosslet fitchée gu
Crest: on a chapeau [purp] turned up erm, a griffin statant with wings elevated and endorsed erm
Motto: Virtus actione consistit
Bookplate "Willm Craven, Esq, 1750," So. Car.

Crawford Gu on a fess erm bet 3 mullets 2 crescents interlaced
Motto: Durum patientia frango
Notepaper Kathleen Beale Crawford, 56th St., N. Y.

Crawford Az a tilting spear in pale, point down, arg
Bookplate Francis Marion Crawford, author. By Paul Avril

Crawford Gu a fess erm
Crest: an ermine arg
Motto: Sine labora nota
Arms are taken from the Crawford bookplate. Crozier's Va. Heral., p. 107

Creagh Arg a chev gu bet 3 fruited branches [vert]. On a chief az 3 bezants
Crest: a horse's head erased and chained, a twig vert at the forehead
Motto: Virtute et numine
Bookplate Arthur Gethin Creagh

Cresseld Impaled by Southack

Crispe Quartered by Andros

Crocker Arg a chev gu bet 3 ravens sa
Bookplate Alice Morgan Crocker, engr. by Hopson, 1902

Crocker Arg a chev engr bet 3 birds sa
Crests: 1: a cup charged with a rose and surmounted by 3 fleurs-de-lis; 2: an eagle's head erased
Bookplate George Glover Crocker, Jr., Boston

Crocker　Arg a chev engr gu bet 3 birds sa
　　Crest: a 2-handled cup or, charged with a rose gu, and 3 fleurs-de-lis on the rim
　　Motto: Deus alit eos
　　Bookplate Lyneham Crocker. S. L. Smith, sc.

Crokatt　Arg a chev az bet in chief 2 mullets az and in base a crescent gu
　　Crest: three spears in pile (?)
　　Motto: Confido
　　Bookplate James Crokatt, So. Car.

Crome　Arg, in chief 3 pierced mullets az, in fess 2 acorns ppr, in base 2 roses
　　Crest: a dexter hand, palm out
　　Motto: Sunt sua praemia laudi
　　Bookplate James Crome, Newburgh, N. Y.

Cromelien　Az a fess arg surmounted of a fess gu met by a half pale arg from the base, surmounted of a half pale gu
　　Crest: a griffin's head erased holding a dead snake in the mouth
　　Motto: Semper fidelis
　　Bookplate Alfred Cromelien, Phila.

Crooke　Arg a heron rising az a chief indented az
　　Tomb of William Crooke, Chirurgeon, "b. at Bigin in Hartfordshire." Lived 22 years in So. Car. and d. April 1723. St. Philip's Churchyard, Charleston, S. C. Seen by L. Park, 1923, Miss Gertrude Gerrish, 1926.

Crookshank　Or 3 boars' heads couped sa
　　Crest: a mailed hand with a short sword
　　Motto: Lege et ratione
　　Bookplate Judge Crookshank of Penn. (Allen No. 189)

Crosby　Az (so engr) on a chev bet 3 rams arg 3 roses
　　Crest: bet the horns of crescent a maltese cross gu
　　Motto: Te duce libertas
　　Ex libris Wm. Lincoln Crosby of Harvard, Mass.

Crosby　Or a cross flory gu. On an inscutcheon arg a chev az bet 3 owls guard (Prescott?)
　　Crest: an arm holding a scimitar
　　Motto: Te duce
　　Bookplate Hiram B. Crosby

Crosby　Sa a chev erm bet 3 rams pass arg
　　Crest: a ram of the field
　　Motto: Meus aequa in arduis
　　Bookplate Judge Hiram B. Crosby, N. Y.

Crown　Per chev [or] and [sa] 3 compasses extended
　　On a seal used by Henry Crown of N. H. on a document dated Aug. 1688. Cartwright arms?

Crouch　Arg on a pale sa within a bordure engr of the last 3 crosses pattée of the first
　　Bookplate Henry Crouch, Charleston, S. C.

Crowninshield　Az a crown gu(?)
　　Crest: an arm emb holding an arrow
　　Bookplate E. A. Crowninshield, Boston

Crowninshield　Gu a crown or
　　On automobile of Francis B. Crowninshield, Peach Point, Marblehead, Mass. Window, Blake Mem. Chapel, Salem, Mass.

Cruger　Arg on a bend az bet 2 greyhounds courant ppr [sometimes sa] 3 martlets ar
　　Crest: a demi-greyhound ppr gorged or
　　Motto: Fides
　　Iron seal brought over by John Cruger in 1688. Also on an urn given 1766 by Bristol to Henry Cruger of N. Y. See Met. Mus. of Art Cat. of Exhib. of Silver, 1911, pp. 69, 85. Owned by T. J. O. Rhinelander. Also on notepaper F. Winthrop coll., 1885. Vermont's Amer. Heral., pp. 36, 163

Cruttenden　[Az] a chev [or] powdered with flames bet 3 estoiles of 6 points pierced [az]. In chief a crescent of the last for diff
　　Crest: an elk's head ppr
　　Bookplate —— Cruttenden, Albany, 1849. A. Tolle. A similar shield is engr. on a coffee pot made by N. G. Owned by Judge Clearwater. Amer. Silver, by C. L. Avery, 1920, p. 46

Cummings　Az a chev arg bet 3 garbs or
　　Crest: two swords in saltire ppr
　　Motto: Courage
　　Framed water color owned by Mrs. Emma L. Cummings, Shirley Mass.

Cunningham　[Arg] a pall [az]. Should the pall be a shakefork?
　　Crest: a unicorn's head
　　Motto: "Youre youre"
　　Engr. on flagon from Nathaniel Cunningham in 1748 to South Church, Boston. Old Silver Am. Ch,. p. 55

Cunningham　Quart 1 and 4: Arg a pall az; 2 and 3: Or a fess chequy arg and az a crescent in chief (Stewart?)
　　Crest: a unicorn's head
　　Bookplate James Cunningham, Jr. Engr. W. A. F. 1794 (Allen, No. 190)

Cunningham Quart 1 and 4: Arg a pall sa; 2 and 3: Or a fess chequy arg and az (Stewart?) all within a bordure engr gu. Impaling: Or 3 crescents sa on a canton of the 2d a ducal crown of the first (Hodges)
Mottoes: 1: Virtute et labore; 2: Virtute et labore verum amicum cole
Bookplate Daniel Cunningham

Curle Vert on a chev or bet 3 fleurs-de-lis a cinquefoil gu
Crest: on a mount vert a hedgehog or
Tomb of Thomas Curle, Gent. Justice of Elizabeth City, Va., buried at Pembroke Farm near Hampton. He d. 30 May, 1700. Crozier's Va. Heral., p. 37

Currey Gu a saltire arg. In chief a rose
Crest: a rose
Motto: Sic curre ut capias
Bookplate G. Currey

Currier Arg on a mount vert a tree. On a chief gu a bezant bet 2 griffins' heads erased of the first
Crest: a cinquefoil arg
Motto: Flecto non frango
Framed water color (not by Coles) owned by Mrs. Geo. A. Anderson, Lunenburg, Mass., niece of John J. Currier, late historian of Newburyport, Mass. These are the arms of Curryer of London. The Curriers of Bow, N. H., had a seal as above, with motto: Flecti non frange

Curry Quart 1: Gu a saltire arg. In chief a rose arg; 2: Az a chev bet 3 pheons or. On a chief gu 3 maidens' heads couped at the breasts (Swain); 3: Arg 3 boars' heads couped sa; 4: Gu a fess engr or charged with a mitre (?) az within a bordure vairé
Crest: a rose
Motto: Sic curre ut capias
Bookplate George Curry, D. D., Commander "Washington Blues," 1812

Curson See also Cushing

Curtin Vert a tilting spear in pale point up surmounted of a stag trippant, bet 3 crosses crosslet, 2 in chief and one in base, and 3 trefoils slipped, one in chief and 2 in base arg
Crest: an Irish harp over 2 tilting spears in saltire, points up
Motto: Books unlike universities are open to all who would read
Roland Gideon Curtin, M. D., Phila., 1904

Curtis Arg a chev sa bet 3 bulls' heads cabossed [gu?]
Crest: a unicorn trippant or in front of three trees
Motto: Gradatione vincimus

Notepaper Hon. Edwin Upton Curtis, mayor of Boston, etc. The bookplate of Ralph Wormeley Curtis bears the Wormeley arms

Curtiss Az a fess dancetté bet 3 ducal crowns or
Crest: a lion issuant ppr supporting a shield of the arms
Old parchment said to have been brought over by Wm. Curtiss, 1632, of Stratford, Conn. On cover of "Curtiss Family," 1903

Curwen Arg fretty gu a chief az
Crest: a unicorn contourné
Bookplate S. Curwen, Salem, Mass. Another "Curwen, Salem," 1799 (Allen, No. 192). George R. Curwen has for motto: "Si je nestoy." Crest not contourné

Curwen Arg a fret gu. On a chief gu a crescent arg. Impaling: Arg a chev sa bet 3 crosses crosslet fitchée (Russell)
Crest: a demi-unicorn erased
Embroidered hatchment, Essex Institute, Salem, Mass.

Curwen Arg fretty gu, on a chief az, a crescent arg
Essex Institute, Salem, Mass. On Rev. Geo. Curwen's portrait

Curwen Quartered by Lynde

Curzon [de] Arg on a bend sa 3 popinjays or, collared gu
Crest: a popinjay rising or, collared gu
Motto: Let Curzon holde what Curzon helde
Seals and plate brought over by Richard Curzon, b. in Eng. 1726. Descendants in Md. Vermont's Amer. Heral., p. 116

Cusack Impaled by Smith

Cushing Quart 1 and 4: Gu an eagle displ or; 2 and 3: Az 3 dexter hands 1 and 2 arg bend sinister ways fingers down, a canton chequy or and az?
Crest: two lions gambs supporting a crown or from which hangs a heart gu
Motto: Virtute et nemine
Framed water color. Miss Margaret W. Cushing, Newburyport, Mass. See N. E. H. & Gen. Rev., Jan. 1865, p. 39, where the hands are 2 and 1, and the form is said to be correct. See Geneal. pub. in Montreal.
Bookplate Livingston Cushing, Boston (numine not nemine). Harvey's Visit. of Norfolk, 1563, gives these arms under the Aldham-Cushin marriage

Cushing   Quart 1 and 4: [Gu] an eagle displ arg (Cushing); 2 and 3: [Gu] two dexter hands couped arg, each bendways fingers up, one in the second quarter, one in the third, a canton chequy [or and az] (Denvers)
Crest: 2 lions' gambs erect erased [sa] supporting a marquis's coronet [or] from which hangs a heart [gu]
"By the name of Cushing." Matthew Cushing of Hingham, Mass., 1638. Granary Burying Ground, Park St. wall, Boston. Heral. Jour., vol. 2, p. 123

Cushing   Quart 1 and 4: [Gu] an eagle displayed [arg]; 2 and 3: [Gu] 2 dexter hands couped [arg] each bendways, fingers up one in the 2d quarter, one in the 3d; a canton chequy [or and az] (Denvers of Co. Norfolk)
Crest: two lions' gambs erect erased [sa] supporting a marquis' cor. [or] from which hangs a heart [gu]
Moulded. Surmounts the portrait of Thomas Cushing as part of the frame. Independence Hall, Phila. (Zieber's Heral., p. 37.) Also embr. hatchment 17 inches square, owned by the Misses Newman, Concord, Mass. Deborah Cushing married Henry Newman, 1781. Cross stitch and petit point. He was great grandfather of Miss Roma Newman of Concord. Another, owned by the Misses Vose, Milton, Mass. In Oct. 1852, H. G. Somerby sent to Hon. Caleb Cushing an ancient c. portrait and two painted arms of Beckham relatives, owned by the legatee of the Hardingham Cushings

Cushman   Sa 3 roses arg 2 and 1 bet 9 crosses crosslet fitchée arg 4, 2, 2, 1 (Arms of Couchman)
Motto: Habeo pro jus fasque
Bookplate Charlotte Cushman, Newport, R. I., actress. Pulini, sc.

Custis   Arg 3 pojinjays vert
Crest: an archer ppr coat vert, shooting an arrow from a bow of the first
Tomb of John Custis at Northampton Co., Va., bears the arms (without the crest). He d. 29 Jan. 1696. Tomb of John Custis, grandson of the above, is also at "Arlington" and bears the Custis arms. He d. 1749. Va. Mag. of Hist. & Biog., July, 1924, p. 239

Custis   [Or] an eagle displ [gu?]
Crest: an eagle's head
Bookplate Geo. Washg Park Custis

Cutbush   Erm a cow statant gu within a bordure sa bezantée
Crest: a mailed arm emb holding a battle axe
Motto: Editando et legendo
Bookplate Edoardi Cutbush, M. D., surgeon, U. S. N., Mass., 1829

Cutler   Arg 3 bends sa.   Over all a lion ramp gu
Crest: a unicorn, horned or, before a sun in splendor
Motto: Spes mea in Deo
Framed water color. "He beareth argent three Benddletts sable over all a Lyon Rampant Gules — by the name of Cutler." N. E. Hist. Geneal. Soc., Boston

Cutler   [Az] 3 griffins' heads erased or
Tombstone Jonas Cutler, who d. 1782. Erected by wife Jemima. Groton, Mass. Green's Epitaphs, p. 89

Cutler   Az 3 griffins' heads [erased or?] a chief arg
Crest: a griffin's head gorged with a mural crown holding a twig
Bookplate Peter Young Cutler, N. Y.

Cutting   Arg fretty gu. On a chief az an escallop [or]
Crest: a demi-griffin [arg] holding an escallop [or]
Motto: Nil desperandum
Bookplate Frank Cutting, Boston

Cutting   Sa on a chev bet 3 roundels each charged with a martlet sa 3 mascles of the last
Crest: a stag's head erased
Motto: Carpe diem postero ne crede
Bookplate Wm. Cutting, N. Y. P. R. Maverick, sc.

Cutts   Arg on a bend engr or wavy [sa?] bet in chief 6 billets paleways and in base 5 billets bendways 3 p ates (?)
In place of a crest the letters I-C
Seal on deed from John Cutt of Portsmouth, 10 Oct. 1679, to Nicholas Morrill, owned by Ralph D. Cleveland, Caponsville, Md.

Cutts?   Arg on a bend engr sa 3 plates
Crest: a bird rising
Embr. hatchment owned by Mrs. Frank E. Peabody, Boston, formerly by Alexander Everett. The framed water color in York Jail Museum, Maine, has for crest a hart's head collared, and motto: Alta pete (?)

Cuyler   Per pale embat gu and az over all an arrow bendways point up [pointed and flighted arg]

Crest: from a mural crown chequy a battle axe erect [or] surmounted of 2 arrows in saltire points up
Motto: Deo nos sagittis fido
Bookplate C. Cuyler
Framed coat at Brandon on James River, Va. The crossed arrows have points down. Seen by L. Park, 1922

Cuyler Vert an arrow in bend point up bet in base an H and in chief a C or
Crest: three arrows points up, one in pale and 2 pilewise
On Hendryk Cuyler's seal used by his widow in her will July 3, 1702. N. Y. Gen. & Biog. Rec., vol. 42, p. 351

D

Dade Gu a chev bet 3 garbs or, in chief a crescent sa for difference
Crest: a garb or, enfiled with a ducal cor per pale gu and az. *See* Va. Hist. Mag., vol. 20, p. 323. Arms used in Eng. on the tomb of Thos. of Tannington, Suffolk, brother of Francis the immigrant to Va.

Dale Gu on a mount vert a swan arg, membered and ducally gorged or
Crest: on a chapeau gu turned up erm a heron arg beaked, legged, and ducally gorged or
Thomas Carter, who married Catherine, dau. of Edward Dale, Gent., used a seal bearing the above crest, 1776. Crozier's Va. Heral., p. 69

Dahlgren Az a plant growing in a flower pot. Issuing from the dexter point a sun in splendor
Motto: Hvad Himlen Föder Ey Afvund öder
Bookplate John Vinton Dahlgren, Admiral

Damon Or a lion ramp az debrused by a fess [gu] charged with 3 martlets arg
Motto: Pro rege, pro lege, pro grege
Notepaper Frederic W. Damon, Arlington, Mass.

Dana On a bend 3 chevrons
Crest: an ox's head cabossed
Bookplate Charles L. Dana, by French

Dana Arg a chev engr gu bet 3 stags trippant
Crest: a fox
Motto: Cavendo tutus
Bookplate Francis Dana, 1743–1811, Charlestown, Mass., N. H., sc. Richard Henry Dana used a field or and unicorns. Gorham Dana of Brookline, Mass., 1916, uses a field or on notepaper

Dana Arg a chev engr az bet 3 stags trippant gu
Crest: a fox
Motto: Cavendo tutus
Carved on frame of Copley's portrait of Richard Dana, 1700–1772

Dana Barry of 6 [   ] and [   ] 3 lions ramp crowned
Crest: an ox head cabossed
Bookplate Charles A. Dana

Dandridge Az a lion's head erased or bet 3 mascles arg
Crest: a lion's head erased, charged with a mascle arg
Tomb of Euphan Dandridge, dau. of the Rev. James Wallace, bears the arms of Wallace impaling Dandridge. She married Capt. Wm. Dandridge of Elsing Green, King Wm. Co., Va., and d. 1717. Va.. Mag. of Hist. and Biog., July, 1924, p. 238. Crozier's Va. Heral., p. 30. Mrs. Ljungs·edt saw a Dandridge stone in St. John's Churchyard, Hampton, Elizabeth City, Va., 1926, with "something rampant" between the mascles

Dandridge *See also* Langborne

Danforth Arg in chief a human eye, in base a lozenge az
(Crest: 3 books)
Motto: Ubi plura offendar maculis nitent non ego paucis
Bookplate of "Danforth" in a book owned by Dr. Samuel Danforth of Boston, N. H., sc. The crest appeare in Dr. Samuel Danforth's bookplats. N. Hurd, sc.

Danforth [Arg] in chief an eye and in base a fusil [az]
Engr. on a tankard from Elijah Danforth, 1736, a physician, to First Church, Dorchester, Mass., E. Ae Jones. Old Sil. Am. Ch., p. 147. *Se. also* a quaint letter in Mass. Hist. Soc. Coll., 5th Series, vol. 1, p. 447

Daniels *See also* Potter

Darling Az guttée or on a fess of the last 3 crosses crosslet fitchée gu
Crest: a female figure ppr habited in a loose robe arg, the body pink, flowing round her a robe az, holding in the hand a cross crosslet fitchée, gu in the sinister a book ppr
Motto: Cruce dum spiro spero
Arms on old seal. Vermont's Amer. Heral., pp. 115, 116

Dart Arg a fess erm a canton of the second. Impaling: Per chev arg and erm in chief 2 boars' heads
Crest: a falcon stooping on a dove
Dart tombstone, Charleston, S. C.

Davenport Arg a chevron bet 3 crosses crosslet fitchée sa
Crest: a stag's head cabossed
Motto: Audentes fortuna juvat
On will of Francis Davenport, Probate Office, Suffolk Co., Boston. Also on letter from Rev. John Davenport to Gov. John Winthrop (Winthrop papers). Also shield on Isaac Davenport's bookplate. Seal on Doc., Mch. 2, 1690–91, of Addington Davenport, Mass. Archives, vol. 36, p. 415. Vermont's Amer. Heral., pp. 46, 163. Heral. Jour., vol. 2, p. 179; vol. 3, p. 177

Davenport Sa a chev gu bet 3 crosses crosslet fitchée [az] as many roses of the field
Crest: a Saracen's head in profile ppr wreathed about the temples, the wreath surmounted of a crescent
On notepaper of Mrs. Geo. H. (Camilla) Davenport, 460 Beacon St., Boston. *See also* N. Y. G. and B. Record, April, 1912, p. 189

Davidson Az on a fess arg bet 3 pheons of the 2d a stag couchant [gu]
Crest: a stag's head erased ppr
Motto: Viget in cinere virtus
Bookplate Duncan Davidson. Henry Davidson has motto: Sapienter si sincere. Same arms used by Sir Wm. Davidson, Boston, 1664, on doc. in Mass. Archives, vol. 60, p. 261

Davie Quart 1 and 4: Sa a fess or bet 3 cinquefoils [erm]; 2 and 3: Sa (?) on a chief or 3 lions heads erased (Richardson)
Crest: a lion sejant arg supporting a column or
Motto: Diu delibera cito fac
Bookplate Wm. R. Davie, 1756–1820, statesman and soldier, So. Car., grad. Princeton, 1776

Davie or **Davis** On a fess 3 lozenges
Seal of Sarah, third wife of Wm. Davis, apothecary, of Boston. Jeffries MSS. N. E. Reg., Jan. 1877, p. 59

Davis Az a fess or bet 3 stars of 6 points arg
Crest: a lion ramp or supporting a ragged staff arg
Water color in So. Car. Hist. Soc.

Davis Erm a chev gu bet 3 roses
Crest: a demi-lion ramp holding a rose
Motto: Quo fata vocant
Bookplate Frederick Willis Davis, Brooklyn, 1907, Fellow N. G. S.

Davis Gu a chev arg bet 3 boars' heads
Crest: a demi-lion rampant
Motto: Auspice Christo
Bookplate H. T. Davis; Admiral Charles H. Davis, Cambridge, Mass.

Davis Gu a chev [or] bet three boars' heads couped [arg]
Crest: a head of the arms
Motto: Fiel pero desdichado
Arms of Dr. Charles A. Davis used on a bookplate by his son, Hon. Charles Thornton Davis, Brookline, Mass.

Davis Or a chev az bet 3 pierced mullets sa
Crest: a swan rising ppr
Also two supporters in liberty caps, brown coats, and blue boots. Embr. hatchment, signed Amy Davis, 1753, "being the arms of E. Davis and is the Paternal Coat Armour of the Right Honorable Thomas Davis, Kt. Lord Mayar of London, Anno 1677." On a stand and used as a fire-screen. There was a Sir Thomas Davies, Sheriff, 1667. Owned by Rev. Glenn Tilley Morse (1920), West Newbury, Mass., earlier by Miss Annie S. Turner of Newport, R. I., then by Mrs. G. von L. Meyer

Davis *See also* Devotion

Davison [Gu] a stag trippant [or]
Crests: a stag's head erased; a stag trippant pierced by an arrow
Bookplate Chas. Stewart Davison, 60 Wall St., N. Y. Spenceley, sc. Some Amer. Coll. Bookplate, 1915, p. 282

Dawes Arg on a bend [az] cotised [gu] bet 6 battle axes [sa] erect 3 swans [or]
Crest: "a halberth erect [or] on the point a flying dragon without legs, tail nowed [sa] bezantée vulned [gu]"
Engr. on silver punch bowl made by Homes for Col. Thomas Dawes of Boston. *See* Mus. F. Arts Bulletin, vol. xi, p. 23. A paten by Jacob Hurd given by Mrs. Ambrose Dawes has crest: a dove with twig

Dawes Arg on a bend gu bet 6 battle axes sa 3 swans ppr. Impaling: Sa a chev or bet 3 roses of the last a chief or (perhaps May)
Embr. hatchment owned 1924 by Arthur Holland, Concord, Mass.

Dawkins Gu a lion pass guard or bet 2 roses in pale arg and as many flaunches of the 2d, each charged with a lion ramp az. Impaling: Gu on a chev bet 3 wolves' heads erased arg 3 oak trees eradicated ppr fructed [or] (Colyear)
Bookplate Henry Dawkins

Dawson Arms used by Ballagh, q. v.

Day Arg a lion ramp. Impaling: Az on a chev arg 3 mullets (Bullard?)
Crest: a sun rising in splendor
Motto: Le matin et le soir le premier jour
Bookplate John Day, Phila. J. Smithers, sc.

Deacon Arg a chev counter compony gu and arg bet 3 rose twigs. Impaling: Arg a chev gu bet 3 stags' heads cabossed (Parker?)
Crest: an eagle's head erased [arg] bet 2 wings [sa]
Motto: Audacter et singere
Bookplate Harleston Deacon

Deane Arg a lion statant. In chief a crescent bet 2 mullets
Bookplate Ruthven Deane, Chicago. Also George Clement Deane, B. E. S. del. 1901

Deane Vert on a chev bet 3 griffins' heads erased [or beaked gu] 5 pierced mullets sa a crescent in chief for diff
Crest: a demi-griffin
Bookplate John Deane

Deas Erm a pale vert
Crest: on a mount vert a bee feeding on a leaved daisy ppr
Motto: Industria
Painting owned by Burrell Boykin of Boykin, sc.

De Berdt Arg a fess az, charged with 3 fleurs-de-lis, or bet 3 griffins' heads erased gu
Crest: a boar's head couped ppr
Framed water color. Under portrait of Dennys de Berdt, agent of Mass. in Eng. State House, Boston. *See* Pub. Colonial Soc. of Mass. for March, 1911

De Blois 3 pales counter vairé. On a chief or a spread eagle
Crest: a griffin's (?) head erased
Bookplate Lewis De Blois. Nathaniel Hurd, sculp. Boston family

De Courcy Arg 3 eagles, displayed gu crowned or
Crest: from a ducal cor or an eagle displayed arg
Motto: Omnia vincit veritas
Framed water color owned by Judge Charles A. De Courcy, Lawrence, Mass., son of John from Kinsale, Ire. Same arms on watch

Degen Sa 2 swords in saltire points up
Bookplate Charles F. Degen, New Orleans, La., about 1800

De Grasse [Or] a lion ramp crowned [sa]
Crest: a coronet
Inscription in St. Mary's (French Catholic) Cemetery, Charleston, S. C., to Amelie and Melanie, daughters of Francis J. P., Count de Grasse, dead in 1799. Seen by Mrs. Milnor Ljungstedt, 1924. *See* Charleston Year Book, 1897, p. 500

Delafield Sa a cross flory or
Crest: a dove rising with olive branch
Mottoes: Fest: Insignia fortuna paria
Notepaper F. Winthrop coll., N. Y., 1885, at Bos. Ath.

Delamare A lion ramp
Crest: a bird
On coffee pot once owned by Mrs. C. W. Eliot. Made c. 1750–75 by B. Burt. Rubbing by F. H. Bigelow

De Lancey Azure a lance in pale, with a flag its point in chief, debruised of a bar or
Bookplate "James De Lancey, Esq., of the Inner Temple." Seal of James De Lancey, Gov. of N. Y., 1753. For crest and motto *see* Godchild of Wash'n, p. 499. Heral. Jour., vol. 4, p. 95, and vol. 2, p. 191

Delano Arg fretty sa on a chief gu 3 wolves' heads erased or
Brought over by Jonathan Delano, Tolland, Ct., 1722. Vermont's Amer. Heral., pp. 47, 163

Delany Gu 3 fishes in pale fessways
Quartered on the bookplate of Rt. Rev. John Delany, D. D., Bp. of Manchester, N. H., 1904. Some Amer. Coll. Bookplates, 1915, p. 226

De Lasset Quartered by De Rosset de Fleury

De Luna Quartered by Renshaw

De Marchado Quartered by Renshaw

Dempster Gu on a semée of guttées arg a sword in bend arg point up debruised by a fess erm
Crest: a leg bone and a quill in saltire ribboned
Motto: Mors aut vita decöra
Bookplate George Dempster

Denham Quartered by Stewart

Denison Arg on a chev engr gu bet 3 torteaux an annulet or
Crest: a cubit arm holding a cutlass
Motto: Domus grata
Will of Major-Gen. Daniel Denison, 1673. Also tombstone of Rev. John Denison, d. 1742, desc. of Maj.-Gen. Daniel Denison. Also tomb of John Denison, 3d, d. 1749. Both in Ipswich, Mass., Burying Ground. Seen by Miss Ethel Stanwood about 1890. Also in John H. Denison's house, Boston, 1890, a painted coat. Heral. Jour., vol. 1, p. 91

Denny Arg (?) a fess sa (?) in chief 3 mullets of the 2d
Seal of Samuel Denny of Maine, adopted 1762 as the seal of Lincoln County and then called "the lawful coat of arms of the said Denny's family." Mass. Hist. Soc. Proc., Mch. 1883, p. 167. Arms of the Dyneley family of Kent?

Denny Gu a saltire bet 12 crosses formée arg (or?)
Crest: a cubit arm holding in the hand ppr 4 ears of wheat [or]
Seal Wm. Denny, Gov. Penn., 1756–59. Sylvan City, 1883, p. 457

De Normandie [Arg] on a fess gu bet in chief 3 martlets and in base 3 [black] birds 2 and 1, sa 3 annulets filled with mullets
Crest: three ostrich feathers
Notepaper Rev. James De Normandie, Roxbury, Mass. André de N. from Geneva in 1708 brought these arms but with bezants on the fess. (*See* Annals, 1901)

Denvers Quartered by Cushing

Depew Or a lion's head erased gu. On a chief az 3 mullets or
Bookplate Chauncey M. Depew, U. S. Senator, N. Y.

De Peyster [Az] a tree [ppr?] eradicated
Silver seal brought over by Johannes De Peyster. Zieber's Heral., p. 69. Also bookplate of Frederick De Peyster, engr. by P. R. Maverick. Crest: a dexter armed arm holding a sword in fess. The tree is in a field. Also bookplate of Johnston L. De Peyster

De Peyster Az on a terrace, a tree vert bet 2 sheep affronté grazing arg
Crest: a tree of the field
Engr. on a tankard marked I V S (Jacobus van der Spiegel, 1668–1716) owned by Frederick Ashton de Peyster of New York, 1922. Photo shown me by F. H. Bigelow

Dering Gu 3 roebucks' heads couped or
Crest: a head of the field
Bookplate Thomas Dering. N. Hurd, sc., 1749. Also of N[icoll] H. Dering

Dering Quart 1: Or on a saltire sa a mullet arg (Dering); 2: Arg a fess az In chief 3 torteaux (Dering); 3: Gu a wyvern (Brent?); 4: Or a chev gu a canton erm (Stafford?)
Bookplate John Thurlow Dering

De Rosset de Fleury Quart 1: Arg a bouquet of 3 roses gu stem and leaves or; 2: Gu a lion or (De Lasset); 3: Quarterly arg and sa (Vissec De la Tude); 4: Az 3 roses or (De Fleury)

Framed painting owned by Mrs. Gabrielle de Rosset Waddell, South Fifth St., Wilmington, N. C. The family also used 3 fleurs-de-lis, for crest a rose bush issuing from a coronet, and motto In Domino Confido

De Saumarez Quartered by Andros

Detcher Erm on a chief dancetté gu 3 crowns
Crest: on a crown a serpent encircling a hand
Framed painting owned by Mrs. Ellen D. F. Arthur, Greenville, N. C.

De Vargas Quartered by Renshaw

Devereux Erm a fess gu. In chief 3 torteaux
Crest: a stag trippant ppr
Window of Eugene Devereux, De Lancey Place, Phila. Zieber's Heral. p. 66

Devlin Az a saltorel or bet 3 stars arg
Crest: a griffin pass [gu] charged on the shoulder with a saltorel as in the arms
Motto: Crux mea stella
Bookplate John Edward Devlin. Spenceley, sc.

Devotion A fess erm bet three cinquefoils
Crest: a bird's head or an arm (?) holding a cinquefoil
Wax seal on a deed from John Devotion of Brookline, Mass., 1706, now in the Public Library. These are not the arms given by Crozier. See Brookline Hist. Pub. Soc., no. 4, p. 42. Mr. J. W. Linzee, Jr., in his Desc. of Peter Parker, p. 335, suggests that this is the Davis coat, as John Devotion's sister Mary married John Davis of Boston

Dexter Arg a fess az debruised by a fess embattled gu bet 3 suns in splendor within a bordure gu
Crest: a sun in splendor
Motto: Sol et sentum Deus
Bookplate George Dexter of Cincinnati. The bookplate of Mary Deane Dexter of Cambridge, Mass., lacks crest and motto. Gregory Dexter of R. I. used as a seal two arrows in saltire, debruised by a heart and in chief an antique crown

Dexter [Arg] 2 chev az a canton gu
Crest: a tree with 2 mullets pendant
Seal ring New York.
On automobile George T. Dexter, Maple St., Sherborn, Mass.

Dexter Gu on a chev bet 3 bezants, 3 daggers points down
Crest: a mailed arm embowed holding a twig
Motto: Esse quam videri

Bookplate Arthur Dexter, F. Gordon Dexter, Samuel Dexter, prominent Bostonians. The gravestone of Samuel Dexter, b. Marlboro, 1756, d. Albany, 1825. (John Evans, maker) lacks the daggers

Dexter Per fess embat gu and az 3 suns in splendor
Crest: a blackbird
Motto: Industria, intelligentia, virtus
Bookplate Georgius Dexter, Cambridge

Dickinson Az a fess erm bet 2 lions pass or
Crest: a demi-lion ramp, per pale erm and az
Bookplate John Dickinson, Prest. Del. and Penn., author. Sylvan City, 1883, p. 442. Hatchment in Phila. Library. Zieber's Heral., p. 318. Philemon Dickinson, Chestnut Hill, Penn., has motto: Esse quam videri
Notepaper John Dickinson, Md., has Esse quam videri

Dickinson Vert a cross az bet 3 hinds' heads couped [or?]
Motto: Esse quam videri
Bookplate Wm. Pliny Dickinson

Dickson Az 3 mullets arg. On a chief sa 3 palets gu
Crest: a hand holding a lance
Motto: Fortes fortuna juvat
Bookplate Frederick S. Dickson, Phila.

Digby Quartered by Lynde and Oliver

Digges [Gu] on a cross arg, 5 double-headed eagles' heads erased [sa]
Crest: an eagle's head
Tomb of Hon. Wm. Digges at Belfield, York Co., Va. He d. 1710. Also tomb of Edward Diggs, with crescent for diff and no crest. Crozier's Va. Heral., p. 32. Also Va. Hist. Mag., vol. 10, p. 377. Also Wm. & Mary Quar., July, 1893, p. 29; Jan. 1893, p. 116

Diggles A lion rampant crowned
Crest: a stag lodged
Bookplate James H. Diggles

Dillman Gu a castle gate with 3 towers
Bookplate —— Dillman

Dinwiddie Per fess. In chief arg an Indian shooting a stag passant reguard in a landscape all ppr. In base arg a sloop sailing toward a fort which flies the British flag. The fort is on the dexter, rocks on the sinister, the sea between
Crest: an eagle rising, holding a guinea pig in the dexter claw
Motto: Ubi libertas ibi patria
Bookplate Robert Dinwiddie, Lt. Gov., Va. Amer. Heral., vol. 2, p. 26

Disney Arg on a fess gu 3 fleurs-de-lis or. In chief a martlet or for diff
Crest: a lion pass guard [gu]
Motto: Vincit qui patitur
Bookplate Samuel Disney, LL.B.

Dix [Az] a lion ramp [or] a chief [or] (Dixie arms)
Memorial tablet to Rev. Morgan Dix in Trinity Church, N. Y. He d. 1908

Dix or **Dickes** 1: Az on a bend or 3 martlets gu. On a chief arg 2 reindeers heads couped gu; 2: Arg a lion ramp sa chained or (Phillips). Impaling: Or on a fess gu 3 dolphins embowed (Lemmon)
Embr. hatchment, very old, made by Mary Dix (Mrs. Harris). Owned 1923 by Misses Emma and Elizabeth Harris, Holyoke Pl., Cambridge

Doane Az crusilly or a unicorn salient arg
Motto: Right onward
Seal Wm. Croswell Doane, Bishop of Albany. Zieber's Heral., p. 208

Doane Az 2 bars arg [embroidered dark] on a bend over all gu, 3 arrows points downward in bend arg [embroidered dark] (Done arms). Impaling: Sa [embroidered bluish] a chev erm [embroidered or] bet 2 lions passant arg [embroidered dark] (Rich arms)
Crest: a sheaf of arrows, points down, or bound [gu]
Hatchment of Hope Doane, 1750–1830, later wife of Samuel Savage of Barnstable, Mass. Embroidery, very elaborate. Inherited 1915 by Henry Savage, Camden, S. C., from Samuel Savage Shaw, Boston. Hope Doane was the daughter of Col. Isaiah and Hope (Rich) Doane of Cape Cod, Mass.

Doane Az a unicorn salient arg bet 8 crosses or 3, 2, 3
Crests: 1: a unicorn's head couped; 2: a bishop's mitre with ribbons
Motto: Right onward
Bookplate George W. Doane, bishop of N. J.

Dodge Barry of 6 or and sa debruised by a pale gu. On an escutcheon of pretence sa a chief nebulé gu charged with 2 martlets and a canton erm
Crest: a demi-horse gorged
Bookplate Murray Witherbee Dodge, engr. by A. W. Macdonald, 1908

Dodge Barry of six or and [sa]. On a pale gu, a plate [arg] dropping tears [or]
Crest: a demi-lion ramp
Used by L. A. Dodge, Groton Inn, Mass., sign and notepaper. On the bookplate of John H. P. Dodge

Doeg Quartered by McFarlan

Done *See also* Doane

Dongan Quart 1 and 4: [Gu] 3 lions ramp or; 2 and 3: 6 roundels 3, 2, 1. On a chief a demi-lion issuant (Molonn or Seys?)
Crest: a lion pass, with paw on a helmet
Motto: Scutum impenetrabile Deus
Bookplate Thomas Dongan. H. Dawkins, sc. Col. Thomas Dongan, 1634–1715, of N. Y. and Hempstead, L. I. For his seal with a lion passant in 3, see Curio, 1888, p. 19

Donnell See also O'Donnell

Doodes On the sea a 17th century ship with 3 masts
Arms of Minor Doodes of Urbanna, Va., on a will, 1677. Crozier's Va. Heral., p. 39

Dorr Per pale gu and az 3 beetles or Dor-beetle, hence dors d'or
Water color of Dorr of Mass. Owned by Mrs. Gordon Wendell of N. Y.

Dorsey Az a semée of crosses crosslet and 3 cinquefoils arg
Crest: on a chapeau gu turned up erm a bull sa
Motto: Un Dieu un Roi
Seal used by John Darcy, Gent., 1749, Maryland. Richardson's Sidelights on Md. Hist., vol. 2, p. 87

Douglas Quartered by Lithgow

Douw On a fess [arg?] bet in chief a slope at the dexter and a tree at the sinister and in base a dove reguard a child holding an anchor in bend lukes up
Crest: a roundel charged with a cross croslet
Motto: Cruci dum fido spiro
Seal of Volckert Peter Douw, mayor of Albany, 1761–70. Also on silver tobacco box, with Susannah and the elders on the reverse side! He d. 1801. Also in the window of the Dutch Church, 1656. (Godchild of Wash., p. 61.) Not the Douw arms described in books

Dove Per chev sa and or [properly az and vert] 3 doves volant [arg]. Impaling: Sa a chev arg bet 3 maidens' faces the necks entwined with ribbons
Crest: a dove rising with a branch
Bookplate Matthew Dove, Va. Crest and motto: "Deus Providebit" used on bookplate of Dr. I. Dove, Richmond, Va. Engraved by —— Brooks

Dowes Impaled by Callaway

Downes Impaled by Franklin

Downing [Barry of ten arg and vert] over all a griffin segreant [or]
Crest: an arm emb holding an arrow

Seal (without barry) of Emmanuel Downing (Winthrop papers, M. H. S. Coll., vol. 36), father of Sir George of London, who impaled a lion ramp possibly for Winthrop. Emmanuel used also arg a chev sa bet 3 griffins' heads. Heral. Jour., vol. 1, p. 164, vol. 3, p. 174

Dous [Or] a chev chequy [arg and az (sometimes sa)] bet 3 greyhounds courant [sa]. Impaling: On a bend 8 lozenges conjoined (Winslow?)
Crest: a head couped
Tombstone of Hon. Jonathan Dous, 1725. Phipps Street Yard, Charlestown, Mass. Heral. Jour., vol. 1, p. 45

Dowse [Or] a chev [chequy arg and az] bet 3 greyhounds courant [sa] collared [gu]
Crest: a wyvern's (?) head
Motto: Labore quæritur gloria
Used by William B. H. Dowse, Boston, on wedding announcement. These arms (no crest) and Virtute et opera appear on a Lowestoft chocolate pot owned by the Groton (Mass.) Historical Society. The shield is arg, the greyhounds brown, and the chev green and white

Drake [Arg] a wyvern with wings addorsed [gu] and tail nowed, the wyvern looks like a cockatrice
Crest: a wyvern of the field on a castle of three embattled towers conjoined
Arms of Richard Drake (d. 1808) and Mary Fearon, his wife (d. 1812). Old St. David's Churchyard, Radnor, Penn. Zieber's Heral., p. 42

Drake [Arg] a wyvern, wings displ and tail nowed gu
Crests: A: an eagle displ gu; B: a dexter arm erect ppr holding a battle axe sa headed arg
Mottoes: A: Sic parvis magna; B: Time tryeth tryst
Arms and crest: A on bookplate of William Walker Drake with motto: Aquila non capit muscas. Vermont's Amer. Heral., pp. 31, 164

Drake Arg a wyvern with wings addorsed and tail nowed gu
Crest: a cubit arm erect ppr grasping a battle axe sa
Motto: Aquila non captat muscas
Water color by Mitchell the gemcutter, Tremont St., Boston, 1905? Framed. The crest and motto used on letter paper. Louis S. Drake, Newton, Mass.

Drake Quartered by Scribner

Draper Quart 1 and 4: Arg on a fess engr gu bet 3 annulets of the last as many covered cups or; 2 and 3: Sa 3 stags trippant [or] (Swift?)

Crest: a stag's head gu charged on the neck with a fess bet 3 annulets or
Motto: Vicit pepercit
Bookplate Eben S. Draper, Gov. of Mass.

Drayton Arg a cross engr gu
Crest: a bird
Motto: Hac Iter Elysium nobis
Engr. portrait of Wm. Henry Drayton, Drayton Hall, Ashley River, S. C.
Notepaper Robert Massey Drayton, Whitemarsh, Pa., has Hac itur ad astra

Drayton Az semée of flames a pegasus arg (?)
Crest: a winged cap gu turned up or above a sun in splendor
Motto: Non nobis solum
Bookplate Wm. Drayton, Middle Temple, S. C., and Fla. Harper's Mo., Dec. 1875, p. 4

Drew Erm a lion pass contourné ppr
Crest: an eagle affronté with wings spread
Motto: Aut nunquam tentes aut perfice
Bookplate William Drew. S. Hill, sc., Boston

Drexel Per bend sin az and vert a demi-stag segreant and issuant arg. Impaling: Gu (sa?) a maunch within a bordure or charged with lions gambs [gu] (Wharton)
Bookplate Lucy Wharton Drexel, engr. by French

Drury Arms used by Chidson, q. v.

Drury See also Chidson

Duane [Erm] a cat passant and in chief two crescents [sa or gu]
Crest: a wolf's head erased ppr
Seal of Rev. Charles W. Duane of Phila., rector Christ Church, Boston.
Also on memorial tablet in Christ Church, Boston

Duane Erm a lion pass sa and in chief 2 crescents gu
Crest: a wolf's head erased ppr
Motto: Nulli praeda
Bookplate James Duane. H. D. Fec.

Dubs Az a pennant in bend sinister. In the dexter chief a fleur-de-lis
Crest: 3 ostrich feathers
Bookplate Joseph S. Dubs, D. D., 1796–1877, Allentown, Pa. Also of Joseph Henry Dubbs, D. D., 1880

Dudley [Or] a lion rampant [az]. In the dexter quarter a crescent for difference
Tablet to Thomas Dudley, 1576–1653, deputy gov. of Mass., and to Paul Dudley, 1675–1751 (Harv. 1690).
There is another coat with no crescent but with a crest, lion's head erased [az],

over the names of Joseph Dudley, 1647–1720 (Harv. 1665), and William Dudley, 1686–1743 (Harv. 1704).
East wall south of chancel, marble.
First Church, Eliot Sq., Roxbury, Mass.

Dudley Or a lion ramp az with forked tail vert
Crest: a lion's head erased az
Motto: Nec cladio, nec arcu
In a window in color, 3d floor, State House, Boston. For Gov. Dudley

Dudley Or a lion ramp double-queued az
Crest: a lion's head erased
Motto: Nec gladio, nec arcu
Seal on will (1654) of Thomas Dudley does not show forked tail but bears a crescent for diff. Seal of Joseph Dudley, son of Thomas, and Gov. of Mass. (1702–1715). Forked tail and no crescent. Vermont's Amer. Heral., pp. 56, 164. See also N. E. Reg., Jan. 1877, p. 59

Dudley [Or] a lion ramp with forked tail [az]
Crest: a lion's head erased [gu]
Motto: Nec gladio, nec arcu
Bookplate Joseph Dudley, 1754, a framed water color of Bailey, Banks & Biddle, Phila. Owned by J. Gardner Bartlett, Boston

Dudley Or a lion ramp az
Crest: a lion's head
Motto: Nec gladio, nec arcu
Gov. Joseph Dudley's arms painted on canvas, 1886. Bostonian Society. Formerly in wooden King's Chapel (an original)

Dudley [Or] a lion ramp [az], in the dexter chief a crescent
Metal ellipse on an altar tomb. Gov. Thomas Dudley "Born in England 1576." Eustis Street Cemetery, Boston

Dudley See also Tyng

Duer Erm a bend gu. Impaling: Or a bend az
Crest: an eagle rising with a green branch
Motto: Esse et videri
Bookplate Alexander Duer, Prest. Columbia Coll., N. Y., 1829

Duffield Sa a chev bet 3 doves arg
Crest: a dove holding an olive branch all ppr
Motto: Deo Reipublicæ et amicis esto semper fidelis
George Duffield, Phila. (?)

Duke Az a chev bet, 3 birds close arg membered gu
Crest: a sword arg hilt or stuck in a plume of 5 ostrich feathers, 2 az 3 arg
Motto: In adversis idem

Seal ring Cliviers Duke, also engr. on old silverware of R. T. W. Duke, Esq. of Charlottesville, a great-grandson of Cliviers Duke. Crozier's Va. Heral., p. 19

Dulany Arg a cross of 8 lozenges conjoined gu. On a chief or a lion pass gu
Bookplate Daniel Dulany, Jr., Esq., Md. Seal on a letter in 1784 seen by E. A. Jones, 1923. Arms of the De Laune family of Blackfriars, London, 1612

Dulany Quart 1 and 4: [Arg] a cross lozengy [gu]. On a chief [or] a lion pass [gu]; 2 and 3: [Az] a saltire bet 4 martlets arg (Smith)
Tomb of Mrs. Daniel Dulany, dau. of Col. Walter Smith. She d. 1737. St. Ann's Churchyard, Annapolis, Md. E. H. Murray's "One hundred yeasr ago" (1895), p. 19. Zieber's Heral., p. 48

Dulany Quart 1 and 4: [Arg] a cross lozengy [gu]. On a chief [or] a lion pass [gu]; 2 and 3: A lion rampant. On a chief two lions rampant [   ]
Crest: a griffin (?)
Seal on a letter reported by E. Alfred Jones

Dumaresq Quart of 6. 1 and 3: Gu 3 escallops or; 2: Sa [ermines?] a cross bow erect charged with an arrow arg (Larbalistier); 4: Sa 3 dolphins emb 2 and 1 arg (De Bagot); 5: Arg 3 trefoils slipped gu (*i. e.* sa) (Payne); 6: Gu 4 fusils in fess arg (De Carteret)
Crest: an ox affronté
Motto: Dum vivo spero
Supporters: Greyhounds ramp
Bookplate Frederika Slade Dumaresq. Julia Jordan Dumaresq used the Jordan arms. *See* Heral. Jour., vol. 3, p. 97

Dummer Az 3 fleurs-de-lis or. On a chief or a demi-lion issuant az
Crest: a demi-lion az holding in his dexter paw a fleur-de-lis or
State House, Boston. In a colored window, 3d floor

Dummer Az 3 fleurs-de-lis or on a chief or a demi-lion issuant sa
Crest: a demi-lion [az] holding in his dexter paw a fleur-de-lis or
Engr. on flagon given by Hon. William Dummer, 1753, to Hollis St. Church, Boston. On a gold snuff box owned by The Misses Loring, 37 Mt. Vernon St., Boston. Old Sil. Am. Ch., p. 81

Dummer Quart 1 and 4: Gu 9 billets 4, 3, 2 arg and in base bezant (Pyldren or Dummer?); 2 and 3: 3 fleurs-de-lis

[or?]. A chief or charged with a demi-lion [sa probably as in the old; az in later coats] (Dummer)
Engr. on "A Prospect of the Colledges in Cambridge," etc. Dedicated by W. Burgis about 1726 to Dummer. Mass. Hist. Soc. *See* Salisbury's Family Memorials, vol. 1

Dumont Az a bend wavy arg bet 2 roses or and in chief a swan's head arg beaked or
Crest: two wings erect and joined arg
Framed water color (modern). Miss Sarah M. Westbrook, 160 Clinton Road, Brookline, Mass.

Dunbar Gu a lion ramp [arg] within a bordure of the 2d charged with 8 roses gu
Motto: Sub spe
Bookplate Charles F. Dunbar, Boston, professor and writer

Duncan Gu a chev or bet in chief two cinquefoils and in base a hunting horn arg [garnished az]
Crest: a ship with three sails spread on fore mast, two on main, and one on muzzin mast
Motto: Disce pati
Embr. hatchment made by Isabella Duncan, daughter of Mrs. Isabella Caldwell Duncan. Owned by Mrs. Richard Morgan, Plymouth, Mass., daughter of Judge Davis

Duncan Gu a chev or bet in chief 2 trefoils and in base a hunting horn [arg] stringed [az]
Crest: a ship with sails and flags
Motto: Disce pati
Bookplate James H. Duncan, Haverhill, 1820

Duncombe A chev bet 3 bugle horns
Crest: on an esquire's helmet a stag's head
Wax seal on will of Thomas Duncombe, probated at Lancaster Court House, Va., 1659. Wm. & Mary Quar., Jan. 1893, p. 121

Dunkin Gu a chev or bet in chief 3 cinquefoils and in base a hunting horn stringed
Crest: a ship of 3 masts
Motto: Disce pati
Bookplate Robert Henry Dunkin [of Phila.]. I. H[utt]

Dunne Arg an eage spread
Crest: a newt before an oak or holly
Motto: Mullach abu
Ex libris Frank Lysaght Dunne. [Az] an eagle displ [or] in Burke

Dupee A fess and in chief 3 patriarchal crosses
Isaac Dupee's tomb. Copp's Hill Yard, Boston, east side. Heral. Jour., vol. 2, p. 81

Dupont Arg a bend gu bet 2 wheels or, on a canton gu a lion ramp or
Framed water color (modern). Miss Sarah M. Westbrook, 160 Clinton Road, Brookline, Mass.

Du Pont Az an Ionic column arg [voided az] [on a base vert?]
Motto: Rectitudine sto
On automobile Francis du Pont, 808 Broome St., Wilmintgon, Del., and 44 the Fenway, Boston, 1916

Dupuy Impaled by Elliston

Durand Sa a fess dancettée or and in chief 3 fleurs-de-lis of the 2d
Crest: a griffin's head erased, pierced with a spear
Bookplate John Durand, Esq.

Durant Quartered by Blake

Durrant Quartered by Gookin

Duryea Arg 3 boars' heads gu each holding a ball
Crest: a boar's head of the field
Motto: Fide et fortitudine
Bookplate Samuel Bowne Duryea, Brooklyn, N. Y.

Duryee [ ] a chev bet 3 crescents
Crest: a bird holding a twig
Motto: La promesse du futur
Bookplate Geo. Van Wagenen Duryee and Margaret Van Nest, engr. by French, 1899

Duvall A chev bet in chief 2 pierced mullets and in base an axe
Crest: a lion pass per pale and holding in the paws a shield of the arms
Motto: Pro patria
Seal of Mareen Duvall of Anne Arundel Co., Md., 1659. Richardson's Sidelights on Md. Hist., vol. 2, pp. 94-96

Dwight Erm a lion pass or. In base a cross crosslet fitchée. On a chief gu a crescent of the 2d
Crest: a demi-lion ramp
Engr. on a silver tankard of Col. Timothy Dwight, who d. Dedham, Mass., 1717, aged 88. A. R. Watson's Some Not. Fam. of Amer.
Bookplate Timothy Dwight, Chicago, 1915

Dyckman Quart 1: Or a dove rising with a branch; 2: Gu a broken chain; 3· Arg a garb; 4: Vert a shovel
Crest: a tree
Motto: Zyt Bestendig
Bookplate J. G. Dyckman. N. Y. G. & B. Record, Jan. 1903, p. 23

Dyer Sa on a fess bet 3 goats pass arg a martlet
Crest: a moor's head in profile ppr with cap or fillet chequy arg and az
Motto: Terre nolo, timere nescio
Seal Anthony Dyer, R. I.

Dymond Gu 3 fusils in fess arg over all a fess of the first
Bookplate John Dymond, N. Y. and Phila.

E

Earle Quart 1 and 4: Paly of 10 or and gu a mullet arg in the center; 2 and 3: Arg a chev sa bet 3 griffins [sa] (Finch?) An inscutcheon quarterly; 1: Earle as above but without mullet; 2: Same as 2 and 3 above; 3: On a bend mascles conjoined; 4: Arg 3 hillocks vert
Crest: a lion's gamb erect and erased, holding an arrow
Bookplate Thomas Earle

Earnshaw Quartered by Marshall

Eastbrook Gu a chev bet 3 cinquefoils
Crest: a dragon sejant
Bookplate John Eastbrook, engr. by French

Easton Per chev gu and or 3 sea dragons counterchanged, those in chief with flaming tongues, that in base with a forked tongue
Crest: a yew tree
Bookplate W. Easton

Eastwick A chev bet 3 bucks statant
Seal of Phesant Eastwick of Portsmouth, N. H., 1687. Jeffries MSS. N. E. Reg., Jan. 1877, p. 59

Eby Az a cornice (?) in bend bet in chief a hunting horn and swallow and in base 3 hills pointed
Crest: a hunter's hat with feather, over 4 arrows in saltire marked 1715
Motto: Be neither tyrant nor slave
Bookplate Simon P. Eby, Lancaster, Pa., 1891. Christian Eby of Manheim, Pa., made tall clocks

Eccleston Arg a cross sa. In the dexter chief a fleur-de-lis [gu]
Crest: a magpie (?) ppr (or a robin)
Bookplate —— Eccleston, N. Y.

Eckley [Gu] 3 swords in fess paleways points upward [arg] hilts and pomels [or] the middle one surmounted by an inscutcheon bearing a dexter hand couped
Crest: a dexter arm embowed and armed
Rev. Joseph Eckley, D. D. Box tomb, 1811, Granary Burying Ground, Boston. Heral. Jour., vol. 2, p. 128. These are the arms of Clarke of Salford, Co. Warwick, Baronet. *See* Clarke

Eckley On a saltire gu a leopard's head pierced by 2 swords saltireways. Impaling: [Sa] a fess [or] lozengy [fretty?] bet 3 fleurs-de-lis of the second (Stiles).
On platter owned by Miss Sarah E. Eustis, Brookline, Mass.

Eden Gu on a chev arg bet 3 garbs as many escallops sa
Crest: a dexter arm in armor embowed couped at the shoulder ppr, the hand grasping a garb bendways
Motto: Si sit prudentia
On tomb of Charles Eden, Gov. of N. C., 1714–22, in St. Paul's Churchyard, Edenton

Edes Az a chev engr bet 3 leopards' faces arg
Crest: a face of the shield
Motto: Nec temere, nec timide
Framed water color owned by Mrs. Henry H. Edes, Cambridge, Mass.

Edes Az a chev engr arg bet 3 leopards' faces arg
Crest: a lion's gamb gorged
Bookplate Dr. Richard H. Edes, 1901

Edgerly Arg on a chev bet 3 cinquefoils gu as many [bezants]
Crest: a griffin segreant
Motto: Memor et fidelis
Bookplate Edwin L. Edgerly, New York City

Edmands "Or a chev az on a quarter of the second a boar's head erased bet 3 fleurs-de-lis or"
Edmands of Leicester, Eng., and Charlestown. The quarter is white. Owned by Mrs. R. S. Southard, Groton, Mass. Framed

Edmands Or a chev az, on a canton az a boar's head couped gu bet 3 fleurs-de-lis sa
Crest: a lion's head erased gu
Bookplate Amos Lawrence Edmands

Edmonds Arg a chev bet 3 garbs gu
Notepaper Mrs. Ida Luella Grady Edmonds, 5639 Rippey St., Pittsburgh

Edmonds Az a chev or bet 3 warriors shields or
Crest: an arm in armor embowed ppr casting a spear [az handle ppr]
Notepaper Franklin Spencer Edmonds, Phila.

Edmonds Per chev embattled gu and sa 3 martlets arg
Crest: a wing arg
Motto: Resurgere tento
Framed water color owned by Miss Deas, Summerville, S. C. Seen by L. Park, 1923

Edolph Impaled by Gookin

Edwards Arg a fess ermines bet 3 martlets or
Crest: on a ducal cor arg a tiger pass or
Seal on will of John Edwards, dated 3 Feb., 1667. Wm. & Mary Quar., Jan. 1893, p. 120

Edwards Arg on a fess bet 3 martlets sa 5 fleurs-de-lis of the field
Crest: a lion pass or
Bookplate Isaac Edwards of No. Carolina

Edwards Arg a fess ermines bet 3 martlets sa a crescent sa in chief for diff
Crest: out of a ducal cor or a tiger passant or
Mottoes: Have wandered; The truth against the world
Bookplate Charles Edwards (b. 1797), lawyer, N. Y.

Edwards Erm a lion ramp az, on a canton gu an eagle displayed or
Crest: a demi-lion ramp az holding a tower
Motto: Sola nobilitas virtus
Bookplate Wm. Edwards Park.
Notepaper Mrs. Helen Edwards Dean Wallace, Pueblo, Colo.

Edwards Per bend sinister erm and ermines, over all a lion ramp or
Crest: a demi-lion ramp or holding bet the paws a castle arg
Motto: Sola nobilitas virtus
Seal of William Edwards, Hartford, Conn., 1639, and on silver willed of Jonathan Edwards. Also on bookplate of Bryan Edwards, Esq., Greenwich Park, Jamaica, historian, Ashby, sc. Motto: "Nosce te ipsum." Vermont's Amer. Heral., pp. 151, 152

Edwards Quartered by Jenks

Edwards *See also* Snell

Eels Arg 3 eels naïant az
Crest: a dexter arm in armour fessways couped holding a cutlass enfiled with a boar's head couped all ppr
Will, dated 1705, of Samuel Eels of Hingham, Mass. Vermont's Amer. Heral., p. 164

Eglintoun Quartered by Montgomery

Elam Gu 2 bars or 3 martlets in chief and 3 in base
Bookplate Samuel Elam, R. I. Like the arms of Ellam but not like those of Elam of Kent

Eldredge Or on a bend raguly sa 3 bezants
Crest: out of a ducal crown 5 peacock feathers
Bookplate: Gift of H. Fisher Eldredge, 1896

Eliot   Arg a fess gu bet 4 cotises wavy az
Crest: an elephant's head ppr collared gu
Framed water color from Sir Isaac Heard, 1784, owned by Samuel Eliot, Boston

Eliot   "He beareth argent a Fesse Gules between two Barrs-Gewelles wavy Sable, Crest: an Elephant's head Sable, by the Name of Eliot"
Motto: Face aut tace
Framed water color by Mrs. Nath. G. Eliot from painting made for her father-in-law (Ephraim Eliot). Size about 10″ x 13″, framed. Owned by Miss Mary L. Eliot, Riverbank Court, Cambridge, Mass.

Eliot   Arg a fess az double cotised wavy gu
Painted on bookcase at Laurence Park's house, Groton, Mass.

Ellacombe   Quartered by Gilman

Ellery   Per chevron az and arg (sometimes arg and az) a bordure engrailed or
Crests: A: (On an old family bookplate) A stag courant; B: (In Burke): A winged globe
Seal of Benjamin Ellery of Newport, R. I. (1669–1746). Also on bookplates, and on silver seal, inscribed B. E., 1749. Vermont's Amer. Heral., p. 108, 109. Heral. Jour., vol. 1, p. 182

Elliot   Gu on a bend engr or a baton az within a bordure or charged with 8 mullets pierced sa (?)
Crest: a dexter hand holding a staff about which a serpent is entwined
Motto: Per saxa per ignes fortiter et recte
Bookplate George Buxton Elliot. The shield on J. B. Elliott's bookplate has no bordure and a cutlass takes the place of the staff and serpent

Elliott   Arg a fess az
Crest: a dragon's.head
Motto: Virtute spernit victa
Bookplate Lt.-Col. Barnard Elliott, S. C.

Elliott   Az a fess or
Crest: a duck rising couped or, with 6 hurts on one wing, one on the other
Motto: Virtute spernit victa
Bookplate Col. Barnard Elliott, Amer. Revol., P. R. Maverick, sc. On cover of Sermons of Rt. Rev. Stephen Elliott. Bookplate John Barnwell Elliott and his wife, Noel Forsyth, by Huger Elliott, 1902

Ellis   Per chev sa and gu a chev or bet 3 fleurs-de-lis arg
Embr. by Elizabeth Ellis, b. 1732, daughter of Dr. Edward Ellis of

Boston. Owned by Henry W. Montague, 32 W. Cedar St., Boston

Elliston   [Per pale gu and vert] an eagle displ [or]. Impaling: Per fess dancettée — and —; 2 lozenges in chief and 2 in base (Dupuy). Broken. One lozenge only shows in base
Crest: from an embattled cor an eagle's head
Motto: Bono n[ec malo?]
Tombstone Dr. John Dupuy, Jr. "M. D. and man mid-wife," d. 1745. Trinity Church vestry wall, New York. Elliston should be impaled instead of Dupuy. See also Dupuy Family (1910), pp. 20, 21

Elliston   Per pale gu and vert an eagle displ or
Crest: an eagle's head erased ppr gorged with a ducal cor [arg]
Motto: Bono vince malum
Bookplate for Robert Elliston's gift to Trinity Church Lib., N. Y. See Dr. A. B. Keep's N. Y. Society Lib. (1908), p. 38. The same coat, crest, and motto are engr. on alms basin given by Elliston to Trinity Church, N. Y. See Jones, Old Sil., p. 335. Elliston was comptroller of the port of N. Y.

Ellsworth   Or a stag's head cabossed sa. On a chief fractured (?) gu a cross pattée arg in the dexter chief
Crest: a stag couchant
Motto: Sans peur et sans reproche
Bookplate ―― Ellsworth

Elwood   Az a chev arg bet in chief 2 annulets or and in base a stag's head cabossed
Crest: an armed arm embowed holding a battle axe
Motto: Fide et sedulitate
Bookplate George May Elwood

Ely   Arg a fess engr bet 6 fleurs-de-lis gu
Crest: an arm erect couped below the elbow, habited arg grasping in the hand ppr a fleur-de-lis sa
On ring brought over by Richard Ely (1660), given by King of France. Nathaniel Ely, his brother, who came 1635, owned an old tankard which bears these arms but has only 3 fleurs-de-lis. Vermont's Amer. Heral., p. 109

Emerson   On a bend engrailed [az] 3 lions bendways pass [arg]. The field should be per fess indented or and vert?
Crest: a lion ramp [vert bezantée] grasping in both paws a battle axe [gu headed arg]
Tombstone Nathaniel Emerson, who d. 1712, Ipswich, Mass., Burying Ground. Heral. Jour., vol. 1, p. 90

Emerson Per fess indented over all a lion ramp [or?] holding a battle axe
Bookplate Henry P. Emerson

Emerson Per fess indented or and vert on a bend engr sa 3 lions passant [arg]
Crest: a lion passant vert holding a battle axe
Motto: Fidem servabo
Bookplate [Rev.] William Emerson, father of Ralph Waldo. S. Hill, sc

Emerson Per fess indented or and vert on a bend engr az 3 lions pass arg
Crest: a lion ramp vert bezantée holding a battle axe gu headed arg
Motto: In te Domine speravi
Tombstone Nathaniel Emerson, who d. 1712, Ipswich, Mass., Cemetery. Vermont's Amer. Heral., pp. 21, 22, 165

Emery Arg 3 bars nebuly gu and in chief 3 torteaux
Crest: a horse collared rising from a mural crown
Motto: Fidelis et suavis
Bookplate Howard B. Emery. Spenceley, sc., 1916

Empson Quartered by Oliver

Endecott Arg on a fess az bet 3 fusils gu a griffin passant or
On portrait of Gov. John Endecott, engr. by D. L. Glover for the N. E. Hist. Gen. Register

Endecott Arg on a fess az bet 3 fusils gu a griffin pass or
Crest: a lion's head erased ppr
Under portrait of John Endecott, Gov. of Mass. Vermont's Amer. Heral., pp. 110, 111, 165

Endicott Arg on a fess az bet 3 fusils gu a griffin passant or
Crest: a lion's head erased or
Framed water color. "By the name of Endicott" and palm branches. Not the original copy which bore the motto: Patria cara carior libertas. Wm. C. Endicott, Marlboro St., Boston, and Danvers, Mass. Also on silver box of his
Bookplate William Crowninshield Endicott the younger (living 1916 Boston), engraved by Henry Mitchell. *See*, however, Heral. Jour., vol. 1, p. 67

English Four martlets 3 and 1
Seal on will of Alexander English, dated 23 Jan. 1685, Lancaster, Va. Wm. & Mary Quar., Jan. 1893, p. 118

Emmet Az a fess engr erm bet 3 bulls' heads cabossed [or]
Crest: from a ducal cor a demi-bull ramp
Motto: Tenez le vraye
Bookplate Thomas Addis Emmet, M. D., New York Public Library

Ensign Sa 3 swords in fess points in chief [hilted or?]
Crest: a sword of the shield
Motto: Fidelitas
Bookplate Joseph R. Ensign, W. F. Hopson, sc., 1899

Eppes Per fess gu and or a pale counterchanged bet 3 eagles displ of the last
Crest: on a chaplet vert flowered or a falcon rising of the last
Engr. on old silver which has been in the family for generations. Crozier's Va. Heral., p. 91

Erving Arg 3 holly branches each of as many leaves ppr banded gu within a bordure chequy vert and of the field
Crest: a dexter arm vambraced and embowed, the hand grasping a sword
Motto: A: Quo fata vocant; B: Flourish in all weathers
Bookplate William Erving (Harris Collection). Heral. Jour., vol. 3, pp. 23, 24

Erving Quart 1 and 4: Arg 3 small sheaves of holly 2 and 1 vert banded [gu] within a bordure chequy arg and vert (Irvine); 2 and 3: Arg an eagle displayed sa [armed gu] within a bordure invected of the second (Ramsay)
Crest: a decussis sa (an X within a circle)
Motto: Sub sole sub umbra virescens
Bookplate —— Erving

Etting Arg on a chev gu 3 roundels (plates)
Crest: a hand holding erect a sword piercing a boar's head couped
Bookplate Frank Marx Etting, historian, Phila.

Eustace Az a bend arg bet 9 crosses crosslet [sa or or?], 4 in chief and 5 in base
Crest: a stag's head couped with the Saviour on the cross bet the antlers
Motto: In hoc signo vinces (another with "Sans Dieu rien)
Bookplate Colonel John Skey Eustace, State of New York

Eustis Az a bend arg bet 6 crosses crosslet or
Crest: a dexter hand ppr couped above the wrist holding a knight's helmet arg
Motto: Cur me persequeris
Framed water color Miss Elizabeth M. Eustis, 1020 Beacon St., Boston

Evans Gu 3 chev arg
Crest: a paschal lamb
Motto: Suum cuique tributo
Bookplate W. E. Evans

Everest Arg a harp gu. In chief per fess az and sa a fleur-de-lis bet 2 roses or
    Crest: a sword erect piercing a mullet
    Motto: Festina lente
    Bookplate Charles William Everest

Everett Gu a chev paly of 8 or and azure bet 3 mullets arg
    Crest: a griffin's head erased sa gorged a "gemel of 3 pieces," middle or, others arg
    Motto: Patria veritas fidès
    Bookplate Edward Everett, Boston, statesman, 1780–1851. The son quartered 2 and 3: Gu a dexter hand couped, thumb and forefinger extended. Cora Elizabeth Everett's bookplate by E. G. Hoyle has "Do ye next thyng"

Ewing Arg a chev embat az bet in chief 2 mullets gu and in base a sun in splendor of the last. From the chev point a British flag, gu a canton per saltire az and arg
    Crest: a demi-lion couped holding a mullet gu in the dexter gamb
    Motto: Audaciter
    Bookplate Maskl Ewing Jun [Maskell Ewing of Trenton, N. J.]. Also used by J. H. Ewing, a Phila. clergyman. Also over a fireplace in Mrs. Ewing's house, Lunenburg, Mass. Euen arms, Craigton, Scot.

Eyre Arg a chev ermines bet 3 escallops gu
    Crest: a demi-lion ramp
    Seal on a letter of John Eyre, H. C., 1718. Jeffries MSS. N. E. Reg., Jan. 1877, p. 59. Vermont's Amer. Heral., p. 121

F

Fagan Or 3 bends sinister compony arg and gu
    Crest: on a ducal cor a swan's head and neck between 2 roundels (?)
    Framed painting seen by Miss Pruden, Edenton, N. C.

Fairbanks Arg on a fess sa bet 3 pellets a bezant
    Crest: three arrows 2 in saltire one in pale, tied with a riband
    Motto: Finem respice
    Bookplate Joseph Fairbanks

Fairchild Bookplate of John Cummings Fairchild by Miss Macleod has the Bartlet arms, which see. Mrs. C. S. Fairchild of Cazenovia, N. Y., uses the Leguard arms and crest with "Per crucem ad stellas"

Fairfax Or 3 bars gemelles gu surmounted of a lion ramp sa
    Crest: on a chapeau or cap of maintenance gu and erm a lion pass guard sa
    Motto: Fare fac
    Bookplate Bryan, 8th Baron Fairfax of Va. The "Survey of Northern Neck of Virginia, 1736–37," owned by W. F. Havemeyer, has the above arms quarterly. See cover of Conway's Barons of the Potomack, 1892. Mrs. Eleanor V. R. Fairfax of N. Y. has the shield, the bars poorly engraved

Falconer Az a falcon displ and crowned bet 3 mullets arg on the breast a human heart gu
    Crest: an angel kneeling in prayer or within a chaplet of laurel ppr
    Bookplate Nathaniel Falconer, first collector port of Phila.

Faneuil A heart in the center, 4 six-pointed stars in chief, 3 like stars below the dexter star, all in pale, and a cross within an annulet in the sinister base
    Crest: a martlet (?)
    Engr. on a paten from Mary, wife of George Bethune and daughter of Benjamin Faneuil, 1791. Christ Church, Cambridge, Mass. Old Sil. Am. Ch., p. 111

Faneuil A heart in the center, 4 mullets (?) in chief, a mullet at the dexter side of the heart and one in the dexter base, and a maltese cross within an annulet in the sinister base
    Engr. on W. Price's View of Boston, dedicated to Peter Faneuil. Mass. His. Soc. Original print and copy. Heral. Jour., vol. 2, p. 121

Faneuil A heart in the center, 4 six-pointed stars in chief, three like stars below the dexter star, all in pale, and a cross within an annulet in the sinister base
    Crest: a martlet (?)
    Peter Faneuil's box-tomb, 1743. Granary Burying Ground, Boston. Heral. Jour., vol. 2, p. 121

Fanshaw See Bloodgood

Farlow Or a lion ramp bet 3 fleurs-de-lis sa
    Crest: a demi-lion ramp holding a fleur-de-lis sa
    Motto: Virtus honoris Janua
    Ex libris John W. Farlow, M. D. E. H. Garrett, 1900, op. 43

Farmer Arg a fess sa bet 3 lions' heads erased gu
Crest: out of a ducal cor a cock's head [gu crested and wattled or]
Motto: Hora e sempre
Bookplate Jasper Farmer

Farnham "Quarterly az and or, a crescent in the first two quarters counterchanged"
Crest: a hawk preying on a coney, both ppr
Framed water color by John Coles, done for Elizabeth Louisa Padelford, who was a Farnham of Providence. Owned by her grandson, F. Apthorp Foster of Martha's Vineyard

Farnham *See also* Reed

Farr Gu a cross moline arg, over all a bend az
Crest: an ostrich ppr holding a horseshoe
Old water color said to have been made by Jonathan Mason. Owned 1923 by Misses Emma and Elizabeth Harris, Holyoke Pl., Cambridge. Arms not under Farr in Burke

Farragut Per saltire arg and gu two horseshoes in pale and two stars of six points in fess counterchanged (?)
Crest: on the sea an antique ship in full sail to the sinister
Bookplate   Loyall Farragut. By Thomas Tryon

Farrington Erm on a chev gu bet 3 leopards' faces sa as many bombs or fired ppr. In chief a hand of Ulster on a shield
Bookplate Rev. Harry Webb Farrington of Newton, Mass., and N. Y. Born Nassau
Arms of Farrington of Cumberland, R. I. (crest a dragon, wings elevated, tail nowed, vert bezanté gorged with a mural crown arg and chain reflexed over the back or, charged on the back with two galtrops fessways of the last) and motto: Le bon temps viendra, on bookplate of Miss Lyslie Moors Hawes of R. I.

Farrow Quart 1 and 4: Sa a chev arg cotised bet 3 hammers; 2 and 3: Or a fess bet 3 eagles displayed sa
Crest: an eagle of the field
Bookplate Blanche Clare Farrow, engr. by A. H. Noll

Fauquier Or a tree on a mound a falcon close in sinister point of base and a human heart in dexter point, in chief 2 mullets
Cres⁚: a falcon close
Bookplate Lt.-Gov. Francis Fauquier of Va., d. 1768
Bookplate "Wm. Fauquier, Esq.,

Jun," younger son of Lt.-Gov. of Va., d. 1805. Oliver's West Ind. Bookplates, 1914, No. 130

Fauquier Quart 1 and 4: Or a tree on a mound, both vert; a falcon close in sinister point of base and a human heart in dexter point; in chief 2 mullets pierced; 2: Gu a bend engr or bet 6 cinquefoils; 3: Gu 3 catharine wheels within a bordure invected arg
Crest: a falcon close
Bookplate Thomas Fauquier

Fawkener Sa 3 pales arg debruised by a bend az charged with 3 trefoils slipped arg
Crest: trefoil of the shield
Bookplate Wm. Fawkener, Esqr.

Fay Arg 6 quatrefoils (properly roses) gu 3 and 3
Crest: a cubit arm holding (in the gauntlet?) a dagger
Motto: Nomine et patriæ asto
Notepaper Mrs. Carl Frelinghuysen Gould (Dorothy W. Fay) of Seattle, Wash.

Fay Arg 6 roses gu 3 and 3. Impaling: Vert a lion ramp within a bordure engr arg (Gray)
Crest: a cubit armed arm holding a battle axe
Motto: Toujours fidéle
Bookplate Dudley Bowditch Fay, Boston

Fay Maubourg Gu on a bend or, a polecat or marten az
On a portrait of Eleanore Florimonde de la Fay Maubourg, wife of Charles D. L. P. Horry. At Mrs. Blackburn Hughes's, 10 Legaré Street, Charleston, S. C. Seen by L. Park, 1923. There is a coronet above the arms which are in an ellipse

Fayerweather Az a tree trunk in bend bet 6 estoiles of 6 points or
Crest: a beaver holding in the mouth a fish all ppr
Carved hatchment in high relief framed under glass. Once owned by Hon. Thomas Fayerweather of Cambridge, Mass., 1723–1805

Fearon Or a chev sa bet 3 horseshoes of the last
Crest: from a ducal cor a falcon's head ppr
Motto: Ut ferrum forte
Bookplate Henry S. Fearon

Feilding Arg on a fess az 3 lozenges or
Wax seal on will of Henry Feilding, who d. in King and Queen Co., Va., 1712. Also engr. on old silver plate. Crozier's Va. Heral., pp. 78 and 79

Feilding Or a lion ramp gu, also arg on a fess az, 3 lozenges or
Seal was used by Edward Feilding, 1684. Ambrose Feilding's will, 1675, has silver spoons and plate marked with "ye Ffeilding Arms." A drawing from old Feilding silver shows 2 shields, one with the lion rampant and the other with gold lozenges on a blue fess. See also Fielding. Crozier's Va. Heral., pp. 80 and 81

Fellowes Az a fess dancettée erm bet 3 lions' heads erased or murally crowned [arg]
Crest: a lion's head of the field charged with a fess dancettée erm
Motto: Justus esto et non metue
Bookplate Miss H. D. Fellowes

Fels Gu a mill rind debrusied by 2 bendlets erm
Crest: an arm emb issuing from the ground and holding a flaming beacon, a mill-rind on the ground
Motto: Feu sert et sauve
Bookplate Robert Fels

Felt Gu a stag's head couped arg attired or
Crest: on an antique crown or a stag trippant ppr
An old water color owned by the Soc. for the Preserv. of N. E. Antiq., Boston

Fendell Paly of 6 arg and gu. On a chief az 3 mullets or
Crest: a stag's head erased gorged with a collar charged with 3 mullets
Motto: Esse quam videri
Bookplate Philip Richard Fendell, Washington, D. C.

Fenwick Gu 3 martlets arg (?)
Crest: a phoenix rising from the flames
Motto: Perit ut vivat
Bookplate J. Smithers, sc.

Fenwycke Quart 1 and 4: Per fess gu and arg 6 martlets, 3, 2, 1 counterchanged, 3 only in chief; 2 and 3: Arg 3 cinquefoils sa
Crest: a pheonix rising from flames gorged with a mural crown
Bookplate Rev. G. C. Fenwycke

Ferguson Az a buckle bet 3 boars' heads or
Carved on oak and in windows of office of Cram and Ferguson (Frank W.), architects, Boston, 1927

Ferrin [ ] on a fess bet 3 birds, 3 annulets
Automobile of Frank Ferrin, 35 Hunnewell Ave., Newton, Mass.

Fetherston Quartered by Wright

Field Gu a chev arg bet 3 garbs
Crest: a cubit arm grasping a baton in bend sinister
Engr. by George Hanners on coffee pot owned by Mrs. Fredk. R. Sears. Amer. Ch. Sil., M. F. A., 1911, pp. 63. 124

Field Sa a chev bet 3 garbs arg
Crest:
Motto: Rien sans droit (?)
Arms on automobile Pierre A. Field, 5 Chestnut St., Boston

Field Sa a chev bet 3 garbs arg
Crest: a garb of the field
Bookplate Eugene Field, Chicago, poet. Also Charles K. Field, engr. by Amer. Bknote Co., but with crest: a four-leaf clover

Field Sa a chev engr bet 3 garbs arg
Crest: a dexter arm [habited gu] issuing fessways from a cloud ppr on the sinister side and holding a sphere [or]
Motto: Sans Dieu rien
Bookplate George Prentice Field; also Maunsell Broadhurst Field and Cyrus W. Field

Fielding Arg on a fess az 3 lozenges or
Crest: on a cor a spread eagle with 2 heads
Motto: Crescit sub pondere virtus
Framed painting owned by Mrs. Lelia Higgs Humber, San Francisco. Also Mrs. M. H. Everett, Palmyra, N. C. See also Feilding

Fielding Quartered by Lewis

Filliol Quartered by Grosvenor

Finch Quartered by Earle

Fisc Chequy arg and gu on a pale sa, 3 pierced mullets or
Crest: a pierced star of 6 points or above a voided triangle
Bookplate —— Fisc

Fish Quart 1 and 4: [Sa] a chev wavy arg bet 3 fleurs-de-lis; 2 and 3: Gu a stag courant ppr. On a chief or a greyhound chasing a hare (Stuyvesant). Impaling: Arg? a chev bet 3 birds
Crests: 1: a tiger's head erased erm; 2: a dolphin embowed; 3: an eagle's head couped with twig in beak
Motto: Deus dabit
Bookplate Hamilton Fish, Stuyvesant Square, N. Y., Gov. N. Y., 1849–51. He married Julia Kean

Fish Sa a chev wavy arg bet 3 fleurs-de-lis [arg]
Crest: a tiger's head erased erm, maned and tusked or
Motto: Deus dabit
Bookplate Augustine H. Fish, M. D.

Fisher   Az in chief a ducal crown, in base a dolphin embowed
   Crest: an eagle rising
   Bookplate Francis Fisher

Fisher   Az a fess embat, counter-embat or, bet 3 dolphins naiant
   Crest: a heron on its nest swallowing a fish
   Bookplate Jabez B. Fisher, Phila.

Fisher   Or 3 kingfishers ppr contourné
   Crest: a stag's head collared and chained contourné
   Bookplate Lindley Fisher, Phila.

Fisk   3 battle axes erect turned to the sinister and in chief a crescent
   Crest: an arrow erect, point down
   "The name of Fisk" below.   Embr. hatchment owned by a grandson of Gen. John Fisk of Salem.   Possibly from a painting by John Coles.   Gibbs arms (?) but not their crest.   Reported to me by Eben Putnam.   In the Essex Institute, Salem, 1919

Fiske   Chequy arg and gu on a fess sa 5 [sometimes only 3] mullets voided of the third or
   Crest: on the point of a triangle sa an estoile or
   Bookplate Samuel Fiske.   Vermont's Amer. Heral., pp. 70, 165

Fiske   *See also* Fisc

Fitch   Vert (?) a chev bet 3 leopards' faces arg.   Impaling: Arg a chev sa bet 3 columbines az (Hall)
   Crest: a leopard's face arg pierced in the mouth by a sword bend sinisterways
   Embroidered achievement found about 1773 at sea in the cabin of a deserted ship by Captain Nicholas Johnson of Newburyport.   Owned by his great granddaughter, Miss Margaret W. Cushing, Newburyport.   Arms of Gov. Thomas Fitch, who married Hannah, daughter of Richard Hall of New Haven

Fitch   Impaled by Jenks

Fitch   Quartered by Oliver

Fitzhugh   Az 3 chevronels in base interlaced or, a chief of the last
   Crest: on a cap of maintenance a wyvern, wings expanded arg
   Tomb of Sarah Fitzhugh and her husband, Edward Barradall, in Bruton Churchyard, Williamsburg, Va., bears the Fitzhugh with Barradall arms impaled.   She d. 1743.   Pair salt cellars, Hall mark 1750, at one time owned by me, but now in possession of a member of the Fitzhugh family.   Letter of D. H. Thomas.   Also Va. Hist. Mag., vol. 2, p. 272; vol. 7, p. 199

Fitzhugh   Az 3 chevronels in base interlaced or, a chief arg
   Crest: a wyvern, wings expanded
   Motto: Pro patria semper
   Bookplate Augustine Fitzhugh of Va. (not Wm. as in Allen, No. 275) but no name on this plate.   Owner, W. E. Baillie, Bridgeport, Conn.

Fitzhugh   Impaled by Barradall

Flattesbury   Quartered by Leigh

Fleet   Quartered by Coote

Fletcher   Az 2 horses' heads erased or, and in base an anchor of the last.   On a chief [wavy or?] 3 hurts [each charged with a pheon arg?]
   On automobile of Frank E. Fletcher, Hotel Princeton, Allston, Mass.

Fletcher   Quart 1 and 4: Sa a cross flory bet 4 escallops arg; 2 and 3: a chev bet 3 crosses (?) Impaling: A chev bet 3 martlets
   Seal of Col. Benjamin Fletcher, Gov. of N. Y., 1692.   Lord Bellomont, a successor, was asked to remove Fletcher's arms from Trinity Church since his birth was so mean and obscure that he was not entitled to bear a coat of arms."   Mem. Hist., N. Y., vol. 1, p. 490.   Heral. Jour., vol. 4, p. 95

Fletcher   Sa a chev engr arg bet 4 plates, each charged with an arrow point down of the first
   Crest: a pheon per pale erm and sa
   Bookplate Fletcher Memorial Library, Ludlow, Vt.

Floebeckher   On a pale [arg?] bet 2 ladders (?) 3 hammer heads az
   Crest: a stirrup (?)
   Bookplate Albert H. Floebeckher, Washington, D. C.

Flood   Vert a chev bet 3 wolves' heads erased arg
   Crest: a wolf's head of the field
   Motto: Vis unita fortior
   Bookplate John Flood

Flower   Per fess arg (?) and [az] in chief 2 fleurs-de-lis [gu] in base one [or]
   Wax seal on bond of George Flower, dated 1712, at Lancaster Court House, Va.   Wm. & Mary Quar,. Jan. 1893, p. 120

Flower   Sa a unicorn pass or, on a chief arg [3 pinks gu stalked and leaved vert]
   Tomb of Jeffrey Flower in Abington Churchyard, Gloucester, Va.   He d. 1726, aged 38 years.   Wm. & Mary Quar., Apr. 1894, p. 230

Fogg Arg on a fess gu bet 3 annulets sa 3 mullets pierced of the first
Crest: a unicorn's head couped [arg]
Motto: Aut pax aut bellum
Bookplate Dr. J. S. C. Fogg, South Boston. Framed photo from painting owned by Mrs. Wm. H. Fegan, Brookline, Mass., 1924. Motto: Fortasse. Joseph Fogg, Alfred, Me., had daughter Kate, who married Wm. F. Hall, parents of Mrs. Fegan. *See* Rogers

Foljambe [Sa] a bend bet 6 escallops [or]
Crest: a leg couped at the thigh, mailed and spurred
Bookplate ⸺ Foljambe, Boston

Foot Arg a chev sa in the dexter point a trefoil slipped of the last
Crest: trees on a mound vert
Bookplate Ebenezer Foot. Maverick, sc.?

Forbes Az 3 bears' heads [arg] muzzled [gu]
Crest: a bear pass [arg guttée de sang] muzzled [gu]
Motto: Omnis fortunae paratus
Bookplate Eli Forbes, 1800. J. M. Furnass, sc.

Forbes Az a cross pattée arg bet 3 bears' heads couped arg muzzled gu
Crest: a cross of the field
Hatchment embr. in silk by Mary Forbes Coffin in Boston, b. 1774, married Henry Phelps, 1795. Owned by Mrs. Charles C. Goodwin, Lexington, Mass.

Forbes Az on a chev bet 3 bears' heads [arg] muzzled [gu] a heart of the last bet 2 daggers meeting in point ppr
Crest: a dagger piercing a man's heart ppr
Motto: Non deest spes
Bookplate Wm. Forbes, Boston

Forbes Gu 2 chev erm bet 3 spread eagles or
Bookplate Susan E. P. Forbes, engr. by Spenceley

Forbes Quart 1 and 4: Az 3 bears' heads couped [arg] muzzled [gu]; 2 and 3: Az 3 cinquefoils [arg] (Lord Pitsligo)
Crest: a falcon rising ppr
Motto: Altius ibunt qui ad summa nituntur
Bookplate John Murray Forbes, Boston

Forbes *See also* Parsons

Forman [Az?] on a chev [sa] bet 2 bars nebulée [arg] 3 martlets [or]. A chief [gu] charged with a lion pass guard or bet 2 anchors erect [or]
Crest: a lion's head couped
Motto: Deo et amicitiae

Bookplate of a Rev. officer "whose estate was near Rose Hill, Charles County, Md." An Ezekiel Forman, Esq., was of Queen Anne County

Forsyth Arg a chev engrailed gu bet 3 griffins segreant [vert]
Crest: a demi-griffin vert?
Framed arms in Founders' Room, Forsyth Dental Infirmary, Boston, James Bennett, George Henry, John Hamilton, and Thomas Alexander Forsyth, brothers, founders. Also shield on invitation to dedication, and cut in stone on the façade
Bookplate John Barnwell Elliott and Elliott and Noel Forsyth, his wife, who was of "Nydrie," Va., with Forsyth shield, crest as above, and motto: "Instaurator ruinae. *See* Elliott

Fortescue Az a bend engr arg cotised or
Crest: leopard pass ppr holding with the dexter paw a shield [arg]
Motto: Forte scutum salus ducum
Bookplate ⸺ Fortescue

Forth Quartered by Winthrop

Forward Arg a castle embattled, with 3 flags
Crest: a mailed arm emb, holding a lance
Motto: Quo fata vocant
Bookplate [Rev. Justus] Forward, Belchertown, Mass. R. Brunton's sc. Bates's Early Conn. Engr., p. 19

Foster Arg 3 hunting horns sa. On a chief wavy vert an eagle rising
Bookplate Charles Chauncy Foster. R. D. Weston-Smith, del. 1900

Foster Arg a chev purpure bet 3 hunting horns, stringed sa
Crest: a stork
Motto: To rock the cradle of reposing age
Bookplate Nathaniel Foster. J. M. Furnas, sc.

Foster Arg a chev bet 3 hunting horns stringed [sa]
Engr. plate from Abigail, wife of John Foster of Boston to Second Church, Boston, 1711. Old Sil. Am. Ch., p. 42

Foster Arg a chev vert bet 3 buglehorns sa, stringed gu
Crest: an arm in armor embowed, holding in the hand a broken tilting spear ppr
Motto: Si fractus fortis
Tombstone, Sarah, wife of Richard Foster, Jr. [1724], Old Burial Ground, Charlestown, Mass. Also on tankard owned by Edward I. Browne, Boston. Here they are beautifully engraved in colors. Vermont's Amer. Heral., pp. 137, 165. Heral. Jour., vol. 1, p. 56

Foster Arg a chev vert bet 3 hunting horns sa
Engr. to show the colors on a large tankard owned in 1865 by Edward I. Browne of Boston. Heral. Jour., vol. 1, p. 56

Foster Arg a chev bet 3 stringed hunting horns [sa] and on a chief 3 leopards' faces
Crest: an armed arm embowed, holding a broken tilting spear
Upright slate stone of James Foster, who d. 1732, aged 82, and Anna, his wife, who d. 1732, aged 68. Dorchester, Mass., Burying Ground, Dudley St.

Foster [Or] 3 bugle horns [vert] stringed [gu]. On a chief wavy az a dove wings addorsed arg in its beak a twig of olive [or]
Crest: on an upturned bugle horn garnished [or] a popinjay with wings addorsed ppr
Motto: Ubi libertas
Embr. on upper right corner of a sangaibushi or christening cloth for Kate Montgomery Foster, daughter of Andrew and Kiku (Kanai) Foster of Yokohama and Boston. Surrounded by pine, plum, and bamboo in gold thread, signifying happiness. Upper left Fujiyama for high ideals. Lower right a white stork flying and gold clouds for long life. Lower left Kanai crest of gold in a broad gold circle: 3 semi-octogon cubes one above another, partially super-imposed. Blue cloth bordered with Turkey red crepe. Owned by Miss Kate Foster (Mrs. Walter W. Purdue) Kuji Machi Ku, Tokyo

Foster Quarterly per fess dancettée arg and sa. In 1 and 4 a hunting horn sa stringed or
Crest: a stag's head erased
Motto: Invidam virtute vincam
Bookplate Ingham Foster

Fowke [Vert] a fleur-de-lis arg, a mullet for diff
Crest: an Indian goat's head erased arg
Seal on deed from Col. Gerard Fowke, Westmoreland Co., Va. Died 1669. See Crozier's Va. Heral., p. 85

Fowle [Gu] a lion pass bet 3 roses [or barbed vert]
A headstone of Welsh slate for Capt. John Fowle, who d. 1711, aged 74. Phipps St. Yard, Charlestown, Mass. Heral. Jour., vol. 1, p. 75

Fowle Gu a lion pass guard bet 3 roses all arg [for or]
Crest: out of a ducal cor gu a dexter armed arm embowed, holding a battle axe az [for or]

Embr. 1784 by Margery Fowle, wife of Col. Loammi Baldwin, when 16, daughter of Josiah Fowle of Woburn, Mass. Owned in Penn.

Fowler Az on a chev arg bet 3 lions pass guard 3 crosses formeé
Crest: a crowned owl
Motto: Ad astra per aspera
On same bookplate: Az 2 bars dancette arg a label of 3 points gu. Crest: a cross arg with 3 plates above. Engr. bookplate by S. L. Smith of Josiah Minot Fowler?

Fowler Erm on a canton gu an owl or (Barton arms)
Bookplate C. Fowler, R. I.

Fowler Quart 1: Az on a chev or bet 3 lions pass guard 3 crosses pattée sa; 2: Per fess or and sa a lion ramp counterchanged; 3: Arg a chev bet 3 griffins' heads sa; 4: Arg a fess gu. In chief a lable az of 4 points
Crest: an owl affrontée ducally gorged
Motto: Watch and pray
Bookplate ——— Fowler, N. Y.

Fowler Quarterly az and or. In the first quarter a flute arg in bend
Crest: a lion's head erased or
Framed water color. "By the name of Fowler" and palm branches. The Samuel Fowler House, Danversport, Mass.

Fox Arg a chev sa bet 3 cocks gu, on a chief az a fox courant or
Crest: a lion sejant guardant or, supporting with the dexter foot a book of the last
Tomb of Isabel Fox, wife of Rev. John Fox, Ware parish, Va. She d. 13 June, 1742, aged 38 years. Crozier's Va. Heral., p. 9

Foxcroft Per chev sa and az a chev bet 3 foxes' heads or
Crest: a head of the arms
Embr. framed arms about 40 x 32 inches. The arms of Coney, sa, on a fess bet 3 conies dormant or as many escallops of the field, occupy the top of the above shield, the 3d coney being placed bet the two foxes' heads. Elaborate roses and lilies about the shield. Owned by the Misses Gertrude and Agnes Brooks, Marlboro St., Boston, daughters of Wm. Gray, Brooks. Francis Foxcroft of Cambridge married, 1722, Mehitable Coney. Their daughter married Lt.-Gov. Samuel Phillips, founder of Phillips Academy, Andover, Mass.

Foxcroft Az a chev or bet 3 foxes' heads erased
Bostonian Society; original formerly

in wooden King's Chapel. On canvas, 1886. Seal on paper dated 3 June, 1684. Seen by Mrs. Ljungstedt in Va.

Foxcroft Az a chev bet 3 foxes' heads erased or
Crest: a head of the arms
Seal used by Francis and Thomas Foxcroft on will of Samuel Williams, 1730. Vermont's Amer. Heral., pp. 98, 165

Francis Per bend sinister sa and or, a lion ramp counterchanged
Crest: out of a ducal cor or a demi-lion sa, holding bet the paws a garb erect or
Memorial window to Anne Francis Bayard (1802–64). Old Swedes' Church, Wilmington, Del. Zieber's Heral., p. 65

Francis Per bend sinister or and sa a lion ramp [counterchanged?]
Crest: a lion ramp holding a garb
Motto: Manet amicitia florebitque semper
Bookplate John Francis. Callender, sc.

Frank Impaled by Vaux

Franklin Arg on a bend bet 2 lions' heads erased [gu] a dolphin embowed arg [bet 2 martlets or]. Impaling: Arg 3 pales gu (Downes)
No crest
Memorial tablet to Elizabeth, wife of Wm. Franklin, Gov. of N. J., in St. Paul's chapel, Broadway, N. Y. She d. 1778. Seen 20 May, 1920, in dim light

Franklin Arg on a bend bet 2 lions' heads erased gu, a dolphin embowed of the field bet 2 martlets close or
Crest: a dolphin's head in pale arg, erased gu, finned or, bet 2 branches vert
Motto: Exemplum adest ipse homo
Bookplate John Franklin, brother of Benjamin. J. Turner, sc. Benjamin Franklin used this coat as his shield, and later William Franklin, Gov. of N. J., used it. Vermont's Amer. Heral., pp. 18, 165

Fraser Az 3 cinquefoils
Crest: a swan's head and wings from a ducal cor, the beak holding a horseshoe
Bookplate J. F. Fraser, scientist, Phila.

Fraunces Erm on a canton sa an Irish harp. Impaling: Or a pile az charged with 3 escallops (Pye arms)
Crest: a garb
Motto: Procurata industria
Bookplate Andrew G. Fraunces. Maverick, sc.

Frazer Az 3 strawberry leaves or frazees arg
Crest: a demi-ostrich ppr
Motto: Je suis pret
On a pitcher made at Hemphill potteries for Persifor Frazer of Phila.

Freeman 3 garbs
Crests 1: a garb; 2: an antelope's head couped
Seal on deed of John Freeman, Sr., July, 1680. Heral. Jour., vol. 1, p. 71. Freeman arms in Burke have 3 lozenges

Freke [Sa] two bars [or]. In chief 3 mullets [of the last]. Impaling: [Arg?] on a bend [gu] bet 3 [pellets] as many swans [of the first?] (Clarke)
Crest: a bull's or talbot's head [sa] collared [or]
"The armes of John and Elizabeth Freke." She was the daughter of Major Thomas Clarke and married in 1661. He was killed in 1675. Granary Burying Ground, Boston, altar tomb. Heral. Jour., vol. 2, p. 130

French Arg a chev bet 3 boars' heads erased az
Crest: a fleur-de-lis
In the possession of the Frenchs of Braintree Manor, N. Y., since their coming over. Ancest. Rec., vol. 2, p. 494

French Arg a chev az bet 3 boars' heads couped
Crest: a fleur-de-lis
Bookplate Frederick W. French. Also Jonathan French. Also Asa French of Mass.

French [Az] a chev bet 3 boars' heads erased [or]
Crest: a fleur-de-lis
Bookplate Hollis French, Boston. Motto: Tuebor

French Az a chev bet 3 boars' heads couped [or]
Crest: a demi-lion ramp
Motto: En Dieu est ma fiance
Bookplate Jonathan French of Boston

Frizell Quart 1 and 4: Arg 3 antique crowns [gu]; 2 and 3: Az 3 cinquefoils arg
Crest: a stag's head [or] bet 2 battle axes addorsed ppr
Motto: Jesu est prêt
Engr. on flagon given in 1723 to the 2d Church, Boston, by John Frizell. See Fraser of Leadclune, Co. Inverness, bart., in Burke. Old Sil. Am. Ch., p. 39

Frost Arg a chev sa bet 3 trefoils slipped vert
Crest: an old man's head in profile bet 2 laurel sprigs vert
Bookplate George H. Frost. D. McN. Stauffer, des.

Frothingham Az a bend arg bet 6 pierced mullets [or]
Crest: a stag trippant ppr [attired gu]
Motto: Frangas non flectes
Bookplate W. Frothingham

Fry Gules 2 horses courant arg
Crest: an armed arm embowed, holding a sword all ppr
Motto: Fidelitas
"Based on the arms of Fry of Exeter, Devon"
Bookplate Charles Fry, engr. by Spenceley

Frye Purpure a fleur-de-lis bet 3 horses courant arg bridled [or]. The shield in Burke is gu
Bookplate Frederick Frye, Andover [Mass.], b. 1760. R. Brunton, sc. Bates's Early Conn. Engr., p. 21

Fuller Arg 3 bars gu
Crest: a lion ramp sa
Motto: Currit qui currat
The crest used on James Fuller's will, Lavenham, Suffolk, 1603, ancestor of A. G. F.
Bookplate Arthur G. Fuller, Groton, Mass.

Fuller [Arg] 3 bars and a canton [gu]
Crest: a cock
Benjamin (d. 1799) and Rebecca (d. 1791) Fuller. Christ Church graveyard, Phila. Zieber's Heral., p. 39

Fullerton Arg a chev or bet 3 otters' heads erased sa
Crest: a camel's head erased [or?]
Motto: Lux in tenebris
Bookplate "Fullerton of Carstairs" of N. Y., engr. by Abel Anderson, Amer. wood engraver

G

Gains Arg a chev az bet 3 doves with wings spread or
Crest: dove with twig
"By the name of Gains." Framed painting. Owned by Mrs. Safford, antique dealer, Fitchburg, Mass., 1914

Gale Arg on a fess bet 3 saltires [az] an anchor bet 2 lions' heads erased [or]
On gravestone of George Gale, at "Tusculum plantation," three miles from Princess Anne, Md. He was b. in 1670, came 1690, d. Aug. 1712. Information from G. W. Maslin, Esq., 1924. Coat 12 x 16 inches. *See also* Hodgson

Gale Gu a griffin segreant or within a bordure gobonated arg and vert
Crest: a unicorn's head paly of six az and or, the horn twisted or and az
Motto: Tiens ta foy
Bookplate Edward Courtland Gale. E. D. French, sc., 1899

Gallatin Az a fess arg bet 3 bezants
Crest: a French count's cor
Motto: Persevere
On seal ring and bookplates of Albert Gallatin, who came 1780
Notepaper F. Winthrop coll., N. Y., 1885, in Bos. Ath., has supporters 2 lions and "Pro patria devoti." Vermont's Amer. Heral., pp. 92, 93, 165

Gallaudet Sa on a chev or bet 3 fleurs-de-lis arg the same number arg. On a chief or 2 swords saltire wise bet 2 maunches
Crest: a demi-rabbit issuing from grass vert
Motto: Ut quiescas labora
Bookplate S. D. Gallaudet, 1894

Gallishan Az a fess bet 3 escallops or
Framed arms. G. Searle, pinx, 1773. Owned by Miss Currier, Newburyport, Mass., 1922

Galvez Quart I. Per pale. 1: Arg a tree vert behind 2 wolves pass sa, one above the other; 2: Arg 3 escallops az. II. Quart 1: or a bend gu; 2: A cross (?); 3: A lion ramp; 4: Or a castle with 3 towers. III. Az a tower supported by 2 lions and above an estoile. IV. Arg 2 goats sa, one above the other
Bookplate or notepaper Dr. Bernardo de Galvez, Gov. New Orleans. Given to the Boston Atheneum by Mrs. Lawrence Park, 1925

Gamble Or bet 2 trefoils slipped a pile gu charged with a fleur-de-lis or a chief erm
Crest: a crane with rose slip in beak bet 2 trefoils slipped
Motto: Vix ea nostra voco
Notepaper Mrs. Eleanor S. Gamble, Haverford, Penn.

Gamble Quartered by Cabell

Gardiner Arg (?) a chev bet 3 bugle horns gu, stringed az
Crest: a dexter armed arm grasping a staff
"By the name of Gardiner." Chippendale bookplate of John Lion Gardiner, 1770–1816. Same arms in china owned by W. M. Ellis of Shawsville, Va.

Gardiner Or on a chev gu bet 3 griffins' heads erased sa 2 lions combatant arg
Crest: a Saracen's face [erased gu]

with a wreath around his temples gu and az, a cap or
Motto: Pro patria mori
Bookplate John Gardiner, Inner Temple. John Philip Gardiner had lions or. Samuel Gardiner had for crest a griffin's head erased. Samuel P. Gardiner used lions guardant. Robert Hallowell Gardiner, Gardiner, Me., used for crest a face ¾ full gu, body or, cap with tassel vert, and motto: Praesto pro patria. R. H. G. of "Oaklands" has same motto and for crest a full face; also John Hays and John Tudor Gardiner

Gardiner Sa a chev erm bet in chief 2 griffins' heads and in base a cross pattée arg
Tombstone of John Gardiner "Third lord of ye Isle of Wight," b. Apr. 19, 1661, d. June 25, 1738. Also of David Gardiner, d. July 4, 1751, aged 61. John was grandson of Lion Gardiner of Gardiner's Island, N. Y. Plate opp. p. 150 of Famous Families of N. Y., vol. 1

Gardiner [Sa] a chev erm bet 2 griffins' heads erased in chief, and a cross [pattée] in base [or]
On a portrait of Lion Gardiner in mail by Marichal. Mass. Hist. Soc. Photograph of an old painting?

Gardner [Az?] a chev [erm?] bet 3 griffins' heads erased [arg?]
Crest: a griffin's head
For Samuel Gardner (H. C. 1732) of Salem. Embr. hatchment by Lois Barnard, made before 1769. Picture in Pickering Geneal. (1897), vol. 1, p. 91. Same arms on a silver teapot owned, 1897, by Col. Henry Lee, Brookline, Mass.

Gardner Gu a chev or bet 3 griffins' heads erased arg, a chief embattled arg
Crest: a head of the field
Engr. on a teapot made by J. Coburn and owned by J. Webb Barton, Hathorne, Essex Co., Mass., son of Gardner, son of John, druggist, and Mary (Webb), son of Samuel and Margaret (Gardner) Barton of Salem, Mass.

Gardner Or on a chev gu bet 3 griffins' heads erased az, 2 lions counterpassant of the field or
Crest: a Saracen's head couped at the shoulders proper. On the head a cap turned up gu and az, crined and bearded sa
Motto: Praesto pro patria
Tomb of Chief Justice John Gardner of R. I. (1767). Vermont's Amer. Heral., pp. 27, 28

Gardner Or on a chev gu bet 3 griffins' heads erased [az] 2 lions counterpassant [of the field]
Crest: a bearded man couped at the shoulders, with a long cap
Motto: Praesto pro patria
Seal, New York

Garland A paly of 6 or and gu. On a chief per pale gu and sa a chaplet [ppr] on the dexter and a demi-lion issuant [arg] in the sinister
Crest: on an embat crown a lion sejant holding a shield arg bearing a garland of the field
Motto: Libertas
Bookplate Charles Tuller Garland

Garlick Arg 3 heads of garlick ppr
Arms of Edward Garlick of Va. engraved on old silver bowl owned by Mr. John B. Minor. Wm. & Mary Quar., vol. 4, p. 270

Garnett Gu a lion ramp [arg] ducally crowned [or] within a bordure engr or
Bookplate John Garnett

Garnishe *See* Gerrish

Garrett A lion ramp
Arms of Garrett, who d. 1727. St. Ann's Churchyard, Annapolis, Md. Zieber's Heral., p. 47

Garter Impaled by Apthorp

Gause Arg 9 mullets gu saltirewise
Crest: a falcon rising
Motto: Se inserit astris
Bookplate H. T. Gause, Wilmington, Del.

Gavell Impaled by Stanton

Gavit Gu a mullet or
Bookplate John E. Gavit, 1817–74, Stockbridge, Mass. Prest. Amer. Bank Note Co.

Gay Az on a fess embat counter-embat bet 3 goats pass arg as many pellets
Crest: a dragon's head bet 2 dragons' wings expanded [gu] guttée d'or
Arms of Gay of Dedham, Mass., on bookplate of Miss Lyslie Moore Hawes of R. I.

Gedney [Or] three eagles displ, 2 and 1 [sa]
Crest: an eagle displayed sa
Bartholomew Gedney's tomb, No. 9, against the Tremont Street fence, King's Chapel graveyard, Boston
Seal used 6 Jan. 1698–9 by Deliverance Parkman and wife Susanna, daughter of John Gedney (Essex Wills). Also on receipt of heirs of Bartholomew Gedney, Dec. 10, 1698. No crest. Heral. Jour. vol. 2, p. 20., vol. 4, p. 170

Gee　[Az] on a chev [arg] bet 3 leopards' faces cabossed or as many fleurs-de-lis gu
　Crest: a fox statant reguardant
　Hatchment, "The armes and tomb belonging to the Family of Gee." Also on silver in Met. Mus. of Art, N. Y., impaling possibly Thornton. Numbered 24, 109, 19A. Copp's Hill Yard, Boston. Rev. Joshua Gee. Heral. Jour., vol. 2, p. 77

Geer　Gu 2 bars arg, each charged with 3 mascles of the field. In a canton or a leopard's face az
　Crest: a leopard's head ducally gorged bet 2 wings displ gu, the head sprinkled with torteaux
　Motto: Sans cause
　Bookplate Walter Geer
　Notepaper.F. Winthrop coll., N. Y., 1885, in Bos. Ath., has crest a stag's head erased and motto: Mentis honestae gloria. Perhaps bars or and mascles az. Geer or Geary

Gerard　Quart 1: Az 3 leaves slipped; 2 and 3: Gu a saltire arg; 4: Az a man's dexter arm embowed, holding a straight sword ready to strike
　Crest: a unicorn's head
　Motto: Invitum sequitur honos
　Bookplate George Gerard

Gerrish　Arg a dart bet 3 escallops sa
　Embr. hatchment by Elizabeth Gerrish. Mrs. Gordon Prince, Boston

Gerrish　Arg (?) 3 escallops and in chief a pheon bladed az hafted or
　Crest: a martlet holding an escallop
　Bookplate John Gerrish, 1735–1829, and John Brown Gerrish. Thomas Johnston, sc.

Gerrish　Quart 1 and 4: A lion ramp; 2 and 3: Three plates
　Seal of Paul Gerrish, Portsmouth, N. H., 1719. Jeffries MSS. N. E. Reg., Jan. 1877, p. 60

Gerrish　Impaled by Barrett

Gervais　Or in the dexter chief a truffle, in the sinister chief an owl, and in base a frog
　Bookplate —— Gervais

Gibbes　3 arrows in pale?
　Seal of Robert Gibbes, Phila., 1709. Gibbs uses battle axes. Jeffries MSS. N. E. Reg., Jan. 1877, p. 60

Gibbes　[Arg] 3 battle axes erect 2 and 1 [sa]
　Crest: 3 broken tilting spears, 2 in saltire and one in pale ensigned with a wreath, hilts down
　Engr. on a teapot, Clearwater collection, made in Newport, R. I., 1750. Dyer's Early Amer. Craftsmen, p. 228. Same arms and crest on the portrait of

Rev. Henry Gibbs of Watertown, Mass., 1668–1723. Owned by Dr. Frederick J. White of Brookline, Mass.

Gibbes　Quart 1 and 4: 3 battle axes in pale, 2 and 1 az; 2 and 3: Arg 2 lozenges in fess gu (Champney)
　Crest: an armed dexter arm holding a battle axe barways
　Motto: Amor vincit patriae
　Bookplate James S. Gibbes, wealthy Charleston merchant, 1819–88. Also on tomb, Magnolia Cemetery. S. C. Hist. Mag., Apr. 1911, p. 98. Shield with charges in relief, attached to a column at right of pulpit, St. James Church, Goose Creek, S. C. Seen in March, 1923, by L. Park

Gibbs　Arg 3 battle axes in fess sa
　Crest: a battle axe of the arms
　Motto: Beware my edge
　Bookplate John Walter Gibbs, Charleston, S. C.

Gibbs　Or 3 pole-axes [sa]
　Crest: an arm embowed, in armour, holding a pole-axe [arg]
　The field is tricked or but is usually arg
　Notepaper Mrs. Henry Lowell Hiscock, Roxbury, Mass., desc. of Lucinda Gibbs of Sturbridge, Mass., b. 1805. Printed in blue

Gibbs　Per fess arg and erm 3 battle axes gu
　Crest: a mailed arm emb, holding a battle axe
　Motto: Tenax propositi
　Bookplate Montgomery Gibbs, law writer, N. Y.

Gibbs　Sa 3 battle axes in pale arg
　Crest: 3 broken tilting spears or, 2 in saltire and one in pale, ensigned with a wreath arg and sa
　Motto: Tenax propositi
　Tombstone of Robert Gibbs (ob. 1769) in the Old North Burial Ground, Providence, R. I. Also on wife's tombstone. Vermont's Amer. Heral., pp. 110, 166

Gibbs　*See also* Fisk

Gifford　Gu 3 lions pass in pale arg
　Bookplate Henry Gifford Hardy. John Giffarde of Lynn, 1683, used a seal. N. E. G. Reg., vol. 13

Gignilliat　Gu a cock passant or wattled gu
　Crest: a cock of the shield
　Water color in So. Car. Hist. Soc.

Gilbert　Az a chev erm bet 3 eagles displ or
　Crest: a lion ramp
　"By the name of Gilbert" and palm branches (?) with pendent chains. An embroidery, framed. Owned by Mrs. Horatio J. Gilbert, Milton, Mass.

Gilbert Arg on a chev sa 3 roses of the field
Motto: Tenax propositi
Bookplate I. H. Grenville Gilbert, Ware, Mass.

Gilbert Gu 2 bars erm and in chief 3 fleurs-de-lis or
Crest: out of a ducal cor or a stag's head ppr
Motto: Tenax propositi
Dinner plate owned by Mrs. Clement S. Houghton, Chestnut Hill, Mass. Gilbert of Gilbertsville, Mass.

Gilbert Impaled by Brimage

Gilchrist Arg a pierced mullet az. On a chief az a sun in splendor rayed or bet 2 crosses pattée fitchée
Crest: a crescent arg
Motto: Fide et fiducia
Bookplate John James Gilchrist, LL.D., Harv. 1828. Chief Just. Court of Claims, Wash.

Giles Per chev arg and az a lion ramp counterchanged
Crest: a lion's gamb erect and erased [sa], holding a fruited branch, leaved vert
Motto: Tourjours le merae '
Bookplate Daniel Giles

Giles Per chev arg and az a lion ramp counterchanged, a label of 3 points for diff
Crest: a lion ramp, holding a rose
Motto: Libertas et patria mea
Bookplate James Giles. Maverick, sc.

Giles Per chev arg and az, a lion ramp counterchanged, collared, or
Crest: a lion's gamb, erased and erect ppr, charged with a baton or, holding an apple branch vert, fructed or
Motto: Libertas et patria
Old drawings of Mountfort family, Boston. Vermont's Amer. Heral., pp. 59, 166

Gillespie Per fess or and az. In the dexter chief a hand couped at the wrist holding a sword. In the sinister chief a cross crosslet fitchée. In base a 3-masted ship, sails furled (period of 1750?)
Crest: a cat segreant
Motto: Touch not the cat but a glove
Seal owned by Mabel A. B. Sawin, Cambridge, Mass.

Gillette Erm on a bend [sa] 3 lucies [arg]
Crest: a lion ramp, holding in his dexter gamb a battle axe ppr
Engr. on notepaper of Hallie C. (Mrs. Edward) Gillette, Sheridan, Wyoming

Gilman Arg a leg embowed [sa]
Crest: on a chapeau a lion rampant
Motto: Si deus quis contra
Bookplate Daniel C. Gilman, Prest. Johns Hopkins Univ.

Gilman Quart 1: Arg a man's leg couped at the thigh sa; 2: On a bend invected az 3 buckles arg bet 2 bendlets gu (case?); 3: Arg a chev engr sa bet 3 stags courant gu (Ellacombe?); 4: Arg on a cross sa 5 fleurs-de-lis
Crest: a demi-lion ramp on a chapeau
Bookplate —— Gilman, N. Y.

Gilman Sa a man's leg in pale, couped at the thigh arg
Crest: out of a cap of maintenance a demi-lion ramp ppr
Mottoes: A: Espérance; B: Si Deus, quis contra
Tablets to Samuel Gilman and his wives, church at Hingham, Mass. Vermont's Amer. Heral., pp. 33, 166. Heral. Jour., vol. 1, p. 151

Gilman [Sa] a horse's head erased [or] bet 3 dexter hands couped arg
Silver teapot made in 1788–89 by W. P. Owned by Jeffrey R. Brackett, 220 Marlboro St., Boston

Gilmer Az a chev bet 2 fleurs-de-lis in chief or, and a writing pen full feathered in base arg
Gilmer bookplate. Crozier's Va. Heral., p. 111

Gilpin Or a boar passant sa
Crest: a mailed arm embr holding a sprig of laurel vert
Motto: Dictis factisque simplex
Bookplate Henry D. Gilpin, Atty.-Gen. U. S. C. G. Childs, sc. Also John F., Wm., and J. Gilpin

Gilpin Impaled by Rogers

Glatfelter [Arg?] two chev
Crest: a hand holding a dagger erect piercing a heart (?)
Over the fireplace in house of Philip H. Glatfelter, Spring Grove, Penn.

Gleason Sa on a bend arg 3 pierced rowels gu
Motto: Vincit amor patriæ
Water color (old) in oval 3¼ x 2¾ in. owned by Benjamin Gleason, geographer, lecturer, Cambridge, 1830. Now owned by Herbert W. C. Browne, 66 Beacon St., Boston. Same arms with Wheildon, water color, framed, by H. W. C. B.

Gleim Arg a wing erect
Crest: a rose seeded bet 2 wings addorsed
Motto: Fides scutum
Bookplate Lilian Frances Gleim. Done 1900 by Huger Elliott, Phila.

Glidden   Arg on a bend gu 3 escallops
Painted on a shield of wood in the
Glidden mansion (with columns), Glid-
den Street, Newcastle, Maine.   Also on
tablet to Wm. T. Glidden (d. 1893) in
St. Andrew's Church

Glover   Sa on a chev erm bet 3 cresc
Crest: a spread eagle ppr
Motto: Surgite lumen adest
Seal ring of Dawson Coleman
Glover of N. Y.   Son of Henry Sheaff
Glover, N. Y., and Fairfield, Conn.
Family from Eng. about 18C1

Goddard   Gu a chev vairé arg and az
bet 3 crescents arg
Crest: a stag's head affrontée ppr
couped [gu attired or]
Motto: Cervus non servus
Bookplate Paul B. Goddard, M. D.

Goddard   Gu an eagle displayed sa
Crest: a demi-lion gu
Motto: In God I trust
Bookplate Lucius P. Goddard

Godfrey   [Arg] a cross potent [or] bet
4 crosses crosslet [or] and Impaling:
a coat apparently paly of ten
Arms on letter from Edward Godfrey to Gov. John Winthrop (Winthrop
papers).   M. H. S. Coll., vol. 37.
Heral. Jour., vol. 3, p. 177

Goelet   Gu a swan in water ppr
Crest: a swan
Bookplate Peter Goelet by Maverick
Notepaper F. Winthrop coll., N. Y.,
1885, has "Ex candore decus"

Goelet   Or a fess erminois bet 3 swans
rising
Crest: on a cor a swan of the shield
Motto: Ex candore decus
Bookplate Robert Goelet, N. Y.

Goldsboro   Quartered by Corbin

Goldsborough   Az a cross flory arg
Crest: a pelican in her piety
Motto: Non sibi
Notepaper   Matthew   Tilghman
Goldsborough, "Otwell," Oxford, Md.

Goldsmith   Or a habited arm erased
from the dexter holding a mallet
Motto: Tu mihi curarum requies
Bookplate Abraham Goldsmith, engr.
by French

Goodrich   Arg on a fess gu bet 2 lions
pass guard sa a fleur-de-lis bet as many
crescents or
Crest: issuing from a ducal cor a
demi-lion ramp sa holding a battle axe
Motto: Fortior leone justis
Bookplate George S. Goodrich.   J.
W. Spenceley, sc., Boston, 1905.   The
same arms used by Isabella Goodrich
in a lozenge

Goodridge   Arg a fess [or, properly sa?]
In chief 3 crosses crosslet fitchée [of
the last]
Crest: a [black] bird ppr
Engr. on a cup given by Walter
Goodridge, Jr., Boston, in 1730, to
Second Church, Boston.   Old Sil. Am.
Ch., p. 36

Goodwin   Arg a lion pass sa.   On a
chief or 3 fusils in fess gu
Crest: a stag trippant or
Motto: Virtute et labore
Bookplate Frank Goodwin, Capt.
Mass. Volunteers.   S. D., sc., 1804

Goodwin   [Gu] 2 bars [or] bet 6 lozenges
arg 3, 2, 1.   Impaling: Quart 1 and 4:
A bend; 2 and 3: 2 bars (?)
On tomb of Rachel, wife of James
Goodwin, Goodwin's Neck, York Co.,
Va., 1666.   Very dim; a lozenge, a
bend and 2 bars still exist.   Wm. &
Mary Quar., July, 1893, p. 25; Oct.
1893, p. 84

Goodwin   Or a fess gu bet 6 lions' heads
erased of the 2d, 3 and 3 in fess
Crest: a griffin sejant
Bookplate Cham[n] Goodwin, S. C.

Goodwin   Or 2 lions pass guard sa.   On
a canton of the last [3 bezants]
Crest: a demi-lion ramp guard sa
holding in the paws [a bezant]
Arms on notepaper of Alice D.
Goodwin, Sunnyslope, Lexington, Mass.

Goodwin   [Or] two lions ramp sa on a
canton of the second three bezants
Crest: a lion of the field
Arms dated 1702, engraved on a
silver snuff box owned by Daniel
Ringe or Rindge of Ipswich, Mass.
(1661–1714), now owned by Arthur
Rindge Wendell, Church St., Rahway,
N. J.

Goodwin   Per pale or and gu a lion
ramp bet 3 fleurs-de-lis, all counterchanged
Crest: a demi-lion
Bookplate "Goodwin"

Goodwin   [Sa?] a lion pass [or?]   on
a chief or 3 mascles voided gu
Crest: a stag trippant
Engr. on a tankard made by Paul
Revere, owned 1916 by Lovell Little,
Brookline, Mass.   Marked on ribbon
"Joseph Goodwin."   Crest on cover

Gooch   Paly of 8 arg and [sa], a chev
[of the first] bet 3 greyhounds of the
second, spotted of the field
Crest: a greyhound pass arg spotted
and collared sa
On the tomb of Major William
Gooch at Temple Farm, York Co., Va.
He d. 29 Oct., 1655.   Va. Mag., April,

1924, opp. p. 125. Ancest. Rec. & Portr., vol. II, p. 731, gives Gooch arms as described in Burke. Sketch in Scribner's Mag., Oct. 1881, p. 811. The dogs look like spaniels

Goode *See also* Morris

Goodman Per pale [erm and or] an eagle displ with 2 heads [sa]
Crest: an eagle of the field
Capt. Walter Goodman, d. 1782. Christ Church graveyard, Phila. The Continent, 25 Apr. 1883, p. 520

Goodyer *See also* Olcott

Gookin [Gu] a chev erm bet 3 cocks
Seal of Maj.-Gen. Dan. Gookin on letter, 1656, to Thurloe. F. W. G.'s Life of Daniel Gookin. Tablet (carved on stone) to Maj.-Gen. Daniel Gookin, 1612–87, placed by the Mass. Soc. Colon. Dames at Jamestown, Va., in 1907

Gookin Quart 1 and 4: Gu a chev erm bet 3 cocks or; 2 and 3: Sa a cross crosslet erm (Durrant). Impaling: Arg on a bend gu 3 mullets or; in chief a bear gu (Edolph)
Crest: out of a mural cor gu (?) a cock or legged sa (?)
Hatchment on wood, owned by N. E. Hist. Gen. Soc., said to have been used at funeral of Thomas Gookin, Ripple Court, Kent, 1625, cousin of the immigrant. Thomas married Jane Edolph

Gordon Az a pheon bet 3 boars' heads erased or
Crest: a stag's head ppr attired or
Motto: Dum vigilo tutus
On a silver tankard of Col. James Gordon, who d. 2 Jan. 1768, now the property of Dr. A. A. E. Taylor of Columbus, Ohio. Crozier's Va. Heral., p. 35

Gordon Az 3 boars' heads couped or
Crest: a stag's head cabossed ppr
Motto: Bydand
On automobile Prue C. Gordon, 857 Main St., Worcester, Mass.

Gordon [Az] 3 boars' heads couped [or]
Wax seal on will of William Gordon, dated 29 Feb. 1684, at Urbanna, Va. Wm. & Mary Quar., Jan. 1893, p. 121

Gordon Az 3 boars' heads couped or within a double tressure flory counter flory with a thistle bet 2 roses on each of the 4 sides or and a fleur-de-lis at each corner
Crest: an arm ppr holding a bow and arrow arg ready to shoot
Motto: Ne nemium
Painting owned by Miss Lena Smith, Scotland Neck, N. C. Bertrand de Gordon shot Richard Coeur de Lion. From Mrs. Everett

Gordon Az 3 boars' heads erased or
Tomb of Samuel Gordon in Blandford Churchyard, Va. D. 14 April, 1771, aged 54 years. Crozier's Va. Heral., p. 10

Gordon Quart 1: [Az] 3 boars' heads couped arg; 2: 3 garbs; 3: [Or] 3 crescents within a royal tressure [gu]; 4: 3 cinquefoils
Crest: an arm embowed, holding a dagger
Seal Patrick Gordon, Gov. Penn., 1726–36. Sylvan City, 1883, p. 457

Gore [Or] 3 bulls' heads 2 and 1 cabossed [sa]
Crest: a bull's head couped at the neck [sa]
Gov. Christopher Gore belonged to the Wiltshire family. Gore Hall, Harvard College. Over the door and on both gate posts. In stone

Gorges Lozengy arg [or?] and az a chev gu
Arms on letter from Thomas Gorges to Gov. John Winthrop (Winthrop papers). M. H. S. Coll., vol. 37. A quarterly coat. *See* Heral. Jour., vol. 3, p. 176

Gough Gu on a fess arg bet 3 boars' heads or a lion pass az
Crest: a boar's head arg holding in the jaws a broken spear gu
Motto: Donat anima virtus
On teapot owned by Miss Mary Carroll Schenck of Baltimore, formerly by Sophia, daughter of Harry Gough of Perry Hall, Baltimore Co., Md., who married James Carroll of "the Mount"

Gould Or on a chev bet 3 roses az 3 pineapples of the first (Gold). Impaling: Quart 1 and 4: Arg a chev sa bet 3 magpies ppr (Kingdon); 2 and 3: Sa 3 crescents or (Boughton)
Crest: an eagle's head erased holding a pineapple
Bookplate George J. Gould of N. Y., engr. by French

Gould Per saltire az and or a lion ramp counterchanged
Carved or painted on bookcase in Archivo de Simancas, Valladolid, Spain, to commemorate gift from Miss Alice B Gould of Boston, daughter of B. A. Gould. Her grandfather had a seal ring with the lion rampant
Mr. Park reports a water color in orig. black and carved gilt frame, by Samuel Blyth of Salem, about 1760, with interrupted palm branches but no scroll. Owned by Mrs. John P. Huntington, Harland Road, Norwich, Conn.

Gourgas Or on a mound with stream sa a tree of the last. On a chief gu a goose in flight

Crest: a goose's head
Motto: Deo omnia plena
Bookplate John Mark Gourgas of London and Milton, Mass. Also of Jean Louis Gourgas, signed P. L. Also of Jⁿ Jˢ Jʰ Gourgas of N. Y., 1837

Gove Arg a cross lozengy bet 4 eagles displ [sa]

Motto: Dum spiro spero
Engr. on notepaper of Mrs. Lottie Gove Norton (Mrs. Charles Oliver Norton), Kearney, Nebraska

Graeme Arg on a fess embat gu bet in chief a rose bet 2 escallops and in base 3 piles or a bird

Bookplate Dr. Thomas Graeme, Phila., used by his daughter, Mrs. Elizabeth Ferguson. Sylvan City, 1883, p. 440

Graham [Or] on a chief [sa] 3 escallops of the field

Crest: 2 wings addorsed [or]
Motto: Nec habe nec careo nec curo
Bookplate Henry Hale Graham, lawyer, Chester, Pa. J. Smither, sc. Engr. arg on a chief or, etc.

Graham Quart 1 and 4: Or on a chief sa 3 escallops of the field; 2 and 3: Arg 3 roses 2 and 1 gu

Crest: a falcon [armed and beaked or] standing on a heron
Motto: Ne oubliez
Bookplate James Lorimer Graham, 1835–76, of N. Y., Consul to Italy. Thomas Haskins Graham has sa a chev arg bet 3 escallops

Grant Arg 3 lions ramp [az] 2 and 1. A chief az

Motto: Stand fast, stand firm, stand sure
Bookplate Percy Stickney Grant

Grant Az 3 lions ramp [arg]. On a chief [arg] a bend [   ] all contourné

Bookplate Rev. Roland D. Grant, Boston

Grant Gu a mullet bet 3 antique crowns [or]

Crest: a burning hill ppr
Motto: Stand sure
Topaz seal of Patrick Grant, fa. of John, fa. of Patrick, fa. of Patrick, fa. of Judge Robert Grant of Boston, writer. Also on family silver

Grant Gu 3 antique crowns 2 and 1

Crest: smoking hills
Motto: Stand fast
Bookplate Madison Grant, engr. by A. W. Macdonald

Gratten Quartered by Cabell

Graves Gu an eagle displ or [sometimes crowned] arg a martlet of the second for diff

Crest: an eagle displ or, winged gu
Motto: Aquila non captat muscas
Tombstone of Thomas Graves, M. D., buried 1746, Charlestown, Mass. Vermont's Amer. Heral., p. 68, 166

Graves Quart 1 and 4: Gu an eagle displ; 2 and 3: Arg a castle bet 2 battle axes sa (Hicks)

Crest: a demi-eagle displ erased [or] environed with a ducal cor [gu]
Motto: Aquila non captat muscas
Bookplate Wm. Graves of Mass. (?)

Gray A barry of 6 arg and az. Over all on a bend gu 3 chaplets

Crest: a dove bearing a laurel branch vert
Motto: In Deo fides
Bookplate —— Gray, Boston
Framed water color, 12 x 14, owned by Mrs. Arthur Moody (Eliz. Gray), Garrison Rd., Brookline. Seen 2 May, 1924, by Dr. Harold Bowditch

Gray A barry of 6 arg and az, over all a label of 5 points gu, each point charged with 3 bezants

Crest: on a ducal cor a bear or
Bookplate Benjamin Gray, Boston

Gray Gu a lion ramp bet 3 cinquefoils arg within a bordure engr of the last

Crest: an anchor and cable in the sea
Motto: Fast
Bookplate —— Gray, Boston. John Gray omitted the cinquefoils and cable. The motto is "anchor fast anchor"

Gray Gu a lion ramp within a bordure engr arg

Crest: an anchor in pale or
Seal brought to America by John Gray, owned by John Bowie Gray, Stafford Co., Va. Croizer's Va. Heral., p. 40

Gray Vert a lion ramp within a bordure engr arg. Impaling: Or on a chev bet 3 maple leaves vert 5 drops

Crest: an anchor erect entwined with a cable
Motto: Anchor fast anchor
Bookplate Francis Gray

Gray Gu a lion ramp arg within a bordure engr of the 2d. Impaling: Sa a chev bet 3 trefoils slipped arg (Lewis)

Crest: a stag trippant
Embr. hatchment by Elizabeth Gray, who married Samuel Alexander Otis, 1764. Her father, Hon. Harrison Gray, married Elizabeth Lewis, 1734. Mrs. John H. Morison, Brimmer St., Boston

Gray Impaled by Fay

Greaves or **Graves** [Gu] an eagle displ [or] a martlet of the second in the dexter chief for diff
Crest: an eagle displ [or winged gu?]
Hon. Thomas Greaves, 1747, Phipps Street Yard, Charlestown, Mass., Tomb 54. Heral. Jour., vol. 1, p. 47

Green "Arg on a fess azure a dragon passant between 2 escallops. Or three lions' heads erased in a circle [*i. e.* in circles] sable. By the name of Green"
Crest: "a woodpecker pecking the stump of a tree"
Framed water color with palm branches (by Coles?) owned by Hon. Samuel A. Green of Groton, 1917

Green Ar on a fess az bet 3 pellets, each charged with a lion's head erased of the first, a griffin pass bet 2 escallops or
Seal on will of John Green of Stow, 1688. (Suffolk Wills.) Heral. Jour., vol. 4, p. 111

Green [Az] a chev bet 3 stags trippant [or]
Crest: a stag's head or
Bookplate Robert Green, very old. John Greene, Jr., of R. I., used seal with 3 stags contourné and a crescent for diff. (Doc. Hist. R. I., vol. 1, p. 233)

Green Az 3 stags trippant or
Crest: a stag's head or
Motto: Nec timeo nec sperno
Bookplate James Ellis Green. Bookplate Gardiner Greene (1635–1753). Ancest. Rec. &. Portr., vol. I, p. 108

Green Sa 3 stags trippant or
Crest: a stag's head
Motto: Labor omnia vincit
Bookplate George Wade Green. Benjamin Green's, Boston, N. H., sc., 1757, has no motto

Green Quart 1 and 4: [Az?] 3 stags trip [or?]; 2 and 3: A chev bet 3 leopards' faces
Crest: a stag's head erased
Motto: Nec timeo sperno
Arms on brass in St. Paul's Church, Norfolk, Va., in memory of John Newport Green, 1843–1902, son of J. N. G. of Newtown House Co., Kilkenny, and his wife, Eliza Arith McGuire of Hereford, Eng.

Greene [Az] 3 stags 2 and 1 trippant [or]
Crest: a dove reguardant holding a twig
King's Chapel graveyard, Boston, altar tomb. Heral., Jour., vol. 2, p. 22

Greene Az 3 bucks trippant or
Crest: a stag's head erased or
Motto: Carpe diem

Bookplate J. S. Copley Greene. Also Thomas Greene, Mason St., Boston, 1705–63 (perhaps Hurd). David Greene, with "Nec timeo nec sperno," engr. by Paul Revere. Margaret M. Q. Greene (wife of B. D. G.) impaled Quincy (a sepia plate). Wm. B. Greene, Jr., Boston, quartered 2: Az 3 covered cups or (Butler); and 3: Arg a chev sa bet 3 stags trippant of the last (Rogers?) and had for motto: Suivez raison

Greene Vert 3 stags trippant [or]
Crest: a stag's head erased [or]
Motto: Nec timeo nec sperno
Bloodstone seal W. M. Greene, New York
Bookplate Roger Edward Green. Brenton Greene changed from azure to vert

Greene Quartered by Tufton

Greenleaf Arg a chev bet 3 leaves erect vert, on the chev a martlet for diff
Crest: a dove holding in its bill an olive branch
Bookplate of William Greenleaf. N. Hurd, sc. Also bookplate of Richard Greenleaf Turner. F. J. Libbie collection. Heral. Jour., vol. 3, p. 22

Greenleaf Arg a chev gu bet 3 green leaves
Bookplate Marion Greenleaf, Saugatuck, H. C. Eno. des. Richard Cranch Greenleaf, Jr., used these arms with the leaves tricked purple

Greenough Arg on a bend engr sa, 3 hunting horns [arg] stringed [or]
Crest: a hunt horn of the field
Bookplate Charles Pelham Greenough, Boston
Motto of W. W. Greenough: "Fide sed cui vide." Arms from Rouge Dragon, 17 Dec. 1840. Gravestone of David Stoddard Greenough, 1844–1924, seen at John Evans & Co.'s, Dec. 1925

Greenway Gu a chev or bet 3 covered cups arg. On a chief arg as many griffins' heads erased az
Crest: a griffin's head erased az holding in its bill an anchor [gu]
Bookplate James Cowan Greenway. J. W. S., sc., 1904

Greenwood [Arg] a fess bet 3 stars of six points pierced in chief, and in base 3 ducks all [sa]. Broken at the left
Crest: a similar star bet a pair of duck's wings expanded [sa]
Motto: Ut prosim
Nathaniel Greenwood from Norwich, Eng., d. 1684. "Tomb 57." Copp's

Hill Yard, Boston. Also a painting.
Heral. Jour., vol. 2, p. 78. Also a
bookplate engr. by Tiffany & Co.
Mullets pierced of Isaac John Greenwood, author

Gregorie Arg on a mound in base vert
a tree in leaf ppr crossed in bend by a
sword ppr hilted or, ensigned on the
point with an antique crown or. In
chief a pierced star of 6 points of the
last. Impaling: Gu 3 lions ramp arg
2 and 1 a mullet in chief or
Crest: a lion's head erased arg
Engr. on a silver waiter owned by
James Gregorie, 1740–1807. Owned
by Edmund Gregorie, Charleston, S. C.

Grew Quart 1 and 4: Arg a fess dancettée sa bet 3 leopards' faces [gu];
2 and 3: Azure a chev bet 3 crosses
crosslet fitchée [within a bordure
engrailed] or (Sturges, Co. Hants)
Crest: a talbot's head couped below
the shoulder or, charged on the
shoulder with a leash knotted in a
double bow
Motto: Esse quam videri
"Armes of Greyve"
Bookplate Henry Sturgis Grew and
Randolph Clark Grew. Spenceley, sc.

Griffin Gu on a fess or bet 3 fusils of
the 2d, each charged with a fleur-de-
lis of the field a half rose bet 2 griffins
segreant [gu]
Crest: a griffin segreant
Motto: Semper paratus
Bookplate George Griffin

Griffin Quartered by Griffin

Griffith Erm a lion ramp or
Crest: a griffin's head erased or
Motto: Omnis a Deo protestas
Bookplate —— Griffith, Phila., and
R. Eglesfield Griffith

Griffiths Arg on a cross sa 5 crescents
In the dexter chief a spear head erect
Crest: a griffin passant
Motto: Benevolentia et justitia
Bookplate William Griffiths of Phila.
Zieber's Heral., pp. 324–5

Grimshaw Az a griffin segreant arg
Crest: a griffin of the field holding
a rose slipped and leaved
Motto: Candide et constanter
Bookplate Wm. Grimshaw, author,
Phila., 1782–1852, b. Ire.

Griswold Arg a fess gu bet 2 greyhounds courant sa. Impaling: Quart
gu and or, on a bend arg 3 lions passant
az (Perry)
Crest: a greyhound courant sa
Motto: Palmam qui meruit ferat
Bookplate Almon Whiting Griswold
of N. Y. City, married Mary Adelaide
Perry. Son Harv. 1881

Griswold Arg a fess gu bet 2 greyhounds sa within a bordure or
Bookplate Daniel P. Griswold

Griswold Quartered by Smith

Gross Per chev arg and az 3 owls
affrontée ppr
Crest: a mailed arm emb, holding a
short sword
Motto: Meditari et agere
Bookplate Dr. Henry B. Gross,
Phila.

Grosvenor 1: [Az] a garb [or] in the
dexter chief a crescent (the arms used
after the controversy with Scrope
which family kept "az a bend or");
Quart 2: [Arg] a chief [az] (Haselwell);
3: [Arg] 2 bars [gu] and in chief 3
cinquefoils gu (Scar-Smith); 4: [Az]
a cutlass in bend [arg] within a bordure
[or] (Tettenhall); 5: [Vairy az and
arg] a canton [gu] (Filliol); 6: [Arg]
a bend [sa] bet 3 mullets [gu] (Clayton);
7: [Arg] on a fess cotised [sa] 3 escallops of the field (Bushbury)
Crest: a talbot statant [or]
John Grosvenor of Roxbury, Mass.,
d. 1691, aged 41, tanner; 3 is Main-
waring an early ancestor, arg 2 bars
gu on a chief gu a lion passant guardant
or; or a late ancestor Scar-Smith, arg
2 bars gu, in chief 3 cinquefoils arg.
The chief shows dots or dents; 4:
In bend is sometimes sinister; 5:
Stanton is the only other possible.
Visitations Stafford, 1614, p. 159, and
Warwick, 1619, p. 384. Herald and
Genealogist, vols. 4 and 5. Drake's
Roxbury has a picture very faulty.
Eustis Street Graveyard, Boston.
Upright slate slab near the street
John was grandson of William of
Bridgnorth, rerhaps grandson of John
of Tettenhall in whose line are all the
quarterings

Grout "He beareth azure on a bend or,
bet 2 mullets argent 3 leopards' faces
gules, by the name of Grout, and was
confirmed by grant the 28th of May,
1587 . . . to Richard Grout of
Walton in the County of Derby, Eng.,
a descendant from an ancient family
of that name in the west of England"
Framed painting. By John Coles?
Henry F. Grout, owner, Fitchburg,
Mass.

Groves Erm a chev engr gu bet 3
escallops or
Crest: a stag trippant
Motto: Propero sed curo
Bookplate Charles J. Groves. S. L.
S., sc., 1896

Grundy Arg on a cross engrailed bet
4 lions pass guard gu 5 martlets [or]
Crest: a demi-leopard ramp guard
sa bezanty

Motto: Sapere aude
Bookplate George Grundy (Baltimore). Ancest. Rec. & Portr., vol. II, p. 591

Grymes [Or] a bordure engrailed [az] on a chief sa 3 escallops arg
Crest: a pair of wings addorsed or
Seal on will of Philip Grymes of Va., dated 1747. Wm. & Mary Quar., Jan. 1893, p. 120. Va. Mag., Oct. 1919

Guerrant Or 3 lions ramp sa langued, membered, crowned gu
Crest: a coronet or
Motto: Flagror non consumor
Water color owned by Mrs. J. L. Clayton, Leaksville, N. C. Also notepaper. Copy by Miss Harriet L. Herring, Spray, N. C. Va. and N. C. family

Guild Az a lion ramp or
Crest: a dexter arm [or] holding a cutlass
Motto: Nous main tien drons
Bookplate Chester Guild, Boston. Benjamin Guild of Boston had a

signet ring with the arms. Gov. Curtis Guild used the crest and motto on notepaper

Guild Per bend or and gu. In chief a demi-wyvern az
Crest: a lion's head or erased langued gu
"By the name of Guild," and palm branches. By Coles? *See* illustration in Burleigh's Guild Family

Guinand Arg a scorpion of 10 legs displ sa (or sanguine)
Crest: a demi-scorpion of the field
Motto: Sans venin (?)
Bookplate Henry Guinand, Balto.

Gunthorpe Impaled by Yeamans

Gurdon Impaled by Saltonstall

Gurney A paly of 6 or and az. On an inscutcheon gu 3 lions ramp arg 2 and 1
Crest: a griffin's head erased
Motto: Spem successus alit
Bookplate Henry Gurney, Phila.

Gwynne Impaled by Vanderbilt

H

Hadley Gu 2 chevronelles bet 3 falcons arg, beaked, legged, and belled or
Crest: a falcon of the field
Motto: God is my help
Water color owned by Francis E. Hadley, 86th St., N. Y., son of Joseph Leonard Hadley, "Hazelbourne," Clapham, Eng.; embroidery by F. E.'s niece, Mrs. E. H. Galbreath

Haggerston Quartered by Maxwell

Haig Quart 1 and 4: Az a saltire arg bet in chief a mullet arg, in fess a decrescent and an increscent of the last, and in base a mullet of the same; 2 and 3: Or a garb [az]. On a chief az a lion ramp [or] (Mackenan)
Crest: a rock ppr
Motto: Tyde what may
Bookplate Dr. George Haig, So. Car.

Haight Arg a millrind gu
Crest: a hound (?) sejant bet 2 wings
Bookplate Frederick Everest Haight

Hains Or on a fess gu 3 bezants and in chief a hound courant sa [az?]
Crests: 1: an eagle displ on a tortoise's back; 2: an eagle displ [az] with a semée of [18] stars of 6 points [arg]
Motto: There is no difficulty to him that wills
Bookplate Andrew Mack Hains, Canterbury, N. H.

Hairston Az a chev or bet 3 keys fessways arg
Crest: a cubit arm ppr bolding a key

Motto: Toujours fidele
By Miss Harriet L. Herring, Spray, N. C., "from drawing or wall plaque"

Hale [Az a chev embat and counterembat or]
Crest: a serpent ppr entwined around 5 arrow shafts [or headed sa feathered arg] one in pale, 4 in saltire-wise
Motto: Vera sequor
Hale memorial bookplate, Keene, N. H., for George Silsbee Hale of Boston. J. W. Spenceley, sc., 1902. The seal of John Hale on will, 1701, (Suffolk Wills) has a crest: a bird rising from a coronet, and Nunquam non paratus

Hale Gu 3 arrows 2 and 1 [or] with shafts az [headed arg]. Impaling: Arg a chev sa bet 3 mullets sa
Crest: a mailed arm embow ppr holding an arrow [arg] by a ribbon around the wrist [gu]
Bookplate John C. Hale

Hale Gu 3 arrows in fess, points down
Crest: a mailed arm embowed ppr, holding an arrow
Bookplate Robert Hale of Beverly, Mass., cir. 1752. In the siege of Louisburg. N. Hurd, sc. Wm. John Hale quartered the above with: Arg in a pale gu a fish's head (?)

Hale [Gu?] 3 arrows points down [or? feathered and barbed arg?]
Crest: an armed arm embowed, holding an arrow

Motto: Cum principibus
Notepaper Samuel Hale, Dover,
N. H., and Dr. Wm. Hale, Gloucester,
Mass.

Hale Quartered by Hobart

Halford Arg a hound statant sa gorged
or. On a chief az 3 fleurs-de-lis or
Crest: a hound's head sa gorged
Bookplate R. Halford

Hall Impaled by Fitch q. v.

Hall 3 tigers' heads (?)
Crest: a lion ramp
On the lid of a silver snuff box
owned by Thomas Hall, Prince George
Co., Va., 1739. The Halls used tal-
bot's heads. Crozier's Va. Heral., p. 30

Hall Arg a chev sa bet 3 columbines or
Crest: a flower of the field
Bookplate F. A. Hall

Hall Arg a chev sa bet 3 columbines
slipped ppr
Crest: a lion's head erased ppr
Very old framed water color, cornstalk pattern, owned by Gen. John H.
Sherburne of Brookline, Mass., desc.
from Elijah Hall of Portsmouth, N. H.,
an officer under John Paul Jones

Hall Arg a chev bet 3 talbots' heads
erased sa
Crest: a talbot's head erased, bezantée
Bookplate James Hall, lawyer and
author, Phila. Heral. Jour., vol. 3,
p. 23

Hall Arg a lion with forked tail ramp
Crest: a peacock couped rising
Motto: Crescit sub pondere virtus
Bookplate James Hall

Hall [Arg?] over a semée of crosses
crosslet [gu] three talbots' heads
erased 2 and 1 [sa] langued [gu?]
Crest: a talbot's head erased
Engr. on a tall cup from Hugh Hall
before 1746, West Church, Lynde
Street, Boston. E. A. Jones. Old Sil.
Am. Ch., p. 87

Hall Erm a chev gu bet 3 stags' heads
couped contourné
Crest: a mason's square and divi-
ders
Bookplate Dr. Timothy Hall, 1758–
1844, of East Hartford, Conn. R.
Brunton, sc. Bates's Early Conn.
Engr., p. 22

Hall Gu 3 bars closeted (3 sets of 3) or;
on a chief erm a lion pass gu. Impaling: Gu 3 bars closeted or, and on a
base erm a lion pass gu
Crest: from a ducal cor a lion's head
erased sa

Motto: Carpe diem
Bookplate George Abbott Hall, Jane
Harris Hall, 1904, So. Car.

Hall Or 3 crescents arg (?) within a
bordure engr erm
Crest: a lion erased or
Bookplate G. Stanley Hall, Pres.
Clark Univ., Worcester, Mass.

Hall Quart 1 and 4: Gu 3 pole-axes in
fess or; 2 and 3: Or on a chev vert bet
3 stags tripp of the 2d 3 cinquefoils or
(Robinson)
Crest: a horse's head in armor arg
surmounted by 2 feathers one gu one
arg
Motto: Vis veritatis magna
On door of automobile of George
Robinson Hall, manager Adams House,
Boston

Hall Quart 1 and 4: Sa 3 talbots' heads
erased arg collared gu; 2 and 3: Sa 3
leopards' heads jessant-de-lys or
Crest: a talbot's head erased sa collared gu
Bookplate William Hall (Harris collection). Heral. Jour., vol. 3, p. 23

Hall Impaled by Fitch

Hall Quartered by Leigh

Hallowell Impaled by Vaughan

Hamblen *See also* Hopkins

Hamersley [Gu?] a chev bet 3 hammers
[or?]
Memorial tablet to Andrew Hamersley who d. in 1819, aged 94. Soame
arms? Trinity Church, N. Y. Not as
in Burke

Hamersley Gu 3 rams' heads, 2 and 1
couped or
Memorial tablet to William Hamers-
ley of New York City in the New Eng.
Hist. Geneal. Society, 9 Ashburton
Place, Boston. "Great grandson of
Sir Hugh, Lord Mayor of London,
1627"

Hamill *See also* Baldwin

Hamilton Gu 3 cinquefoils [arg]
Crest: from a ducal cor an oak tree
transversed with a frame saw ppr
Motto: Through
Bookplate W. Hamilton of Wood-
lands, Phila., a tory. Seal of James
Hamilton, Gov. Penn. 1748–54, 1759–
63. Sylvan City, 1883, p. 457

Hamilton Gu 3 rowels erm. In chief
a bird
Crest: a tree through a mascle
"Capt. Francis Hamilton" of *H. M.
S. Kingfisher*, 1687. On canvas, 1886.
Bostonian Society. Formerly in
wooden King's Chapel

Hamilton [Gu] a mullet pierced bet 3 cinquefoils [arg]
Crest: out of a ducal coronet [or] on a mound [vert] an oak tree "penetrated transversely in the stem by a frame-saw proper; frame [arg]"
Arms of Andrew Hamilton of Phila., engr. on two tankards made by John Myers. The arms on the front and crest on the lid. Andrew's daughter married James Lyle. Mr. C. Hartman Kuhn, who owns the tankards, has also a tray with the Tyllarms and a paten with the Campbell arms. *See* Bulletin Penn. Museum, Fairmount Park, Jan. 1914

Hamilton Quart 1 and 4: Gu 3 cinquefoils, 2 and 1 arg; 2 and 3: Arg a lymphad with her sails furled [sa] (Arran)
Crest: from a ducal cor an oak tree transversed with a frame saw ppr
Motto: Through
Bookplate Henry Hamilton

Hamilton Quart 1 and 4: Gu a mullet arg bet 3 cinquefoils; 2 and 3: Gu a heart or bet 3 cinquefoils
Crest: a dove bearing a twig
Motto: Nuncia pacis
Bookplate Alex^r Hamilton, Esqr

Hammond Arg on a chev sa bet 3 ogresses, each charged with a martlet of the field 3 escallops [or], all within a bordure gu
Motto: Tentenda via est
Bookplate William Churchill Hammond, Holyoke, Mass.

Hampden Impaled by Hobart

Hanchett [Sa] 3 hands couped 2 and 1 arg. Impaling: Arg a chev gu bet 3 boars' heads couped, a cross pattée in the chev point
Bookplate John Hanchett, Hartford, Conn.

Hancock Gu a dexter hand arg couped and on a chief arg 3 cocks gu
Motto: Obsta principiis
On Lowestoft Punch Bowl. Bostonian Soc.

Hancock [Gu] a dexter hand couped erect arg, on a chief or 3 cocks [gu]
Crest: a demi-griffin
Engraved on 6 dishes, given in 1764 by Hon. Thomas Hancock. Brattle Street Church, Boston. Old Sil. Am. Ch., p. 69

Hancock [Gu] a dexter hand couped erect arg, on a chief [of the second] 3 cocks [of the first]. Impaling: A chev sa bet 3 hunting horns of the second. On a chief three lioncelles ramp (Henchman)

Crest: a demi-griffin
Engr. on standing cups given in 1773 by Mrs. Lydia, wife of Thomas Hancock and daughter of Daniel Henchman of Boston. Also on a cup owned 1914 by Fred'k G. May. First Church, Boston. Old Sil. Am. Ch., p. 26. Also engr. on 2 beakers from Thomas Hancock, 1764, owned by First Church or Society, Lexington, Mass. Jones, Old Sil., p. 246

Hancock Gu a hand couped and erect arg, on a chief of the last 3 cocks of the first
Crest: a cock gu holding a dexter hand couped at the wrist arg
Arms on the seal of Gov. John Hancock. On a silver coffee pot given by John Hancock to Mrs. Hancock, who gave it to her grandniece, Mrs. Wm. Greenough, whose son W. W. G. gave it to C. P. Greenough. Vermont's Amer. Heral., pp. 19, 20, 167

Handley A fess bet 6 mascles, 3 and 3
Seal Wm. Handley, Savannah, Georgia, 1769. Jeffries MSS. N. E. Reg., Jan. 1877, p. 60

Hannay Arg 3 stags' heads erased collared or
Crest: out of a crescent a cross crosslet fitchée sa
Motto: Per ardua ad alta
Framed water color, York Co. Jail, Maine

Hanson Az a cross botonné or bet 4 fleurs-de-lis [or] (Rede arms?)
Crest: a bird (martlet ppr?)
Motto: Sola virtus invicta
Bookplate George A. Hanson, Baltimore, author "Old Kent." "Col. Hanson of the Swedish Army was authorized to bear a coat of arms which was preserved by his eldest son, and has been retained by his descendants to the present day." — D. H. Thomas

Hapgood Or an anchor bet 3 fishes naiant az (?)
Crest: a quill and sword in saltire [arg hilt or]
Motto: Inter folias fructus
Bookplate Melvin H. Hapgood, Hartford, Conn., 1887. A framed water color hangs in the Warren Hapgood Gallery, Public Library, Harvard, Mass.

Hardenbrook Sa a fess or bet 3 mascles or, a sword in chief, within a bordure arg charged with 8 estoiles of 5 points
Crest: a hand couped holding a quill
Motto: Favente Deo supero
Bookplate Wm. Ten Eyck Hardenbrook

Harding Or on a bend az 3 martlets arg, a sinister canton [az] charged with a rose of the first bet 2 fleurs-de-lis arg
   Crest: a demi-buck ppr attired [or] holding an anchor [of the last]
   Notepaper Benjamin Fosdick Harding, Milton, Mass.

Harding Impaled by Jones

Harding Quartered by Swan

Hardinge [Arg?] an eagle displ, over all a fess [gu?]
   Crest: a cock
   Motto: Vigilanter (?)
   Bookplate Arline Hardinge by Dougald Stewart Walker, N. Y. *See* arms of Worth of Co. Devon

Hardy Arg on a bend engr gu a crescent bet 2 leopards' faces; on a chief az 3 catharine wheels or
   Crest: a leopard's head couped ppr
   Framed with Simes of Portsmouth, into which Hardy married. Water color in house at Petersham, Mass.

Hardy Sa on a chev bet 3 escallops or 3 dragons' heads erased [sa]
   Crest: a mailed arm embow, holding a dragon's head of the field
   Bookplate Sir Charles Hardy, Colon. Gov. of N. Y.

Harison Or on a chief sa 3 eagles displ or
   Crest: from a ducal cor a talbot's head erm
   Motto: Nec te quaesiverus extra
   Bookplate Wm. H. Harison, engr. by Lewis. Richard Harison of New York had: Quart or and arg on a chief etc. and "Nec te quaesiveris extra." By Maverick

Hark Az in dexter quarter a sun in splendor in sinister base an increscent with a man's face in profile
   Bookplate J. Max Hark, Lancaster, Pa.

Harkness Az 2 bars dancetté the first charged with 2 mullets, the second with a crescent gu, all bet 3 fleurs-de-lis arg
   Crest: ship in a storm
   Motto: Trust in God
   Bookplate Edward Stephen Harkness, engr. by Spenceley, 1906

Harlakenden [Az] a fess erm bet 3 lions' heads erased [or]
   Seal of Richard Harlakenden, Earl's Colne, 1653, on MS in N. E. Hist. Gen. Soc., Boston

Harland Or on a bend wavy vert (?) bet 2 sea lions couchant [sa] 3 stags' heads cabossed [arg]
   Crest: a sea lion [sa] supporting an anchor ppr rising from the sea
   Bookplate Robert Harland

Harman Arg a cross sa bet 4 doves of the field, charged with a stag's head couped arg
   Crest: from a ducal cor [sa] a stag's head of the field
   Bookplate Thomas Leader Harman

Harmon Arg a fess or bet 4 castles sa
   Crest: an American flag
   Framed water color York (Maine) Jail. Done by John Coles?

Harold Gu on an inscutcheon gu bet 2 estoiles [or] an escarbuncle
   Crest: a lion ramp couped, holding a fleur-de-lis
   Motto: Bono vince malum
   Bookplate John Harold

Harpending Az a standing sieve (?)
   Crest: a semi-circular cutter (?)
   Motto: Dando conservat
   Hatchment of John Harpending in Discourse at the Ref. Dutch Church, N. Y., 1856

Harris Gu 3 fleurs-de-lis arg
   Crest: a winged globe surmounted by an eagle rising, both ppr
   Motto: Aquila non captat muscas
   "The same shield is used in America by the Cram family"
   Bookplate Norman W. Harris, Boston. J. W. S., sc., 1896

Harris Sa 3 crescents arg
   Crest: a spread eagle
   Very old water color owned 1923 by Misses Emma and Elizabeth Harris, Holyoke Pl., Cambridge, Mass.

Harris [Sa] 3 crescents [arg]
   Crest: an eagle displayed [or]
   Beautifully engr. on the back of the tombstone at Copp's Hill of Rev. Andrew Eliot, D. D. He bought the stone in Oct. 1770, from Mrs. Samuel Watts, who sold the tomb Nov. 9, 1769, (Suffolk Deeds, vol. 115, p. 256). Her father, Robert Harris of Boston, was the former owner. The arms are of Harris of Radford, Co. Devon. *See* Heral Jour., vol. 2, p. 119, where no family is assigned for the arms. Also bookplate of C. Fiske Harris with motto: Kur deu res pub tra. Also framed water color with crest: a lion ramp sa, in York (Maine) Jail

Harris Quartered by Cabell

Harrison Az 3 demi-lions ramp or
   Crest: a demi-lion ramp arg holding a laurel branch vert
   Seal on deed, Stafford Co., Va., by Col. Burr Harrison, who d. 31 July, 1722. Benjamin Harrison, Jr., used a chevron only. Wm. & Mary Quar., Jan. 1894, p. 159

Harrison Az 3 demi-lions ramp couped [or]
Crest: from a ducal cor [az] a demi-lion [or] holding a laurel chaplet
Motto: In omnia paratus
Bookplate Jones Harrison, N. Y.

Harrison [Az?] 3 demi-lions ramp [or?], a crescent for diff
Arms on letter from Rev. Thomas Harrison of New Eng., 1648, to Gov. John Winthrop (Winthrop papers). He married a daughter of Samuel Symonds of Ipswich. M. H. S. Coll., vol. 37. Heral. Jour., vol. 3, p. 177

Harrison Gu on a chief or 3 eagles displ of the field
Crest: a talbot's head issuing from a ducal cor
Motto: Virtus in arduis
Bookplate Smith Harrison

Harrison Gu [or az] 2 bars erm bet 6 mullets 3, 2, 1. Impaling: Gu on a cross arg 5 eagles displ [sa] (Digges). The mullet in base is missing
Crest: an escallop
Denbigh Church, Warwick Co., Va. On the tomb of Mrs. Mary (Digges) Harrison, who d. in 1744. Zieber's Heral., p. 49. Bellet's Some Prom. Va. Fam., vol. 2, p. 487

Harrison Quarterly or and arg. On a chief arg 3 eagles displ
Crest: from a ducal cor a talbot's head erm
Motto: Nec te quaesiverus extra
Bookplate Richard Harrison, N. Y.

Harstonge Impaled by Weld

Hart Arg a bend gu bet 3 fleurs-de-lis
Crest: a sun dial, top or
Motto: Lumen accipe et imperti
Bookplate Charles Henry Hart, art critic. Phila. and N. Y.

Hart Or 3 hearts 2 and 1 gu
Crest: a deer statant contourné
Motto: Esto fidelis
Bookplate Wm. Henry Hart

Hartwell Sa a stag's head cabossed arg with a cross pattée fitché bet the horns or. In chief a lion pass guard. On a canton erm 2 bars per pale gu and az
Crest: on a mound vert a stag lodged behind 7 pales erm (?)
Motto: Sorte suâ contentus
Bookplate Walker Hartwell

Harvey Gu on a bend arg 3 slipped trefoils voided [vert]. In the sinister chief a crescent on a crescent
Crest: a lion pass guard holding a trefoil of the field
Bookplate Rev. Henry Harvey

Harward A cross fleury
Crest: a stag's head
Wax seal on will of George Harward, dated 5 Jan. 1703, at Lancaster Court House. Wm. & Mary Quar., Ja. 1893, p. 120

Hasell Or on a fess az bet 3 hazel slips ppr 3 crescents of the first
Crest: a squirrel sejant ppr cracking a nut
Motto: Labor omnia vincit
Framed painting owned by Mrs. Thomas Savage Heyward, 48 Legaré Street, Charleston, S. C. Seen by L. Park, 1923

Hasell Vert 3 adders in pale sanguine
Crest: a mailed arm emb holding a mace (?)
Motto: De me praesagia olim
Bookplate James Hasell, acting gov. N. C., prest. council, 1775

Haselwell Quartered by Grosvenor

Haskell Vairy arg and sa
Crest: a fruited bush rising from a field vert
Motto: Vincit veritas
Bookplate Coburn Haskell, Thomasville, Ga.

Haskins Per fess indented or and sa on a bend arg 3 lions pass
Crest: a lion pass holding a battle axe
Motto: Fidem se[r]vabo
Bookplate Samuel Moody Haskins, Rhead des.

Hassell Quartered by Beresford

Hastings Az a maunch sa
Crest: a buffalo's head erased sa gorged with a ducal cor and armed or
Supporters: "Two man-tigers affrontant [or], their visages resembling the human face ppr"
Motto: In veritate victoria
"Arms of the Earl of Huntingdon" Bookplate Frank W. Hastings, Jr. J. W. S., sc., 1898. Also grave Henry Hastings, 1857-1917, Mt. Auburn, Mass., with In veritate victoria. Also engr. on a salver by Jacob Hurd, made for "A. T. H. 1751." Crest: a stag. See Bigelow's Hist. Sil., p. 246

Hastings Quartered by Coote

Hatch Gu 2 demi-lions pass guard couped, in pale or. Over all an inscutcheon per pale ermine and ermines on a chev per pale sa and arg bet 3 fleurs-de-lis or 4 fusils ermine and ermines counterchanged (Addington)
Crest: a lion's face cabossed arg
Motto: Fac alteri ut tibi vis
Bookplate James Hatch

Havemeyer Or a fess sa bet 3 mullets
Crest: two armed arms embowed,
holding a sword erect
Motto: Cultus animi quasi humani-
tatis quidam cibus
Ex libris William Frederick Havemeyer of N. Y. E. D. French, sc. N.
Y. family given in Rietstap as sa a fess
bet 3 mullets or

Havemeyer Quarterly sa and gu, 1
charged with a lion ramp facing sin,
4 with a lion ramp to dex arg (Hugel
arms)
Crest: a crown
Motto: Virtute et industriae
Bookplate H. O. Havemeyer, Jr.
Engr. by Spenceley, 1905

Hawes [Az] on a chev [or] 3 cinquefoils
[gu] a canton erm
Crest: out of a ducal cor or a stag's
head ppr holding in the mouth a sprig
of laurel [vert]
Engr. bookplate Miss Lyslie Moore
Hawes of Providence, R. I., desc. of
Edward of Dedham, Mass.

Hawkes Az 3 bends or, a chief erm
Crest: a hawk on a hawk's lure
Motto: Fortiter et honeste
Engr. on fob-seal. Amer. Heral.,
vol. 2, p. 29

Hawkins Gu a chev bet 3 crosses
crosslet 2 and 1 and 3 wyverns' heads
erased 1 and 2 arg (Howe arms)
Crest: a wyvern, the mouth pierced
by an arrow fessways point to sinister
Notepaper Miss Ethel Hawkins, 257
Pine St., Springfield, Mass.

Hawks Quart 1 and 4: Arg 3 battle
axes erect in fess; 2 and 3: Gu a chev
arg bet 3 horses' heads erased
Crest: an eagle rising
Motto: Never check
Bookplate Rev. Francis Lister
Hawks, prominent N. Y. clergyman
and author. The arms might be
Hicks quartering Tripp

Hay [Arg] 3 inscutcheons 2 and 1 [gu]
Crest: a falcon rising ppr
Motto: Serva jugum
Bookplate Henry Palethorp Hay,
D. D., LL. D.

Hayes Ermine 3 scutcheons gu
Crest: an eagle rising, ducally gorged
Motto: Verite sans peur
Bookplate Harry F. Hayes

Hayne Arg 3 crescents paly wavy gu
and az
Crest: a heron rising
Bookplate Isaac Hayne, 1745–81,
hanged by the British at Charleston,
S. C. Also of Joseph Haynes. Rob-
erts, sc. A drawing at the So. Car.
Hist. Soc. has Tenex propositia

Haynes Arg 3 crescents barry undée az
and gu
Crest: a stork rising ppr
Seal on Winthrop papers (Mass.
Hist. Soc. Coll., 4th ser., vol. 7). Heral.
Jour., vol. 1, p. 51. Gov. John Haynes
family of Conn. The Gov. also used
for crest: a demi-lion ramp supports
a ragged staff. Heral. Jour., vol. 3,
p. 175

Haynes Or on a fess gu 3 bezants and
in chief a coursing greyhound sa
Crest: an eagle displ az powdered
with estoiles or
On brougham of Mrs. John C.
Haynes, Bay State Road, Boston

Hays 3 bucks springing
Crest: a bee-hive
Bookplate Barrak Hays. I. Hutt,
sculp. Browne arms?

Hayward Arg a lion ramp crowned gu
Crest: a griffin's head erased az
Bookplate George Hayward

Hayward [Or] 3 lions ramp [gu] over all
a bendlet [sa]
Seal on doc., 1671, signed by Timothy
Pratt of Boston and witnessed by John
Hayward. Owned by C. P. Green-
ough

Hazelhurst Quart 1 and 4: Arg on a
chev az bet 3 owls guard [sa?] 3 hazel
branches slipped [or]; 2 and 3: Arg a
coursing hound [sa] a canton erminois
(Jacobs)
Crest: a squirrel charged with 3
roundels eating a branch vert
Bookplate —— Hazelhurst, Phila.

Head Arg a chev ermines bet 3 uni-
corns' heads couped sa, the hand of
Ulster in chief
Crest: a unicorn's head couped
ermines
Bookplate [Sir Edmund] Head, Bt.,
Charleston, S. C.

Heard Arg on a chev gu bet 3 water
bougets sa a cor bet 2 estoiles of 6
points arg
Crest: a demi-goat salient ppr
attired or ducally gorged of the last
Motto: Mutare vel timere sperno
Bookplate John Heard, Jr., Boston

Hearn Az a lion ramp holding a slipped
trefoil. On a chief vert a pelican
statant
Crests: 1: a pelican in her piety; 2:
from a ducal cor a pelican's head erased
Mottoes: 1: Virtute non vi; 2:
Ardua petit ardea
Bookplate —— Hearn. Jarrett,
London, sc.

Hearne Sa a chev erm bet 3 herons arg
Crest: a heron's head couped ppr
Motto: Leges, juraque servat
Framed painting owned by C. W.
Hearne, Greenville, N. C.

Heathcote Erm 3 pommes (roundles
vert) each charged with a cross or
Crest: on a mural crown az a pomme
as in the arms bet 2 wings displ erm
Seal of Col. Caleb Heathcote, mayor
of N. Y., 1711. Bolton's Westchester
Co., vol. 2, p. 101

Heley *See also* Reed

Helmershausen [Arg] a helmet ppr
pierced by an arrow bend sinisterways
or, point down
Crest: a demi-lion rampant ppr.
Used by the family of Heinrich
Friedrich Helmershausen of Loben-
stein in Reuss, Germ., who came to
Jefferson, Maine, before the Revolution. Prominent in Weimar

Henchman [Arg] a chev bet 3 hunting
horns [sa]. On a chief [sa] 3 lioncelles
rampant [arg]
Crest: a cubit arm vested, holding
two large spears
Engr. on 2 silver braziers by Jacob
Hurd. Owned by Gov. John Hancock,
whose wife was Lydia Henchman.
Dwight M. Prouty, 8 Louisburg
Square, Boston. A painted copy of
the arms owned by Russell B. Henchman, East Jaffrey, N. H.

Henchman [Arg] a chev bet 3 buglehorns stringed [sa] on a chief [sa] 3
lions ramp [arg]
Hannah Endicott, on a bond dated
13 Sept. 1697, uses this seal. Heral.
Jour., vol. 2, p. 143

Henchman Impaled by Hancock

Henderson Gu 3 piles issuing out of the
sinister side arg, on a chief of the last
a crescent az bet 2 erm spots
Crest: a cubit arm ppr, the hand
holding a star or ensigned with a
crescent az
Motto: Sola virtus nobilitat
On a fire screen by Calvin & Wright,
owned by Miss Helen W. Henderson,
Phila. Engraved on watch used by
Lieut. John Henderson, who d. 1787.
Also in wax on a paper signed by Col.
John, who d. 1824. Both are now
owned by a great great grandson, Dr.
Joseph Lyon Miller, Thomas, W. Va.
Crozier's Va. Heral., pp. 72 and 73

Henkel An anchor
Crest: 3 flowering sprigs
Motto: In hoc signo vinces
Notepaper Lila D. Henkel, States-
ville, N. C.

Henshaw Quart 1 and 4: [Arg] a chev
bet 3 heronshaws [sa]; 2 and 3: [Sa]
three bars [arg] (Houghton)
Crest: a falcon ppr billed [or]
beaked and membered [sa] preying
upon the wing of a bird [arg]
Below heliotype portrait of Col.
William Henshaw, Adjut.-Gen. of
Mass. Militia in 1775. Also on frame
of portrait of Joshua Henshaw, owned
by Sidney W. Hayward (1920), but not
quartered, and bird of crest at rest.
Old South Church, Boston.
Bookplate Samuel Henshaw, Boston,
with heronshaws gu and motto: Esse
quam videri. Zieber's Heral., p. 43.
Heral. Jour., vol. 4, p. 124

Hepburn Gu on a chev arg bet 2 lions
counter passant gu a rose. In base a
buckle arg point up
Crest: a horse's head couped ppr
bridled gu
Motto: Keep tryste
Etching, framed, owned by Andrew
Hopewell Hepburn, Concord, Mass.
Signed A. H. H., 1915

Hepburn Quartered by Livingston

Herben Quartered by Acklom

Herbert Per pale az and gu, 3 lions
ramp arg, armed and langued or
Crest: a bundle of arrows or, headed
and feathered arg, 6 in saltire, one in
pale, girt around the middle with a belt
gu, buckle and point extended of the
first
Tomb of John Herbert of Prince
George Co., taken from family residence, "Puddledock," in Dinwiddie Co.,
Va., to Blandford Churchyard at Peters-
burg. He d. 17 Mar. 1704, aged 46
years. A bookplate of Francis Herbert,
East New Jersey, has for crest a lion
of the shield and for motto: Ung loy,
ung roy, ung foy. Va. Hist. Mag.,
vol. 18, p. 190. Crozier's Va. Heral.,
p. 39. Amer. Heral., vol. 2, p. 23

Herrick Arg a fess vairé or and gu.
Impaling: Or 3 sprigs leaved
Motto: Aut delectare aut prodesse
Bookplate Christine Terhune Her-
rick, writer, N. Y.

Herrick Arg a fess vairé or and gu
Crest: an ox's head guard couped
[arg horned and eared sa?] gorged with
a wreath of roses ppr
Motto: Virtus omnia nobilitat
Bookplate Rev. Samuel Edward
Herrick, Boston

Herrman Per fess. Over all a heart
issuing 3 sprigs of trefoil leaves. In
base 4 arrows points up, 2 in bend and
2 in bend sinister forming a saltire
Engr. on Augustine Herrman's Map
of Virginia and Maryland, 1673, which

has also his portrait. The engraving seems to indicate 4 arrows, but two only may be intended. Herrman was of Bohemia Manor

Herrys *See* Horry

Herter Per pale gu and arg
Crest: out of a ducal cor a demi-horse arg holding an annulet [gu]
Bookplate Christian Archibald Herter, engr. by French, 1894

Heseltine Gu a cross flory or, on a chief az 3 buckles or
Crest: a talbot's head couped and gorged or
Motto: Benigno numine
Bookplate Wm. Keale Heseltine

Hewes Arg on a fess gu 2 gadbees [or]
Crest: a peacock's head erased [az]
Motto: Pro Deo et Patria
Bookplate David Hewes of Orange, Cal.

Hewes *See also* Jewett

Heyman Arg on a chev engr az bet 3 martlets sa, as many cinquefoils or
Crest: a moor full faced, wreathed around the temples, holding in the dexter hand a rose slipped and leaved all ppr
Tomb of Peter Heyman at "Pembroke" near Hampton, Va. He was killed 29 Apr. 1700. Crozier's Va. Heral., p. 44

Heyward Az a chev per pale or and erm bet 3 garbs [or]
Crest: an arm emb, habited [gu], holding a tomahawk blade down ppr
Bookplate Thomas Heyward of So. Car., signer Decl. of Indep. *See also* Curio, 1888, p. 208. Painting of Mrs. Thos. Savage Heyward, 48 Legaré Street, Charleston, S. C. Seen by L. Park

Heyward Az a chev per pale or and erm bet 3 garbs of the second
In a lozenge
Bookplate Maud Heyward. Spenceley, sc.

Heywood Arg 3 torteaux bet 3 bendlets gu. Impaling: Az a fess or bet 3 stags' heads cabossed (Barton)
Crest: a hawk jessed and belled rising from a stump sprouting
Motto: Alte volo
Bookplate Thomas Heywood. J. Buck, sc.

Hibbert Erm on a bend sanguine [sic sa?] 3 crescents [arg]
Crest: a hand ppr erect [vested az cuffed erm] holding a crescent [arg]
Motto: Not decipherable
Bookplate Washington Hibbert

Hibbins A chev bet 3 towers
Crest: broken
Seal on Jonas Clarke's bond, Suffolk Co. Files, Boston, 1672. Probably then owned by Edward Rawson, the witness who had tried to save Ann Hibbins from execution as a witch

Hicks Gu a fess wavy bet 3 fleurs-de-lis or
Probably used at the funeral in 1708 of Hon. Benj. Browne of Salem, Mass., who married Mary, daughter of Rev. John Hicks. Heral. Jour., vol. 4, p. 44

Hicks Gu a fess wavy bet 3 fleurs-de-lis or
Crest: a lion's (?) head [or] couped, crowned with a chaplet
Motto: Tout en bonne heure
Bookplate Elias Hicks, quaker, 1748–1830. P. Maverick, sc. Also of Whitehead Hicks, Esq., with motto: Pro lege et Rege. H. Dawkins, scupl. Another with motto: Judicemur agendo. Rollinson, sc. Also framed water color, Arts and Crafts Society, Park St., Boston

Hicks Quart 1 and 4: Gu a fess wavy bet 3 fleurs-de-lis or; 2 and 3: A ship under sail on the sea, a crescent in the dexter chief
Crest: a lion's head couped crowned with a chaplet
Motto: Pro libertate et commercio
Bookplate Thomas Hicks

Hicks Quartered by Graves

Higginson Or on a fess sa, a tower of the first
Crest: a tower
Seal on will of John Lander, 25 Nov. 1698, witnessed by John Higginson, Jr., John Westgate, and Samuel Beadle, Jr. (Essex Wills). Smoky quartz seal used by Stephen Higginson of Boston, member Continental Congress, owned by Miss Sarah Higginson Bowditch of Milton
Bookplate Waldo Higginson has motto: Deus nobiscum quis contra nos. Heral. Jour., vol. 4, p. 168

Higginson *See also* Tyng

Higgs Arg a chev bet 3 bucks couchant gu
Crest: a buck's head [gu] couped, attired [or], pierced through the neck with an arrow in bend, headed or, feathered arg
Motto: Fide et fortitudine
Notepaper Edward B. Higgs of Greenville, N. C., 1924; framed paintings owned by James A. Higgs, Raleigh, N. C.; Mrs. Laura Higgs Iredell, Norfolk, Va.; Mrs. Moye, Mrs Rouse, Greenville. Information from Mrs. Marguerite Higgs Everett

Hight Arg a fess humetée az bet 3 demi-lions ramp couped and crowned gu
Crest: a lion of the field holding a long sword
Motto: Regarde bien
Bookplate Leroy Lincoln Hight and Clara Webster Hight

Hildreth Arg a cross humettée az bet 4 pheons, in chief a crescent. Impaling: Arg on a chief gu 2 crosses flory voided, a cinquefoil in chief for diff
Crest: a rose branch leaved
Bookplate Eugene W. Hildreth

Hill A lion pass (very fierce, however)
Crest: a demi-lion (?) gorged and issuing from a crown (holding a fleur-de-lis?)
Tomb of Col. Edward Hill, II, at "Shirley," Charles City Co., Va. He d. 30 Nov. 1700, aged 63. judge of Ct. of Admiralty, treas. of Va., councillor, etc. Va. Hist. Mag., vol. 3, p. 157. Stanard's Colonial Virginia, p. 138

Hill Arg a fess az. In chief a mullet sa bet 2 dragons' heads couped az (?)
Bookplate Gov. John F. Hill, Augusta, Maine, engr. by S. L. Smith

Hill Az on a chev bet 3 owls arg, 3 mullets sa, a bordure erm
Seal of Col. Humphrey Hill of Hillsborough, King and Queen Co., Va. Wm. & Mary Quar., Jan. 1894, p. 158

Hill Erm on a fess sa a 2 towered castle ppr
Crest: from a tower 2 branches erect
Motto: Avancez
Bookplate Hamilton Hill

Hill Gu 2 bars erm. In chief a lion pass per pale or and az
Crest: a boar's head and neck sa holding in his mouth a broken spear
Seal of William Hill of Boston, loyalist, 1739–1802. See N. E. H. G. Register, April, 1885, p. 189

Hill Gu a chev bet 3 garbs arg
Crest: a dove with wings expanded and in the beak an olive branch
Notepaper Francis William Hill, Washington, D. C., 1924

Hill Quart 1 and 4: Per pale [or and gu] a lion pass arg; 2 and 3: A saltire bet 4 garbs (?) (supposed to be for Williams)
Crest: out of a cor a demi-lion holding a fleur-de-lis
Hatchment at Shirley on the James, Va. Edward Hill's house. Hillis arms? Cut in Glenn's Some Col. Mansions, vol. 1, p. 242

Hill Impaled by Blount

Hillegas Quart 1: Gu from the base a pineapple (?); 2 and 3: Az a pierced estoile of 8 points arg; 4: Or a stag springing contourné. Over all a fess arg charged with 3 ƒ (like S crossed)
Arms of Michael Hillegas, treas. of U. S. on old silver. His wife Henrietta Boude bore Or 3 chev sa. Zieber's Heral., p. 68

Hilliard Arg a saltire sa on a chief gu 3 pillows of the first (Johnstone arms)
Crest: a spur bet 2 wings
Bookplate Margaret Burgwin and Katharine Haven Hilliard, engr. by A. H. Noll

Hillis See also Hill

Hills Arg a cross az bet 4 crescents [of the second]. A chief az
Crest: a horse courant [gu?] holding a broken spear [sa?] in his mouth, the handle lying behind his hind legs
Carved on wood in Wm. S. Hills Memorial Room, 9 Ashburton Place, Boston

Hilton Arg 2 bars az
Crest: a man's head glorified ppr
Motto: Tanque puis je
Bookplate Wm. Hilton, 1871

Hilton Quartered by Scribner

Hincks A fess bet 3 roses
Crest: "a bust facing forward"
Seal John Hincks, Chief Justice, 1699–1707. Jeffries MSS. N. E. H. G. Reg., Jan. 1877, p. 60

Hines Per bend or and azure in chief 3 crescents 2 and 1
Crest: a plough ppr
Motto: Auctor
Framed painting, Edenton, N. C., seen by Miss Mary Pruden

Hinton Per fess dancettée arg and sa 6 fleurs-de-lis 3 and 3 counterchanged
Crest: an eagle's leg erased entwined by a serpent ppr
Bookplate Mary Hilliard Hinton

Hoadley Quart az and or, in the first quarter a pelican in her piety [or]
Crest: on a ball [or] a dove volant holding an olive branch ppr
Bookplate Charles J. and George E. Hoadley, engr. by Hopson

Hoar [Arg] an eagle displ with 2 heads [sa]
Tombstone Lieut. Daniel Hoar, who d. 1773, aged 93 Hill Burying Ground, Concord, Mass. Hezekiah Usher of Boston in his will speaks of his wife and says: "But as for her daughter Bridget [Hoare], if her mother had not been so undermining and over-reaching for her I should a been willing to have done what I could for her and

I do give her the tumbler with the armes of a spread eagle with two heads but I think one head for a body is enough." Waters's Gleanings, vol. 1, p. 92

Hoar Arg an eagle displ with 2 heads within a bordure engr sa
Crest: a stag's head erased
Motto: Constanter
Bookplate Richard Hoar used reversed colors, "Sa an eagle, etc.," a crescent for diff, and an eagle's head for crest; also Wm. Hoar.

Hoar Quarterly sa and gu an eagle with 2 heads displ [arg] a crescent in chief for diff within a bordure invected gu and sa counterchanged with the field
Crest: an eagle's head erased erm holding an annulet
Bookplate George Hoar

Hobart Quart 1 and 4: Sa an estoile bet 2 flaunches erm; 2: Or 3 bars gu the one in chief indented (Hale but incorrect); 3: Arg a bull pass sa within a bordure charged with 8 plates (?). Impaling: Arg a saltire gu bet 4 eagles displ az (?) (Hampden)
Crest: a bull pass sa charged with estoiles
A very old framed water color of the arms of Sir John Hobart Bart, who married Mary, daughter of the famous patriot Hampden. Oscar Stringer of Hingham, Mass., had it from his mother, Mrs. Elizabeth Loring Hobart. Her husband, Samuel, desc. from Edmund of Hingham

Hobart [Sa] an estoile of 8 points [or] bet 2 flaunches [erm]
Crest: a bull pass
Seal (dim) on bond of Elizabeth Norman of Boston, witnessed by Samuel Hobart, 1685. Owned by C. P. Greenough

Hobart Quartered by Briggs

Hodges Or 3 crescents sa. On a canton sa a ducal crown of the first
Crest: an heraldic antelope ducally crowned
Motto: Ne cede malis
Bookplate George Clarendon Hodges, Boston. Seal ring by Henry Mitchell, engraver, c. 1900. Quarterly 1: Hodges; 2: Arg on a fess sa 3 stags' heads erased or (Bradford); 3: Arg 2 bars sa and in chief 3 lions ramp sa (Howland); 4: Gu a lion ramp arg a chief chequy or and az (Warren)

Hodges Or 3 crescents [sa] on a canton sa a ducal cor [or]
Crest: a crescent [arg] rising from the clouds [az]
Motto: Crescamus
Bookplate Joseph Hodges

Hodges Impaled by Cunningham

Hodgson [Or?] on a fess bet 3 boars' heads couped [gu?] as many lions ramp of the field
Hudson arms on tomb of "Mr. John Hodgson of Whitehaven [County Cumberland, Eng.] commander of the good ship Mary and Frances from thence departed this life ye 22 of July, 1719, aged 27 years and is here interred." Copied by G. W. Maslin from grave slab at Tusculum, near Princess Anne, Md., May 1, 1924. See also Gale

Hodsden A greyhound statant
Seal John Hodsden, Charleston, S. C., 1741. Jeffries MSS. N. E. Reg., Jan. 1877, p. 60

Hoffman (?) Per fess arg and vert. In chief 3 pines
Crest: a cock
Motto: Carpe diem
Bookplate Very Rev. E. A. Hoffman, Gen. Theol. Sem., N. Y., E. D. French, sc. Some Amer. Coll. Bookplates, 1915, p. 243

Hoffman Per fess arg and vert in chief 3 growing trees
Crest: a cock
Motto: Carpe diem
Bookplate Rev. C. F. Hoffman, D. D., LL. D.

Hogg See also Martin

Hoggson Az 3 cutlasses arg [hilted or] 2 points to the dexter and one bet to the sinister. The cutlasses usually are reversed from the above
Crest: "a hand ppr couped below the wrist, holding a broken cutlass arg [hilted or] the broken piece falling from the other"
Bookplate Noble Foster Hoggson. Engr. by Spenceley

Holbrook Or a chev gu surmounted by a cross patté fitchée of the second
In a lozenge
Bookplate Minnie C. Holbrook. J. W. S., sc., 1897

Holden Sa a fess bet 2 chev erm. Above the fess a covered cup [or]. Over all an escutcheon of pretence: Arg a fess chequy gu and sa bet 3 helmets ppr (Whitehall)
Carved over the west door of Holden Chapel, Harvard College, but not now in color Arms of Samuel Holden, M. P., of Roehampton, Co. Surrey, gov. of Bank of Eng. and benefactor. Married Jane Whitehall. He d. 12 June, 1740. Harv. Alumni Bulletin, 3 Feb. 1921

Holland See also Horsford and Sylvester

Holliday [Sa 3 helmets or garnished or within a bordure engr of the 2d] Tomb of James Holliday at Readbourne, Queen Anne Co., Md. *See* Hist. Graves of Md., p. 191. He d. 1747. Mrs. Ridgely writes June 22, 1924: "I recollect several helmets, grouped on the shield"

Hollingsworth Az on a bend arg 3 holly leaves vert
Crest: a stag lodged arg
Motto: Disce ferenda pati
Lyman Hollingsworth, 58 Commonwealth Ave., Boston. Notepaper. Also bookplate A. L. Hollingsworth, Boston. Levi Hollingsworth's early plate has the field sa, the stag erm. Mrs. J. P. Hollingsworth of St. Davids, Pa., used the crest

Holloway Over a paly of 6 arg and or a fess gu bet 3 crescents az a canton ermines
Crest: an antelope's head gu, attired, gorged, and chained or, issuing from a crescent of the last
Motto: Deo lux nostra
Bookplate Horatio F. K. Holloway

Holme [Arg] a stag at gaze [az attired or?]
Crest: a cubit arm holding an arrow
Bookplate John Holme

Holmes Barry wavy of 8 or and az (?) On a canton gu (?) a lion ramp or (?)
Crest: out of a cor an armed arm embowed, holding a trident (?) ppr head or
On a portrait of Gov. David Holmes of Miss. from Va. In Mrs. Rowland's Jackson's Campaign against the British, 1812, p. 46

Holmes Or 3 bars az on a canton arg a chaplet gu
Crest: a lion's head erased
Seal ring of Wm. Edward Holmes, M. D., of Charleston and Boston

Holmes Per chev (the chief per pale) arg and erm a chev gu and in chief 2 dragons' heads erased, the neck pierced by an arrow. An escutcheon of pretence: Per chev and chief per pale a chev gu bet 5 lions passant
Crest: a lion ramp
Motto: Per stabilitas et per fortitudo
Bookplate J. Henry H. Holmes, Va. The chev is engraved pur pure and vert

Holt Arg on a bend engr [sa] 3 fleurs-de-lis (?) arg
Crest: an arm erect, holding a pheon (?)
Seal on deposition before Ryves Holt and others, 1743, Lewes, Del. Seen by M. Ljungstedt at Eastville, Va,

Holyoke Az a chev arg coticed or bet 3 crescents of the second
Crest: a crescent arg
Arms on the will of Elizur Holyoke (1711). Also engr. on cup by Samuel Drowne, Clearwater Collection. In Eberlein & McClure's Early Amer. Arts & Crafts, 1916, p. 143. Same shield with crest: a cubit arm vested [gu] holding an oak branch [vert fructed or], and motto: Duce natura sequor, on bookplate of Edward Augustus Holyoke. A painted hatchment owned in 1911 by Miss Mary W. Nichols of Danvers, Mass., is reproduced in "The Holyoke Diaries, 1709–1856." E. A. Holyoke refers to one in 1744

Holyoke Az a stag's head contourné
Crest: an oak tree couped
Motto: Sacra quercus
Bookplate —— Holyoke

Hooper Arg on a fess vert bet 3 boars pass [az?] as many annulets [of the first?]
Crest: a hound's head erased (?)
Engr. on flagon from Rupert Hooper, 1748–49. First Church, Marblehead, Mass. Old Sil. Am. Ch., p. 261

Homans Vert a chev bet 3 pheons or
Crest: an arrow arg on a drawn bow or bet 2 wings expanded
Motto: Pro Christo et patria dulce periculum
Bookplate John Homans, Boston

Hooke [Arg or sa] a cross bet 4 escallops. Impaling: [arg] 3 boars' heads erased [sa] (Whalley?)
Arms on letter from Rev. William Hooke of New Haven to Gov. John Winthrop (Winthrop papers). M. H. S. Coll., vol. 37. Heral. Jour., vol. 3, p. 177

Hooker Quarterly sa and arg a cross counterchanged paleways and fessways bet 4 escallops counterchanged
Crest: an escallop sa bet 2 erect wings arg
Motto: Esse quam videri
Bookplate John Marshall Hooker. Rev. Thomas Hooker of Conn. used a double-headed eagle

Hooper Arms used by Brightley, q. v.

Hooper Gyronny of 8 az and erm. Over all a tower [arg]
Motto: In Deo et veritate fido
Bookplate Parker Morse Hooper. W. H., W. B., sc.

Hooper Or on a fess bet 3 boars pass az (?) as many annulets of the first
Crest: a boar's head erased
Engr. on a silver sugar bowl made by Hurd and owned by Miss Currier, Newburyport, Mass. Marked $_{R\ R}^{H}$ (Robert and Ruth Hooper)

Hooper *See also* Brightley

Hope Az a chev or bet 3 bezants
Crest: a rainbow issuing from 2 clouds over a globe
Motto: At spes non fracta
Bookplate Alexander I. Beresford Hope, Charlotte, S. C.

Hope Quart 1 and 4: Az a chev or bet 3 bezants; 2 and 3: Erm a mill-rind arg (Mills of Harscombe)
Crest: a rainbow issuing from 2 clouds
Motto: Nemo sine crimine vivit
Engr. on a covered 2-handled cup, which Edward Mills, Jr., gave in 1732 to Henry Hope. Owned 1917 by Miss Una Gray

Hopewell Arg 3 hares playing on bagpipes [gu] 2 and 1
Ex libris John Hopewell. E. B. Bird, des. 1904

Hopkins [Sa] a stag trippant within a bordure indented, a chief indented [or]. Impaling: Erm on a canton gu a cross crosslet [or] (Lello of Herts?)
Gov. Edward Hopkins of Conn. used a seal of Hamblen impaling Lello (?). Heral. Jour., vol. 3, p. 175. Dr. H. M. Buck's attribution. Frame for "Hopkins" coat made 1678 by Nicholas Desborough (Love's Hartford, p. 303)

Hopkins A chev sa bet 3 pistols points down and 3 roses, the roses in chief near the honor point and in base below the pistol
Crest: a castellated tower in flames
Motto: Piety in peace
Bookplate with name H. M. Hopkins in ink

Hopkins Sa on a chev erminois bet 3 pistols ppr 3 roses gu
Crest: a flaming tower
Motto: Pietas est pax
Bookplate Robert Emmet Hopkins, engr. by French, 1900

Hopkins Sa on a chev bet two pistols in chief or and a silver medal with the French king's bust, inscribed Louis XV, tied at the top with a red ribbon, in base, a laurel chaplet in the center, a scalp on a staff on the dexter, and a tomahawk on the sinister, all ppr a chief embattled arg
Crest: on a wreath or and sa a rock, over the top a battery in perspective, thereon the French flag hoisted, an officer of the Queen's Royal American Rangers on the said rock sword in hand, all ppr round the crest this motto
Motto: Inter primos
Granted to Joseph Hopkins of Md., 1764. Berry's Encyc. Heraldica.

Heral. Jour., vol. 1, pp. 36, 71–72. Capt. Hopkins' coat in 1734 apparently derived from early (Visitation) coat of Hopkins family of Coventry, Warwickshire, acc. to account in recent issue (English) Country Gentleman

Hopkinson Arg on a chev gu bet 3 estoiles gu 3 lozenges arg within a bordure vert (so engraved)
Crest: a demi-lion ramp [sa armed gu]
Motto: Semper paratus
Bookplate Francis Hopkinson, signer Decl. Indep. H. Dawkins, sc. Zieber's Heral., p. 321

Hopkinson Vert 3 pillars erm
Crest: an arm embowed and habited, holding a cutlass
Bookplate Edward Hopkinson

Horry Quart 1 and 4: Or on a bend az 3 cinquefoils arg (Herrys arms); 2: Arg 5 fusils sa conjoined paleways within a bordure engr sa (Pinckney); 3: Arg a fess bet 6 annulets gu 3 and 3 (Lucas?)
Motto: Semper honos
Bookplate C. L. Pinckney Horry, Hampton House, S. C.

Horry Quart 1 and 4: Or (gu?) on a bend az 3 cinquefoils or; 2 and 3: Arg 5 (?) fusils conjoined paleways sa
Coat of arms on a portrait of Charles Daniel Lucas Pinckney Horry at Mrs. Blackburn Hughes's, 10 Legaré St., Charleston, S. C. *See also* Fay Maubourg. Seen by L. Park, 1923. This coat is much like that of Spencer. The fret may be 8 or 10 lozenges in pale. Horry is not in Burke

Horsford Per pale indented gu and arg (Holland arms)
Bookplate Cornelia Horsford, Cambridge, Mass. Engr. by French

Horsmanden Quart 1 and 4: Gu a saltire arg. On a fess az 3 leopards' faces or; 2 and 3: Arg an heraldic tiger pass sa
Crest: a lion's face with 2 snakes issuing from the head and the tails from the mouth
Bookplate Daniel Horsmanden, 1691–1778, author, Flatbush, L. I. "De Interior Templo Socius"

Horton Sa a stag's head cabossed gu a canton erm
Crest: a dolphin sa upon a spear point [or] issuing from the waves ppr
Motto: Quod vult valde vult
Bookplate —— Horton

Hoskins Per pale az and gu a chev bet 3 lions ramp or. Impaling: Quart 1: Sa on a cross engr arg bet 4 eagles

displ arg 5 lions pass guard sa 1, 3, 1 (Paget); 2: Sa a swan rising arg within a bordure engr or (More); 3: Az a fess bet 3 griffins' heads arg (Bradford?); 4: Per fess nebuly az and arg 3 antelopes' heads erased counterchanged armed or (Snow)
    Crest: a cock's head erased or charged with 3 pellets
    Motto: Fidem respice
    Bookplate Henry William Hoskins

Hotchkiss Or a lion pass guard
    Crest: a wolf's head erased issuing from flames and vomiting flames
    Bookplate Leonard Hotchkiss, A. M.

Hough Arg a bend sa
    Crest: a bird contourné bet 2 green twigs
    Bookplate Isaac Hough, merchant of Phila.

Houghton [Sa] 3 bars [arg]
    Motto: Malgré le Tort
    Arms on slate tombstone of Azor, eldest son of Timothy and Olive Houghton, who d. 22 Feb. 1825. Also on stone for Oren Houghton, who d. 1 May, 1828. West Cemetery, Bolton, Mass.

Houghton Sa 3 bars arg on an inscutcheon arg 3 battle axes sa
    Crest: a bull passant
    Motto: Malgré le tort
    Bookplate F. S. Houghton. A. W. Clark, des.

Houghton Quartered by Henshaw

Houstoun [Or] a chev [chequy sa and arg?] bet 3 martlets [sa]. Badge of Ulster in chief
    Crest: a sand or hour glass
    Motto: In time
    Sir Patrick Houstoun, Bart., d. 1762. Arms on a marble slab set in a new granite monument at Bonaventure, 4 miles from Savannah, Ga. Georgia's Landmarks, vol. 2, pp. 285, 293. G. E. C. Complete Bar., vol. 4, p. 268

How Gu a chev arg bet 3 crosses crosslet or 2 and 1 and 3 wolves' heads erased of the same 1 and 2
    Crest: "a wyvern or Draⁿg part^d per pale or and vert pierced through ye mouth wth arrow"
    Framed painting. Amer. Anti. Soc., Worcester, Mass.

Howard Arg a bend gu (?) bet 6 crosses crosslet fitché
    Crest: a lion pass guard
    Engr. on a teapot owned by Mrs. Lydia Bowman Taft of Milton. Formerly owned by a son of James Howard, who was sent by Gov. Shirley to Augusta, Maine, to build Fort Western. See North's History of Augusta. Also Bigelow's Hist. Sil., p. 341

Howard Gu on a bend bet 6 crosses crosslet fitchée arg an escutcheon or charged with a demi-lion ramp [pierced through the mouth with an arrow?] within a tressure flory counter-flory of the first
    Crest: on a chapeau gu turned up erm a lion stat guard or
    Motto: Desir na repos
    On tombstone of Joshua Howard of Md. Also his son Cornelius of Grayrock, Md. Henry Howard, 1686, had arms on his seal. Richardson's Sidelights on Md. Hist., vol. 2, p. 146. Letter from Miss Helen W. Ridgely, 1924

Howard [Gu] a bend bet 6 crosses crosslet fitchée [arg]
    Seal on will of John Howard (son of Matthew) of Anne Arundel Co., Md., 1696. Henry of "Collingborne," Baltimore Co., d. 1684, leaving a silver seal to John. (Letter from Francis B. Culver)

Howard Per pale, dexter, az 3 fleurs-de-lis in pale or bet 2 flaunches erm, each charged with a rose gu; sinister, gu a bend bet 6 crosses crosslet fitchée arg. Both for Howard
    Crest: a U. S. flag
    Framed water colors (from original by Cole?) owned by George R. Winsor, 36 Ki'syth Road, Brookline, Mass. Seen by Dr. Harold Bowditch. The American flag over the arms of Katherine Howard, wife of Henry VIII, is John Coles at his best

Howe
    "And in the Parlor, full in view,
      His Coat-of-Arms, well framed and glazed
    Upon the wall in colors blazed.
    He beareth gules upon his shield,
    A chevron argent in the field,
    With three wolf's heads, and for the crest
    A wyvern part-per-pale addressed
    Upon a helmet barred; below
    The scroll reads: By the name of Howe."
                  —Longfellow.
    Owned 1890 by Lyman Howe, The Wayside Inn, Sudbury, Mass.

Howe Gu a chev arg bet 3 wolves' heads 2 and 1 sa, and 3 crosses 1 and 2
    Crest: a wyvern
    Seal of M. A. De Wolfe Howe, LL. D., Bishop of Central Penn., 1871. But see below. Also used by Miss Ethel Hawkins of Springfield, Mass., whose mother was a Howe

Howe [Or] a chev bet 3 wolves' heads erased sa 1 and 2, and 3 crosses crosslet sa 2 and 1
    The flag of a frigate in full sail bears these arms. By B. G. Goodhue
    Bookplate M. A. De Wolfe Howe of Boston. Also silver seal made in Florence for Mr. Howe through Russell Sullivan. The Episcopal seal of Rt. Rev. M. A. de W. Howe of Cent. Penn. has wolves' heads 2 and 1 and crosses crosslet 1 and 2 — an error. Motto: Sine cruce sine luce. Dated 1871

Howe *See also* Hawkins

Howell [Gu] 3 towers [arg]
    Tombstone Major John Howell, who d. in 1686, aged 71. Southampton, Long Island. Also on old silver. Wm. & Mary Quar., Jan. 1894, p. 156. Ancest. Rec. & Portr. vol. II, p. 663, gives "gu 3 towers triple turreted arg"

Howell Quartered by Jenks and Lewis

Howes Arg a chev bet 3 griffins' heads couped sa
    Crest: out of a ducal cor or a demi-unicorn ppr
    Motto: Stat fortuna Domus
    On automobile of H. S. Howes, West Newton

Howland Arg 2 bars sa. In chief 3 lions ramp of the last
    Crest: a lion pass sa [gorged with a ducal cor]
    On an old painting
    Bookplate —— Howland, Buffalo; Meredith Howland, lawyer, N. Y. Vermont's Amer. Heral., pp. 139, 140, 168
    Motto: Fortitudo et fidelitas

Howland [Arg] 2 bars sa and in chief 3 lions ramp sa
    Framed. Pilgrim Hall, Plymouth, Mass.

Howland Quartered by Hodges

Howland *See also* Winsor

Hoyt Arg a mill-rind gu
    Crest: a dog sejant bet 2 wings issuing from a ducal cor
    Bookplate Oliver Corse Hoyt, engr. by A. W. Macdonald

Hubard Sa an estoile of 6 points in chief a crescent arg bet 2 flaunches erm. Impaling: Arg upon a chev gu bet 3 pheons sa 5 mullets arg
    Crest: a Sagittarius statant
    Motto: Fortis and fidelis
    Bookplate James Hubard of Williamsburg, Va., and pasted in book printed 1735. Crozier's Va. Heral., p. 22

Hubbard On a bend [gu?] 3 lions pass reguard [or?]
    Crest: a lion's head erased on a wreath erm
    "Thomas Hubbard's tomb." Granary Burying Ground, Tremont St. side, Boston," 1742. Heral. Jour., vol. 2, p. 134

Hubbard Quarterly arg and sa on a bend over all gu 3 lions pass or
    Crest: a griffin's head erased
    Motto: Nec timeo nec sperno
    Bookplate Gardiner G. Hubbard, 1849; Samuel Hubbard; F. C. Hubbard

Hubbard Quarterly or and arg on a bend over all gu 3 lions pass guard or
    Crest: an elephant's head couped arg (?) holding in the mouth a broken spear, point downward
    Panel with inn and horseman from Wm. Clark House, Garden Court St., Boston, 1712, owned by Maine Hist. Soc.

Hubbard Quart 1 and 4: Quarterly arg and sa on a bend over all gu 3 lions pass or; 2 and 3: Gu on a chev arg 3 escallops or bet 3 ostrich feathers arg
    Crest: on a chapeau gu turned up erm a lion's head erased or charged across the erasure with 3 stars of 6 points
    Motto: Paradisus in sole
    Bookplate John P. Hubbard

Hubbard Impaled by Kay

Huckel Per chev engr arg and az 3 lions ramp counterchanged
    Crest: a lion ramp az
    Motto: His regi sevitium
    Bookplate Earle Wentworth Huckel, Phila.

Hudnut A griffin segreant
    Crest: a tiger crouching (?)
    Book label of Alex. M. Hudnut of Princeton, N. J., and N. Y.

Hugel Quart 1 and 4: [Gu] a lion ramp facing in 1 the sin, in 4 the dexter, holding 3 leaves (a fleur-de-lis?); 2 and 3: or 3 lozenges az 2 and 1
    Crest: a lion of the field
    Motto: Ich habs gewagt
    Bookplate Baron Adolph von Hugel, Phila. and Montreal. Rietstap gives sa 3 lozenges or 2 and 1

Huger Arg a flaming heart gu (?) in chief bet 2 laurel branches fruited in saltire, and in base an anchor erect az bet 2 flaunches az each charged with a fleur-de-lis [or]
    Crest: a Virginia nightingale on a leaved twig all ppr
    Motto: Ubi libertas ibi patria

Bookplate John M. Huger, New Orleans. Grant of arms, 1771, to Huger of S. C.

Hugget Arg a chev gu on a chief az 2 fleurs-de-lis or mill-rinds
Memorial tablet to Eleanor, wife of S'gismund Hugget, in St. Paul's Chapel, Broadway, N. Y. She d. 1795. The N. Y. Gen. & Biog. Record, July, 1872, p. 117, gives a crest: two wings expanded gu, and motto: Dene agendo et cavendo, which I could not see in the dim light

Hughes Arg an eagle with 2 heads displ sa
Crest: an eagle's head erased sa, in the beak a brand raguly sa fired gu
Motto: Fynno Duw Deifydd
By Harriet L. Herring, Spray, N. C., "from drawing or wall plaque"

Hull Arg on a chev az bet 3 demi-lions gu as many bezants on a chief sa 2 piles of the field
Seal on will of Daniel Quincy, 14 Aug. 1690; probably belonged to Samuel Sewell, who married Hannah, only child of John Hull, the mint-master (Suffolk wills). Heral. Jour., vol. 2, p. 90., vol. 3, p. 46

Hulton [Arg a lion ramp gu armed and langued az]
Crest: out of a crown or a hart's head bet 2 branches of hawthorn ppr
Seal of Henry Hulton of Brookline, Mass., before 1775, on papers in Eng. Shield crushed. Seen by E. A. Jones

Humfrey [Gu?] a cross botonnée arg, a crescent for diff
Crest: a leopard pass
Seal of John Humfrey of Sandwich, Co. Kent and N. E. (Winthrop papers). Heral. Jour., vol. 1, p. 192

Humphreys Or a fess az bet 3 griffins' heads couped [   ] and in chief a crescent
Crest: a griffin passant
Motto: Quo fata vocant
Bookplate Maj. Reuben Humphreys, 1757–1832, M. C., of Simsbury, Conn., and Marcellus, N. Y. Bates's Early Conn. Engr., p. 23

Humphries Arg a lion pass guard sa. On a chief sa a pale or bet 2 bezants
Crest: two mailed and spurred legs reversed and addorsed
Motto: Inveniam viam aut faciam
Bookplate Sidney Humphries

Hunt Gu on a fess or bet 3 cinquefoils a lion pass
Crest: a boar's head couped erect bet 2 ostrich feathers
Notepaper used by Lucy Hunt Smith (Mrs. James M. Smith) of Northampton, Mass.

Hunt [Gu] on a fess bet 3 cinquefoils [or] a lion pass guard [of the field]
Crest: a boar's head erect bet 2 ostrich feathers sa
Motto: Vi nulla invertitur ordo
Bookplate Frederick Thayer Hunt. E. B. Bird, des.

Hunt Per saltire 2 hearts in fess
Seal of Richard Hunt of Boston, late of Portsmouth, Eng. "Bisket Baker" on indenture of partnership, 1674. Owned by C. P. Greenough of Boston

Hunter Sa a bugle horn stringed arg
Crest: a greyhound's head erased
Seal of Robert Hunter, gov. of N. Y., 1710. Heral. Jour., vol. 4, p. 95

Hunter [Vert] 3 coursing hounds arg on a chief arg 3 stringed hunting horns [vert] stringed [gu]
Crest: a hound sejant collared
Motto: Cursum perficio
Bookplate Thomas Lomax Hunter, 3d, "Waverly," King Geo. Co., Va.

Hunter Vert 3 coursing hounds arg. On a chief arg 3 stringed hunting horns, vert stringed gu. Impaling: Quart 1 and 4: Or a lion ramp; 2 and 3: Sa 3 horses heads couped
Crest: a hound's head couped arg
Bookplate John Hunter. Another has motto: Dum spiro spero

Huntington Az a harpy with wings disclosed and hair flotant or
Painted and framed. John Coles' style (Mrs. Bolton saw). Mrs. Edward L. Davis, 173 Commonwealth Ave., Boston

Huntington Impaled by Baldwin

Hunton Arg on a chev per pale [gu and az] bet 3 talbots pass [sa] as many stags' heads cabossed [or]
Crest: a demi-talbot [gu] collared and eared [or] holding bet his paws a stag's head cabossed [gu]
Seal, New York

Hurd Azure a lion ramp or. On a chief arg a crane bet 2 mullets sa
Crest: a raven sa on a garb in fess
Bookplate "Name of Hurd. Engr. by N. Hurd? Found with the signature "Isaac Hurd's, 1812"

Hurd Gu a lion ramp or
Crest: on a garb a blackbird ppr
Motto: Bona bonis
Painted arms, the late John Hurd, Boston

Hurry A lion ramp gu and in base 2 rowels az
Crest: a harpy with wings expanded ppr
Motto: Nec arrogo nec dubito
See N. Y. Gen. & Biog. Rec., July, 1904, p. 199. Bookplate

Hutchings Arg 3 lions pass guard 2 and 1 sa
Crest: a lion of the field
Motto: Courage a la mort
Bookplate Col. Wm. Vincent Hutchings, Boston

Hutchins Arg 3 lions pass sa
Crest: a lion pass guard sa
Motto: Courage a la mort
Painted coat owned by Rev. Charles L. Hutchins, Concord, Mass.

Hutchinson Per pale gu and az a lion ramp arg within an orle 12 crosses crosslet or
Crest: out of a ducal cor a cockatrice combed gu
Motto: Libertatem coeo licentiam detestor
Gov. Hutchinson. In color in a window, State House, Boston, 3d floor. On bookplate of Thomas Leger Hutchinson, arms given with 8 crosses crosslet arg. Ancest. Rec. & Portr., vol. I, p. 394

Hutchinson Per pale [gu] and [az] a lion ramp [arg] over a field of crosses crosslet [or]
Engr. dish given in 1711 by Thomas Hutchinson, Boston. Second Church, Boston. Old Sil. Am. Ch., p. 41

Hutchinson Per pale gu and az a semée of crosses crosslet or, over all a lion ramp arg
Painted on the bookcase at "Scottowe," Lawrence Park, Groton, Mass.

Hutchinson Per pale gu and az a lion ramp arg over a semée of crosses crosslet or. Impaling: Chequy or and az a fess erm (Calthrop of Co. Lincoln)
Crest: a wyvern az

Motto: Perge et valeas
Gov. Thomas Hutchinson's decorated octagonal china plate from the Province house. Bostonian Soc.

Hutchinson Per pale [gu and az] a lion ramp arg within an orle of 9 crosses crosslet [or]
Crest: from a ducal cor a wyvern
Engr. on a chocolate-pot, Judge Clearwater collection. Amer. Silver, by C. L. Avery, 1920, p. 22

Hutchinson A lion ramp [arg] over a semée of crosses crosslet [or]
Crest: on a ducal cor a wyvern
Copp's Hill Yard, Boston. Slab on ground, east side
A hatchment (broken) is also mentioned in the Heral. Jour., vol. 2, p. 83. In Doc. Hist. of R. I., vol. 2, p. 93, the seal of Samuel Hutchinson is shown with 7 crosses crosslet

Hutson Per fess embowed and embat or and vert 3 martlets counterchanged
Crest: a martlet holding a twig
Motto: Pro patria
Water color in So. Car. Hist. Soc.

Hutton Gu on a fess bet 3 cushions tasselled or as many fleurs-de-lis of the field
Bookplate Edward Francis Hutton. By E. B. Bird of Boston

Hyslop Arg a stag lodged beneath a tree, ground vert
Motto: Vincit omnia veritas
Bookplate Robert Hyslop

Hyslop Arg 6 lions ramp 3, 2, 1
Crest: a mullet
Bookplate —— Hyslop

I

Ingersoll Gu a fess dancettée erm bet 6 trefoils slipped or
Crest: a griffin's head gu gorged with a fess dancettée erm bet 2 wings displ or
Embr. by Ann Ingersoll, Westfield, Mass., 1758. Hung in hall of Major Edward Ingersoll, Springfield

Ingersoll Or 2 pales gu
Motto: Fama sed virtus non moriatur
Bookplate "Jared Ingersoll, Esqr, of New Haven, Connecticut," 1749–1822

Ingleby Quartered by Middleton

Inglis Az a lion ramp arg. On a chief of the second 3 mullets of the first
Crest: a demi-lion ramp ppr, in the dexter paw a mullet or [arg?]
Mottoes: A: Recte faciendo securus; B: Invictus maneo

Bookplate John Inglis, the emigrant to N. Y. Also on a memorial tablet to the wife of Rev. Charles Inglis, D. D., in St. Paul's Chapel, Broadway, N. Y. (d. 1783), but the lion and chief appear to be or and the mullets gu. No crest. N. Y. G. & B. Record, Jan. 1872, p. 24

Inglis Gu on a bend 3 eagles displ bet 2 (unidentified charges
Wax seal on deed of Mungo Inglis, dated 1700. He was the first Grammar Master of William and Mary College. Wm. & Mary Quar., Jan. 1894, p. 159

Ingraham Erm on a fess gu 3 escallops or
Crest: a griffin's head erased
Motto: Magnanimus esto
Bookplate Edward D. Ingraham, Phila.

Ingraham Erm on a fess gu 3 escallops [or]
Crest: a cock ppr
Supporters: A gazelle gorged (?) and a griffin (?)
Motto: Virtus in arduis
Bookplate Solomon Ingraham, Capt. of Norwich, Conn. R. Brunton, sc. Bates's Early Conn. Engr., p. 25

Innes Arg 3 estoiles az on a bordure az 8 plates
Crest: a man's face in an increscent
Motto: Je recois pour donner
Bookplate Colonel Innes of N. C.

Iredell Erm 2 bendlets gu. Impaling: Arg a stag gu
Crest: an arm embowed arg holding a sword or
Motto: Mens conscia recti
Framed painting and bookplate in N. C. Hall of History, Raleigh, near portrait of Judge James Iredell of Edenton, b. 1751. The bookplate as engraved has 3 arrows bendways on a bend sa and cotised. Mrs. Everett sent me a drawing from the painting

Iredell Quart 1 and 4: Erm a sword gu in bend bet 2 bendlets gu; 2 and 3: Or a stag gu attired arg within a bordure of the 2d
Crest: an arm embowed in armor charged with 2 mullets or and holding a sword arg pomel or
Motto: Mens conscia rectis
Framed painting owned by James and Martha (Higgs) Iredell of West Princess Anne Road, Norfolk, Va. Seal ring of Mrs. Laura Higgs Iredell, same address

Ironside Quart az and gu a cross patonce or
Engr. with the arms of the see of Hereford on a two-handled bowl, 1661. Given by Mrs. George Bromley Ironside of New London, Conn., to Cathedral of St. John the Divine, N. Y. Old Sil. Am. Ch., p. 340

Irvine Or [arg?] a fess gu bet 3 holly leaves vert
Crest: a hand issuing from a cloud holding a thistle leaved vert
Motto: Dum memor ipse mei
Bookplate Pechell Irvine, N. Y.

Irving Arg 3 small sheaves or bundles of holly 2 and one, each consisting of as many leaves slipped vert banded gu
Crest: a dexter arm in armor fessways holding a sword erect hilted and pomeled or
Motto: Sub sole, sub umbra, virens
Bookplate which belonged to William Irving, who came 1763. Vermont's Amer. Heral., pp. 68, 169

Iselin Gu 3 roses
Crest: a rose twig leaved embowed
On notepaper of Mrs. Arthur Iselin, Katonah, N. Y., 1922

Isham Gu 3 piles wavy or, over all a fess of the second
Seal at Henrico, Va. Crozier's Va. Heral., pp. 47 and 48

Ives Arg a chev sa bet 3 moors' heads in profile erased ppr
Embr. arms of Robert Hale Ives, 22 x 15 inches, worked by his sister, Mrs. Rebecca Ives Gilman, 1746–1823. Owned by Mrs. Robert H. Bancroft. Also engr. bookplate (no crest) of Benjn Ives of Beverly, Esqr [Mass.]

Ives Arg a chev sa bet 3 human heads sa couped, earringed, and filleted
Crest: a lion ramp
Motto: Aut tace aut face
Bookplate George B. Ives, Salem, Mass. Also of Thomas Poynton Ives, Brown Univ., but with a label of 3 points

Izard Arg 6 leopards' faces 3, 2, 1 vert
Crests: 1: a dolphin embowed; 2: a helmeted head couped surmounted by 3 ostrich feathers
Bookplate Ralph Izard

Izard Quart 1 and 4: Sa (?) on a bend gu [or?] an annulet sa; 2 and 3: (Izard) arg [or?] 6 leopards' faces 3, 2, 1 gu
Hatchment of Hon. Ralph Izard on wood, framed, hanging in front of slaves gallery in St. James's Church, Goose Neck, S. C. Engraved (perhaps reversed) in Harper's Mag., Dec. 1875, p. 15. He was a U. S. Senator and d. 1804. Sylvan City (1883), p. 469. S. C. Hist. & Gen. Mag., July, 1901, p. 218. L. Park saw and described, 1923. He says the bend in 1 and 4 is or, the field in 2 and 3 or also

Izzard 5 leopards' faces
Crest: an Indian's head plumed
Seal Ralph Izzard, 1779. Chamberlain MSS. N. E. Reg., Apr. 1880, p. 184

J

J T *See* Jordan, Thomas. Seal

Jackson Arg on a chev bet 3 hawks' heads erased [az] 3 cinquefoils arg a martlet in chief for diff
Crest: a horse courant arg gouttée de sang
Bookplate Richard Jackson; Stephen Jackson

Jackson Az 4 escallops arg
Crest: a covered cup
Motto: Bona quae honesta
Bookplate Jonathan Jackson. N. Hurd, sc. Also P. T. Jackson; also James Jackson; also Henry Jackson by S. L. Smith after Hurd. Also on Revere coffee pot — 3 birds (?), and lion rampant for crest

Jackson Gu a fess arg bet 3 shovellers [tufted on the head and breast] arg; [each charged with a trefoil slipped vert]. On an inscutcheon the Badge of Ulster in chief
Crest: a shoveller
Motto: Innocentiae securus
Thomas Jackson's tomb, Granary Burying Ground, by Tremont Building, Boston. Stone is reinforced or reset. Arms of baronets of Beach Hill, Co. Surrey. Heral. Jour., vol. 2, p. 140

Jackson Gu 3 suns or a chief erm
Crest: a lion ramp tongued gu
Ancient water color (with Coles cornstalks) for Jackson of Penn. Copy by Mrs. Arnold Talbot, Lincoln, R. I.
Bookplate Herbert I. Jackson, Boston, engr. by S. L. Smith, 1924, has for crest a dramatic mask to show his tastes

Jackson Quarterly gu and or 4 escallops ppr
Crest: a covered cup or urn
Motto: Bona quae honesta
Framed water color, owned by H. H. Keith, Newton, Mass. Also a "Jackson" engr. bookplate. Also on gold-rimmed china of Walter Jackson, formerly of Newton, now (1917) of Potter's Bar, Leggett's, Herts, Eng.

Jackson Quartered by Lowell and Moreland

Jacobs Arg a chev gu bet 3 wolves' heads erased ppr. Badge of Ulster in chief
Crest: a wolf pass ppr
Bookplate Justin A. Jacobs, 1872

Jacobs Quartered by Hazlehurst

Jacobsen Arg 3 annulets sa 2 and 1 and in chief a figure like an arrow head crossed
Crest: a windmill

Memorial window formerly in the old church at Albany, to "Rutger Jacobsen Commissaris, 1656." Zieber's Heral., p. 66. Heral. Jour., vol. 1, p. 33

Jaeger Per bend sin gu and az a dog gorged and segreant
Bookplate Otto Jaeger, engr. by A. W. Macdonald, 1911

Jaffrey "Jaffrey of Kingswell in Scotland beareth Paly of six arg and sa overall a fess of the first charged with 3 mullets of the second. "For a crest the sun shining through a cloud ppr (not shown)
Motto: Post nubila Pheobus
Water color, small, from an estate in Portsmouth, N. H. W. A. Coffin, owner

Jaffrey Paly of 6 arg and sa surmounted by a fess of the first charged with 3 mullets of the second
Crest: the sun shining through a cloud ppr
Motto: Post nubila Phoebus
On the bookplate of Wm. A. Jeffries of Boston. Also Jeffries MSS. N. E. Reg., Jan. 1877, p. 61. Vermont's Amer. Heral., p. 88

Jagemann Per fess [or?] billety and [arg?]. In chief an anchor, ring down [gu?]. In base a hunting horn [sa?]
Crest: four ostrich feathers
Bookplate Hans Carl Günther von Jagemann, Prof. Harvard Coll. Some Amer. Coll. Bookplates, 1915, p. 302

Jameson Az a saltire or cantoned with 4 ships under sail arg
Tomb of Mrs. Mildred (Smith) Jameson, wife of David, at Temple Farm, Essex County, Va. She d. 11 Dec. 1778, aged 48 years. The arms impale: Az a chev bet 3 acorns slipped and leaved or" (Smith). Wm. & Mary Quar., Oct. 1893, p. 80. Bellet's Some Prom. Va. Fam., vol. 4, p. 17

Jameson Or a castle az
"By the name of Jameson" and palm branches
Framed painting in the hall at the home of Hon. Charles Thornton Davis, Brookline, Mass.

Janney Erm a bend double cotised gu
Crest: on a mailed hand fessways an eagle [or hawk or]
Motto: Ducit amor patriae
Bookplate Thomas Janney, Phila. Notepaper Joseph A. Janney, Jr., of Chestnut Hill, Phila., 1924. Sylvan City, 1883, p. 448

Janvrin A ship bet 2 castles
Seal George Janvrin, Portsmouth,
N. H., 1754. Jeffries MSS. N. E.
Reg., Jan. 1877, p. 61

Jaquelin Or 3 nags' heads gu
Crest: a nag's head
Motto: Comme je trouve
On oil painting of immigrant Edward
Jaquelin, Virginia, 1697. Crozier's
Va. Heral., p. 28 and 29. See, however,
Wm. & Mary Quar., Jan. 1894, p. 159

Jaquelin Quartered by Ambler

Jaquet Az a chev bet in chief 2 mullets
and in base a crescent
Jean Paul Jacquet of N. Y. See
"Jaquett Family," 1907, pp. 73, 74

Jarvis Quart 1 and 4: Az 6 ostrich
feathers 3, 2, 1; 2 and 3: Arg a fess
sa bet 3 lions' heads erased gu (Farmar)
Crest: from a ducal cor a cock's head
Motto: Horae sempre sola salus
servire Deo
Bookplate Samuel Farmar Jarvis,
D. D., son of Bp. Abraham of Conn.

Jarvis [Sa] a chev erm bet 3 doves or
[arg?]
Crest: a demi-hawk rising bet 3
lions' heads erased gu
Bookplate Leonard Jarvis. N. Hurd,
sc.

Jarvis Vert 6 ostrich feathers 3, 2, 1 [sa]
Impaling: A paly of 12 gu and vert
on a chief vert a griffin pass arg
(White?)
Crests: a demi-eagle rising; a lion's
head erased
Motto: Adversis major par secundis
Bookplate —— Jarvis. Not as in
Burke

Jauncey Or 3 chev engr gu a label of
5 points
Crest: an armed arm emb holding a
battle axe (or spear?)
Motto: Quo vocat virtus
Bookplate William Jauncey, N. Y.
merchant (Wm. written in)

Jay Arg a chev gu bet in chief a demi-
sun in splendor bet 2 mullets [arg] and
in base a bird on a rock
Crest: a cross [sa] on a calvary of
2 steps. These are not the usual colors
John Jay's bookplate (Bedford),
engr. by Spenceley, 1907, has an azure
field chev or and the motto: Deo duce
perseverandum. There is also a seal
(Godchild of Wash., p. 94) carved on
Albany Capitol

Jayne Az an eagle displ or
Crest: a swan with wings endorsed
devouring a trout all ppr
Motto: Honore et justitia
Bookplate John P. Jayne, N. Y. City

Jefferds Az on a bend arg double
cotised or a lion pass sa armed and
langued gu
Crest: a lion's head erased or langued
gu
Water color (old) owned by N. E.
Hist. Gen. Soc.

Jeffers Az fretty or. On a chief arg a
lion pass guard ppr. Impaling: Arg
a chev gu bet 6 crosses pattée of the
last (Smith)
Crest: a lion's head erased ppr
langued gu and crowned or
Motto: Post nubila Phoebus
Water color found in a Smith Bible
in Virginia. Copy owned by Mrs.
Ernest W. Bowditch, Milton, Mass.
Used by Admiral. Wm. Nicholson
Jeffers of Penn.

Jeffery Arg 6 billets sa 3, 2, 1. On a
chief of the last a lion pass arg
Crest: a lion's head couped charged
with 3 billets
Motto: In veritate salus (written in)
Bookplate Barth^w Jeffery. Same
in a circle with George Jeffery's name
written in

Jeffries Gu a lion ramp arg bet 3
scaling ladders 2 and 1, all in bend
sinister
Crest: a castle double turreted
Bookplate. Dr. John Jeffries, engr.
by Callender. Also of Dr. B. Joy
Jeffries and W. Lloyd Jeffries. That
of James Jeffry of Phila., 1776, has no
tinctures

Jeffries Sa a lion ramp or bet 3 scaling
ladders of the last
Crest: on a rock arg a castle or, the
2 end towers domed
Motto: Fac recte et nil teme
Used by David Jeffries on a seal
on a snuff box dated 1701, and upon
silver candlesticks mentioned in the
will of John Jeffries of Boston, 1689–
1777, who also used a bookplate with
field gu. Vermont's Amer. Heral., pp.
34, 169. Heral. Jour., vol. 2, p. 166

Jeffries Sa a lion ramp bet 3 scaling
ladders [or]
Crest: a tower embattled with 2
knobbed peaks rising behind the 4
embattlements [or?]
Motto: Fac recte et nil time
Notepaper Mrs. Wm. A. Jeffries,
Marlborough St., Boston. On Mr.
Jeffries's bookplate the tower is on a
mound vert as it should be. The arms
are quartered with Jaffrey. Engr. by
Mitchell, Boston. See also N. E. H.
G. Reg., vol. 31, pp. 56–67

Jekyll Or a fess bet 3 hinds trip sa
Crest: a horse's head couped arg
maned and bridled sa
Gore roll of arms. John Jekyll,
Boston, 1723

Jenings Arg a chev gu bet 3 plummets sa
    Crest: a demi-griffin couped with a plummet sa in its beak
    Motto: Humani nihil alienum mihi
    Bookplate Thomas Jenings, distinguished lawyer, Md. Bookplate Oliver Burr Jennings, engr. by A. W. Macdonald, 1917. Arms similar were used by Abraham Jennings, first owner of Monhegan Island, Maine

Jenkins Quart 1: Or a lion ramp reguard sa; 2 and 3: Sa a chev arg bet 3 fleurs-de-lis; 4: Gu 2 chev arg;.
    Impaling: Gu a chev erm bet 3 garbs (Hill or Baron?)
    Crest: a mailed arm emb, holding a sword by a ribbon at the elbow
    Motto: Non revertur invitus
    Bookplate Lewis Jenkins, 1744. N. Hurd, sc.

Jenks Quarterly of 6; 1: Arg [or?] 3 boars' heads couped sa a chief indented of the last; 2: Per bend sinister erm and ermines, over all a lion ramp or (Edwards?); 3: Gu a lion ramp within a bordure engr or (Talbot or Powell); 4: Gu 3 lions pass or in pale (Howell?); 5: Quarterly 1 and 4: Gu a lion ramp reguard or; 2 and 3: Arg 3 boars' heads couped sa; 6: Arg a lion ramp gu. On a chief sa 3˙ escallops arg (Russell or Kemp). Impaling: Quarterly 1 and 4: Vert a chev bet 3 leopards' faces or (Fitch); 2 and 3: Arg a chev bet 3 crosses crosslet fitchée sa (Rand)
    Crest: a lion ramp reguard arg holding in the gambs a boar's head gu
    Motto: Audax at cautus
    Water color by Wm. Jenks for his son, John Henry Jenks, whose son is C. W. Jenks, owner, Bedford, Mass.

Jenks Vert on a bend engr arg bet 3 arrows 3 hearts of the field
    Crest: a heart engorged with a ducal cor
    Bookplate ——— Jenks

Jenner [Az?] on a cross 5 fleurs-de-lis [or?] within a bordure [engrailed (here ornamented)]
    Crest: a hound sejant [arg?]
    Thomas Jenner, 1765. Tomb No. 51, Phipps Street Yard, Charlestown, Mass. Heral. Jour., vol. 1, p. 56

Jennings Az an inverted chev gu, bet 3 plummets (?) 1 and 2 (billets voided)
    Crest: a wolf's head erased
    Motto: Il buono tempa verra
    Bookplate Edward B. Jennings

Jerdone Arg a saltire and chief gu, the last charged with 3 mullets of the field
    Crest: a spur rowel of 6 points arg
    Motto: Cave adsum

Engr. on silver brought from Jedburgh, Scot., by Francis Jerdone to Virginia. Crozier's Va. Heral., p. 29

Jessup Barry of 6 arg and az, on the first 9 mullets gu 3, 3, 3
    Crest: a dove
    On cover "Edward Jessup and his descendants," 1887

Jett Arg 3 fleurs-de-lis
    Seal on letter of Thomas Jett of Rappahannock River, Va., dated Oct. 1774. Crozier's Va. Heral., p. 8

Jewett Gu on a cross arg 5 fleurs-de-lis
    Bookplate Elizabeth H. Hewes (now Mrs. Tilton), a descendant of the Jewetts. W[eston]-S[mith], del. 1901

Jewett Gu on a cross arg 5 fleurs-de-lis 1, 3, 1 of the field
    Crest: a demi-eagle rising, couped
    Bookplate Stephen S. Jewett

Joachimsen A cross moline (?) and in chief a fusil bet 2 estoiles
    Crest: a hand erect with thumb and 2 fingers raised
    Motto: Manent optima coelo
    Bookplate P. J. Joachimsen, N. Y.

Johnson *See also* Walker

Johnson Arg a bend sa on a chief of the 2d 3 cushions of the first
    Framed arms in a lozenge on copper (?) of Mary (b. 1718) daughter of Baldwin Johnson of Antigua, wife of Thomas Hopkinson of Phila., parents of Francis the Signer. Owned by G. O. G. Coale, Boston. Francis's sister Anne married Samuel Stringer Coale

Johnson Arg a chev gu bet 3 lions' heads couped crowned
    Crest: an eagle rising or
    Motto: Per aspera ad astra
    Bookplate Wm. S. Johnson, Conn., and Miss Sarah E. Johnson. W. L. Johnson, S. C., has crest a pheonix rising from the flames. Also Wm. S. Johnson, LL. D., Prest. Columbia College, 1787–18C1

Johnson Arg an eagle rising, holding in its beak a fruited branch az debruised by an inverted chev gu. In the dexter base a cross pattée
    Crest: a wolf pass holding a fruited branch in the jaws
    Motto: Rien sans peine
    Bookplate Edward Johnson

Johnson [Gu?] on a chev arg? bet 3 fleurs-de-lis as many escallops
    Crest: a cubit mailed arm holding anarrow in bend sinister
    Supporters: Indians with cap and loin cloth of feathers, a quiver at the back, and a bow

Motto: Deo regique debeo
Bookplate Sir Wm. Johnson, com-
missioner Indian affairs, N. Y., 1756

Johnson Gu 3 spear heads or a chief
erm
Crest: two wings erect sa
Framed embroidery called "very
old" seen by Mrs. Harold Bowditch,
1924, 18" x 18", owned by Mrs. Edw.
H. Risley, Waterville, Me., daughter
of Judge Simpson of Newburyport,
whose mother was daughter of Eleazer
Johnson, Jr. E. J. Senior burned tea
there

Johnson Per fess indented gu and
az. Over all a bend arg inscribed
Γνωθι Σεαυτον
Bookplate James D. Johnson

Johnson Per pale sa and az on a
saltire arg bet 3 castles, 1 in chief, 2 in
fess [or], and in base two tilting spears
in saltire [az] 5 cocks sa (?) a plate in
de·ter chief (?)
Bookplate Carnegy Johnson, engr.
by Hopson

Johnson Quart 1 and 4: Arg 2 roses
slipped each with one leaf [gu?]; 2 and
3: Per pale [arg and sa?] a fess dancettée counterchanged, on the base a
lozenge sa (?)
Crest: a tree in leaf
Motto: Suaviter in modo, fortiter
in re
Ex libris Horace Johnson. H. Gregson, sc., 1905

Johnson Impaled by Walker

Johnston Arg a saltire sa. On a chief
gu 3 cushions or
Crest: a winged spur or
Motto: Nunquam non paratus
Bookplate Thomas Johnston of Md.
Maverick, sculpt., N. Y. Seals in the
possession of desc. of Gilbert Johnston
of Va. Robert of Turkey Island had a
bookplate engraved: az a saltire arg,
etc., perhaps an error. Bellet's Some
Prom. Va. Fam., vol. 2, p. 699. The
above with crescent for diff appears on
the bookplate of Gov. Gabriel Johnston
of No. Car. engr. by Andr Johnston.
(No. Car. Booklet, July, 1914.) Also in
St. Paul's Church vestry room, Edenton. (Seen by Miss Mary Pruden)

Johnston Arg a fess gu bet 3 lions'
heads couped
Crest: a mailed arm emb with sword
Bookplate John Johnston, painter,
Boston. Maverick, sc. Also impaling: Arg on a bend az bet 2 unicorns'
heads 3 fusils arg (Beverly or Smith)

Johnston Arg a saltire sa the badge of
Ulster in chief and in base a heart duc
crowned. On a chief gu 3 cushions
vert [usually or]

Crest: a spur bet wings and above it
a mullet gu
Motto: Nunquam non paratus
Bookplate —— Johnston

Johnston Gu 3 spear heads 2 and 1 ppr
a chief erm
Framed water color. "By the name
of Johnston" which suggests John
Coles' work. William E. Barnard,
owner, Shirley, Mass., son of John,
who married, 1835, Sarah, daughter of
Robert Johnston of S. C. (b. 1768) and
Sarah Pierce

Johnstone *See also* Hilliard

Johonnot Erm (?) on a chief az a sun
in splendor
Crest: a dove with a twig in its beak
Engr. on flagon given in 1773 and a
baptismal basin given in 1761 by
Zachariah Johonnot, distiller, Boston.
Hollis Street Church, Boston. Old Sil.
Am. Ch., pp. 82, 83

Jones Arg a lion ramp vert, vulned in
the breast gu
Crest: the sun in splendor or
Motto: Pax hospita ruris
Bookplate Gabriel Jones, "attorney
at law [of Frederick Co.] in Virginia,"
b. 17 May, 1724, d. 1806

Jones Erm 3 lions
Bookplate Robert Jones, King's
Attorney for North Car., 1761–67.
Crozier's Va. Heral., p. 26. A drawing
in color at the So. Car. Hist. Soc. has
erminois 3 lions rampant

Jones Or a lion ramp [az?]
Crest: a goat standing on rocks
Motto: VY: NGWLAD: UN: A:
WASNAETHAV
Bookplate Griffith Jones

Jones Per bend erm and ermines a lion
ramp or, within a bordure of the last
Crest: a demi-lion ramp couped
Motto: Trust in God
Bookplate Samuel Jones of N. Y.
Dawkins, sc. For genealogy *see* Amer.
Heral., vol. 2, p. 25

Jones Per bend sinister erm and er-
mines, a lion ramp or a bordure engr
of the last
Crest: a lion's head erased
Engr. on hilt of sword worn by
Major Cadwallader Jones of Prince
George Co., Va., when aide-de-camp to
Lafayette Crozier's Va. Heral., p. 51

Jones Quart 1 and 4: Gu a stag statant;
2 and 3: Erm on a fess az 3 crosses
crosslet arg (Paul)
Crest: a stag's head erased
Motto: Pro Republica. Two cannon are above the motto, a dolphin on

either side the shield, and above it a lance, sword hilt, cutlass, and anchor

Seal on letter from Commodore Paul Jones on the "Ranger" to John Wendell of Portsmouth, N. H., owned by E. J. Wendell, N. Y. Seal "said to have been given by H. R. H. Marie Antoinette," James Barnes says. The arms were adopted by Paul Jones when knighted by the King of France. The original water color is in the Masonic Library, Boston (Proceedings, June 12, 1912)

Jones Quarterly per fess indented az and or. Impaling: Az a lion pass guard [or] a chief erm
  Crest: a demi-lion ramp couped
  Motto: DUW A DIGON
  Bookplate James Jones

Jones Sa 2 chev interlaced and one inverted arg bet 2 eagles' heads erased
  Crest: eagles' head erased and gorged
  Motto: Ino virtus et fata vocant
  Bookplate Timothy Jones, Esqr, engr. by French. Not as in Burke

Jones Sa a fess or bet 3 boys' heads couped affronté ppr [crined or]. Impaling: On a bend 3 martlets. On a canton sinister a rose bet 2 fleurs-de-lis (Harding)
  Crest: a boy's head couped
  Seal on Col. Frederick Jones's will, No. Car., 1722. Wm. & Mary Quar., July, 1918

Jones Sa a stag statant arg attired or "By the name of Jones." Embr. hatchment, framed, arms of Col. Elisha Jones of Weston, Mass., great grandfather of Henry D. Thoreau, writer. Owned by Concord (Mass.) Antiquarian Soc.

Jones Quartered by Swan

J[ordan?] T[homas?] Az on a base [sa?] a pelican in her piety. In the dexter chief a star of six points and in the sinister chief an increscent
  Crest: above a coronet an arm embowed and vested in fess, holding a scimiter
  Used as a sinker by fishermen in the East River, Guilford, Conn., and brought up in oyster tongs. Impression in wax from Mrs. George H.

Cutler, Guilford, 1917. T. J. engraved on the seal either side the crest. These may be the Allan arms and Jordan crest. Thomas Jordan was treasurer of Guilford plantation, 1643–50, 1652–54. However, Thomas Jones was marshal, 1643–1652. Jordan was a witness to a deed of land on the East River in 1641. (Steiner's Guilford, pp. 31, 45.) An eminent attorney who lived later at Lenham Kent, Eng., and d. about 1705

Josselyn Chequy gu and az on a fess gu an annulet [or?]
  Crest: a bear's head couped and muzzled
  Motto: Faire mon devoir
  Bookplate —— Josselyn

Joy Or on a chev vert bet 3 oak leaves ppr 5 drops of water arg
  Crest: out of a ducal cor or 5 feathers arg
  Motto: Vive la joye
  On seals of several generations of Joys, Boston. The shield in glass is at 86 Marlboro St. (Mrs. C. H. Joy). She has the ancient John Joy (b. 1751) seal with crest: on a stump of a vine with two leafy branches a dove standing, all ppr. No motto

Judah Quart 1 and 4: Vert a chev arg and in base a lion pass guard. On a canton arg scales; 2 and 3: Az 4 fishes' heads naiant couped 2 and 2
  Crest: a whale sa spouting on waves az
  Motto: Fortitudo et justitia
  Bookplate Benjamin S. Judah of N. Y. Maverick, sc.

Judd Gu a fess raguly bet 3 boars' heads couped arg
  Crest: on a ducal cor a cockatrice
  Motto: Deo regnat
  Bookplate Arthur Curtis Judd, by E. H. Garrett, 1900. Clarence Lilley Judd of Saginaw uses the Montford arms on notepaper

Judson Per saltire az and gu [not erm] 4 lozenges counterchanged
  Crest: out of a ducal cor 2 dex arms in saltire hab ppr, each holding a scimitar in pale
  Notepaper Mrs. Henry H. Judson, Seattle, Wash.

Juxon *See* Timson

K

Kay Arg 2 bendlets [sa]. Impaling:
Erm a chevron (Hubbard?)
  Crest: a bird
Seal Nathaniel Kay, Newport, R. I.,
1727. Jeffries MSS. N. E. Reg.,
Jan. 1877, p. 62

Keayne Az an eagle displayed arg
  Reproduced in metal from a seal (?)
of Capt. Robt. Keayne of the Anc. &
Hon. Artil. Co. of Boston. A crest of
mural crown and beacon was devised
by W. L. Willey of Boston. Cayne
family coat. *See* Heral. Jour., vol. 1,
p. 110

Kearney Arg a lion ramp gu. On a
chief of the 2d 3 pheons or
  Crest: a mailed hand couped issuing
from the sinister and holding a sword
erect
  Motto: Semper fidelis
  Bookplate John W. Kearney, Md.

Keeble [   ] A lion ramp on a chief
engr 3 escallops
  Crest: an elephant's head couped (?)
  Wax impression on a deed at Urbana,
Middlesex, Va., dated 1698, and signed
by George Keeble. Wm. & Mary
Quar., Jan. 1893, p. 121

Keene Erm 3 crescents
  Crest: a griffin's head ppr
  Motto: Deus mihi providebit
  Engr. on colonial silver of Rev.
Samuel & Wm. Keene of Maryland.
Richardson's Sidelights on Md. Hist.,
vol. 2, p. 158

Keese Gu a bend sin or bet in chief a
lion ramp and in base a demi-griffin
holding a key in the beak
  Crest: within a wreath a covered cup
garlanded
  Motto: Bello virtus
  Bookplate John Keese. Maverick,
sculpt.

Keith Arg on a chief gu 3 palets or
  Crest: a hart's head erased [ppr]
armed with 10 tynes or, surmounting a
crown or
  Supporters: 2 harts [ppr]. Behind
the shield 2 batons in saltire, the tops
crowned
  Motto: Veritas vincit
  James Keith, Boston. Notepaper.
See Burke's Gen. Armory

Keith *See also* Marshall

Kellett [Arg on a mount vert a wild
boar sa]
  Motto: Ferret ad astra virtus
  Bookplate Wm. Kellett, Larchmont,
N. Y. Not seen

Kellogg Gu a fess bet in chief 2 fleurs-
de-lis or and in base an annulet of the
last
  Crest: a heart [gu] bet 2 wings or
  Motto: Gloria in excelsis Deo
  Bookplate Lois Kellogg. J. W. S.,
sc., 1899

Kelly Arg a chev bet 3 billets gu
  Crest: an ostrich's head arg holding
in the beak a horse shoe or
  Motto: Meliora speranda
  Bookplate William Kelly, Esq.,
Harv. 1767, of N. H.

Kelly Impaled by Belchier

Kemble Sa on a bend erm 3 leopards'
faces sa
  Crest: a boar's head or, couped gu
  Bookplate Peter Kemble of Phila. (?)
J. Lewis, sc.

Kempe Gu (?) a fess erm bet 3 garbs
or all within a bordure of the second
  Crest: from a garb fessways or a
falcon rising erm
  Motto: Labour to rest
  Bookplate John Tabor Kempe, Atty.,
Gen. of N. Y.

Kendrick Erm a lion ramp sa
  Crest: a falcon jessed and belled sa
standing on 3 arrows bound with a
ribbon 2 in saltire and one in fess
  Motto: Dum spiro spero
  Bookplate Edward East Kendrick,
Woore Hall, Shropshire, engr. by
John E. Gavit, Albany, N. Y. Also
Jarvis Kendrick, A. M., with motto:
Virtue is honour

Kennedy Arg a chev gu bet 3 crosses
crosslet fitchée sa
  Crest: a dolphin naiant ppr
  Motto: Avise la fin
  Supporters: Two swans ppr
  Framed water color owned by Free-
man W. Kennedy, Montclair, N. J.

Kennedy Arg a chev gu bet 3 crosses
crosslet fitchée sa within a double
tressure flory counterflory
  Crest: a dolphin embowed
  Motto: Avise la fine
  Bookplate N. Y. Pub. Lib., for John
Stewart Kennedy

Kennet Quartered by Leigh

Kent Quartered by Wright

Kerr Quart 1 and 4: Gu on a chev arg
3 mullets gu; 2 and 3: Az a sun in
splendor (Ker)
  Crest: a sun in splendor
  Motto: Sero sed serio
  Bookplate Rev. B. H. Kerr. Old?

Ketchum Quart 1: A mason's sign; 2: A Bible; 3: A shoemaker's awl; 4: a quill pen
    Crest: an owl holding a bird cage in its beak
    Motto: Ex septem unus
    Bookplate Selas Ketchum, Hopkinton, N. H., 1855. An antiquarian

Kettle Per fess or and az on a fess erm bet in chief 2 stags' heads erased gu and in base a lion pass guard or 3 cinquefoils
    Crest: a double-antlered stag's head erased gorged and chained
    Motto: Cara vita, carior patria, carissima libertas
    Bookplate John Kettle

Keyser Per pale arg and gu issuing from a mount in base az a king robed and crowned holding a sphere and sword
    Crest: two wings raised
    Bookplate Peter D. Keyser, Phila.

Kienbusch Vert a fess or bet 9 mullets pierced 2 in chief 4 and 3 in base
    Crest: a man wearing a hat and having a gun in bend behind him
    Bookplate Carl Otto v. Kienbusch, engr. by A. W. Macdonald

Kilby Arg 3 bars az in chief as many annulets az
    Crest: an ear of maize stripped open
    Gore roll of arms. Christopher Kilby, Boston and N. Y.

Kilham Sa 2 lions ramp combatant guard with a single head arg
    Crest: an otter's head (?) erased
    Painted on satin by Miss Florence Kilham. Owned by Walter H. Kilham, Boston. *See* under Kellam in Burke. Kilham has a morion or helmet

Kneeland A lion ramp or holding in the dexter paw an escutcheon charged with a cross formée
    Crest: a demi-lion
    Gore roll of arms. Thomas Kneeland of Essex, Mass.

Kimball Arg a fess sa within a bordure engr sa
    Crest: a mermaid with glass and comb
    Motto: Nosce te ipsum
    Bookplate David P. Kimball, Boston. Also bookplate of Moses Kimball of Boston. The bookplate of Harold Chandler Kimball bears a shield arg a lion ramp sa on a chief of the last 3 crescents of the first, des. by Claude F. Bragdon

Kimball Gu 3 scythes fessways in pale arg
    Crest: a bull's head couped ppr

On a MS chart of Richard Kimball's family, Ipswich, Eng., and Watertown, Mass. Essex Institute, Salem, Mass.

Kimberly Arg an oak tree eradicated vert fructed [or]
    Crest: a tree of the field
    Motto: Sinceritas
    Notepaper Meta D. Kimberly Musgrave (Mrs. Harrison Musgrave), Chicago

King Arg a lion ramp az crowned gu bet 3 crosses crosslet sa
    Crest: on a ducal cor or a swan az
    Crude water color unframed. "By the name of King." Essex Institute, Salem, Mass. A lion ramp appears on a bill of sale to Asa King of Southold, N. Y., 13 Oct. 1757. N. Y. G. & B. Record, April, 1896, p. 111

King Or 3 pheons
    Bookplate Miles King, b. 2 Nov. 1747, and d. in Norfolk, 19 June, 1814. In 2 books now in the Library of William and Mary College. Crozier's Va. Heral., p. 50

King Sa a lion ramp ermine bet 3 crosses pattée fitchée or
    Crest: a lion's gamb erect and erased sa holding a cross of the field or
    Arms of King of Bromley, Kent, used by Rufus King, statesman, of Jamaica, Long Island, N. Y., on silver. Son of Richard of Watertown, Mass. N. Y. Gen. & Biog. Rec., vol. 41, p. 274

King [Sa] on a chev bet 3 crosses crosslet [or] 3 escallops of the field
    Seal of James King of Suffield, Conn., on a deed, 1721–22. N. Y. Gen. & Biog. Rec.,vol. 41, p. 270

King Sa a lion ramp [or] bet 3 crosses crosslet of the last
    Crest: out of a ducal cor [or] a demi-ostrich arg beak sa wings endorsed
    Motto: Audaces fortuna juvat
    Notepaper F. Winthrop coll., N. Y., 1885, in Bos. Ath.

King Sa a lion ramp ducally crowned or bet 3 crosses crosslet or
    Crest: a demi-swan couped wings displ holding a horseshoe in its beak
    Motto: Loyall au mort
    Bookplate Morris King. A similar coat used by the Kings of Brunswick, Ga., desc. from John of Northampton, Mass. N. Y. Gen. & Biog. Rec., vol. 41, p. 273

King Impaled by Charnock

Kingdon Impaled by Gould

Kingsmill Impaled by Tayloe

Kingston Arg on a fess dancettée sa 3 leopards' heads jessant de lis or, over all an escutcheon az charged with 3 griffins' segreant arg [armed gu]. Impaling the arms on the escutcheon above (Yonge or Wye or Holder) Crest: out of a mural crown a griffin segreant
Bookplate Kingston of Penn? arms of West?

Kinlock Az a boar's head couped bet 3 mascles
Crest: an eagle with wings extended reguardant
Motto: Altius tendo
Bookplate Francis Kinloch, 1755–1826, Capt. Rev. of S. C.

Kip Az a chev or bet in chief 2 griffins sejant, both facing the dexter and in base a sinister hand erect couped [arg?]
Crest: a demi-griffin holding a cross pattée in its claws
Motto: Vestigia nulla retrorsum
Bookplate Leonard Kip, 1768–1843, pres. North River Bank, N. Y. Also tattooed on right forearm of Rev. Leonard Kip Storrs, Brookline, Mass. Dr. Theodore S. Woolsey of New Haven is said to have a tankard bearing the Kip arms

Kirkbride Quartered by Claiborne

Kissam Or on a fess az bet 3 wolves' heads erased of the 2d 3 cinquefoils
Crest: a wolf's head of the field
Motto: Honestum praetulit utili
Bookplate Benjamin Kissam, eminent lawyer, N. Y. H. Dawkins, inv. and sculp.

Kitchen See also Symmes

Kite Arg a chev az bet 3 kites sa
Crest: a kite rising
Ex libris Thomas Kite, Pearl and Walnut sts., Cincinnati, desc. from Sir Geo. Kite, Bart., whose son James came to Penn. in 1680

Klock Gu a fish erect and embowed, the back broken open
Crest: two eagles' wings gu, each charged with a fish of the field
Notepaper and ex libris Max Otto von Klock of Melrose, Mass. An early member of this family, Johannes Jacob Karl Klock, b. 1723 at Sobernheim, Palatinate, Germany, commander the Tryon County regt. of volunteers at the battle of Oriskany. The arms appear on documents at Stuttgardt, dated 1471 and 1491. Mrs. von Klock (nata Laura Fallenstein von

Mühlen) has an ex libris: Paly of eight gu and arg. Crest: a crowned eagle with wings spread. Her mother was Elizabeth Campbell of Redgate

Knauth Arg a saw erect, teeth toward the dexter side [sa], jessant three trefoils slipped [vert]
Crest: from three trefoils [vert] as many lances [or], each bearing a two-forked pennon [gu]
Stone sculpture on the front of No. 302 West 76th St., New York City. This house was owned by Percival Knauth, b. in New York 1851, married 1883 (approximately the date of the house), d. 1900; house sold out of the family in 1922 or 1923. These arms were copied from those on Mr. Knauth's father's house in Leipzig, Germany, still standing 1924. From an oil painting dating from about 1844, in Suhl, Thuringia. Dr. Harold Bowditch, 1924

Knight Sa a griffin segreant [or]
Crest: a tilting spear erect
By the name of Knight. R. Brunton, sc.
Bookplate Jonathan Knight, surgeon of Norwich, Conn., b. 1758. Bates's Early Conn. Engr., p. 27

Knowles Az crusily of crosslets a cross moline voided or
On automobile of Henry A. Knowles, Main St., Dover, Mass.

Knox Gu a falcon rising, jessed and belled, within a bordure engr or
Crest: a falcon of the field on a perch ppr
Motto: Moveo et proficior
Bookplate Wm. Knox. Notepaper S. Elise Leonard-Knox, Allston, Mass., with bordure arg. Bookplate Charlotte D. Knox (in a lozenge) by David M. Stauffer, bordure arg

Koecker Az 3 lions ramp holding a quiver of arrows arg (?)
Crest: a demi-lion of the field gu
Motto: Probitas optimum est consilium
Bookplate Leonard R. Koecker, M. D., Phila.

Krumbhaar Az on a mound in base vert 5 trees. On a flaunch in the dexter chief or a branching sprig, and on a sinister flaunch a sprig reversed
Crest: from a crown a bud slipped bet 2 wings erect
Bookplate George D. Krumbhaar, Phila.

L

Labberton Az a hind salient and at the sinister two trees
  Crest: a demi-doe couped
  A finely engr. seal of Dr. Robert H. Labberton, a Hollander in diplomatic service, owned by his grandson, Robert E. Labberton, Esq., Madison, N. C. A ring has only one tree. Mrs. Wm. Robert Everett of Palmyra, N. C., sent me impressions of both. Said to be in Holland von Hind Loppen

Ladd Or on a fess vert [az?] bet 3 escallops sa 3 shelldrakes arg
  Bookplate —— Ladd, N. H. S. Felwell, sculp.

Lake Quart 1 and 4: [Sa?] a bend bet 6 crosses [crosslet? arg?] a mullet for diff; 2 and 3: [   ] on a bend [   ] 2 mullets
  Mutilated seal on doc. 1657 in Mass. Archives, vol. 2, p. 505a

Lake Sa a bend bet 6 crosses crosslet arg
  Crest: a sea horse's head and neck couped arg
  Drawing by Pierre de C. La Rose, owned by Arthur Adams of Hartford, Conn. Lake family of Great Egg Harbor, N. J., desc. from John Lake, Gravesend, L. I.

Lamar Gu 2 lions pass guard in pale or
  Crest: a mermaid ppr holding in the sinister hand a mirror and in the dexter a comb
  Engr. on old silver and seal. Crozier's Va. Heral., pp. 19 and 20

Lambert Per chev gu and az 3 lambs pass a chief or fretty arg. In the chev point a mullet for diff
  Crest: a lamb of the field
  Motto: Deo et principe
  Bookplate Thomas R. Lambert, Boston? Also Samuel W. Lambert, engr. by French. No motto

Lamprey Az [properly or] in chief 3 cross crosslets fitchée [gu]
  Crest: a hand holding a cross crosslet fitchée in pale ppr
  Bookplate Mrs. Jeannette Lamprey Towle (pronounced Towell) of St. Paul. She a daughter of Uri (long i) Locke Lamprey of N. H.

Lane Per chev or and az a chev gu bet 3 mullets counterchanged
  Crest: a lion pass guard holding a mullet by its point in the gamb
  Motto: Fide et amore
  Bookplate William Lane

Lane Quartered by Corbin

Langborne [Arg] 2 chev [gu]
  Tomb of William Langborne in King William Co., Va. He was b. 1723. Also arms of his mother, Mary Dandridge Langborne: [Az] a lion's head erased [or] bet 3 mascles [arg] (Dandridge). Crozier's Va. Heral., p. 9. Va. Hist. Mag., vol. 15, p. 431

Langton Gu on a chev arg (?) bet 3 lions ramp 7 estoiles
  Crest: a lion of the field
  Notepaper F. Winthrop coll., N. Y., 1885, in Bos. Ath.

Larbalistier Quartered by Dumaresq

Lardner Gu on a fess sa bet 3 boars' heads [arg] a bar wavy arg
  Motto: Mediocria firma
  Bookplate Lyndford Lardner, Phila. Also John Lardner. Not as in Burke. Sylvan City, 1883, p. 449

Larrabee Arg a chev [   ] bet 3 lions ramp [   ]
  Motto: Quo fata vocant
  Engr. on a watch owned by Frederic Larrabee, b. Windham, Conn., 1760. R. Brunton, sc. Bates's Early Conn. Engr., p. 28

Lasinby Gu a fess arg bet 3 cushions [of the same] tasselled [or]. Over all a bend [sa] guttée [d'or]
  Crest: a demi-unicorn holding a heart
  "By the name of Lazinby." Joseph Lasinby of Boston d. 1774, aged 80 years, Granary Burying Ground, Park St. wall, Boston. Heral. Jour., vol. 2, p. 129

Lash Gu 2 axes addorsed arg handles or, each blade charged with a cross az (Loesch)
  Water color in No. Car. Sent by Miss Herring. A desc. of Paul Loesch of Waldoboro, Maine, went to No. Car.

Latané 3 crescents, 2 and 1
  Crest: a crane volant
  Seal on will of Rev. Lewis Latané, 1733. Wm. & Mary Quar., Jan. 1894, p. 156

Latham Or on a chief indented az 3 plates
  Crest: an eagle [or] on a child ppr in swaddling clothes gu lying on a chapeau
  Bookplate W. F. Latham

Latimer See also Norden

Lauder Gu a griffin segreant
  Crest: out of a masoned tower a demi-man in armor with spear in his left hand ppr

Motto: Turris prudentia custos. Ut migraturus habita
Bookplate Geo. Lauder, Jr., engr. by Spenceley

Laughlin [Az] a dexter hand apaumée couped at the wrist, in chief an arrow and in base a sword barways, points to the dexter, arg pommel and hilt or
Crest: a talbot sejant resting his dexter paw on a shield
Photo of modeled coat seen at John Evans & Co.'s, Boston, 1924. Mr. R. D. Weston identified this as possibly the Laughlin family of Pittsburgh and adds: "The dog looks as if he had been overfed for years"

Laurens Sa 3 birds rising arg (?)
Crest: two arms emb holding a chaplet
Motto: Optimum quod evenit
Bookplate —— Laurens, S. C.

Law Two hearts pierced by an arrow and surmounted by a crown
Seal David Law, N. Y., 1704. Not in Burke. Jeffries MSS. N. E. Reg. Jan. 1877, p. 62

Lawrence An eagle with 2 heads displayed. Impaling: A lion ramp
Tomb of Thomas Lawrence, mayor of Phila., d. 1754. Christ Church, Phila. Zieber's Heral., p. 38. Not as in Burke

Lawrence [Arg] a cross raguly [gu]. On a chief [of the second] a lion passant [or]. Impaling: [Sa] a chev bet 3 owls [arg] (Prescott)
Crest: a stag's head cabossed
Motto: Nil desperandum
In white over the fireplace in the long room (late) James Lawrence, Farmer's Row, Groton, Mass. Mr. Lawrence's mother was the daughter of Prescott, the historian Also on Hon. Abbott Lawrence's china now owned by John Lawrence of Groton. Used on notepaper of Miss Eleanora Sears, 1924

Lawrence Arg a cross raguly gu. On a chief of the second a lion pass guard or
Crest: a demi-turbot in pale gu the tail upwards
Motto: In cruce salus
Will of Thomas Lawrence (d. 1703). Also bookplate Charles E. Lawrence, I. Sharp Lawrence. Ashton Lawrence's notepaper, Long Isl., has lion sa not guard; the turbot az (?) A water color by C. Mattoni at the N. Y. G. & B. Soc. has no chief and for motto: Quaero invenio

Lawrence Arg a cross raguly gu. On a chief of the 2d a lion pass guard or
Crest: a stag's head sa antlered or

gorged with a ducal cor and charged with 4 plates
Motto: Nil admirari
Bookplate T. Bigelow Lawrence, Boston. That of Lawrence of Nantucket is charged with 7 plates

Lawrence Arg a cross raguly gu
Crest: a roebuck's head erased
Made of inlaid woods on the end of desk designed by Irving and Casson in 1913, given by churchmen of the Diocese of Mass. to Bishop Wm. Lawrence of Groton and Boston

Lawrence Erm 3 leopards' heads, 2 and 1 or
Crest: a leopard courant or
"By the name of Lawrence" and palm branches. By Coles? Framed water color. Painted for Asa Lawrence (1765–1826) of Groton, Mass. Lawrence Park, owner, Groton, Mass.

Lawrence Sa 2 chev arg
Crest: a griffin's head erased
Motto: Nullius in verba
Bookplate Charles Lawrence. Burke has gu not sa

Lawrence Quartered by Prescott

Lawson Arg a saltire az bet in chief 3 garbs or, in fess 2 estoiles of 6 points, and in base a boar's head erased. Impaling: Arg a fox ramp against a tree and ground vert
Crest: a boar's head erased
Bookplate Francis Lawson

Lawson A chev bet 3 martlets
Will of Rowl:nd Lawson probated in Lancaster, Va., 7 Sept. 1706. Wm. & Mary Quar., Jan. 1893, p. 119

Leach Erm on a chief dancetté gu 3 ducal cor or
Crest: a cubit arm holding a snake gu
Motto: Alla corona fidisimo
On notepaper of Mrs. Eliz. M. Rixford, East Highgate, N. Y.

Leach Erm on a chief indented gu 3 ducal cor [or]
Crest: from a ducal cor an arm couped ppr entwined by and holding a snake vert
Motto: Cavendo tutus
Bookplate John Leach. Callender, sculp. Same in colors framed in a lozenge, owned by Mrs. H. H. Edes, Cambridge, Mass. Also framed water color owned by Mrs. Edward M. Davis, Shirley, Mass., with motto: Virtute et valore

Leavenworth Arg a chev bet 3 leopards pass contourné, a crescent on the chev
Crest: a sinister armed arm emb holding a dagger
Bookplate Capt. Gideon Leavenworth, 1751-1816, of Huntington, Conn. R. Brunton, sc.. Bates's, Early Conn. Engr., p. 28

Leddel Gu on a bend arg 3 pierced mullets
Crest: a griffin's head erased
Motto: Labor omnia vincit
Bookplate I. Leddel. James Turner, sc.

Lee Arg a fess sa bet 3 crescents sa
Crest: from a ducal cor an eagle holding a bird's leg erased
Motto: Fide et constantia
Bookplate Thos. J. Lee, 1836

Lee Az on a fess double cotised [or] 3 leopards' faces [gu]
Crest: a lion passant
Bookplate Edward Lee

Lee Gu 3 antique crowns in pale or
Crest: a pascal lamb carrying the crusaders' flag of England
Bookplate Roger Lee

Lee Quart 1: Arg a fess bet 3 crescents sa; 2: Arg a fess bet 3 leopards' heads sa; 3: Arg on a fess azure bet 3 unicorns' heads erased sa 3 tulips arg (?) 4: Arg a lion ramp azure within a bordure azure charged with 5 fleurs-delis 2 in chief and 3 in base
Crest: out of a ducal cor an eagle on a tower holding a twig in its claws
Motto: Fide et constantia
Bookplate William Lee, M. D.

Lee [Gu] a fess chequy [or] and az bet 8 billets arg 4 in chief and 4 in base
Crest: a squirrel sejant [ppr] holding in his forepaws a [hazel?] branch [vert] fructed [or]
Engr. on a chalice from Hancock Lee, son of Richard Lee, 1711. Wycomico Church, Northumberland Co., Va. Old Sil. Am. Ch., p. 507.
Bookplate Lancelot Charles Lee has 10 billets, 4, 3, 2, 1 and a crescent for diff. The cup given to Queen's College, Oxford, 1658, by Col. Richard Lee's son John has the above shield, but no crest. The arms in wood from Cobbs Hall have a crescent in chief added (Lee of Va., p. 50)

Lee Quart 1 and 4: [Or?] a fess chequy [az?] bet 10 billets; 2 and 3: Arg within a tressure bet 9 crosses crosslet a mullet
Seal Richard Henry Lee. Chamberlain MSS. N. E. Reg., Apr. 1880, p. 184

Leeds See also Bozman

Leeke See also Benson

Leete Arg a fess [gu] bet 2 rolls of matches sa [kindled ppr?]
Crest: three tridents erect
Seal of Gov. Wm. Leete of Conn., d. 1683. Whitmore's Elem. of Heral., p. 65. Heral. Jour., vol. 2, p. 47; vol. 3, p. 177. The rolls resemble screw eyes in fess points to dexter

Lefferts Arg 2 bars sa each charged with a star of 6 points. Impaling: Az a stag's head erased
Crest: a stag's head erased
Motto: Nulla vestigia retrorsum
Bookplate Marshall Clifford Lefferts. E. D. French, sc., 1894

Leftwich Arg on a fess engr az 3 garbs or
Crest: an oak leaf
Motto: Vernon semper floret
Framed painting owned by Louis C. Arthur, Greenville, N. C.

Legg [Az] a buck's head cabossed [arg]
Crest: 5 ostrich feathers [az]? (Broken)
Tombstone in Marblehead of John Legg, Esq., who d. 1718 in 74th year. Also without crest on will of John Legg at Salem. Heral. Jour., vol. 1, pp. 107, 116

Leguard See Fairchild

Leigh Quart of 9: 1, 6, and 9: Arg a lion ramp [gu]; 2: Or 3 boars pass in palé sa (Beram); 3: Arg 3 lozenges gu conjoined in pale (Hall); 4: Quarterly arg and az. In the first quarter a lion pass [gu] a label of 5 points for diff. (Ponseyn?); 5: Quarterly gu and or, a label of 5 points arg for diff (Kennet?); 7: Arg a chev bet 3 lozenges gu (Flattesbury); 8: Arg a fret gu (Saundby?)
Crest: a lion ramp
Bookplate Egerton Leigh, royal attorney-gen. of S. C., married Miss Laurens

Leighton Quarterly per fess indented or and gu
Crest: a wyvern
Motto: Dread shame
From Londonderry, Ireland. (Pronounced Liton.) On notepaper of Leighton Shields, St. Louis. Also bookplate of George B. Leighton, Monadnock, N. H., engr. by S. L. Smith

Lello Impaled by Hopkins

Lemmon [Or] on a fess [gu] bet 3 dolphins embowed [sa] an annulet in the middle chief
Crest: a pelican in her piety
Jonathan Lemmon's tomb, No. 53. From Dorchester, Co. Dorset. Phipps Street Yard, Charlestown, Mass. Heral.

Jour., vol. 1, p. 48. Engr. on baptismal basin from Dr. Joseph Lemmon, 1773. First Church, Marblehead, Mass. York Co. Jail (Maine) has Lemmon shield with a crest: a lion's head erased or a framed water color, called Lyman

Lemmon Or on a fess gu bet 3 dolphins embowed sa an annulet. Impaling: Arg (?) a lion ramp sa in chains or (Phillips)
Crest: a pelican in her piety
Hatchment made of curled paper by Mary Lemmon in 1735. Wife of Joseph Lynde, daughter of Joseph and Elizabeth (Phillips) Lemmon of Charlestown. Owned 1923 by Misses Emma and Elizabeth Harris, Holyoke Pl., Cambridge

Lemmon [Or?] on a fess engrailed vert bet 3 dolphins embowed sa an annulet
Crest: a wolf's head erased
Seal used in 1707 by Joseph Lemmon, the immigrant. Heral. Jour., vol. 1, p. 48

Lemmon Impaled. *See* Dix

Lemon Purpure a fess bet 3 dolphins embowed or
Crest: a pelican in her piety
Motto: Virtutas et labor
Bookplate Edward Rivers Lemon, Wayside Inn, Sudbury, Mass.

Lenney Sa on a chev bet 3 boars' heads erased arg muzzled gu a cinquefoil of the first
Crest: a lion's gamb erased ppr
Said to be quartered on the bookplate of Buchanan of Md.

Lenny Quartered by Buchanan

Le Noble Gu 3 roses arg and in chief an estoile of five points
Seal of Henry Le Noble of So. Car.

Lenox Arg a saltire engr [gu] bet 4 roses of the last
Crest: a lion pass guard crowned
Motto: Auctor pretiosa facit
Bookplate (James) Lenox, N. Y.

Lenox Quart 1 and 4: Arg a saltire engr bet 4 roses gu; 2 and 3: Gu 3 salmon hauriant 2 and 1, each with a ring in its nose (Sprotty)
Motto: Auctor pretiosa facit
Bookplate —— Lenox, Phila. Sylvan City, 1883, p. 455

Lenthall Arg 2 bars sa each charged with 3 pierced mullets or
Crest: a coursing hound
Bookplate John Lenthall. Signed by Thackara. Perhaps Washington, architect

Leonard Or on a fess gu 3 fleurs-de-lis or
Crest: out of a ducal cor or a tiger's head arg
Framed water color from Delano estate, New Bedford. Sold at Libbie's, Feb. 29, 1916. Bookplate of Helen Vernera Drake, engr. by Spenceley, with motto: Memor et fidelis

Leonard [Or] on a fess [gu] 3 fleurs-de-lis of the field
Crest: out of a ducal cor or a tiger's head arg
Seal of W. A. Leonard, Bishop of Ohio, impales the above arms, the crest appearing as a charge on the shield. Zieber's Heral., p. 202

Leslie Quartered by Richardson

Leverett [Arg] a chev bet 3 leverets courant [sa]
Crest: a leveret of the field
Seal of Gov. John Leverett. Also on Prest. John Leverett's altar tomb. He d. 1724. The arms are on a circular disc of lead. Burying ground near Harvard Square, Cambridge, Mass.

Leverett Arg a chev bet 3 leverets courant sa
Essex Institute, Salem. On a portrait of Gov. John Leverett. A ring there also bears the above arms. Used also on an envelope of George V. Leverett, Boston

Leverett [Arg] a chev [bet 3 leverets sa]. Impaling: [Arg?] on a cross [gu 5 bells or] (Sedgwick?)
Crest: a skull
Gov. John Leverett married Sarah Sedgwick and is buried in King's Chapel, Boston in the tomb now marked "Martin Smith." Arms cut on the west face of the tomb in sandstone are nearly gone. The chevron and cross can be seen, and one bell in the honor point can be traced. — C. K. B. *See* Heral. Jour., vol. 1, p. 116

Leversedge Quartered by Lowell

Levy A crescent subverted within a bordure compony
Above the shield "VZ03"
Seal of Judge Moses Levy (pronounced Leevy) of Phila. (1756–1826), son of Sampson Levy. Owned by his great granddaughter, Mrs. Robert H. Bancroft of Boston. The Garter King at arms says these are the Lousana arms in Spain

Lewis Arg on a fess bet 3 hurts a plate
Crest: 3 arrows points down, 2 in saltire and one in pale
Motto:, Finem respice
Bookplate Kenneth and Mollie Lewis, Worcester, Mass.

Lewis   Quart 1 and 8: Arg a dragon's head and neck erased vert, holding in the mouth a bloody hand; 2: Gu 3 towers triple towered arg (Howell); 3: Arg 3 chevronels (not identified); 4: Arg 3 torteaux (not identified); 5: Arg 3 lozenges or a chief az (Fielding); 6: Vert a cross engrailed or (Warner); 7: Az 3 bowls arg out of each a boar's head or (Bowles)
   Crest: arg a dragon's head and neck erased vert, holding in the mou h a bloody hand
   Silver plate of Lewis family. Wm. & Mary Quar., Jan. 1894, p. 156

Lewis   [Sa?] a chev bet 3 trefoils slipped [or?]
   Crest: a griffin sejant [or?]
   Tombstone Jonathan Clark Lewis, d. 1781, Groton, Mass. Green's Epitaphs, p. 86

Lewis   Impaled by Gray

Lidget   Arg a fess wavy or bet 3 estoiles
   Crest: a bust couped at the shoulders affrontée
   Seal Col. Chas. Lidget, Boston, 1686. Jeffries MSS. N. E. Reg., Jan. 1877. On silver candlestick. *See* Buck's Old Plate, p. 120

Lightfoot   Barry of 6 or and gu on a bend sa, 3 escallops arg
   Tomb of Philip Lightfoot, Sandy Point, Charles City, Va. He married Alice, daughter of Henry Corbin. Impaled: "Arg, on a chief or 3 ravens ppr." Crozier's Va. Heral., p. 36.
   Bookplate Thomas Lightfoot has for crest: a griffin's head erased

Lillie   A fess bet 6 roundles
   Crest: a roundel (?)
   On mortgage of Samuel and wife, Mehitable Lillie, to Abigail Arnold, July, 1708. Suffolk (Mass.) Court files No. 7467. Seen by C. K. B. *See also* N. E. H. G. Reg., Jan. 1877, p. 62

Lincoln   Gu a lion ramp or
   Crest: a demi-lion of the field crowned or langued gu issuing from a ducal cor
   Framed water color. Mrs. E. L. Lincoln, Brookline, Mass.

Lindsay   Quart 1 and 4: Gu a fess chequy arg and az; 2 and 3: Or a lion ramp gu, the shield debruised of a ribbon in bend sa over all
   Crest: a cubit arm in armor in pale holding in the hand a sword erect arg on the point a pair of balances of the last
   Motto: Recta sed ardua
   Broken tombstone of Rev. David Lindsay of Yeocomico, Northumberland Co., Va. He d. 3 Apr. 1667. Used

also by William Lindsay of Boston on automobile. Crozier's Va. Heral., p. 43

Lindsley   Or a lion ramp sa bet 8 crosses pattée fitchée sa
   Crest: an armed arm holding a cutlass ppr
   Bookplate Geo. Leonard Lindsley, engr. by A. W. Macdonald, 1905

Lindstedt   Arg a cross humettée. Impaling: Per fess sa and or. In base an anchor
   Crest: from a ducal cor a demi-hawk rising
   Motto: Vincit qui partitur
   Bookplate Frederick W. Lindstedt

Linzee   [Gu] a fess chequy [arg and az] and in chief 3 mullets, in base a hunting horn, all [arg]
   On tablet of crossed swords of Col. Wm. Prescott and Capt. John Linzee, R. N., of the *Falcon* at Bunker Hill Battle. Mass. Hist. Soc.

Linzee   Gu a fess chequy arg and az bet in chief 3 mullets and in base a hunting horn arg
   Crest: an ostrich with a key in the bill
   Motto: Live but (without) dread
   Seal John Wm. Linzee, Boston. "The Linzee Family (1917), vol. 2, p. 664

Lippincott   Per fess embat gu and sa 3 talbots trip arg
   Crest: out of a mural crown gu 5 ostrich feathers alternately arg and az
   Motto: Secundis dubiisque rectus
   Notepaper Walter H. Lippincott, Wynnewood, Penn.

Lisle   Erminois on a chief az 3 lions ramp or. Impaling: Az a fess engr erm bet 3 eagles displ (Margaret?)
   Crest: a lion ramp
   Motto: Legibus vivo
   Bookplate Henry Maurice Lisle, atty.-at-law, Hingham, Mass.

Lister   [Az] on a cross fleury arg [5 torteaux each charged with a mullet or]
   Crest: a stag's head erased [or]
   Wax seal on the will of Edmund Lister, 1709, of Lancaster Co., Va. Part of the cross remains. Wm. & Mary Quar., Jan. 1893, p. 119

Lister   Quartered by Lloyd

Lithgow   Quart 1 and 4: Arg in base a demi-otter ramp rising from waves ppr. In chief 2 roses gu; 2 and 3: Arg a heart crowned gu. On a chief az 2 mullets of the first (Douglas)
   Crests: a palm branch vert (Lithgow); a heart crowned gu bet 2 wings erect (Douglas)

Mottoes: Robori prudentia praestat. Forward
Boókplate R. A. Douglas-Lithgow, Boston Antiquary

Little Arg a saltire engr sa
Motto: Μὴ Φοβοῦ μόνον πίστευε
Bookplate Dr. Geo. T. Little, Libn. Bowdoin College, Brunswick, Me.

Little Sa a cross arg
Painting owned by Luther Little of Sea View, Mass., 1919, a desc. of Thomas Little of Plymouth, 1630. "By the name of Little. *See* "Avery, Fairchild & Park Families," 1919, p. 128

Littlefield Vert on a chev arg bet 3 garbs or as many heads ppr with hair gu
Crest: a bird arg holding an ear of wheat
J. C. Littlefield, tailor, Beacon St., Boston. Painted on his door

Littlejohn Quartered by Adam

Livermore Paly — and — a fess arg bet 3 boars' heads
Crest: leaves issuing from a mural crown (?)
Bookplate John Walton Livermore, engr. by French. Not as in Burke

Livingston Quart 1 and 4: Arg 3 gillyflowers [gu] within a tressure flory counter flory [vert] 2 quart 1 and 4: Gu on a chev arg a rose of the field bet 2 lions passant of the same (Hepburn); 2 and 3: Az 3 martlets or 3 sa a bend bet 6 billets [or] (Callender)
Crest: a ship of 3 masts, top sails set
Motto: Spero meliora
Bookplate Robt. R. Livingston, Esq., of Clermont; Edward Livingston, Maturin Livingston (Maverick sc.); Willm Smith Livingston (Maverick, sc.); Brockholst Livingston, Esq.; William Livingstone of the Middle Temple with motto: Aut mors, aut vita decora; Peter R. Livingston, N. Hurd, sc., and motto: Prestat opes sapiantia; Robert L. Livingston, with spero meliora and the demi-Hercules crest

Livingston Quart 1 and 4: Arg 3 gillyflowers gu within a double tressure flory counter flory vert; 2 and 3: Sa a bend bet 6 billets or (Callender)
Crest: a demi-Hercules wreathed about the head and middle; in his dexter hand a club in bend sinister in the sinister a snake about the arm ppr
Motto: Si je puis
Bookplate John Henry Livinston, Clermont, Tivoli-on-Hudson. Mr. Livingston writes 12 May, 1920: All the old bookplates of the Livingston family are wrong. They all have the Hepburn arms in the 2d quartering. Though there were several marriages between the Livingstons and the Hepburns none of the latter were "Heiresses in their own right." Robert, 1st Lord of the Manor, changed his crest to a "ship in distress with the motto: "Spero meliora," due to a shipwreck; another change was made by converting the ship in distress to a "ship in full sail."

Livingston Quart 1 and 4: Arg 3 gillyflowers [gu] within an orle (properly a tressure flory counter flory) [vert]; 2 quarter quartered 1 and 4 gu a chev arg (incomplete for Hepburn); 2 and 3: [Az] 3 crescents [arg]; 3: [Sa] a bend bet 6 billets or for callendar
Crest: a demi-Hercules, wreathed about the head and middle; in his dexter hand a club in bend; in the sinister a snake nowed, all proper. It is said that the crescents whould be martlets or.
Carved on stone, Capitol, Albany, N. Y. Howell begins "arg 3 lamps," etc. Zieber's Heral., p. 61
Motto: Si je puis
The bookplate of Henry W. Livingston has Hepburn with the lions but no roses, and the martlets instead of crescents, otherwise as above. The Livingston arms are shown in a window of the Commons Room of the Graduate College of Princeton, N. J.

Livius Vert bet 3 pomegranites slipped and leaved ppr on a chev in point embowed a 2d chev gu
Crest: a unicorn's horn erect bet 2 ostrich feathers
Motto: Colendo crescent
Bookplate George Livius, and Barham John Livius. Others with some changes and "Confido" as a motto

Llewellyn Quart gu and or 4 lions pass guard counterchanged
Crest: from a ducal cor 3 feathers
Motto: Symru am byth
Bookplate Wm. David Llewellyn, engr. by A. W. Macdonald

Lloyd Az a lion ramp or
Crest: a demi-lion ramp guard or supporting in the paws an arrow in pale arg
Engr. on silver plate; also on the tomb of Philemon Lloyd of Wye, Md., who d. 22 June, 1685 (but contourné); and Edward Lloyd. The tomb of James Lloyd (d. 1738) has for crest a lion couchant guardant (unusual). *See* Hist. Graves of Md., p. 212; Md. Hist. Mag., Mch. 1922

Lloyd Gu a lion ramp or within a bordure of the last
Crests: A: a bird rising or; B: a pelican or feeding her young ppr

Mottoes: A: I live and die for those I love; B: Please God I live, I'll go On seal attached to will of James Lloyd dated 1684, April 10. Heral. Jour., vol. 2, p. 88. Vermont's Amer. Heral., pp. 135, 136, 171

Lloyd Gu a lion ramp sa (sanguine?) within a bordure or
Crest: a pelican in her piety
Bookplate James Lloyd. Henry Lloyd of Boston, brother of Dr. James, from Queen's Village Manor, Nassau Island, N. Y., used a lion rampant on a seal. — E. A. Jones

Lloyd [Or] 3 lions couchant in pale sa
Crest: a cubit arm erect garnished [or] holding a lizard vert
Bookplate Gamaliel Lloyd

Lloyd Quart 1 and 4: Erm a saltire gu; 2 and 3: Erm on a fess sa 3 mullets or (Lister)
Crest: a boar passant
Motto: Salus et decus
Bookplate Robert James Lloyd

Lloyd Sa 3 roses arg
Crest: a rose twig and 2 wings erect
Motto: Vernon semper viret
Notepaper Stacy B. Lloyd, Bryn Mawr, Penn.

Lloyd Impaled by Bennett

Lloyd See also Neale

Lockwood Arg a fess sa bet 3 martlets az
Crest: on a stump a martlet az
Motto: Tutus in undis
Framed water color owned by Mrs. Alfred Arnold, St. Mark's Sq., Phila. Seen 30 Mch., 1924, by S. K. Bolton

Lockwood Arg a fess bet 3 martlets sa
Bookplate Louise Benedict Lockwood. R. D. W. S. del. Also Hilda Le Grand Lockwood. W. S., 1901

Lodge [Az] a lion ramp arg
Crest: a demi-lion ramp couped sa
Bookplate Abraham Lodge

Lodge Az a lion ramp arg within a bordure arg (?) charged with 8 fleurs-de-lis
Crest: a demi-lion couped
Motto: Spero infestis metuo secundis
Bookplate Henry Cabot Lodge, U. S. Senator from Mass., d. 1924

Logan Or a lion pass suspended by a ring from the points of 3 piles gu in chief
Engr. on old silver owned by A. Sydney Logan of Phila. Zieber's Heral., p. 69. The Loganian Library's bookplate has no ring, piles sa and for crest a stag's head erased gorged and with a cable. Sylvan City, 1883, p.

445, 455. Engr. by Joseph Richardson on sauce-boats with initials S[arah] L[ogan], H[annah] L[ogan] S[mith], E. F. W., and S. G. F., the first two daughters of Gov. James Logan of Stenton, 1674–1751. Met. Mus. of Art, N. Y.

Logan Quartered by Stewart

Lombard "He beareth arg a chevron bet 3 broadswords erect az . . . " "in anno 1603"
"By the name of Lombard," and palm branches. By Coles? Drawn in water color by Mrs. Carleton Hunneman from the original owned by Forham Rogers, Longwood, Mass. Lombards of Truro, Mass.

Lombard Per pale the dexter or a spread eagle sa, the sinister fusily or and sa
Crest: a lion ramp ppr
Motto: Nec opprimere nec opprimi
Bookplate [Herbert Edwin] Lombard, a clergyman of Worcester, Mass. Also his plate engr. by E. D. French, with his church, home, etc. Arms of the County Cork family

Long A lion ramp
Crest: a lion's head
Tomb at Blissland, New Kent, Va., of Mr. John Long of Ramsgate, in the County of Kent, in Great Britain, Commander of the ship "John and Mary," who departed this life 24 July, 1736, aged 25 years. Crozier's Va. Heral., p. 38

Long Sa a lion pass arg. On a chief arg 3 crosses crosslet sa
Crest: from a ducal cor a lion's head [arg] guttée de sang
Bookplate Samuel Long. Charles Long's has a lion contourné

Long See also Moore

Longbottom 1. Per pale gu and az on a chev engr or bet 3 hunting horns a well (?)
Crest: from a boar's head couped a branch issuing
Motto: Labor omnia vincit
2. Az a lamb pendent from a chief sa charged with 3 mullets arg (Town of Leeds)
Crest: an owl
Supporters: two crowned owls guardant
Motto: Pro rege et lege
Bookplate Abram P. Longbottom

Longley Arg a cockatrice sa beaked or
Used by desc. of Wm. Longley of Groton, Mass. See Chandler's Hist. of Shirley, Mass.

Longley Paly of 12 arg and vert per fess counterchanged
Crest: An arm couped at the shoulder resting on the elbow, holding a staff in pale enfiled with a savage's face couped ppr
Framed water color owned by Arthur Longley, Boston

Loomis Arg bet 2 pales 3 fleurs-de-lis a chief az
Crest: on a chapeau gu (?) turned up erm a pelican wounding herself
Motto: Ne cede malis
Bookplate C. B. Loomis, writer

Loomis Or 3 holly leaves points to sinister gu
Crest: a vested hand holding a knife (?)
Motto: Persevera et vince
Bookplate Thomas H. Loomis, Washington, D. C. D. M. S., sc.

Lopez (Lopeaus) Az a wolf's head erased arg
Crest: a lion's head erased or
Embroidery on satin, owned 1923 by Soc. Pres. of N. E. Antiq. Rev. Dr. Mather's daughter Mary married Mr. Blackwell. Their daughter Catherine married John Lopez and had Samuel, John, Andrew, Catherine, and Sarah

Lord Arg on a fess gu bet 3 cinquefoils az a hind pass bet 2 pheons or
Crest: a demi-bird with wings expanded sa. On its head 2 small horns or. The dexter wing gu lined arg. The sinister wing arg lined gu
Seal on will of widow of Thomas Lord, who came 1635. Vermont's Amer. Heral., pp. 22, 171

Loring Quarterly arg and gu. Over all a bend
Engr sa crest: a panache of feathers. Inscription: "Mons[eigneur]: Neell: Loryng: p[ri]m[us]: fund [ato:um]" of the Order of the Garter. Ex libris Augustus Peabody Loring, Jr., Boston

Loring Quarterly arg and gu
Over all a bend engr sa. Impaling: Az a chev or bet 3 towers each charged with a cross humettée (Renton)
Crest: a cubit arm holding a millrind
Motto: Faire sans dire
Bookplate J. Q. Loring, Boston. T. L. Sprague, Brookline, Mass., has 1924 a framed water color done apparently by Coles (palm branches, Amer. flags, etc.) with crest of 5 ostrich plumes or (?) from a bowl arg (?). Seen by Dr. H. Bowditch

Loring Quarterly arg and gu. Over all a bend engrailed sa. Impaling: Az a chev or bet 3 towers arg (Renton)
Lozenge on notepaper of Miss Abby Rand Loring, Auburndale, Mass.

Loring *See also* Winsor

Lorn Quartered by Campbell

Lorne Quartered by McEvers

Lotbiniere Per fess az and arg. In chief 2 birds on a ragged staff or. In base 3 prongs of a cross flory (?), each erect and vert (?)
Motto: Fors et virtus
Bookplate M. le Marquis de Lotbiniere, N. Y.

Lothrop A gyronny of 8 sa and gu. Over all an eagle displ arg
Crest: a cock sa
Framed water color, small. "By the name of Lothrop"

Lothrop Gryonny of 8 sa and gu. Over all an eagle displ
Crest: a cock
Bookplate Henry Wood Lothrop

Lott Vert 2 horses ramp combatant arg
Crest: a horse's head erased arg
Motto: Draagd en verdraagd
Bookplate Abraham Lott, treas. N. Y. Prov. Cong., 1776. Not in Burke

Low *See also* Tylden

Lowell Quart 1 and 4: Sa a hand couped at the wrist grasping 3 darts points down, one in pale and 2 in saltire arg on a chief invected az a crescent arg; 2 and 3: Az in each quarter an escallop arg (Jackson)
Mottoes: Deo dirigente crescendum est. Occasionem cognosce
Bookplate John Lowell, Jr., 1799–1836, founder Lowell Institute, Boston

Lowell Sa a hand couped at the wrist grasping 3 darts points down, one in pale and 2 in saltire arg
Crest: a stag's head cabossed or. Bet. the horns a pheon [az?]
Motto: Occasionem cognosce
Wall tablet to John Lowell, 1769–1840. King's Chapel, Boston. South Aisle. John Lowell, b. Newburyport, 1743, had the same arms and motto, engraved by N. Hurd, and for crest a covered cup. The field as engraved might be considered to be or. D. O. S. Lowell, headmaster Roxbury Latin School, has the above arms and crest on his bookplate with motto in Esperanto: Ne juǧulibron je la kovrilo (Do not judge a book by its cover)

Lowell Quart 1 and 4: Sa a hand couped at the wrist grasping 3 darts, one in pale, and 2 in saltire arg; 2 and 3: Sa a chev or bet 3 dolphins emb arg each with a ball in its mouth (Leversedge)
Crest: A: a stag's head cabossed or. Bet the horns a pheon az
Motto: Occasionem cognosce

Bookplate John Lowell, the author. Bookplate John Amory Lowell; Robert Traill Spence Lowell. Engr. on loving cup owned by Mrs. Edward Rantoul. Also on tea kettle by Jacob Hurd owned by Mrs. Stanley Cunningham. Vermont's Amer. Heral., pp. 20, 172

Lowndes Arg fretty [az] on a canton [gu] a lion's head erased [or]
Crest: a lion's head erased [or]
Motto: Per ardua
Bookplate Arthur Lowndes. On the same bookplate are the Waller arms: [Sa] 3 walnut leaves [or] bet 2 bendlets arg. Crest: on a mount [vert] a walnut tree ppr on the sin side a shield pendent charged with the arms of France. Below, the word Azincourt (six)

Lucas Quartered by Horry

Luckin [Sa] a fess indented bet 2 leopards' faces [or]
Crest: a demi-griffin or issuing out of a tower [paly of six of the last and sa]
Tomb of Alice Luckin, wife of Col. John Page of York Co. in Bruton churchyard, Williamsburg, Va. She d. 22 June, 1698, aged 73. Seen by L. Park, 1922

Ludlow Arg a chev sa bet 3 foxes' heads erased sa
Crest: a lion ramp sa
Motto: Fide sed cui vide
Bookplate Cary Ludlow. W. Smith, sc. See Wm. & Mary Quar., Apr. 1894, p. 267. Roger Ludlow's motto was: Omne solum Forti Patria. The late James D. Ludlow of N. Y. had a coat from Eng. abt. 1875

Ludlow Arg a chev sa bet 3 foxes' heads erased sa. On an inscutcheon gu 3 battle axes arg
Crest: a lion ramp sa
Motto: Nec temere nec timide
Bookplate Abraham Ludlow

Ludwell Gu on a bend arg bet 2 towers or 3 eagles displ sa
Motto: I pensieri stretti ed il viso sciolto
Bookplate dated 1737 of Philip Ludwell of Green Spring in Va. Also used on seal. Wm. & Mary Quar., Oct. 1893, p. 79, Jan. 1894, p. 159. Heral. Jour., vol. 3, p. 95. Thomas Ludwell, Sec. of Va., used: On a bend bet 2 leopards' faces 3 eagles displayed

Lufkin Sa on a chev or bet 3 eagles displ 3 mullets gu (?)
Framed painting at Pierce's Antique Shop, Charles St., Boston, 1924

Lukens Per fess az and arg a cock's head erased counterchanged
Motto: In Domino confido
Bookplate James Lukens. "J. T. fecit" (James Turner?) Penn?

Lunsford Quart 1: Az a chev bet 3 boars' heads couped or; 2: Arg 3 chev gu, over all a label of 3 points purp (Barrington); 3: Or a carbuncle gu (Mandeville); 4: Arg 3 acorns vert fructed gu (Totham)
Crest: upon a wreath a boar's head or couped gu
On a letter of Sir Thomas Lunsford, later of Va., dated 1644. Gent. Mag., July, 1636, p. 34

Lunt Per chev or and gu 3 lions pass counterchanged
Crest: an eagle or displayed
"By the name of Lunt" and palm branches. By Coles? Framed water color, owned by Micajah Lunt, Newburyport, Mass., now owned by Mrs. G. A. Anderson, Lunenburg, Mass.

Lyde Or on a fess bet 2 chev all sa 3 cinquefoils arg
On silver mug, cir. 1790, owned by Miss Sarah E. Eustis, Brookline, Mass.

Lyde See also Byfield

Lydig Gu a chev arg bet 3 sickles or
Crest: two wings spread each charged with a chev bet 3 sickles as on the shield
Bookplate Philip Mesier Lydig, 1903, but done by Spenceley, 1906

Lydius Vert 3 bars within a bordure arg
Crest: two wings erect
Engr. on tankard owned by Francis H. Bigelow, Cambridge, made by Koenraet Ten Eyck (1678–1753), marked IH ∴ G. once owned by Johannes Henricus and Genevieve Lydius (he bp. 1704) of Albany, N. Y. Perhaps careless engr. for Lidius (in Re tstap-Rolland) "or 5 bars gu." If 5 bars then the bordure on each side seems unexplained

Lyman Arg on a fess gu 3 annulets or
Crest: a pelican in her piety
Motto: Esse quam videri
Bookplate C. Frederic Lyman, Boston. Bookplate (lozenge) Annie Lyman, engr. by French A framed water color at York Co. Jail, Maine, has Lemmon arms

Lyman Quart 1 and 4: Per chev gu and arg. In base an annulet gu; 2: Gu a chev arg bet 3 lambs trippant; 3: Quarterly erm and gu a cross arg
Crest: a demi-bull ramp couped
Motto: Quod verum tutum
Bookplate Fredk. W. Lyman; Mary Lyman Kobbé, author

Lynch Az a chev bet 3 trefoils slipped or. On a chief arg 3 roses gu [seeded and barbed vert] a crescent sa for diff, a canton charged with an embattled wall or
    Crest: a wolf coward pass on 2 flags in saltire on a ducal cor
    Motto: Semper fidelis
    Bookplate [Thomas] Lynch, father of signer of Decl. of Indep.

Lynde Gu on a chief or 3 crosses potent gu
    Crest: a demi-leopard holding in the paws a cross potent or
    Tomb of Benjamin Lynde, who d. 1744, aged 79, Salem, Mass. Heral. Jour., vol. 2, p. 29. A framed water color at the N. E. Hist. Gen. Soc., Boston, has a demi-griffin, and motto: Virtute decet nos

Lynde Sa a bend arg bet in chief a mailed arm emb holding a sword and in base 3 fleurs-de-lis in bend
    Crest: a closed helmet
    Motto: Pour le roi et la patrie
    Bookplate Louis F. Lynde, Phila. Not as in Burke

Lynde Quart of 6: 1: Gu on a chief or 3 crosses potent gu; 2: Gu 3 lions'

gambs erased arg (Newdigate) 3: Az a fleur-de-lis arg (Digby); 4: Arg on a bend double cotised sa 3 eagles displayed arg (Browne); 5: Arg fretty gu a chief az (Curwen); 6: Per chev embatt sa and or 3 panthers' faces erased counterchanged (Smith of Buckenham, Norfolk)
    Painting of escutcheon for Benjamin Lynde, Jr., of Salem, Mass., by Thomas Johnston, dated 1740. Whitmore's Elem. of Her., p. 71

Lynde Quartered by Minshull, Oliver, and Walter

Lyon Arg a lion ramp [az] within a double tressure flory counter-flory gu
    Crest: a hand holding the royal thistle ppr
    Motto: In te Domine speravi
    "Based on the arms of Lyon of Glavis"
    Bookplate Frederick Denison Lyon. J. W. S., sc., 1895

Lyon Az on a fess or bet 3 plates, each charged with a griffin's head erased sa a lion passant bet 2 cinquefoils gu
    Crest: a lion's head erased
    Motto: In te Domine speravi
    Bookplate Heber C. Lyon

M

Macartey Or a buck trippant gu
    Crest: a tree and sword in saltire
    Motto: Pro patria semper
    Bookplate Macartey of Va.? No name given. Owned by W. E. Baillie of Conn.

Mack *See also* McKean

Mackenan Quartered by Haig

Mackey Arg a pine tree on a mount vert, over all a sword bendways piercing a crown, all ppr (McGregor arms)
    Crest: a naked cubit arm holding a sword, enfiled with 3 crowns all ppr
    Motto: My might makes my right
    Bookplate Albert J. Mackey, M. D., Charleston, S. C.

Mackarty Arg a buck trippant [gu?]
    Crest: an arm erect grasping a sword impaling a lizard
    Seal of Thaddeus Mackarty, Boston, d. 1705. Jeffries MSS. N. E. Reg., Jan. 1877, p. 62

MacLeod Quart 1: Or a mountain az inflamed ppr; 2: Gu the 3 legs of the Isle of Man, armed ppr, conjoined in the center at the upper end of the thigh, flexed in triangle, the spurs or; 3: Or a galley, sails furled, pennons flying sa;

4: Gu a lion ramp arg. En surtout an inescutcheon party per pale gu and sa a fess bet 3 fleurs-de-lis or
    Crests: A: the sun in splendor; B: a demi-raven sa issuing from a ducal coronet or
    Mottoes: A: Luceo, non uro; B: Quocunque jaceris, stabit
    On the tomb of Malcolm Macleod of Rasay, buried near Bennington, Vt., in 1777. Vermont's Amer. Heral. [1886], pp. 132, 176

Macleod Az a triple towered castle, gate and windows gu
    Crest: a bull's head cabossed
    Mottoes: Hold fast; Murus aheneus
    Ex libris Eldon Macleod, brother of the designer, Miss Macleod

Macomber Arg [az?] in chief 3 dexter hands couped fessways each holding n bunch of arrows, in base a royal crown [or]; all within a bordure gyronny of eight or and sa
    Crest: a boar's head couped pierced by an arrow
    Motto: His nitimur et munitur
    Bookplate Frank Gair Macomber, Boston. Given by Burke under Maconochie

Maconochie *See also* Macomber

Macpherson Arg a lymphad. On a chief or a hand grasping a dagger and a cross crosslet fitchée
Crest: a cat sejant
Motto: Touch not the cat but a glove
Bookplate Margaret Jean Macpherson, by E. H. Garrett, 1918

MacWilliams Per bend arg and gu 3 roses in bend counterchanged
Crest: a fish-weir, or turnstile?
Motto: Recuperatus
Painted coat in oval frame, period of 1780–1800. Owned by John B. Lightfoot, Richmond, Va. Seen by L. Park, 1922

Macy Quart gu and or, 1 and 4 charged with a fleur-de-lis
Crest: a lion's head erased
Bookplate Valentine Everit and Edith Carpenter Macy, engr. by French. Not as in Burke

Magill Vert 3 martlets az
Crest: a phoenix rising from flames
Motto: Perît ut vivat
Bookplate John Magill, Md.

Malbone Or 2 bends company gu and arg
Crest: a lion's head crased gorged with 2 collars company gu and arg
Seal, New York

Mallory Erm a chev arg bet 3 trefoils slipped arg within a bordure engr sa
Crest: a nag's head erased sa
Arms engr. on a teapot at the Museum of Fine Arts, Boston

Mandeville Quartered by Lunsford

Margaret See Lisle

Manigault Az 3 falcons 2 and 1 [or] jessed and belled and hooded (?), in chief a cresc arg for diff
Crest: a demi-savage sa with 5 ostrich feathers on his head a skin about his shoulders, a bow and quiver of arrows
Motto: Perspicere quam ulcisci
Bookplate Charles I. Manigault. S. Clayton, sct. The bookplate of Peter Manigault of South Carolina, by Yates, lacks the crest and crescent

Mann Per fess embat counter-embat arg and [az] 3 goats pass counterchanged attired or
On the tomb at Timber Neck, Gloucester County, Va., of Mary Mann, who d. 18 Mar., 1703–4. Crozier's Va. Heral., 1908, p. 50. Wm. & Mary Quar., Apr. 1894, p. 266

Mann Sa a fess embat counter-embat bet 3 goats statant contourné. Impaling: Arg on a fess cotised gu 3 cocks

Crest: out of a mural crown a demi-dragon sa
Bookplate Roland William Mann, by E. H. Garrett of Boston

Manning [Gu] a cross flory bet 4 trefoils slipped or
Crest: an eagle's head [sa] bet 2 ostrich feathers arg issuing from a ducal cor [or]
Motto: Per ardua stabilis
Notepaper Mrs. W. S. Manning, Jacksonville, Fla.

Manning Quart az and gu. Over all a cross flory arg bet 4 trefoils slipped or
Crest: from a ducal cor an eagle's head sa bet 2 ostrich feathers arg
Bookplate Wm. Manning, Jr. Va.?

Manning Impaled by Vaughan

Manson Per chev arg and gu 3 cresc in chief gu
Crest: a garb or on a chapeau
Motto: Meae memor originis·
Bookplate A. S. Manson, Boston

March Sa a fess componée or and gu bet 3 lions' heads couped 2 and 1, and 3 crosses crosslet slipped 1 and 2 or
Crest: an arm with a coat bendy wavy sinister or and gu holding a rose gu leaved vert over it a goldfinch volant
Motto: Fortis est veritas
Bookplate Charles March, lawyer, Charleston, S. C. Also photo of tapestry in March house at Greenland, N. H.

Marchant Az a chev or bet 3 birds guardant
Crest: from a ducal cor a bird's claw couped
Motto: Patria cara, carior libertas
Bookplate Henry Marchant, attorney-gen. R. I., 1770. N. H., sc. Grave Sarah Marchant Hastings, 1821–84, Mt. Auburn, Mass. The birds are owls

Marion Arg 3 fleurs-de-lis or
Shield in window at Mrs. C. H. Joy's, 86 Marlboro St., Boston, for the Marion family of Salem

Markham Az on a chief or a demi-lion ramp issuant [gu]
Bookplate Thomas Markham, Va.? Harmar, sc., London, 1780

Markham See also Whitebread

Markoe Gu a lion ramp [arg]
Crest: a demi-lion ramp [gu]
Motto: Spem et speravi
Bookplate —— Markoe, Baltimore and Phila.

Marshall [Az?] On a chief or 3 pales gu (Keith arms)
　Crest: a stag's head arg (or?)
　Motto: Ex candore decus
　Bookplate Chief Justice John Marshall, 1755–1835, the grandson of Rev. James Keith

Marshall Quart 1 and 4: Gu 2 bars arg bet 2 flaunches [erm] each charged with a cross crosslet [gu]; 2 and 3: Or a heron sa. On a chief gu 3 plates (Earnshaw). Impaling: Az a wolf's head (?) couped. On a chief arg a shuttle (?) bet 2 bees
　Crest: an armed knight holding a cross crosslet slipped or
　Motto: Utilem pete finem
　Bookplate [Charles H.] Marshall, N. Y. Marshall of Ardwick, Co. Lanc. has 3 annulets or on a chief sa in place of 3 plates

Marston Az a chev embat arg bet 3 crowned lions' heads erased or
　Bookplate John Marston. N. Hurd, sc. Not as in Burke

Marston Az a chev embat bet 3 crowned lions' heads erased or
　Crest: a lion's head erased per chev az and or crowned and langued gu
　Water color by Marjorie Proctor, Lingham, Littleton, Mass., from a drawing in the David Jeffries MSS. Marston of Hertford, 1639

Martin Arg 2 bars gu
　Crest: a star of 6 points gu
　Motto: Sans tache
　Water color, Martin of Providence, R. I., by Mrs. Arnold Talbot

Martin A chev bet 2 fleurs-de-lis. In chief a cresc
　Crest: a bird rising
　Seal of Patrick Martin, Charlestown, S. C., 1711. Jeffries MSS. N. E. Reg., Jan. 1877, p. 63

Martin Arg a chev bet 3 mascles sa within a bordure sa. The arms of Ulster in chief
　Crest: a martlet
　Motto: Initium sapientiae est timor dei
　Bookplate Luther Martin. Also Thomas Martin but for crest a fox pointing

Martin Arg a cresc bet 3 boars' heads couped gu (Hogg?)
　Crest: from a ducal cor a boar's head of the field
　Bookplate Richard Martin, N. Y.

Martin Arg 3 lions ramp
　Crest: an estoile of 6 points
　Bookplate Wm. Bond Martin

Martin Gu a chev bet 3 cresc arg
　Crest: a dexter hand grasping a falchion
　Motto: Pugna pro patria liberta
　Bookplate Hon. Josiah Martin of Antiqua, M. of Council of New York, 1759–62, and d. at Rockaway, Long Island, 1778. Oliver's West Ind. bookplates, No. 77

Martin Gu a chev bet 3 cresc arg. In chief a mullet arg charged with a label
　Crest: a cubit arm with cutlass
　Motto: Pio patria
　Bookplate William Martin, b. London, 1733, d. Portland, Maine, 1814. Trustee Bowdoin College

Martin [Gu] a chev bet 3 cresc arg
　Arms of Col. John Martin of Caroline County, engr. on a silver pint cup, and advertised by him as "stolen" in the Va. Gazette of 20 Nov., 1738. Wm. & Mary Quar., July, 1893, p. 26. Crozier's Va. Heral., 1908

Martin Paly of 6 or and az a martlet in chief for diff. On a chief [gu?] 3 martlets [or]
　Bookplate William Martin

Martyn [Arg] 2 bars [gu]
　Crest: an estoile of 8 [properly 16?] points [gu]. See Martyn in the Visitation of Devon
　Broken stone in Copp's Hill Yard, Boston. The "silver seal" mentioned in Michael Martin's will has for crest a bird. Heral. Jour., vol. 2, pp. 81 and 7

Martyn Arg two bars wavy gu
　Crest: an estoile of 7 points supported from the wreath
　Engr. on a tankard from Sarah, widow of Edward Martyn of Boston, 1724. North Parish, North Andover, Mass. Jones's Am. Ch. Sil., p. 344

Mascarène [Arg] a lion ramp [gu]. On a chief [az] 3 mullets pierced [or]
　Crest: a mullet pierced [or]
　Motto: Non sola mortali luce gradior
　Jean Paul Mascarène, d. in Boston, 1760. Flat stone broken. Granary Burying Ground, Tremont St. side, Boston. Also on silver tray on legs, owned by the Misses Loring, 37 Mt. Vernon St., Boston. Also on silver teapot by Coney, owned by Judge Clearwater. No crest. Perhaps mullets not pierced. Amer. Sil., by C. L. Avery, 1920, p. 40. Also on silver mug owned by Ellery Sedgwick, Boston. Chief az. No motto

Mason Arg on a chev engr gu 3 crosses pattée arg (Peck arms)
　Seal of John Mason (1670), dep. gov. of Conn. Seal on Doc. 1634 of John Mason in Mass. Archives, vol. 30, p. 31

Mason Or a lion with 2 heads ramp az
Crest: a mermaid with comb and glass ppr
Motto: Listo
Bookplate T. B. M. Mason

Mason Per fess embat az and arg on the embattlement a dove, wings expanded arg, beaked and legged gu, in base 3 fleurs-de-lis of the last 2 and 1
Crest: a talbot pass reguard arg, eared sa, hold in the mouth a hart's horn or
Motto: Pro Republica Semper
Col. George Mason of "Gunston" about 1784 sent to London to have arms engraved on the Mason silver quartered with Thompson of Yorkshire. Wm. & Mary Quar., Jan. 1893, p. 117. Crozier's Va. Heral., 1908, p. 42

Mason Per pale or and sa 3 stags' heads counterchanged
Crest: a stag's head erased sa gorged with a ducal cor
Motto: Pro rege, lege et grege
Bookplate William Mason

Mason Per pale arg and sa a chev bet 3 mason's squares counterchanged
Crest: a stag's head erased sa armed and ducally gorged or
Motto: Demeure par la verité
Bookplate Daniel Gregory Mason, Henry Lowell Mason. They were Boston composers

Mason Quartered by Tufton

Masterton Gu a unicorn pass arg
Crest: a unicorn's head erased
Motto: Cogi posse negat
Bookplate Peter Masterton. Maverick, sculpt. Arms of Musterton

Mather Erm on a fess wavy az 3 lions ramp
Crest: lion sejant or on a trunk of a tree raguly (in place of a wreath) vert
Motto: Sunt Fortea notro Pectora
Mather of Salop. Framed painting. Amer. Antiq. Soc., Worcester. A bookplate with the above arms, designer unknown, has for motto: Virtus vera nobilitas est. The shield and crest appear on K. B. Murdock's Portraits of Increase Mather

Matthews Or a lion ramp sa
Crest: on a mount [vert] a moorcock [ppr]
Motto: Afynno dwy y fydd
Bookplate Stanley Matthews, chief justice, U. S. senator. Also, without crest or motto, on gravestone of Anthony Matthewes or Mathewes, b. in London, 1663, d. 23 August, 1735, aged 74. Independent churchyard, Meeting Street, Charleston, S. C. Seen by L. Park, 24 March, 1923

Mauleverer Quartered by Middleton

Mauran Bendy of 6 or and gu. On a chief or a savage's head bet 2 stars of 7 points sa
Motto: Trent à la vérité
Bookplate James Eddy Mauran, Newport, R. I. J. Lawrence Mauran of St. Louis has a seal ring and Isabel Mauran a bookplate

Maverick [Arg] a stag's head cabossed, the horns enclosing a cross moline slipped [gu]. On a chief [az] a crescent bet 2 pierced mullets (arms of Thomson?)
Seal following the signature of Samuel Mavericke. on a letter from Comm'rs to settle Plymouth and R. I. colonies bounds, March 11, 1664, to Gov. of Plymouth. MS. at Boston Athenaeum. See Heral. Jour., vol. 3, p. 176. See M. H. S. Coll., vol. 37, where two other coats used by him are shown

Maxwell Arg on a saltire sa a hedgehog, within a bordure componé or and gu
Crest: a stag lodged before a tree
Motto: Reviresco
Bookplate —— Maxwell. Maverick, sc.

May Gu a fess arg bet 8 billets sa (?), 4 in chief and 4 in base. The billets are tricked sanguine and are properly or
Crest: out of a ducal cor [or] a leopard's head couped ppr
Motto: Vigilo
Tablet to John Joseph May, 1813–1903, south wall of First Church, Eliot Sq., Roxbury, Mass. Wall tablet to Joseph May, 1760–1841, King's Chapel, Boston

May See also Dawes

Mayer Bendy sinister of 7 arg and sa. On a chief gu a phoenix issuing from flames
Crest: a jester with tasselled 2-peaked cap, holding bluebells (?) in either hand
Motto: Effingit pheonix Christum reparabilis ales
Bookplate —— Mayer, Baltimore, Md. Another has paly for bendy, etc.

Mayhew On a chev bet 3 birds 5 lozenges, in chief a mullet for diff
Arms on letter from Thomas Mayhew to Gov. John Winthrop. (Winthrop papers. M. H. S. Coll., vol. 37). Heral. Jour., vol. 3, p. 176

Mayo Az a chev vairé arg and gu bet 3 ducal crowns, a cresc on a cresc in chief for diff
Crest: a unicorn's head gorged with a chev of the field

Motto: Virtus sola nobilitat. Another has: Nec aspera terrent
Bookplate Col. John Mayo; also William Mayo

Mayo Az a chev vairé bet 3 ducal cor [or]
Crest: a unicorn's head [charged with a chev vairé?]
Motto: Nec aspera terrent
Tomb at Powhatan, near Richmond, Va., of Joseph Mayo, d. 25 Mch. 1740, and his son George, d. 1739. Framed picture owned by Geo. D. Mayo, "Belleville," Charlotteville, Va. Seen by L. Park, 1922

Mazÿck Vert on a blasted tree ppr 2 birds or
Crest: a bird holding in the beak an olive branch ppr
Motto: Voici nos liens
See The Exposition, vol. 1, no. 4, p. 130

McAllister Quart 1: Arg a lion ramp [gu]; 2: Or a cubit mailed arm fessways from the sinister holding a cross crosslet fitchée gu; 3: Or a galley with furled sails sa [flags gu]; 4: Vert a salmon naiant in fess arg
Crests: 1: a mailed arm emb holding a sword; 2: a cubit arm as in the 2d quarter holding a cross couped at the end
Motto: Per mare per terras
Bookplate —— McAllister, Phila. Hall McAllister of San Franc., brother of Ward of the "400," used the coat and 2d crest, the flags, the lion in 1 gu and the fish in 4 on a dish

McCall Gu 2 arrows in saltire arg bet 3 buckles 2 and 1 of the last. Over all a fess chequy arg and gu
Crest: a mailed and spurred foot couped half way to the knee
Motto: Dulce periculum
Bookplate John McCall

McCall Gu a fess chequy arg and [gul] surmounting 2 arrows in saltire arg bet 3 buckles of the last, all within a bordure engr or
Crest: a boot with spur
Motto: Dulce periculum
Bookplate —— McCall, Phila. Sylvan City, 1883, p. 453

McCance Gu a bend arg bet 6 crosses crosslet fitchée arg. In the dexter chief on the bend a lion ramp within a tressure flory counter flory (Stewart or Maitland?)
Crest: a lion guard on a chapeau (very ferocious!)
Bookplate James Law McCance. Not in Burke

McCandlish Or a galley sa with furled sails of the 2d, flags gu. On a chief gu 3 mullets arg
Crest: a demi-lion vert
Motto: Sola nobilitas virtus

McCarter Per bend or and vert a stag trip
Crest: a stag's head erased
Motto: Stimulat sed ornat
Bookplate Robert H. McCarter, engr. by French, 1896. Not in Burke

McClellan Or 2 chev sa
Crest: a couped hand holding a moor's head erased [or] on a dagger ppr [hilt or]
Motto: Think on
Bookplate Judge Wm. McClellan, Albany, N. Y.

McComb Az a cross flory arg bet 4 martlets
Crest: a demi-lion ramp
Bookplate John McComb. Plesington arms?

McCormack Gu on a chev bet 3 daggers points down arg 3 torteaux
Crest: a bird
Motto: Sine timore
Bookplate Helen Marsh McCormack, signed Everett, 1920

McCoun Az a chev arg bet 3 trefoils slipped or
Crest: a demi-lion
Motto: Semper paratus
Bookplate Wm. T. McCoun of N. Y. Rollinson, sc.

McCulloch [ ] on a canton arg a stag's head sa
Motto: Vi et animo
Bookplate Joseph Graham McCulloch, engr. by A. H. Noll

McCulloh Erm a fret engrailed gu
Crest: an arm unclothed and embowed throwing an arrow
Motto: Vi et animo
Bookplate Henry Eustace McCulloh, No. Car.

McEvers Quart 1 and 4: A gyronny of 8 sa and or (Campbell arms); 2 and 3: Arg a lymphad and flag sa (Lorne)
Crest: a boar's head couped
Motto: Non obliviscar
Bookplate Bache McEvers, Virginia, 1815. Lewis, 3 Wall St.,sc.

McFarlan Quart 1 and 4: Arg a saltire engr bet 4 roses gu; 2 and 3: Gu a chev arg bet in chief 2 quatrefoils and in base a dagger in pale arg (Doeg)
Crest: a demi-savage with cap couped, holding 5 arrows in the dexter hand, the sinister pointing at a royal crown or

Motto: This I'll defend
Bookplate Frederic McFarlan of Penn. Also Fran. McFarland has the McFarlan arms only, with crest and motto, with "Be Ware" added

McGarrity An oak vert and in chief a pelican in her piety
Crest: an oak
Motto: Comrac anceart
Seal ring Miss Mary McGarrity, Phila., from Connaught to Carrickmore, Co. Tyrone

McGregor *See also* Mackey

MacGregor Arg a sword in bend dexter [az] and an oak tree eradicated in bend sinister ppr. In dexter canton an antique crown [gu]
Crest: a lion's head erased and crowned with an antique crown
Motto: E'en do bait spair nocht
Notepaper Rev. Charles Peter MacGregor, Manchester, N. H.

McHard Gu a dexter hand in fess couped holding a dagger point downwards arg and in chief two spurrowells or
Crest: an armed arm embowed az holding by the blade a dagger arg hilt and guard or the point broken
Water color owned by William McHard of Newburyport about 1790. Owned 1926 by N. E. Hist. Gen. Soc.

McIntosh Quart 1: Or a lion ramp gu; 2: Arg a dexter hand holding a human heart gu; 3: Az a boar's head couped or; 4: or a galleon sa
Crest: a cat salient guard ppr
Motto: Touch not the cat bot a glove
Bookplate Charles L. and Mrs. McIntosh by E. H. Garrett, 1904. Also framed water color by Miss Eliz. Lord, 1925

McIver Quart or and gu over all a bend engr sa
Crest: a cubit arm holding a dagger erect
Motto: Nunquam obliviscar
Notepaper Helen H. McIver, Washington

McKay Az on a bend cotised arg bet 2 demi-lions ramp a rose bet 2 boars' heads couped
Crest: a griffin's head erased
Motto: Delectando pariterque monendo
Bookplate James McKay, Va.

McKean Paly of 8 arg [or?] and gu. On a bend sinister az a decrescent bet 2 spur rowels or (Mack arms)
Crest: a bird rising on a snake
Mott: Mens sana in corpore sano
Bookplate (Thomas) McKean

McKenzie Az a stag's head cabossed, a crescent in chief for diff
Crest: a flaming hill
Mottoes: Luceo non uro; Data fata secutus
Bookplate Francis McKenzie, Esqr. of Va.

McKerrow Quart 1 and 4: Sa 2 crosses crosslet fitchée or in saltire; 2 and 3: Lozengy or and az. On a chev arg 3 roundels gu
Crest: the crosses crosslet of the field
Motto: Crux dat salutem
Bookplate —— McKerrow

McKetchnie [ ] a pale bet 2 lions rampant
Crest: a stork statant
Seal John McKetchnie, Bowdoinham, Maine, 1767. Jeffries MSS. N. E. Reg., Jan. 1877, p. 62

McLanahan Arg in chief a hand holding a cross fitchée, in base 3 mounts gu
Crest: a tower gu
Motto: Virtute aqui.itur honor
Bookplate George Xavier McLanahan and Caroline Duer McLanahan had the above and: Erm a bend gu, impaling or a bend az with the motto: Esse et videri. Of Penn.?

McLean Quart 1: Arg a lion ramp gu; 2: Az a castle arg; 3: Or a mailed arm in fess holding erect a cross crosslet fitchée [az]; 4: Per fess or and vert in chief a galley, in base a salmon naiant arg
Crest: a battle axe erect bet a twig of (laurel?) and one of cypress?
Motto: Virtus Durissima ferit
Bookplate Hugh McLean, Maverick, sc.

McLellan Az 3 doves rising in pale bet 2 mullets or
Crest: a lion ramp
Framed water color owned by Herbert Foster Otis, Esq. of Brookline, Mass. "Granted 1575"

McNair [Or] a lion ramp [gu] bet 3 pheons az
Crest: a mermaid ppr holding in her dexter hand a mirror and in her sinister a comb
Notepaper James B. McNair, Univ. of Chicago

McPherson Per fess or and az. In base a lymphad with oars in action or. In the dexter chief an arm couped holding a sword [gu] and in the sinister chief a cross crosslet fitchée [gu]
Crest: a cat sal'ant guard
Motto: Qui me tanget poenitebit
Motto: Virtutem ante pono honorem
Bookplate Capt. John McPherson, privateersman, Phila.

MacPherson [Per fess or and azure] a lymphad with sails furled in base [or]. In the dexter chief a hand couped grasping a dagger, point up [gu]; in the sinister chief a cross crosslet fitchée [gu]
Crest: a cat sejant ppr
Motto: Touch not the cat bot a glove
Grave of Robert MacPherson, d. 1749. Evergreen Cemetery, Gettysburg, Penn. Zieber's Heral., p. 43

McQueen [Arg] 3 wolves' heads couped [sa]
Crest: an heraldic tiger ramp holding an arrow point downward [arg] pheoned [gu]
Motto: Constans et fidelis
Notepaper Sue Moore McQueen, Wilmington, N. C.

McTavish Quart 1 and 4: A gyronny of 8 sa and or; 2 and 3: A stag's head cabossed gu [attired or]. On a chief gu [az?] a cross crosslet fitchée [or] bet 2 mullets arg (Thomson)
Crest: a boar's head couped
Motto: Non oblitus
Bookplate John McTavish, Baltimore. Not as in Burke

Maxcy Gu a fess bet 3 talbots' heads erased arg
Crest: a talbot's head of the shield
Motto: Nullius in verba
Bookplate Virgil Maxcy of Md.

Maxwell Quart 1: Arg a double-headed eagle sa beaked and membered gu charged on the breast with an inscutcheon arg (?) [bearing a saltire sa?] (Maxwell); 2: Quart 1 and 4: Or a saltire gu; 2 and 3: Arg 3 boars [?]; 3: Quart vairé and gu, over all a bend or (Constable); 4: Az on a bend bet 2 cotises arg billets sa (Haggerston)
Memorial window, St. Mark's Church, Phila., inscribed "Maria Ellwood Davis to Matilda Jessup Maxwell (Letter from Rev. Elliot White)

Mead Sa a chevron erm bet 3 pelicans or
Crest: an eagle ducally gorged
Motto: Toujours prest
Bookplate Mead

Means Gu a chev vairé arg and gu bet 3 lions' faces
Crest: a lion ramp
Bookplate Charles Tracy Means. Also Anne Middleton Means

Meares Arg a ship, 3 masts, sails furled sa
Crest: a mermaid with comb and mirror
Motto: Omnia Providentiae committo

Notepaper Neal Meares, Chicago. Ancestor came 1720 with crest embr. on shirt

Meath Vert an elephant ppr (Button arms?)
Crest: a bush leaved, budded, and flowered
Motto: Vis sapientia pollet
Bookplate Samuel Meath, merchant, Phila.

Mellon Quart 1 and 4: Arg a heron sa 2 and 3: [Gu] on a chev [az] bet 3 armed arms embowed as many 6-pointed stars of the first (Armour?)
Crest: a heron
Motto: Cassis tutissima virtus
Coat of arms said to be in home of A. W. Mellon, sec. of treas. U. S. He writes: "tradition is that it was the coat of arms of the 'Ancient Mellon Family of Ulster.'" Used also by R. B. Mellon, Pittsburgh
Bookplate Wm. Larimer Mellon, des. by Sara B. Hill, 1912

Melton Quartered by Acklom

Melville Quart 1: Az a crown surmounting a thistle; 2: Arg a bend az; 3: Arg a fess gu; 4: Gu 3 decrescents arg within a bordure of the 2d charged with 8 roses of the first
Crest: a hound's head erased and gorged
Motto: Denique coelum
Bookplate John Ward Melville, engr. by A. W. Macdonald

Melville Quartered by Palmer

Menifie The trunk of a tree
Wax seal on deed from George Menifie, dated 21 April, 1638, to Richard Kempe, bears for device the trunk of a tree. W. & Mary Quar., Jan. 1894, p. 159

Mercer Or on a fess gu bet in chief 3 crosses pattée gu and in base a mullet az 3 bezants
Crest: a hound's head gorged
Motto: Per varios casus
Bookplate Carroll Mercer, Washington

Meredith [ ] 2 lions ramp addorsed
Seal on marriage contract of Wm. Meredith, Lancaster, Va., 1706. Wm. & Mary Quar., Jan. 1893, p. 119

Meredith Or a lion ramp sa collared [gu] and chained or
Crest: a demi-lion of the field
Bookplate Wm. Morris Meredith, lawyer, Phila.

Merrick Az a chev bet 3 torches or, flamed gu and in chief a fleur-de-lis bet 2 birds facing one another or
Crest: a tower gu surmounted of a bird as in the arms gu contourné
"By the name of Merrick" and palm branches. A modern copy. Owned by Prest. Wm. F. Warren, Brookline, Mass. (1925)

Merrick Quart 1 and 4: Sa on a chev arg bet 3 staves raguly ppr a fleur-de-lis az bet 3 Cornish choughs ppr; 2: Gu 2 porcupines in pale arg armed or (old Merrick arms); 3: Sa a chev arg bet 3 boys' heads couped ppr crined or, enwrapped about the necks with snakes vert (Vaughan)
Crests: 1: a castle arg surmounted of a chough holding a fleur-de-lis in the dexter claw; 2: a lion's head couped arg wounded with a lance or
Motto: Christi servitus vera libertas
Bookplate Samuel Vaughan Merrick, Phila. Zieber's Heral., p. 326-7

Merrill Arg a fess az bet 3 peacocks' heads erased ppr
Crest: a peacock's head erased ppr
Seal affixed to a deed dated 1726. Vermont's Amer. Heral., 1886, pp. 129, 173

Merrill Arg a fess [az] bet 3 peacocks' heads erased 1 and 2 [ppr]
Crest: a head of the field
Notepaper Mrs. Mae Merrill Buckley, Dorchester, Mass., desc. of Thomas Merrill
Bookplate Sherborn M. Merrill

Merrill Arg a fess az or [sa?] bet 3 birds' heads erased 1 and 2
George D. Merrill's bookplate; also Albert Rowe Merrill

Merrill Az 3 cresc arg
Crest: a dove rising holding an olive branch
Motto: Servata fides cinere
Bookplate Lucie Elizabeth and William Waldo Merrill

Merrill Or a pale engr gu voided of the field bet 2 fleurs-de-lis az
Crest: a peacock's head erased ppr
Motto: Vincit qui patitur
On tablet in the library at Yarmouth, Maine, erected by Joseph E. Merrill in memory of Ezekiel Merrill and his wife. Also on notepaper of Joshua Merrill, Longwood, Mass.
Bookplate [Miss Mary E.] Merrill of Bangor, signed D[orothy] S[turgis] H[arding] of Boston

Merritt On a barry of 6 or and sa a chev erm
Crest: a hound gorged and chained
Motto: Mereo et merito
Bookplate —— Merritt

Mersick Gu 2 hounds combatant or gorged sa
Crest: a lion's head erased, gorged with a ducal cor
Bookplate C. S. Mersick

Messchert Per fess [arg and gu?], in chief 2 flowering rose branches vert, each on a mound and each with 3 roses or. In base 2 fleurs-de-lis in bend and a demi-fess from the sinister per fess gu and or
Crest: on a helmet an eagle with wings spread
Motto: Unica virtus necessaria
Bookplate Huizinga Messchert of Phila. Rotterdam family. Slightly differing from Rietstap

Messinger Arg a chev bet 3 closed helmets sa
Crest: a pegasus courant ducally gorged and chained or
Motto: Agros vigilantia servat
Framed water color owned by Ralph W. Messinger, Oak Bluffs, Mass., 1924. Also bookplate of Marcia Gerard Messenger, engr. by French, 1895. Shield only. Will of Sarah Messenger widow of Henry, 1694 (Mass.) leaves "coat of arms the Messenger arms hanging up in the Parlour" to her son Simeon (Mrs. J. G. Bartlett)

Meyer [Arg?] a pelican in her piety ppr
Crest: a wheel
Also the arms of Appleton: Arg a fess sa bet 3 apples [gu] stalked and leaved [vert]
Bookplate George von Lengerke Meyer, Boston, Secretary of the Navy. Done at Nüremberg. His wife an Appleton

Michie Quart 1: Or a lion ramp sa (?) on a canton arg (?) a hand couped at the wrist hold a cross crosslet fitchée; 2: Arg a chev az bet 3 leaves (or pine leaves?) within a bordure compony arg and purpure; 3: Or a lymphad and in chief a double-headed eagle sa; 4: Per fess arg and vert, in chief a tree, in base a fish naiant
Crest: a hand couped at wrist holding a sword
Motto: Pro patria et libertate
Bookplate James Michie, Esq., of S. C.

Middlecott Az an eagle displ arg on a chief gu 3 escallops or
Crest: a demi-eagle displ holding in the beak an escallop
Gore roll of arms. Richard was of Boston, 1702

Middleton Per pale or and gu a lion ramp within a double tressure flory and counter-flory counterchanged

Crest: a demi-lion issuing from a tower embattled sa
Motto: Fortis et fidus (another with Fortis & fidus)
Bookplate Peter Middleton, M. D., of New York. J. Lewis, sc. Thomas Middleton used one with quarterly gu and or a cross flory in the first quarter arg and a mullet in the center for diff. Motto: "Lesses dire." E. A. Jones, London, writes that Capt. Alex. Middleton, surgeon and loyalist, Va. and Md., 1777, used the above crest on letter in Pub. Record office

Middleton Quarterly of 9: 1: Arg fretty az [sa?] a canton sa (usually charged]; 2: Arg [sa?] 3 coursing hounds in pale sa [arg?] collared [or] (Mauleverer); 3: Sa an estoile of 6 points arg [erm?] (Ingleby of Ripley); 4: Gu a lion ramp arg within a bordure engrailed or (Mowbray); 5: Arg a chev embattled sa [gu?] bet 3 bells sa (Chaumont); 6: Arg a chev bet 3 lions' heads erased gu (Rocliff); 7: Arg a saltire gu [on a] chief [gu] 3 escallops [or] (Talboys); 8: Arg 3 cinquefoils sa [az 3 pilgrims' staves or (Burdon)]; 9: Gu a cinquefoil arg bet 8 crosses crosslet [or] 3, 2, 3 (Umfreville)
Crest: a garb [or] bet 2 wings erect [sa]
Motto: Regard de mon droit
Bookplate John Izard Middleton, 1785–1849, author, b. S. C. Same for Henry Middleton; also John Nathaniel and F. G. has the first quartering and a garb for crest. The end of the tomb of Arthur Middleton, Middleton Place, Ashley River, So. Car., has his arms: No. 1 above with cresc. for diff. and same crest. Seen by L. Park, 1923. There was apparently a Middleton bookplate in which No. 7 has "on a chief gu 3 escallops," and "Regardes mon droit." See So. Car. Hist. & Gen. Mag., July, 1900. Langdon Cheves of Charleston supplies for me the quarterings of Middleton of Stockeld, Yorks, "before the arrival in America"

Middleton See also Moat

Midgley Or 5 bars sa in chief 3 arrowheads sa
Crest: a leopard ramp
Bookplate Henry Midgley

Mifflin Or a chev az. In the sinister chief a star of 6 points arg
Crest: a dove holding in its bill an olive branch
Motto: Nil desperandum
Bookplate George H. Mifflin, Boston publisher. Spenceley, sc.

Mifflin Or a chev az. In the sinister chief a star of 6 points gu
Crest: a bird holding a twig
Seal of John Mifflin, Phila. Zieber's Heral., p. 68

Mifflin Vert a chev az. In the sinister chief a mullet [arg]
Memorial window, St. Mark's Church, Phila. Zieber's Heral., p. 64

Milborn Sa on a bend bet 2 leopards' heads or 3 crosses pattée of the field, on a chief arg as many escallops of the field
Seal on the wills of Isaac Griffin, 1693, John Major, 1702, and William Davis, 1701. William Milborn appears as a witness on all of them. (Suffolk wills.) Heral. Jour., vol. 3, p. 93

Miller Erm a fess or bet 3 wolves' heads erased [gu]
Crest: a wolf's head of the field
Motto: Semper paratus
Bookplate Joseph Miller. N. Hurd, sc. Arms on a silver tankard once owned by Samuel Miller of Rehoboth, Mass., and Milton; in 1900 owned by Mrs. G. Tyler Bigelow of Quincy. Dr. Ebenezer Miller in 1728 had such a tankard with these (Motram) arms

Miller Erm 3 wolves' heads erased gu
Arms of Miller impaling Bolling, on a silver castor, once the property of Hugh Miller of Prince George County, Va. He d. 13 Feb., 1762. Bolling arms: Sa an inescutcheon erm within an orle of 8 martlets arg Crozier's Va. Heral., 1908, p. 55

Milligan Arg a demi-lion ramp bet 2 bars wavy vert and in chief 2 demilions ramp
Bookplate "Robert Milligan, Middle Temple," of Bohemia Manor, Cecil Co., Md. (1754–1806). His son, John Jones Milligan, had a gold seal showing a crest: out of a ducal cor a lion ramp holding a cutlass. The Milligans looked like Napier of Magdala

Millington Arg an eagle displayed with 2 heads sa
Crest: a claw holding a ball gu
A framed water color. Also on silver of Prof. John Millington, b. in England, and a prof. at Wm. & Mary College, Va. Owned by his daughter, Mrs. R. E. Blankenship, 117 So. 3d St., Richmond. Seen by L. Park, 1922

Mills Erm a mill-rind arg a chief gu
Crest: a lion ramp
Motto: Mens conscia recti
Bookplate George Dallas Mills. Also plate King's Chapel, Boston, bearing name of Nath'el Cary. No chief

Mills Quartered by Hope

Milner Per pale or and sa a chev bet 3 horses' bits counterchanged
Crest: a horse's head couped, bridled or
Motto: Scietas scientia virtus
Bookplate James Milner of Va.

Milner Sa a chev bet 3 snaffle bits or
Crest: a horse's head couped arg, bridled and maned or
Tomb of Mary Milner, wife of Col. Miles Cary in Nansemond County, Va. She d. 27 Oct. 1700. Above not seen. *See* Cary family history, 1919

Minns Sa a fess danc per pale arg and gu bet 5 crosses crosslet arg
On cover of "Minns and Allied Families," 1925

Minor [Gu] a fess arg bet 3 [plates]
Crest: a hand o r holding a double-pointed battle axe
On table stone of Ephraim Minor, who d. May 16, 1724 (Taugwonk, part of No. Stonington, Conn.); also of Deacon Manatseh (or Manasseh) Minor who d. Aug. 22, 1728 (Wequete-quock Cemetery, Stonington, Conn); also of Deacon Thomas who d. April 10? 1739 (same place); on watch of George L. Miner. Also on monument to the four founders of Stonington. Also on cover of Thomas's Diary (1915)

Minor *See also* Doodes

Minot Az 2 bars dancettée in chief a label of 3 points gu
Crest: a cross with 3 stars above
Motto: Ad astra per aspera
Bookplate George Richards Minot, historian, Mass.

Minshull Az an estoile of 8 points surmounted by a mullet arg
Crest: two lions' gambs [gu] holding a crescent arg
Bookplate John Minshull

Minshull Quart 1: Az a fess danc or bet 3 spread eagles arg; 2: Gu on a chief or 3 crosses potent ppr (Lynde); 3: Az an estoile of 6 points arg in the horns of a crescent arg; 4: Az a fess gu fretty or bet 2 fleurs-de-lis or
Crest: a lion's head erased
Motto: Fortis que Felix
Framed water color owned by Soc. for the Preserv. of N. E. Antiq., Boston. The Soc. has also Minshull and Leycester

Minturn Az 2 bars arg bet 3 lions pass in pale or
Crest: a bull's head couped [gu] ducally gorged or
Motto: Esse potius quam haberi
Bookplate William Minturn

Mitchell [Sa] a chev bet 3 mascles [or]
Seal ring of Norman Mitchell of Winchester, Mass., son of Henry Mitchell the engraver

Mitchell Sa a fess wavy gu bet 3 mascles or
Crest: a cubit arm holding a ducal cor
Motto: Pour qui sait attendre
Bookplate E. Coppee Mitchell, Phila.

Mitchell Sa a fess wavy gu bet 3 mascles or
Crest: a phoenix rising from the flames
Motto: Spernet humum
Bookplate W. Mitchell

Moat Arg on a bend vert 3 wolves' heads erased of the first. Impaling: Sa 10 plates, 4, 3, 2, 1; on a chief arg a lion pass sa (Bridgman). The badge of Ulster in chief. The arms are Middleton not Moat
Crest: a demi-griffin ramp
Motto: Nil desperando
Bookplate Horatio Shepard Moat

Molineux Az a cross moline pierced lozengeways or
Water color in old frame owned by Miss Marie Ada Molineux, Lynn, 1926. By John Coles, Senior? On back: "From Robert Molineux to his son James Molineux to his son Henry Molineux. Written by Henrietta Molineux Gibson, 1860." She, wife of Geo. Lafayette Gibson, was daughter of James Molineux. Robert married Margaret, daughter of Dr. Philip G. Kast of Salem. A framed description on a shield bears: "Boston, June 27th, 1788. James Dodge Sculpsit." He was "James Dodge junr."

Moloun *See* Dongan

Monckton Gu on a chev or bet three martlets arg as many mullets of the third
Seal of Gen. Rob't Monckton, Gov. of N. Y., 1761. Heral. Jour., vol. iv, p. 95

Monnet Quart 1 and 4: Az a bend or; 2 and 3: Or a lion ramp gu
Crest: a demi-lion ramp gu
Supporters: 2 lions ramp gu
Motto: Florens suo orbe monet
Bookplate Orra Eugene Monnette, Los Angeles. Also in bronze

Monro Or an eagle's head erased gu
Crest: an eagle with wings expanded
Supporters: Eagles with wings expanded
Motto: Dread God

Used by Rev. H. Usher Monro, rector North Andover, Mass. The Lexington Monros. Crest on his notepaper

Montague [Arg] 3 fusils conjoined in fess [gu] bet 3 pellets
Motto: Post tot naufragia portus
Tablet in Christ Church, Boston, in memory of Rev. Wm. Montague, rector

Montford Arg a lion ramp az in a field of crosses crosslet [gu]
Crest: a demi-lion (?) ramp guard
Motto: Non inferiora secutus
Notepaper Clarence Lilley Judd, Saginaw, Mich.

Montgomery Quart 1 and 4: Az 3 fleurs-de-lis arg; 2 and 3: Gu 3 finger rings arg (Eglintoun). All within a bordure or charged with a double tressure flory counterflory [gu]
Crest: a demi-woman ppr holding in the dexter hand an anchor [or] and in the sinister a savage's head couped
Motto: Gardez bien
Bookplate John C. Montgomery

Moody Arg on a chev engr sa bet 3 trefoils slipped vert (?) 3 lozenges or. On a chief az out of a cloud arg 2 arms the dexter gu the other or holding a rose gu
Crest: two arms one vested gu one vert each holding a cutlass arg paneled or
Water color owned by Mrs. Percy Hill, Augusta, Maine

Moody Vert a fess engr arg surmounted of another gu bet 3 harpies of the second crined or
Seal used on will of Elbert Hunt, 1711, witnessed by Jonathan Gulliver, Peter Whyte, and Eliezer Moody. Heral. Jour., vol. 3, pp. 92, 96

Moore Arg 3 greyhounds courant. Impaling: (Long of Jamaica)
Crest: a moorcock, in its beak a sprig
Bookplate Sir Henry Moore, b. 1713 in Jamaica, baronet 1764, Gov. N. Y. 1765, d. 1769. Oliver's West Ind. bk. plates, 1914, No. 484

Moore Az a chev arg bet 3 moorcocks. Impaling: Arg a cross engr sa (Rhett)
Seal of Roger Moore. See The Exposition, vol. 1, no. 4, p. 131

Moore Az on a chief indented or 3 pierced mullets gu
Crest: a moor's head in profile sa ducally gorged or
Motto: Fortis cadere cedere non potest
Bookplate Nanthaniel F. Moore. Maverick, sc. Also J. Owen Moore.

Also Sam'l W. Moore with motto: Non est vivere sed valere vita. *See also* Miss Lyslie Moore Hawes's bookplate

Moore Erm three greyhounds courant gu
Crest: a moorcock, sable
Seal of Sir Henry Moore, Bart., Gov. of N. Y. 1765. Heral. Jour., vol. iv, p. 95

Moore [Or] 10 crosses crosslet [sa] 4, 3, 2, 1
Crest: a moorcock
Motto: Nihil utile quod non honestum
Bookplate John Moore, dep. coll. and receiver-gen. of customs, N. Y. Dawkins (?), sculp. Also of Lambert Moore, Esq., with Virtus interrita pergit

Moore Sa a swan standing arg within a bordure engr or
Crest: a hawk rising with a fish in its beak
Motto: Vis unita fortis (?)
Bookplate Thomas Ewing Moore

Moran Sa (?) a chev bet 3 crosses couped
Christmas card, 1925, of Ed[ward] and Jean Moran, N. Y.

Morby Quartered by Acklom

Mordecai Per bend gu and az. On a bend az bet a lion ramp in chief and a palm tree in base a star of 6 points sa
Crest: a griffin's head erased
Motto: Per aspera ad astra
Bookplate J. Randolph Mordecai

Moreduck Or 2 swords in saltire points down and one in pale point up on which is a chaplet. On a chief embattled az a cross crosslet fitchée
Crest: a demi-lion rampant
Motto: Fortis et fidelis
Bookplate Sarah Moreduck

Morehead Arg on a bend az 3 acorns of the first. A mullet sa in chief for diff
Crest: two hands conjoined couped supporting a sword erect
Motto: Auxilio Dei
Bookplate William Morehead

Morehead Arg on a bend az 3 acorns or, in chief a man's heart ppr within a fetterlock sa, the whole surrounded with an oak wreath ppr acorned or
Crest: two hands conjoined grasping a two-handed sword ppr
Motto: Auxilio Dei
Arms on an old painting in possession of the North Car. branch of the family. Crozier's Va. Heral., 1908, p. 101

Moreland Quart 1 and 4: Gu 3 bars wavy arg, each charged with 3 martlets; 2 and 3: Gu 3 suns in splendor a chief erm (Jackson)
Crest: a falcon ppr [belled or]
Motto: Fides et fortitudo
Bookplate Wm. Wallace Moreland

Morgan Arg a fess bet 3 martlets gu. On a chief az 3 griffins' heads erased arg
Crest: a fox ramp against an oak tree
Motto: Heb Ddvw Heb ddim a Ddvw Digon
Bookplate George M. Morgan

Morgan Arg 3 bulls' heads cabossed sa
Crest: a griffin statant
Bookplate ―― Morgan

Morgan Or 3 stags' heads couped sa
Crest: a lion ramp sa
Motto: Heb Ddow Heb ddim a Ddow Digon
Bookplate ―― Morgan

Morgan Or a griffin segreant sa
Crest: a stag's head erased or armed gu
Motto: Fama praestante praestantior virtus
Bookplate Prof. Morris H. Morgan, Harvard Univ.

Morgan *See also* Betton

Morin *See also* Scott

Morison Arg a fess gu bet 3 young moors' heads [sa]
Crest: three moors' heads on one neck, one facing up, the others to the dexter and sinister
Motto: Praetio prudentia praestat
Seal ring of Everett Austin, Jr., 110 Marlborough St., Boston, and Windham, N. H. His mother's mother was Hannah Morison

Morris [   ] a cat salient with a rabbit in the jaws
Crest: on a shield a cross pattée
Motto: Fides prævalebit
Notepaper Roland S. Morris, Phila. Minister to Japan?

Morris Gu on a chev arg bet 3 lions ramp 3 cinquefoils of the first (Goode arms?)
Crest: a talbot's head erased [gu] crowned [or]
Bookplate Edward Everett Morris, engr. by A. H. Noll

Morris Quart of 6: 1 and 5: Gu a lion ramp reguard or; 2 and 6: Arg 3 boars' heads erased sa (Cadogan); 3 and 4: Sa on a fess arg bet 3 griffins' heads erased arg 3 escallops. An inscutcheon arg a chev bet 3 estoiles
Bookplate Val Morris

Morris Quart 1 and 4: Gu a lion ramp reguardant [or]; 2 and 3: Az 3 boars' heads arg (Cadogan)
Crest: a lion of the field
Bookplate Roger Morris, 1717–1794, who married Mary Philipse, whom Washington loved. Curio, 1888, p. 112. Also of James Morris

Morris Quart 1 and 4: Gu a lion ramp reguard or; 2 and 3: Arg? 3 [torteaux] in fess
Crest: a tower in flames
Motto: Tandem vincitur
Seal of Gov. Lewis Morris of N. J. (1671–1746). The tower is said to be Chepstow Castle. In "Papers of Gov. L. M." the engraving is inaccurate
Bookplate Gouverneur Morris. The shield is engraved azure, the lion guard. Seal of Robert Hunter Morris, Gov. Penn. 1754–6. Sylvan City, 1883, p. 457. Lion is guard

Morris Sa a lion pass bet 3 scaling ladders arg
Crest: an embattled wall with gate bet 2 embat towers
Motto: Proprium decus et patrium
Bookplate Anthony Morris, Phila. Sylvan City, 1883, p. 449

Morse [Arg] a battle axe gu bet 3 pellets
Crest: two battle axes in saltire charged with a wreath
Motto: In Deo non armis fido
Painted on a square wood panel. Rev. Glenn Tilley Morse of West Newbury, from one owned by his great grandfather, Benjamin Morse, b. Fayette, Me., 1791, d. 1852. Also his bookplate

Morse [Arg] a battle axe in pale [gu] bet 3 pellets
Crest: two battle axes in saltire addorsed
Motto: In Deo non armis fido
Seal ring New York

Morse Arg a battle axe in pale gu bet 3 bezants
Crest: two battle axes in saltire [az or ppr?] banded with a chaplet [of roses?]
Motto: In Deo non armis fido
Bookplate Wm. Whitcomb and Bertha Alden Morse, Minneapolis

Mortimer Barry of six or and az. An inscutcheon arg on a chief az a pile or charged with 2 pales az
Crest: a stag's head couped gu faced and antlered or
Motto: Virtutem avorum aemulus
Bookplate Alfred G. Mortimer, Phila.

Morton Arg a coursing hound sa
Crest: a griffin's head erased
Motto: Semper fidelis
Bookplate S. G. Morton, M. D.

Morton Or a lion ramp sa
Crest: a lion's gamb
Motto: Deo tum patria
Bookplate Perez Morton. Paul Revere, sc., 1781

Morton Impaled by Sparrow

Moseley [Gu] an eagle displayed [or].
Strong arms
Motto: Mos legem regit. Mosley motto
Bookplate Frederick Strong Moseley, Boston banker. Engr. by S. L. Smith

Moseley Quart 1 and 4: Sa a chev bet 3 battle axes arg; 2 and 3: Or a fess bet 3 eagles displayed sa
Crest: an eagle displayed sa
Motto: Mos legem regit
William Moseley, who came 1649, brought his arms; his son, Edward Moseley, gave to his son Hilary on the 1 Feb. 1703–4, "My seale, which was my father's, with his coat of arms on it." Wm. & Mary Quar., July, 1893, p. 29

Moseley [Sa] on a chev bet 3 mill picks [arg] 3 mullets [gu]
Crest: an eagle displayed
Motto: Peu a peu
Bookplate Edward Moseley of North Carolina. Framed paintings owned by Mrs. W. T. Lipscomb (nee Moseley), Greenville, N. C., and Moseleys in Raleigh and Charlotte. Also in St. Paul's vestry room. "From 1705 to 1749 the man who was most active in promoting real prosperity and liberty in N. C. was Edward Moseley of Albemarle, N. C."— Mrs. W. R. Everett

Moseley Sa a chev arg bet 3 mill picks or
Crest: an eagle displayed erm
Motto: Mos legem regit
Seal of Capt. Samuel Moseley, who d. in 1680, used on deeds. Vermont's Amer. Heral. [1886], p. 173

Moss Erm on a cross pattée sa a [bezant]
Crest: out of a cor [or] a griffin's head [erm]
Notepaper Frank H. Moss, Bala, Penn.

Motley Gu a tower bet in chief 2 goshawks (?) and in base a helmet [arg?]
Crest: a demi-lion holding a helmet
Motto: Fides leone fortior
Engraved on Thomas Motley's cane, 1888, owned by Mrs. Lawrence Park, Groton, Mass., 1926
Bookplate Edward Preble Motley

Motram *See also* Miller

Mott [Sa] a crescent arg
Crest: an estoile of 8 points
Memorial tablet to Isaac and Adelaide Mott Bell, Trinity Church, N. Y.

Motte Gu on a hill in base 5 trees all within a bordure or
Crest: trees of the field
Bookplate Francis Motte of S. C.

Moulton Arg three bars [gu] bet 8 escallops sa, 3, 2, 1
Crest: on a pellet a falcon rising arg
Notepaper Rev. J. S. Moulton, Stow, Mass. Framed water color at York (Maine) Jail

Moultrie Az on a chev bet 3 escallops arg a boar's head sa [langued gu] bet 2 mullets gu
Crest: a mermaid
Motto: Nunquam non fidelis
Old drawing for a bookplate in So. Car. Hist. Soc.

Mountford *See also* Oliver

Mountfort Bendy of 9 or and sa
Crest: a lion's head erased
Motto: Auxilium ab alto
Bookplate G. Mountfort. In Cocking's Amer. War. 1781

Mountfort Bendy of 9 [or and az]
Crest: a lion's head erased
Jonathan Mountfort's tomb, 1724. Copp's Hill Yard, Boston

Mountfort Bendy of 9 or and az
Crest: a lion's head erased
Painted on canvas, 1886, for use in King's Chapel. Bostonian Society

Movius Gu 3 double eagles displayed
Motto: Quod deus vult fiat
Bookplate Julius Movius, wealthy Jew, formerly called Moses, Buffalo, N. Y. Also of Hallam Leonard Movius, Boston architect, by W. T. Aldrich

Mowbray Quartered by Middleton

Muhlenberg Per chev arg and sa 3 cinquefoils counterchanged, a mullet in chief
Crest: a lozenge or
Motto: Solus minus solus
Bookplate Rev. Henry Melchior Muhlenberg, Trappe, Pa., 1711–1787. From a drawing sent by Mr. W. M. McKee of the Art Inst. of Chicago

Murdoch Arg an arrow fessways pointing to the sinister charged with (or piercing?) 2 ravens
Crest: a raven rising pierced by an arrow in bend sinister
Motto: Omnia pro bono
Bookplate Thomas Murdoch

Murray Az a chev bet 3 mullets arg
Crest: a cock
Motto: Mens sibi conscia recti
Bookplate James Murray, Va.

Murray Az a cross pattée bet 3 estoiles of 6 points arg within a double tressure flory counterflory
Crest: a dexter hand holding a mirror
Motto: Nosce te ipsum
Bookplate Hon. Joseph Murray of New York, who d. in 1757. Maverick, sc.

Murray Az a martlet bet 3 stars of 6 points [arg] within a double tressure flory and counterflory [or]
Crest: a lion ramp holding a battle axe
Notepaper Dr. T. Morris Murray, 21 Marlborough St., Boston

Murray Quart 1: Az an inscut arg charged with 3 mullets pierced sa. In chief a helmet and in base cinquefoils between posts; 2: Within a double tressure per saltire. In chief a hunting horn. Dexter side, 3 mullets above a crescent. Sinister side a crown above a fire ball. In base an ox bow; 3: Gu "Apollyon and Gabriel in combat" with a crown above them; 4: Az a cross bezantée with a bird above and a flaming heart below; in the sinister chief a flaming heart below a crescent and in the dexter base the same
Crest: man with tomahawk, on horseback
Mottoes: Malo mori quam foedari. Juncta virtute fides
Bookplate Rev. John Murray, Marblehead, Mass.?

Murray Quart 1 and 4: Az 3 mullets arg; 2 and 3: Quart 1 and 4: Or a fess chequy arg and az (Stewart) and; 2 and 3: Paly of 6 or and sa (Strabolgi). An escut of pretence gu 3 legs ppr spurred and garnished or, conjoined at the thigh in triangle (Isle of Man)
Crest: on a crown a demi-sailor (or savage?) holding in his dexter hand a dagger, in the sinister a key [or]
Motto: Furth fortune
Bookplate John Murray, Earl of Dunmore, Gov. N. Y. 1770, Va. 1771. Seal in Heral. Jour., vol. 4, pp. 95, 96

Musgrave Az 6 annulets [or] 3, 2, 1
Crest: two mailed arms embowed, hands bare, holding an annulet [or]
Motto: Sans charger
Bookplate Richard Musgrave of New Haven, Conn.

Musterton *See also* Masterton

N

Nagel Or 3 nails sa the points meeting in base (the navel point)
Crest: out of a crown a nail erect sa bet 2 horns, the dexter per fess or and sa, the sinister per fess sa and or
Motto: Der Nagel hält fest
Ex libris Charles Nagel. S. B. Hill, del. 1924. A. J. Downey, sculpt. *Sec* Commerce and Labor under Taft

Nanfan Quartered by Coote

Neale Arg a fess gu in chief 2 cresc of the 2d in base a hunting horn of the last stringed [vert]. Impaled on one lozenge with Lloyd and on another with Bennett
Crest: out of a ducal cor [or] a chaplet of laurel [vert]
On tomb of Henrietta Maria Neale Bennett Lloyd, daughter of Capt. James Neale of Wollaston Manor, Md. Richardson's Sidelights on Md. Hist. vol. 2, p. 184. Hist. Graves of Md., p. 213

Needham Arg on a bend az bet 2 stags' heads cabossed sa an escallop or
Motto: Soyez firme
Framed arms in color owned by Mrs. Edward R. Baird, Pembroke Ave., Norfolk, Va. Seen by L. Park, 1922

Nelson Per pale arg and sa a chev bet 3 fleurs-de-lis counterchanged
Crest: a fleur-de-lis per pale arg and sa
Engr. on the tomb of Thomas Nelson at Yorktown, Va. The crest is still distinct. He d. 7 Oct. 1745. Also on the coach of Mrs. William Nelson, 1773. Also on tomb of Gen. Thomas Nelson, Jr., Grace Episc. Churchyard, Yorktown. He d. Jan. 2, 1789. Seen by L. P. 1922. Sales' Manors of Va., p. 184. Va. Hist. Mag., vol. 3, p. 403

Nelson Quart 1 and 4: Gu a bend az. Over all a cross pattée or; 2 and 3: Az a lion ramp [arg]. In chief a label of 3 points [gu?] (Colvile?). Impaling: Per saltire or and gu 4 plates each charged with a martlet counterchanged (Bidwell)
Crest: a garb
Bookplate George Nelson, Va. (?)

Nelson Sa on a chev or bet 3 fleurs-de-lis arg 3 roses gu
The episcopal seal of the Bishop of Georgia. Cleland Kinloch Nelson impaled the Nelson arms as above. Zieber's Heral., p. 201

Nevill Gu on a saltire arg a martlet of the field
Impaled on ring used by Judge James Russell, son of Richard Russell, whose first wife was a Nevill. Heral. Jour., vol. 4, p. 33

Newberry Sa 3 pales arg on a canton az a lion ramp or
Engr. on Gen. Roger Newberry's sword, 1735–1814. *See* "Ancient Windsor," vol. 2, p. 517. The name was orig. Newburgh bearing or 3 bends az within a bordure engr. gu (J. G. Bartlett)

Newbold Az 2 bends arg a chief of the last
Crest: a cross crosslet flory fitchée az
Notepaper John Sargent Newbold, Phila.

Newbottel *See also* Pease

Newburgh *See also* Newberry

Newcomb Arg a wall embat bet 3 escallops sa
Crest: out of a mural crown a demi-eagle displ
Motto: Non abest virtuti sors
Notepaper F. Winthrop coll., 1885, in Bos. Ath.

Newdigate Quartered by Lynde

Newhall Erm on a fess arg 3 fusils purpure (?)
Crest: a savage with bludgeon and "1500"
Supporters: Lions sejant ramp affrontée
Motto: Diligentia ditat
Bookplate —— Newhall

Newman [   ] 3 demi-lions ramp [   ].
Impaling: (   ) [   ] a lion ramp [   ]
Arms of Roger Newman who d. 1704? On a tomb in Anne Arundel Co., on the Greenberry farm, opposite Annapolis, Md. Ridgely's Historic Graves of Md. suggests that these are arms of Bennett impaling Lloyd. *See* page 7

Newman "Azure a chevron wavy between three Griffons segreant rampant or is borne by the name of Newman, & was confirmed to Gayus Newman of London Gent son of Gabriel son of Thomas Newman of Norfolk Gent & to his posterity by William Camden, Esq. Clarencieuse the 12th of Nov. 1610 in 8th year of the Reign of · King James the first. Boston, Octr 31st 99. A true copy from Heraldry attest J. Coles Herald Painter"
Crest: "a Griffon's head erased or"
Water color in frame black edged with gold, 10⅛ x 14¼ inches. Mant-

ling red and white, open work delicately done. Owned 1924 by Miss Harriet Hancock Newman of Chelsea, Mass., desc. of Robert Newman, sexton of Christ Church, Salem St. (Old North Church). Seen by C. K. B.

Newton Ermines a lion ramp facing the sinister. Impaling: Arg 2 shinbones in saltire, the dexter surmounting the sinister (Newton)
Crest: an armed arm emb holding a battle axe fessways
Motto: Deus non ego
Bookplate Edward Augustus Newton, N. Y.?

Newton [Sa] 2 shin bones in saltire [arg] the sinister surmounting the dexter
Crest: an arm holding a battle axe
Wall tablet to Thomas Newton, warden of King's Chapel, 1704, and attorney-general, d. 1721. King's Chapel, Boston, south aisle

Nicholas Az a chev engr bet 3 owls or
Crest: an owl with wings spread or
Motto: Comme je trouve
On mantelpiece in chamber at "Redlands," Albemarle Co., Va., home of the Misses Carter (pronounced Keartah). They own Stuart's portrait of Gov. Wilson Cary Nicholas of Md. Seen by L. Park, 1922

Nicholson Az a cross arg charged with a mansion house or castle bet 4 suns or
Crest: a man with sword and Bible
Motto: Deus mihi sol
Lieut. Gov. Francis Nicholson. On canvas, 1886. Bostonian Society. Formerly in King's Chapel

Nicholson Az 2 bars erm. On a chief arg 3 suns ppr
Crest: out of a ducal cor or a lion's head erased gu "the erasure showing beneath the coronet"
Motto: Per castra as astra
Seal of Isaac Lea Nicholson, Bishop of Milwaukee. Zieber's Heral., p. 205

Nickerson Az 2 bars erm and in chief 3 wheels
Crest: a bird rising with a twig in its beak
Notepaper Mrs. Wm. G. Nickerson, Hildreth House, Dedham, Mass. The bookplate of Geo. Aug. Nickerson of Dedham has in chief 3 suns in splendor the form given for Nicholson in Burke

Nicklin Sa 3 boars' heads couped in fess arg
Crest: a griffin's head erased arg
Motto: Pro Deo et Patria
Bookplate Nicklin family of Penn., desc. of Joseph of Chester Co., used by J. B. Nicklin, Jr. Chattanooga

Nicoll Or a lion's head bet 3 hawks' heads, all erased gu within a bordure of the last
    Crest: a sun resplendent or
    Motto: Sublimiora peto
    On plate brought over in 1734 by John Nicoll to Orange County, N. Y. Also on old family portrait. Vermont's Amer. Heral. [1886], p. 53, 173

Nicolls [Az] a fess bet 3 lions' heads erased [or]
    Seal on letter from Richard Nicolls, Gov. of N. Y. about 1665, to the Gov. of Plymouth. MS in Boston Athenaeum

Nordeck, Charles, Baron Zur Rabenau [Arg] three trefoils [nenuphar leaves?] 2 and 1 [sa]
    Crest: a trident?
    Nordeck, Baron zur Rabenau, d. 1782, aged 27, of Ditford. A capt. in a Hessian regiment. Flat stone in St. Paul's Churchyard, N. Y. Seen 20 May, 1920. *See also* Zieber's Heral., p. 45 (not Nordeek)

Norden Arg on a fess gu bet 3 beavers pass a cross crosslet fitchée bet 2 fleurs-de-lis or. Impaling: Gu a cross patonce arg (Latimer)
    Crest: a demi-beaver holding in his mouth a branch
    Gore roll of arms. Nathaniel Norden of Marblehead, Mass., married Mary, daughter of Christopher Latimer. Norden d. 1727

Norris 1: Arg a chev gu bet 3 ravens' heads; 2: Sa a cross flory bet 12 billet arg
    Crest: a demi-stag pierced by an arrow
    Bookplate Charles Norris. Jas. Turner, sc.

Norris Arg on a chev gu bet 3 ravens' heads erased sa a mullet or
    Bookplate Isaac Norris, Phila. Jas. Turner, sc.; also of Charles Norris, a son. *See* Art Amateur, Feb. 1894. From Jamaica. Also painted on his carriage.
    Crest: a raven's head of the arms. Amer. Heral., vol. 2, p. 28

Norris Arg on a chev gu bet 3 falcons' heads erased sa, a mullet or
    Crest: a head of the field
    Motto: Ubique patriam reminisci
    Bookplate Joseph Parker Norris, Phila.

North Az a lion passant [or] bet 3 fleurs-de-lis [arg]
    Crest: a dragon's head erased sa, gorged with a ducal cor and chain or (?)
    Motto: Animo et fide

Painting on wood owned by Edwin North Benson, Phila. Zieber's Heral., p. 70

Norton Arg on a bend bet 2 lions ramp [sa] 3 escallops of the first
    Crest: a greyhound's head or gorged with a fess bet 2 bars [gu?]
    For a reproduction of an ancient quartered shield of Daniel Norborne Norton of Magnolia, Va. *See* Bellet's Some Prom. Va. Fam., vol. 1, p. 44

Norton [Arg] a chev bet 3 tuns [sa] hooped [or] standing on their bottoms
    Crest: a griffin's head [or]
    Seal of Capt. Francis Norton of Charlestown, on doc. 1664 in Mass. Archives, vol. 60, p. 258, and also on his will dated 18th June, 1667. Heral. Jour., vol. 4, p. 31

Norton Gu a fret arg, a bend vairé [or and gu] over all
    Crest: a griffin sejeant ppr winged gu beak and forelegs or
    Seal on Rev. John Norton's will, 1663. Norton settled at Ipswich, and succeeded Rev. John Cotton at Boston. Engr. on tankard given by Mrs. Elizabeth Quincy, daughter of Rev. John Norton of Hingham, Mass., to her daughter, Lucy Tufts. In First Ch. Quincy, Mass. *See* Old Sil. Amer. Ch., p. 396. Also Am. Ch. Sil. M. F. A. 1911, pp. 48, 96. Tankard has bend arg and az. M. H. S. Coll., vol. 37, N. E. Gen. Reg., July, 1859, p. 225. Heral. Jour., vol. 2, pp. 5, 177

Norwood Erm a cross engr gu
    Crest: a demi-lion ramp and erased arg holding in his gambs a palm branch vert
    "By the name of Norwood" and palm branches [not by Coles]. Framed embroidery by Judith Norwood of Gloucester, Mass., who d. in 1762. Mrs. J. L. Stevens, Milton, Mass.

Norwood Impaled by Sargent

Nott Az on a bend bet 3 leopards' faces or, as many martlets gu
    Crest: a martlet arg ducally crowned or, in the beak an olive branch ppr
    Arms in Williamsburg Co., Va., on tomb of Edward Nott, Gov. of Va. who d. 23 Aug., 1706, aged 49; buried in Bruton Church. Wm. & Mary Quar., Oct. 1893, p. 78

Noyes [Az] 3 cross crosslets in bend [here sinister] arg
    Crest: on a chapeau gu turned up erm a dove holding in the beak an olive branch ppr
    Motto: Nuncia pacis oliva
    On table tombstone of Rev. James

Noyes (1719) in burying ground, Stonington, Ct. Also bookplate Wm. Curtis Noyes. Hays, sc. N. E. Gen. Reg., 1894, p. 18, 19. 20

Nugent Vert a bend or (?) bet in chief a 3 foil and in base a fleur-de-lis
On automobile of David H. Nugent, Dorchester, Mass.

O

O'Brien Quart 1 and 4: Per pale gu and or 3 lions pass guard in pale counterchanged; 2 and 3: Arg 3 piles gu centered in base
Crest: from a cloud a dexter arm naked holding a broken sword
Motto: Vigueur de dessus
Notepaper F. Winthrop Coll., 1885, at Bos. Ath.

O'Conor Arg on oak tree eradicated and fruited ppr
Crest: a dexter armed arm embowed holding a dagger entwined with a serpent
Motto: A Gaelic motto meaning from the strong hand of God
Bookplate John Christopher O'Conor, 33d St., N. Y. Also on silver cigarette case. His son, Norreys Jephson O'Conor, has an Irish crown of three points in chief on his seal ring

Odell Or 3 crescents [gu?]
Crest: a cock
Motto: Ne quid nimis
Bookplate Rev. Jonathan Odell, a N. J. tory. N. Y. G. & B. Record, April, 1903, p. 99

O'Donnell Sa 2 lions ramp respectant arg supporting a sinister hand [gu] bet 3 mullets of the second (Donnell arms)
Crest: an arm emb holding a spear issuing from a ducal cor
Motto: In hoc signo vinces
Bookplate —— O'Donnell, Washington, D. C.

Offley Arg on a cross pattée flory az, a lion pass guard or bet 4 Cornish choughs ppr
Tomb of Sara Offley, Church Point, Princess Anne Co. She d. 1627, the wife of Adam Thorowgood. Crozier's Va. Heral., p. 12 and 13

Offley *See also* Bernard

Ogden Gyronny of 8 arg and gu. In the dexter chief a sprig of oak fructed ppr
Crest: an oak tree with a lion ramp
Motto: Et si ostendo non facto
Seal on letters of David Ogden seen by E. A. Jones of Pwllheli. Also bookplate of —— Ogden

Ogilby Arg a lion pass guard bet 2 cresc [in chief and a cinquefoil in base gu?]
Crest: a lion ramp grasping a pole (?) with a vine about it

Motto: Toujours pret
Monument to Frederick Ogilby, d. 1813. Trinity Church, N. Y.

Ogle Arg a fess bet 3 cresc gu
Crest: a bull's head couped
Bookplate —— Ogle

Olcott Gu a fess bet 2 chev vairé arg and az within a bordure or (Goodyer arms?)
Crest: a partridge holding in the beak 3 ears of wheat ppr
Motto: Grata manu
Bookplate George Olcott, Jr., Charlestown, N. H.

Olcott Per saltire gu and az a saltire [or?] over all a leopard's head (?) erased contourné. On a chief arg 3 fleurs-de-lis [   ] bet 8 stars of 6 points 2 and 2 sa
Crest: a cock contourné
Bookplate Josiah Olcott of Stratford, Conn. Bates's Early Conn. Engr., p. 33

Oliver Erm on a chief sa 3 lions ramp arg
An escutcheon of pretence on the bookplate of John Proctor Anderdon of Antigua, who married in 1785 Anne, daughter of Thomas Oliver, Lieut. Gov. of Mass. Oliver's West Indian bookplates, 1914, No. 3

Oliver Or 3 garbs gu (Mountford arms)
Crest: a demi-lion holding a garb
Bookplate Peter Oliver, Andover, Mass.

Oliver Quart of 8: 1 and 8: Arg from a cloud at the sinister an arm in fess holding a dexter hand couped at the wrist and dropping blood; 2: Vert a chev or bet 3 leopards' faces (Fitch); 3: Gu on a chief or 3 crosses potent — or mallets? (Lynde); 4: Az a fleur-de-lis arg (Digby); 5: Per bend arg and sa 3 roundels within a bordure all counterch (Pynchon); 6: Arg 2 bends engr sa (Empson?); 7: Gu a chev or bet 3 apples gu leaved vert (Appleton)
Crest: a martlet arg holding a sprig
Motto: Pax in bello
Bookplate Peter Oliver. Also of "Oliver," with Pax aut bellum

Oliver Quart 1 and 4: Arg from a cloud on the sinister an arm in fess holding a dexter gauntlet gu; 2 and 3: Vert a chev or bet 3 leopards' heads [or] (Fitch?)

Crest: a martlet arg holding a sprig
Motto: Pax quaeritur bello
Bookplate Andrew Oliver of Mass.
(engr. by Paul Revere). The bookplate of Chief Justice Peter Oliver,
Boston, 1713–91 had for motto: Fideli
amore. Arms on his portrait. An
early painting impaling Lynde is
engraved in Heral. Jour., vol. 3, p. 3]

Oliver Arg an arm from the sinister
side fessways the hand grasping a
dexter hand couped at the wrist, all
proper
Crest: a martlet arg holding in its
beak a sprig [vert]
Engr. on a paten made by Hurd.
Museum of Fine Arts, Boston, from
Mrs. Ambrose Dawes. The same coat
quartering Fitch (vert a chev bet 3
leopards' faces or) and impaling Lynde
(Gu on a chief or 3 crosses potent) was
engraved as a bookplate, probably by
Hurd. Whitmore's Elem. of Heral., p.
75

Orkney *See* Sinclair

Orme Impaled by Alston

Osborn Arg a bend sa bet 2 lions pass
of the second
Crest: a lion's head under a ducal
cor
Miss Violet Osborn, Hingham, Mass.
Painted by Mrs. C. C. Lane

Osgood Arg [or?] 3 garbs within a
tressure flory. Impaling: Sa a fess arg
bet 3 escallops
Crest: a demi-lion rampant holding
a garb in its paws
Bookplate "By the name of Osgood"

Osgood Or 3 garbs
Crest: a demi-lion ramp holding a
garb
Bookplate Peter Osgood, Andover,
Mass., 1745–1801. Bates's Early Conn.
Engr., p. 34

Osgood Or 3 garbs
Crest: a demi-lion ramp supporting
a garb
Worked in tapestry or worsted and
brought from England by John Osgood
of Andover, Mass. Heral. Jour., vol.
1, p. 8

Otis Arg a saltire engr az bet 4 crosses
crosslet fitchée [?]
Crest: a vested arm gu holding an
ear of wheat
Motto: Sapiens qui vigilat
Bookplate Dr. Jenckes Harris Otis,
U. S. N.

Overing Arg a chev az bet 3 eagles'
heads erased sa. Impaling: Gu a
spear or bendwise bet 2 rowels of 6
points or (Auchmuty)
Seal owned by N. Y. family. Heads
may be griffins. N. Y. Gen. & Biog.
Rec., Apr. 1904, p. 145. Boston
lawyer?

Owen Gu a chev bet 3 lions ramp or
Crest: a lion ramp or
Motto: Honestas optima politia
Notepaper Benjamin Owen, 44 Sted-
man Street, Brookline, Mass.

Owen [Or?] a lion ramp [gu?]
Engr. on tankard from Jeremiah
Owen, 1756, a schoolmaster. First
Presbyterian Church, N. Y. Old Sil.
Am. Ch., p. 336

Oxenbridge Gu a lion ramp arg within
a bordure vert charged with 8 escallops
of the second
Crest: a demi-lion tail forked arg,
langued and armed gu, holding in the
dexter paw an escallop or
Seal on will of Rev. John Oxenbridge, 1674, of the First Church,
Boston. Heral. Jour., vol. 2, pp. 178,
179

P

Paddy Sa an inscutcheon erminois (?)
bet 4 lions ramp or (?)
Crest: a lion pass
Ancient framed water color. William Paddy, treasurer of Plymouth and
selectman of Boston, d. 1658. Mass.
Hist. Society, Boston. Also framed
water color (ancient), Pilgrim Hall,
Plymouth, Mass.

Padelford Vert a lion ramp arg. On a
chief gu a fleur-de-lis bet 2 towers arg
Crest: a leopard sejant
Bookplate Arthur Padelford

Page [   ] a chev bet 3 martlets [   ]
Crest: a demi-griffin
Motto: Spe labor levis

Notepaper David Perkins Page and
grandson, Rufus Willes Page of North
Chatham, Mass.

Page [Arg] a chev sa bet 3 martlets
Crest: from a ducal cor a demi-
griffin
Bookplate Francis Page "of the
Inner Temple, 1703," and of Rosewell,
Va. *See* Sale's Manors of Va., p. 202

Page [Or] a fess dancettée bet 3 martlets [az]
Crest: a demi-horse forcené (or
rearing)
Arms of Col. John Page (d. 1692)
in the vestibule of Bruton Church,
Williamsburg, Va. *See also* his wife

Alice Luckin. Also shield and crest on tomb of Col. Nathaniel Page, Rosewell graveyard, Parish of Abingdon, d. 1703. Also on tomb of Mary, wife of Hon. Matthew, who d. 1707. Arms and crest of Gov. John Page, St. John's Churchyard, Richmond, Va., with motto: Spe labor levis. Seen by S. K. Bolton, 26 Mch. 1924. Also on burnt wood owned by Robert Powel Page of "Saratoga," Clarke Co., Va., with motto: Spe labor levis. Arms and crest on tomb of Mann Page at Rosewell, Gloucester Co., who d. 1730. Impaling: [Arg] a chev bet 3 cartwheels (Carter). The shield has really a fess dancettée across both coats. The Page arms have all 3 martlets in chief 2 and 1. On the tomb of Elizabeth Page, daughter of Matthew of "Timber Neck, 1693, are the arms of Pagett: Sa a cross engr and in the dexter chief an escallop arg. Wm. & Mary Quar., Apr. 1894, p. 266. Page cut on the white marble tablet to the Pages in Gloucester Court House. This, Mann Page, Nathaniel, and Mary, seen by L. Park, 1922. Also on tomb of Capt. Francis Page of Bruton Parish, Va., who d. 10 May, 1692, aged 35, Williamsburg, Va. Seen by L. Park, 1922. Also on tomb of Elizabeth Page, wife of John Page of York and daughter of Captain Francis Page, d. 12 Nov. 1702 in 20th year of her age. Seen by L. P. at Bruton Parish, Williamsburg, Va.

Page Or a fess dancettée bet 3 martlets az within a bordure of the last
Crest: a demi-horse per pale dancettée or and az
Motto: Spe labor levis
Bookplate Logan Waller Page, engineer, Washington, D. C. Framed coat and crest at Miss Mildred Page's, Charlotteville, Va. On carved wood entrance gate, Louis Coues Page, 67 Powell St., Brookline, Mass. Also on ex libris, F. G. Hall, sc.

Page Or a fess gu bet 3 doves arg
Crest: on a ducal cor a griffin segreant or
Motto: Spe labor levis
"By the name of Page" and palm branches. Framed water color, owned by David Page of Newburyport, Mass., from Epping, N. H. First princ. State Normal School, Albany. Now owned by Mrs. G. A. Anderson, Lunenburg, Mass.

Paget Quartered by Hoskins

Paige [Arg] on a bend [   ] 3 eagles displayed
Crest: a demi-eagle couped
Seal of Nicholas Paige, Boston, 1679, on a Mass. Archives doc., vol. 61, p. 196

Pain [Gu] a fess arg bet 2 lions pass arg. Impaling: a barry of six, over all a bend (Mulchester or Gaunt). From St. Kitts or Antigua?
A small stone for Elizabeth, wife of Samuel Pain, near the King's Chapel wall. She d. in 1704. King's Chapel Graveyard, Boston. Heral. Jour., vol. 2, p. 19

Paine Arg on a fess [gu] bet 3 martlets [sa] as many mascles [or], all within a bordure [of the second bezantée]
Crest: [a wolf's head erased az charged with 5 bezants saltireways]
On a letter from William Paine to Gov. John Winthrop (Winthrop papers). M. H. S. Coll., vol. 37. Heral. Jour., vol. 3, p. 178. See Paine Geneal. 1881

Paine Az a bend raguly or bet 6 stars of 6 points sa
Crest: an otter [or?] holding in its mouth a fish [arg?]
Motto: Toujours peine
Notepaper Miss Mary Louise Paine, Newton Center, Mass.

Paine Az a bend raguly or bet 6 estoiles of 6 points
Crest: a demi-officer holding a sword
Motto: Forward
Bookplate Robert Treat Paine, Boston. "Harry Soane, London, 1885," sc. Robert Treat Paine, Jr., has for crest a demi-lion ramp with supporters

Palmer Arg on 2 bars sa 3 trefoils slipped. In chief a greyhound courant sa
Crest: a greyhound sejant sa
Bookplate Clarkson Palmer. That of Josª Palmer has the trefoils vert

Palmer Arg 2 bars sa charged with 3 trefoils slipped of the field. In chief a greyhound courant sa [collared or]. Impaling quarterly 1: Or a lion ramp; 2: Arg an arm issuing fessways from the sinister and holding a heart; 3: Az a wolf's head couped ppr; 4: Or a galley vert, 3 oars on a side erect and crossed, a flag gu
Crest: a greyhound sejant [sa]
Motto: Vix ea nostra voco
Bookplate Thomas Palmer. N. Hurd, sculp.
Thomas Palmer of Boston, 17—, mentioned in Burke's Landed Gentry, 1860, as of Nazing, Co. Essex. N. E. H. Gen. Reg., vol. 43, p. 83. From Wanlip, Leic.

Palmer Arg a chev bet 3 palmers' scrips sa the tassels and buckles or
Crest: an eagle (?) affrontée gu and or
"By the name of Palmer" and palm branches. Framed water color, made

for Ezra Palmer, Ann St., Boston, b. in Newport, R. I., 1781, desc. of Wm. Palmer, who came in the ship *Fortune*. Owned by Mrs. W. B. Stevens, Sr., 98 Mt. Vernon St., Boston

Palmer Or 2 bars gu (?) each charged with 3 trefoils arg and in chief a grey-hound courant sa
    Crest: a demi-panther holding in his paws a holly leaf
    Motto: Palma virtuta (sic)
    Notepaper Mary Ridgeley Palmer, Belvidere Ave., Baltimore

Palmer Quart 1 and 4: Or 2 bars gu, each charged with 3 trefoils arg. In chief a greyhound courant sa; 2 and 3: Gu 3 cresc 2 and 1 within a bordure arg ch. with 8 roses gu (Melville)
    Crest: a demi-lion holding a palm leaf
    Motto: Ultra aspicio
    Bookplate Lowell Melvin Palmer, engr. by French, 1904. Typical of French's heraldry

Palmes [Gu] 3 fleurs-de-lis, 2 and 1 [arg], a chief chequy [prop vairé] a cresc in the fess point
    Crest: a dexter hand vested [   ] holding wheat heads
    On the gravestone of Hon. Charles Chambers, 1743. Tomb No. 50, Phipps Street Yard, Charlestown, Mass. Heral Jour., vol. 1, p. 57. His mother was Elizabeth, daughter of Andrew Palmes of Sherborn, Hants, an ancient family of Naburn, Yorks. Andrew's son, Major Edward, was at New London, Conn.

Palmes Gu 3 fleurs-de-lis arg, a chief vairé
    Crest: a hand holding a palm branch ppr
    Motto: Ut palma justus
    Seal of Edward Palmes, who d. at New London, 1714, in Conn. Archives with cresc for cadency. Heral. Jour., vol. 1, p. 159

Panton Quart 1 and 4: Gu 2 bars erm. On a canton sa a fer-de-Moline [erm] 2: Quart arg and gu, 1 and 4 charged with a stag trippant az, 2 and 3 with the same arg; 3: Arg 3 boars' heads az. Over all an inscutcheon quart 1 and 4: Gu a chev arg bet 3 cinquefoils; 2 and 3: Az 6 bees 3, 2, 1
    Crest: a stag tripp arg
    Bookplate Paul Panton. Francis Panton, Junʳ, of N. Y., had a landscape bookplate with two ducks holding a shield of Panton arms, with crest: a swan rising; and motto; "Spero meliora." By Maverick

Park For arms used by Wm. Edwards Park, *see* Edwards

Parke Arg? 3 stags' heads erased
    Crest: a demi-maiden nude holding in dexter hand a sword and in sinister hand a distaff
    Motto: Terra aut mari
    Bookplate John Parke, Esq., A. M. of Va. Signed I. S[kinner], sculp. Arms not in Burke

Parke Quartered by Corbin

Parker [   ] a chev bet 3 cushions (?) or Bowen knots
    Letter of James Parker of Dorchester and Weymouth to Gov. Winthrop, 1644. M. H. S. Coll., vol. 37

Parker Arg a chev bet 3 leopards' faces or
    Crest: a crane
    Motto: Aude fieri justum
    Bookplate B. Parker

Parker Arg a chev embat and counter-embat sa bet 3 stags' heads cabossed [gu]
    Crest: a talbot holding in the dexter paw a stag's head of the field
    Motto: Fortitude in adversity
    Bookplate George Phillips Parker

Parker Impaled by Deacon

Parkman Az a chev bet in chief a helmet pierced fessways by a sword and in base a ducal cor, all arg
    Crest: a horse courant arg
    Framed water color owned by late Henry Parkman, 30 Commonwealth Ave., Boston

Parks Gu on a pale arg 3 bucks' heads cabossed of the field
    Crest: a talbot's head erased gu charged on the breast with a pheon or
    Motto: Usque ad mortem
    Bookplate —— Parks

Parmele 2 gyrons conjoined in a whorl (?)
    Bookplate Dr. George L. Parmele, Hartford

Parrott On a chev 3 parrots
    Crest: a parrot (?
    Arms on a silver tankard by Nath. Hurd. "Belongs to —— Spalding." Owned by Susan Parker Parrott

Parry Vert a stag tripp ppr
    Crest: a horse's head erased [arg]
    Motto: Gofal Dyn Duw ai Gwerid
    Bookplate —— Parry, Phila.

Parsons Gu 2 chev erm bet 3 eagles displ or
    Bookplate Susan E. P[arsons] Forbes. J. W. Spenceley, Boston, 1905. Also Helen Parsons, by Hopson, 1906

Parsons Gu 2 chev erm bet 3 eagles
displ or
    Crest: an eagle's leg erased at the
thigh or, standing on a leopard's head
gu
    Seal on will of Timothy Prout, 1702,
witnessed by Thomas Hunt, Thomas
Harwood, and Humphrey Parsons.
Heral. Jour., vol. 3, p. 91

Parsons Gu 2 chev erm bet 3 eagles
displ [or]
    Crest: an eagle's leg erased [or]
standing on a leopard's head [gu]
    Motto: Dum spiro spero
    Seal ring New York

Paschall Arg a cross sa bet 1 and 4 a
bird sa and 2 and 3 a lion pass guard sa,
the cross charged with a pascal lamb
arg
    Bookplate Cora Paschall Davis, by
E. D. French

Pasley Az on a chev arg bet 3 roses 3
thistles slipped ppr
    Crest: a mail arm emb holding a
dagger fessways
    Bookplate William Pasley of N. Y.
Maverick? sculpt.

Pasract Quartered by Van Rensselaer

Paterson Arg 3 pelicans in their piety
[or, nests vert]
    Crest: a pelican of the field
    Motto: Such is love
    Bookplate Evan Paterson. F. Gar-
den, sc. Bookplate Walter Patterson
of N. J. and Penn. (J. D. Stout, sc.)
has for motto: I die for those I love

Patteson Quartered by Cabell

Paul Quartered by Jones

Paxton On a semée of fleurs-de-lis a
papal hat or (?)
    Motto: Fidelis morte
    Crest: a mailed arm emb holding a
sword
    Bookplate Wm. Paxton

Payne Quartered by Dumaresq

Payne *See also* Paine

Payne Arg (?) a bend gu (?) bet in
chief a lion's head cabossed and in base
an eagle's leg couped à-la-guise holding
a torteau
    In 1866 in the wall of 14 Beacon St.
covered with earth. I could not find
it in 1914. Edward Payne lived near
by. Granary Burying Ground, Boston. Heral. Jour., vol. 2, p. 134.
Bridgman's Pilgrims of Boston, p. 69.
See Paine Geneal., 1881, p. 73, where
the grave is mentioned as William's,
but another coat claimed for Wm.
Paine

Payson Gu an eagle rising, a chief or
    Crest: a mailed hand holding a lance
in bend with pennant
    Motto: Meum et tuum
    Bookplate Arthur Lithgow Payson

Peabody Per fess nebulée gu and az.
In chief 2 suns in splendor and a garb
in base or
    Crest: an eagle rising or
    Motto: Murus aereus conscientia
sana
    On Bohemian glass pitcher given by
Senator Charles Sumner to Lieut.-Gov.
Wm. Phillips. Bostonian Society. The
same arms appear on a bookplate of the
Peabody Institute, Danvers, for George
Peabody, the great philanthropist.
Also bookplates of N. Peabody (old)
and F. H. Peabody (modern). *See*
Amer. Heral., vol. 2, p. 24, where the
eagle is reguardant ppr

Peabody Per fess nebulée gu and az.
In chief 2 suns in splendor and a garb
in base or
    Motto: Murus aereus conscientia
sana
    Painted on the window of the library
of Prof. Geo. Herbert Palmer by Prof.
J. F. Weir of Yale College. Boxford,
Mass.
    Bookplate May Peabody, engr. by
Hopson, 1895, with motto: "Ne quid
nimis." Window, Blake Mem. Chapel,
Salem, Mass.

Peachey Az a lion ramp double queued
erm, ducally crowned or, a canton of the
last charged with a mullet pierced gu
    Crest: a demi-lion double queued
erm holding in the dexter paw a sword
point upward
    Will of Samuel Peachey, 1711, men-
tions his grandson to whom he leaves
"My great silver tankard and my
sealed ring, having both my coate of
Armes." Crozier's Va. Heral., 1908,
p. 51

Pearce Arg a chev or bet 3 fishes
    Crest: a lion's head erased
    Seal of Henry Ward Pearce of Poplar
Neck, Cecil Co., Md. (b. 1736). His
daughter Mary married Moses Levy.
Owned by Mrs. Robert H. Bancroft,
Boston

Pearmain Or on a chev gu bet 3 escallops azure as many crosses crosslet
of the field
    Crest: a demi-lion ramp
    Motto: Dirige
    Framed water color by Henry
Mitchell of Boston, sealmaker, owned
by Sumner B. Pearmain, Framingham,
Mass. Also shield over fireplace

Pearson *See also* Chapman

Pease Per fess az and erm a fess sa bet in chief 2 escallops and in base a fleur-de-lis
    Crest: a unicorn ramp contourné with paws on mortar and pestle
    Bookplate Dr. Oliver Pease, 1760–1843, Suffield, Conn. Bates's Early Conn. Engr., p. 35

Pease Per fess arg and gu an eagle displayed counterchanged
    Crest: an eagle's head ppr erased holding a branch vert
    Motto: Sic itur as astra. Optime de patria meruit
    Water color. Miss Jospehine M. Stone, Cambridge, Mass. Engr. bookplate (1st motto only) of Miss Ethelwyn Pease of Boston and Chicago. Also Henry Hollister Pease, 1906, by Spenceley. Newbottel arms?

Pechell Impaled by Caillaud

Peck Arg on a chev engr gu 3 crosses formée of the field
    Crest: 2 lances or in saltire headed arg, pennons hanging to them or, each charged with a cross formée gu, the spears enfiled with a chaplet vert
    Motto (of an English branch): Crux Christi salus mea
    Tombstone of Captain Samuel Peck of Rehoboth (d. 1736). Used also by Captain John Mason. Vermont's Amer. Heral. [1886], pp. 108, 175

Peck See also Mason

Peckham Erm a chief quarterly gu and or
    Crest: an ostrich
    Motto: Tentanda via est
    Arms of Peckham of Nyton, Sussex
    Bookplate Antoinette Storrs Peckham

Peel Arg a bend bet 2 mullets [sa]
    On tomb of Samuel and Robert Peel, 1733, in All Hallows or South River churchyard, Md. See Hist. Graves of Md., p. 22. "In a lozenge."

Pelham Az 3 pelicans arg vulning themselves ppr
    Crest: a peacock in his pride
    Motto: Vincit amor patriae
    Seal of Herbert Pelham, d. 1676. Settled in Cambridge, 1638. M. H. S. Coll., vol. 37. Vermont's Amer. Heral. [1886], pp. 18, 175

Pell Erm on a canton az a pelican or vulning herself gu
    Crest: on a chaplet vert flowered or a pelcian of the last vulned gu
    Mottoes: Deus Amicus. Mea spes est in Deo
    Tablet dated 1697 in Trinity Church, New Rochelle. Also on a document found under the cornerstone of the old church at Pelham signed by John Pell and his wife. Heral. Jour., vol. 3, p. 6. Also bookplate Howe and Pell, N. Y., with motto: Deus amici et noi

Pellew Gu a lion ramp guard or. In chief 2 chaplets, a crescent for diff. On a chief wavy a ship at sea, sails furled, before an embat wall with 2 towers, all ppr
    Crest: a ship at sea before a lighthouse, a, cresc for diff, all ppr
    Mottoes: 1: Deo adjuvante. 2: Algiers
    Bookplate George Pellew. See Burke

Pemberton Arg a chev sa bet 3 buckets sa handles and hoops or
    Crest: a dragon's head sa
    Steel seal owned by Henry Pemberton, Phila. Also his bookplate, "H. P." Zieber's Heral., p. 70

Pemberton Arg a chev bet 3 buckets sa
    In a volume of sermons by the Rev. Ebenezer Pemberton, published 1727, is a portrait prefixed, underneath which appears this coat

Pendleton Gu an inscutcheon arg bet 4 escallops or
    Crest: a demi-dragon with wings addorsed or, holding an escallop arg
    Motto: Maneo qualis manebam (not present on all)
    Bookplate Edmund H. Pendleton. Lewis, N. Y., sc. J. D. Stout, N. Y., sc. See Bellet's Some Prom. Va. Fam., vol. 4, p. 224

Pengelly Az 3 escallops
    Bookplate W. G. Pengelly, 1897. This does not appear to be the Pengelly coat

Penington Or 5 fusils in fess az
    Crest: a wildcat pass guard
    Motto: Vincit amor patriae
    Seal on latter from Wm. Pennington, customs officer and loyalist, 1788. Seen by E. A. Jones, London, and Pwllheli. Engr. on silver owned by Mrs. Cookman, Phila. Shield only
    Bookplate Henry Penington, Phila. Sometimes 5 mascles arg voided az. Sylvan City, p. 468

Penn Arg on a fess sa 3 plates
    Crest: a demi-lion rampant gorged with a collar sa charged with 3 plates
    Motto: Dum clavum teneam (or Dum clarum rectum teneam)
    Bookplate William Penn, Esqr. Propr. of Pennsylvania, 1703. Also Sophia Penn (in a lozenge). Zieber's Heral., p. 41

Penn Arg on a fess sa 3 plates. Impaling: Per chev gu and erm, in chief 2 leopards' (?) heads erased
Seal of John Penn, Gov. Penn. 1763–71, 1773–76. Sylvan City, 1883, p. 457

Pennington Or 5 fusils conjoined in fess az
Crest: a crown
Supporters: A lion reguard charged with an acorn leaved and a horse ppr [bridled and saddled or]
Bookplate ——— Pennington, Penn.

Pennypacker A tile erect which rests in the ground and is surrounded by leaves
Motto: Mein Siegel ist ein Ziegel. Pannebakker
Bookplate Samuel W. Pennypacker, Gov. of Pennsylvania. Desc. from Hendrick Pfannebacker, Wm. Penn's surveyor, from Leyden to the Schuylkill in 1674, member of the tile-bakers' guild. (Letter from Henry Pennypacker, Sept. 1924). Usually 3 tiles shown. (Looks like an erect spade with short handle.) Another arg 3 scrolls 2 and 1 gu; crest: a winged scroll

Penrose Arg 3 bends sa, each charged with as many pierced mullets arg
Crest: a trout naiant or
Motto: Ubique fedelis
Engr. on cup brought from England before 1775 by Capt. Joseph Penrose. From Cornwall. Framed water color owned by Mrs. Edward M. Davis, Shirley, Mass.

Pepper Gu on a chev arg bet 3 demi-lions, ramp [or] 3 pellets. In chief a trefoil slipped
Crest: a demi-lion ramp guard or
Motto: Semper erectus
Bookplate Henry Pepper. Also William Pepper, M. D., Phila.

Pepperell Arg a chev gu bet 3 pineapples [vert]. On a canton [gu] a fleur-de-lis [arg]. On an inscutcheon a dexter hand (erroneously) for the badge of Ulster at the center
Engr. on baptismal basin from Sir William Pepperell, Bart., First Church, Kittery, Maine. Sir William's tomb at Kittery Point has the shield, but with no canton (?). Old Sil. Am. Ch., p. 236

Pepperell Arg a chev gu bet 3 pineapples vert. A canton gu charged with a fleur-de-lis arg. Badge of Ulster
Crest: out of a crown a mailed arm holding a banner and over it the word Peperi
Motto: Virtute parta tuemini

On engr. portrait of Sir William Pepperell by J. C. Buttre from original in Essex Institute. Print in Mass. Hist. Soc. Also on a bookplate of Sir Wm. The original arms on parchment made for Sir William are owned by Mrs. Margaret Cutts Judson, Omaha, Neb., a descendant in the 5th generation

Percival Arg on a chief indented gu 3 crosses pattee arg. The badge of Ulster
Crest: a thistle
Supporters: An antelope arg and a stag sa, both ducally crowned and chained
Motto: Sub cruce canto
Bookplate John Percival, Earl of Egmont, 1736, gov. of Georgia

Perine Arg on a chev bet 3 escallops sa 3 crosses pattée [or]
Crest: out of a ducal cor [or] a peacock's head ppr
Bookplate Fred Agens Perine, Detroit. Arms brought over by ancestor Daniel Perrin, Elizabethtown, N. J., 1665. Some Amer. Coll. Bookplates, 1915, p. 321

Perkins Arg a fess indented erm bet in chief 4 billets of the second and in base 6 billets ?, 2, 1
Crest: a pineapple stalked and leaved [vert]
Bookplate George A. Perkins, M. D., Salem, 1880. Also sketch from Harriet Herring, Spray, N. C., "from drawing or wall plaque," with motto "Toujours loyale"

Perkins Arg a fess indented bet 10 billets ermines 4, 3, 2, 1
No crest
On 3 silver tea caddies owned by the Misses Loring, 32 Mt. Vernon St., Boston

Perkins Vert a chev arg bet 3 ostrich feathers erect [arg]
Crest: a demi-man holding 3 ostrich feathers in his dexter hand
Engr. on flagon from Christ'. Perkins, about 1764. Christ Church, Norfolk, Va. Old Sil. Am. Ch., p. 343

Peronneau Az a dolphin bet 3 fleurs-de-lis
Crest: a sun in splendor with human features
Motto: Clarior alter
Bookplate Robert Peronneau of Charleston, S. C.

Perot Quarterly per fess indented or and az a mascle counterchanged
Crest: a sitting hen (parrot?)
Motto: Fama proclamat honorem
Bookplate James Perot

Perrott Three pears
On a seal of Richard Perrot at Middlesex Court House, Va. Crozier's Va. Heral., 1908, p. 55

Perry Quart sa and or. Over all on a bend gu 3 lions pass guard or (?) a cresc for diff
Crest: a hind's head erased
Motto: Virtus vincit invidiam
Bookplate Rev. Joseph Perry, East Windsor, Conn., about 1780. J. Allen, sc.

Peter Gu a bend bet 2 escallops arg
Seal on a letter from Hugh Peter to Gov. John Winthrop (Winthrop papers). M. H. S. Coll., vol. 36, 37

Peters [Gu] on a bend [or] bet 2 escallops [arg] 2 cinquefoils [az]. On a chief [ ] a rose
Crest: two lions' heads erased, endorsed, and gorged, the dexter one [or], the sinister [az] the collars counterchanged
Arms of Judge Richard Peters of the Revolution, stucco. Belmont Mansion, Fairmount Park, Phila. Chamberlain MSS. N. E. Reg., Apr. 1880, p. 185. Sylvan City (1883), p. 466. The Continent, April 25, 1883

Petigru Gu a cresc bet 3 mullets arg
Crest: three ostrich feathers
Motto: Verité sans peur
Bookplate James Louis Petigru, lawyer, Charleston, S. C., 1789–1863

Petty A heart pierced by 2 arrows (Yeoman arms?)
Seal on will of Max'milian Petty, Middlesex Co., Va., 1749. Wm. & Mary Quar., Jan. 1893, p. 122

Peyton Sa a cross engr or
Crest: a griffin sejant or
Major G. A. Barksdale used the Peyton arms on his bookplate

Phelps Arg on a fess az bet 4 lions ramp gu 3 mullets sa
Crest: a lion's head erased ppr
"By the name of Phelps" and palm branches. Evidently from a water color. Used by descendants of Wm. Phelps of Dorchester, Mass. Amer. Fam. of Hist. Lineage, vol. 1, p. 121

Philipse Az a demi-lion [sa] ducally gorged arg and ducally crowned [or]
Crest: a lion of the field gorged by a Viscount's coronet
Bookplate Frederik Philipse, Esq., N. Y. See R. Bolton's Westchester

Phelps Arg a lion ramp sa bet 6 crosses crosslet fitchée gu
Crest: a demi-lion ramp crowned
Motto: Veritas sine timore
Bookplate Charles Harris Phelps

Phillips Arg a lion ramp sa gorged [gu?] and chained [or?]
Crest: a demi-lion ramp guard
Motto: Omnes benevolentia
Bookplate James Phillips

Phillips Or a lion ramp sa gorged and chained
Crest: a lion sejant sa gorged and chained
Bookplate Phillips Academy, Andover, Mass. Another with azure field and a chief erm, the crest a demi-lion ramp guard

Phillips Or a lion ramp gorged sa.
Impaling: Sa on a chev or [arg?] 3 sprigs of broom [vert]. On a canton or a spear head erect [az] embrued [gu] (Bromfield)
Crest: a lion pass sejant
Engr. on flagon from Hon. William Phillips, 1804. Old South Ch., Boston. Old Sil. Am. Ch., p. 56

Phillips Impaled by Lemmon

Phillips See also Dix

Phinney Quart 1 and 6: Vert a chev bet 3 eagles displayed or; 2: Az 3 crosses crosslet arg in bend; 3 and 8: Az a tortoise erect [or] (Cooper); 4 and 7: Az a forked pennant debruised by a fess or; 5: Az bet 2 flaunches erm in chief 3 roundels erm and in base a leopard's face
Crests: 1: a demi-eagle with 2 heads displayed; 2: a tortoise fessways; 3: an armed arm emb holding a pennant
Motto: Prodesse quam conspici
Bookplate Hy Frederick Phinney, Cooperstown, N. Y., son-in-law of Jas. Fenimore Cooper

Phippen Arg 2 bars sa in chief 3 escallops of the second
Crest: a griffin's head erased
Geneal. of Phippen family drawn by John Symonds of Salem, from copy defaced during the Revolutionary War. A bookplate "Fitzpen or Phippen" has for crest a bee. Heral. Jour., vol. 4, pp. 1, 2, 9

Phipps Sa a trefoil slipped bet 8 mullets arg
Crest: a lion's gamb sa holding a trefoil of the field
State House, Boston. In color in a window, 3d floor. On a doc. in Mass. Archives, 1692, vol. 61, p. 330

Phipps [Sa] a trefoil slipped bet 8 mullets [arg]
Crest: a gamb erect holding a trefoil [both sa]
Motto: Virtute Quies

On David Wood's tomb, No. 55, 1762. Phipps Street Yard, Charlestown, Mass. Heral. Jour., vol. 1, p. 47. *See* vol. 4, p. 29, for Samuel Phipps's use of the Bradway arms, a chev bet 3 bunches of grapes

Phipps [Sa] a trefoil slipped bet eight mullets [arg]
    Crest: a lion's gamb erect holding a trefoil
    Engr. on "A Prospect of the Colledges in Cambridge" &c dedicated by W. Price about 1739 to Spencer Phipps. Mass. Historical Society, Boston. *See also* Oliver's West Indian bookplates, 1914, Nos. 696, 697

Phipps *See also* Arnold

Phips Sa a trefoil slipped erm bet 8 mullets arg
    Crest: a bear's paw sa holding a trefoil slipped erm
    Seal on Sir William Phips's will, 1695, in the Suffolk Registry. Heral. Jour., vol. 1, p. 47, 120, 153

Pickering Erm a lion ramp az crowned or
    Crest: a demi-lion
    Motto: Nec timere nec timide
    Embroidered hatchment by [Mrs.] Sarah Pickering [Clarke], 1753. Picture in Pickering Geneal. (1897), vol. 1, p. 11. The will of John Pickering, 1722 (Essex Co. Probate) has a seal with a lion rampant
    Bookplate A. H. Pickering, Shakespeare interpreter. No crest. Col. Timothy Pickering's silver seal. No motto. Tankard by E. Winslow, 1690; arms added about 1695 for W. and H. P.

Pickman Gu 2 battle axes in saltire [or] bet four martlets arg
    Crest: a martlet of the field
    Engr. on tankard from Benjamin Pickman, 1759, to the First Church, Salem, Transferred to North Church, 1772. Window, Blake Mem. Chapel, Salem, Mass. Tomb of the wife of Samuel Pickman, Esquire, who d. in 1761. Salem, Mass. graveyard. On tombstone of Benjamin Pickman, d. 1708, aged 63. (Birds look like doves.) Also on stone to Dr. Thomas Pickman, 1773–1817. Amer. Ch. Sil., M. F. A., Bos. 1911, p. 116. Heral. Jour., vol. 1, pp. 135, 136; vol. 2, pp. 26, 27

Pickman He beareth Gules between two battle axes in saltire or four martlets argent
    Crest: a hand habited gu ruffled arg holding a battle axe in pale or
    Framed water color by S. Blyth in Essex Institute, Salem, Mass. "By the name of Pickman." Cornstalks broken or bent

Pierce [   ] an eagle displ
    Seal of Nathaniel Pierce, Portsmouth, N. H., 1751. Jeffries MSS. N. E. Reg., Jan. 1877, p. 64

Pierce Arg a fess humettée sa bet 3 blackbirds
    Crest: a crane rising
    Motto: In futura spector
    Bookplate Wm. L. Pierce, N. Y. Maverick, sc.

Pierce Arg a fess humettée gu bet 3 ravens rising sa
    Crest: a raven or
    Embr. hatchment by Mrs. Sarah Pierce Nichols, 1796. Misses Nichols, Salem, owners. *See* Picture in Pickering Geneal. (1897), vol. 1, p. 225

Pierce Arg a fess humettée bet 3 blackbirds
    Crest: a bird holding a twig
    Bookplate Henry Hough Pierce

Pierce Gu a chev arg bet 3 roundels
    Crest: an eagle with U. S. shield
    "By the name of Pierce." Framed. Mrs. William E. Barnard, owner, Shirley, Mass.

Pierce Sa a chev erm bet 3 griffins' heads erm
    Crest: a pelican vulning herself
    Motto: Deus mihi providebit
    Bookplate John Timbrell Milward Pierce, Yankton, So. Dak.

Pierpont Arg a lion ramp on a semée of cinquefoils gu
    Crest: a lion of the field
    Motto: Manet amicitia florebitque semper
    Bookplate Charles Pierpont. S. Hill, sc.

Pierpont Impaled by Adams

Pierson Arg 2 chev az bet 3 (beech?) leaves erect vert
    Crest: a doe's head couped [arg] charged with 2 chev az
    Bookplate A. L. Pierson, Mass.

Pietz Per fess arg and gu in chief a key fessways gu (ring to sinister) in base peaks arg
    Crest: a demi-lion arg 2 bars gu holding erect a key of the arms
    Bookplate Adam Pietz of Phila. A. Pietz, sc., 1901

Pigeon Or a chev az bet 3 pigeons ppr
    Water color. Miss Josephine M. Stone, Cambridge, Mass.

Pincham Quartered by Cabell

Pinckney Arg 5 lozenges conjoined in pale sa within a bordure engr sa
    Motto: Non nobis solum
    Bookplate Charles Pinckney, Esq. Also with motto but no crest on tomb

of Henry Laurens Pinckney, son of
Henry L. and Mary S. Pinckney,
b. 26 June, 1850, d. 29 Jan. 1912. In
St. Philip's Churchyard, Charleston,
S. C. Seen by L. Park, 1923

Pinckney   Or four fusils in fess gu
Document under cornerstone of old
church at Pelham signed by John Pell
and his wife, Rachel Pinckney, con-
tains a tricking of these arms and those
of Pell. Heral. Jour., vol. 3, p. 76

Pinckney   Quartered by Horry

Pintard   Az on a fess or bet 3 mullets
arg 3 roses
Crest: three rose twigs leaved
Mottoes: 1: Depressa resurgo; 2:
Fais, bien, crains, rien; 3: Never
despair
Bookplate John Pintard, founder
N. Y. Hist. Soc. Maverick, sc.

Pitkin   Az on a bend arg bet 2 swans
chained about the neck a torteau bet 2
mullets sa
Crest: a knight's helmet
Seal of Wm. Pitkin, Gov. of Conn.
1766. Zieber's Heral., p. 69

Pitsligo   Quartered by Forbes

Pittman   Quart arg and or an eagle
displ with 2 heads gu
Crest: a martlet
Motto: Fortis agendo
Framed painting owned by L. M.
Pittman, Scotland Neck, N. C.; E. B.
Higgs, Greenville, N. C.; E. J. Black-
shear, Dublin, Ga. Reported by Mrs.
M. H. Everett

Plaisted   [   ] a cross bet 4 garbs
Seal of Major Ichabod Plaisted.
Westfield arms? Jeffries MSS. N. E.
Reg., Jan. 1877, p. 64

Plaisted   Arg 3 boars' heads couped, 2
and 1 gu
Crest: a greyhound statant
Engr. on baptismal basin from Col.
Ichabod Plaisted, 1762. First Church,
Salem, Mass. E. A. Jones, Old Sil.
Am. Ch., p. 422

Plaisted   Erm 3 elephants' heads erased
arg
Crest: an elephant's head erased arg
Seal John Plaisted, speaker N. H.
House, 1695. Saunders arms? Jeffries MSS. N. E. Reg., Jan. 1877, p.
64

Plesington   *See also* McComb

Plumptre   Arg a chev bet in chief 2
mullets pierced and in base an annulet
sa
Crest: a pheonix
Motto: Sufficit meruisse
Bookplate John Plumptre

Plumsted   Erm 3 chev sa, the upper one
charged with 3 annulets
Arms of Clement Plumsted, mayor
of Phila., on old silver owned by
Devereux family. Zieber's Heral., p. 68

Poisson   A fess gu (properly or?) and
in chief a fish (dolphin?) naiant. In
base the letters IP interlaced
Crest: a coronet
Drawing (very old) from silver
brought from France. Lent for record
by Mrs. M. A. Empie of Wilmington,
N. C., through Mrs. Everett. Rietstap
has many entries under Poisson. The
field is usually blue or black, the fess
gold, the fish silver

Pollock   Az 3 fleurs-de-lis, 2 and 1 arg
Crest: a boar pierced by an arrow
[the boar quart or and vert?]
Motto: Audacter et strenue
Bookplate A. Russell Pollock

Pomeroy   Or a lion ramp gu holding in
the dexter paw a sphere within a
bordure engr sa
Crest: a lion of the field
Supporters: Wolves gorged and
chained
Motto: Virtutis fortuna comes
Bookplate B. Pomeroy, Southport,
Conn. H. Hays, sc.

Ponseyn   Quartered by Leigh

Poole   [Az] a lion ramp [arg] within an
orle of 7 fleurs-de-lis in the dexter chief
a mullet
Tombstone William Poole, schoolmaster, who d. 1674, aged 81. Dorchester, Mass., Graveyard, Dudley St.
Seen by Mrs. Bolton

Poor   Or a fess az bet 3 mullets [gu]
Crest: a lion's head erased
Motto: Pauper sed non in spe
Engr. on a gold watch and used on
notepaper by Miss Mary M. Poor, 67
Mt. Vernon St., Boston, and Mrs.
James D. Brennan, 677 Dudley St.,
Dorchester, Mass. Also bookplates
Benjamin Poor, Newburyport, and
Henry W. Poor. The bookplates omit
"sed" (old and crude)

Porcher   Per pale barry of 8 arg and gu
counterchanged a cinquefoil erm
Crest: a lion ramp charged with 3
bars gu holding in the paws a cinquefoil of the arms
Motto: Pro rege
Bookplate Henry Porcher, S. C.

Porter   Per chev or (?) and arg 3 church
bells [arg]
Crest: an antelope's head erased
[arg] attired [or] gorged [gu]
Bookplate Horace K. Porter, Phila.

Porter   Per chev sa and arg 3 bells [all, or the 3d] erm
Crest: an antelope's head erased gorged with a collar and bell
Motto: Cor unum via una
Letter paper Frank B. Porter, 116 East 72d St., N. Y.

Porter   Per chev sa and arg 3 bells 2 erm and 1 ermines
Crest: a ram's head erased gorged
Bookplate —— Porter, N. Y.   Also on leather book cover

Post   Arg on a fess bet 3 arches gu a lion ramp bet 2 plates
Crest: a demi-lion ramp [or] holding an arch [gu]
Motto: In me mea spes omnis
Bookplate —— Post. *See* Poston in Burke

Potter   Arg 3 bends gu. On a chief az a cinquefoil bet 2 bezants
Crest: a demi-lion ramp holding a crescent
Motto: Malo mori quam foedari
Bookplate Edwin S. Potter, M. D., Phila.

Potter   Sa a fess erm bet 3 cinquefoils arg
Crest: a sea horse
Bookplate Harold Potter. Also of Donald Potter Daniels of Pasadena. Edmund H. Garrett, del. 1916, op. 76. Motto: Semper fidelis

Potter   Sa a fess erm bet 3 cinquefoils
Crest: a sea horse
Motto: Semper fidelis
Engr. with the name "Potter" on a pewter plate 15 inches wide. Sold at F. J. Libbie's, Boston, April 15, 1915, to a New Yorker. The bookplate of John Sherman Potter has the crest and motto as above, the Potter coat being impaled by Sherman (a rampant lion)

Potter   Sa a fess erm bet 3 cinquefoils or (?)
Seal of Henry Codman Potter, Bishop of N. Y., impales the above arms. Zieber's Heral., p. 201. Carved on wood with crest a sea-horse on house in Trinity Square, Providence, built 1885 by James A Potter.

Poultney   Arg a fess dancetté gu and in chief 3 leopards' faces
Crest: out of a ducal cor a leopard's head erased affrontée
Bookplate Thos. Poultney; also Evan Poultney of Md.

Powel   Per fess arg and or, over all a lion ramp gu
Crest: an estoile of 8 points
Motto: Proprium decus et petrum
Bookplate Samuel Powel, mayor Phila. Also of John H. Powel

Powell   Or a chev gu bet 3 lions' gambs erect [or]
Crest: a lion's gamb of the field
Motto: Laetus in praesens animus
Bookplate Matthew Powell

Power   Arg a bend engr gu. On a chief gu 3 escallops arg
Crest: a stag's head couped ppr
Motto: Impavide
Bookplate James Power of King William County, Va. Price, sc. Va. Hist. Mag., vol. 15, p. 382

Pownall   Arg a lion ramp sa charged on the shoulder with a cross pattée arg. Impaling: Gu (?) a hand in fess holding a dagger in pale bet 2 pierced mullets arg
Crest: a lion's gamb sa holding a key chained
Motto: Videte et cavete ab abaritia. Luke 12. XV. Also: The wicked borroweth & payeth not again
Bookplate Thomas Pownall

Pownall   Quart 1 and 4: Arg a lion ramp sa; 2 and 3: Gu a chev arg bet 3 lions' gambs bendways erased sa within a bordure arg. On a chief arg an eagle displayed sa (Browne). Impaling: Sa a lion rampant arg. On a canton of the last a cross gu (Churchill)
Crest: a lion's gamb gu grasping a key or, to which a chain is fixed
Boston Society. Painted on canvas for King's Chapel, 1886. Thomas Pownall, gov. of Mass. 1757

Prat   Or a pine tree [gu?]
Crest: a wolf's head erased
Motto: Do well and doubt not
Bookplate George W. Prat

Pratt   Arg on a chev sa bet 3 pellets, each charged with a martlet of the field, as many mascles or
Crest: a wolf's head erased per pale arg and sa
Wax impressions of the Pratt arms are found on letters written by various members of the family dating from 1724
Crozer's Va. Heral., 1908, p. 21

Pratt   *See also* Sprague

Preble   Gu on a pale or bet 4 lions' heads 2 and 2, three fusils sa
Crest: a lion's head or
Bookplate —— Preble

Prentis   Per chev or and sa 3 greyhounds courant and counterchanged, collared gu
Crest: a demi-greyhound ramp or, collared, ringed, and lined sa. The line coiled in a knot at the end
Has been handed down from Joseph Prentis, who was judge of the Admiralty court in 1776. Wm. & Mary Quar., July, 1893, p. 26

Prescott Erm a chev sa. On a chief sa 2 leopards' faces [or?]
Crest: a boar's head ducally gorged
Motto: Vincit qui patitur
Bookplate Walter Conway Prescott.
Notepaper Mrs. Prescott, Rockville, Conn.

Prescott Quart 1 and 4: Sa a chev bet 3 owls arg; 2 and 3: Erm a cross raguly arg [gu?] (Lawrence)
Crest: out of a mural crown a head (boar's?) erased
Embr. hatchment 24 x 24 framed, given to Groton (Mass.) Hist. Soc. by Rev. F. J. Walton, whose wife is a desc. of Rev. Daniel Chaplin, who married, 1779, Susanna, b. 1757, daughter of Hon. James and Susanna (Lawrence) Prescott of Groton

Prescott Sa a chev arg bet 3 owls of the last
Crest: an owl
Motto: Nil conscire sibi
Bookplate Wm. H. Prescott. A. and S., sc.

Prescott [Sa] a chev bet 3 owls [arg]
On the tablet of crossed swords of Col. Wm, Prescott and Capt. John Linzee, R. N. Mass. Historical Society, Boston. Also on bookcase, Lawrence Park, Groton, Mass.

Prescott Impaled by Lawrence

Prescott *See also* Crosby

Preston Erm on a chief sa 3 cresc or
Crest: a crescent or
Motto: Lucem spero clariorem
Bookplate Thomas Preston, Phila. 1760

Prevost Az a dexter arm in fess issuing from a cloud in fess point grasping a sword erect ppr, pomel and hilt or
Crest: out of a mural crown or a demi-lion ramp az
Old motto: J'ai bien servi
On imprints of seals and on letter a century old. Vermont's Amer. Heral. [1886], pp. 39, 176

Price [Sa] a lion ramp reguard [or]
Crest: a pelican in her piety
Bookplate Ezekiel Price, Boston notary, 1760. By Hurd

Price Sa a lion ramp reguard or
Crest: a demi-lion ramp or
Two tiles one square, one a long octagon. Rev. Roger Price. Bostonian Society

Pride Arg a mullet gu bet 3 cresc or
Crest: a wyvern
Motto: Libertas
Bookplate Halcott B. Pride. Maverick, sculp.

Pride Quartered by Cabell

Priestly Gu on a chev arg bet 3 towers issuing demi-lions ramp [or] as many grappling anchors
Crest: a cockatrice arg with a spear in bill [or]
Motto: Ars longa vita brevis
Bookplate Joseph Priestly, Penn.

Prime Arg a human leg erased at the thigh sa
Crest: an eagle's leg cap à pis
Motto: Virtute et opere
Bookplate Col. Prime, 17th U. S. Infantry. Frederick Prime's has no crest

Prince Gu a saltire or debruised by a cross erm
Crest: a cubit arm [habited gu] cuffed erm holding 5 sprigs of pineapple
Bookplate —— Prince. Wightman, sc.

Prince "He beareth gules, a saltire or, surmounted with a cross engrailed erm"
"Ye crest a dexter arm issuing out of a ducal coronet or, ye cuff gu, turned up erm, holding in ye hand a Branch of a Pine Tree, proper, fructed or"
A pen-and-ink tricking of arms in the diary of Rev. Thomas Prince, now owned by Rev. Chandler Robbins of Boston. It was written in London, Nov. 29, 1710. Heral. Jour., vol. 1, pp. 7, 8

Pringle Arg on a bend sa 3 escallops [or] within a bordure az, a mullet for diff
Crest: an escallop
Bookplate W. Alston Pringle

Prioleau Paly of six arg and or, a chief gu, a label of 3 points for diff
Crest: a tree
Motto: Pax in bello
Bookplate Dr. Thomas G. Prioleau Charleston, S. C. Also Samuel Prioleau. Orig. Priuli, a son of the doge of Venice

Proby Erm on a fess gu a lion pass or
Crest: an ostrich's head erased arg, ducally gorged or, in the beak a key of the last
Seal on will of Richard Loft, Apr. 25, 1690. Suffolk Wills. Heral. Jour., vol. 2, p. 90; vol. 3, p. 46

Proctor [Arg?] a chev [sa?] bet 3 martlets [gu?]
Tombstone of Capt. Richard Proctor, son of Joseph, d. 1753. Christ Church graveyard, Phila. Zieber's Heral., p. 38

Provoost Arg 3 arrows 2 and 1, points upward, each one enfiled through a pierced mullet [sa].   Impaling: Az a bar bet 2 chev or
  Crest: an arm embowed in armor, the hand ppr grasping an arrow fessways
  Motto: Pro libertate
  Bookplate Samuel Provoost, first Prot. Epis. bishop of N. Y. That with a bishop's mitre was engr. by Maverick. John Provoost used the Provoost arms only. Provoost shield, crest, and motto on salver by Feuter at Met. Mus. of Art, N. Y., cir. 1775–1800

Provoost Impaled by Colden

Pryce Gu a lion ramp reguard az
  Crest: a demi-lion of the field
  Bookplate Charles Pryce, Esq., solicitor in chancery, No. Car. 1770

Pumpelly Az a pile arg debruised by a pale gu charged with a fleur-de-lis bet 2 roses
  Crest: or an eagle displayed sa
  Bookplate Harmon Pumpelly, Esq.

Putman Az a chev vert bet in chief 3 boars' heads arg and in base a lion ramp sa, all within a bordure vert
  Crest: a lion rampant
  On a tile owned by a descendant of Jan Putman in the Mohawk Valley. A copy with the lion arg painted on a wooden plate about 1840 (8 inches

wide) is owned by Eben Putnam of Salem, Mass.

Putnam Sa on a semée of crosses crosslet fitchée a stork arg
  Crest: a wolf's head couped gu
  "Ex libris George Putnam," Boston, clergyman of Roxbury. R. D. Weston drew it in 1914.
  Notepaper Mrs. George J. Putnam, Brookline, Mass.

Pybus Or on a chev gu bet in chief 2 trees vert and in base a negro sanguine balancing 2 piles of cinnamon fagots suspended from a bamboo yoke, all ppr, 3 cinnamon leaves erect or
  Crest: an elephant carrying in its trunk sugar canes
  Motto: Fungor fruor
  Bookplate John Pybus, Esq., West Indies

Pye Impaled by Faunces

Pynchon Per bend arg and sa 3 roundels within a bordure engr all counterchanged
  Memorial tablet in hall, New Eng. Hist. Gen. Soc., Boston, given by G. M· Pynchon, N. Y. banker

Pynchon Quartered by Oliver

Pyne Gu a chev erm bet 3 pineapples [or]
  Crest: a pine tree
  Bookplate Percy Rivington Pyne, engr. by French, 1897

Q

Quappelade Quartered by Bacon

Quincy Gu 7 mascles conjoined 3, 3 and 1
  Crest: an antique crown
  Embroidery, signed 1796, Joanna Q. Loring (b. 1782, daughter Thos. and Joanna Q. Thaxter Loring. Mrs. Loring daughter John Thaxter and Anna, daughter of John and Elizabeth Norton Quincy). Seen by Dr. H. Bowditch. Owned by T. L. Sprague, Chestnut Hill Ave., Brookline, Mass., 1924

Quincy [Gu] 7 mascles 3, 3, 1 [or]
  Crest: three ostrich feathers
  Motto: Discretio moderatrix virtutum
  Bookplate Josiah Quincy, drawn by Eliza Susan Quincy. Shield and motto on gold fob owned by Mrs. M. A.De W. Howe, Boston. The crest perhaps an escallop

Quincy Gu 7 mascles conjoined 3, 3, and 1, or
  Crest: a plume of 3 ostrich feathers
  Motto: Sine macula macla
  On the will of Edmund Quincy, the third. Engr. without crest or motto

on a paten owned by R. T. H. Halsey. Amer. Ch. Sil., M. F. A., 1911, pp. 7, 120

Quincy Gu 7 mascles 3, 3, and 1 or. Impaling: Az a chev bet 3 crosses crosslet fitchée within a bordure engr or (Sturgis)
  Crest: a plume of ostrich feathers (?)
  Embr. hatchment owned by Mrs. Josiah Quincy, Boston. Josiah Quincy married, 1733, Hannah, daughter of John Sturgis of Yarmouth

Quincy [Gu] 9 mascles 3, 2, 3, 1 conjoined [or]
  Engr. on caudle cup from Edmund Quincy, 1697, to the First Church, Braintree.   First Church, Quincy, Mass. Also framed in Quincy homestead, Quincy, Mass.

Quincy Quartered by Adams

Quintard Quart 1 and 4: Az a stag's head couped arg; 2 and 3: Gu an escallop arg. Over all a cross arg charged with 6 pellets. On a chief gu a cross arg
  Motto: Mon Dieu est ma Roche
  Bookplate and seal Charles Todd Quintard, bishop of Tennessee. Zieber's Heral., p. 210

R

Rae [Vert] a chev arg bet [3 roebucks courant ppr]
Crest: [a roebuck at gaze ppr] not visible in 1922
Motto: [In omnia promptus]
Tomb of Robert Rae, merchant of Falmouth, son of Robert Rae of Little Govan, near Glasgow, in Bruton churchyard, Va. He d. 30 May, 1758, aged 30. The chevron can still be seen, also "ptus" of the motto. Seen by L. Park, 1922. Wm. & Mary Quar., Oct. 1893, p. 78

Ramsay Arg an eagle displayed sa, beaked and membered gu
Crest: a unicorn's head couped arg, armed or
Wax seal on the will of Dr. George Ramsay in clerk's office at Norfolk, Va. Will dated 22 June, 1756. See Crozier's Va. Heral., 1908, p. 56
Notepaper Major Wm. Gouverneur Ramsay, Wilmington, Del., with motto: Ora et labora

Ramsay Quartered by Erving and Stewart

Rand Az on a chev or 3 roses on edge a canton erm
Crest: a sword erect bet 2 lions' gambs
Motto: Non mortale quod opto
Bookplate Edward S. Rand. Another with crest: a ducal cor and above a boar's head and motto: Non nobis solum

Rand Quartered by Fitch

Randolph [   ] 3 mullets 2 and 1
Seal of Edward Randolph, collector, Boston, 1683, on doc. in Mass. Archives, vol. 61 p. 260

Randolph Gu on a cross arg 5 mullets pierced [sa]
Crest: an antelope's head couped or, holding a baton or
Motto: Nil admirari
On notepaper of Evelyn Winthrop Randolph (Mrs. James Randolph), Jacksonville, Fla.
Bookplate Herbert Randolph, Esq. (no motto). Also of Thomas Randolph, with a fleur-de-lys in dexter chief for diff. Also of W. K. Randolph, but cross flory and shield left as arg. Also of Ryland Randolph but shield engr. az, a mullet for diff and "Fari qui sentiat"

Randolph Gu on a cross or, 5 mullets of the first
Crest: an antelope's head couped, holding in its mouth a baton or
At the Henrico Court House, Henrico Co., Va., there is a paper dated 1698 which bears a wax impression of the arms of Col. William Randolph, Attorney-General, 1696, of Turkey Island, Va.
Bookplate John Randolph, Middle Temple, Bath, I. Skinner, sc. Also bookplate John Randolph, engr. by "Bath, Skinner." Two mottoes: 1: Nil ad mirari; 2: Fari qui sentiat (has 3 mullets only). A seal has an arrow, not a baton, and "Fari quae sentiat." This motto and the first are on shield and crest as above on a framed coat at Bishop B. D. Tucker's, Stockley Gardens, Norfolk, Va. Crozier's Va. Heral., 1908, pp. 15 and 16. Bellet's Some Prom. Va. Fam., vol. 2, p. 131

Rankin Sa (az?·) on a chev or 3 roses gu a canton erm
Seen 30 Apr. 1924, by Dr. Harold Bowditch, Emmanuel Church, Boston. Ranson arms

Ranson See also Rankin

Rathbone Erm on a fess az bet in chief 2 roses [gu] and in base the Roman fasces erect 3 bezants
Crest: a lion's head erased gorged ppr. Also the faces in fess
Bookplate A. H. Rathbone

Rathbun Arg 3 doves az
Crest: a dove of the field holding a twig in the beak
Bookplate "By the name of Rathbun"
Notepaper Albert Rathbone, Albany, N. Y., has 3 doves as in the crest above

Rattray Az a fess bet 6 crosses crosslet fitchée arg
Crest: an armed arm couped at the shoulder holding a cross crosslet fitchée [or]
Motto: Ex hoc victoria signo
Bookplate John Rattray, Charleston, S. C., Justice of Court of Vice Admiralty, 1760

Ravenel "A field gu with 6 crescents of gold, each surmounted by a star of the same placed 2 and 2, with a gold star at the base of the shield"
Bookplate Daniel Ravenel, Charleston, S. C., 1890. Engr. on cake plate or standing dish, owned by Mrs. William Duane of Boston, daughter of S. Prioleau Ravenel, Esq., of Charleston

Rawle Sa 3 swords erect arg, 2 with points down and the middle one with point up
Crest: an armed arm emb holding a sword
Bookplate (Francis) Rawle, Phila. Sylvan City, 1883, p. 451

Rawson Az a castle arg. Not the usual details
Engr. under portrait of Edward Rawson, from the painting of 1670, owned by R. R. Dodge of East Sutton, Mass., now in N. E. Hist. Gen. Soc.

Rawson Per fess az and sa a castle with 4 towers in perspective or
Crest: a raven's head couped sa, guttée or, in its beak an annulet gu
Motto: Laus virtutis actio
Seal of Edward Rawson, Sec. of Colony of Mass. Bay (1651–1686). Vermont's Amer. Heral. [1886], pp. 87, 176

Rawson See also Brooks

Ray [   ] 3 stags trippant
Crest: a stag at gaze
Motto: J'espere en Dieu
Bookplate Robert Ray, N. Y.

Rayley Quartered by Cole

Raymond Arg 3 bars sa
Crest: an armed arm emb holding a battle axe all ppr
Motto: Rex mundi
Bookplate Thomas Lynch Raymond

Raymond [Sa] a chev bet 3 eagles displayed arg. On a chief erm [or?] a cinquefoil bet 2 fleurs-de-lis [gu]
Crest: a double-headed eagle displayed
Motto: Esperance en Dieu
Bookplate Eliakim Raymond. J. W. Simons, N. Y., sculp. Water color by T. T. Waterman for O. N. Raymond has for crest a demi-griffin

Read Gu on a bend wavy arg 3 shovellers [sa]. Impaling: Arg on a chev sa 3 bezants (Boys?)
Crest: a shoveller
Motto: Indefessus vigilando
Bookplate William Read, Md., 1820. On an altar tomb in churchyard of Emmanuel Church, New Castle, Del. (with another coat, Bond). Ancest. Rec. & Portr., vol. II, p. 490

Read Az a griffin sejant, wings erect
Crest: a demi-griffin holding a baton
Motto: Nec spe nec metu
Bookplate Chas. Read of New Jersey, Esq.

Read Quart 1 and 4: Quart 1 and 4: Gu a saltire orbet 4 garbs [or]. (Read) 2 and 3: Gu 3 lions ramp arg.
2 and 3: Arg a lion ramp sa, gorged and chained or
Crests: 1: a demi-lion rampant; 2: an eagle (?) rising from a growing stump; 3: a demi-lion of the field
Motto: Cedant arma togae
Bookplate Harmon Pumpelly Read

Reade [Az?] guttee, a cross crosslet fitchée [or?]
Crest: a shoveller
On tomb of Thomas Reade, Va., 1739. Also on a silver ewer. Wm. & Mary Quar., Oct. 1893, p. 133

Reade Quartered by Cabell

Rede See Hanson

Redford [   ] 3 bars and a canton
Crest: out of a coronet a lion's head erased and langued
Seal William Redford, Portsmouth, N. H., 1694. Jeffries MSS. N. E. Reg., Jan. 1877, p. 64

Redmond Gu a castle bet 3 woolpacks ppr
Crest: a beacon ppr
Motto: Pie vivere et Deum et patriam deligere
Bookplate William Redmond

Redvers Quartered by Courtenay

Redwood Per bend sa and arg 2 eagles displayed counterchanged
Crest: an eagle rising or
Arms of William Redwood, carved above the delivery room doorway of the Redwood Library, Newport, R. I. Letter from G. L. Hinckley, Libn.

Reed 2 bends wavy, each charged with 3 birds (perhaps shovellers) [within a bordure?]
Crest: a shoveller
Reed d. 1732. Emmanuel churchyard, New Castle, Del. Zieber's Heral., p. 48

Reed [Az] a griffin segreant [or]
Crest: a spread eagle
On linen of George Eaton Reed, Roxbury, Mass., and silver and envelope of Miss Elizabeth Clark Reed, Brookline, Mass.

Reed Gu 4 lozenges in bend conjoined (endwise) erm (Heley arms?). Impaling: Quarterly az (?) and or 4 cresc counterchanged (Farnham arms?)
Crest: a cubit arm holding a serpent
Motto: Tace aut face
Bookplate Thomas S. Reed

Reeve Quart 1 and 4: Arg on a fess engr sa bet 3 escallops az 3 eagles displayed or; 2 and 3: Arg a cross moline gu. Impaling: Arg a chev engr bet 3 martlets sa and in chief 3 towers sa (Webber)
Crest: a squirrel eating
Motto: Re vera
Bookplate Samuel Reeve. Fenner, sc. Thomas Reeve had for motto: Pour sui vez, but no impaled coat

Reid   A chev bet 3 eagles' heads
    Crest: an eagle's head
    Seal on the will of James Reid, merchant, Urbanna, Va., 3 Jan. 1764. The tinctures cannot be distinguished. Wm. & Mary Quar., vol. 4, p. 269

Remington   Gyronny of 8 erm and az. Over all a dolphin emb or
    Crest: a lion's head erased ppr
    Old water color. Arms of "Wm. Remington, Lord Mayor of London, 1500." John Coles type about 1800. Boston dealer

Remsen   Quart 1: Sa 2 pieces of armor for the arms in pale fessways arg; 2: Arg 2 swans in water sa; 3: Arg a swan in water sa; 4: Sa a wheat sheaf or
    Crest: an eagle's head erased
    Motto: Otium ex labore
    Bookplate Henry Remsen of N. Y., mcht. 1762–1845. The colors are conjectures

Remsen   Quart 1: Az 2 dexter mailed arms fessways in pale couped gu; 2: Or 2 swans arg on water vert; 3: Or a swan arg on water vert; 4: Arg a garb vert
    Crest: an eagle's head erased
    Motto: Otium ex labore
    Bookplate ―― Remsen. In color. Also of Simeon Henry Remsen, engraved

Renshaw   Per pale and per chev 3 martlets
    Crest: a decrescent arg and an increscent or adossée
    Bookplate Alfred Renshaw, Noroton, Conn., by Dorothy Sturgis Harding

Renshaw   Quart 1: Or 3 stars of 8 points sa; 2: Arg 5 bars gu (De Marchãdo); 3: Gu a cross humettée arg (De Luna); 4: Az 5 fleurs-de-lis or (De Vargas)
    Memorial window, St. Mark's Church, Phila., inscribed: "Jesu Mercy! Maria Carter Renshaw. March XVI, 1880." The left panel has the Carter arms, arg a chev bet 3 heraldic roses (Letter from Rev. Elliot White)

Renton   Impaled by Loring

Reveley   Arg a chev engr gu bet 3 estoiles of 6 points
    Crest: an estoile
    Bookplate Henry Reveley, F. Kirk, sc.

Revere   [Rivoire, earlier spelling) Arg 3 bars gu, over all a bend sinister (of the field?) charged with 3 fleurs-de-lis sinisterways
    Crest: an annulet
    Bookplate "Paul Rivoire" (Harris collection). There is also a bookplate with a dove rising contourné for crest and for motto: Pugna pro patria, & "Paul Revere." Also slate tablet on Christ Church, Salem St., Boston. Heral. Jour., vol. 3, p. 22

Reynolds   [   ] two bars [   ] bet 3 foxes passant
    Crest: a fox of the field
    On gravestone of Joseph Reynolds, d. Jan. 16, 1759, at Bristol, R. I., aged 83. See pict. in Hist. John and Sarah Reynolds, 1924, p. 11

Reynolds   Or on a chief vert 3 lions ramp of the first
    Crests: a fox's head ? erased, a dove rising contourné
    Mottoes: Sola virtus invicta, 1632; Pugna pro patria, 1625
    Bookplate John Phillips Reynolds III, Boston, His Book, 1887. J. P. R., Jr., Del.

Rhett   Or a cross engrailed sa
    Crest: a dexter arm embowed in armor holding a broken spear
    Tombstone of Col. Wm. Rhett in St. Philip's churchyard (western), Charleston, S. C. He d. 12 Jan. 1722, aged 57. Seen by L. Park, 1923

Rhoades   Arg on a bend az cotised ermines 2 acorns leaved. In chief a lion pass guard [gu]
    Crest: a dexter arm grasping 3 acorns leaved ppr
    Motto: Gwell anguana chywydd
    Bookplate Julius Rhoades. Hall, Packard & Cushman, sculp.

Rhodes   Arg 2 trefoils slipped vert, on a chief sa a lion pass or
    Crest: from a cap of maintenance gu, turned up erm, a male griffin's head sa, langued gu, about the neck a riband arg with ends flying to dexter
    Motto: Coelum non animum
    Framed painting, modern, owned by Walter C. Lewis, Brookline, Mass. Seen by Dr. H. Bowditch

Rhodes   Arg on a cross engrailed gu bet 4 lions ramp gu as many bezants
    Crest: a leopard sejant or, spotted sa
    Bookplate Frederick Leland Rhodes. John Rhodes has the leopard collared and the motto: Ung durant ma vie

Rice   Arg on a chev engr sa bet 3 reindeers' heads couped [gu] 3 cinquefoils [erm]
    Crest: a griffin's head (?) erased
    Water color by J. Coles, reproduced in C. E. Rice's "By the name of Rice," geneal. of desc. of Dea Edmund Rice of Co. Bucks, Eng. and Sudbury, Mass., d. 1663

Rice   Arg a chev sa bet 3 crows ppr
   Crest: a crow of the field
   Motto: Secret et Hardi
   "Ex libris Alexander Hamilton Rice,"
explorer, of Boston.   Tiffany & Co.,
sc.

Rice   Quart 1 and 4: Per pale indented
arg and gu; 2 and 3: Az a lion ramp or
   Crest: a crowned leopard's face (?)
   From seals on 2 deeds of John Rice
and Rebecca, his wife, 1687 and 1686.
Wm. & Mary Quar., Jan. 1894, p. 156

Rich   Gu a chev or bet 3 crosses botonnée of the second
   Crest: a lion's head erased, langued
gu
   "By the name of Rich" and palm
branches
   Water color by Mrs. Carleton Hunneman, Brookline, Mass., from the
original owned by Mrs. Nathaniel
Wilson of Washington.   Rich family
of Truro, Mass.   Also beneath the
portrait of Isaac Rich of Boston,
founder of Boston Univ., 1914

Rich   Impaled by Doane and Willis

Richards   Arg a fess fusilly gu bet 2
barrulets sa
   Crest: a paschal lamb passant arg,
staff and banner proper
   Seal of John Richards, one of His
Majesty's Counsellors of Mass., used
by his father, Thomas Richards of
Dorchester.   Arms also on the tomb-
stone of James Richards of Hartford,
Conn. (1680), "Arg 4 lozenges conjoined
in fess" — Gore roll.   Vermont's Amer-
Heral., [1886], p. 130

Richards   Sa a chev bet 3 fleurs-de-lis
arg
   Crest: a griffin's head erased arg
   Motto: Honore et amore
   Bookplate James Richards, N. Y.,
attorney.   Also of Mrs. Pearl Mary
Craigie, novelist, of London, daughter of
John Morgan Richards of N. Y.

Richards   Sa a chev bet 3 fleurs-de-lis or
   On the tomb of the Rev. John Rich-
ards in the chancel of Ware Church,
Gloucester, Va.   He d. 12 Nov., 1735.
Crozier's Va. Heral., 1908, p. 31

Richardson   Erm on a chief 3 lions'
heads erased
   Crest: from a crown embattled a
lion's head of the shield
   Motto: Pretio prudentia
   Crest engr. and used by Richardson
of Md.   See Richardson's Sidelights
on Md. Hist.

Richardson   Quart of 6: 1 and 6: Arg
[or?] on a fess az bet in chief a bull's
head couped sa and in base a galley

[no oars] [sa?] a saltire couped arg; 2:
Arg a lion ramp within a bordure gu;
3: Az 3 garbs; 4: Arg on a bend az 3
buckles [or?] (Leslie); 5: Gyronny of
8, sa and arg
   Crest: a cubit armed arm holding a
dagger erect
   Supporters: Dexter   a   wyvern,
sinister an eagle, both ppr
   Motto: Virtute acquiritur honos
   Bookplate Edward Richardson of
Lincoln, Mass.   Tiffany & Co., sc.

Richardson   Or on a fess gu bet in chief
a bull's head and in base a galley sa, a
saltire couped sa
   Crest: a lion ramp holding a chaplet
   Motto: Virtute acquiritur honos
   Bookplate Thomas Richardson

Richardson   Sa on a chief arg 3 lions'
heads erased [   ]
   Crest: a cubit arm issuing from a
ducal crown and holding a cutlass
   Engr. on notepaper of Miss Marcia
W. Richardson, Pontiac, Mich.

Richmond   Arg a cross flory bet 4
stars of 6 points gu
   Crest: a tilting spear in 3 parts
encircled by a crown
   Motto· Resolve well and persevere
   Framed water color by Mrs. Arnold
Talbot, Lincoln, R. I.

Richardson   Impaled by Stoddard

Rickets   [Arg?] a lion ramp bet 3 crosses
formée
   Crest: a demi-lion ramp
   Bookplate William Rickets of N. Y.

Ridgely   Arg on a chev sa 3 mullets
pierced arg
   Crest: a stag's head erased or
   Motto: Cave cervum
   Bookplate Nicholas G. Ridgely,
Baltimore.   Arms and crest on tomb-
stone of Ridgely descendant in St.
Ann's churchyard, Annapolis, Md.
(Ancest. Rec. & Portr., vol. I, p. 86).
Motto given: "Dum Spiro Spero"

Ridgeway   Sa 2 wings conjoined erect
arg
   Crest: a dromedary couchant [arg]
maned [sa]
   Motto: Mihi gravato Deus
   Bookplate Jacob E. Ridgeway,
Phila.   Seal ring, without motto, of
Edith Ridgway of Phila. (Mrs. Henry
M. Sperry of N. Y.)

Rindge   See Goodwin

Ring   Arg on a bend gu 3 crescents of
the first (Burke)
   Crest: a hand vested sa, cuffed or,
holding a roll of paper
   Tomb of Joseph Ring, merchant of
York Co., Va., who d. 26 Feb., 1702-3.
Crozier's Va. Heral., 1908, p. 49.   Wm.

& Mary Quar., Oct. 1893, p. 80, gives 3 lozenges conjoined on the bend and in chief a label of 5 points

Ripley   Arg a chev vert bet 3 lions ramp or
Motto: Regard the end
White satin embr. hatchment 21 x 17 inches done by Lucy Ripley at the Female Seminary, Hartford, Conn., in 1802 and signed L. R.   Owned by Miss Laura M. Ripley of Hartford

Risley   Or a saltire gu a chief gu (Bruce arms?)
Bookplate Hanson A. Risley

Roane   Arg 3 stags trip ppr.   Impaling: 3 falconers gloves (Bartelot)
Crest: a stag's head erased ppr attired or holding in the mouth an acorn or leaved vert
Tomb of Thomas Roane at Chaldon, Surrey, 1689, has arms.   Brother of Charles of Glouc. Co., Va.   Crozier's Va. Heral., p. 111

Roberdeau   Sa a chev or, in base a tower bet 2 annulets arg, on a chief arg a cross crosslet gu
Crest: a demi-greyhound ramp ppr
Motto: Ne cede malis
Arms on plate, 1699, brought over by Isaac Roberdeau, who settled in New Jersey.   Vermont's Amer. Heral. [1886] pp. 76, 177

Robert   Arg (?) 2 chev sa, a mullet in chief
Crest: a mullet
Motto: Caton wrth caton Dow a Digon (Heart to Heart God over all)
Bookplate photo.   Santee, S. C., 1686.   From Basle, Switz.

Roberts   Ermines a goat pass bet 3 annulets arg
Crest: a goat in front of a tree eating a green branch
Motto: Ewch Ymlaen
Bookplate H. Wilks Roberts

Roberts   Arg a fess wavy gu (?) bet 3 stags trip sa
Crest: a stag of the field
Motto: Successus a Deo est
Bookplate, 1898, engr. by S. L. Smith

Roberts   Gu 3 estoiles of 6 points or 2 and 1.   A chief wavy or
Crest: a lion rampant holding a flaming sword az
Motto: Quae supra
Bookplate I. B. Roberts.   Also [Job] Roberts, Phila., 1757–1851, with sword wavy?

Roberts   "He beareth Parted pʳ Pale Argent and Gules a Lion Rampant Sable;   Crest, a stag's head Erased Argent Collared Gules, by the Name of Roberts, of Leicestershire."
On the back of the framed coat: "Presented to the Historical & Geneal¹ Society by George Mountfort.   This is the coat of arms of Capt. Richard Roberts of Boston, who married M. Gyles of Boston, but whose family is extinct. Boston, January, 1850.   Virtually these arms appear on the seal of Nicholas Roberts of London, c. 1675 in all his letters to his son in Boston or daughter, Mrs. Shrimpton, owned by C. P. Greenough, 1924

Robertson   Gu 3 wolves' heads erased 2 and 1.   Below the shield a chained man in fess
Crest: a cubit arm holding a crown or
Motto: Virtutis gloria merces
Bookplate Eben Robertson.   Also of John Stuart Struan Robertson.   Also Gilbert Robertson, Phila., 1810

Robeson   Vert on a chev bet 3 stags trip arg 3 fusils gu (Robinson arms)
Seal on will of Andrew Robeson, Sr., 1694, of N. J. and Phila.   See Robeson Genealogy, 1916

Robins   *See also* Rowe

Robinson   Vert on a chev bet 3 stags at gaze [or] 3 suns in splendor [gu?]
Crest: a stag of the shield
Motto: Virtute non verbis
Ex libris C. L. F. Robinson, Newport, R. I.   Engr. by French, 1900

Robinson   Vert on a chev arg bet 3 trippant stags 3 cinquefoils.   Impaling: Arg on a fess sa 3 mullets pierced arg
Crest: a trippant stag
Motto: Celer atque fidelis
Bookplate John Robinson, Esq.

Robinson   Vert on a chev bet 3 trippant stags or 3 cinquefoils [gu?]
Crest: a trippant stag
Motto: Propere et provide
Bookplate Beverley Robinson, N. Y., concerned in Arnold's treason.   *See, however*, Va. Hist. Mag., vol. 15, p. 445; Wm. & Mary Quar., Jan. 1893, p. 122. Christopher Robinson, Middlesex, Va., 1691, used quatrefoils.   Alexander Robinson of Baltimore, 1783, from Co. Armagh, brought a crude painting of his arms with him.   Anc. Rec., vol. 2, p. 599

Robinson   Vert on a chev or bet 3 trippant stags arg 3 trefoils slipped and pierced vert a crescent for diff
Crest: a trippant stag
Motto: Propere et provide
Bookplate William Duer Robinson N. Y.

Robinson Impaled by Bleecker

Robinson Quartered by Hall

Robinson *See also* Robeson

Rockwell Arg on a chief sa 3 boars' heads (not couped short off) [or]
Crest: a boar's head
Bookplate C. W. Rockwell

Rocliff Quartered by Middleton

Rodman Gu a chev arg bet 4 cushions erm tasselled or
Crest: out of a mural coronet or a horse's head arg, maned or
Motto: Garde la foy
Seal ring belonging to Thomas Rodman, Newport, R. I. Ancest. Rec. & Portr., vol. I, pp. 93 and 94

Rodney Or 3 eagles displayed purpure
Crests: 1: a boar's head sa couped gu; 2: out of a ducal coronet or an eagle rising purpure; 3: a demi-talbot arg, eared and langued gu, ducally gorged or. In color
Independence Hall, Phila. Zieber's Heral., p. 37

Roeder Per pale az and sa On the dexter an increscent with a man's profile arg. On the sinister 3 stars of 6 points or in pale
Crest: two wings erect sa and az, each charged with a star of the field
Bookplate A. L. Roeder

Roeding Az 3 wheat stalks bladed and eared [   ]. Impaling: Arg a demi-horse issuing from the dexter [   ]
Crest: a horse ramp
Notepaper Elizabeth Thorne Roeding (Mrs. George C.), Calif.

Rogers Arg a chev gu bet 3 bucks trippant sa
Crest: a buck's head erased
Motto: Ad astra per aspera
Bookplate Henry B. Rogers. Another with the chevron sa and crest a buck of the field. Samuel Rogers of Mass., loyalist, used these arms on a seal, same motto, crest a stag, letter to Geo. Leonard, in A. O. 13/51. Window, Blake Mem. Chapel, Salem, Mass.

Rogers Arg a chev [erroneously engraved party per chev] bet 3 bucks trippant [sa]
Crest: a buck's head couped
Engr. on a tankard from Hopestill Clap, 1748, grandson of Capt. Roger Clap. First Church, Dorchester, Mass. E. A. Jones, Old Sil. Am. Ch., p. 148. Water color, framed, 15″ x 12″ with motto: Justum perficito: nihil timeto; and crest: a buck trip. Owned by Mrs. Wm. H. Fegan, Brookline, Mass.,

1924. Her grandmother, Sarah A. Rogers of Alfred, Me., married Joseph Fogg. Seen by Dr. H. Bowditch

Rogers Arg a chev gu bet 3 stags trip sa
Crest: a stag's head couped
Motto: Nos nostraque Deo
Bookplate I. Smyth Rogers, 1845

Rogers Or a boar gu. Impaling: Arg a chev sa bet 3 stags sa (Gilpin arms)
Crest: an armed arm embowed holding a sprig
Motto: Dictis factisque simplex
Bookplate Fairman Rogers

Rogers Or a fess wavy bet 3 stags trip sa
Crest: on a mount vert a stag trip ppr
Bookplate T. E. Rogers

Rogers Quart 1: Arg on a chev vert bet 3 stags courant sa [5] gold erm spots, a crescent sa for diff; 2: Arg on a fess gu bet 3 griffins' heads couped sa, 3 wings erect [or] (Slocum); 3: Az on a bend arg bet 2 swans stringed and increscent bet 2 mullets pierced sa; 4: Per fess az and or a pale counterchanged charged with 3 fountains 2 and 1, and 3 lions' heads erased gu 1 and 2 (White)
Crest: a stag's head ermines
Motto: Celeriter et jucunde
Bookplate James Slocum Rogers, Phila.

Rogers Quart 1 and 4: Arg a chev bet 3 stags trip sa, a crescent gu for diff; 2 and 3: Arg 3 boars' heads couped sa
Crest: a stag's head erased sa armed or holding an oak branch fruited
Motto: Fide et fiducia
Bookplate Wm. Frederick Rogers. Also Alfred W. Rogers. Also Wm. Beverley Rogers, engr. by French

Rogers Impaled by Beeman

Rogers *See also* Cheever

Rollins Sa 3 swords in fess, points up
Crest: an arm habited resting on the elbow and holding a sword
Bookplate Helen Rollins, engr. by A. W. Macdonald, 1917

Roome Vert an armed soldier with sword, shield and helmet, and dagger
Crest: a man's face bet 2 leaved sprigs
Motto: Virtute et fide
Bookplate John L. C. Roome, N. Y., lawyer, 1774. Roome of Newport had a grant 1772, not like the above

Roosevelt Arg 2 rose-bushes intertwined, the roses gu
Crest: 3 ostrich feathers
Motto: Qui plantavit curabit
Bookplate Theodore Roosevelt, president U. S. Also on his portrait engr.

by Sidney L. Smith and published by C. E. Goodspeed, Boston. Also note-paper F. Winthrop Coll., 1885, N. Y., in Bos. Ath.

Rootes Quart 1 and 4: On a chev bet 3 buglehorns, 3 arrows, points down-wards; 2 and 3: On a cross 5 pheons
Bookplate Philip Rootes, the elder, of "Rosewall," King and Queen Co., Va. He was b. about 1700. Cro-zier's Va. Heral., 1908, pp. 92, 93

Roscow A lion ramp and a ragged staff
Crest: a hand holding a dagger
Tomb of William Roscow, gent., at Blunt Point, Warwick Co., Va. He d. 2 Nov. 1700. Va. Hist. Mag., vol. 7, p. 285

Rose Arg on a base vert or sa (?) a beehive in dexter and a rose bush in sinister with 9 bees
Crest: a unicorn pass contourné
Motto: Tune cede malis
Bookplate Gad Rose, 1756–1837, of West Suffield, Conn. Engr. by R. Brunton, who lived with Rose. Bates's Early Conn. Engr., p. 36

Rose Gu 3 water bougets
Crest: an eagle's head (?) couped
Motto: Fortis et fidus
Bookplate Robt. H. Rose, Phila.

Ross Gu 3 lions ramp 2 and 1 arg
Crest: a cubit arm ppr holding a chaplet of laurel vert
Motto: Spem successus alit
Bookplate John Ross, Phila. Jas. Turner, sc.

Ross Per fess sa and gu 2 water bougets arg in chief and a boar's head couped arg in base
Crest: a water bouget of the field
Motto: Agnoscar eventu
Bookplate James Alfred Ross

Rotch Quart 1 and 4: Arg a lion ramp crowned and with forked tail az; 2 and 3: Two spurs linked or (?)
Crest: on a rock an eagle rising. Over all a cross pattée arg
Motto: Dieu est ma roche

Rous [Sa?] a fess dancettée [or?] bet 3 crescents [arg?]
Crest: a flaming fire (?) The Earl of Stradbroke's crest is a bunch of bay leaves piled in the form of a cone
Finely engr. on a small headstone of Welsh slate for "Mrs. Mary Rous, wife to Capt. William Rous, daughter of Mr. Thomas and Mrs. Mary Peachee," who d. in 1714/15. Phipps Street Yard, Charlestown, Mass. Over-looked by the Heral. Jour.

Rousby [Gu] on a bend arg cotised [or] 3 crosses crosslet [sa]
On the tomb of John Rousby at Rousby Hall, Patuxent River, Calvert Co., Md. See Hist. Graves of Md., p. 60. He d. 1750

Rouse Sa 2 bars engrailed arg a label arg for diff
Crest: a man with bearded face
Bookplate W. J. Shaw Rouse. How-ard Sill, engr.

Rowe Erm a chev sa on a chief sa 2 leopards' faces arg
Crest: a wolf's head duc gorged
Motto: Vincit qui partitur
Bookplate Henry Sherburne Rowe

Rowe Gu 3 paschal lambs 2 and 1 staves and banners arg
Crest: a stag's head erased or
Motto: Libera nos Domine
Embroidered in Exeter, Eng., the shield surrounded by a wreath of flowers caught at the bottom with a bow knot of blue ribbons. Under-neath the ribbon "17 Rebecca Robins 73." Sent to her uncle, John Rowe, the Boston merchant and diarist, who used the paschal lamb as a crest on silver and seal. Mrs. Caleb L. Cun-ningham, Milton, Mass.

Rowe Gu 3 paschal lambs, 2 and 1, staves and banners arg
Crest: a stag's head erased or
Motto: Innocens non timidus
Trinity Church, Boston. E. A. Jones, Old Sil. Am. Ch., p. 86. The same arms with a lamb of the field for crest on covered loving cup by J. Hurd, owned by Mrs. C. L. Cunningham. Amer. Ch. Sil., M. F. A., 1911, pp. 71, 116

Royall [Az] 3 garbs 2 and 1 [or]
Engr. on a two-handled cup from Col. Isaac Royall, 1781. If the en-graver intended his shading to repre-sent tinctures it would be: Arg 3 garbs gu. First Church, Medford, Mass. E. A. Jones, Old Sil. Am. Ch., p. 275
Tomb of William Royall of North Yarmouth, Maine, who d. 1724, aged 85, and his son, Hon. Isaac Royall of Antigua and N. E., who d. 1739, aged 67. Dorchester, Mass., Burying Ground, Dudley St. Heral. Jour., vol. 1, p. 12

Royall Az 3 garbs 2 and 1 [or]
Crest: a demi-lion rampant with a garb [ ] in his paws
Motto: Pectore puro
Engr. on baptismal basin from Isaac Royall, 1747. St. Michael's Church,

Bristol, R. I. Also bookplate ot Isaac Royall, Esq., of Antigua. Old Sil. Am. Ch., p. 97

Rugeley *See also* Ruggles

Ruggles Arg a chev gu bet 3 roses
Crest: a tower [or] flaming ppr pierced by 4 arrows 2 each way in saltire
Painting in color, Virginia Hist. Society, Richmond. Arms of George Ruggles, 1575–1622, a founder of Virginia. *See* N. Y. Gen. & Biog. Record, Oct. 1894, for arms of A. J. Rugeley of New Orleans. A silver pitcher, first owned by Hon. Nathaniel Ruggles (1761–1819) of Roxbury, Mass., bears these coat-of-arms. It passed to his son, Nathaniel Ruggles of Henderson, Kentucky, and is still in possession of his descendants

Ruggles Quart 1 and 4: Arg a chev bet 3 roses gu; 2 and 3: Vert a cross engrailed erm. Over all on a shield. Gu a bend arg charged with 6 leaves vert 2 by 2
Crest: a tower in flames pierced on each side by 2 arrows in bend
Motto: Struggle
Bookplate Henry Stoddard Ruggles, Boston

Rumsey Quart 1 and 4: Az a cinquefoil pierced erm within a bordure erm; 2 and 3: Arg a fess gu in chief a label of 3 points az
Crest: a talbot az [collared or]
Motto: Virtue only has claim to honour
Bookplate James Rumsey, Md., 1743–1792

Rush Gu on a fess or bet 3 horses courant arg 3 roundels vert
Crest: a wolf's head (?) erased vert guttée [arg?]
Motto: Miseris succurrere disco
Bookplate Rush, perhaps Benjamin the Signer

Russell Arg a chev bet 3 cross crosslets, fitchée sa
Crest: a demi-lion ramp collared sa studded or holding a cross of the shield

James Russell, judge of probate, son of Richard Russell, who came to this country in 1611, used these arms on his seal. Also bookplate Thomas Russell, Callender, sc. Also on embroidery in Old Dartmouth Hist. Soc., New Bedford. Vermont's Amer. Heral. [1886], pp. 18, 19, 177

Russell Arg a chev bet 3 crosses crosslet fitchée sa. Impaling: Arg a lion rampant ppr (Russell?)
Crest: a lion ramp ppr
Embr. hatchment (ten inches square) done by Rebecca Russell Lowell (Mrs. Samuel P. Gardner) with the lozenge filled in later with dark foilage by Mrs. Horace Gray (b. 1807). Owned by Russell Gray, Boston

Russell Arg a lion ramp gu. On a chief sa 3 escallops of the first. Impaling: Arg 3 fleurs-de-lis sa
Crest: a goat trip arg armed or
Bookplate Thomas Russell. I. Smither, sc. The Russell coat and crest above are used by Fredk. G. Russell, 131 State St., Boston, on a label with motto: Honi soit qui mal y pense

Russell *See also* Curwen

Russell Impaled by Curwen

Russell *See also* Nevill

Rutgers Arg a lion ramp sa debruised with a bar gu charged with a star of the field. In chief a demi-eagle displayed of the second
Crest: a demi-Hercules, grasping in his dexter hand a club, all ppr
Motto: Tantes da Dir
Bookplate Hendrick Rutgers. Vermont's Amer. Heral. [1886], p. 177

Rutledge Arg on a chev az bet 3. crescents, two lozenges gu
Crest: a crescent
Motto: Progredi non regredi
Bookplate Edward Rutledge, signer of Decl. on Indep., and used as temporary seal of So. Car. by John Rutledge, pres. of the independent gov. set up 1776. The drawing is: Arg a chev compony az and gu bet 3 crescents. Ancest. Rec. & Portr., vol. I, p. 403

S

Sabine Quart 1 and 4: Arg an escallop [gu]. On a chief az 2 mullets arg; 2 and 3: Sa 3 butterflies or 2 and 1 (Sabyn)
Crest: from a mural crown a demi-ox (?) gorged
Motto: Sic vos non vobis
Bookplate John Sabine, Esq.

Sabyn *See also* Sabine

Saffin [Az] 3 cresc [arg] jessant as many estoiles of 8 points [or]
Crest: an estoile of 8 points (properly 16 points)
Dutch beaker inscribed: "Memento Martha Saffin Obijt 11, Dec. [16] 78." She was the daughter of Capt. Thos. Willett, first mayor of N. Y., and wife of Judge John Saffin. Arms of Saffin of Wolf-Hereston Co. Somerset. Old

South Church, Boston. Old Sil. Am. Ch., p. 51

Saffin Az 3 cresc arg jessant as many estoiles or
Crest: on a mural coronet an estoile of 16 rays or
Seal used by John Saffin of Boston on letters to Conn. 1676-7. Also on silver now owned by Leverett Saltonstall, Esq. Heral. Jour., vol. 4, p. 42

St. Barbe Quart 1 and 4: Chequy arg and sa; 2 and 3: Gu a bend bet 6 crosses crosslet or
Crest: a wyvern sa with tail nowed
Framed water color owned by Miss Eliot, Boston

St. Clair Arg a cross engr sa. On a canton arg a St. Andrews cross az surmounted by a crowned escutcheon or charged with a lion ramp gu within a double tressure
Crest: a demi-talbot ppr
Motto: Quo cunque ferar
Bookplate Sir John St. Clair, Bart., officer under Braddock. Signed Ja. Turner, Phila., sculp.

Salisbury Gu a lion ramp bet 3 crescents arg
Crest: a demi-lion ramp
Motto: Sero sed serio
Bookplate Edward E. Salisbury. Theodore S. Woolsey of New Haven has a seal, the crest a martlet, an impression from which I have seen

Salter [Gules] ten billets, 4, 3, 2, 1 or. A bordure engrailed argent charged with eight [hurts and torteaux alternating]. Impaling: Or three piles meeting in the base [azure?] (Bryan)
Crest: a unicorn
Needlework by Mary Salter (Mrs. Henry Quincy of Boston), 1726-55. For picture see Earle's Home Life in Colonial Days, 1898, opp. p. 266. Owned by Mrs. Frank Bolles of Cambridge. Also in N. E. Mag., Oct. 1897

Saltonstall Or a bend bet 2 eagles displayed sa
Crest: from a ducal cor or a pelican's head [az]
Bookplate Hon. Leverett Saltonstall, Boston

Saltonstall [Or a bend bet] 2 eagles displayed [sa]
Crest: out of a ducal coronet [or] a pelican [az] vulning her breast [gu]
Panel shield and crest in Wm. Clark house, Garden Court St. Boston, 1712, road with lovers. Owned by Mrs. F. L. Gay, Brookline, Mass. Hatchment of Gov. Gurdon Saltonstall of Conn., d. 1724. New London, Conn., Family tomb. Also carved on the frame of a

portrait of Sir Richard Saltonstall at the Museum of Fine Arts, Boston (1915). Saltonstall Geneal., p. 213. Richard Saltonstall (Winthrop papers) impaled the Gurdon arms: 3 leopards' faces jessant-de-lys. Heral. Jour., vol. 3, p. 176. Window, Blake Mem. Chapel, Salem, Mass. Seal of Gurdon Saltonstall, Governor of the colony of Connecticut in 1742. Also bookplate Walter Saltonstall, and Leverett Saltonstall, Boston. Jeffries MSS, N. E. Reg., Jan. 1877, p. 64. Vermont's Amer. Heral. [1886], pp. 42, 43, 177. Heral. Jour., vol. 3, p. 22. Engr. on a tankard made by Jeremiah Dummer. The Brooks arms appear on one side and the Cotton arms on the other, which see. Miss Elizabeth H. Brooks, owner, Boston?

Samuels *See also* Yates

Sanborn Quart 1 and 4: A chev or bet 3 mullets pierced gu; 2: Arg 4 lozenges in pale conjoined gu within a bordure az bezantée; 3: Erm a lion ramp guard gu
Crests: 1: a bull's head erased sa holding 3 heads of wheat; 2: a mullet pierced gu
Bookplate John B. Sanborn

Sanderson Paly of 6 arg and az. Over all on a bend sa 3 annulets or
Crest: a talbot pass [eared and spotted or?]
Old drawing owned by the Misses Fanny and Gertrude Sanderson, Littleton, Mass.

Sandford Quart 1 and 4: Quart per fess dancettée [az] and erm; 2 and 3: Per chev sa and erm in chief 2 boars' heads couped or a martlet for diff
Crest: a falcon preying on a partridge ppr
Motto: Nec temere nec timide
Bookplate William Sandford

Sanford Erm on a chief gu 2 boars' heads couped or
Crest: a demi-eagle displayed
Tombstones in the Old Burial Ground at Newport, R. I., dated 1721. Vermont's Amer. Heral. [1886], p. 178

Sargeant Arg three erect flags 2 and 1, two tassels attached to the knob of each staff; 1: Gu a lion ramp holding erect in the dexter paw a sword; 2: Az an anchor erect with chain; 3: Arg 3 escallops 1 and 2 az (?)
Crest: a clock set at 11 and 18 minutes
Motto: Cito pede praeterit aetas
Bookplate Jacob Sargeant, also John, 1796, clockmaker, Hartford, Conn., b. 1761, d. 1843. R. Brunton, sc. Bates's Early Conn. Engr., p. 37

Sargent Arg a chev bet 3 dolphins emb sa
Crest: a dolphin of the field
Bookplate Epes Sargent. Engr. by Revere

Sargent Arg a chev bet 3 dolphins embowed sa
Crest: an eagle rising ppr
Motto: Fortior quo rectior
Bookplate Winthrop Sargent; also of Ignatius Sargent with motto: Nec quaerere honorem nec spernere. Seal of Peter Sargent, 1693, on a power of attorney, now at Salem. One of His Majesty's Council, Prov. of Mass., 1714. A bookplate of Arthur Hewes Sargent with a dolphin of the field for crest was engraved by "S. L. S. after P. Revere 1899." Also on a brougham, Mrs. Winthrop Sargent, Boston. Wm. Durham Sargent and Geo. H. Sargent's bookplate has motto: Nec quaerere nec spernere honorem. Heral. Jour., vol. 1, pp. 118, 123

Sargent Arg a chev bet 3 dolphins emb sa. Impaling: Sa on a chev bet 3 leaves arg as many crosses crosslet of the field (Norwood?)
Crest: an arm erect grasping a serpent
An embroidery marked "Nathaniel and Mary Ellery, Anno Dom. 1745." Mary was Nathaniel's daughter by Abigail Norwood. His second wife was Anne, daughter of Wm. and Ann Sargent. Heral. Jour., vol. 4, p. 42

Satterthwaite Erm on a chief sa 3 roses arg
Crest: a lion's head erased or gorged sa
Bookplate T. B. Satterthwaite

Sattig Quart 1 and 4: Gu on a pale arg a scythe sa; 2 and 3: Arg on a chev az 3 leaves erect
Motto: Aequabiliter et Diligenter
Bookplate Gustave R. Sattig, New Haven, 1895

Saundby Quartered by Leigh

Saunders See also Plaisted

Savage [Arg] 6 lioncelles 3, 2, 1 [sa]
Crest: a lion's gamb
Engraved on baptismal basin given in 1732 by Arthur Savage. Christ Church, Boston. Old Sil. Am. Ch., p. 76. Major Thomas Savage, Boston, d. 1681-2. Table tomb King's Chapel Graveyard, Boston. Also on his portrait, owned by Mrs. Fred C. Shattuck, Boston. Also his four sons used on doc. 1683 in Mass. Archives, vol. 2, p. 58. E. A. Jones, London, refers in a letter to Arthur Savage, Jr., Loyalist, who used the crest and Mori quam

faedari as a motto. Painted on the bookcase at "Scottowe." For Thomas Savage of Boston. Also on a seal ring owned by Mr. Park. Lawrence Park, Scottowe, Groton, Mass.

Savage Impaled by Townsend

Saville Arg on a bend sa 3 owls arg
Crest: an owl arg
Mottoes: 1: Virus sola nobilitas; 2: Be fast
Bookplate James Hamilton Saville, Washington

Sayward A fess bet 3 trefoils slipped
Crest: a ball (?)
A seal on doc. of Jonathan Sayward, July 6, 1772, in Mass. Archives, vol. 25, p. 522. The crest is indistinct. "Sayward" name not in Burke. See also the Gore roll in Amer. Heral.

Scarborough Or a chev bet 3 towers gu
Seal of John Scarborough, Bishop of N. J., impales the above arms. Zieber's Heral., p. 202

Scar-Smith Quartered by Grosvenor

Schenck Az a [double cross or dumbbell?] or
Crest: the figure of the field in front of an escallop inverted az
Bookplate Rev. Noah Hunt Schenck, D. D., rector St. Ann's Church, Brooklyn

Schofield Arg on a pale cotised sa 3 roses. Impaling: Gu 3 roses 2 and 1 arg a chief chequy arg and gu
Crest: a fleur-de-lis
Motto: Vive ut postea vivas
Bookplate Robert Schofield

Schermerhorn Arg a tree ppr on a mount vert which is charged with a beaver (?) ppr
Crest: out of a ducal cor a tree of the shield
Motto: Industria semper crescam
Framed arms in color, owned by E. O. Schermerhorn of Newton, Mass. He has also a seal ring

Schiefflin Tiercé per fess sa and or on 3 piles 2 conjoined and one bet transposed and counterchanged as many crosses crosslet of the first
Crest: pascal lamb with staff and pennon ppr
Motto: Per fidem et constantiam
Notepaper F. Winthrop Coll., N. Y., 1885, in Bos. Ath.

Schuyler Vert issuing from a dexter cloud ppr, a cubit arm in fess vested az holding on the hand a falcon close all ppr
Crest: a hawk close ppr

On plate made before 1650. Also bookplate Philip Schuyler, Esqr., but no cloud

Notepaper F. Winthrop Coll., N. Y., 1885, has no cloud

Schuyler   Vert issuing from the sinister an arm vested [az] holding on the hand a falcon close all proper

Crest: on a crown a falcon of the field gorged with a fillet strings reflexed

Carved on stone, Capitol, Albany, N. Y.   G. R. Howell's Heraldry in new capitol at Albany.   Painted on window of Dutch Church at Albany, with "Filyjp Pietersen Schvyler Commissaris, 1656."   See Heral. Jour., vol. 3, pp. 145, 148.   There seems to have been no crown on the window

Scott   A chev bet 3 dolphins embowed

Crest: a dolphin of the arms

Seal of Gen. Charles Scott, Cumberland Co., Va. and Ky.   Wm. & Mary Quar., Oct. 1893, p. 133

Scott   3 lions' heads erased gu. Impaling: A cannon bet 3 flaming bombs

Crest: a lion's head of the field

Motto: Tace aut face; Autremen tonnerre

Bookplate John Scott, mercator, N. Y., 1702-1733.   Curio, p. 108.   The impaled arms (Morin?) appear on old silver

Scott   Arg a cross crosslet fitchée sa

Crest: an eagle preying on a heron

Bookplate Benjamin Scott

Scott   Or on a bend az a cresc bet 2 mullets arg

Crest: a stag tripp ppr

Motto: Amo

Bookplate Henry Lee Scott, U. S. A.

Scott   Or on a bend az a plate bet 2 cresc arg within a bordure arg charged with 8 roundels [bezants?]

Crest: a bird with a green branch

Motto: Gaudia magna nuncio

Bookplate Mary Scott Townsend, Washington, D. C.

Scott   Or on a bend az a star of 6 points bet 2 increscents arg.   In base a bow and arrow

Crest: a hand holding a battle axe in bend sinister or

Mottoes: 1: Trusty and true; 2: Famam extendimus factis

Bookplate S. P. Scott, Omaha, Neb.

Scott   Or on a bend az a star bet 2 cresc in a bordure arg 8 stars

Crest: a dove ppr

Motto: Gaudia nuncio magna

Tomb of Rev. Alexander Scott, who d. in 1726, at   Dipple, Stafford Co., Va.   See Crozier's Va. Heral., 1908, pp. 67 and 68.   A bookplate of Alexander

Scott has no bordure but a crescent in chief and a stag passant for crest.

Motto: Amo

Scott   Or on a bend az a plate bet 2 cresc within a bordure [gu?] charged with 8 bezants

Crest: a martlet holding a twig

Motto: Gaudia magna nuncio

Bookplate Gustavus Scott, Va., d. 1801. See, however, Wm. & Mary Quar., Oct. 1893, p. 133

Scott   Or on a bend az an estoile of 6 points bet 2 cresc or.   In chief a spear erect ppr

Crest: a cubit arm holding a spear

Motto: Amore patriae

Bookplate Gen. Winfield Scott, Va.

Scott   Or on a bend az an estoile bet 2 cresc of the first

Crest: a lion's head erased

Motto: In God we trust

Bookplate John N. D. S. Scott

Scottow   Arg on a chev sa 5 stars or in chief a book

Crest: a hand couped at wrist holding a quill

Bookplate John Scottow of Boston

Scottowe   Az on a bend or a mullet of the first

Painted by Lawrence Park, Groton, on bookcase at "Scottowe."   Mr. and Mrs. Park both descended from Scottowe

Scribner   Erm on a chief indented az 3 leopards' faces arg (Scribner).   Impaling: Gu on a fess arg cotised or 3 martlets sa

Crest: an arm emb holding a quill

Motto: Veritas securis

Bookplate G. Hilton Scribner

Scribner   Quart 1: Erm on a chief az 3 leopards' faces [or] (Scrivener); Quart 1 and 4:   Per fess vert and or; 2 and 3: Or 3 bars gu bet 9 crosses humetée 4, 3, 2; 3:   Az 2 battle axes in saltire; 4: Gu on a fess arg cotised [or] [3] birds sa (Hilton?)

Crest: an arm emb holding a quill

Bookplate G. Hilton Scribner.   D. McN. Stauffer, sc.

Scribner   Quart 1: Erm on a chief indented az 3 leopards' faces arg; 2: Arg 2 bars gu.   In chief 3 mullets gu (Washington); 3: Sa a fess wavy arg bet 2 estoiles of 8 points arg (Drake); 4: Gu on a fess arg cotised or 3 martlets sa (Hilton)

Crest: an arm emb holding a quill

Bookplate Howard and Anne Scribner.   Des. by Stauffer

Scribner   Quart 1 and 4: Arg a chev bet 3 escallops; 2 and 3: Arg (?) a fess engr sa within a bordure engr sa
Bookplate Sarah Pettingill Scribner

Scripps   [   ] a horseshoe
Motto: Prospicio
Bookplate James Edmund Scripps, engr. by French, 1896

Scrivener   *See also* Scribner

Seabury   Arg a fess engr bet 3 ibexes pass sa
Crest: an ibex of the shield
Motto: Supera alta tenere
Window in Chapel of Berkeley Divinity School at Middleton, Conn., in memory of Bishop Seabury. Also on silver of Mrs. Stanley B. Parker of Cambridge; wedding silver of Mary Seabury, 1870, wife of Henry Ainsworth Parker. Mr. S. B. Parker has a die of the crest used by Bp. S.'s grandson, Samuel Seabury. Vermont's Amer. Heral. [1886], pp. 141, 178

Seabury   Quart 1 and 4: Arg a fess engrailed bet 3 ibexes pass [sa]; 2 and 3: Arg a bear ramp [sa] a canton gu (Beere?)
Crest: an ibex of the field
Motto: Hold to the Most High
Notepaper Katherine E. Seabury (Mrs. W. M.) of Phoenix, Arizona

Searles   Per pale or and gu
Bookplate Edward Francis Searles

Sears   Quart 1 and 4: Gu a chev arg bet 3 eaglets. On a chief erm an escallop bet 2 mullets gu; 2 and 3: Arg a cross gu bet 4 water bougets (Bourchier)
Crest: an eagle displayed
Motto: 1: Annique viresque pariter crescent; 2: Honor et fides
Supporters: A soldier in armor with shield and cross. An Indian with bow
Bookplate David Sears, Boston. Also George E. Sears, with motto 2, and a crown for crest, but no supporters

Sears   [Gu] a chev [arg] bet 3 eaglets ppr
Crest: a demi-eagle displayed with wings inverted
Cut in stone inscribed: "Mansion House erected by David Sears in the year one thousand eight hundred and nineteen. A. Parris, architect." *See* Brief Hist. of the Somerset Club of Boston, 1913

Sears   Gu a chev arg bet 3 eaglets (or pewits) ppr. On a chief erm an escallop bet 2 mullets gu
Crest: an eagle displayed with wings inverted
Mottoes: 1: Exaltat humiles; 2: Honor et fides
Granary Burying Ground, Tremont St. side, Boston

Sedgwick   Or on a cross gu 5 bells of the first. Impaling: Gu a chev or bet in chief 2 thistles and in base a lion ramp
Crest: on a chapeau gu and erm a lion passant
Motto: Confido in Domino
Bookplate Robert Sedgwick. E. D. French, sc., 1896. *See also* under Leverett

Sedgwick   Impaled by Leverett

Seelye   On a bend cotised (?) 5 mullets
Crest: a bird
Motto: Cari Deo nihil . . . carent
Bookplate by Dougald Stewart Walker. Cynthia Eggleston Seelye. Print owned by Mrs. Peck, Lynn

Selby   Az (?) a negro head sa. A chief bendy sa and arg
Sampler 1678, owned by Mrs. Eugene Hale, Ellsworth, Me.

Semple   Arg a chev chequy arg and gu bet 3 hunting horns sa stringed
Crest: a stag's head couped ppr
Motto: Keep triste
Bookplate Anthony Semple

Sener   Per pale az and gu. On the dexter side a lion ramp holding a sword and facing on the sinister side a mailed arm emb holding a sword
Crest: two horns
Motto: Manu forti
Bookplate S. M. Sener, 1855, Penn.

Seton   Or 3 crescents 2 and 1 gu within a double tressure flory counter-flory of the last
Crest: a wyvern
Motto: Hazard zit forward
Bookplate William Seton. Maverick, sculp.

Sewall   Arg a chev gu bet 3 bees
Crest: a bee
Engr. on portrait of Rev. Joseph Sewall, pastor Old South Church, Boston, by Nat. Hurd, 1768. Mass. Hist. Soc., owner

Sewall   Sa a chev arg bet 3 bees arg
Crest: a bee in a wreath (of roses arg leaved vert)
Motto: Vivere est agere
Bookplate Rev. Frank Sewall, Urbana. Framed water color, York (Maine) Jail. Portrait Rev. Samuel Sewall of Boston. Engr. on tankard 1730, Old South Ch., Boston. Chief Justice Sewall used these arms. Old Sil. Amer. Ch., p. 54

Sewell   [Sa] a chev bet 3 bees arg
Crest: a bee arg within a rose wreath arg leaved vert
Used on silver by the Sewells of Md.

Seymour Gu 2 wings conjoined in lure or
Crest: a dove holding a flowering twig
Seal used in 1712 by Capt. Thomas Seymour of Norwalk, Conn., on his will. He was a son of Richard Seymour, who came to Hartford, Conn., 1639. Authority of Geo. D. Seymour, New Haven, Conn.

Seymour [Gu] 2 wings conjoined in lure [or]
Motto: A l'amy fidel pour jamais
Bookplate George Dudley Seymour, Conn. W. F. Hopson, sc.

Seys *See* Dongan

Shanke Impaled by Whitehouse

Sharp Arg a fess az bet 2 crosses crosslet fitchée sa in chief and a mullet gu in base
Framed painting owned by Miss Katherine Nooe, Statesville, N. C.

Sharpless Sa 3 cresc jessant each a mullet arg 2 and 1
Crest: a cubit arm holding a sword ppr
Motto: Pro veritate suffer fortiter
Notepaper T. Wilson Sharpless, Whitemarsh, Penn. Also without crest or motto, bookplate of Nathan H. Sharpless of Phila.

Shattuck A chev bet 3 fleurs-de-lis
Seal on will of Samuel Shattuck, Sr., dated April 6, 1689 (Essex Co. Probate, Mass.)

Shaw Az 3 covered dishes 2 and 1 [or]
Crest: a pheonix rising from flames
Motto: Dum spiro spero
Bookplate T. A. Shaw

Shaw Or on a chev sa bet 3 eagles displayed of the 2d 3 cinquefoils slipped or. The badge of Ulster
Crest: a fawn's head couped az wounded by an arrow [or]
Motto: Te ipsum nosce
Bookplate ——— Shaw, N. Y.

Sheaffe Erm on a chev gu bet 3 pellets 3 garbs or
Seal used in 1713 by Jacob Sheaffe of Boston when he was a witness to James Osborn's will; also on the will of Mathias Smith in 1715, both in Suffolk Registry, Mass. Heral. Jour., vol. 4, p. 81

Sheepshanks Az a chev erm bet in chief 3 roses and in base a lamb arg (?)
Crest: a lamb
Motto: Perseverando
Gold seal owned by the Sproat family, West town, Penn. Zieber's Heral., p. 69.
Bookplate John Sheepshanks

Sheffield Quart 1 and 4: Or a chev bet 3 gauntlets each paleways gu; 2 and 3: Sa a chev bet 3 rowels or
Crest: a demi-lion ramp ppr
A framed canvas of the Sheffields of R. I., about 1700. Now owned by G. Andrews Moriarty of Boston. Burke gives garbs not gauntlets. Painted by "I. P. Halpin"

Sheild Gu on a bend engr or 3 escutcheons sa
Crest: a fleur-de-lis
Motto: Be Traiste
Engr. on old seal and silver plate of descendants of the immigrant, Robert Shield, York Co., Va. Mrs. A. L. Thaw, 421 W. Grace St., Richmond, has a framed coat with bend not engrailed, crest: a boar's head couped; and motto: Be traist. The above is as in Burke. Crozier's Va. Heral., 1908, p. 56

Sheldon Gu a fess bet 3 sheldrakes arg
Crest: an armed arm emb holding a battle axe
Bookplate Henry L. Sheldon, Middlebury, Vt.

Shelley [Sa] a fess engr [or? engraved gu] bet 3 whelk shells [or]
Crest: a griffin's head erased, ducally gorged [or]
Engr. on tankard, Judge Clearwater collection. Owned by Capt. Giles Shelley (1664–1710) of N. Y. Amer. Sil., by C. L. Avery, 1920, p. 20

Shelton Or a griffin pass. On a chief az a star of 6 points
Crest: a lion ramp contourné
Motto: Nil sine Deo
Bookplate Revᵈ Philo Shelton, 1754–1825, Fairfield, Conn. Bates's Early Conn. Engr., p. 39. R. Brunton, sc.

Shepard Erm on a chief gu 3 battle axes arg. Impaling: Arg on a bend gu bet 3 roundels 3 swans, a crescent for diff (Clark)
Crest: a stag reguard trip
Motto: Nec timeo nec sperno
Bookplate George L. Shepard, 1859

Shepley Quartered by Asheton

Sheppard Erm on a chief sa 3 pole axes
Crest: a stag trippant and reguard
Motto: Nec celeri nec forti
Bookplate Edwᵈ Sheppard

Sherburne Quart 1 and 4: Vert an eagle displayed arg; 2 and 3: Arg a lion ramp or
Crest: a unicorn's head arg
"By the name of Sherburne." Embroidery on silk. Owned by Merrill Spalding, Brookline, Mass.

Sherburne Quart 1 and 4: Arg a lion ramp guard vert; 2 and 3: Vert an eagle displayed arg (Bayley). Impaling: Sa a chev bet 3 ox heads cabossed or, a cresc for diff (Bulkeley, but intended for Stanley?)
Crest: a unicorn's head erased [arg armed or]
Motto: Quant je puis
Painted hatchment (very old) owned by Gen. John H. Sherburne, Brookline, Mass., desc. of Henry of N. H. These Sherburnes from Stonyhurst, Lanc., were originally Bayleys; the eagle was used by the Bayleys, but more often by the Winkleys, their neighbors. The Brookline Sherburnes have twelve handsome chairs, Jacobean style, each with the quartered coat. Also Bookplate Kenneth Sherborne of Boston. C. W. Sherborn, sc., 1906. No impaled coat

Sherman Or a lion ramp contourné sa bet 3 sprigs
Crest: a sea lion contourné
Motto: Conquer death by virtue
Bookplate Peter Sherman. R. Brunton, sc. Also Rev. Henry B. Sherman. Bates's Early Conn. Engr., p. 39

Sherman Or a lion ramp sa bet 3 [oak] leaves vert
Crest: a sea lion sejant or
Framed water color owned by Hon. Roger Sherman of Conn., at his death in 1793. See Sherman Geneal., 1920. Notepaper F. Winthrop Coll., N. Y., 1885, in Bos. Ath. with motto: J'espere. Engr. on notepaper Mrs. Cora Sherman Rohlfing, 597 Cass St., Milwaukee, without tinctures indicated

Sherman See also Potter

Sherwin Quartered by Cabell

Sherwood Per bend sinister sa and arg a bull pass reguard erm bet 3 mullets gu
Crest: a cubit arm holding a rose leaved ppr
Motto: Non timeo sed caveo
Fire screen embr. by Mrs. Philip H. Sherwood, Dedham, Mass., Nov. 1923. Also bookplate drawn by Miss Marjorie Bruce

Shipman Gu on a bend arg bet 6 estoiles of 6 points [or] 3 ogresses
Crest: a leopard sejant [arg] spotted [sa] resting his dexter paw on a ship's rudder [az]
Sardonyx ring. F. E. Widmer, 31 West St., Boston

Shippen Arg a chev bet 3 erect oak leaves gu
Crest: a martlet sa holding an oak leaf gu

Iron seal owned by Dr. Edward Shippen, Phila. Zieber's Heral., p. 67. Also bookplate Robert Shippen, S. T. P.
Bookplate "William Shippen," the martlet like a crow

Shirley Paly of 6 arg and sa [properly or, and az] a canton erm. Impaiing: Arg 3 bears' heads erased gu, muzzled [or], in chief 3 torteaux (Barker)
Crest: a bearded face couped at the shoulders
Wall tablet to Frances, wife of Gov. Shirley. King's Chapel, Boston, south aisle. Gov. Shirley stamped on his book covers an S crowned, all within two sprays of laurel (?)

Shirley Paly of six or and az. A canton erm and in chief the arms of Ulster
Crest: a bearded head couped with cap ppr
Bostonian Society. In King's Chapel, 1886. Also in a window, 3d floor, State House, Boston, in color, without badge of Ulster

Shober Arg 3 lions ramp [gu], on a chief az a dexter couped head fessways holding a dagger erect arg hilted [or] bet 2 pheons points down [or] (Carney arms)
Crest: a hand holding a pheon
Motto: Sustine et abstine
Notepaper Mrs. John B. Shober, Phila. Also of Samuel L. Shober, Rosemont

Short He Beareth Sable a Griffon passant argent and a chief ermine
Crest: a demi-griffin
Framed water color, Essex Institute, Salem, Mass. No cornstalk, but a tassel on each side

Shrimpton On a cross five escallops, a crescent for difference
Crest: a demi-lion ramp holding an escallop
On the portrait said to be a Gibbs. The Rev. Henry Gibbs of Newton, Mass., was son of Robt. (1665–1702) and Mary (Shrimpton) Gibbs. Owned by Dr. Frederick J. White of Brookline, Mass. Given in the Gore Roll as Shrimpton, but not so attributed elsewhere. John Cony made a tankard bearing on a cross 5 escallops with an annulet, owned by Mrs. Catharine Abbot Folsom (1918). Mary Shrimpton (b. 1667) married (1) Henry Gibbs in 1692 (2) Samuel Sewall. The tankard has "M. S." Thomas Child in Feb. 1688 sent a bill to estate of Col. Sam. Shrimpton for a hatchment. Seal on a bond of Rowland Story of Boston, 12 Jan. 1687–8, owned by C. P. Greenough. The mark of difference is clearly an annulet

Shubrick Az a chev erm bet 3 estoiles of 6 points or
  Crest: a demi-man with an arrow in his dexter hand sa
  Motto: Inimica tyrannis
  Bookplate Col. Thomas Shubrick, So. Car., 1755–1810. Also seal of the present family

Shute Per chev sa and or. In chief 2 eagles displayed or
  Crest: a griffin pierced by an arrow
  Used to hang in the wooden King's Chapel, Boston. For Gov. Shute

Shute Per chev sa and or. In chief 2 eagles displayed or
  Crest: a griffin sejant or, the breast pierced with a sword and dropping blood gu
  On a window, 3d floor, State House, Boston. Gov. Samuel Shute, 1716–1722. Shield engr. on Price-Burgis view of Boston, 1725

Shuttleworth Arg 3 shuttles sa tipped or 2 and 1
  Crest: an armed cubit arm holding a shuttle ppr
  Bookplate Robert James Shuttleworth

Sibley Per pale az and gu. Over all a griffin bet 3 cresc arg
  Crest: out of a ducal cor a swan's head bet spread wings
  Motto: Esse quam videre
  Bookplate —— Sibley. Sibley and Sybly arms. Carved in stone for Sibley bldg., Rochester, N. Y., by John Evans Co., Boston, 1926

Sidney Or a pheon az
  Crest: a ragged staff and bear muzzled, gorged and chained
  Motto: Quo fata vocant
  Bookplate William James Sidney

Sill Arg a fess sa fretty or. In chief a lion pass gu
  Crest: a demi-griffin ramp ppr
  Bookplate George Imbrie Sill. Also Howard Sill, Hollyday's Choice, Prince George's Co., Md., 1891

Silsbee Gu on a pile az 3 lozenges arg (sic)
  Crest: a lozenge arg
  Framed water color "By the name of Silsbee." Owned by F. S. Whitwell, Boston. Not in Burke. Nathaniel of Salem was a U. S. Senator. Window, Blake Mem. Chapel, Salem, Mass.

Silvester Arg a sea lion crowned [az]
  Crest: a lion couchant [gu]
  Motto: Nec Degener
  Bookplate John Silvester, Esq. Also Peter Silvester, N. Y. Child, sculp.

Simes Az 3 escallops in pale or
  Crest: a hart's head erased ppr
  Framed water color, G. and W. S. Simes (pronounced Sims) of Portsmouth, N. H., in Mr. Simes's house, Petersham, Mass., 1915

Simmons "He beareth Party per pale or and sable three roses counterchanged by the name of Simmons and descends to the name and family. Boston, Sept. 6th, 1805. Copy from Heraldry. Attest (signed) Jno. Coles, Sen'r. Herald Painter"
  Crest: an American flag, red and white stripes and on a blue canton an eagle displayed within an orle of 13 stars. N. E. Hist. Geneal. Society, Boston

Simpson Arg on a chief az 3 cresc arg
  Crest: a lion's head erased
  Motto: Nil nisi bonum
  Bookplate Frank E. Simpson

Simpson Arg on a chief vert 3 crescents. Impaling: 3 crowns in pale
  Crest: a dove rising
  Motto: Alis nutrior
  Bookplate James Simpson, Esq.

Simons Per fess embowed and embat gu and sa 3 martlets or
  Crest: two wings side by side one or and one arg
  Motto: Resurgere tento
  Water color in So. Car. Hist. Soc.

Simpson Arg on a chief vert 3 cresc
  Crest: a bird rising
  Engr. on silver flagon given by John Simpson of Boston to the Old South Church, 1764. Jones, Amer. Ch. Silver, p. 56. Buck, Old Plate, 1903, p. 205

Sims [Erm?] 3 increscents [gu?] (Symmes arms)
  Crest: a demi-dragon (?)
  Motto: In justitia virtutes omnes
  Tombstone, St. Peter's churchyard, Phila., 1773. Sylvan City, 1883, p. 438. The Continent, 25 Apr., 1883

Sims Gu a chev or bet in chief 2 stars of 6 points and in base a battle axe or. Impaling: Quarterly az and gu a cross arg bet 4 pheons. Over all a label of 3 points
  Crest: a demi-lion ramp holding a battle axe or
  Motto: Ferio tego
  Bookplate Henry Augustus Sims, architect, 1832–75. Stauffer, sc. Also (without impaled coat) Clifford Stanley Sims

Sinclair Quart 1 and 4: Az a ship at anchor, oars in saltire and sails furled, within a double tressure flory counterflory or (Orkney); 2 and 3: Or a lion

ramp gu (Spar); 4: Az a ship under sail or, the sails arg (Caithness). Over all dividing the quarters a cross engrailed sa
Crest: a swan arg collared and chained or, beaked gu
Motto: Fight
Silver tankard owned by R. H. Ludlow, N. Y., formerly owned by early Amer. Sinclairs. Vermont's Amer. Heral. [1886], pp. 29, 179

Skaats Gu two schaats (Dutch for skates) sa, quartered with az, a crescent or
Crest: a demi-winged horse salient
In 1858 the family had an ancient coat of arms painted on wood before 1700. Vermont's Amer. Heral. [1886], pp. 138, 139

Skelton Az a fess or bet 3 fleurs-de-lis
Crest: a peacock's head erased ppr, in the beak an acorn or, stalked and leaved vert
Engr. on old silverware owned by the Skeltons of Kentucky. Also bookplate of Reuben Skelton, son of James Skelton, who was living in St. James Parish, Goochland, Va., in 1735; also of Meriwether Skelton, Hanover Co., Va., 1770

Skinner Arg a sea horse sa within an orle and encircled by 16 torteaux
Crest: a demi sea horse
Motto: Droit et avant
Framed paintings owned by Mrs. E. B. Ficklen (Myra Skinner), Mrs. Margaret Skinner Ferguson, Mrs. W. H. Whedbee, all of Greenville, N. C., and Miss Marian Drane, Edenton, N. C., daughter of Rev. Dr. Drane, rector for 47 years of St. Paul's, who married Miss Skinner

Skinner Sa on a chev or bet 3 griffins' heads erased arg a cresc of the first
Crest: a griffin's head erased arg holding in its beak a dexter hand couped gu
Engr. on an alms dish from Richard Skinner, 1727. Second Church, Marblehead, Mass. Old Sil. Am. Ch., p. 268

Skipwith Arg 3 bars gu. In chief a greyhound courant sa [collared or]
Crest: a reel ppr
Motto: Sans Dieu Je ne puis
Bookplate Fulwar Skipwith, Va.

Slacke Az on a cross pattée per bend sinister erm and or a quatrefoil counterchanged
Crest: a lion couchant
Bookplate John Slacke

Slater Or a chev gu bet 3 trefoils slipped sa
Crest: a cubit arm holding a sword
Motto: Crescit sub pondere virtus ventis secundis
Bookplate W. S. Slater of Conn.

Slaughter Arg a saltire az
Seal to the bond of William Slaughter as Sheriff of Essex Co., Va., in 1685. Wm. & Mary Quar., Jan. 1894, p. 157. Bellet's Some Prom. Va. Fam., vol. 4, p. 399

Sleigh *See also* Baer

Slocum Quartered by Rogers

Smith A chev bet 3 leopards' faces
Seal Richard Smith, member of Andros's Council, 1687/8. Jeffries MSS. N. E. Reg., Jan. 1877, p. 65

Smith A chev bet 3 stags' heads couped
Crest: a garb
Motto: Carpe diem
Seal of Rev. Henry Smith, Wethersfield, Conn. Stiles's Anc. Wethersfield, vol. 2, p. 628

Smith Two hands clasped and couped at wrist
Crest: a gamb holding a battle axe
Motto: Je suis pret
On china of Joseph Smith of Penn. (formerly McDonald), owned by Mrs. Arnold Talbot, Lincoln, R. I. (later Phila.)

Smith Arg 3 spears in pale (sa?) a chief chequy arg and (sa?)
Crest: a sea lion passant
Seal of Rev. John Smith, N. Y., 1728. Jeffries MSS. N. E. Reg., Jan. 1877, p. 65

Smith Arg on a bend bet 2 unicorns' heads erased az [armed or] 3 fusils in bend of the last, a trefoil slipped for diff
Crest: an armed arm embowed holding a broken sword
Motto: Nil desperandum
Bookplate "Willm Smith Trin Coll: Camb:" of Va. Also used by Thomas Smith

Smith Arg on a bend bet 2 unicorns' heads erased az [armed or] 3 fusils. Impaling: Per pale or and az a fess counterchanged (Cusack)
Crest: a unicorn's head couped az armed or
Bookplate William Smith, LL. D., Charleston, S. C.

Smith Arg 3 broken lances erect in fess, a chief chequy or and gu
Crest: a sea lion
Motto: Nec aspera terrent
Bookplate Thoˢ Smith Junʳ Esq. Maverick, sculp., of N. Y. Thomas

Smith had the same arms and motto: Mens sibi conscia recti. William Smith had the same arms engr. by Maverick with motto: Tutus si fortis. William Smith, Esqr of N. Y. had these arms engr. by Gallaudet with motto: Optimum est aliena frui insania. The historian, William Smith, A. M., of N. Y. has these arms with motto: Nil utile quod non honestum. (Wilson's N. Y., vol. 2, p. 31 says Tangier Smith family which has also a hatchment.) William P. [Eatree] Smith, A. M., of N. Y. has these arms engr. by Thomas Johnston of Boston and motto: Deus nobis haec otia fecit. Bookplate Samuel Smith, Esq., with motto: Omnes fremant licet dicam quod sentio

Smith Arg a fess dancettée bet 3 roses gu barbed vert
Wax seal on will of Colonel Joseph Smith, 1728, at Tappahannock, Essex, Va. Wm. & Mary Quar., Jan. 1894, p. 156. Also Jan. 1893, p. 123

Smith Arg a chev nebulée double cotised gu bet 3 leopards' faces erased or
Crest: a fusil quartered within a bordure, all arg
Framed water color, very old. "By the name of Smith" and palm branches. The coat is on paper inserted and the surname also. Miss Grace Andrews, 54 Clarke Ave., Chelsea

Smith Az 2 bends wavy erm on a chief or, a demi-lion issuant [sa]
Crest: an ostrich ppr with a worm [or horseshoe] in beak arg
Hatchment of Susanna Smith

Smith Az a chev bet 3 acorns slipped and leaved or
Mildred, daughter of Edmund Smith, married David Jameson. On her tomb at Temple Farm, Gloucester Co., Va., are the Jameson arms, impaling Smith. (*See* Jameson arms.) Crozier's Va. Heral., 1908, p. 14

Smith Barry of 6 erm and gu. Over all a lion ramp sa
Crest: a griffin's head erased sa
Bookplate Chester Ballou Smith

Smith Gu a chev bet 3 griffins segreant or. On a chief of the last as many fleurs-de-lis of the first
Seal and bookplate of Robert D. Weston, Boston, son of R. D. Smith and grandson of Dr. John DeWolfe Smith of Hallowell, Maine

Smith Gu a chev or bet 3 stags' heads couped arg
Crest: a garb
Motto: Carpe diem
Ex libris Richmond and Elizabeth Mayo-Smith. By Mrs. Harding

Smith Gu 5 lozenges conjoined in fess [arg] bet 2 demi-children arg
Crest: a mural tower
Motto: Non est mortale quod opto
Bookplate John Smith

Smith [Or] a chev cotised bet 3 demi-griffins sa, the 2 in chief respectant
Crest: an elephant's head erased [or eared gu] charged on the neck with 3 fleurs-de-lis [az 2 and 1]
Bookplate Major Gen. Robert Smith, Va.

Smith Or a chev cotised bet 3 demi-griffins segreant couped sa, the 2 in chief respectant, a martlet on the chev for diff
Crest: an elephant's head erased or [eared gu] charged with 3 fleurs-de-lis az 2 and 1
Motto: Chacun a son gout
Bookplate William Smith, Mass. Attrib. to Hurd, sc.

Smith Or a chev double cotised sa bet in chief 2 demi-griffins affronté and in base one demi-griffin sa
Crest: an elephant's head or charged with 3 fleurs-de-lis az
Motto: Chacun a son gout
Bookplate William Smith

Smith Or a unicorn salient az
Crest: the unicorn of the shield
Engr. on silver of 16th cent. brought from Amsterdam to Portsmouth, N. H., and Penn., 1740 by Samuel Smith. Amer. Heral., vol. 2, p. 32

Smith Or on a saltire az bet 4 cresc [gu] an escallop
Crest: an escallop
Motto: Quod petis hic est
Bookplate Thomas Hogan Smith

Smith Per chev nebuly sa and arg 3 ounces' faces erased counterchanged
Crest: a horse's head per chev or and sa
Engr. on watch seals of John Smith of Purton, on York River, Gloucester Co., Va. Arms of Smith of Walsham, Co. Suffolk. Pecquet du Bellet's Some Prom. Va. Families, vol. 3, p. 1

Smith 1: Per fess arg and purp. In chief 3 leaves, in base a horn (Not found in Burke); 2: Or on a cross engr gu bet 4 cresc gu a lozenge voided or; 3: Or a lion ramp holding a twig within a bordure engr sa
Motto: Deo juvante
Bookplate Richard and Rebecca Mayes Smith, engr. by Arthur H. Noll, 1916. As engraved

Smith Quart 1 and 4: Arg 10 crosses potent 4, 3, 2, 1; 2 and 3: Arg a unicorn's head erased gu. On a chief wavy gu 3 lozenges or

Crest: a sinister arm mailed embowed holding a long spear
Bookplate William R. Smith

Smith Quart 1 and 4: Gu a chev arg bet 3 garbs; 2 and 3: Arg a fess gu bet 3 coursing greyhounds sa (Griswold?)
Crest: a ship stern to
Supporters: (dexter) a Puritan; (sinister) a Cavalier
Bookplate W. D. Griswold Smith, engr. by A. W. Macdonald

Smith Sa a fess cotised bet 3 martlets or
Crest: a greyhound sejant gorged and chained
Motto: Fidem servabo genusque
Bookplate William Smith, LL.D., Charleston, S. C., 1784–1840. Statesman. Also William Loughton Smith, LL.D., Charleston, S. C. On ring of Thomas Smith, dated 1671, with motto: "Semper fidelis," and same arms used as seal on will of Thomas Smith, 2d, of Carolina. (Ancest. Rec. & Portr. vol. 1, p. 387). *See also* Bellet's Some Prom. Va. Fam., vol. 4, pp. 113, 114, 123, 125. *See* his journal edited by Albert Matthews, in Mass. Hist. Soc. Proc., Oct. 1917

Smith Sa a fess dancettée bet 3 lions ramp each supporting a garb all or
Seal on a deed of Robert Smith and Elizabeth, his wife of Lancaster Co., Va., dated 20 Apr., 1665. Wm. & Mary Quar., Jan. 1894, p. 158

Smith Sa 3 daisies (?) arg
Crest: an open book and a sun in splendor above
Mottoes: Ερεονᾶτε Τὰς ϝραφας
Beauty and grace
Bookplate Hezekiah Smith, Mass.

Smith Sa 3 roses 2 and 1
Crest: a talbot trippant or
Bookplate Edgerton Smith, cir. 1730

Smith Quartered by Adams and Dulany

Smith Impaled by Jeffers

Smith Quartered by Lynde

Smith *See also* Brattle and Weston-Smith

Smyth Sa on a chev engr [or] bet 6 crosses pattée fitchée of the second, 3 fleurs-de-lis az?
Crest: a child's head with wings
Motto: Resurgam
Hatchment Frederick Smyth (died 1806) chief Justice, N. J.; the sinister side sa for the decease of Mrs. Smyth. Christ Church, Phila. Frontispiece to Eberlein & McClure's Early Amer. Arts & Crafts, 1916. Sylvan City (1883), p. 461. *See also* N. Y. Sun,

Feb. 25, 1920, p. 8, for Richard "Bull" Smith, deed 1684, "sealed by Smith's familiar fleur-de-lis of his coat of arms"

Smythe Gu 2 keys in saltire, the dexter surmounted by the other
Bookplate Elizabeth Harris Smythe, Columbus, Ohio, 1898

Snell Erm a lion ramp az on a canton gu a 2 headed eagle displayed arg (Edwards arms?)
Crest: a demi-lion holding a castle arg
Motto: Sola nobilitas virtus
Bookplate Mervin M. Snell

Snelling Gu 3 griffins' heads erased arg, a chief indented erm a mullet for diff
Seal from the will of Dr. Wm. Snelling, Boston, Mass., 1674. Whitmore's Elem. of Her., p. 65. *See, however*, Heral. Jour., vol. 2, p. 10, for variation

Snow Quartered by Hoskins

Soame *See also* Hamersley

Sohier Arg in fess a decrescent (jessant a face) bet 2 mullets and in base an arrow, point to sinister. On a chief gu 2 escallops
Crest: a dexter armed arm embowed holding a cutlass
Motto: Vestigia nulla retrorsum
Bookplate [W. D.] Sohier, Boston, 1787–1871. Lived on Franklin St. This coat has crowned eagles for supporters, each bearing on the breast a harp. The origin of this plate is not known

Sohier Gu a mullet arg
Crest: a cross arg bet 2 stags' horns
Motto: STELLA XPI DUCE
Bookplate George Brimmer Sohier; also Col. W. D. Sohier, 1882; also on notepaper; and on Sevre china made about 1840 for his grandfather, W. D. Sohier, who, however, used a different coat (with arrow) on his bookplate

Solart Az 3 bends compony countercompony gu and or
Crest: a woodcock
A water color unframed of Jean Solart from Piedmont, France, to Wenham, Mass. Left a daughter. Essex Institute, Salem, Mass.

Solly Vert a chev or bet 3 sole fishes anéant of the 2d
Crest: a sole fish anéant
Seal Samuel Solly, Councillor of N. H., 1751. Jeffries MSS. N. E. Reg., Jan. 1877, p. 65

Somerby Per pale arg and vert 3 cresc, 2 and 1 counterchanged
Crest: a hound collared holding an escallop-shell

Motto: Fideliter
Grave Samuel Somerby, 1781–1824,
Mt. Auburn, Mass.
Bookplate —— Somerby

Somervell Quart 1 and 4: Sa a cross humettée wavy; 2 and 3: Gu a cross humettée moline. In the center the badge of Ulster
Crest: a bearded head with shoulders, crowned
Motto: Verite sans peur
Bookplate Wm. Howe Somervell, Washington, D. C.

Sotherton *See also* Sourton

Sourton Arg a fess [gu]. In chief 2 cresc [gu or sa] (Sotherton arms). Impaling ——
Tombstone of Rev. Francis Sourton, Poplar Hill Church, St. Mary's Co., Md., d. 1679. From Devonshire? *See* Historic Graves of Md., p. 48

Southack Arg a fess dancettée gu with 2 spear heads az pointing inward above it. In chief a cubit arm vested gu issuing from a cloud in the sinister chief with cuff arg and dexter hand holding a heart ppr. Impaling: Arg 3 barulets gemelles sa, Caswell, or Creswell, or Cresseld (?)
Crest: a dexter arm counter-embowed, vested gu, cuffed arg, holding a heart ppr
"By the name of Southack" on an apron with blue knots in the upper corners. Very old painted and framed hatchment, owned by Theodore L. Southack, Boston. Capt. Cyprian Southack's arms? *See* Harleian Visitations, vol. 1, p. 59 (Soudeak). *See* Heral. Jour., vol. 2, p. 138, vol. 3, p. 47. Arms on tomb 46 in the Granary, Boston, are all gone except part of the mantling

Southack Arg a fess dancettée gu and above 2 spear heads pointing inward az and in chief a cubit arm vested gu, cuffed arg, issuing from a cloud ppr in the sinister chief and holding a heart ppr
On a marble tablet to Capt. Cyprian Southack, naval officer and chart maker, Boston, 1700. Designed by R. C. Sturgis, 1914. Christ Church, Boston

Southworth Sa a chev bet 3 crosses flory [*i. e.* crosslet?] arg
Crest: a bull's head ppr
Embr. hatchment mentioned in Gov. Wm. Bradford's inventory as "a crest." He married Alice, widow of Edward Southworth. Owned by his desc. Wm. Bradford Goodwin of Lowell, Mass.

Spar Quartered by Sinclair

Spaight Arg on a fess gu 3 pheons
Crest: a dove (?)
Motto: Vi et virtute
Bookplate "Spaight, New Berne," No. Car. Richard D. Spaight, 1758–1802. Gov. No. Car. Abernethy, sc.

Sparhawk Az a fess or bet 3 hawks. The Pepperell arms are on a shield of pretence
On Copley's portrait of Col. Nathaniel Sparhawk, Museum of Fine Arts, Boston

Sparks Chequy or and vert a bend erm
Crest: from a ducal cor a lion ramp guard sa
Motto: In Deo confido
Bookplate Geo. Downing Sparks, engr. by S. L. Smith, 1908

Sparrow Arg 3 roses 2 and 1 gu. A chief gu. Impaling: Arg a chev gu bet 3 buckles sa (Morton)
Crest: a unicorn's head couped arg
Bookplate John Sparrow, Md. (?)

Spaulding Per fess az and arg a pale counterchanged. Over all on a chev arg bet 3 buckles 3 elephants' heads gorged with ducal cor or
Crest: a Bishop's mitre or [banded gu]
Motto: Hinc mihi salus
Bookplate Bishop Spaulding, Colorado

Spenceley "Quart or and az 4 martlets counterchanged; over all a bend sa charged with 3 fleurs-de-lis arg"
Crest: "from a mural cor arg a mailed forearm, the hand grasping a cutlass, all ppr"
Motto: Dieu defende le droit
Bookplate J. Winfred Spenceley. J. W. S., sc., 1896

Spencer Arg on a chief or 3 spears erect
Crest: a demi-lion ramp gu holding a crown
Motto: Nil desperandum
Bookplate Ambrose Spencer

Spencer Quart arg and gu. On 2 and 3 a fret or. Over all on a bend sa 3 fleurs-de-lis
Ex libris Katharine Vosburgh Spencer. W[eston]-S[mith] del. 1900 (R. D. Weston)

Spencer Quart 1 and 4: Arg and in chief a crescent for diff; 2 and 3: Gu a fret or. Over all a bend sa charged with 3 mullets arg
Crest: out of a ducal cor a griffin's head gorged bet 2 wings spread or
Supporters: A griffin and a dragon
Motto: Dieu defend le droit
Bookplate O. M. Spencer, Penn.

Spinney Sa 3 cresc 2 and 1 arg
Crest: a tree
Motto: Esse quam videri
Bookplate Samuel R. Spinney, Boston

Spooner Vert [az?] a boar's head couped or
Crest: a boar's head or pierced by an arrow, point to sinister arg
Motto: Follow reason
Bookplate John J. Spooner, 1782. Also Joshua Spooner. N. Hurd, sc.

Spotswood Arg on a chev gu bet 3 oak trees eradicated ppr a boar's head of the first
Motto: Patior ut potior
Governor Spotswood's silver tea caddy. Stanard's Colonial Virginia, pp. 96, 100

Sprague Erm on a chief arg a lion passant gu
Crest: an eagle displayed charged with a chief paly gu and arg. On a chief az 13 mullets arg
"By the name of Sprague" and palm branches. A copy? Owned by F. T. Widmer, 31 West St., Boston

Sprague Or 3 rose leaves in pale vert bet 2 palets az on a shield of pretence: Arg on a chev sa bet 3 ogresses each charged with a martlet of the first 3 mascles or (Pratt)
Bookplate Mary Bryant Sprague, engr. by French, 1904. Charles Sprague, Ipswich, Mass., used a form of the Blake arms on his notepaper

Sprague See also Chester

Sproat Gu 3 leopards' faces or. On a chief arg 3 mullets sa
Crest: a boar's head couped
Gold seal, Westtown, Penn. Zieber's Heral., p. 69

Sprotty Quartered by Lenox

Spry Per saltire arg and gu 4 cresc counterchanged
Crest: an ostrich feather ppr
Bookplate William Spry, N. Y.

Staats Quart 1 and 4: Gu 2 schaets (Skates) sa; 2 and 3: Az a crescent or
Crest: a demi-winged horse salient
Painted on wood about 1700. In Staats family 1858 and earlier. Geneal. Staats Fam., 1921

Stafford Gu a chev or a canton erm
Crest: a ducal coronet
Mottoes: 1: Virtus basis vitae. 2: Frangas non flectas
Said to have been brought over by Thomas Stafford, Plymouth, Mass., 1626, and Warwick, R. I. Used by Thomas Stafford Drowne of Brooklyn, N. Y.

Stafford Quartered by Dering

Standish Az 3 standing dishes, 2 and 1 arg
Crest: a cock ppr
Motto: Constant en tout
Painting on canvas 2 x 2 feet by S. Ward on steamer *Rose Standish*, Boston

Standish [Az] 3 standing dishes [*i.e.* annulets] 2 and 1 [arg]
Crest: an owl [arg] beaked and legged [or] holding a rat in the dexter claw
Standish Hall, Harvard College. Over the door and on both gate posts. In stone

Standish Sa 3 plates
Crest: an owl on a rat
Bookplate Myles Standish. *See* Mass. Archives, vol. 60, p. 125, for crest used 1661: an owl (?) holding what appears to be a twig

Stanford Sa a chev arg bet 3 hunting horns stringed arg
Crest: a dexter hand holding a hunting horn sa
Motto: Verum dicit
Bookplate Rev. John Stanford, N. E. clergyman

Stanley Arg on a bend [az?] 3 bucks' heads cabossed [or]
Crest: a buck at gaze contourné
Engr. on tankard from William Stanley, 1786, to South or Second Church, Hartford, Conn. E. A. Jones, Old Sil. Am. Ch., p. 209

Stanton Vairé arg and ermines a canton [gu]. Impaling: [Sa] an eagle displayed arg. On a chief [or] 3 pheons sa (Gavell)
Engr. on caudle cup and paten from Rebecca Lady Gooch, 1775, to William and Mary College. Daughter of William Stanton of Hampton, Middlesex, Eng., and wife of Sir William Gooch. Her son, grandson, and brother are buried at York in Va. Christ Church, Bruton Parish, Williamsburg, Va. Old Sil. Am. Ch., p. 496

Stanwood "He Beareth az a Fess bet 3 stars of 8 points or. Granted and Confirmed on the 19th Day of June, 1613, to Sir Ralph Stanwood of Wharton in the County of Lancaster, Bart"
Framed water color owned by William Stanwood, Mere Point, Brunswick, Maine. Not in Burke. By John Coles?

Stanwood A fess bet 4 griffins' heads erased
Crest: a griffin's head erased
"By the name of Stanwood" and palm branches

Framed painting by John Coles? Henry Stanwood, owner, Brunswick, Maine

Stanwood   Or a chev sa bet 3 crosses pattée fitchée gu.   On a chief sa 3 bezants
Crest: an eagle displayed per pale or and sa
Stannard (now Stanwood) of London, Suffolk, and Norfolk. The present spelling appears at Castleacre, Co. Norfolk, in 1682.   Framed water color owned by Edward Stanwood, Brookline, Mass.   Another owned by Mrs. C. K. Bolton, Shirley, Mass.

Stark   Az a chev bet in chief 3 acorns [or] and in base a bull's head erased [or]
Crest: a bull's head of the field. (Another has a dexter hand piercing the neck of a bull's head)
Seal, New York. Also bookplate of James H. Stark, Savin Hill, Boston, with motto: Fortiorum fortia facta

Starr   Az a pair of scales or balances within an orle of 8 six-pointed estoiles
Crest: a lion couchant charged with an estoile [gu]
Motto: Vive en espoir
Seal ring, New York

Stauffer   Az from the sinister an arm emb and vested at the shoulder [or] holding a cup of the second. In the dexter chief a mullet or. From a ground in base a trefoil issuing vert
Crest: a demi-German az with gold cross humettée on his chest, attired in hat and plumes, holding a cup or and sword, hilt or
Motto: Den stauf trage ich
Bookplate D. McN. Stauffer, N. Y., engraver. The bookplate of Florence Scribner Stauffer, 1894, has Stauffer impaling Scribner and the Scribner motto

Stearns   Or a chev sa bet 3 crosses patonce [sa]
Bookplate Foster Waterman Stearns, Librarian Museum Fine Arts, Boston, and Holy Cross College, Worcester

Stearns   Or a chev bet 3 crosses flory pierced sa
Crest: a cock starling
Bookplate Charles Augustus Stearns, Boston. Also Richard H. Stearns, Boston. Also John Lloyd Stearns, engr. by French. Has motto: Sustinebit

Stearns   Or a chev bet 3 crosses flory pierced sa
Crest: an eagle rising
Motto: Absque labore nihil
Bookplate Joseph Barker Stearns. Jarrett, sc. London

Stearns   Per chev embat or and az 3 martlets.   Implaing: Gu a lion ramp coward holding a battle axe
Crest: on a mound vert a martlet
Motto: Firm
Bookplate ―――― Stearns, Mass.

Stedman   Or a cross crosslet vert
Crest: a demi-virgin, gowned vert, her hair dishevelled and holding in her dexter hand a cross crosslet fitchée of the same
Embr. hatchment, owned by the Hist. Soc. of Old Newbury (Mass.)

Steed   Quartered by Tufton

Steel   Arg a bend counter-compony erm and [sa bet 2 lions' heads erased [gu]. On a chief [az] 3 billets [or]
Capt. John Steel, Boston, d. 1768. King's Chapel Graveyard, Boston, by Tremont Street fence, "No. 6". Heral. Jour., vol. 2, p. 20. Engr. shows crest but there is none on the stone

Steel   Arg a bend erm bet 2 lions' heads erased.   On a chief arg 3 wedges gu points to dexter
Bookplate Thomas Steel, York, Pa.

Steenwyck   Sa 2 bars a unicorn's head above, 3 trumpets (?) below
On oil portrait of Cornelis Steenwyck, N. Y., in N. Y. Hist. Soc.

Steer   *See also* Welsteed

Steptoe   Az a fleur-de-lis arg
Crest: out of a ducal cor or a stag's head ppr. But Bellet says: "Crest engraved on the tomb: Knight's head crowned"
Motto: Spes mea in Deo
Tomb of Philip Steptoe at Teddington, on the James River, Va.   Bellet's Some Prom. Va. Fam., vol. 2, p. 714

Stetson   Arg a bend az bet 2 griffins sejant sa
Crest: a demi-griffin or
Motto: Virtus nobilitat omnia
Arms of Robert Stetson, Cornet of first Horse Company raised in Plymouth Colony, Mass., 1658–59. Vermont's Amer. Heral., [1886], pp. 68, 69, 179

Stevens   In chief mountains behind a pine; a river fessways. In base a cow contourné facing 3 garbs
Crest: a stag's head contourné
Bookplate Henry Stevens, Barnet, Vt. Vermont scenery?

Stevens   Arg a chev az bet in chief 2 falcons volant and in base a bear erect and collared
Crest: a ship, sails furled, in a rough sea
Motto: Per aspera ad astra
Bookplate Richard Fowler Stevens

Stevens Per chev az and arg. In chief 2 eagles rising or, a chief gyronny of 8 arg and gu
    Crest: a demi-eagle affrontée with wings displayed or charged on the breast with a mullet sa
    Motto: Ad diem tendo
    Framed water color at Wm. B. Clarke's, 26 Tremont St., Boston, 1915 (?); at C. E. Goodspeed's, 1924

Stevens Per chev az and arg. In chief 2 falcons with wings expanded or (Quarterly of 16)
    Crest: a demi-eagle displayed or
    Motto: Byde tyme
    Bookplate Rev. C. Ellis Stevens, D. C. L., rector Christ Church, Phila. Zieber's Heral., p. 322

Stevens Per pale gu and vert a fess dancettée arg guttée de sang bet 3 eagles displayed or
    Crest: a lion rampant
    Motto: Virtutis amore
    Bookplate I. Austin Stevens, Jr., libn. N. Y. Hist. Soc. 1850

Stewart Or a fess chequy az and arg
    Crest: a lion ramp gu
    Motto: Avito vir et honore
    Supporters: A white horse and a deer
    Framed water color at Brook Hill, Henrico Co., Va. The Misses Stewart. Seen by Lawrence Park

Stewart Or a fess chequy az and arg surmounted by a bend engr arg within a double tressure [gu?]
    Crest: a pelican in her piety [the nest vert]
    Bookplate Charles Samuel Stewart, Phila., 1810

Stewart Quart 1 and 4: Or a fess chequy az and arg within a double tressure gu; 2 and 3: Quart 1 and 4: Or, 3 passion nails conjoined in point sa piercing a man's heart in base gu (Logan); 2 and 3: Arg an eagle displayed sa [properly with 2 heads?] (Ramsey)
    Crest: a demi-lion ramp gu (?)
    Motto: Nobilis ira
    Bookplate Anthony Stewart, Annapolis, Md.

Stewart Quart 1 and 4: Or a fess counter-compony arg and az; 2 and 3: Arg a lymphad sa
    Crest: a horse's head couped
    Motto: Whither will ye
    Bookplate Duncan Stewart, Collector of Customs, New London, Conn. D. 1793 in London. Oliver West Ind. bookplates No. 248

Stewart Quart 1 and 4: Or a fess chequy gu and arg surmounted of a bend gu charged with 3 buckles or, in chief a lion pass gu; 2 and 3: Gu a chev bet 3 cranes' heads erased or (Denham?)
    Crest: a thistle and a sprig of rose-tree in saltire ppr
    Motto: Juvant aspera probum
    Bookplate Redmond Conyngham Stewart. J. W. Spenceley, sc., 1902

Stewart Quartered by Cunningham

Stewart *See also* McCance and Murray

Stickney Ermines 3 lozenges ermine
    On the cover of "The Stickney Family", 1869. Descendants of William of Rowley, Mass.

Stillé Az a lion ramp or holding a wheel arg (?)
    Crest: a demi-lion of the field
    Motto: Innocenter Patienter Constanter
    Bookplate Dr. Alfred Stillé, Phila.

Stith Arg a chev engr bet 3 fleurs-de-lis sa
    Motto: Rather virtue than learning. Βελτιωσαι ου διδασαι
    Bookplate Rev. William Stith, President of William and Mary College in 1752–55. Also on wax seal to a deed of conveyance, Wm. & Mary Quar. Jan. 1894, p. 158

Stobo Az on a chev or bet in chief 2 crosses gu and in base a scimiter in pale arg 2 stars of 6 points of the last
    Crest: a lion statant ppr
    Water color in So. Car. Hist. Soc.

Stockton Or a chev vairé arg and az bet 3 mullets gu
    Crest: a dove holding a sprig
    Motto: Omnia Deo pendent
    Bookplate Samuel W. Stockton. A. M. Not just as in Burke. Another with crest a lion ramp supporting an Ionic column ppr

Stoddard [Sa] 3 estoiles within a bordure arg
    Crest: a demi-unicorn erm issuing from a ducal cor [or]
    A wax impression of old seal on a fan box owned by Miss Elizabeth W. Perkins, Boston, desc. of Anthony Stoddard. She owns also a spoon with Stoddard impaling [arg] on a chief [gu?] 3 lions' heads erased [or?] (Richardson). David m. Elizabeth Richardson, 1713

Stoddart Sa 3 stars of six points within a bordure arg [or gu?]
    Crest: a demi-unicorn erm issuing from a ducal coronet or
    Motto: Festina lente
    Bookplate John F. Stoddart. Same without bordure of E. G. Stoddard, engr. by Hopson, 1895. Vermont's Amer. Heral. [1886], pp. 58, 180

Stokes Quart 1 and 4: Arg 3 lions' heads erased [gu]; 2 and 3: Or 3 daggers 2 and 1 erect. On a canton a passion cross
Crest: a demi-dragon holding a dagger in the dexter claw
Motto: Libertas a legibus
Bookplate —— Stokes

Stokes Sa a lion ramp erm
Crest: a falcon with wings expanded, in its beak a sprig
Bookplate Chief Justice Anthony Stokes of Georgia, 1770. Oliver's West Ind. bookplates No. 156

Stokes Sa a lion ramp erm with forked tail
Crest: a demi-lion of the field
Bookplate Charles William Stokes

Stonard Per fess sa and or a pale engr counterchanged bet 3 eagles displayed counterchanged
Crest: a leopard (?) statant or (?) gorged and chained
Bookplate Jonathan Stonard

Stone [Arg] 3 cinquefoils [sa] on a chief az a sun or
Crest: out of a ducal cor or a griffin's head bet 2 wings exp [gu] bezantée
Motto: Humani nihil alienum
Notepaper Mrs. Stella Stone Welch, Hemet, Calif.

Stone Arg a lion pass guard sa
Crest: an eagle's head erased erm on a ducal cor bet 2 wings expanded
Motto: Mediocria firma
Bookplate Joel Stone, Manchester, 1852

Stone Arg a lion passant sa armed and eyed gu
Crest: a lion of the field
Framed water color owned by Miss Josephine M. Stone, Cambridge, Mass.

Stone Or a chev gu charged with a chevronel arg bet 3 flint stones az in chief a mullet sa
Crest: an eagle with wings extended, the dexter claw on a flint stone
Bookplate —— Stone. The flints are not unlike cinquefoils

Stone Per pale or and sa, a lion ramp counterchanged
An old ring owned by a desc. of Gov. Stone who d. 1695 has the arms engraved upon it. Crozier's Va. Heral. 1908, p. 48

Storer Per fess gu and arg a pale counterchanged and 3 cranes arg
Crest: a crane of the field
Bookplate John Humphreys Storer

Storrow Arg a lion ramp with forked tail vert
Crest: a cubit armed arm ribboned holding a cutlass
Bookplate James J. Storrow, Boston banker

Storrs Or a fess dancettée gu bet 3 stars az
Crest: a unicorn's head erased arg armed and maned or
Seal brought over by Samuel Storrs of Barnstable, Mass., 1663. Vermont's Amer. Heral. [1886], pp. 70, 180

Storrs Gu 2 bars engr erm. On a chief or a lion pass guard [of the first]
Crest: a lion coward holding a crosslet fitchée
Motto: Virtus invidia vincit
Rev. Leonard Kip Storrs, Brookline, Mass. Notepaper

Story Arg a lion ramp purp double queued
Crest: a demi-lion single tail couped
Motto: Fides vincit et veritas custodit
Framed water color owned by F. S. Whitwell, Boston. Also by Edward Gray, Milton (old), and John Lawrence, Groton, Mass. The lion is usually gules as in Mr. Gray's. His has no motto. Arms of Franklin Haven Story, son of Elisha of Boston. Framed. Shield in a window at Mrs. C. H. Joy's, 86 Marlboro St., Boston. Judge Story's daughter married Benj. Joy

Stott Sa 3 pales or on each a torteau on a chief arg a heart gu
Crest: a martlet sa [az?]
Motto: Alta petit
Bookplate Eben. Stott of Va.

Stoughton [Arg] on a saltire [gu] bet 4 door staples [sa] an escallop [or]
Crest: a demi-lion [gu] holding an escallop between its paws
Tomb of William Stoughton, Lt. Gov. of Mass., 1694–99. Dorchester, Mass. Graveyard, Dudley St. Also on two handled covered cup from him to Harvard College, made by John Coney. Seen 1924. Heral Jour., vol. 1, p. 10, vol. 2, p. 6. Vermont's Amer. Heral. [1886], p. 142. Chamberlain MSS. N. E. Reg., Apr. 1880, p. 185

Stoughton Arg on a saltire gu bet 4 door staples sa an escallop or
Crest: a demi-lion gu holding an escallop in his paws
In a window, 3d floor, State House, Boston

Stoughton Arg on a saltire [gu] bet 4 door staples [sa] an escallop [or]
Engr. on 2 tall cups from Gov. William Stoughton, 1701. The saltire appears to be tinctured or. First Church, Dorchester, Mass. Old Sil. Am. Ch., p. 147

Stowe Vert a cross raguly bet 4 leopards' heads or
Crest: over a ducal cor a head of the field bet 2 spread wings vert

Motto: Inter feros per crucem ad coronam
Bookplate Rev. Calvin Ellis Stowe, whose wife wrote Uncle Tom's Cabin

Strabolgi   Quartered by Murray

Stratton   Or a chev az bet 3 birds contourné
Crest: a dog sejant contourné
Motto: Toujours fidele
On automobile Frank B. Stratton, Swampscott, Mass.

Straus   Per pale az and gu 3 lions ramp
Crest: a wyvern
Motto: Un je servirai
Bookplate Herbert Straus, engr. by A. W. Macdonald

Street   Vert a fess bet 3 running horses arg
Crest: an arm embowed holding a bell
Motto: Non nobis solum nati
Bookplate Augustus Russell Street

Strickland   See also Wilbur

Stringer   Arg a cross flory bet 4 martlets sa a canton erminois
Crest: a martlet sa
Bookplate Samuel Stringer, M. D., b. Md., 1734. Lived in N. Y. H. D. fecit

Stringer   Sa 3 eagles displ erminois
Seal seen by Mrs. Ljungstedt, used by John and Hill Stringer, 1687 and 1688, in Va. bond as Sheriff etc.

Strong   Gu an eagle displayed within a bordure engr or
Crest: from a mural crown or a demi-eagle of the field
Motto: Tentanda via est
Bookplate Charles E. Strong

Strong   On a fess bet 6 crosses crosslet fitchée 3 escallops
Tomb of Capt. James Strong of Stepney, Co. Middx., son of Capt. Peter Strong, at Wye, Md., d. 1684. Not Strong as in Burke. Hist. Graves of Md., p. 213. Md. Hist. Mag., Mch. 1922

Strong   See also Moseley

Strother   [Gu] on a bend arg 3 eagles displayed [az]
Crest: a greyhound sejant or
On tombs in Island of Thanet, Va. Wm. & Mary Quar., Oct. 1893, p. 134

Sturges   Az a chev or bet 3 crosses crosslet fitchée sa [or?] within a bordure engr or
Crest: a talbot's head couped
Bookplate John Sturges. R. M. Sculp. That of Rush Sturges by W. T. Aldrich has as a crest: a talbot sejant arg

Sturges   Quartered by Grew

Sturgis   Az a chev bet 3 cross crosslets fitchée within a bordure engrailed or
Crest: a talbot's head or eared sa
Motto: Esse quam videri
Bookplate John H. Sturgis. Russell Sturgis. Framed embroidery made by Mrs. R. Clipston Sturgis, Boston. The emigrant, Edward Sturgis, came to Charlestown, Mass., in 1634 and settled, later, at Yarmouth

Sturgis   Impaled by Quincy

Sturtevant   Gu a lion ramp arg with a bordure of the 2d charged with 8 pheons sa
Ex libris Thomas and Grace Sturtevant, Wellesley, Mass. Drawn by Miss Lane of Quincy

Stuyvesant   Gu a stag courant ppr, on a chief arg a greyhound chasing a hare, both ppr
Crest: out of a prince's crown a demi-stag ppr
Motto: Jovi præstat fidere quam hominé
It is said that the animals should all be contourné (facing the sinister). Carved on stone, Capitol, Albany, N. Y. Also notepaper F. Winthrop Coll., 1885, but with Jovæ, etc. Gov. Petrus Stuyvesant's seal (see also Curio, 1888, p. 18) on a letter in Mass. Archives, 27 Oct. 1659, vol. 2, p. 378a. See also cut in Booth's Hist. N. Y. (1863), p. 129. Carved in Baptistry of Cath. S. John the Divine, N. Y., with Jovæ etc.

Stuyvesant   Gu a stag saliant ppr, on a chief or a hound chasing a hare ppr, all contourné
Crest: out of a cor a demi-stag contourné
Motto: Jovæ præstat fidere quam homine
Bookplate Peter Gerard Stuyvesant

Stuyvesant   Quartered by Fish

Sullivan   Per fess the base per pale in chief [or] a dexter hand couped at the wrist grasping a sword erect [gu], the blade entwined with a serpent ppr bet 2 lions rampant affrontée [gu]; the dexter base [vert] charged with a stag trippant [or], on the sinister base per pale [arg and sa] a boar passant [counterchanged]
Crest: on a ducal cor [or] a robin holding in its beak a sprig of laurel ppr
Motto: Lamh foisdin each an ucechtar [what we gain by conquest we make secure by clemency]
Wall tablet to William Sullivan, 1774–1839, author, son of Gov. James. King's Chapel, Boston, south aisle.

Also on watch of Major James Amory
Sullivan of Boston with hand erect
instead of in fess and motto with
"uachtar" instead of "uœchtar"
    Bookplate Gov. James Sullivan of
Mass., engr. by J. Callendar, with
motto: Modestia victrix, no tinctures,
no coronet, no sprig of laurel, the arm
mailed, the serpent facing sinister, the
boar in the dexter base which is not
per pale. Also of Gen. John and George.
Also an engr. bookplate marked
"Sullivan." See Burke's Herald. Il-
lustr. plate cxxiv where Major James
Sullivan, Chesterfield, Co. Limerick,
uses these arms, 1853

Sullivan Per pale sa and arg a fess bet
2 boars all counterchanged, the boar in
base contourné
    Crest: a robin (?) on an alligator
    Motto: Lám foisdin eac abu
    Notepaper Major James Amory
Sullivan, Boston, Mass., and Asolo,
Italy

Sumner Ermines 2 chev or
    Bookplate George Sumner, brother
Senator Charles Sumner

Sumner Erm 2 chevronels gu
    Crest: a lion's head erminois ducally
gorged or
    Motto: In medio tutissimus ibis
    On bookplate of Increase Sumner,
Gov. of Mass., and Gen. Wm. H.
Sumner. Vermont's Amer. Heral.
[1886], pp. 69, 180

Sumner Ermines 2 chev [or]
    Crest: a lion's head erased ducally
gorged [or?]
    Motto: In medio tutissimus ibis
    Engr. on notepaper of Mrs. Agnes
C. Sumner Stuart, Clarksburg, West
Va.

Suydam Az a rose bet 3 stars of 6
points or
    Crest: a rose enclosed by 2 horns az
    Bookplate Rev. J. Howard Suydam,
D. D.

Swain Quartered by Curry

Swan Az a chev arg bet 3 swans rising
    Crest: a martlet rising holding a
twig in its beak
    Bookplate J. A. Swan

Swan Az a chev erm bet 3 swans arg
    Crest: a demi-talbot salient gu
collared or
    On tomb of Col. Thomas Swan at
Swan's Point, Isle of Wight Co., Va.,
who d. 16 Sept., 1680. Crozier's Va.
Heral., 1908, p. 35

Swan 1: Az a chev erm bet 3 swans arg;
2: [Or] on a bend [az] 3 martlets [arg],
on a canton sin [az] a rose [or] bet 2

fleurs-de-lis [arg] (Harding); 3: [Sa]
a fess [or] bet 3 dogs' heads couped at
the shoulders affronté ppr (Jones)
    Seal on letter of Jane Swan, 1758, to
Uncle Thomas Jones of Va. See
"Capt. Roger Jones of London," p. 15

Swan Sa a fess wavy or bet 3 swans
rising
    Crest: a swan gorged and chained
rising
    Motto: Sit nomen decus
    Bookplate Joseph Swan, Judge, Co-
lumbus, Ohio

Swan Vert 3 swans 2 and 1 or. Impaling: Arg on a bend gu bet 3 roundels
3 swans or. On a sinister canton az
a demi-ram debruised by a baton in
bend bet 2 fleurs-de-lis
    Crest: an armed sinister arm embow
holding a knight's helmet, front open
    Supporters: A Scotchman in tartan
holding on a staff a cap and an Indian
holding a tobacco plant
    Motto: Dum spiro spero
    Bookplate James Swan (Boston Tea
Party). Callender, sc.

Swann Impaled by Bowditch

Sweat Az a chev bet 3 fleurs-de-lis gu
    Crest: a fleur-de-lis gu
    Very old water color (before Coles?)
owned by Very Rev. Edmund Swett
Rousmanière of Boston. Not as in
Burke. Framed with Whitmore

Sweet Six gambs erect erased 3, 2, 1
    Seal used by James Sweet at War-
wick, R. I., upon a letter dated 19 June,
1662. R. I. Hist. Soc. Coll., vol. xi,
p. 100. Apparently not in reference
books

Swett Gu 2 chev bet as many mullets
in chief and a rose in base arg seeded or
    Engr. on a flagon from Joseph Swett
or Sweet, 1759. First Church, Marblehead, Mass. E. A. Jones, Old. Sil.
Am. Ch., p. 263

Swift Quartered by Draper

Sword Sa a bearded face couped at the
shoulders and filleted bet 3 swords
points up ppr [hilted or?]
    Crest: a sword in pale ppr bet 2
wings
    Bookplate William Sword. H. D.
fecit

Sylvester Arg an oak tree vert and in
chief 2 crescents
    Crest: a lion's head erased
    Motto: Aide toi et le ciel t'aidera
    Bookplate Henry H. Sylvester

Sylvester Per pale indented gu and or.
(Holland family?)
    Crest: two sinister wings erect
    Arms on the monument to Nathaniel

Sylvester, Shelter Island, Long Island, N. Y. Used on notepaper of Miss Cornelia Horsford, Cambridge, Mass.

Symes *See also* Bartlett

Symmes Erm 3 increscents gu
Crest: a sun in splendor
Rev. Zachariah Symmes's family, Charlestown? Engr. on mug from Edward Kitchen, 1766, "silver pint cans with the 3 half moons and the sun engraved thereon" Tabernacle Church, Salem. Old Sil. Am. Ch., p. 430. These are the arms of a family at Daventry, Northants. There was some

connection between the Kitchen and Symmes families

Symonds Az a chev engr bet 3 trefoils slipped or
Painted on wood, west parlor mantle, Pound Hill Place, Shirley, Mass. Arms granted to Richard Symonds of Great Yeldham, Co. Essex, father of Samuel of Ipswich, Mass., 1625.
Crest: out of a mural cor or a boar's head arg tusked or crined gu. In writing to Winthrop Symonds used a seal that had no chevron. *See* M. H. S. Coll., vol. 37

T

Tailer Az 2 bars wavy and in chief a lion pass guard arg
Crest: a demi-lion ramp
Bookplate Thomas Suffern Tailer, New York City

Talbot Arg 3 lions ramp az
Crest: a talbot sa
Old framed water color, perhaps by Coles, owned by Arnold Talbot, Lincoln, R. I., desc. of Jared Talbot of Taunton

Talbott Bendy of 10 arg and gu (?) and in the sin chief a canton all within a bordure
Crest: on a chapeau [gu turned up erm] a lion statant or tail extended
Motto: Humani nihil alienum
Notepaper Mrs. Harry Elstner Talbott, Dayton, O.

Talboys Quartered by Middleton

Talmage Arg a fret sa
Crest: a horse's head erased bet 2 wings each charged with ogresses
Motto: Confido conquiesco
Bookplate John F. Talmage, engr. by French, 1899

Taney Az 3 bars arg
Crest: a hind's head erased gu gorged with a cor or
Drawn 1769 by Ignatius Fenwick, Jr., who married Sarah Taney. Anc. Rec., vol. 2, p. 552

Tarrant A lion ramp reguardant
Crest: on an Esquire's helmet a demi-lion ramp
Wax seal on will of Leonard Tarrant, Tappahannock, Essex Co., Va., dated 4 June, 1718. Wm. & Mary Quar., Jan. 1893, p. 122

Tasker Erm 3 lions pass in pale. Impaling: [Gu] 3 chevrons [arg] (Bladen)
Crest: out of a ducal cor a boar's head erect and couped.
Col. Benjamin Tasker, who d. in 1767, was father of the gov. of Md. His

wife was Anne, niece of Gov. Bladen. St. Ann's churchyard, Annapolis, Md. Zieber's Heral., p. 47

Tayloe Purpure [vert?] a sword erect bet 2 lions ramp addorsed [erm]
Crest: a cubit arm holding a sword erect piercing a boar's head couped
Bookplate Benj'n Ogle Tayloe, Md. Also John Tayloe of Mt. Airy, Va. Arms of Teylow. Edward I. Tayloe of Va. on bookplate has a cubit arm habited etc. and motto: Quo Minerva ducit, sequor

Tayloe Vert a sword erect or bet 2 lions ramp addorsed erm
Crest: a cubit arm holding a dagger piercing a boar's head
Bookplate "John Tayloe of Mount Airy, Virginia." On tomb of Elizabeth Kingsmill, wife of Col. William Tayloe, are arms of Tayloe impaling Kingsmill. Wm. & Mary Quar., vol. 2, p. 233

Tayloe [Vert] a sword erect [or] bet 2 lions ramp endorsed [erm]. Impaling: Arg a semée of crosses crosslet [sa] a chev [ermines bet 3 mill-rinds of the second] a chief of the 3d (Kingsmill)
Crest: three stemmed roses (?)
Tomb of Col. Nathaniel Bacon's wife in St. Paul's churchyard, Norfolk, Va. Seen by L. Park, 1922. No mill-rinds visible. Bacon married Elizabeth, daughter of Richard Kingsmill and widow of Col. Wm. Tayloe of Va. She d. 2 Nov. 1691

Tayloe *See also* Kingsmill and Bacon

Taylor Arg a saltire engrailed [sa] bet two cinquefoils in pale [gu] and two hearts in fess [vert]
Crest: a demi-leopard [holding in its dexter paw a cinquefoil?]
Motto: Fide et fiducia
Tomb of John Taylor, merchant from Fintrie, Co. Stirling, Scot., in St. Paul's churchyard, Norfolk, Va. He

d. 25 Oct., 1744, aged 51. Seen by
L. Park, 1922. Restored. Not from
Fintrie it is said. Wm. & Mary Quar.,
vol. 3, p. 18. Crozier reverses cinquefoil and heart

Taylor Az a chev arg bet 3 escallops or
Crest: an arm emb holding a spear
Motto: Acu rem tetigit
Bookplate James Taylor, D. D.

Taylor Erm on a chev gu bet 3 anchors
az erect 3 escallops arg
Crest: a stork with dexter claw on an
anchor of the field
Bookplate George Taylor, Penn.,
signer Decl. of Indep., 1776

Taylor Erm on a chief sa 3 escallops or
Impaled on the bookplate of Dom
Vincent Taylor, O. S. B., of Belmont,
N. C., done by Pierre la Rose. Motto:
Deus adjuvabit

Taylor Gu 3 roses 2 and 1, a chief
chequy arg and sa a crescent for diff
Crest: a lion's head erased [erm]
gorged or (?)
Bookplate Samuel Taylor

Taylor Per saltire or and gu an eagle
displayed
Crest: a demi-eagle displayed gu
double-headed and in each beak a cross
crosslet
Seal of Col. Wm. Taylor, Whitmore's
Elem. of Her., p. 84

Taylor Quart 1 and 4: Arg on a chief
sa 2 dogs' heads of the first; 2: A chief
erm bet 3 coursing hounds; 3: A chev
bet 3 mullets gu
Motto: Consequitur quodcunque
petit
Painting owned by John R. Crawford, Goldsboro, N. C.

Tazewell Arg on a fess sa bet 3 eagles
displayed [az] 3 cresc of the field
Crest: a hawk's head [az] holding a
pine branch [vert] fruited [gu]
Motto: Ne quid nimis
Bookplate John Tazewell of Va.
Framed arms owned by Littleton W.
Tazewell, 711 Stockwell Gardens,
Norfolk, Va. Seen by L. Park, 1922.
Pronounced Tazwell

Tefft Quart 1 and 4: Gu 4 mullets
pierced 2, 1, 1; 2 and 3: Gu a heart bet
3 mullets pierced, all arg
Crest: a boar's head couped
Motto: Ubique fidelis
Bookplate Emma Augusta Tefft

Temple Arg 2 bars sa, each charged
with 3 martlets or
Seal of Sir Thomas Temple, Bart., of
Boston, Mass. Whitmore's Elem. of
Her., p. 65. See Jeffries MSS. N. E.
Reg., Jan. 1877, p. 65

Temple Quart 1 and 4: Or a spread
eagle sa (Earl of Mercia); 2 and 3:
Arg 2 bars sa [each charged with 3
martlets arg] (Temple)
Crest: on a ducal cor a martlet [or]
Motto: Templa quam Dilecta
Memorial tablet to Sir John Temple,
Bart., consul general to U. S., in St.
Paul's Chapel, Broadway, N. Y. He d.,
1798. Noted 20 May, 1920, but hard
to see

Ten Broeck Two pine trees, an ox between, a goat at the dexter and a
horse at the sinister
Crest: a demi-horse
Motto: Perge coepisti
Bookplate John C. Ten Broeck,
general. Maverick, sc.

Ten Broeck Arg 2 trees vert bet 3 deer
ppr, 2 grazing, the dexter stat gua rd
Crest: a horse's head arg
Motto: Sustineo
Framed water color (modern) owned
by Miss Sarah M. Westbrook, Brookline, Mass.

Ten Broeck Per fess or and sa, in chief
2 trees, in base an ox gu bet 2 horses,
the dexter reguard couchant, the
sinister feeding
Crest: a demi-horse salient couped
Painted hatchment on wood, 24 x
24 inches, with "J. T. B." on a scroll.
Very old. Owned by N. Y. Hist. Soc.
The animals are difficult to identify

Ter Beke Quartered by Van Rensselaer

Ternay Sa an eagle with 2 heads displayed arg (?) On a chief gu a cross
arg
Arms of Chevalier de Ternay in
vestibule of Old Trinity Church, Newport, R. I. Zieber's Heral., p. 60

Terry Erm on a pile gu a leopard's head
jessant de lis or
Crest: a four-tongued griffin's head
erased and gorged
Motto: Ex cruce leo
Bookplate Henry K. Terry, Richmond, Va.

Tettenhall Quartered by Grosvenor

Thacher Gu a cross moline arg on a
chief or 3 grasshoppers ppr
Crest: a grasshopper ppr
Bookplate R. W. Thacher, Albany,
N. Y. Seal of Rhodolphus Thacher of
Duxbury, March, 1689/90, on doc. in
Mass. Archives, vol. 11, p. 52. See
N. Y. G. & B. Record, April, 1910,
p. 99, for Thacher heraldry

Thatcher [Gu] a cross moline arg on a
chief [or] 3 grasshoppers ppr
Seal in Suffolk Wills. Thatchers of
Salisbury, Co. Wilts and Plymouth,
Mass. Whitmore's Elem. of Her., p.
88

Thatcher Gu a cross moline arg on a chief or 3 grasshoppers proper
Crests: A: a Saxon sword proper; B: a grasshopper proper
Seal on letter written 1676 by Rev. Thomas Thatcher of Boston to his son, Peter, in London; also on seal of will in Suffolk registry. Seal said to be owned by Boston branch of family. Heral. Jour., vol. 4, p. 77. N. Y. Gen. & Biog. Record, vol. 41, p. 101

Thaxter Gu on a fess or bet 3 lozenges erm a trefoil slipped vert bet 2 cocks' heads gu
Crest: a duck's head couped arg bet 2 leaved branches vert fruited gu
Motto: Semper paratus
Water color owned by Mrs. Walter G. Chase, Brookline, Mass. See Thaker in Burke. Also bookplate (chevron in place of fess) Samuel Thaxter, sec. to John Adams in Paris

Thayer A chev bet 3 ravens. Impaling a lion ramp renversé
Crest: a martlet holding in its beak a rose
Seal Arthur Thayer, Dorchester, Mass., 1791. Jeffries MSS. N. E. Reg., Jan. 1877, p. 65

Thayer Per pale erm and gu 3 talbots' heads erased counterchanged
Crest: a head of the field
Bookplate Mrs. Mary Thayer-Ashman of Milton, Mass., daughter of Nathaniel of Boston, son of Nehemiah of Weymouth

Thebaud "Az a pair of scales in chief and a star in point a chev all arg"
Bookplate Mathilde E. Thebaud. J. W. S., sc., 1899

Thomas Arg a chev lozengy or and sa bet 3 ravens close of the last
Crest: on a branch of a tree fessways a raven rising sa
Motto: Secret et hardi
Seal Elisha S. Thomas, Bishop of Kansas. Zieber's Heral., p. 208

Thomas Arg a chev sa bet 3 Cornish choughs ppr
Crest: a chough rising
Bookplate William G. Thomas

Thomas Arg on a cross sa 5 crescents of the field
Crest: a unicorn
Motto: Never elated never dejected (not on the embroidery)
Embr. hatchment, with "By the name of Thomas." Made by Mary Anne Thomas, b. 1772, d. 1805, daughter of Isaiah Thomas and wife of Dr. Levi Simmons. Owned 1923 by Miss Randall, Boston

Thomas Arg on a cross sa 5 cresc of the field
Crest: a greyhound's head couped or collared and ringed
Motto: Nec elatus nec dejectus
Bookplate Isaiah Thomas, printer, Worcester, Mass. Heral. Jour., vol. 3, p. 22. Also of Isaac Rand Thomas, engr. by S. L. Smith. Also shield on automobile Isaac R. Thomas, 303 Commonwealth Ave., Boston, 1916

Thomas Per pale sa and arg a chev bet 3 Cornish choughs counterchanged
Crest: a chough rising sa bet 2 lances
Framed water color owned by Mrs. Edward M. Davis, Shirley, Mass. Original owned by Mrs. A. Nelson Lewis

Thomas Sa a chev and canton erm
Crest: a demi-unicorn erm armed [or] holding a shield sa
Motto: Virtus invecta gloriosa
On seal and silver of Dr. Philip Thomas's family of Kent Co. and Baltimore, Md. Also seal ring of Douglas H. Thomas, Baltimore. "The above arms engraved on a silver pitcher which belonged to my great grandfather, Dr. Philip Thomas (1747–1815), and now belongs to me, and also his seal which subsequently belonged to my grandfather, John Hanson Thomas (1779–1815), my father Dr. John Hanson Thomas (1813–1881), my brother John Hanson Thomas (1843–1886), and is now owned by his son living in Alabama." Letter of D. H. Thomas, 1917

Thompson Arg a stag's head cabossed. On a chief az a cross crosslet fitchée bet an anchor and a billet
Crest: a cubit armed arm holding a cross crosslet fitchée
Motto: Honesty is good policy
Bookplate engr. by J. J. Butler, N. Y.

Thompson Or on a chev dancettée az 3 estoiles. On a canton az a sun in splendor
Crest: a cubit arm holding 5 straws, heads to sinister
Motto: In lumine luce
Bookplate Prof. A. C. Thompson, Conn.

Thompson Or on a fess dancettée az 3 stars of the field [sometimes arg] on a canton of the second the sun in its splendid proper
Crest: out of a ducal cor a cubit arm erect habited az. In the hand ppr 5 ears of wheat or
Mottoes A: In lumine luce; B: Ante victoriam ne cane triumphum
Bookplates William Thompson and Robert Thompson. The emigrant,

John Thompson, came to Long Island in 1634. N. Y. G. & B. Record, Jan. 1896, p. 1

Thompson Per fess arg and sa a fess embat and counter-embat bet 3 falcons counterchanged
Crest: an armed arm embow holding a broken spear
Motto: Per se
Bookplate William Thompson

Thomson Arg a stag's head cabossed, the antlers enclosing a cross patée fitchée. On a chief a cresc bet 2 mullets
Seal of David Thomson of Charlestown, Mass., used by Abraham Shurt who married his widow

Thomson Quartered by McTavish

Thomson See also Maverick

Thorndike Arg 6 guttées 3, 2, 1 gu. On a chief gu 3 leopards' faces or
Crest: a rose ppr leaved vert and at the base of the stalk a beetle ppr
Notepaper Albert Thorndike, Boston. Ex-libris Sturgis H. Thorndike, Weston, Mass. (No crest.) W[eston]-S[mith] 1900 del.

Thorndike Arg 6 guttées 3, 2, and 1, gu, on a chief of the last 3 leopards' faces or
Crest: damask rose ppr with leaves and thorns vert at the bottom of the stalk a beetle ppr
Motto: Rosae inter spinas nascuntur
Arms on an engraving belonging to George Quincy Thorndike; on bookplate of S. Lothrop Thorndike; also Oliver Thorndike, Boston (no beetle). Heral. Jour., vol. 1, p. 54

Thornton Arg a chev sa bet 3 cherry trees [vert] a mullet in chief for diff
Crest: a lion's head ducally gorged and erased
Bookplate Francis Vansittart Thornton. Wm. Thornton of Va. used 3 hawthorne trees on his bookplate and Deo spes meo. Wm. & Mary Quar., vol. 2, p. 230

Thornton Arg on a bend gu 3 escarbuncles of 8 points [or]. In the sinister chief a mullet sa
Crest: a lion's head ducally gorged and erased
Bookplate J. Wingate Thornton, Boston. Used on Jno. Tuthill's marr. agreement, Southold, L. I., 1690. N. Y. G. & B. Record, Jan. 1896, p. 59

Thornton Arg a chev sa bet 3 leaves
Crest: a dragon's head bet 2 wings issuing from a ducal cor
Motto: Vincit pericula virtus
Bookplate Geo. M. Thornton by E. H. Garrett of Boston

Thorowgood Sa on a chief arg 3 buckles lozengy of the first
Crest: a wolf's head arg collared sa
Said to be on tomb of Sarah, wife of Capt. Adam Thorowgood, in Lynnhaven Church, Va. Va. Hist. Mag., vol. 2, pp. 414–17

Throckmorton
See Va. Hist. Mag., vol. 8, p. 88; Wm. & Mary Quar., vol. 4, p. 129

Thruston Sa 3 buglehorns arg stringed or garnished az
Crest: a heron arg
Motto: Esse quam videri
Will of Malachy Thruston dated 14 Mar., 1698–9, states: "I leave to my son, John Thruston, my signett ring with my coat of arms." Seal mentioned in Bellet's Some Prom. Va. Fam., vol. 4, p. 286. Crozier's Va. Heral., 1908, p. 54. Also bookplates Gates P. Thruston and George A. Thruston

Tilestone See also Tillotson

Tilghman Per fess sa and arg a lion ramp reguard crowned counterchanged
Crest: a demi-lion crowned sa
Motto: Spes alit agricolam
Bookplate James Tilghman, Phila. See Sylvan City, 1883, p. 451. Also of Jacobus Tilghman, arm Annapolis, the lion having a forked tail and in the crest a lion sejant crowned sa and "alet" instead of "alit" a mullet for difference. Hon. Oswald Tilghman of Easton, Md., has bookplate by Zieber, like the preceding but "alit" and no mullet

Tillinghast Sa? a chev or bet in chief 2 masons' triangles of the 2d and in base a shovel palewise of the 2d (?)
On monument near Benefit St., Providence, R. I. Also on notepaper

Tillotson Az a bend or cotised arg bet 2 garbs sa (?)
Motto: Virtus et natale meum
Bookplate Thomas Tillotson. Maverick, sculp. New York. Also in the Gore roll of arms used by Tilestone

Tilton "He beareth az a fleur-de-lis arg"
Crest: an ostrich ppr holding a)
Motto: Deo, non fortuna
In the style of John Coles but modern. Water color owned by Willis P. Tilton, Brookline, Mass.

Timson In chief 2 fleurs-de-lis, and in base a sun in splendor
The tomb of Samuel Timson, who d. 23 Jan., 1694–5, is at Queen's Creek, York Co., Va., and bears the Juxon arms impaling Timson, namely: In the dexter for Juxon of London, Eng. Or, a cross gu bet 4 blackamoor's

heads couped at the shoulders ppr wreathed about the temples of the field Sinister for Timson: charges much defaced representing as above. Wm. & Mary Quar., Oct. 1893, p. 80. Crozier's Va. Heral., 1908, p. 45

Tirrey Sa 3 chevronels bet as many mullets arg
Crest: a demi-roebuck ppr attired and unguled or holding in the mouth 3 ears of corn (wheat) bladed of the first
Tomb of John Tirrey, gent., at "Church Pastures," Prince George Co., Va., a part of the Brandon estate. He d. 20 Aug., 1700. Impaled on the sinister side are arms too worn. Va. Hist. Mag., vol. 7, p. 211

Titcomb A fess bet 3 greyhounds' heads (?) erased and gorged
Crest: a head of the field
Engr. on tankard from Benaiah and William Titcomb, 1731. From Newbury, Berks. First Church, Newburyport, Mass. Old Sil. Am. Ch., p. 295

Tobey Per chev or and [?] a lion ramp debruised by a chev arg. Impaling: Az 2 dolphins embow in pale
Crest: a lion's head erased
Bookplate Phineas S. Tobey

Todd A fox salient
Crest: a bird rising
Motto: By cunning not by craft
Bookplate Henry Alfred Todd, Prof. Columbia Univ.

Toland Gu a lion ramp or
Crest: a lion ramp or holding a rose
Bookplate Henry Toland, Phila.

Toler Arg a cross flory sur mounted of a plain cross arg bet 4 leaves vert
Crest: a fleur-de-lis or
Motto: Regi et patria fidelis
Notepaper F. Winthrop Coll. N. Y., 1885, at Bos. Ath.

Tomlinson Sa a fess arg bet 3 falcons volant [or]
Crest: a griffin's head couped
Bookplate —— Tomlinson (Crude)

Tompkins Az on a chev bet 3 cockpheasants close or as many crosses crosslet sa
Crest: a unicorn's head erased per fess arg and or armed and maned counterchærged gorged with a chaplet of laurel vert
Motto: Principiis obsta
Bookplate Eugene Tompkins, proprietor Boston Theatre. Sculptured in open court of Capitol, Albany. Tompkins was New York State War Gov. during War of 1812. and Vice-President of the United States. Vermont's Amer. Heral. [1886], p. 135

Tooker Barry wavy of 10 arg and az on a chev embattled and counter-embattled or bet 3 sea horses naiant of the first 5 gouttés de poix
Crest: a lion's gamb erased gu charged with 3 billets in pale or and holding a battle axe or headed az
Tomb of Henry Tooker at "Church Pastures," Prince George Co., Va. He d. 20 Oct., 1710. Va. Hist. Mag., vol. 7, p. 211

Torrey Arg on a mound az [vert?] a horse sa saddled [and bridled gu]. On a chief arg a cross crosslet fitchée sa
Crest: a horse's head erased [arg]
Motto: Will God I shall
Bookplate Torrey. George A. Torrey has a cross pattée fitchée

Torrey Bendy of 6 or and \¹vert over all, on a fess arg 3 fleurs-de-lis az
No crest
Very old framed water color once owned by Samuel Torrey who was painted by Badger? Owned by Miss Frances Morse, daughter of Samuel Torrey Morse of Boston, 1921. Not in Burke

Totham Quartered by Lunsford

Towles A lion passant
Wax seal on deed of Henry Towles. His son Henry, Jr., was b. about 1670. Wm. & Mary Quar., Jan. 1893, p. 22

Townsend Az a chev erm bet 3 escallops. Impaling: Arg 6 lioncelles 3, 2, 1 sa (Savage)
Bookplate Frederic De Peyster Townsend, Buffalo, N. Y. R. D. W. S., 1899

Townsend [Az] a chev [erm] bet 3 escallops [or]
Crest: a stag passant
"James Townsend's altar tomb." King's Chapel Graveyard, Boston. Heral. Jour., vol. 2, p. 21

Townsend Az a chev erm bet 3 escallops arg
Crest: a stag trip
Motto: Haec generi incrementa fides
Bookplate James M. Townsend, E. D. F. del. A. Brown, sc., 1910. Notepaper S. V. R. Townsend, N. Y., 1885. No motto

Townsend Quart 1 and 4: Az a chev erm bet 3 escallops arg; 2 and 3: Arg on a chief or 3 spears erect
Crest: a stag trippant ppr
Motto: Haec generi incrementa fides
Bookplate John Townsend. John E. Gavit, sc.

Tracy Arg on a chev gu 3 crosses or
Crest: a semi-circular charge bet 2 wings expanded

Notepaper Mrs. James J. Tracy, Ambler Heights, Cleveland

Tracy   Or 2 bends gu an escallop in the dexter chief
Crest: on a mount vert an escallop [sa] bet 2 wings spread [or]
Bookplate Nathaniel Tracy, Mass. N. H., sc., 1768.
Notepaper F. Winthrop Coll. N. Y., 1885, has chapeau instead of mount and motto: Memoria pii æterna

Trail   [Az] a chev arg bet 2 mascles in chief [or] and a trefoil slipped in base arg
Crest: a column on a rock in the sea proper
Motto: Discrimine salus
John and George Trail, Boston, 1750. King's Chapel Graveyard, Boston. Stone against Tremont Street fence, marked "Gale No. 4." Heral. Jour., vol. 2, p. 18

Travers   Arg on a chev gu 3 griffins' heads erased [or] and on a chief az 3 annulets charged with quaterfoils
Crest: a griffin's head erased [or] holding in the beak a lizard [az]
Motto: Ut prosim
Bookplate John Travers, N. J.

Travers   Arg on a chev gu 3 griffins' heads erased [or] and on a chief az 3 bezants
Crest: a griffin holding a lizard
Motto: Nec temere nec timide
Bookplate John Travers, N. J.

Travis   Gu a chev erm bet 3 martlets
Bookplate John Travis, Scarboro, 1772

Trew   Arg on a chev gu 3 roses, a chief erm
Crest: a rose leaved
Motto: Veritas quasi rosa resplendet
Bookplate William Trew, Canada. Son in California

Tronberg   Arg (?) a tree ppr (?) debruised by a scythe, the blade in pale
Crest: 4 arrows, 2 in bend and 2 in bend sinister
On seal ring of Rev. Petrus Tronberg, rector of church at Christina (Wilmington), known as "Old Swedes," 1742. Ancest. Rec. & Portr., vol. 1, p. 184

Trottman   4 crosses patonce arg. On a canton a lion ramp guardant
Crest: a lion ramp issuant holding a cross between his paws. The Chase arms
Motto: Ne cede malis
Mrs. James F. Trottman, 508 LaFayette Place, Madison, Wis. Notepaper

Truesdell   Arg 3 piles sa debruised by a fess gu, a canton ermines
Crest: a boar's head erect and couped
Ex libris Winfred Porter Truesdell. J. W. Spenceley, sc., 1902. Also H. Gregson, sc., 1904

Trumbull   Arg 3 bulls' heads erased sa breathing flames proper
Crest: bull's head from the escutcheon
Motto: Fortuna favet audaci
Framed water color in reception room of Trumbull Hospital, Allerton St., Brookiine, Mass., size about 10" by 12", signed C. C. Barnett. Said to be the family of Jonathan Trumbull, Gov. of Conn. Arms seen 27 April, 1924, by Dr. Harold Bowditch

Tryon   Az a fess counter-embattled arg bet 3 mullets in chief and 3 in base
Crest: a boar's head erased sa powdered with mullets of the field
Motto: In cruce mea spes
Bookplate James Seymour Tryon. Also "Miss Tryon," crude shield

Tryon   Az a fess embattled or bet six estoiles in orle arg. On an escutcheon of pretence arg two bars gu, in chief three torteaux (Wake)
Crest: a bear's head erased arg powdered with estoiles sa
Seal of William Tryon, Gov. of New York, 1771. The estoiles are sometimes or, the bear's head sa. On comⁿ of John Du Mons in N. Y. Militia, Nov. 15, 1776. E. A. Jones saw in London. Heral. Jour., vol. 4, p. 96

Tryon   Azure a fess embat and counter-embat bet 6 mullets [or?]
Crest: a boar's head sa powdered with mullets [or]
Motto: In cruce mea spes
Ex libris James Seymour Tryon

Tucker   [Az] a chev [or] bet 3 sea horses naiant [arg]
Crest: a lion's gamb erased [gu?] grasping a battle axe [or] head [arg]
Engr. on chalice from Robert Tucker, 1722, Christ Church, Norfolk, Va. Also bookplate Richard Tucker, Va. and Bermuda. The family came from Milton, Co. Kent, Eng. Church of St. Peter at St. George's, Bermuda, monumental inscriptions of Va. Tucker family. The motto is: Suspice Teucro. A Tucker bookplate has: Auspice te ucro

Tucker   Vert a chev arg bet 3 sea horses
Crest: an eagle rising
Bookplate Ichabod Tucker, Salem, Mass., lawyer, 1765-1846

Tuckerman Vert on a bend engr [arg] bet 3 arrows 3 hearts bendways vert
Crest: a heart gu issuing from a ducal crown
Bookplate Edward Tuckerman. Soph. M. Tuckerman used on her bookplate the same arms with the motto: Paratus et fidelis. Bookplate "J. Willard Tuckerman, Jr., and Elsie Morrill Tuckerman" of Brookline, Mass., by Dorothy Sturgis Harding, 1916. Motto: Tout coeur

Tudor Az a lion ramp [or]
Crest: on a mural crown or a serpent nowed [vert]
Bookplate Frederic Tudor

Tudor Or a lion pass [sa] charged on the shoulder with a martlet or, bet 3 annulets [of the second]
Crest: a lion ramp sa
Deacon John Tudor, Boston, 1715. Book cover, "Deacon Tudor's Diary," Boston, 1896. "Corresponds to an old seal recently found among the family papers"

Tufton Quart 1: Arg on a pale [sa] an eagle displayed of the field (Tufton); 2: A fess and in chief 2 hands each holding a ball? (Mason); 3: 3 bucks (Greene of London); 4: [Arg] a fess [sa] bet 3 boars' heads couped [gu muzzled or] (Steed)
Seal of John Tufton, Sheriff of New Hampshire, on document dated August, 1688. Burke for steed gives a chevron

Tuite Quarterly arg and gu
Crest: an angel vested arg holding in the dexter hand a flaming sword ppr and in the sinister a shield of the arms
Motto: Alleluia alleluia alleluia
Bookplate Robert Tuite

Tupper Arg on a fess engr az bet 3 wild boars ppr 3 torteaux (bezants?)
Crest: a hound with dexter paw on a shield
Motto: L'espoir est ma force
Framed water color. M. F. Footer, Ritfield Road, West Somerville, Mass.

Turberville Erm a lion ramp [gu] crowned [or]
Crest: a tower embatt [or?]
Motto: Omnia relinquit servare rempublicam
Bookplate George Lee, Turberville, Va.

Turberville Erm a lion ramp gu, ducally crowned or
Tomb of Frances Turberville on Booth's Plantation, Westmoreland Co., Va. She d. 24 April, 1720. Tomb of Lettice Turberville, who d. 10 Feb., 1732, also bears the arms impaling:

"Ermine on a chief or 3 ravens sa (Corbin). Crozier's Va. Heral., 1908, p. 22

Turner Arg on a cross sa 5 mill-rinds of the first. The badge of Ulster in the dexter canton
Crest: a lion pass guard [gu?] crowned holding a mill-rind [or]
Motto: Dea providentia nostra est haereditas
Bookplate Charles Henry, Paul Dawes, and E. Turner

Turner Erm a cross quarterly pierced [arg?] charged with 4 mill-rinds [sa?]
Crest: a lion passant bearing in the dexter gamb a mill-rind
Motto written in: Tu ne cede malis
Bookplate Geo. Turner, Va. Also tomb of Major Harry Turner of King George Co., Va. (d. 1751). Va. Hist. Mag., vol. 20, p. 438; vol. 21, p. 107

Turner Erm 4 fer de molines sa
Crest: arg a lion holding in the dexter paw a fer de moline sa
Motto: Esse quam videri
Tomb of Major Henry Turner, d. 1757, at Smith's Mount, Westmoreland Co., Va. Crozier's Va. Heral., 1908, p. 65

Turner Sa a chev erm bet 3 mill-rinds arg. On a chief arg a lion pass [gu]
Crest: a lion of the field
Bookplate Alfred Edward Turner. In Paul Dawes Turner's bookplate the lions hold a sprig in the dexter paw; the motto is Esse quam videre; the mill-rinds appear to be or. By "ISL." L. S. Ipsen des. a plate for Wm. Geo. Arthur Turner, 1906, with motto: Carpe diem

Turner See also Greenleaf

Tuthill [Az] on a bend [arg] cotised [or] a lion passant [sa]
Crest: a bird. In Burke "a Cornish chough ppr." Has a long beak
"Mary Tuthill relict of John Tuthill," d. 1705. Altar tomb. Granary Burying Ground, Boston. Painted window in the Charlesgate Hospital, Boston. Heral. Jour., vol. 2, p. 132

Tuttle Az on a bend arg double cotised or a lion pass sa
Crest: a bird (chough?) holding in the beak an olive branch
Gore roll of arms. Zechariah Tuttle of Boston, 1721

Tylden Az a saltire erm bet 4 pheons or
Motto: Scientia est potestas
In a lozenge the arms of Tylden of Co. Kent. Ex libris Adele Tylden Low. J. W. Spenceley, sc., 1897

Tyler Gu on a fess or bet 3 cats pass arg a cross moline inclosed by 2 crescents of the field
Crest: a demi-cat ramp and erased or, charged on the side with a cross crosslet fitchée gu springing from a crescent of the last
Motto: Fari quae sentiat
Bookplate Joseph Tyler (Harris collection) T. Johnston, sc. Gu should be sa? Andrew Tyler's bookplate (N. H. sculp.) has cats or and no motto. Heral. Jour., vol. 3, p. 22

Tyler Quart 1 and 4: Chequy az and or a bend erm; 2 and 3: Or a lion ramp vert (Ward)
Crest: a lion passant
Bookplate R. Tyler. J. D. Stout, sc.

Tyler Quart 1: Az an open book or; 2: Sa an anchor erect with cable; 3: Or a woman erect with babe in arms; 4: Erm a dove with a twig in its bill. Over all a cross purpure
Crest: a sun in splendor above an open book
Motto: Spes mea in Deo
Supporters: Leopards (?) with clubs
Bookplate John Tyler, A. M., rector at Norwich, Conn., b. 1742, d. 1823. R. Brunton, sc. Bates's Early Conn. Engr., p. 40

Tyler Sa on a fess erminois bet 3 mountain-cats passant guardant ermine, a cross formy on either side a crescent gu
Crest: a demi-mountain-cat issuant guardant erminois

On the chart of Tyler of America, recorded at the College, March 2, 1778. A copy is in the possession of Gen. John S. Tyler of Boston. Also bookplate John S. Tyler, 1796–1876. Also his grave, Mt. Auburn, Mass. Heral. Jour., vol. 3, p. 83

Tyng Arg a tower embat (Higginson?). Impaling: Arg a bend cotised sa charged with 3 martlets or
Crest: a martlet
Motto: Esse quam videri
Bookplate Stephen Higginson Tyng

Tyng Arg on a bend cotised sa 3 martlets or
Crest: a wolf's head erased (sa or proper?)
Arms on plate with old hall-marks still in existence. Vermont's Amer. Heral. [1886], pp. 19, 181

Tyng A pale arg charged with a cross bet 4 mullets all sa (Atkins arms), bet or a lion az (Dudley arms), and arg a bend cotised sa charged with 3 martlets or (Tyng)
Crest: a martlet
Motto: Esse quam videri
Bookplate Dudley Atkins Tyng, Mass. Callender, sc.

Tyson Vert 3 crowned lions ramp reguard arg collared or and chains bet legs and over loins
Crest: arm and hand grasping a key (?)
Water color, old, owned by George T. Tyson, Eastville, Northampton Co., Va.

U

Umfreville Quartered by Middleton

Underhill Sa 2 bars arg on a chief or a mount vert
Tomb of Capt. John Underhill of Felgates Creek, York Co., Va., who d. in 1672-3. Too broken, the "2 bars" being distinguishable, however. The tomb is at "Ringfield." Crozier's Va. Heral., 1908, p. 110

Underhill Arg a chev sa bet 3 trefoils slipped [vert]
Crest: a stag statant
Motto: Tibimet ipsi fidem praestato
Bookplate R. C. Underhill, 1853. Brooklyn, N. Y. distr. atty.

Underwood An anvil supporting a hammer ppr
Motto: Aut malleus hodie aut incus cras
Bookplate Francis H. Underwood, writer

Uniacke Arg a lion passant
Crest: a sinister armed arm holding a pistol in fess

Motto: Faithful and brave
Bookplate Richd John Uniacke, Esq., 1801, gov. gen. of Canada

Updike Az 2 bars arg bet 6 fleurs-de-lis arg 3, 2, 1
Crest: a swan's head holding an annulet
Mottoes: Optimum vix satis. Auch tulpen darf man lieben
Bookplate Daniel Berkeley Updike, printer, Boston. "C. W. S.," sculp.

Upton Sa a cross flory arg charged with a trefoil
Crest: two dolphins haurient, and entwined saltireways or [finned az]
Motto: Virtutis avorum praemium
Notepaper Miss Marian Upton Burt, Portland, Maine. Upton of Mass.

Upton Sa a cross flory charged in chief with a trefoil slipped vert
Crest: two dolphins or finned and tailed vert embowed counterpassant
Framed water color owned by Mrs. E. L. Lincoln, Brookline, Mass.

Usher Arg 3 lions' gambs couped and erect sa [armed gu], a cresc for diff

Crest: a lion's paw couped and erect sa (armed gu]
Seal of John Usher, lieut-gov. of N. H., 1692–97. Hatchment painted on wood by Hezekiah Usher for his son, John. In R. I. Hist. Soc. arms and crest as above. Jeffries MSS. N. E. Reg., Jan. 1877, p. 66. On silver candlestick. *See* Buck's Old Plate, p. 120

V

Vail Erm on a bend bet 2 cotises arg, each charged with 3 crosses crosslet, 3 calves statant
Crest: two crosses crosslet in saltire and over all a wolf's head erased bearing in the mouth 3 olive branches
Motto: Qui croit en Dieu croix
Notepaper Louis de Pui Vail, Phila. More like Cooke arms than Vail or Veale

Valentine 3 swords points up, one in pale, two in saltire
Crest: a horse's head couped
On cover of "The Valentines in America"

Van Allen Gu a chev arg
Crest: two wings endorsed gu each charged with a chev of the field
Motto: En tout fidele
Bookplate, notepaper, and seal of Rev. William Harman Van Allen, Boston. A stained glass disc has the crest correctly given but the shield wrong; by Mary Hamilton Frye

Van Berckel Az 3 stars of 6 points arg
Crest: out of a cor 2 horns (?) holding a star of the field between them
Supporters: Savages with garlands about the waists and temples and each holding a long club
Motto: In silentio et spe
Bookplate P. I. Van Berckel. Maverick, sc. of N. Y.

Van Brunt Arg an anchor erect entwined
Crest: an eagle on a globe rising
Motto: Fata sequar
Bookplate Abraham A. Van Brunt

Van Brunt Gu 2 fleurs-de-lis erect in fess
Crest: a talbot's head or
Bookplate C. Van Brunt

Van Buren Arg an anchor entwined with a rope. For bordure a vine
Crest: an eagle rising from a demi-globe
Motto: Fata sequar
Bookplate Ab. A. Van Buren

Vance Arg on a bend gu 3 mullets or. Impaling the arms of England quartering Seymour
Crest: a phoenix rising from a ducal cor
Motto: Foy pour devoir
Bookplate Frank L. Vance, Milwaukee

Van Cortlandt Arg the 4 wings of a windmill conjoined saltirewise sa voided gu bet 5 estoiles placed crosswise of the last
Crest: an estoile gu bet 2 wings displayed, the dexter arg, the sinister sa
Motto: Virtus sibi munus
Seal of Olof Van Cortlandt, who came 1636 to New Netherland. Also a bookplate. Vermont's Amer. Heral. [1886], pp. 13, 162

Vanderbilt Quart 1 and 4: Sa an eagle displayed. Impaling: Or 3 acorns slipped and leaved 1 and 2; 2: Gu a lion ramp reguard [or] (Gwynne); 3: Arg on an inscutcheon azure supporting a ducal cor a fleur-de-lis arg charged with a shield arg a chevron bet 3 roundels
Crest: an acorn slipped and leaved
Bookplate Reginald C. Vanderbilt, N. Y. Van der Bilt colors not as in Rietstap

Van der Kemp On a mound [vert?] a fish before a starved tree
Motto: Moriendum
Seal of Francis Adrian Van der Kemp, 1752–1829, of Holland and N. Y. State. Also on cover of his autobiography (1903)

Van Derlip Or a chev az bet 3 garbs
Crest: five arrows in saltire, points down, intertwined with a serpent and above is the name: Van Deleur
Bookplate Willard C. Van Derlip

Van der poel Gu 3 sheep shears arg 2 and 1
Crest: sheep shears sa bet 2 spread wings
Motto: Esto quod audis
Bookplate S. Oakley Van der poel

Van Guysling Az a chev arg bet 3 eagles
Crest: an escallop (?)
Motto (on chevron)spernit humum.
April 15, 1660
Bookplate Geo. E. Van Guysling

Van Nest Az a fess arg met by a pale from the chief to the fess point, bet 2 stars of 6 points in chief and another in base [or]
Motto: Pro Deo et nobilissima patria Batavorum
Bookplate. Hon. J. P. Van Nest, M. C., N. Y. (name written)

Van Rensselaer Quart 1: Gu a cross moline; 2: Arg a fess couped embat counter-embat sa (Pasraet); 3: Arg 3 antique crowns 2 and 1 (Wenckom); 4: Az 3 chevronelles sa (Ter Beke?)
Crest: a basket issuing flames
Memorial window formerly in the old church at Albany, to "Jan Baptist Van Rensselaer Directeur Colony Rensselaerwÿck, 1656. The Van Rensselaer tomb in the church at Nÿkerk Church, Holland, has the motto: Dulce est pro patria mori. Letter from Rev. P. J. van Melle of Nÿkerk, Mch. 2, 1920, quoting Mr. G. Beernink. W. E. Griffis's Story of New Neth. Also Heral. Jour., vol. 1, p. 33. Kilaen married Nelle van Wenckom, their son Henry married Maria Pasraet; their son Kilaen married Anna van Wely. "Vⁿ Rensselaer" bookplate used by Mrs. Louise Van Rensselaer of Albany. Mrs. M. K. Van Rensselaer's bookplate has the above impaling 1 and 4: Sa a lion ramp arg? bet 3 crosses pattée; 2: arg 3 stags courant gu? 3: Ermine a bend gu impaling or a bend gu. The motto is Nimand zonder
Bookplate Iᴿᴱ Vⁿ Rensselaer, N. Y., with motto: Vertus est vera vetustas. Also of K. K. Van Rensselaer. Maverick, sc., with a motto in writing: "old age is a virtue"

Van Schaick Arg a bull's head cabossed gu 5 feathered arrows, one in bend, one in bend sin points up and one in fess in base point to sinister
Crest: an arrow bet 2 wings
Motto: Amor et amicitia requent
Bookplate John Gerse Van Schaick

Van Sittart Erm an eagle displayed gu [sometimes sa]. On a chief of the second a coronet or bet 2 crosses pattée arg
Crest: an eagle's head couped at the neck bet 2 wings elevated and displayed sa, the latter resting upon 2 crosses pattée arg
Mottoes: A: Fata viam inveniant.

B: Grata quies
Bookplate Nicholas Van Sittart.
Vermont's Amer. Heral. [1886], pp. 78, 179

Van Voorhis Quart 1 and 4: Gu a tower arg; 2 and 3: Arg a green tree
Crest: a tower of the field
Motto: Virtus castellium meum
Bookplate Eugene Van Voorhis

Van Zandt Arg in chief 2 hurts, one charged with a mullet or, the other with a lion ramp or, and in base a cross humettée sa
Bookplate Margaret Van Zandt, 1895. W. F. H[opson] delin.

Varick A woman blindfolded as Justice, a sword in the dexter and scales in her sinister hand
Crest: an open book
Bookplate Col. Richard Varick, mayor N. Y. A. Billings, sc.

Varnum Or on a fess gu 3 garbs (Vernon arms?)
Crest: a boar's head gorged
Motto: Non semper viret
Bookplate James M. Varnum, engr. by French, 1902

Vassall Az in chief a sun in splendor, in base a chalice or
Crest: a ship, sails furled, pointing to the dexter
Motto: Pro Republica semper
Monument erected to Samuel Vassall, M. P., by his great grandson, Florentius Vassal of Jamaica and New Eng., 1766. King's Chapel, Boston, West end

Vassall [Az] in chief a sun in splendor, in base a chalice [or]
Crest: a full-rigged ship, sails furled
Bookplate Henry Vassall. N. Hurd, sc. Dr. Vassall's bookplate has motto: Saepe pro rege, Semper pro patria. Engr. on paten given by Leonard Vassall, 1730, to Christ Church, Boston. Also on tankard from John and Wm. Vassal to Harvard College, ship to sinister, 1729. Curio, p. 21. Also on an American cream jug engraved by Hurd. Owned 1918 by Hollis French. E. A. Jones, Old Sil. Am. Ch., p. 77

Vassall Az in chief a sun in splendor, in base a chalice or
Crest: "a ship without sails or yards sa, at each masthead a pennon and at the poop the ensign flying"
Bookplate John Vassall, Esqʳ., b. Cambridge, 1738, Harv., 1757, d. 1797. Had estate in Jamaica. Oliver's West Ind. Bookplates, No. 547

Vassall [Az] in chief a sun, in base a chalice [or]
Col. John Vassall's altar tomb. The sun in splendor is on metal set into the stone. The chalice is cut into the stone (sunken bas-relief) and the base of the chalice has been broken off. Burying ground near Harvard Square, Cambridge, Mass. Heral. Jour., vol. 2, pp. 15–16. Vermont's Amer. Heral. [1886] pp. 85, 181. Jeffries MSS. N. E. Reg. Jan. 1877, p. 66.

Vaughan Sa a chev arg bet 3 boys' heads couped at the shoulders arg, crined or, each enwrapped about the neck with a snake vert
Crest: a boy's head of the field
Motto: In prudentia & simplicitate
Bookplate Samuel Vaughan, planter Jamaica, settled in Hallowell, Maine, d. 1827. Benjamin Vaughan's bookplate has the above arms impaling: Gu a cross flory bet 4 trefoils slipped [or?] (Manning), and the motto: Prudenter et simpliciter. Oliver's West Ind. Bookplates, No. 558. Another impaling Hallowell: Arg on a chev sa 3 bezants and motto: Christi servitus vera libertas

Vaughan Quartered by Merrick

Vaux Or a fess chequy gu and or bet 3 garbs gu. Impaling: Vert a saltire engr arg charged with 5 fleurs-de-lis vert (Frank)
Crest: an eagle's head couped
Bookplate Edward Vaux, Phila. A seal of John Vaus of Va. is similar. See Wm. & Mary Quar., Jan. 1893, p. 121

Velasquez de la Cadena Quart 1: Or and (?) 2: Gu a castle chained; 3: Per fess arg and az. In chief 2 cows statant; in base 3 fleurs-de-lis or; 4: Gu an inscutcheon arg charged with 13 hurts within an orle of 8 saltires couped
Crest: a plumed helmet
Motto: Fidem servat, vinculaque solvit
Bookplate Mariano Velasquez de la Cadena, Columbia College, N. Y. He also used 1 impaling 2

Verney See also Williams

Vernon Or on a fess az 3 garbs of the field
Crest: a demi-Ceres ppr vested az, in the dexter hand a sickle also ppr, in the sinister hand a garb or, wreathed about the temples with wheat or
Motto: Semper ut te digna sequare
Tombstones of the Vernon family, Old North Burial Ground, Newport, R. I. (1721–1737). Vermont's Amer. Heral. [1886], p. 134

Vernon See also Varnum

Verster Az a fess arg bet in chief a fruited oak branch fessways and in base 3 stars of 6 points or 2 and 1
Bookplate Jane F. Verster, 1894

Vincent Az 3 quatrefoils arg 2 and 1
Crest: a demi-ram arg
Motto: Vincenti dabitur laurea
Bookplate Richard Vincent

Vissee de la Tude Quartered by De Rosset de Fleury

Vose Erm a chev bet 3 roses gu
Crest: a demi-lion ramp holding a rose
Motto: Quo fata vocant
Letter paper of the Misses Vose, daughters of Rev. James G. Vose of Providence, R. I. Also bookplate Isaac D. Vose with cinquefoils

W

Waddell Gu on a chev counter-embat bet 3 martlets arg an eagle displayed enclosed by 2 escallops [sa]
Crest: a horse's head couped
Motto: Mens conscia recti
Bookplate Albert Rosenthall Waddell, N. C.

Waddington Arg a fess sa bet 3 fleurs-de-lis [gu]. In chief a martlet for diff
Crest: an arm embowed holding a battle axe [az?]
Motto: Redde suum cuique
Bookplate George Waddington

Wade Az on a saltire bet 4 fleurs-de-lis or 5 escallops
Bookplate Caroline Dupee Wade, Chicago

Wadham Gu a chev bet 3 roses [arg] a mullet for diff
Crest: a stag's head erased [or] gorged with a collar charged with 3 bezants, all bet 2 rose branches erect, flowered arg, stalked and leaved [vert]
Notepaper Charles K. Wadham, Dalton, Mass.

Wadsworth Az on a bend erm 3 lions ramp or
Framed water color (old). "By the name of Wadsworth," but the name changed to Wordsworth on the scroll. Bent palm branches. Dealer in antiques, owner, Pemberton Square, Boston, 1915

Wadsworth [Gu 3 fleurs-de-lis [arg]
Crest: an eagle's (?) head erased

A seal ring owned by Harold J. Coolidge, Boston. Christopher Wadsworth's family?

Wadsworth   Gu 3 fleurs-de-lis arg
Crest: an eagle rising [or] on a winged globe ppr
Motto: Aquila non captat muscas
Bookplate —— Wadsworth
Notepaper F. Winthrop Coll. N. Y., 1885, in Bos. Ath.

Wainwright   [Gu] on a chev [arg] a lion ramp bet 2 fleurs-de-lis [of the field] all within a bordure engrailed [sa]. In chief a crescent
Tomb of Col. Francis Wainwright who d. 1711. Ipswich, Mass. Burying Ground. Also on deed of Stephen Minor, 1728. Heral. Jour., vol. 1, pp. 89, 110

Wake   See also Tryon

Walcott   Arg a chev bet 3 chess rooks erm
Crest: out of a ducal cor [or] a buffalo's head cabossed arg bet 2 wings erect
Motto: Sis justus et ne timeas
Notepaper Nancy Walcott (Mrs. Lewis) Watson, Indianapolis

Waldo   Az on a bend sinister or 3 leopards' faces, each pierced fessways by an arrow contourné. In the dexter chief on a canton arg a fleur-de-lis
Crest: a leopard pass contourné
Motto: Nil sine Deo
Bookplate D. Waldo, 1762–1863, minister in Conn.   Bates's Early Conn. Engr., p. 41

Waldo   Or a bend az bet 3 leopards' faces gu
Crest: a leopard's head erased ppr "By the name of Waldo." Owned by Waldo Lincoln of Worcester, Mass. This was owned by his great uncle, Daniel Waldo. Swinging sign, antique shop of Frederick Waldo, Phillips St., Boston, 1926, with motto: Nihil sine Deo

Waldoe   Arg a chev bet 3 birds sa beaked and legged or
Wax seal at Lancaster court-house on will of Edward Waldoe, dated 1693–4. Wm. & Mary Quar., Jan. 1893, p. 118. Waldoure?

Waldron   [Arg] 3 bulls' heads cabossed horned [or]
Seal Richard Waldron, Boston, 1691. Jeffries MSS. N. E. Reg., Jan. 1877, p. 66
Said to have used 3 fleurs-de-lys in 1683

Wale   See also Walley

Wales   Sa on a chev or bet 3 griffins' heads erased 3 estoiles of 6 points sa
Crest: a griffin's head couped
Motto: Cura et industria
Bookplate G. W. Wales (of Boston?), Thenard, sc.

Walker   Arg a chev az bet 3 eagles rising
Crest: a stag trippant
Motto: Nec temere nec timide
Bookplate George Walker

Walker   Ar on a chev sa bet 3 hurts 3 crescents arg
Crest: a sun rising in clouds all ppr
Bookplate John Walker

Walker   Gu a cross raguly bet 4 lions' heads erased arg, crowned or
Crest: a dove rising ppr holding in its beak a branch vert
"By the name of Walker" and palm branches. Framed water color. The Misses Cummings, 16 Kennard Road, Brookline, Mass., descended from Ezekiel Walker of Boston. "This coat granted 20th of Dec. 1660"

Walker   Gu a cross raguly bet 4 lions' heads erased arg crowned or. Impaling: Arg a fess counter-embat bet 3 lions' heads erased gu, crowned or (Johnson)
Crest: a lion's head erased arg, crowned or
"Walker and Johnson" and palm branches. This Walker was a cousin of Pres. Walker of Harvard College. Framed. A. G. Fuller, Groton, Mass.

Wall   Az a chev erm bet 3 eagles displayed arg. On a chief embat or 3 roundels [sa?]
Motto: Par pari refero
Bookplate —— Wall (Allen, No. 903) J. D. Stout, N. Y., sc.

Wallace   Gu a lion ramp arg
The tomb of Euphan, daughter of Rev. James Wallace of Elizabeth City, Va., bears the arms of Wallace, impaling the arms of her husband, Col. Wm. Dandridge of Elsing Green, King William Co. Crozier's Va. Heral., 1908, p. 30

Wallace   [Gu] a lion ramp arg
Crest: an ostrich head and neck ppr holding a horseshoe in the beak or
Tomb of Rev. James Wallace, St. John's churchyard, Hampton, Elizabeth City, Va. He d. 3 Nov., 1712. From Erroll, Perthshire. Seen by Mrs. Ljungstedt, 1926

Wallace   Gu a lion ramp debruised of 2 bars
Crest: a lion's head ppr collared arg
Motto: Aut omnes aut nullus
Notepaper Matilda Wallace, Brookline, Mass.

Wallace Gu a lion ramp arg within a bordure caboney az and arg
Bookplate —— Wallace. W. G. Mason, Phila., 1840, sc.

Wallace Gu a lion ramp [arg] within a bordure compony of the last and az
Crest: a demi-lion of the field
Motto: Pro patria
Arms of John Wallace, b. 1717, d. 1783, at Hope Farm, N. J. St. Peter's churchyard, Pine St., Phila. The Continent, 25 Apr. 1883, p. 522. Sylvan City (1883), p. 470

Wallace Gu a lion ramp arg within a bordure compony of the first and last
Crest: an ostrich's head and neck ppr holding in the beak a horseshoe
Motto: Sperandum est esperance
Bookplate Walter Thomas Wallace, South Orange, N. J. By R. B. Jr.

Waller Sa on a bend cotised arg 3 walnut leaves ppr
Crest: a walnut tree ppr, on the sinister side an escutcheon pendent charged with 3 fleurs-de-lis
Motto: Medio tutissimus ibis
Bookplate Benjamin Waller, Va. Ancest. Rec. & Portr., vol. 2, opp. p. 794

Walley Arg on a cross sa 5 lions ramp or (Wale arms)
Crest: a lion ramp affronté holding a sword point down
The cut in Bridgman's Pilgrims of Boston, p. 33, seems to have been taken from a hatchment. An embroidered hatchment is owned (1916) by Mrs. A. W. Lamson, Dedham, Mass. The lion does not seem to be affronté

Walmsley Gu on a chief erm 2 hurts
Crest: a lion crowned statant guard erm
Bookplate I. Walmsley, 1792

Walmsley Gu on a chief erm a trefoil slipped vert bet 2 hurts
Crest: a lion crowned statant guard erm
Motto: En Dieu est mon espèrance
Bookplate Morris Walmsley; also Jas. Elliott Walmsley, Prof. Winthrop Coll., Rock Hill, S. C.

Walter Az a fess dancettée or bet 3 eagles displayed [arg]. Impaling: Gu on a chief or 3 crosses potent of the first (Lynde)
Crest: a lion's head couped
Motto: Fortis que felix
Bookplate J. W. Walter, architect, Phila.

Walters Az a squirrel sejant [or]
Crest: a squirrel of the field
Motto: Sit dux sapientia
Bookplate Frank Walters

Walton Arg a chev gu bet 3 hawks' heads erased sa
Crest: a savage with loin wreath, holding in dexter hand a trefoil slipped vert, and in sinister hand an oak tree
Motto: .A la volante de Dieu
Bookplate William Walton, N. Y.

Walworth Gu a bend raguly arg bet 2 garbs [or]
Crest: a cubit arm vested, holding a sword dropping blood
Motto: Strike for the laws
Bookplate —— Walworth

Wanton [Arg?] a chev [sa?]
Tomb of wife of George Wanton (1726) in Old North Burial Ground, Newport, R. I.; also on official seals of Gov. John Wanton, 1734, and his son, Gov. Gideon Wanton, 1745, both of R. I. Burke gives these arms, but the tinctured seal gives az a chev erm etc. Heral. Jour., vol. 3, pp. 8, 64. Vermont's Amer. Heral., p. 136

Wanton Az a chev erm bet 3 griffins' heads couped gu
Crest: out of a mural crown a griffin's head gu
Motto: Virtus sola nobilitas
Arms on portraits of William Wanton, gov. R. I., 1732–33, and John Wanton, gov. R. I., 1734–40. State House. Early R. I. Wanton seal owned by Edward Wanton Gould, 5 Nassau St., N. Y. (No motto.) Burke says arg a chev sa

Ward Az a cross flory or
Crest: a wolf's head erased ppr langued gu
Mottoes: Non nobis solum. Sub cruce salus
Tombstone of Gov. Richard Ward of R. I., in old Newport churchyard. Vermont's Amer. Heral., pp. 85, 86, 181

Ward Az a cross moline arg
Crest: an eagle's head
Bookplate Henry Ward

Ward Erm on a chev vert bet 4 martlets a horse's head erased or
Crest: on a stump or sprouting branches a pelican vulning herself
Motto: Audacter et sincere
Bookplate —— Ward, Phila.

Ward Quart 1 and 4: 3 quatrefoils; 2 and 3: 3 water-bougets, on the fess point a crescent for diff
Arms on a letter from Nathaniel Ward to Gov. John Winthrop (Winthrop papers). M. H. S. Coll., vol. 37. Heral. Jour., vol. 3, pp. 175, 176

Ward Quartered by Tyler

Wardlow   [Az] 3 mascles [or]
   Crest: an estoile [or]
   Motto: Familias firmat pietas
   Arms of Wardlow, Co. Antrim, Ire.,
and Pawtucket, R. I., on bookplate of
Miss Lyslie Hawes of R. I.

Wardwell   Arg on a bend gu bet 6
martlets 3 plates
   Crest: a hand holding a spear
   Motto: Avito viret honore
   Bookplate J. Otis Wardwell, Mass.,
by E. H. Garrett, 1899

Ware   [Or] two lions pass [az] contourné
within a bordure of the 2d charged
with escallops of the first
   Crest: a dragon's head pierced
through the neck with an arrow bend
sinister ways
   Engr. on side of teapot made by
Josiah Austin of Mass. and marked
by a former owner $\overset{S}{RE}$. Owned by
Shreve, Crump & Low, Boston, 1920

Waring   Quart 1 and 4: Sa 3 peacocks'
heads erased arg; 2: Arg on a chief
indented sa 3 martlets of the field
(Levins); 3: Arg on a fess sa 3 escal-
lops of the field (Blythe?)
   Crest: an eagle's head bet 2 wings
   Motto: Nec vii nec astutia
   Bookplate T. Pinckney Waring

Warner   Vert a cross engr or
   Old silver of descendants of Col.
Augustine Warner, "Warner Hall,"
Va., 1628.   Crozier's Va. Heral., p. 58.
Wm. & Mary Quar., Jan. 1894, p. 156

Warner   Quartered by Lewis

Warren   Gu a lion ramp or a chief
chequy or and az
   Crest: a demi-griffin
   Bookplate Dr. John C[ollins] Warren,
Boston (H. C. 1797), and Dr. J[ohn]
Collins Warren [H. C. 1863] same
plate, shield against a rock; also bookplate of Dr. J[ohn] Mason Warren,
whose seal (crest and shield) is 5/16 in.
high.   The seal of Dr. John Warren,
founder Harvard Med. Sch., gold
and carnelian, is 13/16 in. high and
still used.   Also bookplate Sullivan
Warren.   Also on cover of "Remi-
niscences of My Life" by Annie C.
Warren, 1910

Warren   Gu a lion ramp arg.   A chief
chequy arg and gu
   Crest: a griffin's head couped
   Bookplate George Washington War-
ren.   Also Lucius Henry Warren.
Also engraved on a tall teapot.   Mu-
seum of Fine Arts, Boston, from Dr.
Buckminster Brown

Warren   Quarterly per fess indented or
and gu

   Crest: a wyvern
   Motto: Dread shame
   Notepaper Mrs. Wm. Marshall
Warren, wife of dean of B. U.   Brook-
line, Mass.

Warren   Quartered by Hodges

Washburn   On a bend 3 roses
   Motto: Labora et spera
   Bookplate Charles D. Washburn,
Worcester, Mass.

Washburn   Arg on a fess bet 6 martlets
gu 3 cinquefoils arg
   Crest: on a wreath a coil of flax arg
surmounted by another wreath arg and
gu, thereon flames ppr
   Motto: Persevera deoque confides
   Water color, framed, owned by Dr.
G. H. Washburn, 238 Com. Ave.,
Boston.   The shield, done by R. D.
Weston, is on a match box owned by
Dean Henry B. Washburn, Cambridge,
Mass.

Washington   Arg 2 bars gu.   In chief
3 mullets gu
   Motto: Exitus acta probat
   Painted by Carlotta Reed Stuart.
Framed.   Mt. Vernon, Va.

Washington   Arg 2 bars gu.   In chief
3 mullets gu
   Crest: out of a ducal cor an eagle
rising or (?)
   Motto: Exitus acta probat
   Bookplate Bushrod Washington. The
President's plate has an eagle sa and
apparently a bordure gu.   John, son of
Robert, left his armorial seal to his son,
Wm. Henry, 1785.   Va. Hist. Mag.,
vol. 23, p. 99.   The catalogue of the
Wm. Lanier Washington sale, N. Y.,
April 19, 1917 (Anderson Galleries)
gives a picture of G. W.'s gold seal
with the shield and crest as above, the
bars only tinctured.   Although the
President's bookplate shows as a crest
a bird like a raven or dove the Boston
Transcript, Feb. 21, 1920, shows on
the stained glass at Fawsley Church
(formerly at Sulgrave) an eagle, also
at Thrapston (Sir John) and at Cambridge, Eng. (Rev. Godfrey)

Washington   [Arg] 2 bars [gu] and in
chief 3 mullets [gu].   Impaling [az?]
a chev bet 3 covered cups [or?] (Butler)
   Lawrence Washington, father of the
immigrant. Butler of Tees, Co. Sussex.
Slate facsimile of slab in State
House, Boston

Washington   Arg 2 bars and in chief
3 mullets (pierced?) gu
   Motto: Virtus sola nobilitas
   Bookplate Jane Washington and
Felix Grundy Ewing of Glenarm, engr.
by A. H. Noll

Washington [Arg] 2 bars and in chief 3 mullets. The bars dotted as if or Robert Washington (d. 1622) uncle of the immigrant to Va., with a cresc. for diff. Slate facsimile of slab st Sulgrave, Co. Northants in State House, Boston, Mass.

Washington Quartered by Scribner

Waterman A paly of six arg and gu, 3 crescents counterchanged
Crest: a lion ramp
Motto: Mare ditat
Bookplate Thomas Waterman, Boston, 1855

Waters Az a chev erm bet 3 griffins' heads erased arg
Crest: a griffin sejant holding a mirror framed az
Bookplate Edwin Forbes Waters

Waters Quart arg and az a saltire engr counterchanged
Crest: a talbot arg holding an arrow bendways in its mouth [gu]
Motto: Toujours fidele
Bookplate —— Waters

Waters Sa on a fess wavy arg bet 3 swans of the 2d two bars wavy az
Crest: a demi-talbot arg, in the mouth an arrow gu
Motto: Toujours fidele
Water color sketch owned by Col. H. J. Waters, Princess Anne, Md., seen by G. W. Maslin, 1924. Lieut. Edw. Waters from Middleham (?) Yorks, 1622

Waters Sa 3 bars wavy bet 3 swans arg
Crest: a talbot arg holding an arrow bendways in its mouth [gu]
Motto: Toujours fidele
Bookplate Wilson Waters, Boston

Watkins 10 six-pointed stars 4, 3, 2, 1
Crest: crescent with star above
Motto: Immotus
Notepaper Mrs. Pearl B. Watkins, Oklahoma

Watkins Az on a chev arg bet in chief 2 leopards' faces arg and in base a Cornish chough of the same 3 fleurs-de-lis gu
Crest: a talbot's head gu gorged with a collar arg
Motto: Flydd lawn Bunydd
Watkins of Woodstock, Conn., and Vt. Framed glass, owned by Walter K. Watkins, Boston

Watkins Gyronny of 8 erm and sa, over all a lion ramp or
Crest: a hound pass
Motto: Fortis et fidelis
Bookplate John W. Watkins, A. M. Rollinson, sc.

Watmough Sa a chev bet 3 fleurs-de-lis or
Crest: a mailed arm emb resting at the elbow and holding a dagger erect
Motto: Spes meliora
Bookplate —— Watmough, Phila. Not the arms in Burke. *See* Sylvan City, 1883, p. 460

Watson Arg 3 bars gu charged with 3 crescents 2 and 1 erm. In chief 2 tilting spears crossed and broken
Motto: Ferio tego
Bookplate Eleanor Whitney Watson in lozenge, 1906, by Spenceley. Also of Margery Willard Watson, 1908

Watson Az [arg?] on a chev or [az?] bet 3 martlets ppr [sa?] 3 crescents or
Crest: a lion's head erased or
Embroidery on satin, owned 1923 by Soc. Pres. N. E. Antiq. Wm. Watson of Cambridge, son of Dea. Isaac, m. Catherine, daughter of John and Catherine (Blackwell) Lopez, and had Samuel, Dr. Abram A., and Catherine (Mrs. Allen), whose daughter, Elizabeth Allen, d. 1923 leaving this and the Lopez arms

Wayne Gu a chev erm bet 3 inside gauntlets or
Crest: a stag's head erased ppr
On seal ring of Capt. Anthony Wayne of Easttown, Chester Co., Pa. Glenn's Some Colon. Mansions, vol. 2, p. 281

Webb Gu a cross engr and couped bet 4 falcons or
Crest: an eagle rising from a ducal cor or
Motto: Principia non homines
Bookplate I. Watson Webb, editor, Conn.

Webb Gu a cross humettée engr or bet 4 falcons jessed and belled or
Crest: a demi-eagle displayed issuing from a ducal coronet
Bookplate W. B. Webb, Washington

Webber Az billety or a lion ramp or
Crest: out of a mural crown 2 sprigs
Motto: Je m'en souviendray
Bookplate and car Franklin R. Webber, 2d, Boston

Webber Impaled by Reeve

Webster Az on a bend arg bet a plate pierced by an arrow bend sinisterways and a demi-lion erm a rose [gu] bet 2 boars' heads couped sa
Crest: a horse's head couped
Motto: Vero pro gratis
Bookplate Hon. Daniel Webster, Senator, Mass. Also on Dartmouth College Library bookplate. Also on auto of Pearl Bates, 66 Crystal Ave., Springfield, Mass.

Webster Gu on a fess or bet 3 horses courant 3 roundels vert
  Crest: a horse's head erased
  Motto: Omnia Deo pindent
  Engr. on Daniel Webster's silver service owned by the Somerset Club, Boston. His name also appears. Seen

Weeks Arg on a pale endorsed sa 3 greyhounds heads erased or gorged with a bar-gemelle gu
  Crest: a greyhound's head of the field holding in his mouth a man's leg couped above the knee arg
  Motto: Cari Deo nihilo carent
  Bookplate John Wingate Weeks, U. S. Senator from Mass. and Sec. of War. J. W. Spenceley, 1902

Welch Arg a saltire bet 4 annulets sa a bordure gu
  Crest: on 3 grieces arg a long cross sa
  Motto: Auspice numine
  Bookplates Berthe L. Welch and A. Welch. Spenceley, sc.

Welch Arg a saltire sa bet 4 pellets within a bordure gu
  Crest: a cross calvary with 2 grieces
  Motto: Auspice numine
  Bookplate B. d'Alté Welch, engr. by Spenceley

Welch Az 6 mullets 3, 2, 1 within a bordure caboney arg and gu
  Crest: an antelope's head erased [az]
  Bookplate Charles A. Welch, Boston

Weld Az a fess embat bet 3 crescents erm
  Crest: a wyvern erm [sa guttée d'or?]
  Motto: Verum atque decens
  Bookplate Isaac Weld, writer on America. Not an American (Allen 920)

Weld Az a fess nebulée bet 3 crescents erm
  Crest: a wyvern [sa] guttée [d'or] ducally gorged or
  Bookplate Charles Goddard Weld, Boston. J. W. S., sc., 1899. Ex libris B. C. & M. S. Weld. (No crest.) W[eston] S[mith], 1900

Weld Az a fess nebulée bet 3 crescents, all erm. Impaling a chev [   ] bet 3 garbs (Harstonge)
  Crest: a wyvern
  Motto: Non est mortale quod opto
  Engr. on circular dish, with scalloped edge, owned by First Church, Boston. Made 1720–21. Old Sil. Am. Ch., p. 34

Weld Az a fess nebulée bet 3 crescents erm
  Crest: a wyvern vert gouté de sang, langued gu, gorged and chained or
  Motto: Nil sine numine

Rev. Thomas Weld, b. Sudbury, Suffolk, B. A. Trinity Coll., 1613, vicar of Terling, Essex, 1624–32, minister First Church, Roxbury, 1632–41. Enameled in color on brass, east wall, under the pulpit. First Church, Eliot Sq., Roxbury, Mass.

Weld Purpure a fess dancettée bet 3 crescents erm
  Crest: a wyvern
  Motto: Nil sine numine
  Bookplate Richard Harding Weld, Jr.

Wellman Arg a chev bet 3 dolphins emb sa
  Bookplate Sargent Holbrook Wellman. Sidney Smith, sc., 1914

Wells Arg 3 demi-hurts flaming 2 and 1 (Flat side down)
  Crest: a dove with raised wings contourné
  Bookplate Noah Wells, Conn. R. Brunton, sc. Bates's Early Conn. Engr., p. 43

Wells Or a lion ramp sa
  Crest: an ostrich ducally gorged with a horse's shoe or in beak
  Motto: Nec temere nec timide
  Bookplate John Dagworthy Wells, Phila., lawyer

Wells Or a lion ramp sa with 2 tails
  Crest: a demi-lion of the field
  Motto: Semper paratus
  Bookplate George Doane Wells

Welsh Az 6 mullets or 3, 2, 1. Impaling: a chev bet 3 crescents [   ]
  Crest: a demi-unicorn
  Tomb of Samuel Welsh, who d. 1702. Christ Church, Phila., north aisle. Zieber's Heral., p. 40

Welsteed Az a bend chequy arg and gu (Steer arms)
  Crest: fruit and leaves (?)
  Engr. on a flagon from Rev. William Welsteed to the Second Church, Boston, 1753. The Welsted arms did not resemble these. Old Sil. Am. Ch., p. 40

Wenckom Quartered by Van Rensselaer

Wendell Az an arm embowed in fess holding a cutlass arg bet 3 plates
  Crest: two arrows in saltire arg, points down or, bet 2 ensigns or, cloth out
  Patent of arms from King of Sweden (?) to Christopher Adolph Wendel, 1690, soldier of fortune, near Copenhagen, and Rockport, Mass. Parchment owned by Charles J. Wende.l, Skowhegan, Maine

Wendell Within a window of 12 panes, in the eighth pane the shield, per fess az and arg in chief a ship in full sail toward the dexter; in base 2 anchors in saltire sa rings down. In pane 5 the helmet and above in pane 2 the crest: a ship in full sail toward the sinister. On a riband in panes 10, 11, 12

Evert Jansen Wendell Regerend en dijaken 1656

Conjecturally restored from the window in the Old Dutch Church, Albany, then lost but since recovered. There are 9 panes, the inscription is cursive, the name spelt Eevert Jansen Wendel, the sea blue but not the sky, and the anchors slender

Bookplate Barrett Wendell, Boston (d. 1921), E. D. French, sculp. Here the galleon of the crest sails to the sinister. B. W's drawing had ship to dexter. The window was traditionally put in when Wendel was ruling elder in 1656. When the church was demolished a century ago the window went to the Wendells of Schenectady and lately to Miss Wendell's nephew, Mr. Case of New Brunswick, N. J. It has been photographed; and a seal cut from the photograph shows the crest to be a ship of the field. The Soc. for the Preserv. of N. E. Antiq. has a silver covered bowl with the Wendell ship and ship-crest (both to dexter), given by Ann Wentworth to Ann Wendell, but the anchors were not engraved on the shield

Wendell Per fess az and arg. In chief a ship in full sail of the second, and in base 2 anchors in saltire rings downwards sa

Framed water color. Barrett Wendell, Portsmouth, N. H. John Wendell of Portsmouth used a notarial seal dated 1767, bearing a galleon to dexter as a device. America Heraldica has the ship to sinister in the illustration. Cornelius Wendell's bookplate had the crest a galleon of the field. A memorial tablet to be (1922) in St. John's Church, Portsmouth, N. H., has Wendell as above with crest: ship to dexter, impaling Barrett: Erm on a fess gu 3 lions ramp arg. Designed by A. W. Longfellow

Wensley Erm on a bend gu 3 escallops or

Crest: a man's head in profile

"These arms appertain to the name and family of John Wensley merchant" Ancient framed water color in Mass. Hist. Soc. See also Paddy

Wensley Sa on a bend gu 3 escallops or

Crest: a bearded man's head

Old water color, framed, in Pilgrim Hall, Plymouth, Mass.

Wentworth Sa a chev or bet 3 leopards' faces arg

Crest: a griffin pass

Motto: En Dieu est tout

Bookplate —— Wentworth of New Hamp. N. Hurd, sc. Seal Samuel Wentworth, Portsmouth, N. H., 1757. N. E. Reg., Jan. 1877, p. 66. Seal of Benning Wentworth, 1743, on commission of Jeremiah Sandburne of Hampton, N. H. (no motto)

Wesselhoeft Per chev gu and or a griffin's head erased bet 3 cinquefoils arg

Crest: a cinquefoil enclosed by 2 wings

Bookplate Wm. P. Wesselhoeft, Mass.

West Arg on a fess dancettée sa 3 leopards' faces jessant de lis

Tomb of Major Charles West at Onancock, Accomac Co., Va. He d. 28 Feb., 1757. Va. Hist. Mag., vol. 2, p. 434

West See also Kingston

Westbrook Gu a leopard's head, jessant de lis or

Crest: an armed leg couped above the knee arg, purfled or, spur sa

Framed water color (modern), Brookline, Mass.

Westfield See also Plaisted

Weston-Smith [Gu] a chev bet 3 griffins segreant [or]. On a chief of the last 3 fleurs-de-lis of the first (Smith, Co. Bedford)

Bookplate R. D. Weston, Cambridge, Mass. "R. D. Weston, del. 1907"

Westwood Sa a lion ramp arg crowned with a mural crown bet 3 crosses crosslet fitchée or

Crest: a stork's head ppr erased and gorged with a mural crown or

W. J. Westwood, Richmond, Va. has coat. Wm. & Mary Quar., July, 1893, p. 27

Wetmore Arg on a chief az 3 goshawks

Crest: a goshawk rising

Motto: Tentanda via est

Bookplate William Wetmore. Revere, sc. Also Thomas Wetmore. Callender prob. sc.

Wetmore Arg on a chief az 3 goshawks

Crest: a goshawk

Motto: Virtus libertas et patria

Bookplate Charles H. Wetmore, Conn. Doolittle, sc. Also Samuel Wetmore, William S. Wetmore

Wharton [Sa] a maunch [arg]
Crest: a bull's head arg
On a doc. signed by Richard Wharton, 1686. Mass. Archives, vol. 126, p. 32. Seen by Samuel Morrill

Wharton Impaled by Drexel

Whatley Gu a lion ramp [arg]. On a chief or 3 mullets gu
Crest: a bull's head cabossed
Bookplate Joseph Whatley

Wheelock Arg a chev bet 3 catherine wheels sa
With other arms on Dartmouth College Library bookplate. This is at the lower left. The lower right is Webster, the upper right is Dartmouth, the upper left is Berkeley

Wheelwright Erm on a fess or bet 3 wolves' heads erased 3 roundels
Crest: a wolf's head erased
At top of the slab "No. 7" at bottom "John Wheelwright," 1740. King's Chapel Graveyard, Boston, by Tremont Street fence. Miss Mary Wheelwright says that at the Ursuline Convent, Quebec, there is a piece of silver with crescents, not roundels. Left for Esther by her nephew, Nathaniel. Mrs. E. R. Warren has candlesticks with Wheelwright (Nath.) impaling Apthorp (Ann)
Bookplate Nathaniel Wheelwright, Mass.

Wheildon Gu on a chev arg bet 3 pears stalked and leaved or 3 crosses couped sa. On a chief erm a lion pass guard ppr
Crest: on a mill-rind [sa] a parrot [vert] holding a pear [Burke has a pheon] in the dexter talon, all within 2 oak branches leaved ppr
Motto: Virtus praestantior auro
Bookplate [W. W.] Wheildon of Boston and Concord, Mass., 1870. Also water color by Herbert Browne from original owned 1850 by Hon. W. W. Wheildon

Whipple Sa on a chev bet 3 swan's heads erased arg as many crescents of the first
Crest: a head of the shield
Engr. on a teapot by Hurd about 1750. Owned by the Cleveland Museum of Art

Whitcomb Paly of 6 or and sa 3 eagles displayed counterchanged
Crest: out of a ducal cor a demi-eagle displayed per pale sa and arg with wings counterchanged
Motto: Aquilla non captat muscas
Bookplate Ernest Miller Whitcomb

White [Arg] on a chev bet 3 wolves' heads erased gu a leopard's face
Memorial window to Rt. Rev. William White, Christ Church, Phila. Zieber's Heral., p. 40

White [Az] on a fess bet 3 greyhounds courant [or], collared [gu], as many roses of the last slipped ppr
Crest: an eagle rising ppr
Motto: Virtus omnia vincit
In plaster, library ceiling house of George Robert White, 285 Com. Ave., Boston. Seen by me

White Gu a chev bet 3 boars' heads erased arg
Crest: out of a mural crown a head of the shield
Motto: Sit justus et ne timeas
Bookplate by Sara B. Hill. Also old water color, framed, in Pilgrim Hall, Plymouth, Mass., without crest or motto

White Gu on a canton erm a lion ramp sa all within a bordure sa charged with 8 estoiles or
Crest: a lion ramp holding a mullet
Motto: Vix ea nostra voco
Notepaper F. Winthrop Coll., N. Y., 1885, in Bos. Ath.

White Paly of 12 az and or. On a chief az a griffin passant
Shield in window at Mrs. C. H. Joy's, 86 Marlboro St., Boston, for White family of Salem. Seen

White Per fess az and or a pale counterchanged 3 fountains 2 and 1 ppr and 3 lions' heads erased 1 and 2 [gu]
Crest: a lion's head of the field
Motto: The right and sleep
Bookplate Richard Grant White, N. Y., the Shakespeare commentator

White Per fess gu and arg a pale counterchanged. Over all 3 fountains 2 and 1, and 3 lions' heads erased 1 and 2, gu
Crest: a lion's head of the field
Bookplate Herbert Hill White, Brookline, Mass.

White Per fess sa (?) and or a pale counterchanged, 3 fountains or and vert 2 and 1, and 3 lions' heads erased 1 and 2 [gu]
Crest: a head of the shield
Motto: Maximum proeli impetum et sustinere
Bookplate Rev. Erskine N. White, N. Y., formerly without the motto used by Amos White, merchant, East Haddam, Conn. R. Brunton, sc. Arms of John White, Lord Mayor of London, 1563. Bates's Early Conn. Engr., p. 44

White Sa a pale gu bet 2 fleurs-de-lis in chief and over all 3 chevronels or
Crest: on a ducal cor a bird
Motto: Demum
Bookplate Lillian E. White, Phila.

White Vert 3 roses arg
Crest: a lion's head couped [or]
Seal ring of Henry White of N. Y., whose father came from Md. Henry married Eva van Cortlandt (1737–1836), and as a tory went to Eng. about 1781. Owned by Augustus Van Cortlandt of N. Y., 1920

White Impaled by Jarvis

White Quartered by Rogers

Whitebread Az on a chief or a demilion ramp issuant gu (Markham arms)
Crest: a lion of St. Mark sejant, guard, winged or, circled round the head arg, supporting a harp of the first
Motto: Pro lege et rege
Bookplate William Whitebread of N. Y. H. Dawkins fecit

Whitehall *See also* Holden

Whitehead Az a fess bet 3 fleurs-de-lis or
Motto: Ad finem fidelis
Seal Cortlandt Whitehead, D. D., Bishop of Pittsburgh. Zieber's Heral., p. 207

Whitehead Az on a chev bet 3 buglehorns or 3 martlets of the field
Crest: out of a celestial crown or a buglehorn bet 2 wings
Seal on a deed of Richard Whitehead for 5,000 acres granted 24 Oct., 1673. Also on deed of Philip Whitehead of King William Co., Va., and Elizabeth, his wife, 13 May, 1701. Crozier's Va. Heral., pp. 27 and 28

Whitehouse Gu on a bend arg 2 greyhounds pass sa. Impaling arg a spread eagle sa
Crest: a lion's gamb
Bookplate Francis Meredyth and Mary Armour Whitehouse. In the F. Winthrop Coll. of monograms, etc., Whitehouse has motto: Cito et cento and impales Shanke: Gu on a fess arg a hawk's lure gu bet in chief a cinquefoil and in base a hawk's leg jessed and belled arg

Whitin Five shields: 1: Sa 3 swords points up, 2 in saltire debruised by one in pale; 2: Per fess or and gu. In chief 3 crosses potent gu; 3: Azure a fleur-de-lis; 4: Gu 3 lions gambs; 5: Or a lion ramp
Bookplate Sarah Elizabeth Whitin. E. D. F., sc., 1901

Whiting Gyronny of 4 az and erm. Over all a leopard's head or at the fess point and in chief 3 bezants
Crest: a lion rampant
Motto: In Deo confido
Bookplate —— Whiting. S. B. Congdon, sc.

Whiting On a chev bet 3 leopards (or wolves) heads as many trefoils
Crest: a wolf's head erased
Tomb of Catherine Washington, Highgate, Gloucester Co., Va. She was the daughter of Col. Henry Whiting and the wife of Major John Washington. She d. 7 Feb., 1743. Wm. & Mary Quar., Jan. 1894, p. 157. Also vol. 2, p. 235. Va. Hist. Mag., vol. 18, p. 357

Whiting Per saltire az and erm a leopard's face in the center point or and 3 bezants in chief
Crest: a lion's head erased or
"By the name of Whiting" and palm branches. Framed. Owned by Arthur G. Fuller, Groton, Mass. Another owned by F. S. Whitwell, Boston (plates not bezants). Original (very old) said to be owned by Dwight Whiting, Los Angeles

Whiting Per saltire az and erm a lion's head erased or in chief 3 bezants
Crests: A: a lion's head erased or. B: a bear's head proper
Bookplate in the Lichtenstein collection. Slightly different coat on seal (1687) of William· Whiting of Hartford, emblazoned thus: Az 2 flaunches erm, etc. Vermont's Amer. Heral. pp. 71, 72, 182

Whiting Per saltire az and erm a leopard's face in the fess point and 3 plates in chief
Crest: a leopard's gamb ppr
"By the name of Whiting" and palm branches. Framed water color, the Misses Cummings, 16 Kennard Road, Brookline, Mass., descendants of Charles Whiting of Boston. "Granted the 28th of May, anno 1587

Whitman Per fess or and sa a maunch counterchanged
Crest: a stag on a branching stump
Motto: Per vias rectas
Bookplate William Whitman, mill owner, Brookline, Mass.

Whitmore Vert fretty or
Crest: a mullet
Very old framed water color (before days of Coles?) owned by Very Rev. E. S. Rousmaniére of Boston. "By the name of Whitmore." Framed with Sweat, which see

Whitney Az a cross chequy or and gu
Crest: a bull's head couped arg
The arms differ from those of the Whitneys of Co. Hereford
Bookplate Margaret F. G. Whitney. B. G. Goodhue, des. 1902. J. W. Spenceley, sc. Also Eli Whitney, engr. by Hopson, 1903. Also Stephen

Whitney. On automobile Nelson Whitney, 26 Braemore Road, Brighton, Mass., but with 2 feathers for crest (?) Bookplate Eleanor Whitney Davis in a lozenge. W. S., 1900

Whitney Paly of 6 or and gu a chief sa
Crest: a bull's head couped sa armed or
Framed water color, by Mrs. Mary Lovering Holman. Owned by Mrs. Susan Cotton Tufts, Brookline, Mass.

Whittingham Arg a fess az over all a lion ramp [gu]
Crest: a passion cross purpure
Motto: Pro ecclesia
Bookplate William R. Whittingham. Wm. Rollinson, N. Y., sc.

Whittingham Arg a fess vert over all a lion rampant gu
Crest: a lion's head erased gu langued az
Descendants of the Brattle family have the Whittingham's coat made of narrow rolls of colored papers, pasted on a flat surface. Heral. Jour., vol. 4, p. 43

Whittle Gu a chev erm bet 3 talbots' heads erased or
Crest: two arms embowed, habited arg, cuffed erm, holding bet the hands ppr a garb or
Framed arms owned by Mrs. John Newport Greene, 317 Boush St., Norfolk, Va., who was a Miss Whittle. Seen by L. P., 1922

Whitwell Az 3 griffins' heads erased or
Engr. on alms dish from Admiral Sir Matthew Whitwell, 1749, of a family from Oundle, Northants. This family assumed the arms of Griffin. Christ Church, Norfolk, Va. Old Sil. Am. Ch., p. 342

Whitwell *See also* Ashwell

Wickham Arg 2 chev sa bet 3 roses gu [seeded or barbed vert]
Crest: a bull's head sa armed arg charged on the neck with 2 chev arg
Motto: Manners makyth man
"Arms of Wickham of Abingdon, Co. Berks"
Bookplate Adrienne Adams Wickham. J. W. S., sc., 1899. Also on embr. hatchment owned by Mrs. Helen West Ridgely of Towson, Md., but with crest: an arm embowed holding a cutlass. From Cape Cod. There is some evidence that there are three chevrons

Wiener Vert 5 mullets 2, 1, 2
Crest: a dragon holding something? Bookplate Rose K. Wiener, engr. by A. W. Macdonald

Wigglesworth 3 arches of stone with keystones
Crest: an armed arm embowed holding a spear
Bookplate John Wigglesworth, possibly English

Wilbur 1: Sa a fess bet 2 boars arg (Wilbur)
Crest: a boar's head couped, transfixed by a sword
2: arg 3 escallops sa (Strickland!)
Crest: a stag's head cabossed with a saltire bet the horns
Motto: Volonté de Dieu
Bookplate Nannie Lamberton Wilbur. The bookplate of James Benjamin Wilbur of Manchester, Vt., has on the fess a spear head sa and the motto: Audaces fortuna juvat

Wilk *See also* Wilkes

Wilkes Or a chev bet 3 ravens' heads erased sa. In chief a crescent sa (Wilk arms)
Crest: on a mound vert a crossbow erect [or]
Motto: Arcui meo non confido
Bookplate Capt. Charles Wilkes, U. S. N.

Wilkinson Or 3 goats ramp sa within a bordure of the last
Crest: a goat's head erased, armed and collared sa, langued gu
Confirmation of arms in R. I. Hist. Soc.   Burke gives these arms to Thorold of Co. Lincoln, 1631

Willard Arg a chev ermines bet 3 open baskets or
Crest: a griffin's head erased or
Motto: Gaudet patientia duris
Framed water color owned by Miss Theodora Willard, Berkeley Place, Cambridge, 1920

Willard Arg a chev ermines bet 3 baskets
Crest: a griffin's head erased [or]
Motto: Gaudet patientia duris
Engr. on notepaper of "Major Simon Willard. Descendants association." From Horsmonden, Co. Kent

Willard Arg 3 leopards' heads or
Crest: leopard's head
Made about 1780–90. Miss Susanna Willard, the donor, calls this imaginary. Embr. hatchment by Miss Mary Willard, daughter of Joseph, President of Harvard College in Quincy Homestead, Quincy, Mass.

Willard Gu over a pale arg a maltese cross charged with a roundel bearing a studded crown
Crest: an eagle's head erased
Motto: Litteras ne despice
Bookplate Ashton Rollins Willard, author, Boston

Willey Arg on 2 bars gu 3 martlets or
Crest: a demi-lion ramp gu
Motto: Tenax et fidelis
Seal ring cut for Tolman Willey of
Boston about 1870. Owned by Wm.
Lithgow Willey, Boston, 1922. Also on
mahogany fire screen

Williams A lion ramp [   ]
Crest: a cock
Bookplate —— Williams of Mass.
Robert Williams' grandson, Rev. Wm.,
had these arms on silver, and Dr. Thos.,
brother ot Col. Ephraim, had them on a
silver seal ring. Seal Jonathan Williams, Jr., U. S. agent, 1777. N. E.
Reg., Apr. 1880, p. 185. Seal of Rev.
John Williams's petition, 1705, to
Mass. Gen. Court to repay money
advanced by Capt. Sam. Vetch, vol.11,
p. 198c. *See* beyond

Williams A lion ramp, in chief a
label of 3 points
Ex libris Bertram Williams, 1901.
R. D. W[eston] S[mith] delin. Ex
libris Bertram & Olive Williams. R.
D. W. S., 1900 (No label)

Williams A griffin's head erased holding
a dexter hand in its beak
Crest: a dexter arm mailed holding
a cutlass
Notepaper Miss Cornelia and Miss
Anna P. Williams, 1362 Astor St.,
Chicago

Williams A lion ramp within an orle
of 9 pheons
Seal on a letter from Roger Williams
of R. I. to Mrs. Sadleir, owned by
Trinity College, Cambridge. The
Roope family use a lion and 8 pheons.
Heral. Jour., vol. 3, p. 175. O. S.
Straus's Roger Williams, N. Y., 1894

Williams A lion ramp within a bordure
Crest: a cock
Tablet to Robert Williams, who came
to Roxbury 1638 and d. 1693. Marble,
east wall, north of pulpit in First
Church, Eliot Sq., Roxbury, Mass.

Williams Arg 2 foxes salient counter
salient in saltire, the dexter surmounting
the sinister gu
Crest: a spread eagle
Motto: Fructu non foiiis
Notepaper Mrs. Wentworth Williams Leech, Phila.

Williams Arg a griffin segreant con-
tourné sa
Crest: a griffin's head contourné
Bookplate William Williams, S. T. B.

Williams Az a lion ramp
Crest: a cock
Motto: Cognosce occasionem
Bookplate John C. Williams, Mass.
N. H., sc. Another has: Pauca
respexi pauciora despexi

Williams Az 3 eagles displayed 1 and 2.
On a canton arg a sinister hand ruffled
erect
Motto: Amicitia cum libertate
Bookplate Azarias Williams. N. Y.,
1795. Rollinson, sc.

Williams Erm on a chief sa 3 talbots'
heads erased erm (Barrell arms)
Crest: a head of the field
Motto: Integer audax promptus
Bookplate —— Williams

Williams Gu a chev erm bet 3 men's
bearded heads in profile couped at the
neck ppr
Crest: a bearded face with shoulders
Motto: E Pursimuove (?)
Bookplate Edmund Sydney Williams. Also of Sidney Williams, without crest and motto

Williams Gu on a cross arg 5 pierced
mullets of the first (Verney arms)
Crest: a goat holding a nail
Motto: Nil admirari
Bookplate James Skelton Williams,
engr by French, 1899

Williams Or a lion ramp gu. On a
chief az 2 doves rising arg
Granted 1767 to Williams, Boston,
N. E. *See* Papworth's Alphab. Dict., p.
104. Used by Williams of Phila. with
crest an eagle rising, claw on ball.
Sylvan City, 1883, p. 451

Williams Or a lion ramp gu. On a
chief az 2 doves rising
Crest: an eagle rising with dexter
claw on a sphere or and holding a cross
pattée
Bookplate Henry I. Williams, lawyer,
Phila. Also of John Williams. J.
Callender, sc.

Williams Quart 1 and 4: Or a lion
ramp gu. On a chief az 2 doves rising
or (?); 2 and 3: Az a fess erm bet 3
bells or (Bell)
Crest: a dove rising, the foot on a
sphere charged with a cross
Embr. hatchment owned by Frederick C. Cobb, Dedham, Mass., 1926,
done by a daughter of Henry Howell
Williams of Noodles Island (East
Boston) 150 years ago. Desc. of
Robert of Boston

Williams Sa a lion ramp arg [armed
and langued gu]
Crest: a tufted bird
Engr. on 2 "bellied" mugs given by
Deacon Jonathan Williams of Boston,
son of Robert, and Margery, in 1737,
to First Church, Boston. Old Sil.
Am. Ch., p. 32

Williams Sa a lion ramp contourné
Crest: a bird with 3 tufts contourné

Mottoes: Floriferis ut apes in salti-
bus. Omnia libant omnia nos
Bookplate John Williams, Esq.,
1762–1840. Lawyer Wethersfield,
Conn. R. Brunton, sc. (Allen 939).
Also with lion not contourné and bird
not tufted. Bates's Early Conn. Engr.,
p. 44

Williams Quartered by Hill

Williamson Arg (?) a maple branch
[vert?] and in chief a cross
Bookplate E. S. Williamson

Williamson Arg a chev gu bet 3 trefoils slipped sa
Crest: out of a ducal cor gu a dragon's head
Motto: Constare in sententia
Embr. hatchment 11¾ inches by
9 inches, owned by Mrs. Henry H.
Edes, Cambridge, Mass. The Misses
Stewart, Brook Hill, Henrico Co., Va.,
have a framed water color, the shield or
the motto "God help us." The dragon
is entire and or

Willis Arg 3 griffins passant sa, a bordure engrailed gu bezantée
Tomb of Anne Rich, wife of Col.
Francis Willis, in the chancel of Ware
Church, Gloucester, bears the above
arms impaling Rich: "Gu a chev bet
3 crosses botonnée or." She d. 10
June, 1727. Crozier's Va. Heral., p.
49 and 50

Willis Arg a chev sa bet 3 mullets gu
Crest: a falcon, wings expanded ppr,
belled or
Seal of Samuel Willis (1684) and on
the portrait of George Willis, sec. of
Conn. (1735–1796). Also on Willis
bookplate, 1751. John Willis of Middlesex, Va., 1688, used a seal with
chevron, now defaced. Wm. & Mary
Quar., Jan. 1893, p. 122. Anne Willis
of Groton, Conn., used 1648 a seal:
a chev bet 3 crescents (M. H. S.)

Willoughby [Or] fretty [az]
Crest: vague. N. E. H. Gen. Reg.,
Jan. 1856, p. 51, says old man's head
(or lion's head) bet wings
Seal of Francis Willoughby, Charles-
town, 1664, on doc. in Mass. Archives,
vol. 60, p. 270. He was deputy gov. of
Mass., 1665

Wilmer Gu a chev vairé az and arg
bet 3 eagles displayed or
Crest: an eagle's head or bet 2 wings
expanded vairé
Motto: Fac et spera
Framed water color. Wilmer of
Co. Northampton and of Md. Henrietta Wilmer (b. Kent Co., Md., 1814),
married Mr. Coombe and had Cora (b.

Smyrna, Del., 1834), married Thos. L.
Poulson whose son, Harper W. Poulson,
Boston, uses the Wilmer arms

Wilson [Per pale arg and az] 3 lions'
gambs erased fessways in pale [coun-
terchanged]
Crest: a lion's head [arg guttée de
sang]
Seal on will of Rev. John Wilson,
First Church, Boston, d. 1667. His
grandfather William had a grant 1586.
Heral. Jour., vol. 2, p. 182. Bostonian
Soc. Pub., vol. 6, p. 49. Vermont's
Amer. Heral. [1886], pp. 73, 182

Wilson Sa on a cross engr bet 4 cherubim or, a human heart of the first,
wounded on the left side ppr, and
crowned with a crown of thorns vert
Tomb of Capt. Willis Wilson in
St. John's churchyard, Hampton, Va.
He d. 1701, aged 28. Cary family
history, 1919

Wilson Sa 3 dragons' heads erased arg
on a chief or 3 stars of 6 points
Motto: Res non verba
Bookplate Chas. Robt. Wilson, engr.
by S. L. Smith. In a corner the Winslow (?) arms, crest, and motto

Wilson Sa a wolf salient or (?) on a
chief [of the last?] 3 estoiles of 6 points
Crest: a demi-wolf
From gold watch charm owned by
John C. Wilson, 1784–1832, Somerset
Co., Md., desc. of Ephraim Wilson,
Ireland and Somerset Co., Md., 1664–
1733. Wax from Geo. Wm. Maslin,
1924

Wilson *See also* Bradshaw

Winchell Arg 3 eagles' wings erect sa (?)
Bookplate Winchell Lib. of Geology,
Univ. of Minn. Some Amer. Coll.
Bookplates, 1915, p. 147

Winckley Per pale arg and gu an eagle
displayed counterchanged
Crest: a demi-eagle per pale as in
the arms
Motto: Tendit in ardua virtus
Bookplate Thomas Winckley

Wingfield Arg on a bend gu enclosed
by 2 cotises sa 3 pairs of wings joined
in lure of the field
Crest: an eagle rising arg looking at
the sun in its glory
Supporters: Two pegasi winged,
maned, and hoofed or
Motto: Fidelite est de Dieu
Seal of John Henry Ducachet Wingfield, D. C. L. Bishop of Northern
Calif. He adds a mitre in the sinister
chief and a key and staff in saltire in the
dexter base. Zieber's Heral., p. 207

Winn Erm on a fess vert 3 eagles displayed or
Crest: a lion's head erased ppr
Motto: Virtute et labore
Bookplate Woburn, Mass. Public Library. Also on swinging sign

Winslow Arg on a bend gu 5 lozenges conjoined [or?]
Crest: trunk of a tree with new branches ppr
Motto: Decoptus floreo
Notepaper Mrs. Geo. S. Winslow, 47 Chestnut St., Boston. On side of John Winslow's table tomb, 1674. King's Chapel Graveyard, Boston. Slate, and looks modern. Heral. Jour., vol. 2, p. 21

Winslow Arg on a bend [gu] 7 lozenges conjoined [arg?]
Crest: a branch with growing twigs
On an engr. portrait of Edward Winslow, the gov. Mass. Hist. Soc. The Gov. used a pelican only. His seal is owned by Pelham Winslow Warren of N. Y. (1917). Framed oil painting in Pilgrim Hall, Plymouth, Mass. No crest

Winslow Arg on a bend gu 7 lozenges
Crest: on a stump with growing twigs, a strap with buckle
Slate slab in Pilgrim Hall, formerly tombstone of Hon. Josiah Winslow, Gov. of New Plymouth, d. Dec. 18, 1680, aged 52; Penelope, his widow, who d. in Dec. 1703, aged 73; and Hon. Isaac who d. Dec. 14, 1738, aged 67. Also in Pilgrim Hall a framed water color as above. At N. E. Hist. Gen. Soc. Old water color by Isaac Child with motto En Dieu est tout

Winslow Arg on a bend gu 7 lozenges conjoined or
Crest: on a sprouting stump an annulet gu
Bookplate Samuel E. Winslow, Stonewall Farm, Leicester, Mass.

Winslow Per pale arg and gu a fess counterchanged
Crest: two wings erect
A very curious seal with "F. B." on the reverse, and enclosed in an escallop shell. John Winslow of Boston, 1674, used the shield on his will. See Heral. Jour., vol. 3, p. 91. Shown by Hollis French. Owned by Mrs. C. W. Hubbard, Weston, Mass.

Winslow Impaled by Dous

Winslow Quartered by Bernard

Winsor Gu a buck's head cabossed
Motto: Je me fie en Dieu
Howland: Az on a semée of crosses couped a lion ramp [arg]; Winsor:

Gu a saltire arg bet 4 crosses crosslet or; Loring: Quarterly gu and arg over all a bend sinister engr sa (reversed?)
Bookplate Justin Winsor, historian, libn. Harvard Coll. Engr. in Paris, 1855

Winston Sa a plate bet 3 towers [arg]
Crest: a dexter arm embow holding 4 arrows ppr
Motto: Virtute non verbis
Bookplate —— Winston
Framed painting and notepaper of Judge Robert W. Winston, Raleigh, N. C., and Judge Francis E. Winston, Windsor, N. C.

Winterbotham Az 11 guttées d'eau 3, 2, 3, 2, 1 arg Impaling: Arg a chev embat bet 3 battle axes sa (Bambridge)
Crest· a lion ramp gu on a ducal cor
Motto: Confide recte agens
Bookplate J. B. Winterbotham

Winterbotham Az 11 guttées d'eau 3, 2, 3, 2, 1 [arg?]
Crest: a leopard's face above a ducal cor
Motto: Prævisa mala pereunt
Bookplate H. S. P. Winterbotham

Winthrop Arg 3 chev gu, over all a lion ramp [sa]
Crest: on a mound [vert] a hare courant ppr
Engr. on baptismal basin given in 1706 by Adam Winthrop, great grandson of Gov. John, Second Church, Boston. Same arms "past by patent by Garter, 1594" in Grantees of arms, p. 283. E. A. Jones. Old Sil. Am. Ch., p. 40.
Bookplate William Winthrop with motto: Spes vincit terrorem. S. Hill, sc. Adam Winthrop used: Spes vincit thronum. Vis. 1612 (Evidence of the W⁴ of Groton, p. 1–10) 2 chev not crenellés. Confirm. to Jno. son of Adam, 1592, 3 chev crenellés

Winthrop Arg 3 chev crenellated gu, over all a lion ramp sa
In a lozenge
Bookplate Marie Winthrop. J. W. S., sc., 1902

Winthrop Arg (but engr az) 3 chev crenelles gu, over all a lion [rampant] sa
Crest: on a mount vert a hare courant ppr
Motto: Spes vincit thronum
Bookplate Henry Roger Winthrop. J. W. S., sc., 1903. Bookplate Frederic Bayard Winthrop, engr. by Mussett, London

Winthrop Arg 2 chev gu embat or
over all a lion ramp ppr
Framed MS. Pedigree by Richard
St. George, dated March 1, 1610, seen
1924 at Mrs. Robert C. Winthrop's,
Walnut St., Boston. As borne by
Adam who married Jane Burton.
Adam who married Agnes Sharpe had
chev not embattled

Winthrop Arg 3 chev [gu]. Over all
a lion ramp [sa]. A label of three
points
Crest: on a mound [vert] a hare
courant ppr
Gov. John Winthrop used this coat
from 1620 to 1648 as I notice on his
papers. His will 1620 is quarterly
with no crest. His son John used the
same. The Gov. used often a crest
alone: a hawk (a dove-like one) holding a spray of wheat (Fownes). He
used also: a chev embat bet 3 towers
(Nov. 16, 1646), possibly the Hibbins
seal used by Rawson. The chev
crenellé was on a grant but is not the
ancient Winthrop form. See Heral.
Jour., vol. 1, p. 59; vol. 2, p. 6

Winthrop Arg 3 chev embattled gu.
Over all a lion ramp sa [armed and
langued az]
Motto: Spes vincit thronum
Portrait of John Winthrop, b. 1587,
engr. by Jacques Reich, in Bostonian
Soc., Boston

Winthrop Quarterly of 8: 1 and 8:
Arg 3 chev embat gu over all a lion
ramp sa; 2: 2 bends (Forth); 3:
Per pale az and arg 3 lions ramp; 4:
Arg a cross gu; 5: Az 3 fleurs-de-lis;
6: Arg a lion ramp or; 7: Sa a chev
bet 3 heads couped and entwined by
snakes
Crest: a hare ppr
Motto: Spes vincit thronum
Framed water color in home of Mrs.
Robert C. Winthrop, Boston, 1924.
"Winthrop and Forth, 1603"

Wiseman Sa a chev erm bet 3 cronels
(spear heads) arg
Crest: a sea horse contourné
Bookplate Joseph Wiseman, Penn.
Vallance, sc.

Wistar Arg on a bend az 2 stars of 6
points of the first. Impaling lozengy
arg and sa a fess or
Crest: a demi-eagle displayed sa
issuing from a cor [or] and holding in
the beak a sprig of six olives
Bookplate the Wistar Institute of
Anatomy and Biology, Phila.

Withers Arg a chev gu bet 3 crescents
sa
Crest: a rhinoceros or
Descendants of A. W. Withers of
Gloucester Co., Va., have an old

armorial emblazoning, on the back of
which is: "The arms of the family of
Withers as granted to and confirmed
to Sir Richard Withers of East Sheen,
the ancestor of the poet, and registered
in the Coll. of Arms, London. Va.
Hist. Mag., vol. 7, p. 91

Witthaus Per bend sinister az and gu.
In the dexter chief 2 swords in saltire
points down. In the sinister base a
chaplet
Crest: a hawk rising
Motto: Fama semper vivet
Bookplate Rudolph August Witthaus

Wolcott [Arg] a chev erm bet 3 chess
rooks
Bookplate Oliver Wolcott (in MSS.).
Crudely engraved

Wolcott Arg a chev erm bet 3 chess
rooks [sa?]
Crest: a buffalo's head (?) erased
(gorged with a star?)
Motto: Nullius addictus jurare in
verba magistri
Oliver Wolcott. Engr. by F. Halpin
from a painting by Earle in 1782.
Mass. Hist. Soc. A seal which appears
to bear these arms is on a letter from
Gov. Leverett, July 6, 1675, to Gov.
Josiah Winslow. MS. at Boston Athe-
naeum. On a silver tankard, 1756.
Wolcott Memorial, p. 120

Wood Arg on a mount ppr a wolf stat
in front of an oak tree
Crest: out of a mural crown a demi-
savage wreathed about the temples
and waist with oak leaves, the sinister
hand holding a club erect and in the
dexter an oak tree eradicated
Motto: Perseverando
Bookplate Frank Wood, Boston.
E. B. Bird, des.

Wood Az an oak tree on a mound ppr
bet a 3-masted ship in the dexter and
sinister quarters
Crest: a ship with main and mizzen
mast main sails furled
Motto: Tutus in undis
Bookplate W. Wood, Prest. Bd. of
Educ., N. Y. City. R. Gray, sc.

Wood Or on a mound vert a wolf stat
sa under an oak tree vert
Crest: from a mural crown a demi-
man holding in the dexter hand a
griffin's head erased sa and in the
sinister a club sa (?)
Bookplate Col. Joseph Wood, Revolutionary Army

Wood *See also* Phipps
David Wood's tomb bears the Phipps
arms

Woodbridge Arg on a bend gu 3 chaplets ppr
Crest: a chaplet of roses ppr
Motto: Virtus se coronat
Bookplate "Dudleius Woodbridge," Revolutionary period. Mass.

Woodbury Barry of 15 arg and az, over all 3 lions ramp gu [crowned or]
Crest: a bundle of 5 arrows encircled by a serpent ppr
Bookplate John P. Woodbury of Boston. E. D. French, sc. Mrs. C. A. Pratt, Little Rock, Ark., uses a barry of 10 on notepaper but no crest or motto (vera sequor). Her mother was Marietta Woodbury

Woodford Sa 3 leopards' faces or, jessant de lis
Crest: 2 lions' gambs erased or
Engr. on a seal of Gen. William Woodford, prior to 1780. Crozier's Va. Heral., p. 18

Woodman A man holding a club (?)
Crest: an animal statant
Seal of Edward Woodman, Boston, 1694, on doc. in Mass. Archives, vol. 61, p. 450

Woodward Arg 2 bars azure debruised by 3 stags' heads cabossed or
Crest: from a ducal cor a boar's head [couped arg]
Motto: Virtus semper viret
Bookplate John Woodward

Woodward A barry of 6 or and az
Crest: a stag's head or
Motto: Virtus semper viret
Bookplate Wm. Woodward

Woodward A barry of 6 or and az. In a canton gu a demi-man holding a club.
Crest: a squirrel eating a green branch
Motto: Gardez bien
Bookplate Samuel B. Woodward

Woodward A barry of 6 arg and az. 3 stags' heads cabossed [or]
Bookplate Edith Woodward; also of Sarah Rodman Baldwin, engr. by E. D. French

Woodward *See also* Bull

Woolsey Gu on a cross engr arg a lion passant guard gu bet 4 leopards' faces gu. On a chief arg a rose bet 2 birds gu (the birds Cornish choughs?)
Crest: an arm embowed coulped holding a shin bone, all ppr
Motto: Manus hoec inimica tyrannis
Bookplate Edward J. Woolsey, Jr. *See* Woolsey arms in Burke. Theodore S. Woolsey of New Haven has a bread basket, 1737, with these arms: shield sa, faces az, lion gu. No crest

Wooten Arg a cross formé fitchée at the foot sa
Crest: an estoile or above a ducal cor
Framed painting owned by Dr. John Wooten, Greenville, N. C., Mr. C. S. Wooten, Mrs. Evelyn Wooten, Mt. Olive, N. C., and others

Worcester Arg 10 torteaux 4, 3, 2, 1
Framed water color owned by A. G. Fuller, Groton, Mass.

Wormeley Gu on a chief dancettée arg, 3 lions ramp sa
Motto: Nunc mihi nunc alii
Bookplate Ralph Wormeley of Rosegill, Va. The family came from Dedham, Co. Essex. Also of Ralph Wormeley Curtis

Worthington Arg 3 dung forks sa
Crest: a goat passant arg, holding in his mouth an oak branch vert fructed or
Motto: Virtute dignus avorum
Arms on plate very old, owned by desc. of Nicolas Worthington, Saybrook, 1650, later Hartford, Ct. He d. in Mass. 1683. Vermont's Amer. Heral., p. 102

Worthington Gu 3 leopards' faces 1 and 2
Crest: an armed arm emb holding a sword
Bookplate Erastus Worthington, 1761–1831 (?), bookseller Colchester, Conn. R. Brunton, sc. Bates's Early Conn. Engr., 'p. 45

Wray Az on a chief or 3 martlets gu
Crest: an ostrich or
Motto: Et juste et vray
Tomb of Capt. George Wray, in St. John's churchyard, Hampton, Va., bears the arms. He d. 19 Apr., 1758. Va. Hist. Mag., vol. 10, p. 213

Wright Arg a cross az, 3 leopards' faces in the dexter chief
Crest: a leopard's head winged
Seal of Mrs. S. M. Wright, Bar Harbor, Me., and 1903 Walnut St., Phila.

Wright Az 2 bars engr arg and in chief 3 leopards' faces arg
Crest: out of a ducal cor a wolf's head
Motto: Tam arte quam marte
Bookplate Eben Wright, Boston

Wright Quart 1 and 4: Az a chev bet 3 axes arg; 2 and 4: Az a lion pass guard or a chief erm (Kent)
Crests: 1: from a cloud a mailed arm emb holding a cutlas; 2: a lion's head erased and gorged
Notepaper F. Winthrop Coll., N. Y., 1885, in Bos. Ath.

Wright Quart 1: Sa a chev engr or bet 3 fleurs-de-lis; 2: Per pale erm and ermines on a chev counterchanged bet 3 fleurs-de-lis or 5 fusils counterchanged (Addington); 3: Gu on a chev arg bet 3 ostrich feathers as many annulets [sa] (Fetherston); 4: Sa on a fess arg bet 8 guttées in chief and 8 in base 3 martlets, a crescent in chief
   Crest: a griffin's head couped or
   Motto: Garde le droit
   Bookplate Christopher Wright

Wright Sa on a chev arg bet 3 fleurs-de-lis [or] a mullet. On a chief arg 3 spear heads sa
   Crest: a griffin's head couped
   Bookplate James Wright, royal gov. Ga. Also Sir J. Wright, Bart. with badge of Ulster in centre

Wright Sa a chev engr arg bet 3 fleurs-de-lis or. On a chief of the last as many spear-heads ppr. All within a bordure, wavy erm
   Crest: on a mount vert and within an annulet or a dragon's head couped at the neck arg semée of annulets sa and murally ɔ ɔ r ged gu

Motto: Mens sibi conscia recti
Bookplate Sir James Wright, last royal gov. of Ga. Here the chevron is not engrailed and there is a mullet for diff. The crest is a plain dragon's head. Vermont's Amer. Heral., p. 183

Wynkoop On a mound ppr a vine with grapes at sinister and beside it a man in colonial dress with white plumes on hat, dress and hat vert, holding glass in dexter hand. At dexter a cask az and boy vert holding a staff in dexter hand
   Crest: eagle wings spread
   Supporters: Thinly clad bacchantes holding glass and bottle
   Bookplate Augustus Wynkoop, N.Y., also Peter Wynkoop. Also Richard Wynkoop, the man's coat purpure and vert, cask gu
   Motto: Virtutem hilaritate colere

Wythe Az 3 griffins passant or 2 and 1
   Crest: a demi-griffin
   Motto: Secundis dubiisque rectus
   Bookplate George Wythe, Va.

Y

Yardley Arg on a chev az 3 garbs or. On a canton gu a fret [or?]
   Crest: a stag courant gu [attired or]
   Motto: Nunquam non fidelis
   Bookplate Samuel Swan Yardley, engr by A. W. Macdonald

Yarnall Az a cross engrailed or
   Bookplate Francis C. Yarnall, Phila.

Yates Arg a fess bet 3 gates sa
   Crest: from a ducal coronet a goat's head ppr
   Motto: Ne parcas nec spernas
   Bookplate Stephen S. Yates, Brooklyn. The Yates arms are said to have been used on James Samuel's Bookplate with the motto: L'un pour l'autre, and signed H. Dawkins, Philada. fecit. Bookplate Peter W. Yates, Esqʳ. by Dawkins has for crest a garb

Yates Or a chev bet 3 gates sa
   Crest: a mailed arm embowed holding a pennant perhaps az
   Motto: L'un pour l'autre
   Bookplate Chˢ Yates (in MS.) by Dawkins, Phila.

Yates Per fess embat or and sa 3 gates
   Bookplate Anah Yates

Yeamans Gu a chev bet 3 spear heads arg. Impaling: Gu on a bend bet 2 lions' heads erased arg 3 leopards' faces or (Gunthorpe)
   On silver cream jug owned by Mrs. Barrett Wendell, Boston, from her relative Shute Shrimpton Yeamans of Boston and Antigua, who married Matilda Gunthorpe. Jas. W. Gerard has a plate, less clearly tinctured, but with crest: a dexter arm holding a broken spear

Yeoman *See also* Petty

Yonge Ermine a lion ramp
   Seal on will of Col. John Yonge of Southold, L. I. *See* The Morris Manor, by Lucy D. Akerly, ɒ. 13. Yonge of London used the lion

Young Arg on a bend sa 3 eagles' heads erased
   Crest: an eagles' head erased in a chaplet
   Motto: Pro libertate
   Bookplate William Young, Esq.

Young Az 3 piles sa the middle pile charged with a mullet. On a chief gu 3 annulets or
   Crest: a demi-lion holding a sword in the dexter gamb
   Motto: Robori prudentia præstat
   Bookplate Rev. Alexander Young, Boston

Young Or 3 piles sa on a chief or 3 annulets of the 2d
   Crest: a dexter arm holding an arrow
   Motto: Press through
   Bookplate William Young

Young Per pale or and purpure, in chief 2 leopards' faces counterchanged and in base a lion ramp
Crest: two arms vested vert holding a scroll marked Labore, the dexter holding also a quill
Bookplate William Young

Youngs Arg on a bend sa 3 eagles' heads erased of the first within a bordure invected sa charged with 8 bezants
Crest: an eagle's head erased within a chaplet

Ex libris Wm. J. Youngs, Dist. Atty., N. Y.

Yuille Arg on a fess bet 3 crescents sa a garb or banded [gu]
Crest: an ear of wheat ppr
Motto: Numine et virtute
Tomb of John Yuille, Merchant, in Bruton churchyard, Williamsburg, Va. He d. 20 Oct., 1746, aged 27, son of Thomas Yuille of Darleith in Scotland. The fess not the garb is banded, as seen by L. Park, 1922. Wm. & Mary Quar., Oct. 1893, p. 78

INDEX

A

B

C

Hills

3 hills	Brinckerhoff
Mount inflamed	Macleod
Mountains in chief and pine	Stevens

Horns

Bugle horn argent	Hunter
Hunting horn	Foster
3 horns	Bellingham, Bude
3 buglehorns argent	Thruston
3 horns and on chief	Foster

Horseshoes

Horseshoe	Scripps
2 horseshoes in pale and stars	Farragut

Inscutcheons

Inscutcheon within martlets	Bolling
Inscutcheon bet 4 escallops	Pendleton
Inscutcheon bet 4 lions ramp	Paddy
Inscutcheon charged with 3 mullets	
	Murray
On an inscutcheon bet crosses pattée	
	Bartram
On an inscutcheon bet 2 estoiles	Harold
3 inscutcheons	Hay, Hayes

Keys

Key fessways in chief and in base peaks	
	Pietz
2 keys in saltire	Smythe

Lance

Lance in pale	De Lancey
3 lances erect a chief chequy	Smith

Leaves

Hazel leaves	Baldwin
3 holly leaves	Loomis
3 leaves in chief	Burnet
3 leaves in chief in base a horn	Smith
3 leaves slipped	Gerard
3 rose leaves in pale bet 2 palets	Sprague
3 strawberry leaves	Frazer

Leg

Human leg	Prime
Leg embowed	Gilman

Lozenges

2 lozenges	Champney
3 lozenges	Bigelow
3 lozenges ermine	Stickney
3 lozenges and a chief	Fielding
4 lozenges counterchanged	Judson
4 lozenges in bend	Reed, Heley
5 lozenges conjoined in pale	Pinckney
5 lozenges conjoined bet 2 demi-children	
	Smith

Mallets

3 mallets	Browne

Man or Woman

Man holding a club	Woodman
Man holding fuse	Cannon
Soldier armed	Roome

Indian

Indian shooting a stag	Dinwiddie

Justice

Justice, woman as	Varick

King

King crowned	Keyser

Mascles

Mascle counterchanged	Perot
Mascle within bordure	Shepley
3 mascles or	Wardlow
7 mascles	Quincy

Mason's sign

Mason's sign, Bible, etc.	Ketchum

Maunch

Maunch	Hastings
Maunch bet cinquefoils	Acklom
Maunch counterchanged	Whitman
Maunch within bordure	Wharton

Millrind

Millrind	Haight, Hoyt
Millrind and chief gules	Mills
Millrind debruised by bendlets	Fels
4 millrinds	Turner

Monsters

Cockatrice

Cockatrice	Longley

Griffin

Griffin and chief ermine	Short
Griffin and on chief star	Shelton
Griffin bet 3 crescents	Sibley
Griffin segreant	
Baker, Collins, Coolidge, Downing,	
Griffin, Grimshaw, Hudnut, Knight,	
Lauder, Morgan, Read, Sherwin,	
	Williams
Griffin segreant within bordure	Gale
Griffin sejant	Baldwin
3 griffins pass or	Wythe
3 griffins pass within bordure engr	Willis

Harpy

Harpy	Huntington

Pegasus

Pegasus	Caverly, Drayton

Phoenix

3 phoenix	Brown

Sea dragon

3 sea dragons	Easton

Sea horse

Sea horse within an orle	Skinner

Sea lion

Sea lion crowned	Silvester

Unicorn

Unicorn	Smith
Unicorn pass argent	Masterton
Unicorn salient	Doane
Unicorn and a chief	Flower

Wyvern

Wyvern	Brent, Drake

Mullets

Mullet	Ashton, Claghorn, Gavit, Sohier
Mullet and canton	Assheton
Mullet and a chief	Gilchrist
Mullet bet 3 crescents	Pride
Mullet bet crosses crosslet	Adam
Mullet bet 3 crowns	Grant
Mullet bet 3 cinquefoils	Hamilton
Mullet bet 3 plates	Smith
Mullets counterchanged	Apthorp
3 mullets	Murray, Randolph
3 mullets and on a chief 3 palets	Dickson
3 mullets in chief	Crome
3 mullets within tressure	Murray
4 mullets	Bigger
4 mullets pierced	Tefft
6 mullets or	Welsh
6 mullets within bordure caboney	Welch
9 mullets	Gause, Jessup
10 mullets	Alston

Nails

3 nails	Nagel
3 passion nails piercing heart	Logan

Pale

Pale	Clement, Deas
Pale and 3 fountains	White

MOTTOES

Recorded as found. Spelling and grammar not corrected

A

A prendre amourir — Browne
A la volante de Dieu — Walton
A l'amy fidél pour jamais — Seymour
Absque labore nihil — Stearns
Acu rem tetigit — Taylor
Ad astra per aspera — Fowler, Minot, Rogers
Ad diem tendo — Stevens
Ad finem fidelis — Beck, Whitehead
Ad mortem fidelis — Chandler
Adversis major par secundis — Jarvis
Aequabiliter et Diligenter — Sattig
Afynno dwy y fydd — Matthews
Agnoscar eventu — Ross
Agros vigilantia servat — Messinger
Aide toi et le ciel t'aidera — Sylvester
Algiers — Pellew
Alis nutrior — Simpson
Alla corona fidisimo — Leach
Alleluia alleluia alleluia — Tuite
Alta pete (?) — Cutts?
Alta petit — Stott
Alte volo — Heywood
Altius ibunt qui ad summa nituntur — Forbes
Altuis tendo — Kinlock
Amat victoria curam — Clarke
Amator de virtus — Case
Amicitia cum libertate — Williams
Amicus amico — Bellingham
Amo — Scott
Amo probos — Blair
Amor et amicitia requent — Van Shaick
Amor vincit patriae — Gibbes
Amor y Amistad — Amory
Amore patriae — Scott
Anchor fast anchor — Gray
Animo et fide — North
Animus nisi paret imperat — Bernard
Annique vivesque pariter crescent — Sears
Ante victoriam ne cane triumphum — Thompson

Aquila non captat muscas — Drake, Graves, Harris, Wadsworth, Whitcomb
Arcui meo non confido — Wilkes
Ardua pet¡t ardea — Hearn
Arma (?) Libertatis — Bigger
Ars longa vita brevis — Priestly
Aspire persevere trust — Adams
At spes non fracta — Hope
Auch tulpen darf man lieben — Updike
Auctor — Hines
Auctor pretiosa facit — Lenox
Audaces fortuna juvat — King
Audaces fortuna juvat timidosque repellit — Ambler
Audaces juvo clarior hinc honos — Buchanan
Audaciter — Ewing
Audacter et sincere — Ward, Deacon
Audacter et strenue — Pollock
Audax at cautus — Jenks
Audax bona fide — Bull
Aude fieri justum — Parker
Audentes fortuna juvat — Davenport
Auspice Christo — Davis
Auspice numine — Welch
Auspice te ucro — Tucker
Aut delectare aut prodesse — Herrick
Aut malleus hodie aut incus cras — Underwood
Aut mors, aut vita decora — Livingstone
Aut nunquam tentes aut perfice — Drew
Aut omnes aut nullus — Wallace
Aut pax aut bellum — Fogg
Aut tace aut face — Ives
Auxilio Dei — Morehead
Auxilio Dei supero — Chapin
Auxilium ab alto — Mountfort
Avancez — Hill
Avisela fin — Amory, Kennedy
Avito viret honore — Stewart, Wardwell

B

Be fast — Saville
Be just and fear not — Arnold
Be neither tyrant nor slave — Eby
Be steady — Butcher
Be traist — Sheild
Bear and forbear — Bernard
Beata Downs, custodita sic cuja Deo, Domino est — Brasher

Beauty and grace — Smith
Bello virtudo — Keese
βελτιωσαι ου διδασαι — Stith
Benevolentia et justitia — Griffiths
Benigno numine — Heseltine
Beware my edge — Gibbs
Bona bonis — Hurd
Bono n[ec malo?] — Elliston

C

Bona quae honesta	Jackson
Bono vince malum	Elliston, Harold
Books unlike universities are open	
to all who would read	Curtin

By cunning not by craft	Todd
By sea and land	Campbell
Bydand	Gordon
Byde tyme	Stevens

Candide et constanter	
	Cooley, Grimshaw
Cara patria carior libertas	Clinton
Cara vita, carior patria, carissima	
libertas	Kettle
Cari Deo nihil carema	Cary
Cari Deo nihilo carent	
	Seelye, Weeks
Carpe diem	
Greene, Hall, Hoffman, Smith,	
Turner	
Carpe diem postero ne crede	Cutting
Cassis tutissima virtus	Mellon
Caton wrth caton Dow a Digon	
(Heart to Heart God over all)	
	Robert
Cave adsum	Jerdone
Cave cervum	Ridgeley
Cavendo tutus	Dana, Leach
Cedant arma togae	Read
Celer atque fidelis	Robinson
Celeritas viritus fidelitas	Carpenter
Celeriter et jucunde	Rogers
Certamine summo	Beeman
Cervus non servus	Goddard
Chacun à son goût	Smith
Christi servitus vera libertas	
	Merrick, Vaughan
Cito et cento	Whitehouse
Cito pede praeterit aetas	Sargeant
Clarior alter	Peronneau
Clibor ne sceame	Cleborne
Coelum non animum	Rhodes
Coelum tueri	Ball
Coelumqui tueri	Ball
Cogi posse negat	Masterton
Cognosce occasionem	Williams
Colendo crescent	Livius
Comme je trouve	
Ambler, Cary, Jaquelin, Nicholas	
Comrac Anceart	McGarrity

Conanti dabitur	Conant
Conanti nihil difficile est	Conant
Confide recte agens	Winterbotham
Confido	Boyd, Crokatt, Livius
Confido conquiesco	Talmage
Confido in Domino	Sedgwick
Conquer death by virtue	Sherman
Consequitur quodcunque petit	
	Taylor
Consilio non impetu	Agnew
Constans et fidelis	McQueen
Constans fides et integritas	
	Brinckerhoff
Constant en tout	Standish
Constanter	Hoar
Constare in sententia	Williamson
Cor unum, via una	Brightley, Porter
Courage	Cummings
Courage à la mort	
	Hutchings, Hutchins
Crescamus	Hodges
Crescit sub pondere virtus	
	Chapman, Fielding, Hall
Crescit sub pondere virtus ventis	
secundis	Slater
Cruci dum fido spiro	Douw
Cruce dum spiro spero	Darling
Crux Christi nostra corona	Barclay
Crux Christi salus mea	Peck
Crux dat salutem	McKerrow
Crux mea lux	Brockett
Crux mea stella	Devlin
Crux mihi grata quies	Adam
Cultus animi quasi humanitatis	
quidam cibus	Havemeyer
Cum principibus	Hale
Cuneus genuem trudit	Coolidge
Cur me persequeris	Eustis
Cura et industria	Wales
Currit qui currat	Fuller
Cursum perficio	Hunter

D

Dabit otia deus	Brisbane
Dando conservat	Harpending
Dat Deus incrementum	Bancroft
Data fata secutus	McKenzie
"De Interior Templo Socius"	
	Horsmanden
De me praesagia olim	Hasell
Dea providentia nostra est haere-	
ditas	Turner

Débonnaire	Bethune
Decoptus floreo	Winslow
Delectando pariterque mo nendo	
	McKay
Demeure par la verité	Mason
Demum	White
Den Stauf trage ich	Stauffer
Dene agendo et cavendo	Hugget
Denique coelum	Melville

Deo adjuvante — Pellew
Deo dirigente crescendum est — Lowell
Deo duce perseverandum — Jay
Deo et amicitiae — Forman
Deo et principe — Lambert
Deo favente cresco — Bartlett
Deo juvante — Smith
Deo lux nostra — Holloway
Deo, non fortuna — Tilton
Deo nos sagittis fido — Cuyler
Deo omnia plena — Gourgas
Deo ragnat — Judd
Deo regique debeo — Johnson
Deo Reipublicæ et amicis esto semper fidelis — Duffield
Deo spes meo — Thornton
Deo tum patria — Morton
Depressa resurgo — Pintard
Der Nagel hält fest — Nagel
Desir na repos — Howard
Deum cole regem serva — Cole
Deus adjuvabit — Taylor
Deus alit eos — Crocker
Deus amici et noi — Pell
Deus Amicus — Pell
Deus clypeus meus — Biddle
Deus dabit — Fish
Deus dat incrementum — Bancroft
Deus mihi providebit — Keene, Pierce
Deus mihi sol — Nicholson
Deus nobis haec otia fecit — Smith
Deus nobiscum quis contra nos — Higginson
Deus non ego — Newton
Deus Providebit — Bond, Dove
Deus vivat — Black
Deux dux certes — Brimage
Dictis factisque simplex — Gilpin, Rogers
Dieu avec nous — Berkeley

Dieu défend le droit — Bancker, Spenceley, Spencer
Dieu est ma roche — Rotch
Dieu te garde et regarde — Bernon
Difficiles sed fructuosæ — Appleton
Diligentia ditat — Newhall
Dirigat Deus — Allan
Dirige — Pearmain
Disce ferenda pati — Hollingsworth
Disce pati — Duncan
Discite justitiam moniti — Camm
Discretio moderatrix virtutum — Quincy
Discrimine salus — Trail
Diu delibera cito fac — Davie
Do well and doubt not — Prat
Do ye next thyng — Everett
Domus grata — Denison
Donat anima virtus — Gough
Draagd en verdraagd — Lott
Dread God — Monro
Dread shame — Leighton, Warren
Droit et avant — Skinner
Duce natura sequor — Holyoke
Ducit amor patriae — Bull, Janney
Dulce est pro patria mori — Van Rensselaer
Dulce periculum — McCall
Dum clavum teneam (or Dum clarum rectum teneam) — Penn
Dum memor ipse mei — Irvine
Dum spiro spero — Ahmuty, Collet, Gove, Kendrick, Parsons, Ridgely, Shaw, Swan
Dum vigilo curo — Cranston
Dum vigilo tutus — Gordon
Dum vivo spero — Dumaresq
Durate — Aolfsen
Durum patientia frango — Crawford
Duw a digon — Jones
Dux vitae ratio — Bloodgood

E

E Pursimuove (?) — Williams
Ecce ferunt calathis musae mihi lilia plenis — Cram
Editando et legendo — Cutbush
E'en do bait spair nocht — MacGregor
Effingit pheonix Christum reparabilis ales — Mayer
En Dieu est ma fiance — French
En Dieu est mon espérance — Walmsley
En dieu est tout — Connolly, Wentworth, Winslow
En Dieu ma foy — Cheever
En tout fidéle — Van Allen
Ερεσνᾶτε Τά s'Τραφας — Smith
Espérance — Gilman

Espérance en Dieu — Raymond
Esse guano videri — Fendell
Esse et videri — Duer
Esse et videri of Penn — McLanahan
Esse potius quam haberi — Minturn
Esse quam videri — Archdeacon, Beal, Bryan, Dexter, Dickinson, Grew, Henshaw, Hooker, Lyman, Sibley, Spinney, Sturgis, Thruston, Turner, Tyng
Esto fidelis — Hart
Esto quod andis — Van der poel
Esto quod esse videris — Chew
Et juste et vray — Wray
Et si ostendo non facto — Ogden
Et vi et virtute — Burrows

Ewch Ymlaen	Roberts
Ex candore decus	Goelet, Marshall
Ex cruce leo	Terry
Ex hoc victoria signo	Rattray
Ex malo bonum	Appleton

Ex septum unus	Ketchum
Exaltat humiles	Sears
Exemplum adest ipse homo	Franklin
Exitus acta probat	Washington
Exstant recte factis proemia	Coffin

F

Fac alteri ut tibi vis	Ha tch
Fac et spera	Wilmer
Fac recte et nil teme	Jeffries
Fac recte et nil time	Jeffries
Faire mon devoir	Josselyn
Faire sans dire	Loring
Fais, bien, crains, rien	
	Colden, Pintard
Fais ce que dois advienne que	
pourra	Clapp
Faithful and brave	Uniacke
Fama candida rosa dulcior	Ames
Fama praestante praestantior	
virtus	Morgan
Fama proclamat honorem	Perot
Fama sed virtus non moriatur	
	Ingersoll
Fama semper vivet	Witthaus
Famam extendimus factis	Scott
Familias firmat pietas	Wardlow
Fare fac	Fairfax
Fari aude	Child
Fari quae sentiat	Randolph, Tyler
Fari qui sentiat	Randolph
Fast	Gray
Fata sequar	Van Brunt, Van Buren
Fata viam inveniant	Van Sittart
Fatti Maschii Parole Femine	Calvert
Favente deo et sedulitate	Collins
Favente des supero	Hardenbrook
Feil pero desdichado	Davis
Fenein respice	Bowman
Ferio tego	Sims
Ferret ad astra virtus	Kellett
Fest	Delafield
Festina lente	
	Abbott, Everest, Stoddart
Feu sert et sauve	Fels
Fide et amore	Lane
Fide et constantia	Lee
Fide et fiducia	
	Gilchrist, Rogers, Taylor
Fide et fortitudine	
	Barton, Duryea, Higgs
Fide et sedulitate	Elwood
Fide sed cui vide	
	Greenough, Ludlow
Fidei coticula crux	Chesebrough
Fidelis ad mortem	Buckler
Fidelis et suavis	Emery
Fidelis morte	Paxton

Fidelitas	Ensign, Fry
Fidelitas vincit	Chidson, Cotton
Fidélité est de Dieu	Wingfield
Fideliter	Somerby
Fidem libertatem amicitiam	
retinebis	Adams
Fidem respice	Hoskins
Fidem servabo	Emerson, Haskins
Fidem servabo genusque	Smith
Fidem servat vinculæ solvit	Cadena
Fidem servat, vinculaque solvit	
	Velasquez de la Cadena
Fides	Cruger
Fides et fortitudo	Moreland
Fides leone fortior	Motley
Fides prævalebit	Morris
Fides scutum	Bruen, Gleim
Fides vincit et veritas custodit	Story
Fidite virtuti	Bard
Fier mais sensible	Burt
Fight	Sinclair
Finem respice	
	Aspinwall, Fairbanks, Lewis
Finis coronat opus	Blight
Firm	Stearns
Flagror non consumor	Guerrant
Flecto non frango	Currier
Florens suo orbe monet	Monnet
Floriferis ut apes in saltibus	
	Williams
Flourish in all weathers	Erving
Flydd lawn Bunydd	Watkins
Foedere non vi	Barnard
Follow reason	Spooner
Forget not	Campbell
Fors et virtus	Lotbiniere
Fortasse	Fogg
Forte scutum salus ducum	Fortescue
Fortes fortuna juvat	Dickson
Forti et fidele nihil difficile	Allen
Fortior leone lustis	Goodrich
Fortior quo rectior	Sargent
Fortiorum fortia facta	Stark
Fortis agendo	Pittman
Fortis cadere cedere non potest	
	Moore
Fortis est veritas	Barton, March
Fortis et fidelis	
	Burnham, Hubard, Moreduck, Watkins
Fortis et fidus	Middleton, Rose

Fortis et judus — Middleton
Fortis que felix — Minshull, Walter
Fortiter! Ascende! — Caldwell
Fortiter et fideliter — Brown
Fortiter et honeste — Hawkes
Fortiter gerit crucem — Allen
Fortitude in adversity — Parker
Fortitudine — Barry
Fortitudini juncta fidelitas — Bogart
Fortitudo — Archer
Fortitudo et fidelitas — Howland
Fortitudo et justitia — Judah
Fortuna favet audaci — Trumbull

Fortune, infortune, une fort une — Brewster
Forward — Lithgow, Paine
Foy pour devoir — Vance
Frangas non flectas — Stafford
Frangas non flectes — Bourne, Frothingham
Frange, lege, tege — Bolton
Fructu non foliis — Williams
Fungor fruor — Pybus
Furth fortune — Murray
Fynno Duw Deifydd — Hughes

G

Garde la Foy — Chaloner, Rodman
Garde le droit — Wright
Gardez bien — Montgomery, Woodward
Gaudet patientia duris — Willard
Gaudia magna nuncio — Scott
Gaudia nuncio magna — Scott
Giving and forgiving — Biggar
Gloria in excelsis Deo — Kellogg

Glorior in cruci Christi — Burder
Γνωθι Σεαυτον — Johnson
God is cortuer — Bull
God is my help — Hadley
Gofal Dyn Duw ai Gwerid — Parry
Gradatione vincimus — Curtis
Grata manu — Olcott
Grata quies — Van Sittart
Gwell anguana chywydd — Rhoades

H

Habeo pro jus fasque — Cushman
Hac Iter Elysium nobis — Drayton
Haec generi incrementa fides — Townsend
Hagard zit forward — Seton
Have wandered — Edwards
Heb Ddvw ddim a Ddvw — Digon
Morgan
Hinc labor et virtus — Allison
Hinc mihi salus — Spaulding
His nitimur et munitur — Macomber
His regi sevitium — Huckel
Hold fast — Macleod
Hold to the Most High — Seabury
Honestas optima politia — Owen
Honestum praetulit utili — Kissam
Honesty is good policy — Thompson

Honor et fides — Sears
Honor et justitia — Antill
Honor et justitia manet amicitia florebit semper que — Bayard
Honor virtutis proemium — Bell, Brearly
Honore et amore — Richards
Honore et justitia — Jayne
Hora e sempre — Farmer
Horæ sempre sola salus servire deo — Jarvis
Honie soit qui mal y pense — Russell
Humani nihil alienum — Stone, Talbott
Humani nihil alienum mihi — Jenings
Hvad Himlen Föder; Ey Afvund öder — Dahlgren

I

I live and die for those I love — Lloyd
I pensieri stretti ed il viso sciolto — Ludwell
Ich habs gewagt — Hugel
Il buono tempa verra — Jennings
Imitari quam invidere — Child
Immersabilis est vera virtus — Coddington
Immotus — Alston, Watkins
Impavide — Cabell, Power
In adversis idem — Duke
In altum — Alston

In cruce mea spes — Tryon
In cruce salus — Brigham, Lawrence
In Deo confido — Sparks, Whiting
In Deo et veritate fido — Hooper
In Deo fides — Gray
In Deo non armis fido — Morse
In Deo sola salus — Barker
In Deo solo confido — Converse
In Domino confido — Assheton, De Rosset de Fleury, Lukens
In fide et in bello fortes — Carroll

In futura spector	Pierce	Industria, intelligentia, virtus	Dexter
In God I trust	Goddard	Industria semper crescam	
In God we trust	Scott		Schermerhorn
In hoc signo vinces		Inimica tyrannis	Shubrick
Eustace, Henkel, O'Donnell		Initium sapientiae est timor dei	
In justitia virtutes omnes	Sims		Martin
In lumine luce	Thompson	Innocens non timidus	Rowe
In me mea spes omnis	Post	Innocenter Patienter Constanter	
In medio tutissimus ibis			Stillé
Cary, Sumner		Innocentiae securus	Jackson
In omnia paratus	Harrison	Insignia fortuna paria	Delafield
[In omnia promptus]	Rae	Insperata floruit	Claghorn
In prudentia & simplicitate	Vaughan	Instaurator ruinae	Forsyth
In te Domine speravi	Emerson, Lyon	Integer audax promptus	Williams
In time	Houstoun	Inter feros per crucem ad coronam	
In veritate salus	Jeffery		Stowe
In veritate victoria	Hastings	Inter folias fructus	Hapgood
Ino virtus et fata vocant	Jones	Inter primos	Hopkins
Indefessus vigilando	Read	Inveniam viam aut faciam	Humphries
Indure but Hope	Barrell	Invictus maneo	Inglis
Industria	Deas	Invidam virtute vincam	Foster
Industria et frugalitas	Cheever	Invitum sequitar honos	Gerard

J

J'ai bien servi	Prevost	Jovæ præstate fidere quam ho-	
J'avance. Foy en Dieu	Bartram	mine	Stuyvesant
J'espère	Sherman	Jovi præstat fidere quam homine	
J'espère en Dieu	Ray		Stuyvesant
Je me fie en Dieu	Winsor	Judicemur agendo	Hicks
Je m'en souviendray	Webber	Juncta virtute fides	Murray
Je ne l'oublierai jamais	Baldwin	Juste rem para	Apthorp
Je n'oublierais jamais	Appleton	Justi velut lumen astrarum	Checkley
Je n'oublierais pas	Baldwin	Justum perficito, nihil timeto	Rogers
Je reçois pour donner	Innes	Justus esto et non metue	Fellowes
Je suis prêt	Frazer, Smith	Juvant aspera probum	Stewart
Jesu est prêt	Frizell	Juvo audaces clarior hinc honos	
Jouir en bien	Beckwith		Buchanan
Jour de ma vie	Conarroe		

K

Keep triste	Semple	Kur deu res pub tra	Harris
Keep tryste	Hepburn		

L

L'espoir est ma force	Tupper	Laus virtutis actio	Rawson
L'un pour l'autre	Yates	Law and Right	Allen
La promesse du futur	Duryee	Le bon temps viendra	Farrington
Labor ipse voluptas	Belcher	Le matin et le soir le premier jour	Day
Labor omnia vincit		Lege et ratione	Crookshank
Green, Hasell, Leddel, Longbottom		Leges, juraque servat	Hearne
Labore quæritur gloria	Dowse	Legibus vivo	Lisle
Labour to rest	Kempe	Lesses dire	Middleton
Laetus in præsens animus	Powell	Let Curzon holde what Curzon	
Lám foisdin eac abu	Sullivan	helde	Curzon
Lamb laidir an nachdar	Bryan	Liber ac sapiens esto	Bradley
Lamh foisdin each an nœchtar	Sullivan	Libera nos Domine	Rowe
[What we gain by conquest we make secure by clemency]		Libertas	Garland, Pride

Libertas a legibus — Stokes
Libertas et patria — Giles
Libertas et patria mea — Giles
Libertatem, amicitiam, retinebis et fidem — Boylston
Libertatem coeo licentiam detestor — Hutchinson
Liberté toute entière — Barker
Liberty above all things — Brewster
Linquenda tellus — Boucher
Listo — Mason

Litteras ne despice — Willard
Live but (without) dread — Linzee
Look through — Acklom
Loyal au mort
Adams, Belcher, Chatterton, King
Loyal jusqu'à la mort — Belcher
Loyalté n'a honte — Clinton
Lucem spero clariorem — Preston
Luceo non uro — MacLeod, McKenzie
Lumen accipe et imperti — Hart
Lux in tenebris — Fullerton

M

Magnanimus esto — Ingraham
Major virtus quam splendor — Baillie
Malgré le Tort — Houghton
Malis fortiter obsta — Appleton
Malo mori quam foedari
Barnwell, Beale, Blackwell, Chrystie, Murray, Potter
Manent optima coelo — Joachimsen
Maneo qualis manebam (not present on all) — Pendleton
Manet amicitia florebitque semper
Francis, Pierpont
Manners makyth man — Wickham
Manu forti — Sener
Manus haec inimica tyrannis
Clark, Woolsey
Mare ditat — Waterman
Maturity — Bartlett
Maximum proeli impetum et sustinere — White
Mea spes est in Deo — Pell
Meae memor originis — Manson
Medio tutissimus ibis — Waller
Mediocra firma — Bacon
Mediocria firma — Lardner, Stone
Meditari et agere — Gross
Mein Siegel ist ein Ziegel — Pennypacker
Meliora speranda — Kelly
Memor et fidelis
Brewer, Edgerly, Leonard

Memoria pii æterna — Tracy
Mens conscia recti
Beekman, Iredell, Mills, Waddell
Mens conscia rectis — Iredell
Mens sana in corpore sano — McKean
Mens sibi conscia recti
Murray, Smith, Wright
Mentis honestae gloria — Geer
Μή Φοβοῦ μόνον πίστευε — Little
Mereo et merito — Merritt
Meum et tuum — Payson
Meus aequa in arduis — Crosby
Meus in ardues æqua — Abercrombie
Mihi gloria sursum — Arnold
Mihi gravato Deus — Ridgeway
Miseris succurrere disco — Rush
Mon Dieu est ma Roche — Quintard
Mori quam faedari — Savage
Moriendum — Van der Kemp
Mors aut vita decöra — Dempster
Morte triumpho — Arnold
Mos legem regit — Mosley motto
Moseley
Moveo et proficior — Knox
Mullach abu — Dunne
Murus aereus conscientia sana — Peabody
Murus aheneus — Macleod
Mutare vel timere sperno — Heard
My hope on high — Bedlow
My might makes my right — Mackey

N

Ne cede malis
Appleton, Chase, Hodges, Loomis, Roberdeau, Trottman
Ne jugulibron je la kovrilo (Do not judge a book by its cover) — Lowell
Ne nemium — Gordon
Ne oubliez — Graham
Ne parcas nec spernas — Yates
Ne quid nimis — Odell, Tazewell
Ne tentes aut perfice — Burnham

Nec arrogo nec dubito — Hurry
Nec aspera terrent — Mayo, Smith
Nec celeri nec forti — Sheppard
Nec cladio, nec arcu — Dudley
Nec Degener — Silvester
Nec elatus nec dejectus — Thomas
Nec gladio, nec arcu — Dudley
Nec habe nec careo nec curo — Graham
Nec opprimere nec opprimi — Lombard
Nec quaerere honorem nec spernere
Bell, Sargent

Nec quaerere nec spernere honorem   Sargent
Nec spe nec metu   Read
Nec sperno nec timeo   Coggeshall
Nec te quaesiveris extra   Harison, Harrison
Nec temere nec timide
   Bulkley, Combe, Cradock, Edes, Ludlow, Pickering, Sanford, Travers, Walker, Wells
Nec timeo nec sperno
   Brown, Green, Greene, Hubbard, Shepard
Nec timide nec temere   Bridgman
Nec vii nec astutia   Waring
Nec virtus suprema fefellit   Butler
Negata tentat iter via   Card
Nemo nisi Christus   Apthorp
Nemo sine crimine vivit   Hope
Never check   Hawks
Never despair   Colton, Pintard
Never elated never dejected   Thomas
N id cyfoeth ond boddlondek   Comstock
Nil admirari   Lawrence, Randolph, Williams
N il conscire sibi   Prescott
Nil desperando   Moat
Nil desperandum
   Bedell, Cutting, Lawrence, Mifflin, Smith, Spencer
Nil facimus non sponte Dei   Atkinson
Nil nisi bonum   Simpson
Nil sine Deo   Shelton, Waldo
Nil sine numine   Weld
Nihil utile quod non honestum   Moore, Smith
Nimand zonder   Van Rensselaer
Nobilis ira   Stewart
Nomine et patriæ asto   Fay
Non abest virtuti sors   Newcomb
Non crux sed lux   Black
Non deest spes   Forbes

Non est mortale quod opto   Smith, Weld
Non inferiora secutus   Montford
Non mortale quod opto   Rand
Non nobis solum   Drayton, Pinckney, Ward
Non nobis solum nati   Street
Non oblitus   McTavish
Non obliviscor   McEvers
Non revertur invitus   Jenkins
Non semper viret   Varnum
Non sibi   Goldsborough
Non sifficit orbis   Bond
Non sola mortali luce gradior   Mascarène
Non timeo sed caveo   Sherwood
Non vi sed voluntate   Boucher or Bouchier
Non nostraque Deo   Rogers
Nosce te ipsum   Edwards, Kimball, Murray
Not always so   Barrell
Not laws of man but laws of God   Balch
Nous maintiendrons   Guild
Nulla dies sine linea   Bolton
Nulla Pallescere Culpa   Byrd
Nulla vestigia retrorsum   Lefferts
Nulli praeda   Duane
Nullius addictus jurare in verba magistri   Wolcott
Nullius in verba   Banks, Lawrence, Maxcy
Numine   Bowie
Numine et virtute   Yuille
Nunc mihi nunc alii   Wormeley
Nuncia pacis   Hamilton
Nuncia pacis oliva   Noyes
Nunquam non fidelis   Moultrie, Yardley
Nunquam non paratus   Betton, Hale, Johnston
Nunquam obliviscar   McIver

O

Obsta principiis   Hancock
Occasionem cognosce   Lowell
Old age is a virtue   Van Rensselaer
Omne bonum desuper   Burnham
Omne solum Forti Patria   Ludlow
Omnes benevolentia   Phillips
Omnes fremant licet dicam quod sentio   Smith
Omnia Deo pendent   Stockton, Webster
Omnia libant omnia nos   Williams
Omnia pro bono   Murdoch

Omnia Providentiae committo   Meares
Omnia relinquit servare rempublicam   Turberville
Omnia vincit veritas   DeCourcy
Omnis a deo protestas   Griffith
Omnis fortunae paratus   Forbes
Opinionem vincere omnium   Antill
Optimum est aliena frui insania   Smith
Optimum quod evenit   Laurens
Optimum vix satis   Updike
Otium ex labore   Remsen

P

Palma virtuta (sic)	Palmer
Palmam qui meruit ferat	
	Bult, Griswold
Par pari refero	Wall
Paradisus in sole	Hubbard
Paratus et fidelis	Tuckerman
Parva segessatis est	Cole
Patior ut potior	Spotswood
Patria cara, carior libertas	
	Brown, Endicott, Marchant
Patria veritas fides	Everett
Pauper sed non in spe	Poor
Pax aut bellum	Oliver
Pax et amicitia	Cowell
Pax et amor	Backhouse
Pax et copia	Claiborne
Pax in bello	Oliver, Prioleau
Pax in terris	Codman
Pax hospita ruris	Jones
Pax quaeritur bello	Oliver
Pectore puro	Royall
Per ardua	Clark, Crabb, Lowndes
Per ardua ad alta	Hannay
Per ardua stabilis	Manning
Per aspera ad astra	
	Johnson, Mordecai, Stevens
Per castra as astra	Nicholson
Per crucem ad stellas	Fairchild
Per fidem et constantiam	Schiefflin
Per mare per terras	McAllister
Per saxa per ignes fortiter et recte	
	Elliot
Per se	Thompson
Per stabilitas et per fortitudo	Holmes
Per varios casus	Mercer
Per vias rectas	Whitman
Perge coepisti	Ten Broeck
Perge et valeas	Hutchinson
Perit ut vivat	Fenwick, Magill
Persevera decque confides	Washburn
Persevera et vince	Loomis
Perseverance	Bell
Perseverando	
	Balmanno, Sheepshanks, Wood
Persevere	Gallatin
Perspicere quam ulcisci	Manigault
Peu a peu	Moseley
Pie vivere et Deum et patriam	
deligere	Redmond
Pietas est pax	Hopkins
Piety in peace	Hopkins
Placidus semper timidus nunquam	
	Catlin
Please God I live, I'll go	Lloyd
Post hominem animus durst	Bridge
Post nubila Phoebus	Jaffrey, Jeffers

Post tenebris speramus lumen de	
lumine	Coffin
Post tot naufragia portus	Montague
Pour le roi et la patrie	Lynde
Pour qui sait attendre	Mitchell
Pour sui vez	Reeve
Poussez en avant	Benjamin
Praesto pro patria	Gardner
Praetis prudentia praestat	Morison
Prævisa mala pereunt	Winterbotham
Press through	Borland, Young
Prestat opes sapientia	Livingston
Pretio prudentia	Richardson
Principia non homines	Webb
Principiis obsta	Tompkins
Pro aris et focis	Bloomfield
Pro Christo et patria dulce peri-	
culum	Homans
Pro Deo et nobilissima patria	
Batavorum	Van Nest
Pro Deo et Patria	Hewes, Nicklin
Pro ecclesia	Whittingham
Pro lege et Rege	Hicks, Whitebread
Pro libertate	Provoost, Young
Pro libertate et commercio	Hicks
Pro patria	
Duvall, Hutson, Martin, Wallace
Pro patria et libertate	Michie
Pro patria mori	Gardiner
Pro patria semper	Fitzhugh, Macartey
Pro rege	Porcher
Pro rege et lege	Longbottom
Pro rege et patria	Champion
Pro rege et populo	Bassett
Pro rege, lege et grege	Mason
Pro rege, pro lege, pro grege	Damon
Pro Republica	Jones
Pro Republica semper	Mason, Vassall
Pro veritate suffer fortiter	Sharpless
Probitas laudatur et alget	Antill
Probitas optimum est consilium	
	Koecker
Probitas verus honos	
	Batterson, Corbin
Probitate et industria	Bridgen
Procurata industria	Fraunces
Prodesse quam conspici	Phinney
Progredi non regredi	Rutledge
Propere et provide	Robinson
Propero sed curo	Groves
Proprium decus et patrium	Morris
Proprium decus et petrum	Powel
Prorsum et sursum	Boker
Prospicio	Scripps
Providentia sumus	Blatchford
Prudenter et simpliciter	Vaughan

Pugna pro patria, 1625 — Reynolds
Pugna pro patria, & "Paul Revere" — Revere

Pugna pro patria liberta — Martin
Purus sceleres — Carter

Q

Quae supra — Roberts
Quant je puis — Sherburne
Qui croit en Dieu croix — Vail
Qui me tanget poenitebit — McPherson
Qui plantavit curabit — Roosevelt
Quo cunque ferar — St. Clair
Quo fata vocant
 Bay, Davis, Erving, Forward, Humphreys, Larrabee, Sidney, Vose
Quo Minerva ducit, sequor — Tayloe
Quo vocat virtus — Jauncey
Quocunque jaceris, stabit — MacLeod

Quod deus vult fiat — Movius
Quod ero spero — Booth
Quod fieri non vis alter ne feceris — Cock
Quod non pro patria — Bowie
Quod petis hic est — Smith
Quod severis metes — Bliss
Quod sis esse velis nilque malis — Champion
Quod tibi vis alteri feceris — Bathurst
Quod verum tutum — Lyman
Quod vult valde vult — Horton
Quondam his vicimus armis — Bowman

R

Rather virtue than learning — Stith
Re vera — Reeve
Recta sed ardua — Lindsay
Recte faciendo securus — Inglis
Rectitudine sto — Du Pont
Recuperatus — MacWilliams
Redde suum cuique — Waddington
Regard de mon droit — Middleton
Regard the end — Ripley
Regarde bien — Hight
Regardes mon droit — Middleton
Regi et patria fidelis — Toler
Res non verba — Wilson

Resurgam — Smyth
Resurgere tento — Edmonds, Simons
Reviresco — Maxwell
Rex mundi — Raymond
Rien sans droit (?) — Field
Rien sans peine — Johnson
Right onward — Doane
Robor et agilitas — Baker
Robori prudentia præstat — Lithgow, Young
Rosae inter spinas nascuntur — Thorndike

S

Sacra quercus — Holyoke
Saepe pro rege semper pro patria — Clarke
St. Callawy ora pro me — Callaway
Salus et decus — Lloyd
Sans cause — Geer
Sans charger — Musgrave
Sans crainte — Belmont
Sans Dieu Je ne puis — Skipwith
Sans dieu rien — Eustace, Field
Sans tache — Martin
Sans peur et sans reproche — Ellsworth
Sans venin — Guinand
Sapere aude — Baer, Buckle, Grundy
Sapiens qui vigilat — Otis
Sat cito si sat tuto — Clerk
Scientia est potestas — Tylden
Scietas scientia virtus — Milner
Scutum impenetrabile Deus — Dongan
Se inserit astris — Gause
Secret et hardi — Rice, Thomas

Secundis dubiisque rectus — Lippincott, Wythe
Semper caveto — Ball
Semper constans et fidelis — Barker
Semper cor caput Cabot — Cabot
Semper erectus — Pepper
Semper idem — Clark
Semper fidelis
 Allen, Cromelien, Lynch, Kearney, Morton, Potter, Smith
Semper honos — Horry
Semper paratus
 Bleecker, Blodgett, Clifford, Griffin, Hopkinson, McConn, Miller, Thaxter, Wells
Semper ut te digna sequare — Vernon
Semper presto servire — Bostwick
Semper vigilans — Alcott
Sero sed serio — Kerr, Salisbury
Serva jugum — Hay
Servata fides cinere — Merrill
Si deus quis contra — Gilman

Si fractus fortis	Foster	Spes alit agricolam	Tilghman
Si je n'estoy	Curwen	Spes anchora vitae	Boas
Si je puis	Livingston	Spes durat avorum	Bowditch
Si sit prudentia	Eden	Spes et fides	Chamberlain
Sic curre ut capias	Currey, Curry	Spes mea in Deo	
Sic itur as astra. Optime de patria			Cutler, Steptoe, Tyler
meruit	Pease	Spes meliora	Watmough
Sic parvis magna	Drake	Spes vincit thronum	Winthrop
Sic vos non vobis	Sabine	Stand fast	Grant
Sicut quaercus	Chaloner	Stand fast, stand firm, stand sure	
Silenzio ad concordia	Baird		Grant
Sinceritas	Kimberly	Stand sure	Grant
Sine cruce sine luce	Howe	Start in time	Brooks
Sine Deo careo	Cary	Stat fortuna Domus	Howes
Sine labora nota	Crawford	Stella xpi duce	Sohier
Sine macula macla	Quincy	Stimulat sed ornat	McCarter
Sine timore	McCormack	Stolz und treu	Cram
Sine virtute vani sunt honores		Strike for the laws	Walworth
	Bozman	Struggle	Ruggles
Sis justus et ne timeas		Suaviter in modo, fortiter in re	
	Walcott, White		Johnson
Sit dux sapentia	Walters	Sub cruce canto	Percival
Sit nomen decus	Swan	Sub cruce salus	Ward
Sol et sentum Deus	Dexter	Sub sole, sub umbra, virens	Irving
Sola bona quae honesta	Alexander	Sub sole sub umbra virescens	Erving
Sola nobilitas virtus		Sub spe	Dunbar
	Edwards, McCandlish, Snell	Sublimiora petamus	Bancker
Sola virtus invicta, 1632		Sublimiora peto	Nicoll
	Bispham, Hansom, Reynolds	Sublimis per ardua tendo	Chauncy
Sola virtus nobilitat	Henderson	Successus a Deo est	Roberts
Soli deo gloria et honor	Boudinot	Such is love	Pateson
Solus minus solus	Muhlenberg	Sufficit meruisse	Plumptre
Sorte sua contentus	Hartwell	Suivez raison	Browne, Greene
Soyez firme	Needham	Sunt Fortea notro Pectora	Mather
Spe labor levis	Page	Sunt sua praemia laudi	Crome
Spem et speravi	Markoe	Supera alta tenere	Seabury
Spem successus alit	Gurney, Ross	Surgite lumen adest	Glover
Sperandum est esperance	Wallace	Suspice Teucro	Tucker
Sperate et vivite fortes	Bland	Sustinare	Brooks
(on chevron) spernit humum		Sustine abstine	Belcher, Belchier
	Mitchell, Van Guysling	Sustine et abstine	Shober
Spero	Chalmers	Sustineo	Ten Broeck
Spero infestis metuo secundis	Lodge	Sustinere	Brooks
Spero meliora	Livingston	Suum cuique tributo	Ashenden, Evans
Spes alet agricolam	Tilghman	Symru am byth	Llewellyn

T

Tace aut face	Reed	Tenax propositi	Gibbs, Gilbert
Tace aut face; Autremen tonnerre	Scott	Tenex propositia	Hayne
Tam arte quam marte	Wright	Tenez le vraye	Emmet
Tandem vincitur	Morris	Tendit in ardua virtus	Winckley
Tanque puis je	Hilton	Tentanda via est	
Tantes da Dir	Rutgers	Hammond, Peckham, Strong, Wet-	
Te duce	Crosby	more	
Te duce libertas	Crosby	Terra aut mari	Parke
Te ipsum nosce	Shaw	Terre nolo, timere nescio	Dyer
Templa quam Dilecta	Temple	The entrance to an enchanted	
Tenax et fidelis	Willey	world	Clapp

The right and sleep White
The truth against the world Edwards
The wicked borroweth & payeth
  not again Pownall
There is no difficulty to him that
  wills Hains
Think on McClellan
Think well Clement
This I'll defend McFarlan
This I'll defend. Be Ware
  McFarlan
Through Hamilton
Tibimet ipsi fidem praestato
  Underhill
Tiens ta foy Binney, Gale
Time tryeth tryst Drake
To rock the cradle of reposing age
  Foster
Touch not the cat but a glove
  Gillespie, McIntosh, MacPherson
Toujours fidèle
  Fay, Hairston, Stratton, Waters
Toujours le merae Giles

Toujours loyal Brown
Toujours peine Paine
Toujours prest Mead, Carmichael
Toujours prêt Ogilby
Toujours propice Ballagh
Tout cœur Tuckerman
Tout d'en haut Ballou, Bellows
Tout en bonne heure Hicks
Trent à al vérité Mauran
Trewe Bolton
Trust in God
  Benson, Harkness, Jones
Trusty and true Scott
Try Brazer
Tu mihicurarum requies Goldsmith
Tu ne cede malis Turner
Tuebor French
Tune cede malis Bradshaw, Rose
Turris prudentia custos. Ut migra-
  turus habita Lauder
Tutus in undis Lockwood, Wood
Tutus si fortis Smith
Tyde what may Haig

U

Ubi libertas Foster
Ubi libertas ibi patria
  Dinwiddie, Huger
Ubi plura offendar maculis nitent
  non ego pancis Danforth
Ubique fidelis Penrose, Tefft
Ubique patriam reminisci Norris
Ultra aspicio Palmer
Un Dieu un Roi Dorsey
Un je servirai Straus
Ung durant ma vie Rhodes

Ung loy, ung roy, ung foy Herbert
Unica virtus necessaria Messchert
Usque ad mortem Parks
Ut aquila versus coelum Bowdoin
Ut ferrum forte Fearon
Ut palma justus Palmes
Ut prosim Greenwood, Travers
Ut quiescas labora Gallandet
Ut vivas vigila Arnold
Utere mundo Blackly
Utilem pete finem Marshall

V

Vera sequor Hale
Veritas et fidelitas Coggeshall
Veritas liberabit Adams
Veritas quasi rosa resplendet Trew
Veritas securis Scribner
Veritas sine timore Phelps
Veritas vincit Keith
Vérité sans peur
  Hayes, Petigru, Somervell
Vérité soit ma garde Brewster
Vérité soyez ma garde Brewster
Vernon semper floret Leftwich
Vernon semper viret Lloyd
Vero pro gratis Webster
Vertus est vera vetustas
  Van Rensselaer
Verum atque decens Weld
Verum dicit Stanford
Verus et fidelis semper Alward

Vestigia nulla retrorsum
  Kip, Sohier
Vi et animo McCulloch, McCulloh
Vi et armis Armstrong
Vi et virtute Brownell, Spaight
Vi nulla invertitur ordo Hunt
Vicit pepercit Draper
Videte et cavete ab abaritia.
  Luke 12. XV Pownall
Viget in cinere virtus Davidson
Vigila Amderson
Vigilantes (?) Hardinge
Vigilantia praestat Coxe
Vigilo May
Vigueur de dessus O'Brien
Vincenti dabitur laurea Vincent
Vincit amor patriae
  Boardman, Gleason, Pelham, Pen-
  ington

Vincit omnia veritas	Hyslop
Vincit pericula virtus	Thornton
Vincit qui patitur	
Chester Colt, Disney, Lindsgeht,	
Merrill, Prescott, Rowe	
Vincit veritas	
Berry, Coote, Chambers, Haskell	
Virescit vulnere virtus	Burnet
Virtue is honour	Kendrick
Virtue, liberty, and independence	
	Barton
Virtue only has claim to honour	
	Rumsey
Virtus actione consistit	Craven
Virtus basis vitae	Bull, Stafford
Virtus castellium meum	Van Voorhis
Virtus Durissima ferit	McLean
Virtus est dei	Briggs
Virtus et notale meum	Tillotson
Virtus honoris Janua	Burr, Farlow
Virtus in arduis	
Cockayne, Harrison, Ingraham	
Virtus invecta gloriosa	Thomas
Virtus invidia vincit	Storrs
Virtus libertas et patria	Wetmore
Virtus mille scuta	Bradford
Virtus nobilitat omnia	Stetson
Virtus omnia nobilitat	Herrick
Virtus omnia vincit	White
Virtus praestantior auro	Wheildon
Virtus se coronat	Woodbridge
Virtus semper viret	Woodward
Virtus semper viridis	Corey, Cory
Virtus sibi munus	Van Cortlandt
Virtus sibi proemium	Catherwood
Virtus sola nobilitas	
Saville, Wanton, Washington	
Virtus sola nobilitat	Blake, Mayo
Virtus vera nobilitas	Chesebrough
Virtus vera nobilitas est	Mather
Virtus vincit invidiam	Perry
Virtutas et labor	Lemon
Virtute aquiritur honor	
McLanahan, Richardson	
Virtute dignus avorum	Worthington
Virtute et fide	Roome
Virtute et fortuna	Andrews

Virtute et industriae	Havemeyer
Virtute et labore	
Cunningham, Goodwin, Winn	
Virtute et labore verum amicum	
cole	Cunningham
Virtute et nemine	Cushing
Virtute et non vi	Bradstreet
Virtute et numine	Creagh
Virtute et opere	Prime
Virtute et valore	Leach
Virtute invidiam vincas	Cleborne
Virtute non verbis	
Robinson, Winston	
Virtute non vi	Hearn
Virtute parta tuemini	Pepperrell
Virtute Quies	Phipps
Virtute spernit victa	Elliott
Virtutem ante pono honorem	
	McPherson
Virtutem avorum aemulus	
	Mortimer
Virtutem hilaritate colere	Wynkoop
Virtutis amore	Stevens
Virtutis avorum praemium	Upton
Virtutis fortuna comes	Pomeroy
Virtutis gloria merces	Robertson
Vis sapientia pollet	Meath
Vis unita fortior	Flood
Vis unita fortis (?)	Moore
Vis veritatis magna	Hall
Vita sine litteris mors est	Allen
Vive en espoir	Starr
Vive et vivat	Atkinson
Vive la joye	Josselyn
Vive ut postea vivas	Schofield
Vive ut vivas	Abercrombie
Vivere est agere	Sewall
Vivere recte est	Cooley
Vivo et morior pro quibus amo	
	Chandler
Vix ea nostra voco	
Campbell, Gamble, Palmer, White	
Voici nos liens	Mazyck
Volo et valeo	Charles, Clarke
Volonté de Dieu	Wilbur
Vulnus opemque fero	Addison
Vy: ngwlad: un: a: wasnaethav	Jones

W

Watch and pray	Fowler	Will God I shall	Torrey
Whither will ye	Stewart		

Y and Z

Youre youre	Cunningham	Zyt Bestendig	Dyckman

CORRECTION

On page 129 Pepperell *should read* Pepperrell